Encyclopedia of Folk, Country and Western Music

T5-AQQ-374

Books by IRWIN STAMBLER

Battle for Inner Space
Encyclopedia of Popular Music

DISCARDED
Goshen Public Library

ENCYCLOPEDIA
of
FOLK, COUNTRY
and
WESTERN MUSIC

by Irwin Stambler and Grelun Landon

ILLUSTRATED WITH PHOTOGRAPHS

PUBLIC LIBRARY
GOSHEN, INDIANA

ST. MARTIN'S PRESS *New York*

R
781.7
STA

Copyright © 1969 by Irwin Stambler and Grelun Landon
All Rights Reserved
Library of Congress Catalog Card Number: 67-10659
Manufactured in the United States of America

To those creative individuals,
heralded and unheralded,
who have contributed to the world heritage
of folk, country and western music.

Baker 4-70 1250

PICTURE CREDITS

The authors and publisher are grateful to the sources listed below for permission to reproduce the illustrations that appear on the pages indicated.

3: Howard Risk; 4: WSM Archives; 5: WSM Grand Ole Opry; 9: Decca Records; 13: RCA Victor Records; 17: RCA Victor Records; 24: Columbia Records; 26: RCA Victor Records; 31: Midwestern Hayride; 38: Columbia Records; 48: RCA Victor Records; 49: WSM Grand Ole Opry; 57: Capitol Records; 60: RCA Victor Records; 62: Elektra Records; 67: Country Music Association; 69: RCA Victor Records; 75: RCA Victor Records; 81: Capitol Records; 84: Columbia Records; 87: Mercury Records; 89: Columbia Records; 92: Folklore Productions; 95: Columbia Records; 99: Capitol Records; 110: WSM Archives; 111: WSM Archives; 112: WSM Grand Ole Opry; 113: WSM Photo by Les Leverett; 119: Diana J. Davies, from Insight; 120: Photographer unknown, picture supplied by Peter J. Welding; 124: RCA Victor Records; 127: Berkeley Folk Music Festival; 130: WSM Archives; 131: WSM Archives; 133: Agency for the Performing Arts; 135: Matt Hinton; 137: RCA Victor Records; 139: Sam "Lightnin' " Hopkins; 145: Mississippi John Hurt; 147: Capitol Records; 152: Capitol Records; 155: Capitol Records; 157: RCA Victor Records; 158: WSM Grand Ole Opry; 163: Folkways Records; 167: Acuff-Rose Publications; 173: RCA Victor Records; 178: RCA Victor Records; 179: RCA Victor Records; 181: Louvin Brothers; 185: WSM Photo by Les Leverett; 187: Ewan MacColl; 191: RCA Victor Records; 196: Ed McCurdy; 198: WSM Archives; 201: AVCO Broadcasting; 202: AVCO Broadcasting; 204: Smash Records; 206: Bill Monroe; 215: Folkways Records; 221: A & M Records; 222: RCA Victor Records; 225: Decca Records/Grand Ole Opry; 229: Elektra Records; 232: WSM Archives; 234: Capitol Records; 240: RCA Victor Records; 242: Columbia Records; 252: WSM Photo by Les Leverett; 259: RCA Victor Records; 263: Milene Music, Inc.; 266: Elektra Records; 273: Columbia Records/Leventhal; 274: Capitol Records; 275: Capitol Records; 277: Si Siman; 287: RCA Victor Records; 294: Columbia Records; 298: Jimmy Tarleton; 300: David Gahr; 301: Warner Brothers Records; 308: WSM Archives; 309: WSM Archives; 321: Dan Seeger; 324: RCA Victor Records; 326: Marianne Pfältzer; 328: Josh White; 329: Imperial Records; 330: WSM Archives; 334: Acuff-Rose Publications, Inc.; 335: Boone Record Company; 343: RCA Victor Records; 345: Mercury Records.

Introduction and Acknowledgments

In preparing this work, we have been conscious of the difficulties in adequately covering a field with a long, honorable history that has also received a minimum of literary attention. The problems of surveying any broad field within the confines of a single book are obvious, but they are compounded when documentation is spare and often conflicting. In the end, editorial judgment must apply, both in the selection of entries and, in many instances, resolving which of several conflicting reports of dates, incidents, and the like to accept. We have naturally made every effort to insure that all material in the book is as accurate as possible, and believe in the main to have succeeded. However, it would be foolhardy, under the circumstances, to hope that some errors of fact have not crept in, and for them we ask the forbearance of the reader.

We hope that this Encyclopedia will serve as an important landmark in the field of folk, country and western music. This music, which is one of America's major contributions to music in general, is at last beginning to receive the close attention of both scholars and laymen that it merits. Our goal has been to present a readable, balanced picture of this dynamic part of our musical heritage; the selection process this entails unavoidably may result in omission of items or career descriptions that are as deserving of mention as any included in the book.

If our efforts to make this a definitive volume have succeeded, our success is due in no small part to the suggestions and cooperation of many people and organizations. We are particularly thankful to Bill Anderson, Sam Hinton, and Ed Kahn for their article contributions, and to Bob McCluskey and Acuff-Rose for permission to include some of their catalog of folk and country standards.

We are also indebted to Dr. D. K. Wilgus and the Edwards Memorial Foundation of UCLA and Jo Walker of the Country Music Association for providing access to their files and supplying data of great importance to our efforts. We would also like to thank Irwin Silber for sending us issues of "Sing Out!" magazine and the many folk music volumes published by Oak Publications.

We would also like to thank the following for their help: Eddy Arnold; Bess Lomax Hawes; Steve Sholes; Ken Nelson; Ted Daffan; Pat Faralla; Ron Tepper; Lee Delaney and Capitol Records; Herb Helman and RCA Records; Tammy Owens and

Columbia Records; Moses Asch and Folkways Records; Vanguard Records; Mercury Records; Elektra Records; Frances Preston and BMI, Nashville; Juanita Jones, ASCAP, Nashville; the staff of Station WSM, Nashville, and the Grand Ole Opry; Paul Ackerman, Billboard; Carol Ann Muñoz; Chet Atkins; Rod McKuen; Randy Sparks; Jack Speirs; Charles Williams; Joe Nixon; Tom Riney, Liberty Records; Biff Collie; Hubert Long; Hal Neely; Don Robertson; Cliffie Stone and Central Songs, Inc.; Roy Horton, Southern Music Publishing Co.; Cindy Walker, Music City News; Smiley Wilson; Scotty Turner; Jack McFadden (OMAC); Bernie Pearl, Ed Pearl, and the Ash Grove; Newport Folk Festival; Academy of Country & Western Music; and Dick Broderick.

We would also like to thank Bob Jones, Art Director of RCA Records, for preparing the color transparencies for the jacket.

Irwin Stambler and Grelun Landon
Hollywood, California
April 1969

Contents

A–Z of Folk, Country and Western Music

ACADEMY OF COUNTRY AND WESTERN MUSIC: Western-based awards association, founded 1964.

The concept of special awards for creativity in the entertainment media seems to have its strongest roots in California. Such events as the Academy Awards of the Academy of Motion Picture Arts and Sciences and the Grammy Awards of the National Academy of the Recording Arts and Sciences originated in the Golden State. Thus the environment was right for creation of a new series of country and western awards in the 1960s.

The new Academy grew out of discussions in 1964 between trade journal publisher Tommy Wiggins (D.J.'s Digest) and three other country enthusiasts, Eddie Miller, Mickey Christiansen, and Chris Christiansen. Their original goal was to promote greater interest in country and western music in the western states. It was decided to invite industry executives and performers to informal meetings. One aim of the meetings was to provide forms of recognition for those in the field.

Interest in the idea spread rapidly, resulting in the holding of the first Awards event in late 1964. Locale was the Red Barrel nightclub, a leading country music club in the Los Angeles area. Wiggins' publication underwrote the evening and Tex Williams served as master of ceremonies. In 1965, a second Awards Dinner was held, sponsored by V.I.P. magazine.

The Academy concept caught on quickly. As membership soared, it was decided to form a continuing organization to handle future Academy progress. A dues plan was instituted so that sponsorship of Awards dinners could be handled by the Academy itself. The first official Awards Show of the Academy of Country and Western Music was held at the Hollywood Palladium in February 1966.

By the time the second Annual Awards Dinner was held at the Beverly Hilton, Beverly Hills, California, on March, 6, 1967, the Academy had elected its first officers: Tex Williams as president, Eddie Dean as vice president, Bettie

Song of the year for 1967 in the Academy of Country & Western Music Awards voting was "It's Such a Pretty World Today." At the awards banquet in March 1968, presenter Doug McClure (center) presents awards to the song's publisher, Cliffie Stone (right) and vocalist on the hit recording, Wynn Stewart.

Azevedo as secretary and Herb Eiseman as treasurer.

(For Award winners, *see* Appendix.)

ACKERMAN, PAUL: Editor, writer. Born New York, New York, February 18, 1908.

Communicating is obviously at the heart of entertaining. The performer must communicate with his audience. In addition, the written part of communicating is also vital. News reviews in trade publications, critical reviews in papers and magazines all are part of the chain that binds artist and listener together. One of these important, often unheralded communicators is the leading music journalist and editor Paul Ackerman.

Paul was born and raised in New York City. His interest in the world of music was strong during his years at William and Mary College, Virginia (B.A.) and Columbia University in New York (M.A.). After finishing college, he eventually satisfied his combined interest in journalism and music by joining the staff of

Billboard, "The International Music-Record Newsweekly."

Over the years, Paul became one of the best informed observers of the music scene. He covered all aspects of show business, from legitimate theater to radio and music, advancing up the ladder until he was appointed music editor of Billboard. During his career, Paul had a particularly close tie to country music and was one of the staff members best versed in the subject. By the mid-1960s, he had contributed much journalistically to the country music field both for Billboard readers and in material presented for public view in the Country Music Hall of Fame in Nashville.

As he writes (personal communication, 1967): "I have edited and compiled Billboard's annual World of Country Music; I am the recipient of the Connie B. Gay President's Award for outstanding service to the country field. I have served on the CMA board, written the script of CMA's film on country music; written most of the historical material used in the Country Music Hall of Fame in Nashville—and have been a country music buff many years."

In 1963, Paul's overall accomplishments were recognized by the award to him of the Jesse B. Neal Editorial Achievement Award. Paul's credits also included serving as editor of a book, *This Business of Music,* by S. Shemel and M. W. Krasilovsky.

ACUFF, ROY: Singer, fiddler, band leader, m.c., songwriter, record company executive. Born Maynardsville, Tennessee, September 15, 1903. Elected to Country Music Hall of Fame, 1962.

So great was Roy Acuff's impact on the country music scene that his name became almost synonymous with the Grand Ole Opry, despite the fact that the Opry went back a decade and a half before he joined. From 1940 on, he provided nationwide Opry audiences with some of the most acclaimed renditions in country music history, including his versions of the "Wabash Cannonball," "Crash on the Highway," "Great Speckled Bird," "Shout, Oh Lulu," and "Night Train to Memphis."

Acuff's success was all the more noteworthy for his late start in the field. Until he was almost

The Crazy Tennesseans, Roy Acuff's band of the 1930s

[4]

30, he had no intention of having a career in music. As a boy in Maynardsville, Union County, he dreamt of becoming a star athlete. When not thinking along these lines, he considered following the law some day. This was in emulation of his father, who was both a successful lawyer and a missionary Baptist minister.

In high school in Knoxville, sports seemed to win out. Roy was a three-letter man, starring in baseball and football. When he left school, he played minor league ball for a number of years. In his mid-twenties, he was considered a prime prospect for the big leagues. Unfortunately, he developed a susceptibility to sunstroke. He suffered sunstroke on three occasions, the last occurring just when he was on the verge of signing a contract with the New York Giants.

The stroke was so bad that Roy was invalided home. For several years he worked at odd jobs as he slowly recovered his full strength. As Roy said, "I had to pick me out a new career." His father helped point the way. Acuff, Sr., was a talented country fiddler who collected records of famous fiddlers. Roy soon began to listen closely to the records for hours on end. He perfected his fiddle playing and also learned a number of the lyrics to the country ballads. In 1932, he was once more hale and hearty. Now approaching 30, he joined a medicine show that was touring Virginia and eastern Tennessee. After two years of this, he settled down in Knoxville as a regular on stations WNOX and WROL. That same year, he also turned out the first record of a career that was to cover hundreds of recording performances.

From 1934 to 1940, Roy continued to increase his following with audiences throughout Tennessee. Besides his radio show, he sang at many country events in other parts of the south. In 1940, this led to a contract with the Grand Ole Opry in Nashville. Uncle Dave Macon had been undisputed king of the Opry, up to this point, but before long, Roy became as popular as Uncle Dave. By 1942, Roy Acuff's name was number one with almost every country music fan from coast to coast. Soon after joining the Opry, he also organized his famous band, the Smokey Mountain Boys.

Roy's records were on best-selling lists almost every month throughout the 1940s. On Vocalion Records, he turned out such songs as "Steamboat Whistle Blues," "New Greenback Dollar," "Steel Guitar Chimes," "Wabash Cannonball," "The Beautiful Picture," "The Great Shining Light," and "The Rising Sun." His output on Okeh included such songs as "Vagabond's Dream," "Haven of Dreams," "Beautiful Brown Eyes," Living on the Mountain," "Baby Mine," "Ida Red," "Smoky Mountain Rag," "Will the Circle Be Unbroken," 'When I Lay My Burden Down," Streamline Cannonball," "Weary River," "Just to Ease my Wearied Mind," "The Broken Heart," "The Precious Jewel," "Worried Mind," "Lyin' Women Blues," "Are You Thinking of Me Darling," "Wreck on the Highway," "Night Train to Memphis," "Don't Make Me Go to Bed and I'll be Good," and "It's Too Late to Worry Anymore."

Roy's recordings for Columbia were even greater in number than his combined total for Vocalion and Okeh. His Columbia list included many of the songs listed earlier plus such others as "Beneath That Precious Mound of Clay," "It Won't Be Long," "Branded Wherever I Go," "Do You Wonder Why," "The Devil's Train," "The Songbirds Are Singing in Heaven," "I Saw the Light," "Unloved and Unclaimed," "Mule Skinner Blues," "Not a Word from Home," "Waiting for My Call to Glory," "I Called and Nobody Answered," "Golden Treasure," "Heartaches and Flowers," "Tennessee Waltz," "Sweeter Than the Flowers," "Polk County Breakdown," "I'll Always Care" and "Black Mountain Rag."

In 1944, Roy was nominated to run for gover-

Hall of Famer Roy Acuff addresses some pretty Opry misses of the 1940s.

nor of Tennessee. He lost in the primary, but was nominated again in 1946 and '48. In 1948, he won the Republican primary by an eight-one margin, but lost in the final election.

In the 1950s and '60s, Roy continued to appear on the Opry and on occasional tours, but he spent more time on his expanding business enterprises. The most successful of these was the music publishing firm he formed in 1942 with Fred Rose. The Acuff-Rose company grew to be one of the largest in the country. In the post-World War II decades, the country and western top 10 was peppered with songs bearing the Acuff-Rose banner. He also operated Roy Acuff Hobby Exhibits, Dunbar Cave Park and Recreation Center near Clarksville, Tennessee, and became part owner of a growing record firm, Hickory Records.

Many of Roy's LPs of the 1960s appeared on the Hickory label, including "King of Country Music," "American Folk Songs," "Once More," "World Is His Stage" and "Stars of the Grand Ole Opry." Harmony Records also produced a number of his LPs, such as "Roy Acuff" ('58), and "That Glory Bound Train" ('61). In the '60s, he was also represented on Capitol with "Best of Roy Acuff" ('63) and "Great Roy Acuff" ('64); on MGM with "Hymn Time" ('62); and Metro with "Smokey Mountain Boys" ('65).

Roy continued to tour widely until he was hurt in an auto accident in 1965. Many of his tours were to entertain American troops, starting with a trip to Berlin during the 1949 blockade and continuing with shows in Korea in the 1950s and the Dominican Republic and Vietnam in the 1960s.

By the time Roy was nominated to the Country Music Hall of Fame in 1963, his total record sales were well over the 30-million mark.

ADAMS, DERROLL: Singer, banjoist, songwriter. Born Portland, Oregon, November 25, 1925.

In a field in which there are many rugged individualists, it would still be hard to find a more bizarre career than that of Derroll Adams. His is a life replete with many psychological problems, broken marriages, bouts with alcoholism, drugs, and poverty. It is a life in which his exposure to the music public has been limited to only sporadic appearances with many years of public silence between. Despite this, Adams achieved a legendary reputation, particularly with European fans and fellow folk music art-

ists, for artistic integrity and great creative ability.

Adams' childhood hardly was calculated to contribute to his stability. His father, Tom Thompson, an ex-vaudeville juggler, was often drunk until Derroll's mother, Gertrude, left him. She left her next husband, Jack Glenn, a truck driver, because the man beat young Derroll with a belt buckle. Finally, she achieved a stable marriage with an inventor and salesman from Washington, George Adams. Adams succeeded in getting a civil engineering degree at night school.

Young Derroll (whose real name was Derroll Lewis Thompson) spent many of his boyhood years traveling throughout the west with his parents. His father worked part time on the Bonneville Dam power line and, when things were slack, drove throughout the region seeking fruit picking work for himself and Derroll's mother. Derroll's first interest in music came from listening to the Grand Ole Opry, which his parents always listened to on the car radio. He also enjoyed listening to the other fruit pickers sing when his parents were working. In time, Mrs. Adams bought her son a harmonica, his first instrument.

Later, the family settled in one place for a while and Derroll went to school. He wore cowboy clothes and identified with Buck Jones and other heroes of western movies.

After the Japanese bombed Pearl Harbor, Derroll, then 16, faked his age and enlisted in the Army. His parents found him and agreed to let him stay, but soon after he was given a minority discharge. Later in the year, he married a school classmate and succeeded in enlisting in the Coast Guard. He suffered a nervous breakdown, however, and tried to attack an officer with a knife. After spending some time in a naval hospital on Treasure Island, San Francisco, he was discharged, and stayed with his family for a while until his recovery was completed. From a blind lady, his mother bought him a banjo to occupy his time. Derroll managed to teach himself to play the instrument, but with some unorthodox methods of tuning.

In Portland in the late '40s he began to study art at Museum Art School, part of Reed College. In his spare time he tried many things, from drugs to joining the Vedanta Society. By now he had grown a beard to go with the earring he had affected in the service.

Politics now engrossed him. He held Marxist classes in his studio and became deeply interested in Henry Wallace's 1948 bid for the Presidency on the Progressive Party ticket. He had learned to play the banjo from listening to records and attending college concerts of such artists as Josh White. He now began to get performing experience singing such songs as "Little Brown Jug" and "I Don't Want Your Millions Mister" at Wallace rallies in the northwest.

After leaving his first wife, and marrying and breaking up with a second, he married again and headed for Mexico to study art. The journey was halted at San Diego, California, when it was found Derroll's wife was pregnant. For the next few years, Derroll supported his family with many jobs from taxiing Marines cross-country during the Korean War to driving a truck for Max Factor. A fellow driver helped bring him to the attention of a small Los Angeles booking agency, World Folk Artists. By now, Derroll had lost interest in politics, but was still painting and singing for his own pleasure.

He moved his family to Topanga Canyon, near Los Angeles. There he met many folk artists of note who lived nearby, including Bess and Butch Hawes, Woody Guthrie, and Jack Elliott. Adams' new acquaintances were deeply impressed with his ability as a performer and with some of his original songs. This helped encourage him to continue as a performer, resulting in an assignment to play banjo for the Elmer Bernstein sound track for the film "Durango." Derroll turned out a song titled "Portland Town" that became one of the folk standards of later years.

Derroll and Jack Elliott became close friends and singing partners. Until Elliott married and moved to Europe, the two traveled up and down the West Coast singing at many small spots. In 1957, Derroll was again single and accepted an invitation to join the Elliotts in Europe. There Derroll recorded some songs for the English Topic Records and spent many months on a performing tour throughout Europe with the Elliotts. He became one of the best known folk artists on the Continent though almost unknown in the U.S. outside folk artist circles.

Adams left the Elliotts and went on a drinking spree. After recovering, he moved to Paris where he met and married the daughter of a French aristocrat. Her family disowned her and they moved to Brussels, Belgium. There Derroll's new wife established a highly successful decorating business. In 1958, Derroll appeared in a sensationally successful engagement at the

Brussels World's Fair with the Elliotts. Other than that, however, he stopped performing and helped his wife run the business until the mid-1960s. Again, his marriage broke up, and by 1966 Derroll was once more showing audiences why he had achieved the status of a legend. He settled in England at this time, became a close friend of Donovan, and toured throughout the country. Trouble still followed him: some clubs banned him because of the off-color nature of some of his lyrics.

ADCOCK, EDDIE: *See* Country Gentlemen

ALLEN, REX: Singer, guitarist, fiddler, actor, songwriter. Born Willcox, Arizona, December 31, 1924.

The nickname "The Arizona Cowboy" was a natural one for Rex Allen. Unlike many actors who starred in western movies, he was raised in cattle country and spent some years after high school graduation as a ranch hand and rodeo contestant.

Rex was born and raised in Willcox, Arizona. He completed both grade and high school there. He learned to rope and ride as a normal part of growing up. Along with this came a love for cowboy songs and an early interest in learning to play guitar and fiddle. Rex began to take part in local rodeos while still in his teens. He also found a ready audience among fellow cowboys for his songs. By the time he neared his twenties, singing began to seem a more remunerative career than bulldogging or bronc riding.

Rex's travels took him to California, where he completed a course in electronics, and back east to New Jersey where he gained his first radio job on station WTTM, Trenton, during 1944-45. During the same period, he also performed on station WCAU in nearby Philadelphia, Pennsylvania. Rex quickly achieved local star stature which resulted in a bid to join the cast of the National Barn Dance in Chicago. From 1945 to 1950, Rex was a featured member of the cast. In 1949, though, he began to commute to Hollywood, where CBS had given him his own show. The Rex Allen Show became a national favorite in the early 1950s, ranking seventh nationally for the 1949-50 season.

Rex signed with Decca and had a number of songs on the best-seller lists in the 1950s. In 1953, he had a top 10 winner in "Crying in the Chapel." He was signed to a long term movie contract by Republic in 1950. Between 1950 and 1957, he was starred in 32 films for Republic. In the 1960s, he was featured in "For the Love of Mike" for Twentieth Century Fox, "Tomboy and the Champ," for Universal, and several Walt Disney films. His TV activities during the late 1950s and 1960s included regular status on the Town Hall Party show from Compton, California, guest shots on the Red Skelton Show and star billing on a TV series, Frontier Doctor.

Rex's LP albums for Decca included "Under Western Skies" and "Mister Cowboy" ('58). He switched to Mercury in the early 1960s and scored a national hit in 1962 with "Don't Go Near the Indians." In early 1962, Rex was represented on the Walt Disney Buena Vista label with "16 Favorite Songs." Later that year Mercury produced one LP, "Faith of a Man," and in 1963 turned out a second album, "Rex Allen Sings and Tells Tales." Some of the songs in the albums were part of Rex's songwriting total of more than 300 numbers.

Songs recorded by Rex during his career included "The Trail of the Lonesome Pine," "Old Faithful," "Invitation to the Blues," "Money, Marbles and Chalk," "Sleep Little Moses," "On Top of Old Smoky," "The Last Round-Up," "Softly and Tenderly," "Lonesome Valley," "Rarin' to Go," "Blue Dream," "Blue Light Waltz," "Little White Horse," "Durango," and "Flowers of San Antone."

ALLEN, ROSALIE: Singer, guitarist, disk jockey. Born Old Forge, Pennsylvania, June 27, 1924.

The east's gift to country and western, Rosalie Allen, became the "Queen of the Yodelers" over her family's vehement objections. She decided on a musical career at an early age, memorizing songs and lyrics from radio programs and records. An older brother had learned how to yodel and play the guitar and he, in turn, taught her.

In high school, Rosalie performed at school events. When she suggested earning a living at singing, her parents argued against it. First prize in an amateur contest when she was 17 made her sure she could succeed. Soon after, she was featured on a local radio station. This led to the chance to do weekend dates and one-night stands through most of the eastern states. On one of these tours, singer Denver Darling heard her and invited her to join his Denver Darling "Swing Billies" show on a New York station. She was featured on the show until it was disbanded due to World War II.

In July 1944, she was offered the chance to run her own show, which was well received and ran for several years. Later she was also a member of the Zeke Manners show which starred another yodeler, Elton Britt. This led to a number of recordings with Elton in the late '40s and early '50s on Victor, including "Soft Lips," "The Game of Broken Hearts," "Tennessee Yodel Polka" and "Tell Her You Love Her." In 1950, they had a best-seller in "Quicksilver." Rosalie's solo efforts on Victor included "Mountain Polka," "Rose of the Alamo," "Yodel Boogie" and the most popular of her renditions, "He Taught Me How to Yodel."

In the 1950s, she was often invited to the Grand Ole Opry TV show and also had her own show on a New York TV station. She also established a successful record shop, Rosalie Allen's Hillbilly Music Center. Her activities in the 1960s included running her own disk jockey show on WOV radio in New York.

ALMANAC SINGERS, THE: Vocal group, active in the early 1940s.

At the end of the 1930s many talented folk artists lived or entertained in New York. These performers, including Woody Guthrie, Lee Hays, and Burl Ives, had gravitated there from many parts of the U.S. The climate was not too favorable for folk music at the time and most had to work at other trades to make ends meet.

From this trying situation grew a new group called The Almanac Singers. It was a loosely knit gathering of fellow artists to gain the enjoyment of singing with each other and, in time, to present their songs before whatever audiences they could find to listen. The original members of the group included Pete Seeger (who called himself Pete Bowers at the time), Woody Guthrie, Lee Hays and Millard Lampell. During its early stages in New York, Burl Ives regularly joined the sessions.

After a while, the group decided to go across the U.S., singing on street corners, college campuses, or anywhere support could be found for their material. For roughly two years at the start of the '40s, the Almanacs crisscrossed the country on a number of informal tours. At various times they were joined by such other performers as Cisco Houston, Josh White, Bess Lomax (Hawes), Butch Hawes and Earl Robinson. Part of the time, the Almanacs consisted of only Pete Seeger and Woody Guthrie.

The group emphasized union songs, performing before many union organizations. They also sang anti-war songs until Hitler attacked Russia, at which time the emphasis switched to U.S. involvement. A good part of their material, though, was of traditional folk music. The group did record a number of albums during its brief period of existence. These included "Dear Mr. President," "Talking Union," "Sod Buster Ballads," and "Deep Sea Shanties." The albums are considered classics of the folk music genre of the mid-twentieth century.

U.S. entry into World War II resulted in the breakup of the Almanacs in 1942. Some of its members joined the armed forces, some enlisted in the Merchant Marine, and others returned home to help in the war effort. The group never reformed after the war, but it did serve as the forerunner of that great postwar group, The Weavers.

AMERICAN FOLK FESTIVAL (MOUNTAIN DANCE AND FOLK FESTIVAL): Annual festival presented at Asheville, North Carolina.

One of Bascom Lunsford's major contributions to America's folk heritage was the organization of the state festival at Asheville in 1928. Still functioning in the 1960s, this continued as one of the oldest such festivals in operation. Goal of the festival was to present traditional folk music and dances of America with restrictions against introduction of "popular" folk material.

The continued inroads of the post-World War II popular folk boom caused stresses on the festival concept. In the early 1960s, this led to a reorganization of the affair to try to minimize these outside influences. The Chamber of Commerce of Asheville assumed sponsorship with the help of a special advisory board. The original board members included Lunsford, Lunsford's son, the late Carl Sandburg, Alan Lomax, John Jacob Niles, Harry Golden, and Paul Green.

Over the years, the festival grew from a small local event to one in which hundreds of performers and crowds of 10,000 and more were the rule. Many major folk artists were introduced to the public here.

ANDERSON, BILL: Singer, guitarist, actor, songwriter. Born Columbia, South Carolina, November 1, 1937.

The 1960s might almost be called the Anderson Decade in country and western music. It's been a rare week when an Anderson song, recorded either by himself or by another major artist, has not been on the national country hit charts. At times, there have been two or three Anderson numbers on the charts at the same time.

Bill was born in South Carolina, but his family moved to Georgia when he was quite young. He spent his growing-up years in Decatur and Commerce, Georgia. He was already leading his own band and writing songs while in high school. He won a talent contest in Avondale High School with one of his compositions. He had already worked as a DJ on local stations when he entered the School of Journalism of the University of Georgia. While on the way to his B.A. degree in journalism, he continued to perform at local affairs and won one talent contest after another at school.

After graduating, Bill had a dual career for a while as performer and DJ and as a sports writer. By 1959, his air credits included spots on WEAS, Decatur; WBGE, Atlanta; and WQXI-TV, Atlanta. He worked as a scribe at the DeKalb *New Era* in Decatur, Georgia, and on the famed Atlanta *Constitution*. It was pretty certain, though, by the late 1950s, that Bill would concentrate on music. In 1958, a solid indication was the hit Ray Price scored with the Anderson song "City Lights." In 1959, Ray's record of Bill's "That's What It's Like to Be Lonesome" was a top 10 entry. Bill meanwhile had signed with Decca and his version of the last-named song also was a success.

Bill Anderson

From then on it was a series of hits in all areas for Anderson. He became both top country artist and songwriter as well. In 1960, he made the hit record of his song "Tips of My Fingers," and saw Jim Reeves' version of his "I Missed Me" reach the top 10 too. His 1961 roll included "Happy Birthday to Me" sung by Hank Locklin and Bill's records of "Po' Folks" and "Walk Out Backward." The following year, Kitty Wells and James O'Gwynn hit, respectively, with Bill's "We Missed You" and "My Name Is Mud." Bill hit the charts with his record of "Mama Sang a Song."

The year 1963 was a banner one for Anderson. Roy Clark was successful with a new record of "Tips of My Fingers" and Porter Wagoner scored with "I've Enjoyed as Much of This as I Can Stand." Bill's record output included "8 x 10," a song co-authored with Walter Haynes, and the number one hit, "Still." Anderson's 1964 successes included a rare song written by someone else, Alex Zanetis' "Me." Two other Anderson hits of this year were his record of "Five Little Fingers" and Roy Drusky's version of "Peel Me a Nanner." During 1965, records of an Anderson song, "Strangers," by two different artists, Merle Haggard and Roy Drusky, both were hits. Keeping his own hand in, Bill sang "Three A.M." to the top 10 list. Bill's 1966 hits were his own record of "I Love You Drops" and Connie Smith's "Nobody But a Fool."

Through the 1960s, Bill guested regularly on just about every major TV music show in the U.S. His own group, the Po' Boys, were signed to appear in all fifty states and Canada. In addition, Anderson's syndicated TV show was featured on stations throughout the country. Besides all this, Bill began a career in the movies, appearing in such films as "Country Music on Broadway," "Forty Acre Feud," "Las Vegas Hillbillies" and "The Road to Nashville."

Bill's talents were recognized by many major awards in the 1960s. These included Top Songwriter of the Year in C&W for 1963, '64, and '65; Top Male Vocalist of the Year for 1963; and Record of the Year for 1963.

ANGLIN, JACK: Singer, guitarist, songwriter. Born Columbia, Tennessee, May 13, 1916; died near Madison, Tennessee, March 8, 1963.

The team of Johnnie and Jack was one of the most popular country acts of the post-World War II period. The two members of the team were both Tennessee born and bred with strong family backgrounds in traditional country music. The closeness of Jack Anglin and Johnny Wright made them an inseparable act for more than two decades. It was only after Jack's untimely death that Johnny went on to establish a reputation as a solo performer.

Jack was born and raised in a town of 16,000 about fifty miles south of Nashville. His family and friends all were interested in country music sings and square dances and many were expert fiddlers, guitarists, and banjoists. Like most boys of his area, Jack was interested in learning a stringed instrument at an early age. He became a proficient guitarist by the time he was in his teens.

He continued to pick up experience at local dances and clubs as he grew toward manhood. In time, he headed to the big city, Nashville, for a try at a radio assignment. In 1936 he joined station WSIX, Nashville, where he met many other aspiring young performers, including Johnny Wright. Two years later, he and Johnny formed their own team. Eventually they added their own musical group, The Tennessee Mountain Boys.

Johnnie and Jack toured many parts of the south and played on many radio stations during the '40s, including WCHS, Charleston, West Virginia; WEAS, Decatur, Georgia; WPTF, Raleigh, North Carolina; and WAPI, Birmingham, Alabama. The group was temporarily sidetracked by World War II, but came back strong in the late 1940s. In 1949, Johnnie and Jack began to gain national attention when they joined the cast of the KWKH Louisiana Hayride in Shreveport.

In the early 1950s, the team was asked to join the Grand Ole Opry. Over the rest of the decade they scored many national hits, many of which were their own compositions. Their best sellers included "Crying Heart Blues," "Poison Love" ('51); "Beware of It," "Goodnight, Sweetheart, Goodnight," "I Get So Lonely" ('54); "South of New Orleans" ('53); and "The Moon Is High and So Am I." RCA Victor featured the boys on a number of LPs, including "Hits of Johnnie and Jack" ('60); "Johnnie and Jack" ('63); "Sincerely."

During the 1950s and early 1960s, the boys toured all parts of the country and guested on most of the top network country and western shows. Their song output during this period exceeded 100 original compositions. In 1963, Jack Anglin's career was abruptly ended when he was killed in an automobile crash while on the way to funeral services for Patsy Cline and three other Grand Ole Opry stars killed in a plane crash.

APO, PETE: *See* Travelers 3

APPALACHIAN DULCIMER (MOUNTAIN DULCIMER): Musical instrument.

Though not as common as the guitar or fiddle, the dulcimer has long been an important instrument in the folk and country music field. The term dulcimer in this case, however, does not refer to the classic European dulcimer, but to a completely different instrument.

Outside of the fact that both are stringed instruments, there is little resemblance between the two. The classic European dulcimer consists of a flat box with many metal wires stretched across the top. The wires are attached to adjustment pegs along the sides and are played by being struck with small wooden or cork mallets. This form of dulcimer, which is of ancient origin—the Persians or Arabians are credited with its invention—is a direct forerunner of the piano.

The Appalachian (also called mountain or American) dulcimer is a smaller instrument usually with only three or four strings. (Mountain dulcimers have been made, however, with five or six strings.) The strings are plucked instead of hammered and are tightened by pegs in the instrument's scroll. A feature of the mountain dulcimer is a long hollowed fret block extending the length of the instrument and serving as part of the sound box.

The body of the mountain dulcimer is long and narrow with flat top and bottom. The flatness of these surfaces provides one point of similarity to the classic dulcimer. The contour of these surfaces varies. Most recent ones are roughly in the form of an elongated hourglass, but others are used that are of diamond or oval shape.

The origins of the mountain dulcimer are obscure. Many experts believe it is of European origin, possibly from Scandinavia. However, the absence of concrete references to this type of instrument in ancient documents leads some experts to feel it is of American origin.

The hammered dulcimer has been used in hill country music in the past. However, the use of this form of dulcimer has been very limited compared to the mountain or Appalachian instrument.

ARIZONA COWBOY, THE: *See* Allen, Rex

ARKANSAS FOLK FESTIVAL: Folk festival held in April in Mountain View, Arkansas.

The first annual Arkansas Folk Festival was held in 1963. Producer of the festival was Jimmy Driftwood, aided by the Rackensack Folklore Society. The Society title is derived from the Indian word for the Arkansas River. As Driftwood pointed out in reviewing the festival in Sing Out!, Sam Houston's pet name for this part of the Ozark Mountains was "Land of the Rackensack."

The first festival in the region was held in 1941, but the effort was abandoned because of World War II. The idea remained dormant until Driftwood and other folk artists and enthusiasts helped revive it in the early '60s. Though new in point of time, the goal of the founders was to preserve the folk music heritage of the region. For example, amplified instruments, bass fiddles, and drums are specifically barred.

Talking of the '66 concert, Driftwood wrote in Sing Out! (April/May '66, p. 14), "There will be ballad singing, old time revival singing, Sacred Harp, Christian Harmony, fiddling—both picking and bow, banjo frailers, pickers and thumpers, mandolin ticklers, guitar strummers, and occasional tunes from the gourd, dulcimer, and the jawbone of the wild jackass. There will be early American play-party games and old time square dances. And when the 'fiddle gets tickled' there will be spontaneous jig dancing like you never saw before. . . ."

Performers at the event include many amateur artists and groups as well as some better known performers such as Driftwood and Glenn Ohrlin. Among the traditional singers who have sung at the festival and also provided material to folklorists are Ollie Gilbert, Neal Morris, Bookmiller Shannon, Absie Morrison and Almeda Riddle. A typical local group at one of the events was the banjo picking Vergil Johnson family, including three generations from Mr. and Mrs. Johnson to their grandchildren. The more than 100 members of the Rackensack Folklore Society, which Driftwood helped organize, also are a regular part of the program.

In 1966, Congress, impressed by a Washington concert of the Society, appropriated $1,-431,000 to construct a Folk Cultural Center of America in Mountain View. A parcel of

1,000 acres in the Ozark National Forest region was purchased as the site for the new facility.

ARKIN, ALAN: Actor, songwriter, singer, guitarist, teacher. Born Brooklyn, New York, March 26, 1934.

In the 1960s, Alan Arkin was best known as one of the most promising new performers in movies and on the stage. During the 1950s and early 1960s, though, he was better known for his important contributions to folk music as a performer and arranger.

He was born and spent most of his early years in Brooklyn. When it came time to go to college, however, he wandered farther afield, spending time at Bennington College in Vermont and Los Angeles City College and Los Angeles State in California. By the time he was in college, he had gained some knowledge of folk music partly from records and reading. He also found time to learn to play the guitar.

He returned to New York in the mid-1950s and worked as an arranger as well as a folk artist. Elektra Records put out an LP album of his singing, "Folksongs—Once Over Lightly," that included such songs as "A Knave Is a Knave," "Kisses Sweeter Than Wine," "Tom-With-A-Grin," "Crawdad Song," "Colorado Trail," "Tobacco Union," "Great Grandad" and "Ann Boleyn." When Erik Darling formed The Tarriers folk quartet in 1956, Arkin was one of the members. For the next few years he toured with the group and sang in many of the eastern states and Canadian provinces as well as some European countries. For two years he sang with The Tarriers and also did much of their arranging.

When The Tarriers broke up in the late 1950s, Arkin spent more time acting while also studying music and teaching a course on basic theory and folk guitar. As time went on, acting became his main endeavor and he joined the Compass Theatre in St. Louis and the Second City group in Chicago. When the Second City moved to a lengthy engagement in New York in 1961, Arkin was one of the major performers. By now he was receiving close attention from Broadway directors and producers. He soon won major roles in two Broadway comedy hits, "Enter Laughing" and "Luv." His work in "Luv" won him nationwide notice and bids to play in important movie roles. When his contract for "Luv" was up, he was quickly signed by Hollywood. In a short time he gained widespread critical approval for his performance in the 1966 movie hit, "The Russians Are Coming, The Russians Are Coming!" For his performance in this film, he was nominated for an Oscar in the Best Actor category.

Arkin also found time over the years to write music. His output included background music for two plays and a number of songs, including "Cuddle Bug," "That's Me," and "Best Time of the Year."

ARNOLD, EDDY: Singer, guitarist, songwriter, Born near Henderson, Tennessee, May 15, 1918. Elected to Country Music Hall of Fame, 1966.

If anyone could lay claim to the title of king of country and western music, it would have to be Eddy Arnold. No one dominated any segment of popular music the way Eddy did from the late 1940s through the 1960s. Over more than two decades, despite changing public moods, his efforts were as sure to gain hit status as in the first years of success. More than that, by the mid-1960s he had moved beyond the country and western field to recognition as one of the nation's top popular entertainers.

Eddy came by his nickname of "The Tennessee Plowboy" naturally. Born and raised in rural Tennessee, he performed farm chores from his boyhood. In later years, he continued to maintain interest in farming with his own large operation in Brentwood, Tennessee. He began to show interest in music while he was in Henderson Elementary School. His father was an old-time fiddler and encouraged Eddy's efforts to learn the guitar when the boy was ten.

When Eddy entered Pinson High School there, he quickly showed his skill as both singer and guitarist. He had to leave high school, however, in the early 1930s to help on his family's farm. For a while, music was mainly a sideline. He played for local affairs, riding to and from the events on a mule with his guitar slung on his back, but earned his living as a farmer and an assistant in a mortuary.

Gradually, however, Eddy's talent brought more and more chances to perform. In 1936, he made his radio debut on a Jackson, Tennessee, station. In the early 1940s, he rapidly became one of the most popular artists in his part of Tennessee. In 1942, he joined WTJS radio station in Jackson, Tennessee. For six years he was one of the top features of the station. By the late 1940s, Eddy was rapidly achieving national attention from his first records with RCA Victor. He soon had star status on such programs as the Grand Ole Opry.

Eddy's popularity snowballed as the decade came to an end. Almost every record he turned out made the hit charts and most made the top 10. From 1948 to 1952, it wasn't unusual for two or three of his records to be in the top 10 at the same time.

In 1948, he had no less than nine top 10 records, five of which were ranked number one for several weeks each. Eddy showed his multi-faceted talent by writing or co-writing many of these early hits. His 1948 output included "I'll Hold You in My Heart" (written with Horton and T. Dilbeck); number-one-ranked "Just a Little Lovin' Will Go a Long Way" (written with Zeke Clements) and "Then I Turned and Walked Slowly Away" (co-writer, Fortner). Other 1948 hits included number-one songs "A Heart Full of Love," "Bouquet of Roses,"

"Any Time," "Texarkana Baby" and top 10 hits "My Daddy Is Only a Picture" and "What a Fool I Was to Cry Over You."

The 1949 hit lists included such Arnold co-authored songs as "C-H-R-I-S-T-M-A-S," "I'm Throwing Rice at the Girl I Love," "One Kiss Too Many," and "Will Santa Come to Shanty Town." Other '49 hits included number-one-ranked "Don't Rob Another Man's Castle," "Show Me the Way to Your Heart," "The Echo of Your Footsteps" and "There's Not a Thing I Wouldn't Do for You." Eddy's 1950 hit roster included "Cuddle Buggin' Baby," "Love-bug Itch," "Mama and Daddy Broke My Heart," "Take Me in Your Arms and Hold Me," "Why Should I Cry" and "Enclosed, One Broken Heart."

As the 1950s went by, Eddy continued to turn out chart-making songs with monotonous regularity. In 1951, he had such number-one-

Eddy Arnold displays several dozen of his albums, an array that indicates why he was elected to the Country Music Hall of Fame in 1966.

[13]

ranked songs as "Kentucky Waltz," "There's Been a Change in Me," and "I Want to Play House with You." In top 10 ranks were "Heart Strings," "May the Good Lord Bless and Keep You," "Somebody's Been Beating My Time" and "Something Old, Something New." The following year, Eddy scored with an original composition, "Easy on the Eyes." His other 1952 hits included "Bundle of Southern Sunshine," "Full Time Job" and "Older and Bolder." His other hits of the 1950s included number-one-ranked "Eddy's Song," "Mama, Come Get Your Baby Boy" ('53), "Hep Cat Baby," "I Really Don't Want to Know," "My Everything," "This Is the Thanks I Get" ('54); number-one-ranked "Cattle Call," "I've Been Thinking," "Richest Man," "That Do Make It Nice," "Two Kinds of Love" ('55); "Trouble in Mind," "You Don't Know Me" ('56); and "Tennessee Stud" ('59).

During the 1950s Eddy's name became known to more and more people outside country and western music. He was a featured guest on such network TV shows as Arthur Godfrey, Milton Berle, Perry Como, Bob Hope and Dinah Shore. He was also in demand for engagements in all parts of the country at everything from county fairs to major nightclubs. Eddy also had his own show for several years on NBC and ABC networks. He also was starred in a syndicated TV series, Eddy Arnold Time.

The Arnold magic remained as good in the 1960s as it had been the previous decade. He turned out several dozen chart hits from 1961 to 1967. These included such top 10 successes as "A Little Heartache," "After Loving You," "Tears Broke Out on Me" ('62); "I Thank My Lucky Stars," "Molly" ('64); "Make the World Go Away," "What's He Doing in My World" (both number-one-ranked hits) ('65); number-one-ranked "I Want to Go with You," "The Last Word in Lonesome Is Me," "Tips of My Fingers," "Somebody Like Me" ('66).

Eddy's single-record success was naturally duplicated in LP sales as well. His best-selling RCA Victor albums included "Any Time"; "All Time Favorites"; "Chapel on the Hill"; "Wanderin' "; "Dozen Hits"; "Praise Him, Praise Him" ('58); "Eddy Arnold," "Have Guitar, Will Travel," "Thereby Hangs" ('59); "More of Eddy Arnold," "Sings Them Again," "You Gotta Have Love" ('60); "Memories" ('61); "One More Time" ('62); "Country Songs," "Cattle Call,"

"Our Man Down South" ('63); "Folk Song Book," "Eddy's Songs," "Sometimes I'm Happy," "Pop Hits" ('64); "I Want to Go with You," "My World," "The Last Word in Lonesome" ('66).

Eddy's personal appearances in the 1960s took him to all fifty states and throughout the world. He continued to be a regular visitor to many major network TV shows. His stature was illustrated again in October, 1967, when sellout crowds greeted his first engagement in Los Angeles' famed Cocoanut Grove.

ASH GROVE: Coffee house, center of folk music entertainment in the Los Angeles area.

During the great vogue of coffee houses in the late 1950s and early '60s, probably well over a thousand came into existence across the country. These all played an important part in the development of folk music during these years. The listing of even the most important of these usually short-lived spots would require a book in itself, and is not properly a part of this Encyclopedia.

The Ash Grove, however, would seem to merit special mention because it has been more of an institution than a place. In fact, a number of folk songs have been written either about the Ash Grove or mentioning it in passing.

The Ash Grove was founded on July 15, 1958, by Edward Pearl. Located in a section of small shops on Melrose Avenue, it was almost unnoticeable to passing strollers or motorists. With no marquee and few distinguishing features in front, it became known by word of mouth as the mecca of true folk music in the Los Angeles area. As John Cohen noted in Sing Out! ("The Ash Grove Saga, or 'The Perils of Pearl,'" July 1964, p. 45), "By virtue of its tenacity rather than its commercial success, (it) is now the oldest club in the area under continuous management." Three years later, when most coffee houses had long since disappeared, it was still presenting artists ranging from Flatt & Scruggs to Brownie McGhee and Sonny Terry to local audiences.

The importance of Pearl's enterprise was its presence in the area as a stable source of good folk entertainment. This helped provide a prop to the careers of many rising young artists, as well as seasoned folk performers just coming to public attention.

In the first few years of its existence, the Ash Grove presented such artists as McGhee and

Terry, Guy Carawan, Bud and Trav, Jesse Fuller, Sam Hinton. Stan Wilson, Bess Lomax Hawes, and Lou Gottlieb. By the end of its first decade of life, the Ash Grove had played host to almost every artist of note in the folk field as well as many important names in the country music field. The country artists featured in the '60s included Mother Maybelle Carter, Flatt & Scruggs, Doc Watson, Bill Monroe and Roscoe Holcomb.

The blues also received continued attention from the Ash Grove. Such performers as Bessie Jones, Mance Lipscomb, Joe Williams, the Gospel Pearls, Memphis Slim and many others played to enthusiastic audiences over the years.

As Cohen noted, during its lifetime the Ash Grove ranked as the greatest employer of folk talent in the west.

ASHWORTH, ERNIE: Singer, guitarist, songwriter. Born Huntsville, Alabama, December 15, 1928.

Ernest "Ernie" Ashworth was born in the town that spawned America's first satellite and the boosters that will take man to the moon. For a time it was touch and go whether Ernie would become a country and western star or a member of the U.S. military booster program.

At the time of Ernie's birth, of course, the space age had not yet arrived. Huntsville was a sleepy southern town where the greatest noise resulted from country music. Contributing to this sound were many of Ernie's relatives in Huntsville and, before long, little Ernie was being taught the basics of guitar playing. By the time he was high school age, he was good enough to play on local stations in Huntsville.

When Ernie reached his twenties, he felt he was ready for the big time and moved to Nashville. Things looked good for him when he was signed to work on station WSIX radio and TV. He also won many club dates for his band. Some of the major country artists also took note of some of Ernie's compositions. Both Carl Smith and Little Jimmy Dickens recorded Ernie's songs in 1954. The next year, Wesley Rose of Acuff-Rose Publishing Company won an MGM recording contract for Ernie. Ernie made a number of records for MGM under the name Billy Worth.

But then things slowed down for him. His records were not selling well and club dates were hard to find. Finally, in 1957, he moved back to his home town to take a job in the

Army missile program at Redstone Arsenal. For the next three years, music became only a spare time thing for Ernie. Wesley Rose had faith in him, though, and won Ernie a second chance in 1960 recording for Decca. This time the fates smiled and Ernie scored a top hit with his first Decca single, "Each Moment." He followed with another top 10 number of 1960, "You Can't Pick a Rose in December." Two other records were hits, just missing the top 10 bracket in nationwide charts.

In 1962, Ernie moved over to Hickory Records. The first Hickory disk, "Everybody But Me," was a hit as was his next one, the 1963 "I Take the Chance." In 1963, Ernie finally hit the number one spot with "Talk Back Tremblin' Lips." The song was one of the gold record hits of the year and stayed on the charts for 36 weeks. One welcome result was a bid to join the Grand Ole Opry cast in March 1964. He also won the Most Promising C&W Artist award two years running, 1963 and '64, from both Billboard and Cashbox.

His 1964 hits included "A Week in the Country" and "I Love to Dance with Annie." In 1965, he made the top 10 with "The DJ Cried." Other Ashworth hits include "Pushed in a Corner," "Because I Cared," "Sad Face," and "At Ease, Heart." Ernie's first movie effort, "The Farmer's Other Daughter," was released in 1965. By the mid-1960s, Ernie was in demand for personal appearances in all the U.S. states. He also was roundly applauded in engagements in major cities of Canada and Germany. By 1967, his TV credits included not only Grand Ole Opry, but such shows as Porter Wagoner's, Wilburn Brothers, Flatt & Scruggs, Bobby Lord and the American Swing-Around.

ATCHER, BOB: Singer, guitarist, songwriter, m.c. Born Hardin County, Kentucky, May 11, 1914.

The country music king of the Chicago area for many years was James Robert Owen "Bob" Atcher. Atcher came by his country music abilities in the normal course of events, since his family had a rich Kentucky folk heritage. His grandparents knew many hill country ballads and used to sing them to their little grandson, and his father was a local fiddle champion.

The boy was precocious—so much so that his father traded a coon dog to buy Bob a guitar when he was only four. While still grade school age, Bob accompanied his father and three brothers at local square dances and other mountain functions. Bob's intelligence showed in other ways besides music. He had the educational background to qualify for Kentucky State University when only fourteen. He attended for several years as a pre-med student. However, he abandoned medicine for a chance to sing on station WHAS in Louisville.

He soon began to receive bids to work in many major midwest cities. In addition, his composing abilities resulted in records of his music by a number of entertainers in the mid-1930s. In 1938, Bob accepted an offer to sing on station WBBM, Chicago, starting a long relationship between the Windy City and the Kentucky artist. Bob remained in Chicago, gaining an ever wider audience during the five year period 1938-43. He also signed with Columbia, turning out many successful disks for them over the next few decades.

His career was interrupted by Army service in World War II. During his 25-month hitch in the Pacific Theater, he sang for the Armed Forces Network and performed in many shows at hospitals and military bases. In 1946 he returned to Chicago, starring first on radio and then, during the late 1940s and throughout the 1950s, as one of Chicago's favorite TV artists.

Atcher's repertoire ranged from pure folk music to popular and country and western. One of Columbia's albums of the early 1950s was "Early American Folk Songs," including such numbers as "De Ladies Man," "Methodist Pie," "Old Smoky," "Young Rogers, the Miller" and "The Hunters of Kentucky." Another album of this period was "Songs of the Saddle," including such classic western ballads as "Home on the Range," "Strawberry Roan," "Red River Valley," "Little Joe the Wrangler," "Bury Me Not on the Old Prairie," "The Cowboy's Dream" and "The Old Chisholm Trail." In early 1965, Columbia turned out an LP of many of Atcher's hits called "Bob Atcher."

Some of Atcher's other recordings, including some of his own compositions, were "Money, Marbles and Chalk," "Time Alone," "Don't Let Your Sweet Love Die," "Tennessee Border," "Don't Rob Another Man's Castle," "The Warm Red Wine," "Why Don't You Haul Off and Love Me," "You Are My Sunshine," "Walkin' the Floor Over You," and "Foggy, Foggy Dew." Atcher also recorded for Capitol, including such songs as "Peek-A-Boo," "Chain Around My Heart," and "Ain't You Ashamed."

ATKINS, CHET: Guitarist, composer, recording manager, singer. Born Luttrell, Tennessee, June 20, 1924.

From the Clinch Mountain country near Knoxville, Tennessee, Chet Atkins went on to international fame. Atkins' early years were spent in and around his home town of Luttrell where his father gave piano and voice lessons. The wind-up phonograph in the house had its store of Jimmie Rodgers records and it was music that filled the home a good part of the day.

By the time he had finished high school Atkins had acquired respectable proficiency on the guitar—somewhere along the way he traded an old pistol for his first one—and was broadcasting from WNOX, a twenty-mile run from Luttrell. He played with Bill Carlisle and also filled in with a group billed as the Dixieland Swingsters. He stayed in the Knoxville area for three years. He then played jobs on the radio circuit, as a solo act or as part of a band, on such stations as WLW, Cincinnati; WPTF, Raleigh, North Carolina; WRVA, Richmond, Virginia; KWTO, Springfield, Missouri; and KOA, Denver, Colorado.

RCA Victor's man in charge of country music—it was called hillbilly then—was Steve Sholes. Sholes heard Atkins on a Mutual radio show that originated in Springfield, but was unable to locate him immediately as Atkins kept going from one radio station job to another. Si Siman of KWTO sent a transcription of one show on which Atkins played guitar to Al Hindle, who ran the custom records business out of Chicago for RCA Victor.

Hindle forwarded the transcription to Sholes in New York who recognized both the name and the performance and knew he had finally located Atkins. In Atkins' words:

"By that time I had been fired in Springfield and was working KOA in Denver with Shorty Thompson and his Rangers. Steve called me and asked if I wanted to record for RCA and I said sure. He mailed me a contract. A couple of months later on I mortgaged my car, borrowed some money, and went to Chicago where I met Steve and we recorded—two sessions in one day, one morning, one afternoon—eight sides."

What is not generally known is that five of the eight songs were vocal cuts by Atkins. Three were instrumentals. The vocals included "I'm Gonna Get Tight," "Standing Room

Symphony conductor Arthur Fiedler of the Boston Pops and Chet Atkins work out arrangement for their RCA Victor collaboration, "The 'Pops' Goes Country."

Only," and "Don't Hand Me That Line." Atkins liked the instrumentals more than the vocal efforts. He has quietly broken each vocal master he could find since then.

The instrumentals, "Canned Heat," "Bug Dance," and "Nashville Jump," received good airplay but limited sales and it was not until 1949 that sales started to increase with releases of "Gallopin' Guitar," "Main St. Breakdown," "Country Gentleman," and others.

It was around this time that he started working with the Carter Family and moved with them to Nashville and the Grand Ole Opry. His first appearance on the Opry had been in 1946 with Red Foley.

Atkins recalls another incident of that first

Chicago session. Sholes had asked Hindle to find a good rhythm guitar player to back Atkins. Hindle came up with the legendary George Barnes, one of Atkins' idols. The youngster felt all thumbs trying to play with Barnes watching him.

Sholes started using Atkins around 1949 as studio guitarist for RCA Victor sessions in Nashville. Atkins would offer a few softly expressed suggestions here and there which always turned out very well and to which all the other musicians listened attentively.

Atkins was made a part-time producer for RCA Victor in Nashville in 1957 for Sholes, whose Nashville operation consisted of a small studio and office. Atkins, Juanita Jones, his secretary (who now heads the ASCAP office in Nashville), and engineer Jeff Miller combined with Sholes to help further the "Nashville sound" of the era. Later that year Atkins was made full-time manager when Sholes was promoted to pop A&R in New York.

"The hit artists Chet's found for us," according to Sholes, "include Don Gibson, Floyd Cramer, Connie Smith, Dottie West, etc. (Don't forget he got Roger Miller on the label, Boots Randolph, Roy Orbison—but you never know at what point in their careers an artist will hit.) Although I was lucky enough to bring Jim Reeves in, Chet did all the successful recordings with him.

"Chet plays finger-style guitar. He doesn't pick, he just *touches* the strings, pushes down on them and lets his fingers up—except for his thumb—he has a pick on his thumb and that's generally for the bass strings. He can play other styles too—Spanish, classical, everything else. But the style that first got me intrigued was his finger-style playing. I had never heard it before. There are few people who play that way now."

Finally settled in Nashville, Atkins proved a worthy successor to Sholes. He still managed to play personal engagements, in addition to recording a roster of more than 40 artists for RCA Victor, and appeared in Europe, where he is recognized as an eminent jazz guitarist. He performed as guest soloist with the Atlanta Symphony, Nashville Symphony, the 1960 Newport Jazz Festival and at the Press Photographers' Ball at the White House in 1961 for the late President John F. Kennedy.

Slender and silent, Atkins is the subject of many anecdotes in the country music business. His reticence to elaborate beyond minimal communication catches many city hucksters off guard. One New York music publisher sent a representative to Atkins to play some demos for recording consideration. The downcast man returned to New York to report Atkins' reaction to one song in particular. "All he said was that he liked it," he sighed, "and I pitched him on it for fifteen minutes, really pitched hard." The New York publisher just smiled. The record that resulted was Hank Locklin's "Please Help Me, I'm Falling," a world-wide hit.

If not verbose, Atkins listens closely along with studying the speaker's eyes and mannerisms. He applies the same concentration to his

studies of music, history, philosophy, poetry, psychology and physics, tempering a natural tendency toward strong convictions with a self-taught tolerance.

His knowledge of physics has resulted in a new concept for an instrument to aid guitarists. The invention is of the "electronic brain" principle which he has tagged a "magic bass." It plays the precise bass note at the right time without need for foot pedals or button pushing. He has a complete personal sound studio in his home where, when time allows, he works on his guitar techniques, researches new material, and tinkers with the equipment.

His researches into electronics are closely watched by country artists as a portent of the future in country music in the same way that Atkins' past activities helped form the patterns of the 1960s.

AUTOHARP: Musical instrument; derived from the harp.

The harp is considered by most experts to be the oldest of the stringed instruments. Murals, stone friezes, and other remnants from ancient times show musicians playing harps of one form or another. The frame of a 4,500-year-old harp from ancient Sumeria, a culture that existed in the southern Euphrates Valley, has been unearthed by archaeologists.

Early harps were relatively small so that they could be held in the lap or cradled in the performers' arms to play while walking or standing up. From the ninth century A.D. on, European instrument makers gradually increased the harp size until the large in-place instrument usually associated with the name today was derived. However, small harp designs continued to be built by instrument makers in rural areas. In the 1800s, one form of the small harp called the autoharp was made in several parts of the Appalachian region.

Though not a widely used instrument, the autoharp continued to be favored by some highly skilled rural artists throughout the first four decades of the twentieth century. One of those who performed widely with the autoharp was Maybelle Carter of the famed Carter Family. As traditional music began to be overwhelmed by the advances of the technological age, the instrument seemed in danger of extinction. However, with the folk song revival of the post-World War II period, a number of major artists, the Seegers in particular, brought

the autoharp to the attention of both audiences and performers.

Mike Seeger used the autoharp on many of his recordings of the 1950s and '60s. In addition, he collected tapes of country artists for a Folkways LP, "Mountain Music Played on the Autoharp."

The autoharp consists of a series of 40 to 50 metal wires secured at one end and fastened to movable tuning pegs at the other end of the frame. A series of chord bars are attached across the lower part of the frame. In the Appalachian Autoharp produced by one company in the 1960s, 15 of these chord bars were used. Pressing on the button for a particular chord bar controls the strings so that moving a pick across them produces the desired sound. The autoharp's strings are stretched across a frame that is positioned over a sound box that operates like that of a guitar or violin, rather than the open-string arrangement of the conventional harp.

AUTRY, GENE: Singer, guitarist, songwriter, actor, business executive. Born Tioga, Texas, September 29, 1907.

Few entertainers in any field can say they own a major-league ball club, and fewer still can claim to have a town named for them. Orvon "Gene" Autry can note both distinctions and more besides: he is owner of a chain of radio stations and hotels, interests in newspapers, TV films, etc. All of these were the fruits of a talent few other western performers were blessed with.

In his boyhood, the idea of a music career hardly occurred to him. Gene naturally heard cowboy songs and country musicians during the years he was growing up in Texas and Oklahoma. He was born in Texas, but spent some years in Oklahoma before graduating from Tioga, Texas, High School in 1925. Though he learned some western songs over these years, music as a profession was far from his mind when he took his first job after high school. He signed on as a railroad telegraph operator and began work in Sepulpa, Oklahoma.

As he later noted, a night job such as this is lonely, with long hours between messages. To while the time away, he bought a guitar and learned to play it. One night, a stranger came in to write a telegram while Gene was playing. The man waited until Autry finished the song, then said, "Young feller, all I can say is that you're wasting your time here. You ought to quit and try radio." The name on the telegram sheet was Will Rogers.

Gene took this advice and soon after gained a job with station KVOO as "Oklahoma's Singing Cowboy." The audience took to him and he became known beyond state borders by 1929. That year, he was signed to make several cowboy records, among the first cowboy songs ever recorded, for the old American Record Company. One of the firm's labels on which Gene was featured was Okeh. In 1930, Gene was given his own program on station WLS, Chicago. He rapidly became one of the best known artists in the midwest, remaining on WLS until 1934.

By the start of the 1930s, Gene was recording both traditional cowboy material and new songs of his own. One of his first original compositions in 1931 was "That Silver Haired Daddy of Mine." The song was one of the top hits of the early 1930s and sold over 5 million copies in succeeding years. From 1930 on, Gene wrote more than 250 songs, including such other hits as "You're the Only Star in My Blue Heaven" and "Dust" in 1938; "Tears on My Pillow" and "Be Honest with Me" in 1941; "Tweedle O Twill" ('42); and "Here Comes Santa Claus" ('48).

In 1934, Gene moved to Hollywood to act in his first film. This was a bit singing role in a Ken Maynard western, "In Old Santa Fe." After this, Gene rapidly became a star in his own right, pioneering the singing western. By the end of the 1950s, he had been seen by untold millions in film audiences all over the world in 82 feature-length musical westerns; by 1968 the total exceeded 100. His popularity was enhanced throughout the '30s by personal appearances in all parts of the world. These included another first, the initial appearance of a movie cowboy as star of the World Championship Rodeo in New York's Madison Square Garden. During the '30s, he was also honored by having the town of Gene Autry, Oklahoma, named for him.

When World War II broke out, he enlisted in the Army Air Corps as a technical sergeant on July 26, 1942. His service career took him to the Far East as a flight commander and first pilot. For some time with the Air Transport Command he ferried planes, cargo, and supplies to India, North Africa, and Burma. After his discharge on June 17, 1945, he returned to Hollywood to resume an even more dynamic career.

He made new movies and also soon had his own network radio show, Melody Ranch, that remained one of the top features into the 1950s. Its TV successor of the same title was still going strong at the end of the 1960s.

Until the mid-1940s, Gene continued to record for the Okeh label. His output included such songs as "Mexicali Rose," "I'll Go Riding Down That Texas Trail," "Louisiana Moon," "The Yellow Rose of Texas," "El Rancho Grande," "I'll Never Let You Go, Little Darlin'," "Deep in the Heart of Texas," and "Maria Elena."

In the late 1940s, Gene signed with Columbia Records. Among the dozens of records he made for that label in the 1940s and '50s were several that became all-time standards. These included such top 10 hits as "Buttons and Bows" and "Here Comes Santa Claus" ('48); "Rudolph the Red Nosed Reindeer" ('49); "Frosty the "Snow Man" and "Peter Cottontail." These and other best-sellers in his list of LP albums included, in the 1960s, "Greatest Hits" (Columbia—'61); "Golden Hits" (RCA Victor—'62); and "Great Hits" (Harmony—'65).

During the 1950s, while continuing his entertaining activities in movies, records, and TV, Gene began to move into many other fields. He started to put together a chain of stations that, by 1962, included KOOL-TV, Phoenix; KOLD-TV, Tucson; KSFO, San Francisco; and KMPC, Los Angeles. He also became head of his own record firm, Challenge Records, and established a TV production company, Flying A Productions. In the early 1960s, he performed in a series of 52 half-hour TV shows for Flying A. He also had many other endeavors, including a hotel chain, music publishing firm, etc.

At the start of the 1960s, Gene combined forces with sportsman Bob Reynolds to bid for an expansion franchise in the American League. In 1962, their bid was accepted and Gene was part owner of the Los Angeles Angels. In 1966, he proudly took part in ceremonies opening the Angels' new stadium in Anaheim, California.

BAEZ, JOAN: Folksinger, guitarist. Born Staten Island, New York, January 9, 1941.

In 1960, Vanguard records issued the first LP of a new folk artist and was surprisingly snowed under with orders in a short time. Titled "Joan Baez," it rocketed this quiet 20-year-old to national stardom. Vanguard officials could still say, several years later, "It is the highest-selling individual female folk album in the history of long-playing records."

The girl who was to be called "Queen of the Folksingers" blends Latin and Anglo-Saxon ancestry. Her father, physicist Dr. Albert V. Baez, was born in Mexico and her mother, Joan, was the daughter of an Episcopal minister who also taught dramatics. Her parents had great interest in classical music, but young Joan was rebellious and refused to take piano lessons. At 12, though, she took up the guitar, but not for folk music. Instead, she became a rock 'n' roll addict. She did show wider musical interest in high school in Palo Alto, California, to which the family moved when Dr. Baez changed jobs. She was an A student in music and also sang in the school choir.

The family moved back across country in early 1958 just after Joan was graduated from high school. Dr. Baez now taught at MIT. He took his daughter to Tulla's Coffee Grinder coffee house one evening and Joan decided folk music was her main interest. Though she enrolled in Boston University Fine Arts School of Drama, she soon left to concentrate on folk singing. One of her first songs was "House of the Rising Sun." Gradually, she built up her repertoire and began to sing in local coffee houses, including the Golden Vanity, Ballad Room, and Club 47. Her name became well known, but, still strong willed, she turned down an offer from Harry Belafonte to join his troupe.

A brief appearance at the Gate of Horn Club in Chicago resulted in a bid from folksinger Bob Gibson for her to appear at the 1959 Newport Folk Festival. Her name was not on the program, but she won wild applause from the Newport crowd and also started close friendships with Odetta, The Weavers, and the Seeger family. Record offers came, but Joan turned them down, to go back to Boston coffee houses. After another successful appearance at the 1960 Newport Folk Festival, though, she finally signed with Vanguard.

After the reception of her first album, she was in demand all over the U.S. In 1961, she went on a triumphal tour of college campuses and concert halls, receiving critical acclaim everywhere. Despite this, Joan has refused to follow the usual success pattern, limiting her personal appearances and turning down bids for TV shows, movies, and nightclub stints. In 1963, she was one of the artists who refused to appear on ABC-TV's Hootenanny unless Pete Seeger was invited. In the mid-1960s she was the center of controversy about her refusal to pay part of her federal income tax because of opposition to the Vietnam War.

In 1961, Joan Baez moved to California, living first in a rough cabin at Point Sur and later in a more conventional home in Carmel. She continued to limit her performances, spending more time in free appearances at charity events, UNESCO affairs, and civil rights rallies than in concert halls. Her goal was to keep concert tours down to two months in the year and record-making to one LP a year. Her LPs include "Joan Baez, Volume 2," "Joan Baez at Newport," and "Joan Baez in Concert."

BALSLEY, PHIL: *See* Statler Brothers

BANJO: Stringed musical instrument.

One of the major instruments of folk music, the banjo has a long and ancient lineage. A banjo-like instrument called the rebec was played in Arabian countries for well over a thousand years. Many experts believe the origin of the banjo as far as the U.S. is concerned is West Africa. An instrument called the bania, believed derived from the rebec, is played there. Conjecture is that Negro slaves brought this kind of instrument with them. In fact, Thomas Jefferson in 1785 in his "Notes on Virginia" stated that the "banjar" was the main instrument played by American Negroes.

However, there is another theory that a form of banjo was derived from a European instrument called the bandore. The latter is a stringed instrument similar to the lute. Obviously, there is a close similarity of the word banjo to both "bania" and "bandore."

The conventional banjo of the 1700s and early 1800s was a four-string banjo. In the 1800s, though, an "American" banjo was invented which used five strings. The five-string banjo's invention is credited to Joe Sweeney who is believed to have built the first one in 1830. Sweeney was born and died in Appomattox, Virginia (1810-1860). The five-string banjo is the one associated with Bluegrass style.

As Louise Scruggs, wife of Bluegrass banjo great Earl Scruggs, wrote in the Tennessee Folklore Society Bulletin in 1961, "The fifth string is the blend in the banjo. It is plucked by the thumb in various intricate and ingenious ways while the other fingers are busy on the other four strings. No other instrument in the world is strung like the American five string banjo, and entirely new playing methods were invented that are unique to the instrument."

The banjo was one of the most popular instruments in America throughout the 1800s. In the 1900s, though, it began to fall into disuse. In particular, the five-string banjo gave way to a new four-string tenor banjo in popular music groups such as ragtime and jazz bands. The tenor instrument had a shorter neck and larger head than previous banjos.

The low point in banjo playing was reached in the 1930s when only a few popular artists, such as Uncle Dave Macon and Grandpa Jones, still used it. However, both the old style long-neck four-string banjo and the five-string banjo made a comeback both in the Bluegrass revival sparked by Bill Monroe and, later, Flatt & Scruggs, and in the folk music genre. One of those responsible for its wide use by folk artists in the post-World War II era was Pete Seeger.

The banjo might be considered a cross between a drum and a stringed instrument. The head is a round wooden hoop across which is stretched a skin, or drumhead. The head tension is regulated by a screw device. The strings are fastened at the bottom of the head and run over a supporting bridge part way up the head the length of the narrow neck to tuning pegs. The banjo is played with the fingers or a pick.

BARE, BOBBY: Singer, guitarist, songwriter, actor. Born Ironton, Ohio, April 7, 1935.

Bobby Bare burst upon the country and western scene in 1963 with a million-selling record of "Detroit City." Since then, he has gone on to become one of the most successful performers in both country and western and popular music.

The suddenness of Bobby's success overshadowed the fact that it took him many years of toil and struggle to reach the top. He was born on a farm in Ohio near the Kentucky border. His family was poor and his mother died when he was five. Though his father struggled to made ends meet, the family was forced to put Bobby's sister out for adoption because there wasn't enough money to feed everyone.

Bobby had to do heavy chores and odd jobs from his earliest years. Finally, at 15, he had to leave school and go out on his own. He worked for a time as a farm laborer and in a clothing

[21]

factory as a bundle boy. Following the same pattern, when Bobby became interested in music, he built his own guitar and learned to play it by himself. The materials for his first homemade instruments included an old coffee can, a stick, and some string.

By his mid-teens, Bobby was performing before local audiences. He started by singing with a country band in the Springfield-Portsmouth area, for no pay. He continued to gain experience without financial return at local clubs and on small radio and TV stations in Ohio and Kentucky. Some of the songs he sang were his own compositions.

In the 1950s, Bobby headed for California with only $25 in his pocket to see if he could hit the big time. He was only in the Golden State a short time when he was called for military service. The day before he left, he rented a studio with some friends to tape some songs. Driving to the studio, he thought of a new one and included it in the session. The tapes were sent to record companies after Bobby was in the Army. His song became a best-seller, "All American Boy," but he had sold the rights for only $50.

Bobby picked up the threads of his career in the early 1960s after receiving his discharge. In mid-1963, "Detroit City" hit the number-one spot in the nation in all popular music categories. The song won Bobby a Grammy in the 1964 NARAS (National Academy of Recording Arts and Sciences) awards. In 1963, Bobby also hit with "500 Miles Away from Home," with Charlie Williams. Bobby continued his string of successes in 1964 with top 10 spots for "Four Strong Winds" and "Miller's Cave." The following year he scored with "It's Alright" and, in 1966, with "The Streets of Baltimore."

Through 1967, Bobby had written more than 200 songs of which 100 were recorded by major artists. Because he can't read a note of music, he records his compositions by singing into a tape recorder. He also added another string to his bow in 1964 with a major acting role in the Warner Brothers film "A Distant Trumpet."

BARKER, HORTON: Singer. Born Laurel Bloomery, Tennessee, August 23, 1889.

A folksinger from the old school, Horton Barker thought of music as an enjoyable hobby. In fact, it was his love for music that helped ease the burden of total blindness, the result of a boyhood accident. He earned his living in other ways and sang mostly at local functions or for friends and neighbors. The result was that his name long was better known to scholars of folk music than to the general public.

Barker had the advantage of growing up in a region where old-time folk song was a tradition. Though born in Tennessee, he moved to Staunton, Virginia, at an early age. In Staunton, nestled in the Shenandoah Valley between the Shenandoah and Piedmont mountain ranges, many people sang the old ballads descended from those sung in the British Isles centuries before. Young Horton learned some of these from his mother and others from his neighbors and school friends. Though Barker had never heard of Professor Francis Child of Harvard, by the time he was graduated from Staunton's high school he could sing many of the songs listed in the Child Ballads. He was an unusual performer in that he never learned to play the guitar or any other folk instrument.

In the 1920s, Barker's name became known to many of the people in the region as that of a fine folk artist. His reputation was built up mainly by word of mouth, since he would only play for friends and resisted suggestions that he become a performer. He was finally persuaded to appear at the White Top Mountain Folk Festival, near Marion, Virginia. His first performance in August, 1933, was well received and led to his appearing at many other folk music festivals throughout the Appalachian region in the following three decades. He was particularly interested in White Top and often sang there, since festival officials strove to present material based only on traditional Anglo-Saxon folk music.

During the 1930s, Barker recorded a number of his songs for the Archive of American Folk Song of the Library of Congress. The first commercially available LP album of Barker was produced by Folkways Records in the 1950s. The excellent critical response to the record helped Horton's friends persuade him to show his talents to a wider national audience. One result was his highly successful appearance at the first annual University of Chicago Folk Festival in 1961.

BEAVERS, CLYDE: Singer, guitarist, songwriter. Born Tennga, Georgia, June 8, 1932.

Clyde Winfrey Beavers was born on the borderline between Tennessee and Georgia, but it turned out there was nothing marginal about his musical ability. Life was far from easy on his parents' farm in the Depression years. Finally, his parents gave up fighting the battle to keep their farm going and the children were sent to different friends. Clyde managed to finish basic schooling despite having to work at many chores and odd jobs. He finally escaped from the cycle of hard luck that beset his family by enlisting in the Air Force.

During his two-year hitch he saw a good deal of the U.S. His travels brought out a desire to write descriptions of the people and places he encountered. By the time he was discharged, he had begun to write country and western songs. He brought these to the attention of some performers and finally managed to get some of them recorded. This introduction to the music field served to get him his first job as a disk jockey. His first DJ activities were in the Atlanta area. From here he moved on to announcing and occasional performing work on country music radio shows in Tennessee.

By the start of the 1960s, Clyde was spending more and more time as an artist and less as a DJ. In addition, his songs were in demand among many leading artists. Clyde's following increased steadily among country fans, resulting in a call to join the Grand Ole Opry in 1961. Since then, he has been a regular on the show and has been greeted with enthusiasm by audiences in most of the major cities of the country.

His output includes a number of hit records of his own and a list of hit records of his songs by other stars. The latter include George Jones' rendition of "My Mom and Santa Claus" and Paul and Paula's "Crazy Little Things." Clyde's record successes include "I'd Rather Fight Than Switch," "That's You," "Still Loving You" and an English-language version of the Japanese hit "Sukiyaki."

BEE, MOLLY: Singer, actress. Born Oklahoma City, Oklahoma, August 18, 1939.

Showcase for many promising new performers in the 1950s was Cliffie Stone's Hometown Jamboree TV show in Los Angeles. One of the youngsters who went on to fame in country music was a pretty blonde, blue-eyed teenager named Molly Bee (real name: Molly Beachboard).

Though only eleven when she started work on the Jamboree, Molly was already a veteran performer. She began to sing country music at six under guidance of one of her brothers. Soon after, the family moved from Oklahoma to Tucson, Arizona. There little Molly concentrated on dancing lessons rather than singing. She learned rapidly and soon danced in local children's shows, church events, etc. When she was ten, cowboy artist Rex Allen heard her sing "Lovesick Blues" in a school show. Shortly after, she debuted on his Tucson radio program.

She moved to Hollywood with her family the following year and was soon signed for the Cliffie Stone show. She continued as a featured performer on the Jamboree until she was in her late teens. In short order, she was asked to appear on national TV, starting with a job on the Pinky Lee show when she was thirteen. After three years with Pinky, she was signed as a regular cast member on the Tennessee Ernie Ford daytime TV show for another two years.

From then on, she was also a featured guest artist on many TV programs, including Ernie Ford's nighttime show, Ed Sullivan, Roy Rogers, Jimmie Rodgers, Jackie Gleason, Jack Benny, Bob Hope and Jimmy Dean. She also was in demand for personal appearances at fairs and rodeos and in nightclubs across the country. Her first personal appearance at Mesker Auditorium, Evansville, Illinois, broke a six-year attendance record. Her credits in the late 1950s and during the 1960s included many stints in Las Vegas at such well known spots as the Thunderbird, Desert Inn, and Flamingo. Other appearances were at the Moulin Rouge in Los Angeles, Shamrock Hotel in Houston, Harrah's Club and the Mapes in Reno, and the Crystal Bay Club in Lake Tahoe. In 1967, she added a successful tour of Japan to her accomplishments.

During the 1960s, Molly received many requests to star in musical comedy. Her first role was in "The Boy Friend" at the Garden Court Theater in San Francisco's Sheraton Palace Hotel. She later starred with Alan Young in "Finian's Rainbow" at Melodyland, Anaheim, California, and with Buddy Ebsen, of Beverly Hillbillies fame, in "Paint Your Wagon" at the Valley Music Theater, Woodland Hills, California.

Her recording career began with Capitol in the 1950s and continued under the MGM label in the mid-1960s. Among her successful singles were such songs as "Single Girl," "Losing You," "Hate to See Me Go" and "Miserable Me." Her

LPs included the 1967 MGM album "Swingin' Country."

BEERS FAMILY, THE: Vocal group, Robert Harlan "Fiddler" Beers, born Clearfield, Pennsylvania, October 1, 1920; Evelyne Christine Sauer Andresen Beers, born Chicago, Illinois, May 3, 1925; Martha Christine Beers, born Chicago, Illinois, 1945.

In the classic tradition of folk music, Robert "Fiddler" Beers founded what promises to be a continuing tradition for his family. After forming a folk song team, he and his wife later added the voice of their daughter Martha in the fashion of such other groups as the Ritchies and the Carter Family.

In one way or another, all three Beerses had a close association with upstate Illinois. Though Robert was born in Pennsylvania, his family moved to Joliet, Illinois, when he was nine and he completed grade school there. Evelyne meanwhile was growing up in Chicago. Though the Beerses met and married in St. Louis, they returned to Chicago by the time Martha Christine was born.

Both Robert and Evelyne were exposed to folk influences in their youth. Robert became interested in fiddle playing from listening to his grandfather. Evelyne's mother sang Danish folk songs, as well as light opera, to her daughter and encouraged young Evelyne's interest in music. Robert went on to take classic violin lessons from professional instructors first in Joliet and later in St. Louis, Missouri, to which his family moved in 1935.

While attending Kirkwood High School in a St. Louis suburb, Robert became concertmaster of the school orchestra. His musicianship was highly polished in those years and he tried out and won a place in the St. Louis Symphony. He played with the orchestra in many local engagements, including radio broadcasts. After graduating from Kirkwood, he went on to enroll in the School of Music at Northwestern University, Chicago. While he was moving to Chicago, Evelyne's family was going the other way—to St. Louis. Evelyne had shown increasing interest in singing, and in St. Louis she became a soloist at her church. A few years later Robert Beers, visiting his family in St. Louis, heard her sing "Sweet Little Jesus Boy."

In 1944, he asked for her hand. After their marriage, the Beerses moved to Chicago where their daughter Martha was born. Robert, whose

The Fiddler Beers Family

college career had been interrupted by wartime service, was graduated from Northwestern in 1947.

The Beerses decided to move west. Robert worked with symphonic groups in the Montana-Wyoming region, eventually becoming concertmaster of the Symphony Orchestra of Billings, Montana. He held this position from 1951 to 1955. His wife also sang at local functions. Robert's interest in folk music revived when he devised an "Old Time Fiddler" sketch for the Judith Mountain Players. Before long, he and his wife were spending their spare time traveling through Montana and Wyoming collecting folk material. During the early 1950s they began to give folk recitals, in which Robert accompanied his wife on the fiddle and such exotic instruments as psaltery and fiddlesticks. The reception was excellent and they decided to devote more and more time to the folk genre.

As their stature increased, they were asked to appear at major folk festivals, including the Ozark Festivals of 1957 and '58 and the National Folk Festival at Oklahoma City in 1957. In the 1960s, they gave nationwide concerts and also appeared at the Newport Festival. By this time, their daughter was a regular participant.

In 1965, all three Beerses were featured on their first Columbia Records LP, "Introducing the Beers Family." The Beerses had turned out a number of LPs on other labels prior to this, including some solo renditions by both the Fiddler and Evelyne. Evelyne was featured on

[24]

a Prestige LP, "The Gentle Art," and Robert on the same label in "The Art of the Psaltery." Other LPs of the Beerses were the 1961 Prestige album "Walkie In The Parlor" and Folkways' "Fiddler Beers and Evelyne Songs."

In the mid-1960s, the Beers family moved to Fox Hollow, New York, to a house with spacious grounds. Here they instituted an annual Beers Family Festival of the Arts.

BELAFONTE, HARRY: Singer, actor, TV producer. Born New York, New York, March 1, 1927.

For a time, Harry Belafonte was so closely identified with calypso music that many people thought he had been born in one of Britain's Caribbean islands. He helped to dissipate this image with his demonstration of great versatility as an actor and singer of a wide variety of folk music.

Born in New York, Harry George Belafonte spent his first eight years there. He did have an authentic heritage of the West Indies, since his mother came from Jamaica and his father from the French-speaking island of Martinique. In 1935, his mother returned to Jamaica and took young Harry with her. For the next five years, he built up a background of familiarity with the island culture that was to be of great value in his career.

By 1940, his mother returned to New York and Harry attended parochial school and George Washington High School in upper Manhattan. When World War II erupted, he left high school to enlist in the U.S. Navy. After several years in the service, he was discharged. Still not sure of what he would do, he got a job as a janitor in a New York building. A tenant gave him tickets to the play "Home Is the Hunter." Impressed by the drama, Harry decided to use the G.I. Bill to study acting.

He enrolled in Erwin Piscator's Dramatic Workshop. One of his roles called for him to sing. In the audience for one of the performances was the owner of the Royal Roost, a Broadway nightclub. Working in the garment district pushing dress carts for a living, Harry was offered a two-week engagement that was so well received it was extended to 20 weeks.

As a singer of popular songs, Harry soon seemed on the way to the top. He was offered engagements in many other cities across the country. In addition, Capitol Records gave him a recording contract. In 1950, however, Harry

stopped short. This career didn't please him. To the amazement of show business experts, he quit and dropped from sight.

After thinking things over, Harry decided he was most interested in folk music. He combined with some friends to open a small folk spot in Greenwich Village where Harry hung around, listening to other folk musicians and singing when the mood struck him. He also made many trips to Washington to study the material in the Archive of American Folk Music. In the early 1950s, he had a considerable repertoire of American as well as West Indian folk songs. Now he joined forces with a close friend, guitarist Millard Thomas, to work up an act.

They opened at the Village Vanguard in New York for the familiar two-week stand. Once more they had to be held over. Critics came to hear Harry and went back to write ecstatic reviews. People flocked to the Vanguard for another 12 weeks to applaud this new talent. Other engagements followed, including a highly successful one at New York's Blue Angel. Soon after, Harry went to Hollywood for his first film part in "Bright Road."

He was then asked to join the cast of "John Murray Anderson's Almanac." When the show opened in New York in December 1953, Harry's singing of "Hold 'Em Joe" and "Acorn in the Meadow" stopped the show. This resulted in a bid in 1954 to play the lead role of Joe in Oscar Hammerstein's version of "Carmen Jones." Late in the year, he toured the country in "Three for Tonight," leaving audiences breathless from his 14 folk song renditions.

The night of June 23, 1955, a television adaptation of the show catapulted Harry to national stardom. The CBS-TV program helped increase the growing national interest in folk material. Harry went on to guest spots on just about every major TV network program. During the late 1950s and through the 1960s, he was featured a number of times on the Ed Sullivan Show. His other appearances included both singing and dramatic roles. One of his non-singing roles that won major attention was on the General Electric Theatre's "Winner by Decision." In the 1960s, Harry went on to produce some of his own NBC specials, hour-long shows on the broad subjects of Negro music, folk music, and Negro humor. His shows won critical praise and high audience ratings.

In 1956 and '57, Harry turned out a series

Harry Belafonte

many important folk artists to national attention, including Miriam Makeba and Greece's Nana Mouskouri. His tours extended throughout the world and to every state in the Union. Following his initial appearance at New York's Carnegie Hall in the late 1950s, he returned several times thereafter to cheering, sellout audiences. He also set attendance records in major cities in other parts of the country. A prime example was his every-other-year summer engagement at Los Angeles' Greek Theatre where he was the first artist to fill the house for three weeks, instead of the conventional two-week stands.

BELEW, CARL: Singer, guitarist, songwriter. Born Salina, Oklahoma, April 21, 1931.

One of the most sensational record hits of the mid-1950s was Elvis Presley's version of "Lonely Street." Before long, there were dozens of versions of the song by many different artists available in record stores. The song brought Carl Belew little public notice at the time, but it helped clear the way for his future record hits under his own name.

Born on a farm in the southwest, Carl spent many hours listening to country music as a boy. While still of elementary school age, he began to spend more and more of his time piecing out chords and simple tunes on an old guitar. He had a strong desire to leave the farm, and a career as a country and western performer seemed a glamorous way to do it. By the time he was in his teens, Carl's singing and playing were good enough to win him several engagements in his home area.

The way to the top in music, though, is usually not that easy. Carl spent many years of grueling one-night stands, playing county fairs and small clubs, before he gained a regular spot on the top ranked KWKH Louisiana Hayride program in Shreveport. In the early 1950s, he had become known to fans in all parts of the country who heard syndicated versions of the show.

By the mid-1950s, Carl was turning out more of his own material. After "Lonely Street," he had requests for original songs from many performers. In 1958, he provided the team of Johnnie and Jack with a top 10 hit, "Stop the World" (co-author, W. S. Stevenson). Meanwhile, Carl had signed with Decca Records. He wrote and recorded a major hit of 1959 for them, "Am I That Easy to Forget." In the

of recordings that brought about a calypso boom in the U.S. His hits included such stirring songs as "Jamaica Farewell," "Day-O (Banana Boat Song)," "Matilda," "Brown Skin Girl," and "Come Back, Liza." His RCA Victor LP "Calypso" became one of the label's top sellers. As the years went by, Harry was represented by dozens of other hit albums, some in a calypso vein but most in other kinds of music from spirituals and traditional American folk ballads to smooth (but not conventional) popular vocals.

His output included "Evening with Belafonte"; "Harry Belafonte Sings of the Caribbean"; "Mark Twain and Folk"; "Love Is a Gentle Thing"; "Harry Belafonte at Carnegie Hall" ('59); "Harry Belafonte Returns to Carnegie Hall"; "What a Mornin'"; "Harry Belafonte Sings the Blues"; "Swing Dat Hammer" ('60); "Jump Up Calypso" ('61); "Midnight Special"; "Many Moods" ('62); "Streets I Walked" ('63); "Harry Belafonte at the Greek Theatre" ('64).

By the mid-1960s, Harry had helped bring

[26]

early 1960s, he switched to RCA Victor. He provided them with a major hit in 1962 with his recording of "Hello Out There." The song went on to bring Carl another slice of royalties, becoming a major national "pop" success. Some of Carl's other singles of the 1960s were "You're Driving You Out of Your Mind," "Boston Jail," and "I Spent a Week There One Day."

Among his LP successes were "Carl Belew" (Decca—'62); "Carl Belew" (Wrangler—'62); and, on RCA, "Hello Out There" ('64) and "Am I That Easy to Forget" ('66).

BIBB, LEON: Singer, guitarist. Born Louisville, Kentucky, 1935(?).

During the post-World War II decades, several singers made their mark in both musical comedy and folk music. These included Burl Ives, Theodore Bikel, and Leon Bibb.

Bibb was born and raised in Louisville. He had a fine voice as a child and sang in his church choir. He also took part in singing gospel songs with friends and neighbors. His interest in music increased when he entered high school. During his high school years, he sang in the school chorus, sometimes taking solo parts. He went on to take several music courses in college before leaving for several years in the Army.

After his Army discharge, he decided to go to New York to study voice. Once in the big city, he began to sing in small clubs, then went on to various roles in off-Broadway productions. In 1958, he was given the key role of the Leader in a revival of Kurt Weill's "Lost in the Stars." His excellent critical reception insured that he would move ahead in the music field after this. Over the next few years, he played various roles in such musicals as "Annie Get Your Gun," "Finian's Rainbow," and "Living the Life."

Meanwhile, drawing on his earlier background in gospel and other folk music, he began to give concerts in this field. His concerts sometimes involved a mixture of musical comedy favorites and folk music. He usually accompanied himself on the guitar, an instrument he had mastered during his teens. In the late 1950s and early 1960s, he was featured in concerts and festivals across the country, including appearances at the Village Gate in Greenwich Village, the hungry i Club in San Francisco and New York's Town Hall. In 1959, he was one of the artists at the first Newport Folk Festival.

He also gained his first major record contract in the late 1950s from Vanguard. One of his first Vanguard LPs was the 1959 album "Leon Bibb Sings Folk Songs." This included such numbers as "Sinner Man," "East Virginia," "Turtle Dove," "Darlin'," "Rocks and Gravel," "Poor Lolette," "Look Over Yonder," "Red Rosy Bush," "Take This Hammer," "Skillet," "Jerry," "Dink's Blues" and "Irene." In 1960, he was represented on two more Vanguard LPs, "Leon Bibb Sings Love Songs" and "Tol' My Captain." In 1960, he was also featured on the Washington Record label with "Oh Freedom and Other Spirituals." In the early 1960s he turned out several LPs on Liberty label including "Leon Bibb in Concert" and "Cherries and Plums." His first Columbia LP, "Leon Bibb Sings," was issued in 1961 and included such songs as "Joey, Joey, Joey," "John Hardy," "Oh Shenandoah," "On My Way to Saturday," "Bonnie Wee Girl" and "Lost in the Stars."

During the 1960s he continued to tour widely, including a 1964 three-week tour of Russia accompanied by guitarist Stuart Scharf.

BIG D JAMBOREE: Variety show broadcast over station KRLD, Dallas, from 1947 to early 1960s.

For more than a decade, the southwest's major contribution to country music entertainment was the Big D Jamboree. The show reached audiences throughout the country over the CBS network on Saturday night. The original show on station KRLD, Dallas, lasted from 8:15 to 12 P.M., though maximum rebroadcast length in most areas outside the southwest was an hour.

Many of the best known names in country and western music in the 1950s and '60s were graduates of this show, including Ray Price, Sonny James, Merle Kilgore, Hank Locklin, Carl Perkins and Billy Walker. Also a regular cast member for a while was country music great Hank Snow.

The Jamboree originated from the large Sportatorium in Dallas. It was founded in 1947 and remained a prime attraction of CBS until the temporary recession in country music, caused by rock'n'roll, led to its demise at the start of the 1960s.

Some of the other cast regulars over the years included Johnny Hicks, Slim Willett, Gene Vincent, Homer, Ronnie, and Walter Callahan, Charlene Arthur, Benny and Bobby Belew,

Dough Bragg, Dick Burnet, Paul Buskirk, Bert Carrol, Riley Crabtree, Orville Couch, Dianne and Gus Foster, Artie and Darrell Glenn, Dewey Groom and the Texas Longhorns, Jimmy and Johnny, Okie Jones, Eddy McDuff, Marvin Montgomery, Gene O'Quinn, Peach Seed, Le-Fawn Paul, Wilford Roach, Bob Roy, Sunshine Ruby, Georgia Slim, Howdy Forrester, Billy Jack Saucier, Al Turner, Bobby Williamson.

Many of the performers were also featured on another major KRLD show, the late Pappy Hal Horton's daytime Cornbread Matinee.

BIKEL, THEODORE: Singer, guitarist, actor, author. Born Vienna, Austria, March 2, 1924.

Someone who can speak 17 languages would seem a natural for folk music, particularly if he can sing. Theodore Bikel can do both of these things as well as many others, including acting of the highest calibre.

Bikel started his language curriculum at home, where he learned Yiddish and Hebrew to go with his homeland's German. He expanded his language studies in school, but his schooling was momentarily cut short by the rise of Hitler. His family fled to Palestine in 1938 and became British subjects. In Palestine he spoke English while continuing his studies aimed toward teaching linguistics. While doing this, he started work as a laborer on a communal farm. His ability in reciting Shakespeare led to reassignment to the library and spare-time work directing and staging local pageants.

In 1943, he left the farm to join Habimah Theater in Tel Aviv. In 1945, he left Habimah to form the Tel Aviv Chamber Theater with four other young actors. Within two years he had outgrown local production and went on to the Royal Academy of Dramatic Arts in London. By 1949, he was gaining attention from work in little theater groups in that city. Sir Laurence Olivier liked young Bikel's capabilities and signed him for the first European production of "A Streetcar Named Desire" that opened in London September 27, 1947.

Bikel's work in the play brought him a close look from movie makers. The first of a long series of major support roles was that of a German sailor in the 1951 film "The African Queen." That same year he played a Russian officer in a hit London stage play, "The Love of Four Colonels." He appeared in many films in the 1950s, including "Moulin Rouge" ('52); "Melba" ('53); "A Day to Remember," "Love Lottery" and "The Little Kidnappers" (all '54); and "Divided Heart" ('55).

In 1955, he came to New York. His first vehicle did not last long, but the second, "The Lark" (November, 1955), won praise for him from the critics. In December '56, he debuted on TV in Hallmark Hall of Fame's "There Shall Be No Night." As in Europe, he soon began another round of film roles, including "Vintage" ('57); "The Pride and the Passion" ('57); "The Colditz Story" ('57); and "The Defiant Ones" ('58). In the last-named, his performance won an Academy Award nomination for best supporting actor.

He had been collecting and singing folk music throughout his life and by 1958 had a contract with Elektra Records. His reputation was enough to insure a sellout audience for his first solo concert at New York's Town Hall on October 5, 1958. The Elektra LP of the concert is called "Bravo Bikel." Among his many LPs are such titles as "Folk Songs of Israel"; "Songs of a Russian Gypsy"; "An Actor's Holiday"; and "Folk Songs From Just About Everywhere." After 1958, Bikel was in demand for folk song concerts throughout the U.S. and the world. His singing also pleased radio and TV audiences. In the early 1960s, he had his own music show, called "At Home with Theodore Bikel," on FM stations in New York, Los Angeles, and San Francisco.

Bikel changed the pattern from supporting to lead roles in August '59 when he won the part of Baron George von Trapp in "The Sound of Music." When the Rodgers and Hammerstein show opened on Broadway on November 16, 1959, Bikel's performance as actor, singer, and guitarist won unanimous favor with the critics. In the late 1960's he starred as Tevya in "Fiddler on the Roof," in Las Vegas.

BLUE BOYS, THE: *See* Reeves, Jim

BLUEGRASS: Traditional style of country music playing.

The word Bluegrass refers to a modern derivative of one of the oldest forms of country music, a style of playing that goes back to the first origins of string music in rural America. In form, the Bluegrass style involves the use of unamplified instruments with the lead handled by banjo, mandolin, or fiddle rather than guitar. It reflects the fact that in "old-timey" string music, the guitar often was not used or provided accompaniment rather than lead.

The leading exponents of Bluegrass music in the 1950s and '60s were Flatt & Scruggs with their Foggy Mountain Boys. Bill Monroe, however, holds the title of twentieth century "Father of Bluegrass." Monroe and his group, the Bluegrass Boys, made their style of playing nationally famous in the 1930s and '40s. The word Bluegrass springs from the Kentucky origins of the Monroe brothers. Flatt and Scruggs, as well as most other Bluegrass stars of the 1950s and '60s, are alumni of Monroe's band.

Bluegrass as exemplified by Flatt & Scruggs featured Scruggs' unique three-finger "arpeggio" picking style on a five-string banjo. Peter J. Welding, writing in Saturday Review (June 10, 1961), analyzed Flatt & Scruggs' instrumental work as follows:

[Columbia Records' "Foggy Mountain Banjo"] ". . . shows that instrumentally Bluegrass is a charging, heavily syncopated dance music, much like New Orleans jazz in that it is primarily a polyphonic ensemble style, replete with 'breaks' and solos. Each of the instruments, moreover, has a specific and well defined role that is strictly adhered to: guitar and bass are used for backing, and one or occasionally two fiddles, a mandolin and a five string banjo are used for lead or solo playing. These last three generate an amazing contrapuntal complexity in the ensemble passages, just as the clarinet, trumpet and trombone do in traditional New Orleans styles. . . ."

Scruggs' playing was reviewed thusly by Robert Shelton in The New York Times (December 4, 1961): "Scruggs' picking is a three fingered, heavily syncopated line that sharply accents the melodic line to make it stand out in a shower of notes. Moving at gasping tempos, it is dominated by a brilliant technical shine and employs 'Scruggs pegs,' cams that slacken and tighten a banjo string to provide some dazzling effects." (See also FLATT, LESTER; MONROE, BILL; SCRUGGS, EARL)

BLUEGRASS BOYS: See Monroe Brothers

BLUE SKY BOYS: Vocal, instrumental duo, the Bolick brothers, both born Hickory, North Carolina, Earl, December 16, 1919; Bill, October 28, 1917.

The names that were bywords in country music families in the late 1920s and early 1930s are almost unknown to country and music fans today. The great names included Jimmie Tarleton, Gid Tanner, Riley Puckett, Uncle Dave Macon and the brother act called the Blue Sky Boys. Most of the "classic" performers were dead or old by the time the folk music surge revived interest in the country music of earlier decades. To the surprise of many folklorists, when the Blue Sky Boys returned to the performing arts in the mid-1960s, they were only in their forties.

The boys were weaned on country music in their youth in North Carolina. Records of such performers as Gid Tanner and his Skillet Lickers and the great old-time fiddlers were often played in their home. The brothers learned to play stringed instruments and had collected a considerable number of country songs of the 1920s and earlier by the time they were in their teens.

In their early teens, they were in demand for dances and local affairs in Hickory. Word of their talents spread to other parts of the state and helped gain them a job on station WWNC, Asheville, North Carolina, in 1935. Within a short time they were prime favorites in many parts of their home state. Their rising popularity brought them a recording bid and they cut their first sides on June 16, 1936. The records helped spread their names to other parts of the country until they were one of the best known country teams of the late 1930s.

The boys were featured on many stations in the 1940s and made personal appearances in many parts of the south. In the late 1940s they were regulars on station WNAO, Raleigh, North Carolina.

Styles had changed, however, and country and western fans wanted more commercial songs rather than the older material which was often close to classical folk balladry. Many country performers swam with the tide, but the Bolicks felt the old way was best. Rather than play in a different style, they retired from the music field in 1951.

Their name continued to ring in the memories of many fans. Their records also were collected by folklorists at many schools, including Dr. D. K. Wilgus and Ed Kahn of UCLA's Edwards Collection. They were instrumental in a new search for the Bolicks in the 1960s.

When the Blue Sky Boys were rediscovered, efforts were made to have them perform at major folk festivals. At first they turned these bids down. Finally, they agreed to play at a fall '64 concert sponsored by the University of Illinois Campus Folksong Club. Their performance was awarded a loud ovation and was followed by requests for more appearances. In 1965, the Bolicks were starred at the UCLA Folk Festival, and the New York Folk Festival in Carnegie Hall. They also began to play in other festivals and college concerts throughout the country.

In 1965, they were represented on records again. Capitol issued the LP called "The Blue Sky Boys." Typical of the brothers' repertoire, the record included such songs as "Corrina, Corrina," "Jack o' Diamonds," "The Unquiet Grave," "Wild and Reckless Hobo," "Midnight Special," "Poor Boy," "Who's Gonna Shoe Your Pretty Little Feet," and "Oh Those Tombs."

BOGGS, DOCK: Singer, banjoist. Born Norton, Virginia, February 7, 1898.

"I was born Feb. 7th, 1898, place of birth, Dooley, Virginia. Long time done away with. I was named after the 1st phisician ever was in Norton, Va. My dad nicknamed me 'Dock' and it has stuck with me ever since."*

It took retirement to bring Dock Boggs to the forefront of the folk music revival of the 1960s. Many folk song experts had enthused about rare recordings he had made decades earlier and wondered what had happened to him. As he later related, his wife had thought working as a miner a more honorable way to make a living, and to please her he had abandoned his music until he completed 41 years in the mines in 1954.

Dock (given name, Moran L.) heard folk music played while he was a child by his older brothers and sisters. The banjo was the main instrument in the Boggs home, and Dock began to play it in traditional "knockdown or claw hammer style" (i.e., with one finger and thumb) when he was 12. At the same time, he started his long career as a miner, first as a helper on a coal cutting machine and progressing rapidly to machine operator.

Dock had been playing the banjo only a short time when he was introduced to a different way of playing. As he wrote in Sing Out! (July 1964, p. 32), ". . . My younger brother Rosco brought a colored man home with him one evening that used to be around Norton.

I heard him play 'Alabama Negro.' He played with his forefinger and next finger—two fingers and thumb." From that time on, Dock developed that style of playing to a fine art.

Dock's banjo playing slowed down after he married in 1918. Though devoted to her husband, Mrs. Boggs came from religious training that held folk music to be sinful. Dock continued to play for his own enjoyment for most of the 1920s and his ability gained much notice among people of the region. Thus when representatives of Brunswick Records came to Norton in 1927 to look for country music talent, Dock was urged to apply. He finally agreed to go to the tryout in the ballroom of the Norton Hotel. He played his favorite type of "lonesome songs": "Country Blues," "Down South Blues," and "Mean Mistreatin' Mama." The record executives signed him to play 24 songs. The contract increased his wife's unhappiness, however, and Dock agreed to put his banjo aside.

When Dock began to draw his miner's pension and Social Security in 1954, there was no longer a bar to his banjo playing. He took it up again and also enjoyed attending folk festivals throughout the region. At one of these he met Mike Seeger who encouraged Dock to try his hand as a performer. Audiences were as impressed with him as Seeger had been, and he soon became a regular on the folk music circuit, playing in concerts at major halls and at colleges across the U.S. By the mid-1960s he was a star performer at most folk festivals, including the ones at Newport.

In 1964 Dock was again represented on records with a Folkways LP, "Dock Boggs." Another album of his songs came out on the Disc label in 1965.

BOLICK, BILL: *See* Blue Sky Boys

BOLICK, EARL: *See* Blue Sky Boys

BOND, JOHNNY: Singer, guitarist, songwriter, actor. Born Enville, Oklahoma, June 1, 1915.

A 98-cent ukulele started Johnny Bond on the path to success in country and western music. At the time, Johnny was a boy on his parents' farm in Marietta, Oklahoma, to which the family had moved a few years after his birth in Enville. Taking time out from his chores one day, he glanced through a Montgomery Ward catalog and saw the ad which stated a booklet

---

* Letter to the authors, August 21, 1968.

came with the ukulele that taught the instrument in a matter of minutes.

Johnny sent for the uke and learned to play after a fashion. From then on, though, he became more and more interested in music. By the time he entered Marietta High School in 1930, he was well along to mastering the guitar. During his four high school years, Johnny performed at many school dances and other local events. In 1934, he made his radio debut on a station in Oklahoma City.

Bond had some thoughts of going on to college, but these were Depression years and he stuck with music. Later on (1937-38) he did get in some time at a university in Norman, Oklahoma. By that point, however, he'd had several years of experience as a performer in Oklahoma City theaters, hotels, and ballrooms. This resulted in a bid, in 1937, to join the Jimmy Wakely Trio on CBS radio. He stayed with the Trio until 1940, when Gene Autry heard the group and signed them to join his network Hollywood show, Melody Ranch. Johnny remained as a featured performer and a contributing songwriter for 14 years. He also found time to appear on the Hollywood Barn Dance from 1943 to 1947.

His arrival in Hollywood in 1940 also resulted in a contract from Columbia Records. He was a mainstay of Columbia's western catalog until 1954, the same year the Melody Ranch Show closed its doors. Among Bond's many records for Columbia were "Divorce Me C.O.D.," "Smoke! Smoke! Smoke!," "Oklahoma Waltz," "Sad, Sad and Blue," "Cimarron," "Tennessee Saturday Night," "Cherokee Waltz," "Steppin' Out," "Cream of Kentucky," "Wildcat Boogie," "Barrel House Bessie," "A Petal from a Faded Rose," and "Til the End of the World." In the 1960s, Johnny recorded for Starday, gaining a major hit in 1965 with "10 Little Bottles."

Johnny's songwriting activities resulted in an output of more than 400 songs through the mid-1960s. One of his earlier compositions was an all-time western standard, "Cimarron." Other Bond compositions are: "Glad Rags," "Jim, Johnny and Jonas," "Tomorrow Never Comes," "Gone and Left me Blues," "I'll Step Aside" and "I Wonder Where You Are Tonight."

After 1940 Johnny also appeared in movies with many of the top cowboy stars. He worked in many films with Gene Autry, for whom he often was special guitar accompanist. Some of his film credits are: "Kansas City Kitty," "Duel in the Sun," "Gallant Bess," "Cowboy Commandos," "Six Lessons" and "TV Ranch Party." His movies included non-western roles as well; an example is "Wilson."

In the 1950s and '60s Bond appeared on many TV shows, including some of Autry's; The Spade Cooley Show; and the Jimmy Wakely Show. In 1953, he began a long association with the Town Hall Party show, telecast from Compton, California.

Johnny's LP album output for Starday included "Live It Up and Laugh It Up" and "Johnny Bond" ('62) and "Songs That Made Him Famous" ('63). In 1964, Harmony produced an LP called "Johnny Bond's Best."

BONNIE LOU: Singer, yodeler, guitarist. Born Bloomington, Illinois, 1926.

For more than twenty years after World War II, one of the favorites of midwest country western audiences remained the Midwestern

Longtime sweetheart of the Midwestern Hayride, Bonnie Lou

Hayride's inimitable Bonnie Lou. Her presence on the show came about by a chance conversation in a club car between a Hayride executive and an enthusiastic country music fan.

At the time, December 1944, WLW talent department head Bill McCluskey and Billboard executive Bill Sachs were traveling to Chicago for the International Showman's Convention. In the club car, a salesman raved about Sally Carson, a teenage singer and yodeler on station KMBC, Kansas City, Kansas. McCluskey told the man to send records of her songs and some pictures. Back in Cincinnati, McCluskey found them on his desk and was impressed. He then asked her to make a recording of "Freight Train Blues." She complied and the WLW staff agreed it was a sensational effort. Sally Carson was hired, moving to Cincinnati in 1945.

From then on, under her new name of Bonnie Lou, she rapidly became one of the favorite artists of the Midwestern Hayride. During the 1950s and '60s many of her songs became top local favorites and some made national ranking. The latter group included two major top 10 hits, both in 1953, "Tennessee Wig-Walk" and "Seven Lonely Days."

Her other songs on King Records included "Teenage Wedding," "Papaya Mama," "I'm Available," "The Texas Polka," "No Rock 'n' Roll Tonight," "Daddy-O," "Boll Weevil," "Miss Bobby Sox," "No Heart at All," "Tennessee Mambo," "Runnin' Away," "Dancing in My Socks," "Miss the Love," and "Waiting in Vain," as well as an LP album, "Bonnie Lou Sings."

BONYUN, BILL: Singer, guitarist, teacher. Born Brooklyn, New York, April 15, 1911.

Though a New Englander only by adoption, William "Bill" Bonyun ranks as one of the foremost exponents of whaling songs and other ballads of the region. Bonyun was born and spent his early years in Brooklyn, New York, where such music was heard only on records, if at all. Later, he attended school in Summit, New Jersey, and Silver Bay, New York. Finishing high school in the late 1920s, he went on to attend several universities, including Wesleyan, University of Connecticut, and Columbia University.

He had some interest in folk music by the time he gained his master's degree in the 1930s. He enjoyed listening to folk records and could play the guitar. It was not until 1940, however, that folk music became a major part of his life. In that year, Bonyun obtained a farm in Maine where he spent part of the year farming. His folk song bent whetted his interest in songs of the region. He began to collect as many traditional songs as he could from old-timers and other folk song buffs of Maine. He also continued to build up his repertoire from other singers, books, records and other sources.

Teaching social science had been an early objective of his. As he built up his collection of folk music, he came up with the idea of presenting special programs to school children. By careful selection of ballads, he theorized, children could learn much of the country's social heritage. In 1949, he made his first appearance in this role at a grade school in Holbrook, Long Island. From then on, he spent a good part of the school year touring New York and New England singing and telling stories to school children.

In the 1950s, he continued this routine, operating from a home base in Brookhaven, Long Island, New York. He added a new string to his bow in 1955 by spending several months of the year singing on the green at the historical landmark of Old Sturbridge Village in Sturbridge, Mass. His impromptu concerts proved a highlight of visits to the reconstituted New England town of the 1800s by tourists from all over the country.

Bonyun's growing reputation in schools led to recording and film projects in the 1950s. Life magazine engaged him to provide the sound track for the documentary film "Hands That Built America." He also recorded an album for Folkways in the mid-1950s called "Who Built America?" This included such songs as "Waly Waly," "Santy Anno," "Boll Weevil," "Green Mountain Boys," "Erie Canal," "Government Claim," "Salangadou," "Drill Ye Tarriers," "Jesse James," and "Shoot the Buffalo."

In 1957, he and Gene Bonyun recorded "Yankee Legend" for Heirloom Records. This was designed for use in school history or social science programs and was intended as the first in a series of LPs. In this record, Bonyun drew more heavily on some of his New England collecting efforts. Some of the songs in the album were "Katie Cruel," "Riflemen of Bennington," "Blow the Man Down," "The Herring," "The Connecticut Peddler," "Song of the Fishes," "The Young Man Who Couldn't Hoe Corn," "The Frog in the Spring," and "Three Jolly Rogues of Lynn."

Bonyun continued his school performances and also extended collecting tours in the 1960s. In 1961, another Heirloom LP was issued titled "Songs of Yankee Whaling."

BOTTA, MICHAEL: *See* Travelers 3

BOWES, MARGIE: Singer, guitarist. Born Roxboro, North Carolina, March 18, 1941.

Combining a good sense of humor with a first-rate singing voice, Margie Bowes was charming audiences at an age when many girls still played with dolls. She performed in school events when still in elementary school. When she was 13, she branched out to perform on radio and TV. Her TV efforts consisted of frequent guest shots on a North Carolina program. During this period, she also was featured on a weekly show emanating from Virginia.

In 1958, she felt ready to move into the big time. She traveled to Nashville, Tennessee, to compete in the Pet Milk Company's nationwide talent competition. She won first prize going away and was soon featured on major TV shows in both the country and popular fields. Her rhythm songs won several appearances on Dick Clark's American Bandstand. For several years, she also performed for network audiences on Red Foley's Jubilee U.S.A.

Soon after her Pet Milk triumph, Margie signed with Hickory Records. In 1959, she turned out a top 10 national hit, "Poor Old Heartsick Me." In the 1960s, she switched to Decca. Her hits on that label included "Big City," "Understand Your Gal," "Overnight," "Our Thing," "Lost" and "Look Who's Lonely." By this time, Margie had moved to Nashville and was appearing on many country music shows from that city, including guest spots on the Grand Ole Opry.

During the 1960s she also made her first movie, "Gold Guitar." Personal appearances during this decade took her to all fifty states and, on two occasions, on international tours. She was also signed for several more movie roles in the mid-1960s.

BOWMAN, DON: Comedian, guitarist. Born Lubbock, Texas, August 26, 1937.

The title "world's worst guitarist" is an odd one, but Don Bowman wears it proudly. It signifies his success as one of the top comedians in the country and western field, carrying on the heritage of such stars as Minnie Pearl and The Duke of Paducah.

Don became interested in singing at an early age in his home state of Texas and sang in church recitals. As he grew up, he added guitar playing to his repertoire. Presumably he played well, though it's not something he can now admit to anymore than Jack Benny admits he can play the violin with great proficiency. His monologue on this part of his career goes something like, "I think my parents wanted to discourage me; they kept hocking my guitar."

His interest in music remained strong through high school and three years of college. While still in school, he worked as a disk jockey, a career that he went into full time after quitting college. His other sometime occupations during his early years included picking cotton, selling hub caps, and working as a part time meter painter. During his disk jockey chores, he began to work in comedy routines with his record spinning. In time, he began to appear in local clubs in the south and southwest. His comedy performance, based on material he wrote himself, began to attract attention. In the mid-1960s, RCA Victor Nashville artist and executive Chet Atkins heard Don and signed him to a record contract.

The result was a major comedy hit for Don, "Chit Atkins, Make Me A Star." He followed this up with "Wrong House." By this time Don was in demand for many major shows, including the Grand Ole Opry. In 1967, he was given the Billboard Award for favorite country and western comedian of 1966.

BOYD, BILL: Singer, guitarist, band leader, m.c., movie actor, songwriter. Born Fannin County, Texas, 1911(?).

Though he gained a reputation as the "Cowboy Rambler," William "Bill" Boyd really wandered too far from his native Texas. In fact, his daily show on station WRR, Dallas, Texas, set some sort of record for longevity. Starting in November 1932, the show was still going strong more than thirty years later in the 1960s.

Boyd had a legitimate cowboy background. He was born and raised in ranching country and could rope and ride at an early age. He also learned to play the guitar and sing many of the old western ballads while still a boy. By the time he was in his teens, he was performing in local events and had made his radio debut. His reputation had gone beyond state limits by 1935, resulting in a recording contract from RCA Victor. This too was a long-term arrangement, lasting more than twenty years and encompassing over 300 records of Boyd and his group.

From the start of his WRR program, "Bill Boyd and His Cowboy Ramblers," he had a hand in almost every aspect of the show. Besides singing, leading the band, and being the m.c., he helped produce the program and provided many of his own compositions for the band. Among Boyd's song output over the years were "Boyd's Blues," "David's Blues" and "New Fort Worth Rag." Among Boyd's recordings from 1935 to the 1950s on both RCA Victor and Bluebird labels were such songs as "Oklahoma Bound," "Homecoming Waltz," "Shame on You," "Don't Turn My Picture to the Wall," "Get Aboard That Southbound Train," "Old Fashioned Love," "New Spanish Two Step," "The Train Song," "Southern Steel Guitar," "Drifting Texas Sand," "Lone Star Rag" and "Pass The Turnip Greens."

In the 1930s and '40s, Boyd left his home state from time to time for feature roles in Hollywood westerns. The movies expanded his reputation to a national one and insured his presence on late late TV shows for the post-World War II era. In 1939, the Boyd reputation for rambling began in earnest with tours to every part of the country. For the next twenty years Boyd spent a good part of each year on the road, performing at theaters (often in combination with his western films), fairs, nightclubs and on guest spots on radio and TV.

BRAND, OSCAR: Singer, guitarist, banjoist, songwriter, author, m.c. Born Winnipeg, Canada, February 7, 1920.

From the wheatfields of Canada, Oscar Brand went on to become one of the major forces in the folk song world of New York. Over the years, his modest program on the city-owned radio station helped present dozens of new names to audiences all over the world.

Born on a wheat farm, Oscar did get a little feel for the wonders of living close to nature before his family moved to Minneapolis. He was seven when this occurred and not much older when they moved again, first to Chicago and then to New York. He completed his grade schooling in Brooklyn and went on to graduate from that borough's Erasmus Hall High School in 1937. Partly because it was still the Depression era and partly because of remembrances

from his early years, he literally hit the road for the next few years. He worked his way across country as a farm hand, picking up folk songs along the way to play on the banjo he had brought along.

Having sown his wild oats, he returned to Brooklyn College to work for a B.A. degree with a major in abnormal psychology. World War II interrupted this, however, and he entered the Army to work his way up to section chief of a psychology unit. After his discharge in 1945, he decided to try to earn a living in music. For a while, he toured as a singer with the Herb Shriner Show. But in late 1945 he struck deep roots in New York when he was named coordinator of folk music for station WNYC.

He also started his own program on the station, Folksong Festival. From then on, the show was a mainstay of Sunday evening radio at 6:00 P.M. In the mid-1960s, the show was still going strong. Over its decades of existence, the show presented records and "live" performances by everyone from Woody Guthrie and Richard Dyer-Bennet to Bob Dylan. In the 1950s and '60s, the show was rebroadcast overseas by the U.S. Information Service. In the mid-1960s, his government-sponsored show The World of Folk Music was broadcast every week over 1,880 stations.

During the decades after World War II, Brand built a major reputation in many fields. As a performer, he won rave reviews at concerts in almost every city in the country. He also appeared at most of the major folk festivals and was appointed a member of the board of directors of the Newport Folk Festival. His abilities attracted sellout crowds to many major nightclubs over the years, including the Troubadour in Los Angeles, Exodus Club in Denver, and Bitter End in New York. In the 1960s, his TV engagements included the ABC-TV Hootenanny and the NBC-TV Tonight and Today shows.

His network efforts included the job of musical director of many major shows. In the early 1960s, he was music director of NBC-TV's Exploring show that won the Peabody and Edison Awards for contributions to education. The years 1966–67 found him as both music director and the head of the cast of NBC-TV's The First Look. Brand also gained major attention on Canadian TV where he performed as star and host on CBC-TV's weekly show Let's

Sing Out from 1962 into the mid-1960s. During 1966–67, he signed for the same role on CTV-TV's weekly show, Brand New Scene.

In addition to all of this activity, he managed to find time to make more than 52 LP folk albums (as of 1967) and write songs and major movie, TV, and stage show scripts. One of his earliest song hits was "A Guy Is A Guy," based on a bawdy Army ballad. His 45 film scripts won him awards at the Venice and Edinburgh Festivals and Golden Reel, Valley Forge, and Scholastic Awards.

Among his TV output of scripts, narrations, and scores were contributions to Invisible Journey, Highway by the Sea, The Farmer Comes to Town, Agnes de Mille's The Gold Rush on CBS-TV, and Frederick Remington's Bay at the Moon. He also wrote more than 50 scripts for the National Lutheran Council.

His LPs were produced by many different labels, including Elektra, Impulse, Decca, ABC-Paramount, Tradition, Folkways, Audio and Riverside. His Riverside output included such LPs as "Give 'Em the Hook," "Riddle Me This," "Drinking Songs," "Children's Concert" and "G.I." He recorded eight volumes of "Bawdy Songs" for Audio. Folkways LPs of Brand's include "Election Songs" and "Town Hall." Among his Elektra albums are "For Doctors Only," "Courting's a Pleasure," "The Wild Blue Yonder," "Boating Songs" and "Every Inch a Sailor."

The six-foot-two Canadian's prodigious output also included a number of books. The earliest of these, *Singing Holidays,* was published in 1957. Later he wrote *The Ballad Mongers,* one of the basic histories of folk music in the U.S.

The year 1966 also found him represented on Broadway with "A Joyful Noise" starring John Raitt. Brand provided music and lyrics for the musical. Earlier, he had made his mark on the musical theater with a critically acclaimed off-Broadway production, "In White America."

BRAZOS VALLEY BOYS: *See* Thompson, Hank

BRITT, ELTON: Singer, guitarist. Born Marshall, Arkansas, July 7, 1917.

One of the top stars of the country and western field during the 1940s and '50s, Elton Britt (real name: James Britt Baker) literally sprang from behind the plow to stardom.

During World War II, his reputation was such that no less a person than President Franklin D. Roosevelt sent Elton a personal invitation to perform at the White House.

Elton's half Cherokee Indian-half Irish background was symbolic of a country musical heritage. Though born in Arkansas, he was brought up in the Osage Hills of Oklahoma where family sings were a tradition. In Elton's case, his mother brought many melodies from her girlhood home in the Ozark Mountains while his father was one of the top old-time fiddlers of Oklahoma and Arkansas. When Elton was still grade school age, his father bought him a $5 guitar from Sears, Roebuck and taught him three chords. Elton continued to add to his singing and playing ability after that by listening to country and western records. Before he was in his teens, he occasionally entertained at local parties or dances.

Though he enjoyed performing, Elton expected to make his living as a construction engineer. He started high school with this in mind. Times were tough, though, and he had to work during these years at various chores, including digging potatoes, hoeing corn, picking cotton and milking cows. The first job he was paid for, however, was plowing corn, for which he received 75¢ a day.

In early summer of 1932, some talent scouts came through the region looking for a real country boy who could sing and yodel. They were directed to Elton. They found the 14-year-old plowing, listened to him sing, and promptly signed him to a year's contract with station KMPC in Los Angeles. Elton was rushed to California and, in a few days, was singing on his first radio program. Before the year was up, Elton had created quite a stir among local country and western fans and was soon featured on several network radio shows.

His following continued to grow, resulting in a recording contract with RCA Victor in 1937. Elton turned out to be one of the most durable of RCA's recording stars, turning out 672 single records and 56 albums in a relationship that lasted 22 years. In the 1960s he also recorded for several other labels, including Decca, ABC-Paramount, and Ampar.

During World War II, Elton became one of the nation's most popular recording artists, turning out a number of million-selling records. His top hit during this period was "There's a Star Spangled Banner Waving Somewhere," which sold more than 4 million copies through the 1960s. His other top 10 hits included "Chime Bells" in 1948, "Candy Kisses" in 1949, and, with Rosalie Allen, "Quicksilver" in 1950. Some of his other successful RCA records were "Detour," "Someday," "Blue Texas Moonlight," "I'd Trade All of My Tomorrows," "I Hung My Head and Cried," "Roses Have Thorns," "Born to Lose," "Cowboy Country," "Roses of Yesterday," "It Is No Secret," "Oklahoma Hills Where I Was Born." His duets with Rosalie Allen included such songs as "Soft Lips," "Game of Broken Hearts," "Tennessee Yodel Polka," "Tell Her You Love Her," and "Cotton Candy and a Toy Balloon."

In 1948, Elton signed with Columbia Pictures for several films. His first one, in 1949, was "Laramie." Later he also starred in such movies as "The Prodigal Son" for Universal International. During the 1950s and '60s, Elton appeared on many network shows, including the Grand Ole Opry, WWVA Wheeling Jamboree and the George Hamilton IV TV show. His LPs available in the 1960s included an RCA Victor album, "Yodel Songs," and ABC-Paramount's "Wandering Cowboy," "Beyond the Sunset," and "I Heard a Cowboy Praying." In 1968 he hit with his composition "The Jimmie Rodgers Blues," released in April, the 40th anniversary of Peer Southern International Organization, publisher of Rodgers' songs.

BROONZY, BIG BILL: Singer, guitarist, fiddler, songwriter. Born Scott, Mississippi, June 26, 1898*; died Chicago, Illinois, August 14, 1958.

Considered one of the greatest country blues performers of all time, William Lee Conley "Big Bill" Broonzy was famous in Europe when hardly any of his fellow countrymen knew his name. Like so many folk artists, Bill led a hand-to-mouth existence until the last few years of his life. For all that, he managed to maintain his good nature and sense of humor, showing a driving energy and zest for living even when singing his saddest songs.

As one of a family of 17 children, Bill knew hard work from his earliest years. His family wandered between Mississippi and Arkansas during the first 15 or 16 years of his life. In 1915, he farmed on a share-cropping basis, but gave it up in 1916 when drought wiped out his crops.

* Broonzy himself gave the year as 1893; after his death, his twin sister produced a birth certificate giving it as 1898, the currently accepted year.

Bill grew up in a singing environment. He heard his people sing spirituals in church, listened to wandering blues singers, and heard and sang work songs in the fields before he was 10, at which time he decided to learn to play an instrument. He made himself a makeshift fiddle from a cigar box and a guitar out of a goods box. With a friend he played for picnics, including "two stage ones." In a two stage picnic, the white people danced on one side of the stage and the colored on the other.

World War I provided a turning point in Bill's life. He enlisted in the Army and went overseas in 1917. He returned home in 1919, with a restless urge to move on to bigger and better things. In the early 1920s he went north to Chicago, where he got a job with the Pullman Company and also perfected his guitar playing with veteran musician Papa Charlie Jackson.

The pattern of Broonzy's life in Chicago was the general story of all his life. He worked at various jobs to earn a living and gained his main enjoyment, and a little extra money, from part-time jobs in music. For a good part of the 1920s, he entertained at Saturday night "house rent" parties. One of his first original compositions of these years was a guitar solo called "Saturday Night Rub." Among the many musicians he performed with in Chicago were Sleepy John Estes, Shorty Jackson, Blind Lemon Jefferson, Blind Blake, Lennie Johnson, Shorty George, Jim Jackson and Barbecue Bob.

In 1923, he made his first two records of his own material, "Big Bill Blues" and "House Rent Stomp." The $100 payment for these, though, was wangled away by a friend and he received nothing for his effort. Bill managed to make a little on some of his later efforts of the 1920s, such as "Date with an Angel Blues," "The Walking Blues," "Big Bill Blues No. 2," "House Rent Stomp No. 2," "Bull Cow Blues," "Milk Cow Blues," "Serve It to Me Right Blues" and "Mama Let's Cuddle Some More."

In the 1930s, things began to look up for him. He had gained a reputation as a top country blues artist and was starting to find work in Chicago nightclubs. He made a number of records with various performers on the Champion label in the early 1930s. In 1932, he was in New York with one of several bands he organized. He soon made a number of recordings on such labels as Vocalion, Oriole, and Melotone, including such songs as "Too Too

Train Blues," "Worryin' You Off My Mind," "Shelby County Blues" and "Mistreatin' Mama Blues."

He was soon back in Chicago, spending most of the 1930s in the midwest at a succession of daytime jobs and an increasing number of club engagements. During these years, he turned out dozens of recordings of commercial blues and country blues, but gained little monetary return from them. However, the folk music field had become increasingly aware of his talents. In 1939, he won rousing critical acclaim for his appearance at the "Spirituals to Swing Concert" in New York's Carnegie Hall.

During the 1940s, Bill toured much of the country playing to various audiences from segregated ones in small southern towns to college concert halls. He still supported himself through work as a cook, piano mover, porter, molder or any of a half dozen other "trades."

Though more and more folk enthusiasts avidly looked for his recordings, Bill did not seem to be getting anywhere. In 1950, he almost gave up his music career. At this point, however, he was swept up in the post-World War II folk revival. He joined a new group formed by Chicago folk artist Win Stracke called "I Come for to Sing." The group met wide acceptance as it toured major college campuses. After one visit to Iowa State College at Ames, Bill's financial health was illustrated by his willingness to stay on for a time working as a janitor.

In 1951, he was offered a tour of Europe. European audiences could not believe he was almost unknown in the U.S. His tour was a triumphal one and his name was one of the best known in European music circles by the time he went home. Slowly his career began to move ahead back home. He was featured on dates with many top artists, including Pete Seeger and his old friends Sonny Terry and Brownie McGhee. He also began to receive requests to perform on radio and TV. During the 1950s he extended his overseas tours to Africa, South America, and the Pacific region, meeting with great response everywhere he went.

The sales of his new LP recordings also began to go up. Folkways Records issued several of these, including "Big Bill Broonzy Sings Country Blues," and "Big Bill Broonzy's Story." Ironically, though, his LP output increased sharply after his death. In 1959, Folkways issued a blues album by Bill, Sonny Terry, and Brownie McGhee. Verve turned out a five-LP set called

"Big Bill Broonzy's Story" and another, "Big Bill's Last Session," in 1961. In 1962, he was represented by the Folkways release "Big Bill Broonzy Sings," in 1963 by Mercury's "Memorial" album, and in 1964 by Mercury's "Remember Big Bill."

In 1953, the acceptance of Bill's talents had finally permitted him to devote full time to his music. He savored this late windfall for several more years. By 1958, however, he was dying of cancer, finally passing away on August 14.

He recounted his career to Belgian writer Yannick Bruynoghe in 1954. It was issued in book form in 1955 as *Big Bill Blues: Big Bill Broonzy's Story as told to Yannick Bruynoghe*. The book was revised and updated in a 1964 edition by Oak Publications.

BROTHERS FOUR, THE: Vocal group, Bob Flick, born Seattle, Washington; Michael Kirkland, born Everett, Washington; John Paine, born Wenatchee, Washington; Richard Foley, born Seattle, Washington.

One of the most successful folk-pop groups of the 1960s, The Brothers Four played almost every college campus across the U.S. They were naturally at home in this environment, since their group name does not refer to direct kinship, but to the fact that they met as fraternity "brothers."

All four of the group were born in the state of Washington in the 1939–40 time period. They attended elementary and high schools in different sections and then went on to the University of Washington at Seattle. Their choice of majors was varied, Bob opting for radio and TV production, Mike for pre-med, Dick for electrical engineering and John for political science.

Their meeting resulted from their joining the same fraternity. As Mike reported in a Columbia Records release, "The guys at the fraternity house did a lot of singing, usually in a gang—no really worked-out arrangements. We decided to get together a small group, with maybe a little instrumental backing, just for fun. By Christmas time, we were performing some place or other every weekend." For their first professional date at Seattle's Colony Club in 1958, they received $5 each.

In 1959, the group prepared a tape of some of their folk renditions and sent it to Columbia Records in New York. Company executives enthused over the demonstration and signed them in July 1959. A few weeks later, Columbia released the record "Greenfields," which became one of the major national hits of the year and is still a standard. Later in the year, similar success was achieved by the group's first LP, also called "Greenfields," produced by Bob Morgan.

In the 1960s, the Brothers became one of the top national singing groups. In the 1961–62 season, their schedule included a 90-day personal appearance tour of 100 colleges. In 1962–63, their college tour ranged over 200 campuses. In April of 1962, they had a wild welcome from crowds of admirers during their first tour of Japan.

One of their major hits of the early 1960s was "Green Leaves of Summer." They were invited to sing it as part of the 1961 Academy Awards presentations, on network TV. Their TV appearances during the 1960s included most major network shows, including Mitch Miller's Sing Along, Today, Bell Telephone Hour, the Chevy Show and Bob Newhart. They were also featured a number of times over the years on the Ed Sullivan Show. Their agenda included

nationwide concert and nightclub work. In New York, they were headlined several times at Basin Street East.

Their LP output for Columbia included: "Brothers Four," "Rally 'Round" ('60); "Brothers Four On/Off Campus," "Roamin'," "Song Book" ('61); "Greatest Hits," "In Person" ('62); "Cross Country Concert," "Big Folk Hits" ('63); "Brothers Four Sing of Our Times," "More Big Folk Hits" ('64).

BROWER, CECIL: *See* Light Crust Doughboys, The

BROWN, BONNIE: *See* Browns, The

BROWN, FLEMING: Singer, banjoist, folk music collector. Born Marshall, Missouri, 1926.

One of the phenomena of the mid-twentieth century is the urban folk movement. A great number of folk performers of the 1950s and '60s were from the large cities with little personal background in the environment from

The Brothers Four

[38]

which traditional folk music was derived. Most of these performers therefore had only limited success with critics or folk music followers. One of the major exceptions is Fleming Brown. Unlike most of his urban contemporaries, Brown has achieved note with his peers, though not overwhelming popular acclaim.

Brown was born in the small town of Marshall, Missouri. When he was four, his family moved to Glen Ellyn, near Chicago, and Brown grew up in the Chicago area during the Depression years, attending local schools and finding more interest in swing bands and popular music than other forms. In his teens, however, exposure to some of Burl Ives' recordings led to a new interest in folk material.

He decided to learn to play a stringed instrument. He found an old five-string banjo at a local junk shop and found a teacher in the person of Kentucky musician Doc Hopkins. By the end of the 1940s, Fleming was performing for local groups in the Chicago area. He became known as a fine folk artist and was asked to sing at the 1950 National Folk Festival in St. Louis.

During the 1950s he continued to make progress in the music field. However, his talent in commercial art paid most of his bills. He spent much of his free time collecting folk music of the Appalachian region, until he was considered one of the foremost collectors of this kind of material.

In 1953, he replaced one of the members of the Chicago-based "I Come for to Sing" folk music program. During the next few years he toured many parts of the country with the group, singing in concerts and at major folk festivals. During the 1950s and '60s he also appeared as a solo performer at many festivals, including several sponsored by the University of Chicago. Brown's first LP record was issued by Folk-Legacy Records in 1962 titled "Fleming Brown Sings Folk Songs."

Soon after Win Stracke founded his "Old Town School of Folk Music" in Chicago, Brown was asked to join the faculty. During the 1960s, Brown taught banjo and also sang and helped organize some of the many festivals and concerts sponsored or aided by the school.

BROWN, FRANKIE: *See* Daffan, Ted

BROWN, JIM ED: *See* Browns, The

BROWN, MAXINE: *See* Browns, The

BROWNS, THE: Vocal trio, Maxine, born Sampti, Louisiana, April 27, 1932; Jim Edward, born Sparkman, Arkansas, April 1, 1934; Bonnie, born Sparkman, Arkansas, July 31, 1937.

It was the fall of 1967 in Nashville and the annual WSM-Country Music Association-disk jockey convention was in full swing. The Browns had just finished performing their spot on the Grand Ole Opry to a rousing ovation. Moments later, the audience received the surprising news that the group was breaking up. Bonnie, in tears, announced that after 13 years with the family trio, she was retiring to spend all her time with her growing family and her busy doctor-husband, Gene Ring. Maxine, too, said she had decided to follow the same route.

Thus one of the best known groups of the 1950s and '60s was reduced, momentarily, to a single, for Jim Edward Brown soon after decided to go it alone.

The Browns actually started as a duo in the early 1950s. Ella Maxine Brown teased her brother into entering a local amateur contest in which he won first prize. This success encouraged him to team up with Maxine to appear at local events. For a time, Jim considered a non-show business career. He majored in both music and forestry at Arkansas State Teachers College, the latter course being in line with a possible job in his father's sawmill business.

When Jim and Maxine won the talent show on Barnyard Frolic on station KLRA in Little Rock, though, the die was cast. They followed up with a successful guest appearance on KWKH's Louisiana Hayride in Shreveport. In 1955, younger sister Bonnie made it a trio, completing the vocal blend that made them regulars on the Ozark Jamboree in Springfield, Missouri.

They caused disk jockey excitement on Fabor Robinson's Abbott Records label with "Draggin' Main Street" and "I was Looking Back to See." In 1955 Jim Reeves, who joined RCA Victor after recording for Abbott for a while, brought them to the attention of Steve Sholes and Chet Atkins and The Browns also moved to RCA.

Soon after this, Jim Edward was called for Army service. While he was in uniform, baby sister Norma Brown filled in for him on personal appearances. Meanwhile, he hoarded passes and leaves for recording dates.

Though their records attracted some attention, The Browns were largely unknown as the

1950s came to a close. In 1959, they became interested in a song called "Jimmy Brown," for obvious reasons. They couldn't find the copyrighted music because, as it turned out, the basic title was "Three Bells." (The song originated in France.)

In a phone conversation with Grelun Landon, vice president of Hill and Range Songs, Inc., Bonnie mentioned the song. Landon tracked it down and obtained copies from Peer International's Roy Horton. The music was sent to The Browns in time for their next recording session. Almost as soon as their recording (the "Jimmy Brown" version) came out, it hit sales rates of 100,000 a week. In a short time, The Browns had their first million-seller and a nationwide reputation.

In between a mushrooming series of bookings in all parts of the nation, Bonnie eloped with Gene Dale Ring. (Earlier, Maxine had married attorney Tommy Russel.) Soon after her marriage, the group hit paydirt again with "Scarlet Ribbons" and "The Old Lamplighter." The songs were hits in the pop category as well as country and western.

Between 1960 and 1963, The Browns started a supper club and catering service in Pine Bluff, Arkansas, appeared on many national TV shows, including the Grand Ole Opry, and went on personal appearance tours of the U.S., Europe, and Asia. In 1963, The Browns became regulars on the Opry. Though the Opry contract added a little more stability to their lives, the girls finally decided they wanted to spend more time with husbands and children, leading to the disbanding of the trio in 1967.

Under the guidance of agent Hubert Long, Jim Edward started a series of intensive solo appearances. His first solo effort for RCA, "Regular on My Mind," was a 1967 country hit. He followed with such others as "Pop-A-Top" and "The Enemy." He prepared a new act which successfully debuted in Atlanta, Georgia, in early 1968, followed by an immediate bid for a long engagement at the Sahara Tahoe's Juniper Lounge in Lake Tahoe, Nevada.

Retirement proved difficult for Maxine, though. In 1968, she started a career as a single on a limited basis, signing with Chart Records.

As of 1968, Bonnie lived in Dardanelle, Arkansas, Jim Edward in Brentwood, Tennessee, and Maxine in Little Rock, Arkansas.

BRUMLEY, TOM: *See* Buckaroos, The

BRYAN, CHARLES FAULKNER: Singer, composer, folklorist, educator. Born near McMinnville, Warren County, Tennessee, July 26, 1911; died Pinson, Alabama, August 7, 1955.

In the past few decades, an increasing number of scholars have given breadth and depth to folk, country and western music. Such people as Alan Lomax, John Lomax, D. K. Wilgus and Charles Faulkner Bryan helped trace the roots of today's music while also preserving songs, stories, and other important parts of this musical legacy. In Bryan's case, not only did he provide such research, particularly on the Appalachian Mountain dulcimer, but he also wrote orchestral scores and operas based on folk music background.

Bryan heard much of the old-time folk and country music during his early years in Tennessee. He leaned towards classical music, though, and enrolled in the Nashville Conservatory of Music in 1930. While completing the four year course for his B.A., he organized and conducted the Nashville Junior Conservatory Orchestra for two years. During this period, he also worked as an arranger and soloist at station WSM, home of the Grand Ole Opry.

After graduation, he headed the music department at Tennessee Polytechnic Institute from which he received a second degree in 1939. His next position, a teaching fellowship at George Peabody College for Teachers, introduced him to one of the country's leading collectors of spirituals, the late George Pullen Jackson. Jackson's insight brought about a deep interest in folk music on the part of Bryan. Before long, Bryan went on tour with Jackson's "Old Harp Singers."

After receiving his M.A. from Peabody in 1940, Bryan worked for several years on the Federal Music Project and, later on, as a consultant to the Office of Civil Defense. During these years, he collected folk material and expanded his knowledge of the Appalachian dulcimer. Bryan became very proficient at playing this classic folk music instrument.

After World War II, he moved to Yale University to study under composer Paul Hindemith for a year. In 1946, he wrote a folk cantata that was performed at Carnegie Hall in New York by the Robert Shaw Chorale, called "The Bell Witch." With this experience under his belt, he returned to Peabody from 1947 to 1952 as a teacher of voice, theory, and choral music. He continued his activities as both a folklorist and composer. His compositions included "Cumberland Interlude 1790" and "White Spiritual Symphony." In 1952, he left for a new position at the Indian Springs School for Boys at Helena, Alabama. He remained there until his death in 1955.

In the few years left to him, Bryan performed at many folk festivals and concerts. He also wrote a book now widely used in schools across the U.S., *American Folk Music for High Schools and Other Choral Groups*. His music output included the "Birmingham Suite" ('53), a musical folk play, "Strangers in This World," and an opera, "Singin' Billy." The year before his death, he traveled through Europe collecting data on the origins of the Appalachian dulcimer.

BRYANT, BOUDLEAUX AND FELICE: fiddler (Boudleaux), song writing team, Boudleaux, born Shellman, Georgia, February 13, 1920; Felice, born Milwaukee, Wisconsin, August 7, 1925.

In country and western, the song is the thing. Thus songwriters have long been as important as performers in this field. So it was that C&W artists of the post-World War II decades beat a path to the door of the great husband-and-wife writing team of Boudleaux and Felice Bryant. Even when rock 'n' roll caused a near depression in the country field, the Bryants proved the latent value of good material by helping the Everly Brothers dominate the pop field in the late 1950s.

Boudleaux, born in Shellman but raised in Moultrie, Georgia, had an excellent classical background. He began to study violin when he was five and continued until he was eighteen with the goal of becoming a concert violinist. In 1938, he played a season with the Atlanta Philharmonic.

Then he met a man from Atlanta station WSB in a violinmaker's shop. The man needed a fiddle player for a country band. Having also played country music for his own pleasure, Boudleaux took the job. After several years as a country fiddler, Boudleaux joined a jazz band and toured through many parts of the country. In 1945, while playing in Milwaukee, he met Felice. She was an elevator starter at the Shrader Hotel and had been born and raised in Milwaukee.

After their marriage, Felice traveled with Boudleaux. Sometimes they made up country and western songs just for fun. They eventually decided to try to place some. In 1949, at the suggestion of a friend, performer Rome Johnson, they sent a song called "Country Boy" to Fred Rose of Acuff-Rose in Nashville. Rose bought it and Little Jimmy Dickens soon turned it into a top 10 hit. The following year, at Rose's suggestion, the Bryants moved to Nashville.

From this time on, it was rare that one of their songs wasn't on hit charts. Many of their compositions made it in both country and western and popular fields. An example was "Hey Joe," a top 10 hit for Carl Smith in 1953 and a million-seller for Frankie Laine in the pop domain. For some years, the Bryants worked closely with Carl Smith. Smith's top 10 successes from the Bryants' pen included "It's a Lovely, Lovely World," "Our Honeymoon" ('52); "Hey Joe," "Just Wait 'Til I Get You Alone," "This Orchid Means Goodbye" (the last named co-written by Boudleaux and Carl) ('53); and "Back Up, Buddy" ('54).

In 1955, Eddy Arnold was given two Bryant hits, "I've Been Thinking" and "Richest Man." In the mid-'50s, the Bryants began to work up a close relationship with a rising young brother act, the Everlys. The combination of Bryant songs and Everly renditions soon had a major impact on both popular and country charts. In 1957, the Everlys had number-one-ranked records on both charts, "Bye Bye Love" and "Wake Up Little Susie." Webb Pierce also had a top 10 hit with "Bye Bye Love" in the country field. The following year, the Everlys were given two more number-one-ranked songs, "All I Have to Do Is Dream" and "Bird Dog." In 1958, the Bryants also were represented on the top 10 list with Jim Reeves' version of "Blue Boy."

In 1961, Boudleaux had a worldwide hit with an instrumental composition, "Mexico." The song won a gold record in Germany. During the 1960s, the Bryants could concentrate again on material for country artists. The top 10 hits to their credit included Bob Luman's "Let's Think About Living" ('60); "My Last Date" (written by Boudleaux with several co-authors, including vocalist Skeeter Davis) ('61); Sonny James' "Baltimore" and Ernest Ashworth's "I Love to Dance with Annie" (both '64).

BUCKAROOS, THE: Buck Owens' band. As of 1968, Buckaroo members were: Don Rich, born Olympia, Washington, August 15, 1941;

Tom Brumley, born Powell, Missouri, December 11, 1935; Doyle Holley, born Oklahoma City, Oklahoma, June 30, 1936; Willie Cantu, born Corpus Christi, Texas, May 26, 1943. (*See* OWENS, BUCK)

BURGESS, WILMA: Singer. Born Orlando, Florida, June 11, 1939.

Though born in the south, Wilma Charlene Burgess never fell into the usual country music pattern. A city girl, brought up in Orlando, she had a closer affinity to popular music than rural ballads. It was not until she was in high school that she really became aware of the country music heritage of the region. She attended a concert given by Eddy Arnold and found his renditions of country and western standards much to her liking.

While not abandoning other forms of music, she began to spend more and more time listening to records and radio programs of country material. She memorized the lyrics of many songs and sometimes sang them to her friends. However, a music career was not in her plans when she enrolled as a physical education major at Stetson University in Florida. She did sometimes sing along with fellow students at parties and impressed them with her vocal ability.

Soon after she finished college, a friend who wrote country music asked her to go to Nashville to sing some of the songs for prospective publishers. This was in 1960 and one of the people for whom she demonstrated the material was Charlie Lamb of Sound Format publications. Lamb was more interested in her voice than the music. He offered to bring her ability to the attention of some recording executives.

Owen Bradley, a Decca Records executive, agreed with Lamb's estimate and signed Wilma. The result was a move to Nashville by Wilma, where she was soon featured on several of the TV shows emanating from there. She turned out some songs that stayed on the charts for a number of weeks in the early 1960s. In 1966, she made the top 10 nationally with her hit record "Baby." In 1967, she had a top-rated single in "Fifteen Days," and a top 10 LP, "Wilma Burgess Sings Misty Blue." Her single "Parting" made the charts in 1969.

BURNS, KENNETH C.: *See* Homer and Jethro

BURTON, ROBERT JAY: Music executive, attorney, past president, Broadcast Music, Inc.

Born New York, New York, September 21, 1914; died Vancouver, British Columbia, Canada, March 29, 1965.

The part of any field that meets the public eye is much like an iceberg. Behind every major public figure or group of figures there are many others who provide the basis for the artist's success. Two organizations that provide major support for the growth of country and western music are ASCAP and BMI.

One of the pioneers in the formation of the latter was Robert Jay Burton. He was born in New York and attended public schools in Larchmont. He also added a tinge of European culture to his background at the Chateau de Bures, France. He was graduated from Columbia University in 1935 and went on to gain his law degree from Columbia Law School in 1937.

When BMI began operations, Burton became resident attorney of the new music organization. He increased his activities with BMI as it grew into one of the major representatives of composers and related artists in various fields of modern music. His important contributions to BMI included much work in the field of copyright law as it affects music. Over the years he became a major authority in this field, serving on many committees of the Bar Association and lecturing and teaching at Columbia, New York University, Yale Law School and the College of the City of New York.

He found time in his schedule to serve as Acting City Judge of his home city of New Rochelle, New York, from 1960 to 1963. Meanwhile he had advanced from secretary to vice president of BMI. Upon his election to president of BMI in 1963 he resigned his judgeship. He remained as head of the corporation until his death. At the time of his passing, he was chairman of the Copyright Committee of the American Patent Law Association and a trustee of the Copyright Society of the U.S.A.

Burton's untimely end came as a result of a hotel fire while he was attending a convention in Vancouver, Canada.

BUTLER, CARL: Singer, guitarist, songwriter. Born Knoxville, Tennessee, June 2, 1927.

Carl Roberts Butler discovered how to cram two successful performing careers into a lifetime: add your wife to the act. For more than a decade, he had had star status as a solo performer and songwriter. Then in 1962 he was joined by his wife Pearl to form an act that won them the nod in a disk jockey poll as the number-one new vocal team of 1963.

Carl was born and raised in Knoxville, Tennessee, a hotbed of country music activity. He followed the Opry and other country and western programs eagerly as a boy and learned to play guitar before he reached high school age. In 1939, he was accomplished enough for his first show date, picking for a square dance and singing between the sets. By the time he was graduated from Stair Tech High School in the mid-1940s, he had a number of engagements at local clubs and dances to his credit.

During the next few years he appeared in shows in other parts of the southeast. He also was featured on radio on such stations as WROL and WNOX, Knoxville, and WPTF, Raleigh, North Carolina. In 1948 he was asked to join the Grand Ole Opry, the start of a long association with the show. He was featured on a number of TV shows in the 1950s, including appearances on WATE-TV and WBIR-TV in Knoxville.

In the 1950s, Carl moved ahead in the industry as both performer and songwriter. His own compositions were performed by such top artists as Roy Acuff, Carl Smith, Rosemary Clooney, Bill Monroe and Flatt & Scruggs. He wrote some songs with Earl Scruggs, including "Building on Sand" and "Crying My Heart Out Over You." Some of Carl's other efforts included "If Teardrops Were Pennies," "My Tears Don't Show," "Crying Alone," "Grief in My Heart," "Loving Arms," "A White Rose," "I Like to Pretend," "So Close," "Hold Back the Dawn," "Guilty Conscience" and "Country Mile."

Carl's recording efforts began with a contract with Capitol in 1951. In 1953, he switched to Columbia Records. Among his recordings during the 1950s and early 1960s were "Borrowed Love," "Angel Band," "Walking in God's Sunshine," "Hallelujah, We Shall Rise," "Only One Heart," "Through the Windows of Heaven," "Watching the Clock," "Cry You Fool, Cry," "If Teardrops Were Pennies," "River of Tears," "I Know What It Means to Be Lonesome," "I Know Why I Cry" and "You Don't Steal Pennies from a Poor Man."

Close harmony had long been a private enjoyment of Carl and his wife, Pearl. In 1962 they decided to try their hand as a show business team. They soon had a top 10 hit of 1962, "Don't Let Me Cross Over." Now a hit act, they

were featured on the Opry and such other network shows of the '60s as Porter Wagoner's. They also appeared in a movie, "Second Fiddle to a Steel Guitar." In 1964 they hit a new career high with another Carl Butler composition, "Too Late to Try Again." The song remained on the hit charts for many weeks, a good part of them in the number-one-ranked position.

Among Carl's LP total were such successes as "Carl Butler" ('63) and "Loving Arms" ('64).

BUTLER, PEARL: Singer, guitarist. Born Nashville, Tennessee, September 20.

A husband-and-wife team hailing from Knoxville and Nashville would seem a natural for country and western music success. The combined backgrounds helped move Mrs. Carl Butler from the kitchen to front and center on the Grand Ole Opry.

Growing up in Nashville, young Pearl Dee Jones naturally had a youthful interest in country and western music. As a girl she sang in school choruses, but also enjoyed singing some of the Grand Ole Opry hits for her own pleasure. When she completed schooling in Nashville, she had both an excellent singing voice and a solid reputation as one of the best cooks in her class.

Later, she added to the latter among country and western artists after her marriage to a young, rising performer, Carl Butler. For a good many years she remained in the background as Carl won his spurs as a top songwriter and musician. When Carl had time away from his profession, he and Pearl often took a busman's holiday, singing together at home or at family get-togethers. In the early 1960s, after Carl completed a new song called "Don't Let Me Cross Over," they decided to record it as a duet for Carl's label, Columbia.

The song became a top 10 hit of 1962, and the new team of Carl Butler and Pearl was on its way to regular status on the Grand Ole Opry. Carl and Pearl recorded such other well received songs as "Forbidden Street," "I'm Hanging Up the Phone," "Just Thought I'd Let You Know," "We'll Destroy Each Other," "Wrong Generation," "Little Mac," "Little Pedro," "Call 29" and "Same Old Me." In 1964, Carl wrote "Too Late to Try Again"; Carl and Pearl's recording became number one in the nation for several weeks in 1964.

The Butlers also turned out a number of hit

LPs during the mid-1960s, including "Don't Let Me Cross Over," "Greatest Country and Western Hits," and "Old and the New." In nationwide demand for personal appearances, they performed in all fifty states between 1962 and '67, as well as many parts of Canada and Europe. The Butlers also appeared in the movie "Second Fiddle to a Steel Guitar."

Carl and Pearl were awarded the title of best new vocal team of 1963 in the annual disk jockey poll. In 1967, their many years of effort for the Salvation Army resulted in their receiving that organization's Meritorious Service Award.

CAGLE, BUDDY: Singer, guitarist. Born Concord, North Carolina, February 8, 1936.

Country music often expresses the sadness and pain of everyday life. Buddy Cagle could understand the feeling in such songs from his own experience. Born in Concord, North Carolina, he spent his growing-up years in the Children's Home in Winston-Salem, North Carolina. When he was old enough to go out on his own, he enlisted in the Air Force for a four-year hitch.

He had always enjoyed country music, but had never thought much about making a career in the field. He still had no idea of going this route when he received his discharge in the late 1950s. A few years later, though, some of his friends suggested he had a good voice. He took this idea to heart and began to try to find work as a vocalist in the Southern California area.

Before long, he had several jobs under his belt and could call himself a professional. He met other country artists who were impressed with his ability. Some of them began to call him to the attention of local record companies. At the urging of Wynn Stewart and Don Sessions, Capitol signed him. In the early 1960s he turned out a number of well received records, including "The Gold Cup" and "Sing a Sad Song." Another of his efforts, "Your Mother's Prayer," was on the national charts for many weeks.

In the mid-1960s, Buddy toured widely with Hank Thompson and the Brazos Valley Boys. He embarked on three successful tours of Europe, playing in Germany, France, and Spain. He also performed on a number of TV shows in California and other parts of the country.

He moved from Capitol to Imperial Records

in the mid-'60s. One of his first efforts on the new label was "Tonight I'm Coming Home," which was high on the hit charts for 18 weeks. He also turned out "Apologize," which remained on the lists for 10 weeks.

CAMPBELL, ARCHIE: Singer, comic, narrator. Born Bulls Gap, Greene County, Tennessee, November 7, 1914.

Archie Campbell grew up in Bulls Gap which shows up on some maps of upper East Tennessee in the foothills of the Great Smoky Mountain country, next to a railroad line. He grew up liking what he saw around him in the world, a fine and mellow place for Campbell.

He studied art and has sold his works along with accepting commissions for his portrait paintings. It wasn't the art world that claimed him exclusively as he decided that the entertainment business was for him. His first major assignment was a spot on the Mid-Day Merry-Go-Round radio show on WNOX, Knoxville, where he worked with Roy Acuff, Chet Atkins, PeeWee King, Eddie Hill, Homer and Jethro and The Carlisles.

A Navy hitch during World War II was followed with his own television show, Country Playhouse, on WROL-TV, Knoxville, which helped launch Carl Smith, Carl and Pearl Butler, and Flatt & Scruggs. He joined the Prince Albert portion of the Grand Ole Opry in 1958 and was signed by RCA Victor. Campbell's versatile approach includes a series of comic routines with a wry touch as well as ballad singing and recitations, both serious as "Old Doc Brown" and humorous as "Beeping Sleauty." He also performs rocking gospels and is an accomplished after-dinner speaker for organizations, including charitable institutions.

He has bridged from the comedy era of the blackface Jam Up and Honey days to the Don Bowman approach of the 1960s. His recordings for RCA Victor include "Trouble in the Amen Corner," "Pee Little Thrigs," "Rindercella" and two albums, "Bedtime Stories for Adults" and "Have a Laff on Me."

CAMPBELL, GLEN: Singer, guitarist. Born Delight, Arkansas, April 10, 1938.

Instantaneous stardom is not unusual in rock 'n' roll ranks, but the way to the top in country and western usually calls for many years of seasoning. This accounts, perhaps, for the smooth showmanship of many first-rank country artists. Thus when youthful Glen Campbell became a national favorite in 1967, he had served an apprenticeship going back to six years of age.

He actually began his career as a musician at four. He was the seventh son of a father who also had been number seven in his own family. Sensing an interest in music in his child, Campbell senior gave Glen a Sears, Roebuck guitar when the boy was four. Within two years, Glen had mastered the instrument to the point where he achieved a regional reputation playing on radio programs in Arkansas and two neighboring states.

In the late 1950s, teenaged Glen accepted a bid to play with the western band of his uncle Dick Bills in Albuquerque, New Mexico. After a stint with Bills, Glen organized his own band and played in the southwest for several years. Finally feeling he was ready for more challenging things, he took off for Hollywood.

His skill as a twelve-string guitarist led to many offers for studio work. From 1960 on, he was a sideman at recording sessions for many top artists, both C&W and popular, on almost every major label. He signed with a local label and turned out a song that made the 1961 charts, "Turn Around—Look at Me." The success of the number resulted in a seven-year contract offer from Capitol Records. Soon after signing with Capitol he again made the charts with "Too Late to Worry—Too Blue to Cry."

However, despite some limited record successes, not too much happened to Glen's career for most of the 1960s. He continued to be in great demand as a sideman and appeared as a performer on many local C&W in-person shows. Capitol felt he had potential and turned out several LPs, including "The Astounding 12-String Guitar of Glen Campbell" and "Burning Bridges."

In 1967, during a visit to Nashville, Glen became acquainted with the work of a new country writer-performer, John Hartford. He turned out a record of "Gentle on My Mind" that made a major mark on the national scene. This was followed by a hit LP of the same title. Then, in late '67, Glen followed up with a recording of a number written by 21-year-old songwriter Jim Webb. The song, "By the Time I Get to Phoenix," his number one on all national popular lists, a feat equaled by the LP of the same title.

Now a firmly established star, Glen was featured on TV and in nightclubs and concerts throughout the country. His guest appearances in 1967-'68 included Boss City, Groovy, Dick Clark's American Bandstand, Red Skelton, Pat Boone, Woody Woodbury, Mike Douglas, the Tonight Show and The Smothers Brothers Show. In mid-1968, Glen had another successful LP, "Hey Little One," and the job of m.c. for the CBS-TV show called "The Summer Brothers Smothers Show." He won gold records in 1968 for "Wichita Lineman" and 1969 for "Galveston," and won his own show on CBS-TV.

CANSLER, LOMAN: Singer, guitarist, folk music collector. Born near Long Lane, Missouri, September 6, 1924.

As a teacher of American history, Loman Cansler could appreciate the close relationship between traditional folk music and the development of the country. He could point to a rich heritage of folklore going back to his childhood days in his home state of Missouri.

He was born and raised on a farm in Dallas County near Springfield, Missouri. His parents and grandparents were all musically inclined and sang many old ballads around the house or during family gatherings. Young Loman also heard many songs from the neighbors and family friends in the days when sings were prime sources of community entertainment. By the time he finished the grades at Northview Rural School, he knew many songs by heart and had begun to pick out chords on the guitar. During the late 1930s, he and his brother Ralph sometimes entertained at local events.

He did not continue his formal schooling after grade school and might have concentrated on farming except for the outbreak of World War II. Loman entered the Navy and was assigned to programs that helped prepare him for college. When he was discharged, he decided to take the entrance exams for the University of Missouri. He was accepted in 1946 and attended the University until 1950. While in college, his interest in folk music grew and deepened. He made several tours through Missouri and Illinois, during vacation periods, collecting material.

In 1949, he made his first major public appearance before a church retreat near Lake of the Ozarks, Missouri. After finishing college, he began his teaching career at Fayette, Missouri. In two years he moved to a new job as teacher of American history at North Kansas City

High School, Missouri. During the 1950s, he was asked to perform many times before local groups. He also took part in concerts in other parts of the country. Some of his most pleasing performances were before history classes in his own and other schools and colleges.

Besides collecting folk music, he also wrote a number of articles for scholarly publications, including the Southern Folklore Quarterly, Missouri Council of Social Studies Bulletin, and Rayburn's Ozark Guide. His reputation extended beyond his home state by the late 1950s, resulting in a bid from Folkways Records to make an LP album. The album, issued in 1959, was titled "Missouri Folk Songs." It included such songs as "When I Leave for to Take My Leave," "Judgement Day," "The Blue and The Gray," "Far Away," "Charles Guiteau," "I Told 'em Not to Grieve After Me," "Kickin' Mule" and "Arthur Clyde."

CANTU, WILLIE: *See* Buckaroos, The

CARAWAN, GUY: Singer, guitarist. Born Los Angeles, California, July 28, 1927.

One of the many young folk artists who rose to fame on the coffee house circuit of the 1950s was Guy Carawan. Like many of these performers, he was a political activist, singing both classical ballads and protest songs and also taking a major role in many of the civil rights demonstrations of the late 1950s and early '60s.

Carawan's family moved to Los Angeles from the Carolinas, and Guy was born and brought up in the land of sun and surf. He entered the University of California at Los Angeles in the late 1940s and went on to complete his master's degree in sociology in 1953. He had learned to play the guitar, and entertained in school activities. When he finished college, he decided to travel through the south and southwest to collect folk material. In the mid-1950s he began to attract attention as a promising folk artist with his work in such bellwether locations as New York's Greenwich Village and the Ash Grove Coffee House in Los Angeles.

In 1957, he went to the World Youth Festival in Moscow as did the Seegers and other folk performers. Significantly, he continued his travels through Red China as well as Europe in the following year. He returned to the U.S. to perform at many major concerts and festivals in the late 1950s. In 1959, he also worked at the Highlander Folk School in Monteagle,

Tennessee, which included as students many people in the civil rights movement. During this period and in the 1960s, Carawan spent a good part of his time helping with sit-ins and protest marches. Besides entertaining the marchers, he also collected songs from the movement. Among the songs he helped make one of the symbols of civil rights was "We Shall Overcome."

By the late '50s, he had also turned out a number of recordings of folk material. In 1959, Folkways produced a three-LP album of his work.

Besides performing, Carawan also worked to develop the talents of Negro folk artists. In 1963, this led to organization of the Sea Island Singers on Johns Island, South Carolina. The group was set up to perform many of the traditional songs of Negro culture and was featured at several Newport Folk Festival concerts in the mid-1960s.

In addition to performing at major folk festivals throughout the world, Carawan also found time to lecture. In the spring and summer of 1968, he taught classes at Pitzer College, Pomona, California.

CARLISLES, THE: *See* Carlisle, Bill and Cliff

CARLISLE, BILL AND CLIFF: Singers, instrumentalists, comedians, songwriters, Bill Carlisle, born Wakefield, Kentucky, December 19, 1908; Cliff Carlisle, born near Taylorsville, Kentucky, May 6, 1904.

To sports fans, the name Carlisle means the famed Indian school for which Jim Thorpe played. The Carlisles of Kentucky were no relation to the school, but their star began to rise about the time Carlisle College went out of business. For more than three decades, the name, as borne by Cliff Carlisle and his younger brother Bill, meant some of the best contributions to country music and country humor.

Both boys learned to play the guitar during their school days in Wakefield, Kentucky. Clifford Raymond Carlisle preceded his brother at Ashes Creek Grade School near Wakefield, attending from 1912 to 1915. William Carlisle began school about the time Cliff started his courses at Doe Run Grade School in Wakefield. Cliff went to Doe Run from 1916 to 1920 and then finished his schooling (1922) at Jacob's Addition Grade in Louisville, Kentucky, after the family moved there in 1921.

By the time the family moved to Louisville,

young Bill could take full part in Carlisle Sunday sings with his four brothers and two sisters. Cliff, by this time, was beginning to perform professionally. When Bill finished school some years later, he decided to follow in Cliff's footsteps and try for a career in country music. As the Carlisle Brothers, Cliff and Bill were featured on many shows in the Louisville-Cincinnati area from the late 1920s through the 1940s.

The brothers' first radio exposure was on station WLAP, Lexington, Kentucky, in 1931. They moved to a Louisville station in 1937. Over the next decade, though spending much time in their home region, they played throughout the midwest and were featured for a time on a station in Charlotte, North Carolina.

One of the top hits of Cliff and Bill was "Fresh from the Country." This was also the title of their King LP album of 1959. In the late 1940s the brothers began to go their separate ways, touring with their own groups at times, though still performing together at others. Bill was featured on station WSB, Atlanta, in 1949 and soon after formed a new group called The Carlisles.

The Carlisles soon became one of the most popular humorous groups in the country and western field. Their first radio engagement in Cincinnati, at the start of the 1950s, was avidly followed by local audiences. Their comic rendition of "Rainbow at Midnight" was soon turned into a national record hit. They followed up in the early 1950s with two more successes in the same vein, "No Help Wanted" and "Too Old to Cut the Mustard," both of which were written by Bill. After several guest appearances on the KWKH Louisiana Hayride, The Carlisles accepted a bid to perform on station WNOX in Knoxville. They added two top 10 hits to their earlier 1953 Mercury record success, "No Help Wanted," with "Is Zat You Myrtle" and "Knothole." Bill wrote the latter himself and the former in collaboration with the Louvin Brothers.

In 1954, Bill and The Carlisles were asked to join the cast of the Grand Ole Opry. The group remained major cast members for many years. After it disbanded, Bill was still an Opry regular in the 1960s. In 1966, his Opry audiences roared at his new hit, which became a top 10 national favorite, "What Kinda Deal Is This."

During his long career, Bill recorded for Bluebird, RCA Victor, Mercury, King and, in the mid-1960s, Hickory. Some of his other songs on these various labels were "Rattlesnake Daddy," "I'm Rough Stuff," "Do You Need Any Help?" "Shake a Leg," "Business Man," "Gettin' Younger," "The Girl in the Blue Velvet Band," "Wedding Bells," "Maggie," "Rainbow Follows Rain," "Lost on a Sea of Sorrow," "Dollar Bill Mama Blues I and II," "Tramp on the Street," "Poor Man's Riches," "Skip to My Lou," "Old Joe Clark," and "I Hope You See the Same Star I Do." In 1967, Bill was featured on a Hickory LP, "Best of Bill Carlisle."

CARSON, MARTHA: Singer, guitarist, songwriter. Born Neon, Kentucky, March 19, 1921.

Martha Carson has a rare talent for pleasing a range of audiences from posh supper clubs to the more exuberant country fairground crowds. Her ability is attested to by a number of awards for her entertaining and songwriting ability by music business trade magazines, such as Cashbox and Billboard.

Born in the implausibly named Neon, Kentucky, a name that symbolized Martha's future success, but not the town's night life, Martha spent most of her growing-up years in the Bluegrass state. She performed in local programs when she was little and learned to play first class guitar by the time she was in her teens. In the late 1930s, young Martha was already pleasing audiences at dances and other events in the border states region. The year 1939 brought her first radio experience, over station WHIS, Bluefield, West Virginia.

In 1940, her name became known to listeners in many other states as she was featured on several of the top country and western radio shows of the period. These included the Renfro Valley Kentucky Barn Dance and the WSB Barn Dance from Atlanta, Georgia. During the 1940s she toured widely, winning applause from crowds in many parts of the country.

By the start of the 1950s, she was well established as a major country and western artist. She had also begun to write songs in both country and gospel vein. In 1950 she joined the cast of the Tennessee Barn Dance, WNOX, Knoxville. Two years later she was asked to join the Grand Ole Opry. Late in the decade, she spent some time in California as a member of the Town Hall Party Show on Channel 11 in Compton, California.

[47]

During the 1950s, some of her recordings gained national attention in popular as well as country and western markets. Her own composition "Satisfied" was one of these that helped win bids to appear on many major network TV programs. During the 1950s and '60s, her credits included guest spots on the Ed Sullivan Show, Tennessee Ernie Ford's Show, NBC-TV's Tonight, Ray Bolger's Washington Square Show, the Arlene Frances Show, and the Galaxy of Stars Show. She was also featured on such country and western programs as Jubilee U.S.A. and Jimmy Dean.

Her diversity was shown by the locations of some 250 personal appearances she made yearly in the mid-1960s. The list included country fairs, college auditoriums, and such supper clubs as the Waldorf Astoria, Chez Paree, Chase Hotel and Latin Casino.

Her record output in the 1950s and early '60s included songs on three different labels, RCA Victor, Capitol, and Cadence. Among her recordings were such numbers as "Light of Love," "Rock-A-My-Soul," "Journey to the Sky," "Amen," "Shadrack," "Who Built the Ark," "That Ain't Right," "Get on the Heavenly Road," "Ac-cent-tchu-ate the Positive," "Gonna Shout All Over God's Heaven," "Get That Golden Key," "Music Drives Me Crazy," "Get on Board Little Children," "He's Got the Whole World in His Hands," "Let the Light Shine," "This Ole House," "Dixieland Roll" and "Be Not Discouraged." Her albums included "Rock-A-My-Soul" and "Journey to the Sky."

Besides "Satisfied," her list of more than 100 compositions includes such songs as "I'm Gonna Walk and Talk with My Lord" and "I Can't Stand Up Alone."

In 1967, Martha signed a new recording contract with Decca Records.

CARTER, A. P.: *See* Carter Family

CARTER, ANITA: *See* Carter, June; Carter, Mother Maybelle

CARTER FAMILY: Vocal and instrumental group, originally consisting of Alvin Pleasant "A.P." Carter, born Maces Spring, Virginia, died Maces Spring, November 7, 1960; Sara Carter, born Wise County, Virginia, July 21, 1899; Maybelle Carter, born Nickelsville, Virginia, May 10, 1909.

On August 1, 1927, a historic event took place in the border city of Bristol, Tennessee. In the upper story of a three-story house at 410 State Street on the Tennessee side (the state line between Virginia and Tennessee runs down the middle of the street), Ralph Peer, RCA Victor talent scout, supervised the first recordings of the soon-to-be-famed Carter Family. It was a doubly important day, for the first cuts of another legendary artist, Jimmie Rodgers, were also made.

The Carter Family had come down from their home in Maces Spring, Virginia, near Clinch Mountain, in response to an advertisement in *The Bristol Herald*, offering auditions to local musicians. The Original Carter Family consisted of A.P. Carter, his wife Sara, and Carter's sister-in-law, Maybelle Carter. For the first session, Maybelle and Sara played guitar and sang in support of A.P.'s bass singing. The first six songs recorded that day, which were soon to make the Carter Family well known in many parts of the country, were "Bury Me Under the Weeping Willow," "Little Log Cabin by the Sea," "The Poor Orphan Child," "The Storms Are on the Ocean," "Single Girl, Married Girl" and "Wandering Boy."

The Carters' singing had been distilled from many years of country music heritage. Long before this date, they had performed for church socials, school parties, and other local events. Both Sara and Maybelle had become expert at the guitar and autoharp when they were little girls, and they and A.P. had learned many old hill-country ballads from their parents and friends. Music was one of the prime pleasures of A.P. and Sara's lives after their marriage on June 18, 1915. (Sara's maiden name was Dougherty.)

In a short time after Peer completed the first Carter cuts, RCA came back for more. By

The Original Carter Family (l. to r.): Maybelle (Mother Maybelle), Sara, and A. P. Carter

Two generations of Carters are shown in this 1938 picture. Standing, from left, are A. P. Carter, Jeanette (daughter of Sara and A. P.), radio announcer Bill Rinehart, Sara, Maybelle. In front are Maybelle's three daughters, Helen, Anita, and June.

the end of the 1920s, the group was known from one end of the country to the other. In the 1930s, their fame continued to spread, resulting in many more record releases and personal appearances at county fairs and city auditoriums and on radio in many parts of the U.S.

The popularity of the Carters kept them together as a group even though increasing problems cropped up in the marriage of A.P. and Sara. They were divorced in 1936, but continued to perform together until the early 1940s.

Among the many Carter recordings were such songs as "Keep on the Sunny Side," "Foggy Mountain Top," "Room in Heaven for Me," "Soldiers Beyond the Blue," "The Titanic," "Where the Sunset Turns," "False-Hearted Lover," "On the Rock Where Moses Stood," "The Homestead on the Farm," "On a Hill Lone and Gray," "Anchored in Love," "Meeting in the Air," "Pickin' in the Wildwood," "Worried Man Blues," "Gathering Flowers from the Hillside," "Forsaken Love," "You Are My Flower," "Western Hobo," "I Shall Not Be Moved," "Carter Blues," "Beyond the River," "The Wayworn Traveler," "Angel Band," "Dixie Darling," "Waves of the Sea," "Sunshine in the Shadows," and "My Clinch Mountain Home." From their first session in August 1927 to their last record date on October 14, 1941, the original Carters recorded more than 250 songs.

Typical Carter Family songs that became country standards were their version of "Wabash Cannonball" and A.P. Carter's original compositions, "I'm Thinking Tonight of My Blue Eyes," "Lonesome Valley," and "Jimmy Brown the Newsboy." The Carter Family left the border region in 1938 to accept a daily program on station XERA, Mexico, near Del Rio, Texas. Also taking part in some of the group singing by now were A.P. and Sara's children, Jeanette and Joe. The Family stayed in Del Rio until 1941, when they moved to station WBT in Charlotte, North Carolina. In 1943, the original members went separate ways and A.P. returned to Maces Spring.

Maybelle formed a new act with her three daughters, June, Helen, and Anita, and moved to Richmond, Virginia. From 1943 to 1948, Maybelle and the Carter Sisters were featured on station WRVA in Richmond, Virginia. Soon after this, they accepted an offer to join the Grand Ole Opry. In the 1950s, the girls went their separate ways, but Maybelle remained a regular on the Opry into the 1960s. (*See also* CARTER, JUNE; CARTER, MOTHER MAYBELLE)

CARTER, FRED F.: Singer, guitarist, songwriter, recording director. Born Winnsboro, Louisiana, December 31, 1933.

The "Nashville Sound" is one of the great elements of country and western music in the post-World War II decades. The term refers to the improvisations provided by studio musicians in the Nashville area that provided a new depth and originality to modern music. The success of the "Nashville Sound" thus is due to talented artists such as top-flight guitarist Fred Carter.

Carter was brought up in Louisiana, where he was exposed to many of the traditional forms of country music. He gained a deep interest in it at an early age and could play proficient guitar in his teens. In the early 1950s, he began

to gain experience the hard way, starting on the fringes as a sideman in small local bands and playing recording dates for small record companies.

He began to gain notice as a guitarist's guitarist, resulting in a position with the Conway Twitty contingent in the late 1950s. His backing was so effective that he was soon asked to help turn out demonstration records for both publishers and songwriters. Since he had a good singing voice, he served as both vocalist and instrumentalist for these. By the 1960s, he was receiving regular demo work from both Nashville and New York writers and publishers.

In the 1960s, he made Nashville his base. Besides his continued supporting work, he was given a recording contract by Monument Records. His recordings included some of his own compositions, many of which were also recorded by major country and western artists. The importance of Carter to the "Nashville Sound" was shown by the fact that he played guitar on close to 90 per cent of all Nashville record sessions in the mid-1960s. By 1967, Carter also had the post of artist and repertoire director for the Country Music Division of ABC Records.

CARTER, HELEN: *See* Carter, June; Carter, Mother Maybelle

CARTER, JUNE: Singer, autoharpist, actress, comedienne, songwriter. Born Maces Spring, Virginia, June 23, 1929.

One of the royal families of folk and country music, the Carter Family was well represented in several areas of show business into the second generation. In the case of June, one of the three daughters of Mother Maybelle Carter, she made her mark not only as a singer and musician, but as a star of a number of TV series.

As a child, June had the chance to hear many performances of her mother, aunt, and uncle. Like her sisters, she exhibited musical talent at an early age. Her mother, who brought renewed attention to the autoharp as an important folk-country instrument in the 1930s, also taught June to play. June enjoyed singing with her sisters, Helen and Anita, and the three girls began to appear as the Carter Sisters in 1943. During the 1940s, the girls toured many parts of the country and, with Mother Maybelle, were featured on such stations as WBT, Charlotte,

North Carolina, WRVA, Richmond, Virginia, and WNOX, Knoxville, Tennessee. In the late 1940s they reached a wide audience over Si Siman's station KWTO, Springfield, Missouri. Besides singing and playing the autoharp, June also displayed a talent for comedy in the Carter Family act.

In 1950–51, the Carter Sisters and Mother Maybelle were asked to join the Grand Ole Opry and moved to Nashville. June remained with the group for several years, but found a growing interest in dramatics. She struck out on her own after a while, attending drama school in New York. By the late 1950s, she was well launched into a career of her own. She guested as a singer on such shows as Tennessee Ernie Ford, Jack Paar, and Garry Moore. As an actress, she began to appear on several TV series, including "Jim Bowie" and "Gunsmoke." Her credits also include a part in the movie "Country Music Holiday."

She turned out a number of her own records over the years in addition to recording with her mother and sisters. Her renditions on Columbia and RCA Victor labels included "Tennessee Mambo," "Time's a Wastin'," "He Don't Love Me Anymore," "Leftover Lovin'," and "Love, Oh Crazy Love." In 1949, she showed her talents as a singing comedienne, vocalizing with Homer and Jethro in the top 10 parody of "Baby, It's Cold Outside."

During the 1950s and '60s, June's name showed up on the credit line of a number of hit songs. In the 1960s, she was particularly successful in writing material for, and in some cases with, Johnny Cash. In 1963, for example, she co-authored "The Matador" with Johnny, one of his major hits of the year. June also teamed with Merle Kilgore in 1963 to write a great standard, "Ring of Fire." In 1966, the writing combination of June, Merle, and Johnny brought Cash a top 10 success, "Happy to Be with You."

In 1967, June teamed with Johnny on several songs that became top hits in both country and western and popular markets. These included "Jackson" and "Guitar Pickin' Man." Soon after, June married Johnny. (*See also* CARTER FAMILY; CARTER, MOTHER MAYBELLE; CASH, JOHNNY)

CARTER, MOTHER MAYBELLE: Singer, autoharpist, guitarist, songwriter. Born Nickelsville, Virginia, May 10, 1909.

The artistry of the Carter Family had become a living legend in both folk and country music circles by the end of the 1930s. More than two and a half decades later, it was still represented by an original member of the group, the redoubtable "Mother" Maybelle Carter. The continued vitality of the Carter tradition was confirmed by the rousing ovation given her performance at the Country Music & Blues session of the 1967 Newport Folk Festival.

Born and raised in southwestern Virginia, Maybelle began to sing traditional hill-country ballads almost as soon as she could talk. She learned to play both the guitar and the autoharp before reaching her teens and won much applause from friends and relations at local sings. Before she was out of her teens, she married Ezra Carter on March 23, 1926, and set up housekeeping with him in Poor Valley, Virginia, about 25 miles from Bristol, Tennessee.

Ezra also came from a musical family. His brother A.P. and A.P.'s wife Sara were particularly skilled musicians, and in the mid-1920s Maybelle joined them to perform at many local events. On August 1, 1927 (*see* Carter Family), A.P. took his own family and Maybelle to Bristol to answer an RCA Victor ad for recording talent. The results of the first records soon made the Original Carter Family the royalty of American country music. In the years that followed, Maybelle joined A.P. and Sara in nationwide tours and many more recording sessions in such places as Camden, New Jersey, Chicago, Illinois, New York City, Atlanta, Georgia, and Memphis, Tennessee.

When the Carters accepted a bid to broadcast a daily program on station XERA near Del Rio, Texas, Maybelle and her own family moved there. In 1941, she and the other Carters headed north again to a new show on station WBT in Charlotte, North Carolina. The Original Carters were joined for many performances by their children, including Maybelle's three daughters, Helen, June, and Anita. In 1943, after A.P. returned to Maces Spring and Sara (who had divorced A.P. in the late 1930s and married Coy Bayes in 1939) settled permanently in Angels Camp, California, Maybelle and her daughters moved on to Richmond for their own show on station WRVA. For the next five years, Maybelle and the Carter Sisters starred on WRVA and also made personal appearances in many sections of the country.

In 1949, Maybelle and the girls moved to

[51]

PUBLIC LIBRARY

GOSHEN, INDIANA

Nashville, where they became featured stars on the Grand Ole Opry. Among the songs they recorded for Decca and Columbia Records were "Amazing Grace," "Wabash Cannonball," "Are You Afraid to Remember Me," "Wildwood Flower," "Gold Watch and Chain," "Blood That Stained the Old Rugged Cross," "Gethsemane," "How About You" and "Softly and Tenderly." They also treated Opry audiences to some of Maybelle's own compositions, such as "A Jilted Love" and "Walk a Little Closer." Their repertoire also included songs co-written by Maybelle, including "I've Got a Home in Glory," "The Kneeling Drunkard's Plea," "Don't Wait," and "A Rose Covered Grave."

When the girls went their own ways in the 1950s, Maybelle continued to star on the Opry. In 1967, still an Opry regular, she was also in demand for personal appearances on both the folk and country music circuits. Her repertoire by then included songs of such "new wave" folk artists as Bob Dylan and Johnny Cash.

Her LP output included such titles as "Songs of the Famous Carter Family" (Maybelle and Flatt & Scruggs) on Columbia; "Mother Maybelle" on Briar Records; and "Mother Maybelle Carter" on Smash Records ('64).

CARTER, SARA: *See* Carter Family

CARTER, WILF (MONTANA SLIM): Singer, songwriter, guitarist. Born Guysboro, Nova Scotia, December 18, 1904.

Wilf Carter is a cowboy, no doubt about it. He has covered the rodeo circuit regularly and is in the Horsemen's Hall of Fame. He was brought up in Canadian ranch country, later shifting around from job to job, picking and singing.

After Merle Anderson hired him as a cowboy in 1924, Carter combined two professions into one. Anderson, who still enters a chuck wagon into the races at the Calgary Stampede each year, was influential in encouraging Carter to entertain along the rodeo circuit.

Carter's radio experience started in Calgary (Ontario), Canada, in 1933 on CFCN. Shortly after another program for Radio Vancouver, he moved to New York for a CBS radio show. It was around this time that Bert Parks introduced him as "Montana Slim," which he adopted.

His recording career has been with Bluebird, Decca, and more recently with Don Pierce's Starday label in Madison, Tennessee. His repertoire is predominantly campfire-and-roundup-flavored—plaintive ballads and yodels with overtones of Jimmie Rodgers' influence.

"I'm Hittin' the Trail" and "Swiss Moonlight Lullaby" are among the five hundred-plus songs written by Carter. In the late 1960s, Wilf was in professional semi-retirement, living in Winter Park, Florida. He kept his cowboy roots going with an interest in a Canadian ranching operation. A visit to New York to see Roy Horton of Peer-Southern Organization in 1967 resulted in a recording session that provided an LP, "Montana Slim–Wilf Carter," released on Starday.

CASH, JOHNNY: Singer, guitarist, songwriter. Born Kingsland, Arkansas, February 26, 1932.

Troubled, talented, dynamic John R. "Johnny" Cash was an erratic comet across the horizons of American music in the mid-twentieth century. His genius showed through in performances and original compositions that made him a top name in not only country and western, but folk and popular music too.

Some of the answers to his complex personality lay in the poverty and daily fight for survival of his youth. The Ray Cash family was proud, though bent by years of sharecropping, tragedy, and near tragedy. Johnny was born and almost died of starvation in his infancy in Kingsland, Dyess County, Arkansas. Life consisted of a dirt farmer's shack, five brothers and sisters, cotton patches to be hoed and weeded, and a fundamentalist Bible rearing by a determined mother and a work-wearied father. Undertones of all this break through often in fragments of his songs and attitudes toward life.

The family stayed together, but when Cash was in his early teens, another blow struck the sensitive youngster. Sudden death claimed two brothers, leaving Johnny, Reba, Joann and Tommy to work the fields with their parents.

Johnny finally began to break away from his old ties when he enlisted in the Air Force at 22. After his discharge in the mid-1950s, he scratched for a living as an appliance salesman in Memphis. In his spare time, he took a radio announcing course as a gesture toward a more creative existence. In Memphis he met Luther Perkins, who played an amplified guitar, and bass player Marshall Grant.

They got together and practiced with the

ultimate objective of auditioning for Sam Phillips of Sun Records, discoverer of many young country and western artists. The audition finally arrived, resulting in a recording contract and a 100,000-record sale of Johnny's initial "Hey, Porter"/"Cry, Cry, Cry" release. These were followed with "Folsom Prison Blues" and such top 10 hits, in 1956, as "So Doggone Lonesome," "There You Go" and "I Walk the Line," all three original Cash compositions.

Johnny quickly became one of Sun Records' all-time successes. In 1957, he scored with such top 10 originals as "Train of Love" and "Next in Line" and a co-authored hit, "Home of the Blues." The following year, Johnny had six top 10 hits, including two number-one-ranked songs, "Guess Things Happen That Way" and "Ballad of a Teenage Queen." The other four records included three he wrote or co-wrote, "You're the Nearest Thing to Heaven," "What Do I Care" and "All Over Again" plus "The Ways of a Woman in Love."

By now his first manager, Bob Neal, had booked Cash and the "Tennessee Two" into personal appearances throughout the country and the money came easier. (This later became the Tenessee Three with the addition of Bill Holland on drums.) In 1958, Cash moved from Sun to Columbia Records and his first release, his composition "Don't Take Your Guns to Town," sold past the half-million mark and stayed in number one spot for many weeks. His first Columbia LP scored an impressive 400,000. Sun Records released more of his material in 1959 and had another top 10 record in "Luther Played the Boogie." Columbia hit pay dirt with Johnny's original versions of "Frankie's Man Johnny" and "I Got Stripes."

Going into the 1960s, Cash had a growing national reputation. He was featured on both country and western and major network variety shows. As the 1960s went by, he also became a favorite with folk music audiences, starring at many major folk festivals and performing in folk-oriented clubs in many parts of the country.

Success did not bring smooth sailing, though. Johnny's moods sometimes caused him to retreat from the world in an effort to erase memories of present and past. At other times, he presented a different face, one of boundless energy and a deep preoccupation with first one, then another subject—to a point of obsession. At times, his driving approach to his career came close to the "burnout syndrome" of legendary Jimmie

Rodgers and Hank Williams.

Despite these problems, some of which resulted in occasional negative mentions in newspaper columns, Johnny continued to turn out records and songs that had music fans crying for more. His top 10 hits of the 1960s included "Seasons of My Heart" ('60); "In the Jailhouse Now" ('62); "The Matador," and one of Johnny's greatest hits, number-one-ranked "Ring of Fire" ('63); "Bad News," "It Ain't Me Babe," "The Ballad of Ira Hayes," number-one-ranked "Understand Your Man" (written by Cash) ('64); "Orange Blossom Special," "The Sons of Katie Elder" ('65); "Happy to Be with You," "The One on the Right Is on the Left" ('66); "Jackson," and "Guitar Pickin' Man" ('67). The last two were made with June Carter, who became Mrs. Cash in 1967.

His Columbia LPs, most of which were bestsellers, included "Songs of Our Soil," "Johnny Cash," "Hymns" ('59); "Ride This Train," "There Was a Song" ('60); "Hymns from the Heart," "Sound of Johnny Cash" ('62); "Blood, Sweat and Tears," "Ring of Fire" ('63); "I Walk the Line," "Bitter Tears" ('64); "Orange Blossom Special" ('65); "Everybody Loves a Nut," and "Mean as Hell!" ('66). In 1968 Johnny scored of his greatest successes with his gold record LP, "Johnny Cash at Folsom Prison."

Johnny's contribution to America's musical heritage was recognized by inclusion of one of his guitars in the U. S. exhibit at Expo 67. (*See also* CARTER, JUNE)

CHANDLER, LEN: Singer, guitarist, songwriter. Born Akron, Ohio, May 27, 1935.

"Len Chandler—acutely contemporary and emotionally individual—a superb ear for varied and idiomatic speech, edited into stories of real power and poignancy—an evocative and husky sound, which is passionate in expressing both virility and vulnerability—his impact comes from a fusion of qualities: voice, intelligence, integrity and lyrics of flesh and bone."

So said Nat Hentoff in reviewing Len Chandler's first Columbia LP, "To Be A Man," in the June 1966 issue of Hi-Fi Stereo Review. He referred to a man whose songs had been accepted by folk music fans and his brethren of the civil rights movement as folk classics. By the time he was 25, Chandler had written more than 50 folk songs, many of which were soon believed to have been of the folk music domain for decades.

[53]

Born and brought up in Akron, Chandler first was introduced to music at nine when his mother sent him to chamber-music recitals. He enjoyed classical music and took lessons on the oboe and French horn in high school. He continued his studies at the University of Akron. At the same time, he was an accomplished musician and a member of the city's symphony orchestra. While he was at the university, a visiting professor from New York, Walter Lehrman, introduced him to the folk recordings of such great artists as Guthrie, Broonzy, and Leadbelly.

Len became deeply interested in this form of music, an interest that increased when he gained a scholarship to Columbia University in New York. While earning his master's degree, he began to frequent folk music locales in the city. Before long he had learned the guitar and was performing at some of the clubs himself.

By the late 1950s, he also was active in civil rights movements. When the civil rights marches began, he journeyed throughout the south to take part in them. His activities included entertaining the marchers with folk songs, both classical and ones he had written himself.

He continued his activities in the 1960s, appearing at many folk music concerts and performing in coffee houses all over the country. His compositions, such as "The Wicked Weirs," were now being performed by most of the folksingers of the country. In the summer of 1963, the power of his music was demonstrated at a street hootennany in Cambridge, Massachusetts. Chandler played his songs commemorating civil rights martyr Medgar Evers of Mississippi and, as *The New York Times* reported, "galvanized a throng of 11,000. . . ."

Chandler suffered a near-fatal accident in 1963 when he knocked on the wrong door late at night in Greenwich Village. The people in the apartment assumed that Chandler was a mugger and hit him on the head with a lead pipe. Physicians had to perform a delicate six-hour brain and nerve operation to save his life and the use of his left hand. Fortunately he came out of it able to continue his career. Late in 1963, he began a series of Sunday Broadside Hoots at the Village Gate in New York with other major folk artists.

Chandler LPs appeared on various labels in the 1960s. In 1966 he signed with Columbia. By mid-1967, he had turned out two LPs on the Columbia label, including the well received "To Be A Man."

CHARLES, ROOSEVELT: Singer, songwriter. Born Louisiana, 1919*.

"Back in 1937, times was hard and work was hard, the boss was very hard. The inmates they were very cruel sometime themself. You get out on the job sometime early in the mornin'; we'd be drowsy, feelin' bad. The leader of Number One would go to hollerin' "John Henry." That mean pick your tools up high an' let 'em fall together. Boys, then the life would hit the gang an' they would start to rollin' on.

"Every now an' then you'd call the water boy and the water boy he'd look around at the boss. The boss would tell him, 'Ya can carry him water if ya wanta, an' if ya don't, ya don't hafta because they get water outa the tools.' They mean by gettin' water outa the tools you'd hafta drink the sweat from yo' top lip."

So Roosevelt Charles described the background of his life and the source of his music to Harry Oster. It was Oster who collected the blues and work songs of Charles for the few recordings available of this folk artist.

As Oster points out, most of Charles' life has been spent in prison. He was born in rural Louisiana and never knew his parents. Charles told Oster he was "raised by the buzzard and hatched by the sun." When he was nine years old, he tried to escape from the hard work and misery of Louisiana by grabbing "an armful of freight" and bumming his way to Los Angeles.

Los Angeles was no kinder to him than Louisiana and he was back in the south by the time he reached his teens. Charles had a natural talent for music and for creating lyrics, but his main way of existing was through criminal acts. In 1937, he was sentenced to notorious Angola prison in Louisiana for killing a man in a drunken brawl. By 1959, he was on his third sentence at Angola when Oster heard of his musical talent and taped some of Charles' songs. When Charles was released on parole shortly after, Oster paid him to perform odd jobs at his house in Baton Rouge and also continued taping Roosevelt's music. By 1961, Charles was back in prison again for the fourth

* Exact month and day of birth not available.

[54]

and presumably last time, since a four-time loser is not eligible for parole.

The few joys and many sorrows of this kind of life are evident in Charles' Vanguard LP, "Blues, Prayer, Work and Trouble Songs." The album includes such numbers as "Mean Trouble Blues," "Mule Blues," "Pick 'Em Up Higher," "Greenback Dollar Blues," "That Ole Ship o' Zion," "Freight Train Blues" and "Wasn't I Lucky." An example of a talking blues composed in part by Charles is "The Boll Weevil and the Bale Weevil."

CHILD, FRANCIS J.: Folklorist, author, educator. Born Boston, Massachusetts, February 1, 1825; died Boston, Massachusetts, September 11, 1896.

Harvard University isn't a strange place to be associated with folk music in the post-Korean War era. To many, though, it does seem odd to connect the austere image of the Harvard of the 1800s with the field. However, not only is this so, but it was at Harvard that the groundwork was laid for the world-wide folk scholarship of the current century.

The man responsible for this was a brilliant professor of English at Harvard, Francis James Child. Child's youthful goal was to go to the great university of his home town, and he achieved this despite his father's meager income as a sailmaker. His obvious gift for learning won him a series of scholarships that brought a degree from Harvard in 1846. A few years later, in 1851, he was appointed Boylston Professor of rhetoric, oratory, and elocution. By the time he gained this position, he was deeply immersed in literature studies in Berlin and Gottingen. This work occupied his time from 1849 to 1853. It helped establish his reputation as a scholar in Europe and, eventually, led to a book contract that changed his life.

In 1855, he increased his stature by editing a five-volume edition of the works of British poet Edmund Spenser. He was then asked to prepare a study of Anglo-Scottish ballads as part of a series covering British poets. The result was an eight-volume set, "English and Scottish Ballads," published in 1857–58. Child was not satisfied with the short period of time given him to prepare the material, particularly since he became intensely interested in the subject during his researches. From then on, his thoughts turned more and more to doing a

proper study. Eventually, he was determined to spend years, if necessary, to compile a work covering all authentic old folk ballads.

He began to collect materials on ancient British folk music, increasing his efforts as time went on. He did not abandon his studies of English literature, however. In 1863, he wrote a famed treatise called "Observations on the Language of Chaucer." The University recognized his great contributions in 1876 by appointing him Professor of English. By this time, he had provided the University library with hundreds of manuscripts, song sheets, and other material on English and Scottish ballads. (He had secured a publisher for his projected new work in 1872.) This was to make Harvard one of the world's major repositories of information on folk music in later years.

From 1872 on, Child went at his task in earnest. He wrote to educators the world over for possible material, and collected songs and verses from many states in the U.S. His deep interest in the subject was from the standpoint of the poetry of the verses, for he was not deeply interested in music nor is there any indication he ever tried his hand at singing.

In 1882, the first part of his work was completed. Between this time and the mid-1890s, Child continued to sift and judge hundreds of songs to turn out a work that included only authentic material. He had completed the last of ten parts of the work before his death in 1896, although the final volume did not appear until 1898.

Shortly after, the total collection of 305 ballads, covering such titles as "The Elfin Knight," "Sir Andrew Barton," "Sir Patrick Spens" and "The Marriage of Sir Gawain," was published in five quarto volumes. The work was called "The English and Scottish Popular Ballads." A cryptic note of Child #10, 20, 100, or whatever the case may be, after ballad references in the world's folk music literature testifies to the genius and effort of the great Harvard scholar.

CIMARRON BOYS: *See* McAuliff, Leon

CLANCY BROTHERS, THE: Vocal and instrumental group—Patrick, Liam and Tom—all born Carrick-on-Suir, Ireland.

The Clancy Brothers, by themselves or in combination with Tommy Makem, provided a unique and welcome addition to the American folk music scene from the mid-1950s on. Their separate achievements, which range from acting honors to a successful record company, add up to almost as impressive a list as their combined vocal successes.

Patrick, the oldest of the brothers, though not of the nine Clancy children, was the first to leave the home fields of Tipperary. Partly as part of his two years of service in the R.A.F. and partly on his own, he traveled to England, Canada, Wales, Venezuela and India in the early 1950s. His occupations over these years included painter, insurance salesman, welder, cab driver, diamond hunter and actor. It was his acting background that stood him in good stead when he came to the U.S. in the mid-1950s. He soon found work with the Cleveland Playhouse and then in plays by Yeats, O'Casey, and Synge on and off-Broadway.

His knowledge of Irish folk music resulted in bids to edit and arrange songs for such labels as Folkways and Elektra. This gave him the idea of forming his own company. He scraped together enough cash to start Tradition Records and soon had signed Odetta, Oscar Brand, Josh White and Carolyn Hester.

Soon after this, a second Clancy, Tom, arrived in New York. Tom also served in the R.A.F. and then won attention in Ireland as a pop band vocalist. He too had a flair for acting and appeared with an English Shakespearean repertory company and in many Irish plays before crossing the Atlantic. In the U.S., he quickly found work in summer stock and in New York productions.

He continued his acting career right along with his later vocal chores. His credits as of 1969 exceeded 150 roles on Broadway and on almost every major dramatic TV show. His most noticed work included appearances with Orson Welles in "King Lear," with Siobhan McKenna in "St. Joan," and with Helen Hayes in "A Touch of the Poet." He also won critical praise for portraying Dylan Thomas on the Camera Three show of CBS-TV.

Last of the Clancys to come to America was the youngest of the brothers, Liam. Liam had formal dramatic training at the National College of Arts in Dublin. He was asked by Pat to collect material for Tradition Records and this led to a meeting with Tommy Makem. The two decided to go to the U.S. together in the late 1950s. Liam too found acting roles starting at the Poet's Theatre in Cambridge,

Massachusetts. He then appeared in New York in Frank O'Connor's "Guests of the Nation," with Julie Harris in "Little Moon of Alban" (and in the TV version of this as well), and in Brendan Behan's "The Quare Fellow."

In New York, the three brothers and Tommy Makem often got together on weekends to sing "out of the sheer joy of·it." Before long, they made their first record on Tradition and followed this up with a hit engagement at the Circle in the Square in Greenwich Village. The audience reception was so favorable, the group was signed to an uptown engagement at the Blue Angel nightclub. Here the critical praise both in papers and magazines gave them a national reputation. In short order, they were featured at the hungry i Club in San Francisco, the Village Gate in New York, Gate of Horn in Chicago and on such network TV shows as Ed Sullivan, Tonight, and Arthur Godfrey.

Clancy Brothers Tradition LPs soon were high among the album sales leaders including "Rising of the Moon," "Fill Your Glass" ('59) and "Clancy Brothers and Tommy Makem" ('61). In 1961, the boys signed with Columbia Records and their LPs hit even higher sales volume. Their Columbia output included "Clancy Brothers with Tommy Makem" ('61); "Hearty & Hellish" and "The Boys Won't Leave the Girls Alone" ('62); "In Person" ('63); "First Hurrah" ('64); and a two-record set titled "The Irish Uprising" ('66).

During the 1960s, the Clancy Brothers and Tommy Makem were featured on almost every major TV show and in concerts throughout the U.S., Canada, Ireland, Britain, and Australia. Their overseas work included TV appearances on the BBC and in Ireland and Australia. In the early 1960s, they played to sellout audiences in Carnegie Hall, leading to a series of regular twice-a-year concerts there, in November and on St. Patrick's Day.

In 1966, Tom Clancy directed and staged all the concerts at the Newport Folk Festival and accepted a bid to stage the International Dublin Folk Festival in September 1967. The brothers' 1967 activities included filming a one-hour color special in Ireland and planning a Broadway stage show. (*See also* MAKEM, TOMMY)

CLANCY, LIAM: *See* Clancy Brothers, The

CLANCY, PATRICK: *See* Clancy Brothers, The

[56]

CLANCY, TOM: *See* Clancy Brothers, The

CLARK, ROY: Singer, instrumentalist (banjo, 12-string guitar), comedian. Born Meaherrin, Virginia, April 15, 1933.

As Jimmy Dean, a longtime friend of Roy Clark's, put it, "Everybody loves him. When he walks out on stage with his bungling attitude as though he didn't know what was going to happen next, the audience is immediately on his side. It's like cheering for the underdog or the hometown boy." This rapport is important, for it permits Clark to pull off the rare feat of switching from comic routines into serious musicianship without losing his audience.

Roy began to gain experience as a performer at an early age. His father, a Virginia tobacco farmer, played guitar and helped Roy learn while his son was still public school age. Before he was ten, Roy became even better with the banjo. In the late 1940s, he won the National Country Music Banjo Championship two years in a row. After his first victory, he made his TV vocal debut in 1948 on a regional show called The Hayloft Conservatory of Musical Interpretation. His second win provided a trip to Nashville and an appearance on the Grand Ole Opry.

In the early 1950s, Roy moved to Washington, D.C. Before long he was appearing locally with another young performer, Jimmy Dean. When Dean had his own TV shows on ABC network, Roy was one of his featured artists. By the mid-1950s, Roy had a top reputation as an instrumentalist with country music insiders and a growing following among country and western fans. He was introduced to a wider audience in 1956 when he made his first appearance on the Arthur Godfrey Show.

During the late 1950s, Roy continued to add to his experience with cross-country tours and radio and TV exposure. In the 1960s he began to move into the top ranks of not only country, but also more general entertainment categories.

In 1960, he joined the Wanda Jackson show at Las Vegas' Golden Nugget. He backed her on a number of recordings in the early 1960s, work that soon led to a solo recording contract for him with Capitol Records. In 1961, Roy was signed as a feature act with the Hank Thompson show. He appeared with Hank at Harrah's Club in Reno, Nevada, and the Thunderbird Hotel in Las Vegas, as well as touring much of the country with the show.

Roy Clark

One of his first Capitol LPs was the 1962 "Lightning," a record that helped increase his national stature still more. In January 1963, Roy made his first appearance on Johnny Carson's Tonight show on NBC-TV. The response to this resulted in several more appearances with Carson in the mid-1960s. Later that year, Roy was represented in the national country and western top 10 with his hit recording of "Tips of My Fingers." He was equally successful with the LP of the same title released in October 1963.

During 1964 and '65, Roy toured the state fair circuit with the Andy Williams show. He was also featured on Williams' TV show in the mid-'60s, as well as on many others, including Jimmy Dean's and the Opry. He also joined the cast of the syndicated Swingin' Country show. He won sustained applause in 1966 as a member of the Andy Griffith Spectacular in Las Vegas.

As comic and performer, he appealed to a wide range of audiences in the mid-1960s, from

[57]

county fairs to sophisticated nightclubs. His nightclub engagements included the Chicago Playboy Club and a 1967 stint at the newly-opened Century Plaza Hotel in Los Angeles. His repertoire at these shows ranged from a skilled 12-string guitar performance of "Malagueña" to such comic renditions as "I Am a Great Pretender," a parody of "Dear John Letter," "Kansas City Star," and "I Had You at the Tips of My Fingers, But I Let You Slip Out of My Hand." The latter he called "a medley of my hit record."

By 1967, Roy was represented by several more successful LPs, such as "Happy to Be Unhappy" and "The Lightning Fingers of Roy Clark."

CLAYTON, PAUL: Singer, guitarist, dulcimer player, author, folk music collector. Born New Bedford, Massachusetts, March 3, 1933.

As befits a descendant of New England sailing families, Paul Clayton helped preserve much of the heritage of whaling songs and sea chanteys from this region. But his lengthy list of recordings showed his range from New England ballads to folk songs of every type and description. Many of these songs were the results of collecting expeditions to far-flung parts of the U.S. and Canada.

Clayton early received encouragement in his musical interests from his parents who both played instruments. His father strummed the banjo and his mother was a pianist. The folk music bug bit him early and he was listening to records by many artists before he was in his teens. When he was 11, he got his first guitar and soon could play many of the classic folk songs on it.

His early school years were varied, for his family moved to several different parts of the country, including New Hampshire and Florida. When he was ready for high school, though, they were once more settled in New Bedford. When he was a high school sophomore, he was skilled enough to gain his own folk music program on a hometown station. He was given a 15-minute weekly program that he wrote, produced, and performed himself starting in April, 1948.

He continued his deep interest in folk music after he was graduated from New Bedford High. He attended the University of Virginia next, which gave him the opportunity to collect new material from the southern hill country.

His mentor at Virginia, as Professor Raymond Lawless notes, was "the distinguished folklorist and archivist, Professor Arthur Kyle Davis, Jr."

When he finished college, he was set for a career in folk music. His performances at concerts and festivals quickly won critical attention for him and, in 1954, he turned out the first of hundreds of recordings. Through the 1950s and '60s he was represented on many LP labels, including Stinson, Riverside, Tradition, Elektra, Folkways and Monument. He continued his collecting tours throughout the '50s, including one tour with Liam Clancy, youngest of the three singing Clancy Brothers.

His Folkways LP credits as of the mid-1960s included: "Bay State Ballads," "British Broadside Ballads in Popular Tradition," "Cumberland Mountain Folksongs," "Foc'sle Songs and Shanties," "Folk Songs and Ballads of Virginia," "Folkways-Viking Record of Folk Ballads," "Folk Ballads of the English Speaking World," and "Dulcimer Songs and Solos." On Tradition, he turned out the LP "Whaling and Sailing Songs from the Days of Moby Dick." This included such songs as "Ranzo," "The Mermaid," "Johnny's Gone to Hilo," "Sally Brown," "Shenandoah," "Admiral Benbow," "Boney Was a Warrior" and "Santy Anna."

Other Clayton LPs include: "Bobby Burns' Merry Muses of Caledonia" and "Unholy Matrimony" (Elektra—'58); "Bloody Ballads," "Concert of British and American Folksongs" ('58); "Timber-r-r!" and "Wanted for Murder" (Riverside); "Waters of Tyne" and "Whaling Songs and Ballads" (Stinson). In 1965, he turned out an LP titled "Folk Singer" on the Monument label.

During the 1950s and '60s, Clayton performed in most of the U.S. east of the Mississippi and in many parts of Canada and Europe. He was featured on radio shows in many foreign countries, including appearances on the BBC. His contributions included folk song material for the American Archive of Folk Song and the Helen Hartness Flanders Ballad Collection, Middlebury, Vermont.

CLEMENTS, VASSAR: *See* Virginia Boys

CLINE, PATSY: Singer, pianist. Born Winchester, Virginia, September 8, 1932; died Camden, Tennessee, March 5, 1963.

During her tragically short lifetime, Patsy Cline (real name: Virginia Patterson Hensley) scored more musical successes than many performers do in a full career. Even though she was only thirty-one when a light plane accident took her life, Patsy had been performing for close to twenty years. Her first success was at four when she won first prize with a tap dance in an amateur contest in her home town of Winchester. By the time she was in grade school, she had expanded her musical interest to include singing as well.

At eight, she started learning to play the piano after she was given a new one for her birthday. Knowledge of the basic patterns of music gained from her piano lessons helped improve her vocal efforts. While still in public school she was a featured singer with her church choir, continuing to sing with it through her teens. In high school, she sang in school plays and also began to make some appearances in local clubs. Her reception increased her confidence in her singing ability.

When she was 16, Wally Fowler of the Grand Ole Opry was starring in a touring show at the Winchester Palace Theater. Patsy gained an audition and impressed Fowler enough to win a guest spot on the bill. Through his intervention, her parents helped her to go to Nashville to try to break into the big time. Though she did appear in some small clubs, she finally decided she was not quite ready and returned to Winchester.

She kept at her music and soon after won a new chance, a bid to appear on Arthur Godfrey's Talent Scouts program. The song she chose for her network debut on January 21, 1957, was "Walkin' After Midnight." The Godfrey audience applauded wildly when she finished. The result was first prize and a contract with Decca. "Walkin' After Midnight" was one of the top country and western hits of 1957 and Patsy was on her way to stardom. In the early 1960s she became one of the top recording artists as well as a featured performer on Grand Ole Opry.

In 1961, she scored another number-one hit with "I Fall to Pieces" and a top 10 number with "Crazy." In 1962, she had two hits with "When I Get Through with You You'll Love Me Too," and the best-selling "She's Got You." Her 1963 output included the major successes "Faded Love," "Leavin' on Your Mind," and "Sweet Dreams (of You)." With seven hit songs in three years, Patsy seemed on the way to setting a new record of success for female country and western vocalists—until the tragedy that shocked Grand Ole Opry fans across the United States.

On March 5, 1963, Patsy died in an airplane crash 85 miles west of Nashville. With Cowboy Copas, Hawkshaw Hawkins, and Copas' son-in-law Randy Hughes (pilot of the private plane), she was returning to Nashville from a benefit performance in Kansas City, Kansas, for the family of DJ Cactus Jack Call, who had been killed in a traffic accident.

Her voice continued to appeal to country music enthusiasts long after her death. Her LPs were still selling briskly in the mid-1960s. Among them were such titles on Evergreen Records as "Golden Hits"; "In Memoriam" ('63); "Patsy Cline Legend" ('64); and "Reflections" ('65). Decca also issued several LPs, including "Patsy Cline Story" (two records— '63); "Patsy Cline Portrait" ('64); and "How a Heartache Begins" ('65).

COCHRAN, HANK: Singer, songwriter. Born Greenville, Mississippi, August 2, 1935.

In the 1960s, Henry "Hank" Cochran was a man all country artists wanted to be in close touch with. For, as the hit charts indicated, Hank had a way with words and music that provided performers with nationwide successes. Through 1967, dozens of his compositions made the charts and four of them remained in the number one spot for many weeks.

Hank was born and raised in Mississippi. In his late teens, after finishing school, he moved to New Mexico. From 1955 to 1957, he worked in the oil fields there. Having gone that far west, he decided to go all the way and traveled to California. As in New Mexico, he earned his living by the sweat of his brow. But he had long enjoyed singing country music and he began to work in his spare time in small local clubs. This led to other jobs on local radio and TV. Among the material he played were some of his own songs. Gradually he shifted away from manual work and spent more time as a performer. He teamed up with Eddie Cochran in a duo called The Cochran Brothers.

In 1958, they both decided to go their separate ways. Hank landed a job in Stockton, California, with a TV show called The California Hayride, where he was a regular for two years. He left when the show was discontinued and, in January 1960, moved east to Nashville. He made demonstration records of his songs and

Hank Cochran

Jones' success with "Make the World Go Away." This time the record became number one in the nation for many weeks. The same position was held by Arnold's recording of Hank's "I Want to Go with You" in 1966. Jeannie Seely also gained top 10 ranking in 1966 with "Don't Touch Me."

Meanwhile, Hank starred on many network shows in the 1960s. He signed with RCA Victor in 1964. His first release was his composition "What Kind of Bird Is That?" He also turned out "Going in Training." Victor produced the LP "Hank Cochran" in 1965. In 1966, Hank recorded his own version of some of his best-selling songs for the LP "Hits from the Heart."

COHEN, JOHN: Singer, guitarist, folk music collector, author, movie producer. Born New York, New York, 1932.

In folk music groups, the sum has often been greater than the parts. An example is the New Lost City Ramblers. While winning notice as one of the best traditional revivalists of the 1960s, all of its members also carried on rewarding careers in several other creative tasks. John Cohen, one of the original founders of the group, wrote important articles and criticism on the folk field in general, showed great talent for photographic arrangement, and also produced some of the most sensitive film footage dealing with the origins of folk music.

Cohen was raised in New York and was exposed to folk music at an early age due to the interest of his older brother Mike. Mike was one of the early urban folk performers of the post-World War II era, playing with a group called The Shantyboys. Mike's influence led John to learn to play several stringed instruments and a basic repertoire of folk songs.

By the time John entered Yale in 1952, he was well prepared to take part in hootenannies. At first, he had little company in such ventures. Folk music was frowned upon by most of the students in those years. By the time Cohen was graduated, however, he found himself playing before sizable audiences at college hoots.

For the next few years, Cohen played at coffee houses in the New York area, meeting many of the new breed of folk artists coming to the fore. He also took off on several trips to the border and southern states to collect folk material. Among the artists with whom he formed firm friendships were Mike Seeger

made the rounds of artists and publishers while also seeking work as a performer. By 1961, his star was rising in both categories.

He worked on one song with the great country composer Harlan Howard that made the number one spot nationally in 1961. The song was "I Fall to Pieces," the singer, Patsy Cline. That same year Hank signed with Liberty Records and his second release, "Sally Was a Good Old Girl," was widely played.

Hank continued his winning ways as a songwriter with a sensational year in 1962. Five of his songs were top 10 successes. One of these, Patsy Cline's version of "She's Got You," was number one in the nation for a good part of the year. The other four included two hits for Burl Ives, "A Little Bitty Tear" and "Funny Way of Laughing," and Eddy Arnold's "Tears Broke Out on Me" and Shirley Collie and Willie Nelson's record of "Willingly."

Artists who scored hits with Cochran songs in 1963 were Ray Price with "Make the World Go Away" and George Jones with "You Comb Her Hair." In 1965, Eddy Arnold repeated and Tom Paley. They all had a deep interest in the traditional folk, country and western music.

The result was the formation of the New Lost City Ramblers in the summer of 1958. In the years that followed, the group became one of the best known on the folk circuit. They were featured in coffee houses and concerts across the U.S. The group also was regularly invited to play at the Newport Folk Festival.

Cohen continued his collecting tours, sometimes by himself and sometimes accompanied by others of the group. He helped discover or rediscover many country artists. One of his major contributions was the introduction of Roscoe Holcomb to folk audiences. In the early 1960s, he began a documentary film dealing both with Holcomb's life and the general environment of the hill country. Released in 1964, the film, "The High Lonesome Sound," was hailed by critics as one of the finest of its kind ever made.

John's activities included articles for folk journals throughout the country. He contributed critical reviews, biographical sketches of performers, discussions of musical techniques, etc., regularly to Sing Out! magazine. His literary output included the 1964 *New Lost City Ramblers Song Book,* edited for Oak Publications by John and Mike Seeger. The book included a selection of 125 songs played by the group.

COLDER, BEN: *See* New Lost City Ramblers; Wooley, Sheb.

COLLIE, BIFF: Disk jockey, singer, trumpeter, booker, promoter. Born Little Rock, Arkansas, November 25, 1926.

Hiram Abiff "Biff" Collie started full time at KMAC in San Antonio, Texas, at the age of 17. Since that time, 1943, he has been in the radio field in Texas and California, closely identified with country music in several areas. While in the service he held mike-side duties at KBWD, Browning, Texas, near Camp Bowie, moving on to Alice, Texas, in 1947 with KBKI.

The following year was the start of bigger things for Collie when he joined Houston's KNUZ and became the top jockey on the top show in town. He moved over to KPRC in Houston and duplicated the same feat. It was during this Houston stint that Collie, a "Personality Jockey," started making personal appearances at the Magnolia Gardens. This activity

taught him the rudiments and refinements of booking artists for appearances and handling the advance promotion that guaranteed box office sales.

Collie was named manager and master of ceremonies of the Philip Morris Country Music Show which toured 37 states in 1957–58. The tour, coupled with weekly broadcasts of these shows on Mutual and CBS radio, helped open up additional territories for country music. A trumpet player, Biff also played with various bands in clubs and helped pioneer the brass sound in several country units. In the 1960s, Biff settled down near KFOX in Long Beach, California. As a key staff member, he helped make KFOX one of Southern California's main country and western stations.

Some artists with whom he associated in show business in their early days are Tommy Sands, Elvis Presley, Tennessee Ernie Ford, Sonny James and Hank Williams. Collie served on the board of directors of the Country Music Association for several years. He was also named in the Top Ten disk jockey polls, conducted by Billboard and The Music Reporter, for 12 consecutive years. In 1967, he produced the Academy of Country and Western Music show in Beverly Hills. His activities by the late 1960s had grown to include various interests in syndicated tape shows, music publishing, and record shop operations. He also wrote some widely read trade music columns.

COLLINS, JUDY: Singer, guitarist. Born Seattle, Washington, May 1, 1939.

One of the most beautiful of the folk song protest brigade of the 1960s is blue-eyed Judy Collins. Donald Mullen of UPI referred to her singing abilities in early 1967 (Los Angeles Times, February 4, 1967) as follows: "Folk singer Judy Collins has a voice that makes the 10-year-old want to go out and protest something, the 30-year-old restless in his dark pin stripes and the 40-year-old wonder what happened to those dreams of living in a Left Bank garret."

Her early upbringing was far from a protest environment. Not long after her birth in Seattle, the family moved to Boulder, Colorado. Her first introduction to music took the form of classical piano lessons. In grade school and the first years of high school, she was considered a child prodigy and a brilliant classical career was predicted for her.

Judy Collins

New York's Town Hall. Wild applause greeted her renditions of such songs as "Winter Sky," "Tear Down the Walls," "Wild Rippling Water," "The Lonesome Death of Hattie Carroll," "Coal Tattoo" and "Hey Nellie Nellie." The LP album "The Judy Collins Concert" produced by Elektra Records was one of the best-selling folk albums of the year. In 1969, she had one of the year's major singles, "Both Sides Now."

By the mid-1960s, Judy was in demand for concerts at campuses, theaters, etc., across the U.S. Her songs of the 1966–67 period included a heavy sprinkling of the "New Left" protest and anti-war songs. In 1967, she stressed, "I don't have the young rebel image. I'm trying to make statements as a woman. My message is my music—what one woman is doing. One of my new songs is 'The Dove.' It says war is wrong. You have to answer 'yes.' There's no way to say 'yes . . . maybe.' "

COLLINS KIDS, THE: Vocal and instrumental duo, Lawrence Albert "Larry" Collins, born Tulsa, Oklahoma, October 4, 1944; Lawrencine May "Lorrie" Collins, born Tahlequah, Oklahoma, May 7, 1942.

Youthful singing teams are not too unusual in country and western music. Unlike rock 'n' roll, where such teams often fall by the wayside after a year or two of success, a good many of the country and western youngsters remain in the limelight for long periods of time. An example of this staying power is the team of Larry and Lorrie Collins, who first became country favorites in their pre-teen years and were still stars more than a decade later.

Both Collins children were introduced to country and western music almost as soon as they could walk. This was only natural, since this kind of music was avidly followed by most people in their home state of Oklahoma. By the time Larry and Lorrie were ready for public school, their family was living in Sapulpa, Oklahoma. Lorrie began at District 36 school in Sapulpa in 1948 and Larry started there two years later. They showed musical aptitude even at this early age and were already playing guitar and singing by the time they moved over to Pretty Water Grade School (Sapulpa).

They were brought to the attention of the directors of the Town Hall Party program in Compton, California, and made their debut on the show in 1953. For a while they commuted between California and Sapulpa, but in 1954

When she was 16, though, she decided the guitar was the instrument she preferred. Though rock 'n' roll guitar-playing dominated radio and TV, Judy sought a sweeter idiom and soon spent many hours memorizing folk songs. At 19, she felt ready for bigger things and auditioned at a Boulder nightclub. As she told Mullen, "The manager said, 'I hate folk music. I'm sorry your audition was such a great success because the demand is so popular I'm going to have to hire you for $100 a week.' "

For several years Judy played in her home area, but gradually she began to perform in other clubs and coffee houses in other cities. By the beginning of the 1960s she was appearing in folk music clubs in New York, where she received more and more attention from audiences and music critics. She also became increasingly interested in civil rights and was a regular participant in fund-raising events and civil rights marches. By 1964, her name had become one of the better known ones in the folk song boom. On March 21 of that year, she scored a major hit in her concert debut at the family settled in California. The children, now regulars on the Town Hall Party, continued their schooling at the Hollywood Professional School. They already had a growing reputation in the entertainment field in 1954 and were introduced to national audiences on the Grand Ole Opry and Red Foley's Ozark Jubilee.

Their careers moved forward rapidly after this. By 1956, they were signed to a long-term contract by Columbia Records. Their efforts for the label in 1956 included "Beetle Bug Bop," "Hush Money," "Make Him Behave," and "Rock Away Rock." In 1957 they began to turn out records of some of their own compositions, such as "In My Teens" and "My First Love." Their record credits for the rest of the 1950s included such songs as "They're Still in Love," "Rock and Roll Polka," "Move a Little Closer," "Party," "Rock-Boppin' Baby," "Sugar Plum," and "Kinda Like Love." Their output included such other original compositions as "Go 'Way Don't Bother Me," "Hop, Skip and Jump," "Young Heart," "Heart Beat," "Whistle Bait," "Mercy," and "Sweet Talk."

Their growing success resulted in appearances on such shows as Steve Allen and Tony Bennett, repeat appearances on the Opry in 1958 and in the '60s, the Ozzie and Harriet Show, Dave Garroway, George Burns, and the Bob Crosby Show. The Kids were also featured in the Screen Gems 1957–58 Ranch Party TV series and in the 1956 Universal film "Music Around the World." In 1957, the Collinses were voted the "Best New Instrumental Group" in the Country and Western Jamboree poll.

During the late 1950s and in the '60s, The Collins Kids made personal appearances throughout the U.S. Their credits ranged from the World Championship Rodeo at New York's Madison Square Garden to the Sahara and Showboat Hotels in Las Vegas and the Deauville Hotel in Miami, Florida.

Their musical output included a number of albums, such as "Country Spectacular" ('57) and "Town Hall Party" ('58).

COLLINS, LARRY: *See* Collins Kids, The

COLLINS, LORRIE: *See* Collins Kids, The

COLLINS, TOMMY: Singer, guitarist, songwriter. Born Oklahoma City, Oklahoma, September 28, 1930.

Among the many artists who helped make Bakersfield the western capital of country and western music, a goodly contingent came from Oklahoma. In Tommy Collins' case, he arrived not only with a guitar, but with a suitcase full of original music. He added to this after settling in California until, by 1968, his total included 800 compositions of which more than 400 were published. The list of performers who recorded some of Tommy's material included many of the top names in country music.

As a boy, of course, Tommy had never heard of Bakersfield, much less planned to visit there. Country and western music, though, was a constant companion in most homes in Oklahoma. Tommy could play the guitar and sing many folk and country ballads by the time he was in high school. His interest in music intensified while he was attending Oklahoma Central State College in Edmond. He performed at local clubs and increased his radio credits to include appearances on such Oklahoma stations as KLPR, KBYE, KOCY, WKY, and WKY-TV. In the early 1950s, his increasing stature as a performer resulted in a recording contract with Capitol.

By now Tommy was aware of the growing concentration of country artists in Bakersfield. The result was a move west and a continuation of radio and TV work on local Bakersfield stations. The success of his records brought Tommy's name to attention of people across the country. In 1953, he scored his first major success with "If You Ain't Lovin', You Ain't Livin'," which sold more than 300,000 records.

In 1954, Tommy really made the big time with a series of hits that won him awards from BMI, Billboard, and Cashbox. These included "Whatcha Gonna Do Now," "You Gotta Have a License," and "You Better Not Do That," all of which were original compositions. The last of these sold more than 500,000 records. In 1955, Tommy was voted the "Most Promising Male Vocalist" and a "Top 10 Recording Artist for 1954" in disk jockey polls. In 1955, Tommy had another top 10 hit with "It Tickles," also one of his own songs. Among his other Capitol recordings of the 1950s were such songs as "Words and Music Country Style," "I'll Be Home," "High on a Hilltop," "Boob-I-Lak," "Smooth Sailin'," and "Love A Me."

One of Tommy's first LPs for Capitol was a religious album, "Light of the Lord." In 1959, Tommy was represented on Capitol with an LP of some of his best received songs, "This Is Tommy Collins."

During the 1950s and 1960s, Tommy entertained in most of the states. In addition, his performances took him to twelve other countries. His audiences heard such other original compositions as "Little June," "I'll Stop Loving You," "How Much Are You Mine," "Whole Hog or None," "Just Married," "I Need a Little Help," and "I Believe in Lovin' 'Em."

In the mid-1960s, Tommy signed with Columbia Records. In 1965 he had a chart hit, "Sam Hill," and in 1966 he wrote himself another top 10 success, "If You Can't Bite, Don't Growl."

COOKER, JOHN LEE: *See* Hooker, John Lee

COOPER, STONEY: Singer, fiddler, songwriter. Born Harman, West Virginia, October 16, 1918.

No better testimonial to the contributions of the team of Wilma Lee (Leary) and Stoney Cooper could be had than their selection by the Music Library of Harvard University in 1950 as the most authentic mountain singing group in the U.S. Stoney Cooper and his wife began conveying their background in traditional country music to audiences throughout the world in the mid-1930s, and were still going strong at the end of the 1960s.

Stoney was born and raised on a farm near Harman, West Virginia. Harman is in Randolph County, the location of Valley Head, home of the singing Leary Family. Stoney received much background in hill country music from his own family, which had long provided both farmers and teachers for the region. At an early age he learned to play the fiddle and, when he was 12, taught himself the guitar as well. By the time he finished school he was well versed in what today is called Bluegrass music.

About this time, Stoney joined the Leary Family and performed at church functions and on radio programs with them. He soon became fond of young Wilma Leary and, before long, proposed marriage. The Coopers stayed with the family group for a time, then left to go into show business on their own.

They gained singing jobs on several stations in the late 1930s, starting in Fairmont, West Virginia, and continuing to Harrisonburg, Virginia, and Wheeling, West Virginia. Times, however, were difficult and their income from performing was not enough to pay the bills, particularly after their daughter, Carolee, was

born. For a while, Stoney had to work in a beverage company in Wheeling.

In the early 1940s, things were a little better as they went on to other areas of the midwest. The Coopers played on stations in Grand Island, Nebraska, and Indianapolis, Indiana; station WJJD in Chicago, and in Blytheville, Arkansas, and Asheville, North Carolina. While in Chicago during this period, Stoney added to the family income by working in a defense plant in Gary, Indiana.

In 1947, they moved back to West Virginia as regular cast members of the WWVA Jamboree in Wheeling, broadcast over 19 other major stations in various parts of the country. The Coopers remained on WWVA until 1957, also starring on the Saturday WWVA Jamboree from 1954 to 1957, when they moved to Nashville as regular members of the Grand Ole Opry. They were still featured on the show as of 1967. During their many tours of the country and overseas, the Coopers were backed by their own musical group called the Clinch Mountain Clan.

From 1947 on, the Coopers were regularly represented on radio programs across the U.S. by many hit recordings. Many of their songs were original compositions. (*See* Wilma Lee Cooper.) In 1959, they scored one of their biggest years, turning out three top 10 hits on the Hickory label, "Come Walk with Me," "There's a Big Wheel," and "Big Midnight Special." In 1961 they had another top 10 hit with a revival of Dorsey Dixon's "Wreck on the Highway."

Some of their other recordings included: "The Golden Rocket," "West Virginia Polka," "Just for a While," "Legend of the Dogwood Tree," "How It Hurts to Be Alone," "Please Help Me If I Am Wrong," "I want to Be Loved," "Cheated Too," "Each Season Changes You," "Thirty Pieces of Silver," "This Crazy, Crazy World," "Walking My Lord Up Calvary's Hill," "Tramp on the Street," "Rachel's Guitar," "Diamond Joe," "The White Rose," "Not Anymore," "We Make a Lovely Couple," "Row Two, Seat Three," "This Thing Called Man," "Is It Right?," "Come Walk with Me," and "Canadian Reel."

COOPER, WILMA LEE: Singer: guitarist, banjoist, organist, songwriter. Born Valley Head, West Virginia, February 7, 1921.

Country music is a way of life for many of

[64]

its practitioners, and so it has been in the careers of the husband-and-wife team of Wilma Lee and Stoney Cooper. Wilma Lee Leary was fated for a music future from birth. She was born into one of the best known church-singing families in the hill country, the Leary Family of Valley Head, West Virginia. As soon as she was old enough to carry a tune, she joined the other members of the family, comprising several generations, in entertaining at local events and at regional folk and country festivals.

Her first public performance came when she was five. From then on, she sang regularly with the Leary Family on many radio and church programs. In 1938, the family was featured at a national folk festival sponsored by Mrs. Eleanor Roosevelt. Despite all this, Wilma Lee did not allow her singing interests to keep her from a good education. She went on from high school to complete work for a B.A. degree in banking at Davis & Elkins College in Elkins, West Virginia.

The music cycle continued to dominate her life, though, for she was courted by a new member of the Leary Family group. This was guitarist-singer Stoney Cooper from Harman, a town in Randolph County, the same county in which Valley Head is located. After their marriage in the late 1930s, they remained with the Leary Family for a time, then went out on their own. They sang at local events for a while, then were hired to sing on a station in Fairmont, West Virginia. From Fairmont, they went on to perform on stations in Harrisonburg, Virginia, and in Wheeling, West Virginia.

During the 1940s, the Coopers had to go further afield to find entertainment work. They were heard by audiences over stations in Grand Island, Nebraska, Indianapolis, Chicago (station WJJD), Blytheville, Arkansas, and Asheville, North Carolina. By the late 1940s, they had built up a following of fans in many parts of the border states. The result was their first major break, a bid to join the regular cast of the WWVA Jamboree in Wheeling, West Virginia, in 1947. That same year, they also received their first record contract as a team.

From 1947 to 1957, they were prime favorites of audiences who listened to the Jamboree on 19 stations throughout the country. From 1954 to 1957, they also appeared on the Saturday WWVA Jamboree. In 1957, they were asked to move to Nashville to join the regular cast of the Grand Ole Opry. More than a

decade later, they were still starred on the Opry TV show. During these years, the Coopers toured every state in the union. In the mid-1960s they were acclaimed by West European audiences during several international tours.

The Coopers turned out dozens of best-selling records for Columbia, Hickory and, in the mid-1960s, Decca Records, between 1947 and 1967. (*See* Stoney Cooper for records.) Many of the songs were written by Wilma Lee herself or by the Coopers jointly. These included: "Cheated Too" ('56); "I Tell My Heart," "Loving You," "My Heart Keeps Crying" ('57); "He Taught Them How" ('58); "Heartbreak Street," "Tomorrow I'll Be Gone," and "Big Midnight Special" ('59).

COPAS, COWBOY: Singer, guitarist. Born Muskogee, Oklahoma, July 15, 1913; died Camden, Tennessee, March 5, 1963.

The fortunes of Lloyd "Cowboy" Copas took many strange turns. In 1948, he was at the top of country and western music, voted number one entertainer by Cashbox. A few years later he was considered a has-been. Then, after almost ten years out of the limelight, he returned to the pinnacle in full glory, only to have his new career ended by a plane crash.

Cowboy was born and brought up on a small ranch in Oklahoma. His grandfather loved to tell him about frontier days in the west and some of the others on the ranch often played western songs. Long before he was 10, Cowboy had taught himself to play an open-string guitar. By the time he was in his early teens, he was one of the most popular boys in the region. His friends loved to listen to his intricate guitar playing on his flattop instrument.

When he was 16, Lloyd decided to try for a career in music. His travels took him to Cincinnati where he met a young Indian fiddler named Natchee. Natchee talked him into entering an amateur fiddling contest as an accompanist. Natchee also got Cowboy to try his hand at singing as well as guitar playing. The boys won the contest and soon were off on a series of one-night stands all over the country, playing at nightclubs, fairs, local dances, etc. As an added attraction, they began to hold fiddling contests of their own. To help promote the contests, Copas began to take guest spots on local radio shows. This was the start of his record of appearing on 204 different stations in the U.S., Canada, and Mexico between 1938 and 1950.

In 1940, Natchee and Copas separated and the Cowboy gained a regular spot on a Knoxville station. Later in the '40s, he returned to Cincinnati as a featured performer on station WLW's Boone County Jamboree which later was retitled the Midwestern Hayride. He was becoming well known to midwest audiences by now and King Records signed him up. One of his first records for King was a major hit of the World War II period, "Filipino Baby." Some of his other well received recordings for King were "Juke Box Blues," "Texas Red," "Sundown and Sorrow," and "Honky Tonkin'." In the mid-1940s he had two major hits in "Tragic Romance" and "Signed, Sealed and Delivered."

By 1945, Cowboy had become a close friend and co-worker of PeeWee King. In late '45, PeeWee asked Cowboy to join his band as a sideman on the Grand Ole Opry. Cowboy's Opry chores started in 1946 and before long he had scored two major hits with "Tennessee Waltz" and "Kentucky Waltz." These won him the title of "Waltz King of the Grand Ole Opry." To join his "Tennessee Waltz" as a top 10 hit of 1948, Cowboy also scored with "Tennessee Moon." In 1949 he had another major hit in "Candy Kisses," and won again in 1951 with "Strange Little Girl."

As rapidly as fame had appeared, it vanished. Cowboy's record sales went down, and personal appearance requests as well. By the early 1950s, he was reduced to working in small, local shows. In 1959, though, a second chance came in the form of a new contract from Don Pierce of Starday Records. The result was a record called "Alabam" that became one of the major hits of 1960, remaining on the charts for 40 weeks. In 1961, Cowboy followed with two more hits, "Flat Top" and "Signed, Sealed and Delivered."

Now once more a star on the Opry and in demand for appearances across the country, Cowboy seemed to have things well in hand. Then his career abruptly closed when a private plane carrying him, as well as country stars Patsy Cline, Hawkshaw Hawkins, and pilot Randy Hughes, crashed near Camden, Tennessee.

COUNTRY GENTLEMEN: Vocal and instrumental group, Charlie Waller, born Jointerville, Texas, January 19, 1935; John Duffey, born Washington, D.C., March 4, 1934; Eddie Ad-

cock, born Scottsville, Virginia, June 17, 1938; Jim Cox, born Vansant, Virginia, April 3, 1930.*

One of the more popular Bluegrass groups of the 1960s, the Country Gentlemen, came into being accidentally. Its genesis occurred when a mutual friend asked Charlie Waller, then working in Baltimore, and John Duffey, then at station WFMD, Frederick, Maryland, to fill in for a sick musician at a date in the Baltimore area on July 4, 1957. The two enjoyed playing together and decided to continue their association.

Before their paths crossed, Waller and Duffey both had become proficient in guitar playing many years earlier. Waller, though born in Texas, went to Los Angeles with his family while still little. When he was 10, he obtained a $15 guitar and learned to play. By the time he reached Baltimore in the mid-1950s, he was an accomplished guitarist with a leaning toward Bluegrass style. Duffey was raised almost entirely in the Washington area in nearby Bethesda, Maryland. At 17, a neighbor persuaded him it would be worth while to learn to play the guitar.

Duffey and Waller expanded their group to a trio in a few months' time. Jim Cox joined them as bassist and banjoist in early 1958. Raised on a farm, Jim mastered the banjo before he reached his teens. In June 1960, Eddie Adcock was added, lending a stronger Bluegrass tone to the group. Adcock learned to play the mandolin at 12 and became a regular on a gospel program on station WCHV, Charlottesville, Virginia, in his teens.

In the 1960s, the Country Gentlemen gained a nationwide reputation among Bluegrass fans. They were featured on many network TV shows as well as in personal appearances at county fairs, nightclubs, and a number of major folk festivals.

The group turned out a number of albums on Folkways and Starday labels. Their Folkways output included "Audience Participation" and a two-record set, "Country Gentlemen" ('61). Starday LPs were "Bluegrass" ('62) and "Country Gentlemen" ('65).

COUNTRY MUSIC ASSOCIATION: Industry trade organization, based in Nashville, Tennessee.

One of the important forces behind the

* Roster as of the early 1960s.

growing popularity of country and western music from the start of the 1960s is the Country Music Association. The CMA was formed in 1958 by industry executives and artists to promote this form of music and try to combat the temporary depression caused by the rise of rock 'n' roll. In November 1958, a series of meetings led to the organization's formation with an original leadership of nine directors and five officers. Connie B. Gay was elected to the first two-year term as CMA president with Wesley Rose, president of Acuff-Rose, as CMA board chairman.

At the first annual meeting in November 1959, the Board of Directors was increased to eighteen and officers to nine. The meeting confirmed the continued work of Mrs. Jo Walker as executive secretary. The membership was divided into nine categories: Artist-Musician, Artist-Manager, Booker, Promoter, Agent, Ballroom Operator, Composer, Disk Jockey, Music Publisher, Radio-TV and Record Company Personnel, Trade Publication Representative, and Non-Affiliated. Each category is entitled to elect two Board members; the Board, in turn, appoint the officers.

Functions of the CMA include worldwide promotion of country and western music, conducting industry surveys to provide useful data to members, and informing members of industry news. Most ambitious project of the CMA was establishment of the Country Music Hall of Fame (*see* Country Music Hall of Fame) in which CMA offices are now located.

COUNTRY MUSIC HALL OF FAME AND MUSEUM: Building in Nashville, Tennessee, housing plaques of members elected to Hall of Fame and collections of exhibits, historical data, etc.

In 1967, an impressive monument to country music was open to the public at 700 16th Avenue South, Nashville, Tennessee. The structure was the culmination of years of work by

Country Music Hall of Fame

the Country Music Foundation toward a repository of information about the field. The idea for the center had been proposed by the Foundation in 1961. Funds had been collected from country artists, music fans, firms, and others.

The building consists of a modernistic barn-shaped center section flanked by two flat wings. A "Walkway of Stars" leads up to the center entrance, consisting of brass emblems with names of leading country artists on them embedded in concrete blocks. The right wing houses a 50-seat theater in which films on the history of country music and videotapes of major artists are shown. The other wing includes the "Artists' Gallery," a series of pictures of important performers below which are earphones for listening to some of their important recordings.

The hall also houses other exhibits of importance, a library of tapes, books, and publications, and material from the John K. Edwards Memorial Foundation. The latter is a collection of information about country and western music considered one of the foremost of its kind in the world.

Each member elected to the Hall of Fame is represented in the center hall with a bronze plaque giving biographical data and including an image of the person. Selection of Hall of Fame members is by annual vote of a committee of 100 members selected from the Foundation roster. Each member votes for the 10 people he or she considers to have made the most important contribution to the field from 1925 on. To be elected to the Hall of Fame, the subject must receive 75 per cent of the votes cast.

The first six members of the Hall of Fame included three living artists, Ernest Tubb, Roy Acuff, and Tex Ritter, and three deceased, Jimmie Rodgers, Hank Williams, and Fred Rose. (For complete list of Hall of Fame members, *see* Appendix.)

COWELL, HENRY DIXON: Pianist, composer, author, folklorist. Born Menlo Park, California, March 11, 1897; died New York, New York, December 10, 1965.

Though best known as a composer of symphonies and other orchestral music, as well as a commentator on classical music, Henry Cowell made major contributions to the field of folk music. In fact, he was one of the foremost authorities on folk music around the world. This was reflected in the inclusion of many folk themes in his compositions, from Irish fiddle tunes to rhythms of Africa and the Far East.

Cowell, who was largely self-educated, was a child prodigy. He could already play melodies on the piano when he was five. He made his professional debut playing his own piano compositions when he was 15 in San Francisco. Soon after, he began formal music studies at the University of California at Berkeley. He continued to compose and, in the early 1920s, played concerts in many parts of the U.S. His playing was so unusual that he became nationally known. He struck large numbers of notes together to produce, as the World Encyclopedia states, "dense and dissonant effects which he called 'Tone Clusters.'" He explained his theories in a book, *New Musical Resources,* first published in 1919 and revised in 1930.

In 1923, he went to Europe on the first of five tours over the next decade. During his visits, he studied folk music of the Continent; in 1931 he spent some time at the University of Berlin. In 1927, he founded the "New Music Editions" for the "circulation of experimental scores." Cowell's overseas trips included a tour of Russia in 1928 during which he compiled a considerable library of Russian folk music. Cowell incorporated his folk discoveries into his concert and lecture tours of the U.S. which he began in 1920 and continued until 1936. After a four-year break, they were resumed from 1940 to 1956.

During World War II, Cowell served as senior music editor for the Office of War Information. One of his tasks was to provide authentic musical background propaganda material for broadcasts to try to disrupt the Japanese war effort.

Cowell's first published music consisted of 22 piano pieces in 1922. He made his European debut as a concert pianist in Leipzig, Germany, in 1923 and his New York debut in 1924. The first major orchestra performance of one of his longer works was by the Philadelphia Orchestra in 1932. During the next three decades, he was commissioned or performed major works not only in the U.S., but in Europe, Asia, and Latin America. In recognition of his work, Wilmington College, Ohio, awarded him an honorary doctorate in music in 1953.

Cowell became one of the country's most

distinguished lecturers on all phases of music, including folk. In 1956–57 he went to Asia under a Rockefeller grant to combine study of Asian music with a lecture series. He later returned to give lectures in several Asian nations in 1961. He joined the New School in New York as a lecturer in 1928 and remained on the staff almost until his death. In 1951, he was also appointed adjunct professor at Columbia University in New York.

Over the years, he turned out a considerable number of compositions based directly on folk music. These included 25 works of his American hymnody. He also turned out such pieces based on foreign folk material as the "Toccanta," "Ongaku," "Homage to Iran," and the "Persian Set." His 1962 "Icelandic Symphony" (No. 15) is an example of his use of folk themes in larger works. He also turned out such LPs for Folkways Records as "Music of the World's People" and "Primitive Music of the World."

In his long career, Cowell was responsible for many important articles, critical reviews, and books. His book output included *American Composers on American Music* in 1933 and *Nature of Melody* in 1938. In 1941 he married Sidney Hawkins Robertson, a distinguished folklorist in her own right. In 1954, he and Sidney collaborated on a biography of their good friend, American composer Charles Ives, titled *Charles Ives and His Music.*

After a long illness, Henry Cowell died in New York on December 10, 1965.

COX, JIM: *See* Country Gentlemen

CRAMER, FLOYD: Singer, pianist. Born Shreveport, Louisiana, October 27, 1933.

Shreveport was lucky for Floyd Cramer. It was his birthplace and, later in life, the starting point for a highly successful career in country music. In between, though, he spent most of his developing years in the small Arkansas sawmill town of Huttig.

It was in Huttig that he showed musical talent at a very young age. His parents bought him an old piano when he was five. From then on, he often spent hours experimenting and teaching himself how to play. When high school years came along, young Floyd was already one of the best pianists in town. In high school, he began to pick up experience playing for school dances and with friends in local clubs. When

Floyd Cramer

he finished high school in 1951, he felt encouraged to try for a career as a musician.

That year, he went back to Shreveport to audition for the KWKH Lousiana Hayride. He was accepted and joined such other embryo national stars as Webb Pierce and Faron Young. In the early 1950s, Floyd rapidly became one of the most popular supporting players for many recording artists. He played for recording sessions of Jim Reeves and The Browns for the Shreveport Abbott Record firm. During this period, he cut his first solo record on Abbott. Between 1952 and 1955, he toured a good part of the country with such performers as Hank Williams and Elvis Presley.

He also went to Nashville on several occasions to play in recording sessions. While there, he met Chet Atkins who urged him to move to Tennessee. In January 1955, Floyd took him up on this. In Nashville, he was in even greater demand as an individual performer and sideman than before. He played for dozens of sessions in Nashville studios and continued to tour most of the major cities of the U.S. He also was a regular performer on the Grand Ole Opry from the mid-1950s on.

Before long, Chet Atkins had signed him to a recording contract for RCA Victor. Throughout the late '50s and the 1960s, Floyd continued to increase his stature as a performer. In 1960–61, he scored a major national hit with "Last Date." He also was featured on many successful LPs, including one in 1964 titled "Floyd Cramer" and the 1966 "Class of 66." In 1966, Cramer was nominated for Favorite Instrumentalist of the Year in Billboard's Country Music poll.

CRUM, SIMON: *See* Husky, Ferlin

CURLESS, DICK: Singer, guitarist. Born Ft. Fairfield, Maine, March 17, 1932.

The road to success in any part of the music field is often rocky. In Richard "Dick" Curless' case, he seemed on the way to stardom in his teens, then a has-been in his twenties. After a half dozen years in obscurity, however, he returned to national ranking in the mid-'60s.

Born and raised in New England, he learned to play the guitar before he reached his teens. During those early years, young Dick appeared in a number of shows in the region. In 1948, as "The Tumbleweed Kid," he gained his own radio show in Ware, Massachusetts. His singing efforts were rewarded with bids to tour throughout the New England and Atlantic states. What first seemed an interruption of his career, Army induction during the Korean War, added to his lustre. He was sent to Korea as a performer instead of a soldier. As the "Rice Paddy Ranger," he became a favorite with the servicemen via his show over the Armed Forces Korea Network.

Back in the States after the war, he continued his career with rising success. In 1957, his version of "Nine Pound Hammer" won first place on the Arthur Godfrey Talent Scouts TV show. From this point, however, things went down instead of up. A series of personal problems and little luck with his record efforts resulted in his returning to Maine. He settled down to what looked like a permanent job as a performer in a local club in Rockland.

Things went on with little change for more than half a dozen years. Then in 1965 he met a songwriter named Dan Fulkerson. Dan talked Dick into paying for a record of Dan's song, "A Tombstone Every Mile." They released it on their own Allagash label and it began to move. Soon after, Tower Records, a subsidiary of Capitol, bought the master. The song quickly became one of the major hits of 1965. Dick's second Tower release, "Six Times a Day," also rated high on the charts as did his 1966 effort, "Tater Raising Man." In 1967, he came up with another well received song, "Travelin' Man." Tower also released two LPs, "Tombstone Every Mile" and "Travelin' Man."

In 1966, Dick was voted the best new country singer of 1965 in two different disk jockey surveys. He was also signed as a regular cast member of the Buck Owens American Music Show for tours of the U.S., Europe, and the Far East.

DAFFAN, TED:[*] Singer, guitarist, songwriter. Born Houston, Texas, September 21, 1912.

"My father, Carrol Eugene Daffan, grew up in Houston, Texas. While following sawmill work in Louisiana he met my mother, Della Brown, and married her. I was born in Beauregarde Parish, La. While I was still a child we returned to Texas and I graduated from Jeff Davis High School in Houston in 1930. Altho born in Louisiana, I consider myself a Texan.

"I was twenty years old when I first saw someone play the Hawaiian guitar. (Now called 'Steel guitar') The next day I purchased a guitar from a pawn shop for five dollars. Six months later I had a small Hawaiian group called 'The Blue Islanders' and we played over radio station KTRH in Houston. A few months later I was teaching guitar in a large downtown music studio and four months later I started my own music studio and was quite successful. After teaching for a year I was invited to join a local country group, 'The Blue Ridge Playboys.' I did join them altho I had never played country music. I could sight read with a pop band, knew almost every Hawaiian song, played some classical on the steel but I found country music extremely difficult for the first few months. Floyd Tillman was lead guitarist with this band and we became friends and have remained so all these years.

"A year or so later I joined the 'Bar X Cowboys,' another very successful Houston string band, and remained with them for several years. While with the Bar X Cowboys I formed

[*] Autobiography from a letter to the authors, dated July 10, 1967.

a small group for the purpose of recording. I created a style quite different from anything on the record market. We made demo records and I pestered every A&R man who came down Texas way. (By the way, most of the country records were made in Texas in those days.)

"Altho I did not get my own group on, Decca records accepted some of my songs and the first one released, 'Truck Drivers Blues' became the biggest country record of 1939. This song was such a big hit that the other two record companies, RCA and Columbia, both had to cover it. Art Satherly of Columbia remembered me from the name on the song and flew down to Houston and signed me up to record my own group. This was the start of 'Ted Daffan and His Texans.'

"Then like in the story books, my first record for Columbia, 'Worried Mind' (my own song of course), became an even bigger hit than 'Truck Drivers Blues.' 'Worried Mind' was only second best seller in 1940. It was topped by the fantastic million seller by Bob Wills, 'San Antonio Rose.'

"Several 'Best sellers' of this period were 'Blue Steel Blues,' 'Always Alone' and 'I'm a Fool to Care.' World War Two broke up the band and stopped all record production by Columbia Records. We did do a final record session before the band broke up. We recorded twenty-four sides, all my songs, and Uncle Art suggested I use a pen name on some of the songs. As he put it, 'We couldn't take twenty-four songs at once from one song writer even from Irving Berlin.' I selected my mother's maiden name, 'Brown,' and pulled a first name out of thin air, 'Frankie.' As a result two of my biggest songs have the pen name 'Frankie Brown' on them.

"Columbia was able to resume record production in 1943 and my first record was 'No Letter Today' and 'Born to Lose' back to back. Both were my own songs, of course, but both had my pen name 'Frankie Brown' on them. Both songs were smash hits and were on almost every Juke Box in America all thru 1943, 1944, and still on many of them in 1945. Columbia gave me a gold record for this one. After hitting a million seller Uncle Art decided it didn't matter how many Ted Daffan songs Columbia recorded so the pen name, 'Frankie Brown,' was never used again.

"In 1944 I accepted a contract to lead a band at the huge Venice Ballroom at Venice Pier, Los Angeles, California. I built a new band and the attendance soon reached five thousand or better every Saturday night. During this period I had the following hit records, all my own songs. (I consider any country record that sells over one hundred thousand a hit.)

" 'Look Who's Talkin' '; 'Time Won't Heal My Broken Heart'; 'Beyond the Shadow of a Doubt'; 'Baby, You Can't Get Me Down'; 'Bluest Blues'; 'Trouble Keeps Hanging 'Round My Door'; 'Heading Down the Wrong Highway'; 'Broken Vows'; 'Shut That Gate'; 'You'd Better Change Your Ways.'

"In 1946 I left the band in California under the leadership of one of the boys in the band and returned to Texas. I moved to Arlington, a small town between Ft. Worth and Dallas, built a new band and worked in Fort Worth and Dallas for the next four years. In 1951 I moved back to my old home town, Houston, Texas, the only town in America where I was not a star.

"Things did not go well at all until 1954 when Les Paul and Mary Ford recorded my old song, 'I'm a Fool to Care,' and it became one of their big hits. This was the start of another series of hits, this time by artists other than myself. These included 'I've Got Five Dollars and It's Saturday Night' by Faron Young, and 'Tangled Mind,' by Hank Snow. All three of these last named songs were citation winners.

"In 1958 I moved to Nashville and Hank Snow and I became partners in a music publishing company. During this period I wrote two more hit songs for Hank, 'Last Ride' and 'Rocking Rolling Ocean.'

"At the end of 1961 I returned to Houston and so far, I am still here. In 1962 Ray Charles recorded the fabulous 'Modern Sounds of Country Music.' Two of my songs, 'Worried Mind' and 'Born to Lose,' were in this album. 'Born to Lose' was coupled with the smash 'I Can't Stop Loving You' and this along with the Album accounted for over four million mechanicals (royalties on records or albums). Later Ray Charles did two more of my songs as singles, 'I'm a Fool to Care' and 'No Letter Today.' Since then I have had over fifty singles and over one hundred and fifty albums by the top artists in both Pop and Country.

"Here are a few statistics on my songs compiled from royalty statements: 'Worried Mind'— over two million; 'No Letter Today,' over two million; 'I'm a Fool to Care,' over two million;

'Born to Lose,' over seven million; total mechanicals on all my songs, over sixteen million."

DAILY, PAPPY: Music executive, record producer. Born Yoakum, Texas, February 8, 1902.

One of the most colorful and successful executives in the country and western music field after World War II was Texas-born Harold W. ("Pappy") Daily. Pappy's management helped propel many artists to stardom in the 1950s and '60s, including George Jones, Melba Montgomery, and Gene Pitney. For most of his career, despite the lures of Nashville, Pappy succeeded in running his various music businesses from his home base in Houston.

Born and brought up in Texas, Pappy was imbued with the spirit of adventure. When World War I came along, he managed to enlist in the Marine Corps despite being under age. When the war was over, he returned home and started a career in business. During the 1920s he gained a broad and successful background as a businessman, though not in the music field. Pappy continued active in veterans' affairs as well, resulting in his election as Commander of the American Legion in 1931 and 1932.

Pappy had long been a fan of country and western music. This finally led him to enter the record business in a small way in 1933. During the 1930s and '40s, he slowly increased his experience in the field and, in the early 1950s, started a small record company in Houston called Starday. Pappy's main interest was in finding talent and producing their material, and he looked for a partner to help handle the sales part of the business. He found his man in 1952 in the person of young Don Pierce, who had helped 4 Star Records of California become a major factor in the country and western field.

The Starday fold soon included such artists as George Jones and Arlie Duff. These and other performers and songwriters (the Starday operation included a music publishing section) soon made the name well known nationally. Between 1952 and 1955, Pappy and Don Pierce had such hits as Arlie Duff's record of "Y'all Come" ('53) and George Jones' "Why, Baby, Why" ('55).

In the mid-1950s, Mercury Records approached Don and Pappy with an arrangement under which the two would handle the production of all country and western material for the label. The agreement was accepted and Pappy and Don concentrated on this job, allowing Starday to lie dormant. Things were slow in the country field in the late 1950s and, in 1961, the Mercury arrangement was cancelled. Pappy and Don then divided up the assets of their own firm, each taking half the songs and masters. Pappy took the name of the publishing catalog, Starright, and Don gained the Starday record name. For a time, Pappy had his own new record firm, D Records, in Houston.

In 1961, Pappy moved over to United Artists as Country and Western Director. He provided UA with a number of hits during the next four years, such as George Jones' top 10 "A Girl I Used to Know"; Judy Lynn's "Footsteps of a Fool"; Jones' number-one-ranked hit "She Thinks I Still Care"; and several hits by a new singer named Melba Montgomery.

Pappy left UA in 1965 to start a new firm, Musicor. By the mid-1960s, Musicor had such stars as Jones, Melba Montgomery, Ricky Sears, Floyd Tillman, Gene Pitney, Benny Barnes, Myrna Lorrie and Jack Gray on its roster. Among the top 10 hits in 1965 and '66 on Musicor were "Take Me," "Things Have Gone to Pieces," "I'm a People," and "Baby, Ain't That Fine." Besides serving as vice president of Musicor, Pappy's titles included president of Glad Music and Starright Publishing Company.

DANE, BARBARA: Singer, guitarist. Born Detroit, Michigan, May 12, 1927.

"Away With Rum" (the song of the Salvation Army) had the shabby walls of the Ash Grove shaking with a rhythmic beat while the audience laughed or clapped hands in time with the music. It was a rousing climax to an evening of folk singing that ran the gamut from lowdown blues to classic folk ballads to comedy. The time was the late 1950s and the singer a good-looking, husky-voiced woman named Barbara Dane. The name has since become familiar to folk and folk-blues fans the world over.

Barbara (real name: Barbara Spillman) started with a folk music heritage. Her parents had moved from Arkansas to the motor city of Detroit where Barbara was born. But they wanted to forget the struggles and slights of their humble origin and carefully avoided any mention of southern customs or music. They were interested in more sedate music, though, and saw that their daughter had piano and voice lessons. Young Barbara sang in the church choir and school glee club.

In her late teens, Barbara worked in a Detroit plant and joined the union. When the union went on strike, she began to learn her first folk songs, including some from a stirring performance by Pete Seeger. The Seeger union concert caused her to teach herself the guitar from a "'25 easy lessons' book and from records in the Detroit public library" (Sing Out! April-May 1964).

After getting nowhere trying to find radio work in Detroit, she went to Berkeley, California, in 1949. Folk songs still weren't in vogue, so she got a job as a popular singer on a program called "Sweet and Mellow." She then tried out for the Horace Heidt Amateur Hour but didn't make it. Her first TV appearance was as the winner of a San Francisco bathing suit-talent contest. She kept up her folk efforts, though, and finally was given her own show, Folksville, U.S.A., on KGO-TV. In 1952, she moved to KPFA. On one show she learned one of her most popular songs, "San Francisco Bay Blues," from blues singer Jesse Fuller. From Bessie Mercer she learned such songs as "Don't Sing Love Songs," also known as "Silver Dagger." Another song she learned during this period was the "Spiritual Trilogy."

Soon after, she was asked to join the Dixieland band of Dick Oxtot. She sang many blues numbers and began to achieve notice for her blues work far beyond the bounds of San Francisco. By the early 1960s, she had performed in concerts and at coffee houses in many major cities. In October 1963, she returned to a scene of her earlier triumphs but now as a folk-blues artist. The result was a rousing ovation night after night from sellout crowds.

By the mid-1960s, she had been featured on many major TV shows and concert stages. These included a Timex TV special with Louis Armstrong, the Newport Jazz Festival, UCLA Jazz Festival, Playboy Penthouse and PM West. She also starred on a cross-country tour with comedian Bob Newhart. Over the years, Barbara turned out LP albums for a number of labels. The titles included "Trouble in Mind"; "Living with the Blues"; "Night at the Ash Grove"; and "When I Was a Young Girl."

DARLING, ERIK: Singer, guitarist, banjoist. Born Baltimore, Maryland, September 25, 1933. The big hit of early 1963, "Walk Right In,"

brought Erik Darling to the fore for a moment of national attention. It was somewhat unusual for a gifted artist who tended to remain in the background. Many of the major achievements of the folk music boom of the 1950s and '60s involved Darling, but in most cases as a member or co-worker of a famous group or performer.

Darling's early years were certainly ones of variety. His family moved many times and his education was divided into small periods at different schools. By the time he was in his late teens, his family had finally settled in New York. He was graduated from Rhodes School in New York and entered New York University in the early 1950s.

Some years earlier, he had learned to play the guitar and five-string banjo. At 15 he had begun to sing folk music, and performed at high school functions from time to time. His interest in music grew and deepened until he decided to leave NYU after a year and try for a career in folk music.

He began to sing in local coffee houses and then started to travel through the country, appearing in clubs or coffee houses in most of the states. His reputation with folk artists increased and he began to receive requests to accompany some of them in recording sessions. In particular, Ed McCurdy liked Darling's guitar or banjo assistance. Among the LPs on which Darling accompanied McCurdy were "A Ballad Singer's Choice," "Barroom Ballads," and "When Dalliance Was in Flower."

In 1956, Darling organized a new group called The Tarriers. For the next few years, the quartet gained an enthusiastic following in the folk field. One of their early recordings was a hit version of "The Banana Boat Song." Harry Belafonte turned the song into a national hit as part of his calypso repertoire. Darling also formed a group called The Folk Singers in the late 1950s that provided the Elektra LP "Run Come Hear" in '58.

Darling was not ignored as a solo performer, however. He turned out a successful LP for Elektra called "Folksongs" in August 1958. This included such renditions as "Salty Dog," "Cumberland Mountain Bear Chase," "Oh What a Beautiful City," "Pretty Polly," "Hard Luck Blues," "Banjo Medley," "Swannanoa Tunnel," "Boll Weevil," and "Candy Man." On Vanguard label, he later recorded two more solo LPs, "True Religion" and "Train Time!"

When The Weavers were faced with the problem of replacing Pete Seeger in 1958, they called Darling in. For the next few years, he worked with this legendary group in concerts throughout the world. Among Weaver recordings on which Darling performed are versions of such songs as "So Long, It's Been Good to Know Ya," "Tzena, Tzena, Tzena," "Kisses Sweeter Than Wine" and "Wimoweh."

After several years with The Weavers, Darling once more felt the urge to organize a group of his own. The result was the formation of the Rooftop Singers in 1962. This trio, besides Darling, comprised Lynne Taylor and Bill Svanoe. In early 1963, the Rooftop Singers scored a gold record success with "Walk Right In." The hit single was followed with an LP of the same title, featuring such other songs as "Stagolee" and "Ham and Eggs." During the mid-1960s, the Rooftop Singers toured the U.S., Canada, and Europe, playing concerts and club dates and appearing on radio and TV in many cities. Their second LP, "Good Time!," was released in 1964.

DAVIS, JIMMIE: Singer, guitarist, songwriter, educator, public official. Born Quitman, Louisiana, September 11, 1902.

Few country and western greats achieved more honors than Jimmie H. Davis. He won many awards as one of the nation's foremost gospel and country performers. He also won national attention for some of his compositions, particularly the western standard "You Are My Sunshine." But his most important honors came in the form of the backing of the people of his home state, who twice elected him governor.

Davis was born and raised in rural Louisiana, completing elementary and high school in his home town of Beech Springs. He grew up in an environment where singing country music and gospels was an integral part of everyday living. In high school, he already had a considerable repertoire of songs and had learned to play the guitar. Singing, however, remained a hobby in these years. After finishing high school, he concentrated on continuing his education rather than pursuing an entertainment career.

Jimmie completed work on his B.A. at Louisiana College in Pineville in the early 1920s. He went still further, completing work on a master's degree at Louisiana State University in Baton Rouge. Later in the decade, he gained a post as professor of history at Dodd College. He con-

tinued to expand his musical activities during these years, particularly in the gospel field. As word of his ability spread through the southwest, he had more and more invitations to perform.

In the 1930s, a good percentage of his time was devoted to music. In time, Jimmie spent a good part of each year touring the country singing both country and gospel music. However, he never completely abandoned his interest in public affairs. He held several public posts during the 1930s, including a year and a half as a public service commissioner and a period of time as a criminal court clerk.

By the end of the 1930s, Jimmie was one of the best known performers in the country and western field. Besides his public appearances and radio work, he also was gaining a reputation as a recording artist for RCA Victor and as a songwriter. In the early 1940s, this led to a bid to appear in a movie, "Louisiana," released by Monogram in 1944. Two of the compositions he co-authored, "You Are My Sunshine" and "It Makes No Difference Now," helped make Gene Autry a top recording star. Jimmie's songwriting credits as of the 1960s included such other songs as "Doggone That Train," "Someone to Care," and "When It's Roundup Time in Heaven." He co-authored a number of others, including "When We All Get Together Up There" and "I Dreamed of an Old Love Affair."

In 1944, Jimmie was offered the nomination for governor on the Louisiana Democratic ticket. He combined discussions of state problems with country music fare to win the election. Jimmie completed his term in 1948 and returned to spending much of his time as a singer, though he devoted more time to gospel work than popular singing. His religious work in the 1950s won him a number of national awards, including the American Youth Singers award as Best Male Sacred Singer of 1957.

First for RCA and, in the 1950s and '60s for Decca, Jimmie turned out a great variety of recordings over the years. A few of his many records were: "You Are My Sunshine," "Suppertime," "Lord, I'm Coming Home," "Get On Board," "Aunt Susan," "Honey in the Rock," "The Great Milky Way," "Alimony Blues," "You've Been Tom Cattin' Around," "Somewhere There's a Friend," "The Lord Has Been Good to Me," "Take My Hand, Precious Lord," "Worried Mind," "I'm Bound for the Kingdom," "Columbus Stockade Blues," "When I Prayed Last Night," "It Makes No Difference Now,"

[74]

"I Won't Have to Cross Jordan Alone," "There's a Chill on the Hill Tonight," "I Hung My Head and Cried" and "Down by the Riverside."

When the state political pot began to boil in the late 1950s, Jimmie was asked to run in the 1960 primary. Amid cross-currents of racial strife and arguments about the Long political machine, Davis managed to win the primary against several opponents. Once again he occupied the executive mansion as governor of Louisiana from 1960 to 1964.

As his term came to an end in 1964, he was represented in the LP field by a newly issued Decca LP, "Jimmie Davis Sings." Still in stock at the time were such earlier Decca albums as "Someone to Care" (mid-'50s) and "You Are My Sunshine." Reflecting his gospel work, a dozen of his religious LPs on Decca were available in the late '60s, including "Near The Cross"; "Highway to Heaven"; "Hymn Time"; "Songs of Faith"; "Suppertime"; "Sweet Hour of Prayer"; "The Door Is Always Open" ('58); "Hail Him with a Song" ('59); "No One Stands Alone" ('60); "Watching Over You" ('61); "How Great Thou Art" ('62); and "Beyond the Shadow" ('63).

He was nominated for the Country Music Hall of Fame in 1968.

DAVIS SISTERS, THE: *See* Davis, Skeeter

DAVIS, SKEETER: Singer, songwriter. Born Dry Ridge, Kentucky, December 30, 1931.

One of the great country and western female vocalists of the 1960s, Skeeter Davis (born Mary Frances Penick), gained a reputation among her fellow artists for taking stardom in stride. Booked out of Hubert Long's talent agency in Nashville, she put some unusual restrictions on where she would perform. In particular, she asked the agency not to book her where liquor is served. This was not due to an objection to others drinking. Rather it reflected her view that she did not want her non-drinking fans drawn into a situation where they might be tempted.

Skeeter learned humility and restraint from her family life in Kentucky. Music was one of the main pleasures of the Penick clan, which included four girls and three boys. In her teens, Skeeter enjoyed singing with one of her close friends, Betty Jack Davis (born Corbin, Kentucky, March 3, 1932), and, in time, formed a duo with her. Calling themselves the Davis Sisters, they performed at small clubs in Lexing-

ton, Kentucky, then broke into radio in 1949 on station WLAX of that city. In the next few years they were featured on WJR, Detroit, WCOP and WKRC-TV, Cincinnati, and WWVA, Wheeling, West Virginia.

The Davis Sisters were signed for RCA Victor in the early 1950s by Steve Sholes. His judgment was verified in 1953 when the girls scored a number-one-ranked hit, "I Forgot More Than You'll Ever Know." Things seemed to be moving at a happy clip when tragedy struck. While returning to Cincinnati from an appearance on WWVA on August 2, 1953, the girls' car was struck by another which crossed over the dividing line. Betty Jack was killed.

After several months of mourning, Skeeter began performing once more with Betty Jack's sister, Georgia. By 1955, though, she went out on her own as a single act. She began to record under the watchful eyes of RCA Nashville A&R man Chet Atkins.

In 1959, her growing audience provided her with a top 10 hit, "Set Him Free." She followed in 1960 with "I'm Falling Too." Then came

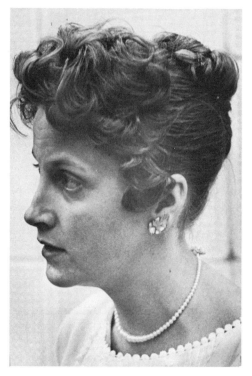

Skeeter Davis

such top 10 country and western hits as "Optimistic" in 1961 and "Where I Ought to Be" in 1962.

Her gingham dresses got a little fancier as she was signed for appearances on the Dick Clark Show, the Duke Ellington Show, and with Sammy Davis, Jr., and the Rolling Stones. By this time she was featured regularly on Nashville's Grand Ole Opry. In 1963, RCA's Nashville office received an excited call from its Houston distributor. Skeeter's latest record, "The End of the World," had sold 10,000 records for him in a few weeks' time. It was the start of her biggest hit to that point, a record that went to the top of popular music charts in the U.S. and overseas as well. The success of this song made her a top name in many European countries as well as America. Among her many personal appearances in the 1960s, throughout the world, one of the most memorable was her debut in New York's Carnegie Hall.

Skeeter scored another top 10 hit in 1963, "I'm Saving My Love," and followed in 1964 with "Gonna Get Along Without You Now." Some of her other RCA successes of the 1960s were "Dear Judge," "Am I That Easy to Forget," "I Can't Stay Mad at You," "He Says the Same Things to Me" and a song which she co-wrote, "Homebreaker."

Skeeter also turned out many hit LPs. Through the mid-'60s, these included: "Hits with the Davis Sisters" and "Jealous Love" on the Fortune label; "I Forgot More" (Camden—'64); and, on RCA, "Songs" ('60), "Skeeter Davis" ('61), "End of the World," "Cloudy" ('63), "Let Me Get Close" ('64), "Skeeter Davis Sings Standards," "Singin' in the Summer Sun" ('66), "My Heart's in the Country," "Skeeter Davis Sings Buddy Holly," "What Does It Take?" ('67), and, with Bobby Bare, "Tunes for Two" ('65).

DEAN, JIMMY RAY: Singer, instrumentalist (guitar, accordion, piano, harmonica), songwriter. Born Seth Ward near Plainview, Texas, August 10, 1928.

"Oh, I was a hardworkin' little boy. Pullin' cotton, shockin' grain, cuttin' wheat, loadin' wheat, choppin' cotton, cleanin' chicken houses, milkin' cows, plowin'. They used to laugh at my clothes, my bib overalls and galluses, because we were dirt poor. And I'd go home and tell mom how miserable I felt being laughed at. I dreamt of havin' a beautiful home, a nice car, an' nice clothes . . . I wanted to be somebody."

So Jimmy Dean described his childhood to Edith Efron of TV Guide (January 4, 1964). He had, by then, achieved his desires and then some.

Though his family was poor, it was not unhappy. His mother managed to earn enough to keep things going by running a barber shop. She also learned how to play the piano by correspondence and taught Jimmy when he was 10. He, in turn, used this knowledge of music to help teach himself to play the guitar, accordion, and harmonica.

For a while, though, a career in music seemed far off. He tried irrigation engineering at 16, but left this for a two-year stint in the Merchant Marine. After this, he enlisted in the Air Force. While stationed at Bolling Air Force Base outside Washington, D.C., he formed the Tennessee Haymakers with three friends. They gained spare time employment in local honkytonks. When Jimmy left the service in 1948, he continued to perform in Washington and its vicinity.

Several years later, impresario Connie B. Gay heard him and asked to represent him. In 1952, Gay sent Jimmy on a tour of U.S. bases in the Caribbean. Jimmy and his new group, the Texas Wildcats, were then placed on station WARL, Arlington, Virginia. In 1953, they gained national attention with their hit recording of "Bummin' Around."

By 1955, Jimmy had his own TV show, Town and Country Time, on WMAL-TV. It was soon expanded to Town and Country Jamboree. Tapes of the show were featured on stations all over the country. This led to a contract with CBS for a network morning spot, The Jimmy Dean Show, starting April 8, 1957, on WTOP-TV, Washington. Thousands of letters poured in, but sponsors wouldn't back the show. In 1958, an afternoon network show from New York was planned for Dean, but a dispute arose and Jimmy left.

For the next few years, Jimmy toured the U.S., winning tremendous audience acceptance. He also had a Columbia Records contract. In 1961, while on a plane to Nashville for a recording session, he tried to select a song to fill a gap in the schedule. He decide to write his own. The song, his first composition, was "Big Bad John," which sold more than 2,000,000 records. That same year, he hit again with "Dear Ivan." He continued his recording success in 1962 with "The Cajun Queen," "P.T. 109," and "Gonna Raise a Ruckus Tonight" and a best-selling LP, "Big Bad John."

His singing success led to a new TV show on ABC starting in 1963. The show, after a slow start, became a feature of afternoon TV from 1963 to 1966. Jimmy had less success with an hour-long evening show (1964–1966). Mail was heavy but the Nielsen ratings were low. In the meantime, he kept up his recording work with a different label, RCA Victor. For RCA he provided such hits as "Stand Beside Me" in '66 and "I'm a Swinger" in '67.

His output on Columbia included such albums as "Hour of Prayer," "Big Bad John," "Jimmy Dean Portrait" ('62); "Everybody's Favorite" ('63); and "Songs We Love" ('64). He was also represented on King with "Favorites" ('60) and on Mercury with "Television Favorites" ('65). His RCA LPs included "Jimmy Dean Is Here" and "Most Richly Blessed" ('67).

Over the years, Jimmy was a guest star on most major TV networks and made personal appearances in all parts of the country. His 1967 engagements, for example, included appearances on the Ed Sullivan Show, Daniel Boone Show, Hollywood Palace and at Harrah's Club, Reno; Valley Music Hall in Salt Lake City; Circle Star Theatre, San Carlos, California; Midland Empire Fair, Billings, Montana; Shoreham Hotel, Washington, D.C.; Holiday House, Pittsburgh; and a stint with the Ice Capades.

DELMORE, ALTON: *See* Delmore Brothers, The

DELMORE BROTHERS, THE: Vocal and instrumental duo, songwriters, both born Elkmont, Alabama, Alton Delmore, December 25, 1908, died Nashville, Tennessee, July 4, 1964; Rabon Delmore, born December 3, 1910, died Athens, Alabama, December 4, 1952.

Long-time favorites on the Grand Ole Opry for more than twenty years, The Delmore Brothers provided some of the all-time standards in the country field. In their many decades together, Alton composed better than 1,000 songs while Rabon turned out in excess of 200. Among their collaborations was the major hit "Blues Stay Away from Me," while Alton composed "Beautiful Brown Eyes" with Arthur Smith.

Both brothers were farm bred and sang for pure enjoyment when their boyhood chores were through. They learned many songs from family and friends in the constant round of local sings that were an important part of rural life in the early part of the century. The boys learned to play the fiddle at an early age and, in their teens, entered many fiddle contests in their region. Their performance in these began to gain them a reputation in many parts of Alabama. Though starting on the fiddle, the brothers also mastered the guitar and were considered as good on this instrument as the other.

After playing for some years for local events, the boys auditioned for Columbia Records in 1931. It was their first time before a microphone and led to their first records for that label. Soon after, they were signed by the Grand Ole Opry. Unlike most artists, who spend years trying to make the Opry, the Delmores' radio debut was on the Nashville program in 1932. In the later '30s and throughout the 1940s, the brothers appeared on many other stations besides WSM, including WPTF, Raleigh, North Carolina; WFBC, Greenville, South Carolina; WAPI, Birmingham, Alabama; WLW, Cincinnati; WIBC, Indianapolis; WMC, Memphis; and KWHN, Ft. Smith, Arkansas.

In the 1940s and 1950s, the brothers were represented on King Records. Their output included such songs as "Prisoner's Farewell," "Sweet, Sweet Thing," "Midnight Special," "Why Did You Leave Me Dear," "Don't Forget Me," "Midnight Train," "Freight Train Boogie," "Boogie Woogie Baby," "Harmonica Blues," "Barnyard Boogie," "Used Car Blues," "Peachtree Street Boogie," "Take It Out on the Captain," "Fifty Miles to Travel," "Shame on Me," "Calling to That Other Shore," "The Wrath of God," "Weary Day," "Blues Stay Away from Me" (a top 10 hit of 1949), "Pan American Boogie," "Trouble Ain't Nothin' But the Blues," "Blues You Never Lose," "I Swear by the Stars," "Sand Mountain Blues," "Life's Too Short," "I Let the Freight Train Carry Me On," "Please Be My Sunshine," "Field Hand Man," "Gotta Have Some Lovin'," "Everybody Loves Her," "Lonesome Day," "The Girl by the River," and "There's Something 'Bout Love."

Their output included several sides with

Grandpa Jones, including "Darby's Ram" and "Take It Out on the Door."

DELMORE, RABON: *See* Delmore Brothers, The

DENNY, JAMES R.: Manager, publisher, talent booker. Born Buffalo Valley, Tennessee, February 28, 1911; died Nashville, Tennessee, August 27, 1963. Elected to Country Music Hall of Fame, 1966.

Horatio Alger, Jr., would have been pressed to create a hardship story more tear-jerking than that of James R. (Jim) Denny. He was born in Buffalo Valley, described as being "near Cookeville, Tennessee." Denny, the youngest of three brothers, was shipped off to an aunt in Nashville when his family was reduced to survival-each-day status during the Depression years. He arrived in Nashville with forty cents jingling in a small tobacco sack and eleven years of life in the world.

Living with his aunt didn't work so he sold newspapers in the downtown section and delivered telegrams between editions. His bed was several freshly bound bundles of newspapers in a corner of the pressroom. He was a hustler, though, and his ingenuity was noted by one of his newspaper route customers, National Life and Accident Insurance Company, which owned WSM and staged the Grand Ole Opry. National Life hired him as a mailroom clerk at the age of 16 and Denny soon worked himself into a side job as "gopher" on the Opry. A gopher, or helper, was told to "go for" messages or coffee or do other chores, including ushering.

Denny took an evening course in business at Watkins Institute and gradually moved up the National Life ladder, being named to head the accounting and systems division. During this time he also worked with the Opry organization. In 1951, this gained him the job of Opry talent director. Working closely with top country and western artists, Denny saw the great opportunity there would be in setting up a publishing business. In 1954 he took the plunge, establishing the Cedarwood Publishing Company.

Jack DeWitt, WSM president, had seen young Denny literally rise from the streets. Still, he felt that Denny must give up his publishing company or be relieved of his position as Opry manager. Denny could see no conflict between the positions but was dismissed. WSM had been serving as a booking office for most of the top country and western acts. Denny now felt no compunction about setting up his own booking office, the Jim Denny Artist Bureau.

Because of his knowledge of the WSM operation, Denny had no problem in gaining clients. Goldie Hill (now Mrs. Carl Smith) was the first artist to sign and others soon followed. Other booking agencies started and prospered. Denny's pioneering in the booking business is credited with bringing new talent to Nashville, opening doors that had been closed to newcomers. Carl Smith and Webb Pierce became closely associated with Denny in his business ventures and he soon teamed with Pierce to purchase three radio stations.

Denny parlayed his music publishing enterprise into an international organization with offices in London and Berlin. Some 54 BMI awards and Billboard's Triple Crown for "Love, Love, Love," "I Don't Care," and "More and More" followed. His 18-hours-a-day work schedule and tight hand on his enterprises and artists/writers was a personal way of living for him. He seldom looked back at the newspaper boy but retained that same boy's fighting spirit. Denny could look back on industry honors: Billboard's "Man of the Year" for 1955, Ralph Peer Award in 1957, and Music Reporter's "Outstanding Service Award."

In the 1960s, another honor came his way, one he did not live to see. He was voted into the Country Music Association's Hall of Fame in 1966.

DENNY, J. WILLIAM: Publisher. Born Nashville, Tennessee, August 25, 1935.

The name Denny is a great one in country and western music, even if it is little known beyond the field's professional circles. In the years after World War II, it was the "behind the scenes" executive that helped make Nashville the country music capital of the world. No one did more in this regard than the Denny family, the late James R. Denny and his son, J. William Denny.

The younger Denny was introduced to country music operations by his father almost as soon as he could walk. As a youngster, he worked Saturday nights at the Grand Ole Opry and traveled with a carnival during summer vacations. In high school, he was both a prop man and a cameraman at WSM-TV. He also gained insight into the performing end of the business by working as a disk jockey on stations WSM and WMAK in Nashville.

He majored in business administration at Vanderbilt University and, in 1956, became road manager for the Philip Morris Company Music Show, handling advance publicity and promotion; he later became director of the Philip Morris Country Music Show. He then worked for an advertising agency and trained for two years in the banking business. In 1956 he joined Columbia Records, Inc., as Nashville studios manager, developing Columbia's custom record pressings operation.

He became general manager of Cedarwood Publishing Company in 1963 shortly before his father's death and was elected president that fall, monitoring the worldwide Cedarwood interests since that time. In 1962 he was recipient of Nashville's Area Junior Chamber of Commerce "Spotlight Award," and in 1965 was voted "Man of the Year" by the Nashville Jaycees. In the mid-1960s, still in his twenties, he served as president of the Country Music Association, youngest ever to hold the position. He was also the youngest member ever named to the Board of Trustees of the National Academy of Recording Arts and Sciences (NARAS). Denny represents the young wit and intelligence that keeps country music rolling for and into Nashville.

DE WITT, LEW: *See* Statler Brothers

DEXTER, AL: Singer, guitarist, organist, songwriter. Born Jacksonville, Texas, May 4, 1902.

In the mid-1940s, one song swept the nation. It was on every list of hits in every popular music category. The song remained one of the most-played songs of all time for many years afterward. The song, "Pistol Packin' Mama," catapulted the man who wrote and recorded it into nationwide fame. For Al Dexter, it was a far cry from his one-time occupation of house painter.

Al was born Albert Poindexter in Jacksonville, Cherokee County, Texas. His interest in music started in high school. At 15, he was already playing the guitar and performing for school affairs. Soon after, he began to play with the first of many local groups with whom he appeared in the 1920s and '30s. He also wrote a number of hymns; his first composition was called "Going Home to Glory." For a while, though, music was a spare time thing and he

worked at house painting and other odd jobs for his living.

By the early 1930s, he had decided to concentrate on music and organized his own group, the Texas Troopers. Their first record, in 1934, helped make them one of the most popular bands in the East Texas area. His early records were for Vocalion and Okeh, but in the 1940s he was featured on Columbia.

By the time he joined Columbia, Al had begun to make a reputation as a songwriter as well as a performer. He turned out two major hits in the early 1940s, "Honky Tonk Blues" and "Rosalita." "Rosalita" was written in 1942 but before Al could record it, the industry was hit by the struggle between ASCAP, BMI, and the radio stations. The song was popular with audiences, but no record could be made for many months. When the ban was lifted, Al and the record executives were sure they had a great hit. Since a new song seemed a good idea for the flip side, Al was asked to write one. The result, "Pistol Packin' Mama," surprised everyone by becoming an all-time best-seller. The song and Al's followup records resulted in Dexter's receiving the Juke Box Operator's award as leading artist of 1946.

Among the many other recordings turned out by Dexter and the Troopers were "Too Late to Worry," "Guitar Polka," "Saturday Night Boogie," "Car Hoppin' Mama," "One More Day in Prison," "Down at the Roadside Inn," "New Broom Boogie," "Triflin' Gal," "Rose of Mexico," "Little Sod Shanty," "Alimony Blues" and "Sundown Polka."

During the 1950s and '60s, Dexter continued to entertain enthusiastic audiences at his own nightclub, the Bridgeport Club in Dallas. In 1962, a new LP of Dexter music, "Pistol Packin' Mama," was issued by Harmony Records.

DICKENS, LITTLE JIMMY: Singer, guitarist, songwriter. Born Bolt, West Virginia, December 19, 1925.

"I'm Little But I'm Loud," went a hit song "Little" Jimmy Dickens wrote about himself. His voice certainly had plenty of strength for his four feet, eleven inch build, but it certainly did not seem "loud" to his many fans. His warm tones and infectious smile made him one of the favorites of audiences across the U.S.

Jimmy was raised on a farm in Raleigh County, West Virginia. He attended local schools and went on to enroll in the University of West Virginia. By the time he was in his teens, he had learned to play guitar and entertain his friends with country and western songs. When he was 17, he auditioned at station WJLS in Beckley, West Virginia, and won his first commercial singing job. He called himself Jimmy the Kid and worked with Johnny Bailes and His Happy Valley Boys. His early efforts included work on another West Virginia station, WMNN in Fairmont.

After serving his apprenticeship locally, Jimmy moved further afield in the mid-1940s and began to sing on his own rather than as a member of a group. He toured many of the eastern and midwestern states and performed on several midwest stations. The latter included WKNX, Saginaw, Michigan; WING, Dayton, Ohio; and WLW in Cincinnati. More and more country fans began to take notice of the diminutive Jimmy, and by the late 1940s he had a sizable following. The result was a bid to join the Grand Ole Opry in 1948 as a regular cast member. From then through the 1960s, Jimmy was a star performer on the Nashville TV classic.

Dickens signed with Columbia Records and his name was constantly on the hit charts in the years following World War II. One of his first top 10 successes was the 1949 "Take an Old Cold Tater." The same year provided his second major hit, "Country Boy." He scored again in 1950 with "A-Sleeping at the Foot of the Bed" and "Hillbilly Fever." Some of his other popular recordings were "Just When I Needed You," "My Heart's Bouquet," "I Got a Hole in My Pocket," "Out Behind the Barn," "Conscience," "I Can't Help It," "Lovin' Lies," and "Salty Boogie." His own songs include "Sea of Broken Dreams" and "I Sure Would Like to Sit a Spell with You."

In 1965, Jimmy turned out his all-time best-selling record for Columbia Records, the number-one-placed "May the Bird of Happiness Fly Up Your Nose."

Jimmy's albums include the 1957 Columbia LP "Little Jimmy Dickens," the '61 "Big Songs" and '62 "Behind the Barn." Two of his LPs were produced by Harmony Records, "Best of Little Jimmy Dickens" in 1964 and "Old Country Church" in '65.

DILLARD, DOUG: *See* Dillards, The

DILLARD, ROD: *See* Dillards, The

DILLARDS, THE: Bluegrass group, Douglas "Doug" Dillard, born Salem, Missouri, March 6, 1937; Rodney "Rod" Dillard, born Salem, Missouri, May 18, 1942; Dean Webb, born Indianola, Missouri, March 28, 1937; Mitch Jayne, born Hammond, Indiana, July 5, 1930.

One of the results of the folk boom of the post-World War II period was a wide interest for the style of folk-country music known as Bluegrass. Even when the nationwide folk rage subsided, Bill Monroe, Flatt & Scruggs, and other Bluegrass practitioners continued to draw enthusiastic audiences. The door was thus opened for popularity of newer groups, such as The Dillards.

The originators of the group were Doug and Rod Dillard who learned to play Bluegrass style on banjo and guitar while still in elementary school. Their interest in the music increased when they reached high school and they began to perform at school events and for local folk sings. In 1958, they decided to try for a wider audience. They went to St. Louis and found a backer for their first recording. They took some disks home and won support from their friend Mitch Jayne. Jayne, disk jockey on Salem station KSMO, played the record a number of times. Though it was a good record, it didn't come close to becoming a nationwide hit.

However, Jayne, who played banjo, joined the Dillard boys in playing local school events, square dances, etc. Soon after, a fourth member was added, mandolin player Dean Webb. After several years of working in the Missouri region, the group began to move further afield. One of their first engagements in the early 1960s was in the Buddhi Club in Oklahoma City. They played other clubs and coffee houses, building up a reputation as a coming group.

In a short time they signed their first major recording contract with Elektra Records. Elektra issued their LP, "Bluegrass," in July 1963. The resulting attention won bids to play in eastern clubs and at a number of folk festivals. The group also was featured on several folk-type TV shows. In November 1964, Elektra issued a second LP, "The Dillards Live!"

In 1965, the group moved its base of operations to California. They soon were appearing in clubs up and down the coast, including the leading folk nightclub, the Troubadour. They were featured on eight TV shows in 1965, in-

The Dillards, Bluegrass favorites of the 1960s. Leader Doug Dillard holds his trusty banjo.

cluding a Judy Garland special and the Andy Griffith Show. The group also signed a new recording contract that year with West Coast based Capitol Records.

DIXON BROTHERS, THE: *See* Dixon, Dorsey

DIXON, DORSEY: Singer, guitarist, songwriter. Born Darlington, South Carolina, October 14, 1897.

Dorsey Murdock Dixon was one of the most talented of the older generation of country music artists and writers. His song "Crash on the Highway" is one of the standards of country music and one of the all-time hits of Roy Acuff. Dorsey and his brother Howard also formed one of the oft-remembered teams of the 1930s, The Dixon Brothers. (Howard was born in Darlington, South Carolina, June 19, 1903 and died March 24, 1961.)

Despite this, Dorsey gained little but enjoy-ment from his music. He was born too soon, and his active career came at a time when there was little money in the country field. In fact, though many of his songs were widely played, he had sold the rights and received no additional royalties in most cases. Thus Dorsey spent almost his entire life as a mill hand, able to devote more than a few hours a day to music only in his years of retirement.

Dorsey Dixon was one of seven children of a textile mill family. His father worked for the Darlington Cotton Manufacturing Company as a steam engine operator and the children followed suit. Dorsey's older sister started work for eight cents a day as a spinner in the mill at the age of eight. Dorsey was a bit luckier; he started there at 12.

But though life was hard, the family was close knit and happy. Music was a prime way of adding meaning to their life and Dorsey learned spirituals and hill country ballads from his mother from the time he was five. Dorsey

[81]

got his first guitar when he was 14 and quickly taught himself to play. He also learned to play the fiddle from a local teacher at the same time. He soon performed at local Sunday schools. In his later teens, he teamed with his brother Howard to play duets in the Rockingham movie theater.

During World War I, Dorsey worked as a railway signalman on the Atlantic Coast Line in Darlington. When the war ended, he returned to mill work and remained a mill hand from 1919 to 1951. His jobs over the years took him to Lancaster and Greenville, South Carolina, and East Rockingham, North Carolina. In 1947, he also worked for a time in a New Jersey rayon plant before going back to southern mills. In 1951, he left the mills and worked in a munitions plant box factory in Baltimore.

Over these years, Dorsey continued to develop as an artist and writer. During the 1920s, he and his brother played at many local dances and affairs, but never for pay. In the late 1920s, Dorsey finally began to write some of his own music. One of his first efforts (1929) was "The Cleveland Schoolhouse Fire," originally a poem that his mother and brother began to sing to an old country tune. In the early 1930s, Dorsey and Howard met the legendary Jimmie Tarleton when he worked briefly in East Rockingham, and learned many new tricks with the guitar.

The Dixon Brothers branched out into show business in 1934 by appearing on J. W. Fincher's Crazy Water Saturday Night Jamboree over station WBT in Charlotte. This led to a record date with RCA Victor two years later, the first of five such sessions between 1936 and 1938. The Brothers recorded more than 60 songs during this period, but their income was still not enough to permit working as fulltime artists. Some Dixon songs were later turned into national hits by other performers.

For a long time, the Dixons settled back to their work in the mills. Occasionally a song showed up on the country hit charts with Dorsey's name on it. In the 1960s, he was rediscovered, this time by folk music collectors. He was asked to appear at the 1963 Newport Folk Festival. He listened to some of his songs performed by others and sang some himself. In the years that followed, he sang at a number of folk concerts as well as returning to Newport several times. Among the songs he presented were "Weave Room Blues" and "Will the Circle Be Broken."

His 1963 Newport performance was presented on the Vanguard LP "Old Time Music at Newport." He also recorded an LP for Piedmont Records in 1963. In November '63, and the following January, he provided 38 songs for the Library of Congress American Folk Song Archive. In 1966, Testament Records released a new Dorsey Dixon album called "Babies in the Mill."

DIXON, HOWARD: *See* Dixon, Dorsey

DOBRO: Stringed instrument, basically a guitar with raised strings.

One of the more exotic versions of the guitar that began to be widely used in the decades after 1930 is the dobro. It is an instrument that uses a special resonator cone in combination with a raised string arrangement to produce a sound something like that of a Hawaiian guitar.

The instrument was originally devised by a brother team of Czechoslovakian origin, the Dopyeras. John Dopyera, the oldest, started by making a guitar with raised strings in 1925–26. This was later modified to the square-necked form used by most dobro players today. In 1929, John and his brothers Ed and Randy started the Dobro Guitar Co. The name of the instrument is derived from its inventors' family name: DOpyera BROthers. The word means "good" in the Slavic language.

The basic dobro uses a 12-inch diameter concave resonator cone to reinforce the sound. The cone can be adjusted by changing the tension on the bolt holding the cone and bridge together. A spider of 4, 6, or 8 strings is mounted between bridge and resonator.

The Dopyeras initially were the only dobro manufacturers. In 1932, they sold rights to the instrument to National Music Co., which marketed a modified version called the National Dobro. In 1954, National was bought out by Valco Company, which continued to produce a type of dobro.

DOLAN, JIMMIE: Singer, guitarist, band leader. Born Missouri, October 29, 1924.

Born and raised in rural Missouri, Jimmie Dolan was a western film addict as a youngster in the 1930s. He enjoyed listening to country and western music on the radio and sometimes dreamed of touring the west as a singer and bronc rider. When he was 14, a mail advertise-

[82]

ment for a combined guitar and mail order instruction course caught his eye. He sent for the instrument and managed to teach himself to play.

In his mid-teens, he knew enough about the instrument to begin to play for local events. It wasn't too long before he was auditioning for work on radio stations. In the late 1930s, he won a job with station KWK in St. Louis. He quickly gained a following and continued to work on the show until the start of World War II.

Jimmie laid aside his cowboy suit and joined the Navy as a radioman in the early 1940s. He served for five years throughout the South Pacific. He took his guitar along, and spent some of his overseas time entertaining troops in advance bases. The many rousing receptions given him during these shows made him feel that he should try for a wider audience when he returned to the States.

On his discharge in 1946, he decided to settle in Los Angeles. He gathered his own group and soon was featured on several stations in Southern California. Billed as America's Cowboy Troubadour, he played engagements at many clubs in the Los Angeles area. By the late 1940s, he was given a recording contract by Capitol Records. Starting in 1949, he turned out a number of well-received records on the label. Some of his first recordings were "I'll Sail My Ship Alone," "I'll Hate Myself Tomorrow," "Wham! Bam! Thank You Ma'am," "I've Got the Craziest Feeling," "A Load of Trouble" and "I'll Make Believe."

In 1951 he scored a top 10 national hit, "Hot Rod Race." This resulted in bids to tour many parts of the country with his group. During the early 1950s he continued to turn out new Capitol recordings, such as "Tennessee Baby," "Goodbye My One and Only," "All Alone in Texas," "Lost Love Blues," "Many's the Time," "Wine, Women and Pink Elephants," "SOS Save My Heart," "The Spider and the Fly," "Juke Box Boogie," "Sailor's Blues," "That Last Love Letter" and "Until I Die."

DOLLAR, JOHNNY: Singer, guitarist, songwriter. Born Kilgore, Texas, 1936.

The road to success in any field of music is often a rugged one. So it was for Johnny Dollar, who performed in many small towns and recorded many excellent records that received little play for lack of exploitation. At one

point, he gave up music for a while before finally working his way to the big time.

Johnny was born in Texas, and raised partly there and partly in Oklahoma. As a boy, he listened avidly to the Grand Ole Opry on the family's old cabinet radio. When he got to public school, he joined the choral group and also was choir leader at the rural church his family attended. Still, he didn't think much about making music his life's goal during his youth.

When he was in his late teens, the onset of World War II caused him to enlist in the U.S. Marines. When he was discharged, he stopped off in Denver during a slow journey home. A $14 guitar caught his eye and he bought it. He went back to the Oklahoma-Texas border region and learned how to play it. Then with the guitar slung over one shoulder, he hitchhiked throughout the Texas-Oklahoma-New Mexico region, performing wherever he could and auditioning for many talent shows.

After many weary miles of this, he heard of a small swing band that needed a vocalist. He sought them out and soon was made leader. Called Johnny $ Dollar and the Texas Sons, they made a name for themselves in West Texas. This finally helped win them a job with the Big D Jamboree in Dallas. Not long after, Johnny accepted a bid from the Louisiana Hayride in Shreveport. Once there, Johnny also got a job as DJ with KZEA radio.

In Shreveport, Johnny began to spend more time writing his own music. Many of his songs were co-authored with fellow artist Shelby Singleton. Johnny had been given a recording contract by the small Dee label. He recorded a number of his and Shelby's songs, including "Lonesome Trains," "West Texas," and "Crawling Back to You." The records were good, but made little headway in the national market.

After five years in Shreveport, Johnny threw in the towel in the mid-1950s and accepted a job with an Oklahoma investment firm. Things were slack at this time in country music, thanks to the rock 'n' roll boom. For three years Johnny stayed in Oklahoma.

Then, as things began to pick up in country and western in the late 1950s, Johnny couldn't keep from trying again. He went back on tour, appearing in many shows in the south and southwest. In the early 1960s he turned out a new composition, "Lumberjack," on the Winston label that began to move. It caught on enough to win him a contract from Columbia Records. Going into the mid-1960s, Johnny began to find things moving his way. One of his first Columbia records, "Tear Talk," made the national charts. In 1966, he scored one of the top hits of the year with "Stop the Start." By 1967, he had three more successful numbers to his credit, "Your Hands," "Watching Me Losing You," and "The Wheels Fell Off the Wagon."

DONOVAN: Singer, songwriter. Born Glasgow, Scotland, February 10, 1946.

In the 1960s, a young, gentle-seeming singer-composer from Scotland became close to a legend while still in his early twenties. His songs had a poetic ring to them that attracted the attention not only of young folk music fans the world over, but of many well known poets as well. Some of his compositions, such as "Universal Soldier," helped add fuel to the many protest movements of the decade.

Born Donovan Leitch to a working class family in Glasgow, he had anything but a gentle childhood. His first ten years were spent in the Gorbals area of the city, which is one of the roughest in Scotland. Things were a little easier for him when the family moved to the outskirts of London in 1956. However, his poetic and artistic temperament often puzzled his teachers. In his biography for Epic Records he recalled, "At school, the teachers thought I was a little strange because I wrote a lot of fear and horror stories and drew sketches for them. One was about this man who got locked in a drain when it rained."

For a while, during his teens, art was his main interest, though he also learned to play guitar. He finished the English equivalent of high school and began taking art in college. However, he didn't have the money to continue his education and left after a year. With a friend, Gypsy Davy, he then began to wander throughout England, hitching rides on trucks, beachcombing, and observing people. "We weren't working out the problems of the world [he wrote]; we were letting our days fill up with strange encounters. We didn't talk much, but we moved fast a lot." During the months on the road, Donovan wrote stories and songs and often played his guitar.

Back in London again, in 1964, he settled in a small basement studio. He taped some of his songs and took them to music industry execu-

Donovan

tives. Some of them were impressed with his ability and the end result was an appearance on the BBC-TV show, "Ready, Steady, Go." The audience response was so great that he was signed for two more appearances.

His first recording, "Catch the Wind," soon appeared and rapidly made the number two spot on English hit charts. Two more hit compositions followed, "Colors" and "Universal Soldier." These were well received all over the world, including the U.S. His first two LPs, "Catch the Wind" and "Fairytale," also created an international stir.

In 1965, this led to an invitation to appear at the Newport Folk Festival. Donovan's U.S. debut was sensational; rapt critical approval from Newport was quickly followed by sellout engagements at Carnegie Hall, Cornell University, and the Hollywood Bowl. In 1966, he repeated his triumphal U.S. invasion with standing-room-only performances at a Los Angeles club, The Trip. Other visits to the States in later years were similarly well received, including a sellout show at the new Anaheim, California, convention center.

In the mid-1960s, he was signed for U.S. record rights by Epic. In 1966 his first effort for the label, "Sunshine Superman," was a best-seller, as was his next U.S. Epic release, "Mellow Yellow." Though given a certain amount of popular notoriety for his "message" songs, most of his work tends to be basically along poetic, descriptive lines. In "Sunshine Superman," his composition covered such topics as children, love, fairy tales, beaches and a girl who entangles her hair in a Ferris wheel.

In 1968, Epic issued a two-LP special of Donovan's work, "Gift from a Flower to a Garden."

DRAKE, PETE: Guitarist, band leader. Born Atlanta, Georgia, October 8, 1932.

If you're a guitarist, a song like "Talking Steel Guitar" seems natural enough. For Pete Drake, it came so easily that it propelled him into the national spotlight in 1964. The success of this record won him the Cashbox Award for number one instrumentalist of the year in both the pop and country fields. It also won him the nod from Record World as "Fastest Climbing Instrumentalist of the Year."

Born and raised in Atlanta, Pete took an early interest in country music. He enjoyed listening to the music on records and radio, but didn't try to go any farther during his grade and high school years. All this changed in 1951 when he learned to play the steel guitar. Within a year, he could play one of the best guitars in the Atlanta region. That same year, he formed his own band, The Sons of the South. The group played local clubs and soon were featured on Georgia stations. During most of the mid and late 1950s, the group broadcast regularly on WLWA in Atlanta and WTJH in East Point, Georgia.

In 1959, Pete moved to Nashville. He was soon established as one of the best sidemen in the business for local recording sessions. During the '60s, he backed such artists as Jim Reeves, Porter Wagoner, Norma Jean, Roy Drusky, Carl Butler, Elvis Presley, Bonnie Guitar, Teresa Brewer, Bobby Vinton, and Bob Dylan.

Before long, Pete was also playing for his own record sessions. In the mid-1960s he hit first with "Talking Steel Guitar" and, soon after, with the million-selling "Forever." His output on Smash label included several LPs and such other songs as "I'm a Fool to Care" and "Mystic Dream."

DRIFTWOOD, JIMMY: Singer, guitarist, fiddler, banjoist. Born Mountain View, Arkansas, June 20, 1917.

In 1958, a folk song took the U.S. by storm. It was called "The Battle of New Orleans" and its strident rhythms dominated both the popular and country and western charts for many weeks. The best-selling record bore the name of Johnny Horton as the artist; the composer's name, which appeared on an excellent version of his own, was Jimmy Driftwood.

The song was one of many derivations of early American folk songs given new life by Jimmy. He had gained his background in the music naturally from his upbringing in the Ozark Mountains. His family (he was born Jimmy Morris) all played and sang songs of the hill country, as did many of their friends and neighbors. He learned to play banjo, fiddle, and guitar while still of grade school age. His favorite instrument was a homemade guitar, given him by his grandfather Morris. As Raymond Lawless notes, Jimmy said the guitar was made "of fence-rail, ox-yoke and bedstead."

Jimmy learned his Three R's at a country school in Mountain View. He went on to take three years of high school there before finishing his senior year at nearby Marshall. In high school he performed at local dances and picnics. He continued his spare time music activities after graduating from high school and starting work as a teacher in Arkansas rural schools. Another spare time avocation was eking out enough credits for his college degree. After years of taking courses, mostly during vacation, at several local colleges, he won his B.S. in education from Arkansas State Teachers College, Conway, in the early 1940s.

Over the years he continued to collect folk material and his presence was felt in a number of regional folk festivals, including the Ozark Folk Festival at Eureka Springs. By the 1950s, he was invited to appear at folk concerts and festivals in many of the states. The growing interest in folk music eventually led to wider exposure of Jimmy's songs. RCA Victor signed him for an LP in 1958 called "Newly Discovered Early American Folk Songs."

One of the songs, "The Battle of New Orleans," began to receive more and more plays from disk jockeys across the country. This led to the hit single of 1959. Other songs in the album were "Unfortunate Man," "Fair Rosamond's Bower," "Soldier's Joy," "Country Boy," "I'm

[85]

Too Young to Marry," "Pretty Mary," "Sailor Man," "Zelma Lee," "Rattlesnake Song," and "Old Joe Clark." Also in 1959, Driftwood's song "Tennessee Stud" provided a major hit for Eddy Arnold.

In the 1960s, Jimmy Driftwood was a familiar figure at many major folk festivals, including several years at Newport. He also helped get the new Arkansas Folk Festival underway in 1963 and served as its director, a role he still was fulfilling in the late 1960s. The success of the festival and its emphasis on traditional music helped win the support of Congress for establishment of a national folk music center in this region.

DRUSKY, ROY: Singer, guitarist, songwriter, disk jockey. Born Atlanta, Georgia, June 22, 1930.

The Cleveland Indians' and veterinary medicine's loss is the country and music field's gain. Though Roy showed the ability for both these careers, the result was a happy one for music since Roy became one of the major performers and songwriters of the 1960s.

Roy Frank Drusky had little interest in country music while attending Tech High in Atlanta. Instead, he was a star athlete, particularly as a second baseman for the school's baseball team. After graduation, he signed up for a two-year Navy hitch. While on the *U.S.S. Toledo,* he became intrigued with the western style band some of his shipmates had formed. When he got the chance, he bought a guitar and taught himself to play it.

Though interested in music, he felt it best to try for a degree in veterinary medicine at Emory University when he returned to Atlanta in 1950. In his spare time, he and some friends got together and had country music sessions. In 1951, Roy decided to form a professional band. His new group, The Southern Ranch Boys, started with local dates, then won a 15-minute daily show on WEAS, Decatur, Georgia (now WGUN). Soon after, Roy became a featured disk jockey on the station. This work, in turn, led to a solo singing job at the Circle H Ranch in Atlanta. For three years, Roy and his band, whom he brought in after a few months, drew record crowds to the club. During this period, Roy made his TV debut on WLWA (now WAIA) in Atlanta.

Roy's first record for Starday came in 1953. It was a hit called "Such a Fool" and led to a

Columbia Records contract. The Columbia setup did not produce best-sellers, but the success of the Starday disk provided him with bids to work across the country in such places as the Ocean Pier Casion in 1954. In 1955, Roy broke up his band and returned to DJ ranks on station KEVE, Minneapolis. Once again the DJ job helped gain a singing role, this time at the Flame Club.

While at the Flame, he began to write his own songs. Many guest artists appeared at the Flame over the years and liked Roy's material. In the late 1950s, Webb Pierce thought enough of Roy's "Alone with You" to suggest to Decca that Roy record it on their label. Faron Young covered the song and the result was a top 10 hit of 1958. Decca then suggested Roy move to Nashville to be closer to the country music production scene.

After a short apprenticeship, Roy began to hit the best-seller lists regularly both as songwriter and performer. In 1960, two records of his own compositions, "Another" and "Anymore," were in the top 10 part of the year. In 1961, he worked with V. McAlpin and J. Felrod on two more Decca hits, "I Went Out of My Way" and "I'd Rather Loan You Out." His singing of the Ray Pennington-Sonny Thompson "Three Hearts in a Tangle" also was a bestseller of 1961. Roy's next three record successes were by other writers. These included "Second Hand Rose" in 1963; "(From Now on All My Friends are Gonna Be) Strangers," 1965; and his first number-one hit, "Yes, Mr. Peters," in 1965. The last song was performed with Priscilla Mitchell on the Mercury label to which Roy moved in 1964. In 1966, he scored with "White Lightning Express," title song for a country and western film. Drusky also starred in two other country and western films, "Forty Acre Feud" and "The Golden Guitar." By the mid-1960s, he was also receiving ovations from European audiences on annual overseas singing tours.

DUDLEY, DAVE: Singer, guitarist. Born Spencer, Wisconsin, May 3, 1928.

An arm injury that wiped out one promising career led to the beginning of a second, successful one in music for Dave Dudley. The injury, which occurred in 1950, finished his chances as a right-handed pitcher. He had been invalided home from the Gainesville, Texas, Owls to Stevens Point, Wisconsin. While recovering, Dave was asked by his next door neighbor to

[86]

come down to station WTWT where the neighbor worked. At the station, Dave dropped in one morning on DJ Vern Shepherd who had just bought a guitar. Dave, who had played guitar in high school, began playing along with the records. Shepherd liked Dave's style, asked him to come the next morning to sing "live" on WTWT, and a new career was born.

Dave grew up in Stevens Point. When he was 11, his dad used part of his World War I veteran's bonus to buy his son a guitar. Dave managed to learn to play the instrument by watching Saturday performances at the local Fox Theater. Though he kept at it, he never was more than a backup guitarist in school groups.

But he was a star baseball pitcher. When the six-foot-two Dudley finished high school, he played semi-pro ball for a while, then made the Wausau, Wisconsin, team in the Wisconsin Valley League. In 1949, his 15-3 record won a call to the higher Gainesville Owls. Then the arm injury caused him to switch to music.

In the fall of 1950, Dave channeled his energies into a new morning show on WTWT. His fan mail grew and he moved on to a new DJ and singing show at KBOK, Waterloo, Idaho, in 1951 and then to KCHA, Charles City, Idaho, in 1952.

In 1953, Dave took a deeper plunge into the music world by forming his own trio. For the next seven years, the Dudley Trio played nightclubs and lounges in most of the midwest states. Audiences liked them, but nothing sensational occurred. In 1960 they had to disband the trio in Minneapolis. Soon after, the new Gay Nineties Club in Minneapolis needed a group and Dave formed the Country Gentlemen* with three other musicians and a girl vocalist. He gained enough of a following in the city to gain a midday DJ spot on KEVE. He was also hired as m.c. of a new country format for the Flame nightclub.

Just when things looked bright again, Dave was hit by a car after finishing work at the Flame on December 3, 1960. This time Dave was in bed for six months. For another six months after this, he was only able to work a little each week. It looked as though his second career was over, but Dudley decided to make one more try. He bought time at a local studio to record a song a friend from Decca had pro-

Dave Dudley

vided, called "Six Days on the Road." He took the dubbing to a friend, Jim Madison, who supplied jukebox records. While Dudley was on a trip to the Dakotas, the record came out on the Soma label. The song caught on and Dudley returned to find himself a national artist.

From then on, Dudley kept his name on the hit charts with a series of best-selling recordings. He scored a second hit in 1963 with "Cowboy Boots." In 1964, he signed with Mercury Records and turned out "Mad" and "Last Day in the Mines." His new four-piece group, The Roadrunners, were guests on most national TV country shows, including the Grand Ole Opry. In 1965 he added two more hits, "Truck Drivin' Son-of-a-Gun" and "What We're Fighting For." His career took a new turn in 1967 with an invitation to the Newport Folk Festival.

DUFFEY, JOHN: *See* Country Gentlemen

DUKE OF PADUCAH, THE: *See* Ford, Whitey

---

* Not the Bluegrass group of the same name.

[87]

DULCIMER: *See* Appalachian Dulcimer

DUNN, EDDIE: *See* Light Crust Doughboys, The

DURHAM, JUDITH: *See* Seekers, The

DYER-BENNET, RICHARD: Singer, lutist, guitarist, composer. Born Leicester, England, October 6, 1913.

The goal of the "Twentieth Century Minstrel," as Richard Dyer-Bennet is called, has been to bring a new dimension to American folk music. His aim was to revive the art of minstrelsy in North America as it had been practiced in ancient times in Europe. He implemented his plans in the late 1940s by establishing the first School of Minstrelsy at the summer music camp at Aspen, Colorado.

Dyer-Bennet, son of a British father and an American mother, spent his early years in Canada. His family moved to the U.S. in 1925. (He chose to claim American citizenship when he came of age, completing naturalization in 1935.) In 1932, he enrolled at the University of California at Berkeley, majoring in English and music. During his undergraduate years, 1932-'35, he also excelled in sports and was a member of the school's tennis and soccer teams.

While in college, he delved deeply into the history of folk music and, in 1934, began singing with Gertrude Wheeler Beckman. His outlook on folk music was given its direction on a European trip during the summer of 1935. He traveled to Sweden to meet the dean of European folk music, 75-year-old Sven Scholander. Scholander sang many minstrel lays while accompanying himself on the lute. Dyer-Bennet decided to become Scholander's disciple in bringing this kind of music to prominence in the Western Hemisphere. From the Swedish artist, he learned 100 folk songs in German, French, and Swedish.

On returning to the U.S., Dyer-Bennet increased his musical activities, performing for many college audiences across the land. Through 1941, he performed with Miss Beckman. At first, Dyer-Bennet accompanied himself on the lute, but he soon switched to the Spanish guitar. He credited Rey de la Torre with teaching him improved fingering techniques for the classic guitar in 1944.

By the early 1940s, Dyer-Bennet was already recognized as a major innovator in folk music.

His first recording sessions were for the folklore department of Harvard University. These were the forerunner of many recordings for different labels including Decca, Mercury, Concert Hall Society, Disc, Vox and Asch. In the mid-1950s, he turned out LPs on his own label.

During World War II, Dyer-Bennet sang on a number of broadcasts for the Office of War Information, in addition to appearing on commercial radio programs. In March 1944, the time seemed propitious for his first recital in New York's Town Hall. The concert's success was such that he had to give another one a month later. From that time on, his Town Hall recital became an annual event in New York's music schedule. In 1946, a booklet containing twenty of his songs was published by Leeds Music.

In the post-World War II era, LPs of Dyer-Bennet's music were among the steadiest sellers in the folk field. On Stinson label, he was represented by such albums as "Ballads," "Richard Dyer-Bennet, 20th Century Minstrel." Among the songs performed on these are: "Barbara Allen," "I Once Loved a Girl," "The Three Ravens," "Gentle Johnny My Jingalo," "Olde Bangum," "Lord Randal," "The Ghost of Basel," "Lincolnshire Poachers," "Come All Ye," "The Lass from the Low Country," and "The Charleston Merchant."

Many of the songs he performed at concerts in the 1950s and '60s were represented by albums on the Dyer-Bennet label. These LPs include "Gems of Minstrelsy" ('60); "Dyer-Bennet" ('62); "Songs in the Spirit of 1601" ('63); and "Of Ships and Seafaring Men" ('65).

DYLAN, BOB: Singer, guitarist, pianist, harmonica player, songwriter. Born Duluth, Minnesota, May 24, 1941.

"On the slow train time does not interfere and at the Arabian crossing waits White Heap, the man from the newspaper and behind him the hundred Inevitables made of solid rock and stone—the Cream Judge and the Clown—the doll house where Savage Rose and Fixable live simply in their wild animal luxury. . . ."

These words from the liner notes by Bob Dylan for his 1965 album "Highway 61 Revisited" are typical of the complex imagery of this Pied Piper of the 1960s. They pose such questions as whether it's all a put-on, a meaningless parody of liner notes, or simply a special kind of code for the initiated or, on the other hand, poetry in the footsteps of such symbolists as T. S. Eliot or Ezra Pound. In the same way, Dylan has sometimes intrigued and sometimes enraged observers from all sides of the musical —and political—spectrum. In the end, it is almost impossible to exactly define Dylan except as an important and multi-faceted creative artist.

His way to fame as composer and performer was a troubled one almost from Dylan's earliest years. He was born Robert Zimmerman in Duluth; soon after, his family moved to Hibbing. Though his parents were in comfortable circumstances, young Bob soon gained a great distaste both for Hibbing and for his conventional home life. He learned to play the guitar when he was 10, and two years later began a pattern of escape from an environment he did not feel adjusted to.

He ran away from home almost as soon as he learned the guitar, but did not get far before being returned. At 12, he tried once more without success. When he was 13, he succeeded in evading the authorities for some months, traveling with a carnival through upper Minnesota, North Dakota, and South Dakota.

He was sent home again. But he kept breaking away at regular intervals, running away when he was 15, 15½, 17 and 18. Although he got as far as Kansas and California on some of these adventures, his family located him each time until, at 18, they gave up the attempt. Meanwhile, gaining experience from his trips, Bob spent more and more of his energy in expanding his musical background. At 15, he learned to play the harmonica and autoharp. He also wrote his first song, dedicated to French screen siren Brigitte Bardot.

Despite his escapades, Dylan finished high school with honors and a scholarship to the University of Minnesota. He entered in the spring of 1960, but stayed only six months. This brief sojourn still had a major effect on his musical career. Previously, he had been influenced by a combination of rhythm and blues performers (Bo Diddley, Chuck Berry), Negro folk artists (Leadbelly, Mance Lipscomb), and country and western artists such as Hank Williams and Jimmie Rodgers. At the University, he heard some of Woody Guthrie's songs and became an avid fan of the great folk musician.

While at Minnesota, Bob sang for a while with the regular group at The Scholar coffee house. He finally left school in the fall to go back to New York to try to see Guthrie, then ill at Greystone Park Hospital, New Jersey. He managed to see Woody, who had never heard of him, and they became friends.

Once in New York, Bob began to try to make his living in folk music. For a while he led a hand-to-mouth existence, performing only now and then for little money and sometimes sleeping in the subways. Then he was discovered by Columbia Records executive John Hammond who heard him by accident during a rehearsal session of another folk artist.

Hammond signed Dylan and soon set up Bob's first recording sessions. Meanwhile, things began to look up for Dylan. In early 1961, he played at the Gaslight coffee house in New York's Greenwich Village. In April, he appeared opposite blues singer John Lee Hooker at Gerde's Folk City. The critics raved about Dylan's work, as Bob later noted in some of the lyrics of his "Talkin' New York," and soon Bob was "in."

In an amazingly short period of time, he had

Composer, folksinger, pioneer of folk rock, Bob Dylan

a reputation that began to rival such giants of folk music as Guthrie and Pete Seeger. He was signed for concert appearances in all parts of the U.S., appeared on major network TV shows, and from 1962 to 1965 was the object of much attention at the Newport Jazz Festival. He also starred on the opposite coast in the Monterey, California, Folk Festivals. In rapid succession he composed dozens of folk songs that became standards. These included such compositions as "Blowin' in the Wind," "The Times They Are A-Changin'," "Masters of War," "Don't Think Twice, It's All Right," "Mister Tambourine Man," "Spanish Harlem Incident," "Chimes of Freedom," and "Like a Rolling Stone."

During the mid-1960s, Dylan often was represented on the popular charts with hit singles. Each new LP increased his following, starting with his first in 1961, "Bob Dylan." In the early 1960s he soon had such others as "The Freewheelin' Bob Dylan," "The Times They Are A-Changin'," and "Highway 61 Revisited."

By 1965, a definite change could be noted in Dylan's material. The last-named album is an example. It included such songs as "Tombstone Blues," "It Takes a Lot to Laugh, It Takes a Train to Cry," "From a Buick 6," "Ballad of a Thin Man," "Queen Jane Approximately," "Highway 61 Revisisted," and "Desolation Row." The lyrics of most of these were complex, symbolic, but strangely compelling.

Dylan's trend to avant-garde lyrics and folk-rock caused a split in his following. His former strong supporter, editor Irwin Silber of Sing Out!, wrote an open letter implying that Dylan had abandoned the cause of folk music. At the 1965 Newport Folk Festival, Dylan's presentation won ecstatic approval from part of the audience and vocal opposition from others.

As always, Dylan ignored external criticism and went his way. He did not appear in the Newport event in 1966. For a time, he was hampered by an injury received in a motorcycle accident. (One of his main non-musical hobbies was cycling.) He managed to make several highly successful European tours in the mid-1960s. One of these, to England, was filmed by Donn Pennebaker. Released in mid-1967, the film, called "Don't Look Back," won almost unanimous critical approval as one of the best movies of the year.

In 1968, Dylan moved in still another musical direction. His hit album "John Wesley Harding" was in the country music style, as was his 1969 LP "Nashville Skyline."

EDMONDSON, DIAN: *See* Greenbriar Boys

EDMONDSON, TRAVIS: *See* Gateway Singers

EDWARDS, JOHN, MEMORIAL FOUNDATION: Collection of country and western (plus some folk) material, maintained at the University of California at Los Angeles.

At this writing, probably the most complete collection of country and western material in the United States is housed in the Folklore & Mythology Center at UCLA. Heart of the collection is the compilation of records, tapes, correspondence, photographs, biographical and discographical material made by the late John Edwards. Edwards, ironically, was a native of Australia who never visited the United States to talk to performers or record companies in the country and western field.

Edwards established himself as one of the major authorities on country and western music of the period 1923-1941 mainly through correspondence. By 1960, he had gathered together more than 2,000 78rpm records of the earlier period, as well as a number of magnetic tapes. In addition, he had documented many important facts about the careers of pioneer performers in an accumulation of letters to and from the performers, their acquaintances, and music industry executives. His collection included taped interviews with many of them.

Born in 1932, John Edwards died in an automobile accident near his home in Cremorne, Australia, on December 24, 1960. In his will he requested that his collection be sent to the United States to be used for scholarly purposes. The material was shipped to his designated trustee and friend, Eugene W. Earle, then in New Jersey. In 1962, Earle arranged for the collection to be located at UCLA. Though the Foundation is housed on the campus, it is supported solely by outside contributions.

The John Edwards Memorial Foundation, Inc., was chartered as an educational, non-profit corporation in California on July 19, 1962. Initial charge of the collection was given to folklorist Dr. D. K. Wilgus, who served as secretary of the Foundation. Present at UCLA when the material arrived was a graduate student, Ed Kahn, who also became closely associated with the Foundation. As of 1968, he held the titles of treasurer and executive secretary. Other initial Foundation directors included Earle as president, Archie Green, 1st vice president, and Fred G. Hoeptner, 2nd vice president.

Additions to the Foundation included almost 10,000 records from the combined holding of all the directors. Other collections were added in the mid-1960s, including one comprising 487 song folios. Various publications and industry mementos, including musical instruments of several important performers, have also been contributed.

Foundation goals include continued collecting of new material, archiving, cataloging and indexing the old and new information, and publishing and distributing scholarly articles on various aspects of the field. It is also planned "To sponsor and promote field collections of such music, to stimulate academic research in this area, and to instruct and educate the public to the value of such music as part of its cultural heritage."

The importance of the Edwards collection was recognized by the Country Music Hall of Fame when its new Nashville building was opened. A grant was given to the Foundation to copy the original material for a second Edwards collection in Nashville.

ELIRAN, RON: Singer, guitarist, violinist, songwriter. Born Haifa, Israel, 1940.

The folk music phase of the 1960s led to introduction of a number of overseas artists to the U.S. public, not the least of whom was Ron Eliran. Eliran was born under the British Mandate rule in Palestine, now Israel. He showed talent in his youth as a violinist and studied classical violin for a number of years.

When he took part in the Israeli-Egyptian campaign of 1957, he was in his teens. He had by this time gained an interest in classical guitar. After serving as a combat photographer, he returned to civilian life and concentrated on improving his guitar playing. Before long he had gained an excellent repertoire of Israeli folk songs as well. He also studied at a university in Jerusalem during these years. In the 1950s, he began to make a name for himself as a folk singer in his homeland.

At the start of the 1960s, word of his ability reached the U.S. Eliran was signed to make his first U.S. TV appearance on the Ed Sullivan Show. He followed this with a successful tour of the U.S. and Canada, singing in nightclubs and in concerts on college campuses. He also was given a U.S. recording contract by Prestige

International which released a number of LPs of his singing. These included "Golden Songs of Israel," "Ladino (Jewish Songs)," and "New Sounds of Israel."

Ron settled in New York for a while and studied at New York University. He completed work for his B.A. in television and motion picture directing at NYU. In later years he directed several film shorts. His performing work in this period included an engagement at New York's Village Vanguard and a tour with the Ford Motor Company show "Jazz and Folk Wing-Ding."

Eliran returned to Israel in the mid-1960s to become one of the country's leading artists. He performed many songs that he composed as well as folk material from all parts of the world. When the 1967 Arab-Israeli War flared up, he returned to the service and took part in the brief campaign. He also composed the song "Sharm El Sheikh," which became the number-one war song in Israel. In September 1967, he introduced his version of the song to American TV audiences on the Johnny Carson Show. Following this, he also gave a number of concerts in the U.S.

ELLIOTT, RAMBLIN' JACK: Singer, guitarist. Born Brooklyn, New York, August 1, 1931.

A cowboy from Brooklyn? This seems a little incongruous, but it is perhaps no more so than a matador or flamenco dancer from the same benighted territory. Elliott is indeed from the big city, as are many others of the urban folk movement of the 1950s and '60s. However, most critics agree that his music has the true flavor of the plains and the hills.

As Elliott told an English interviewer (quoted in "Ramblin' Jack Elliott" by Bill Yaryan, Sing Out!, November '65, p. 26), "People (in the U.S. would) . . . just laugh their heads off at the idea of a kid from Brooklyn singing cowboy songs. So I invented this Oklahoma thing to keep 'em quiet. Said I was born on a ranch."

Elliott gained his initial interest in cowboys from watching countless movie westerns in his home town. Though born Elliott Charles Adnopoz, son of a doctor, he began to think of himself as "Buck Elliott" by the time he was high school age. When he was 16, he ran away from home to join Col. Jim Eskew's rodeo. His family notified the authorities and Buck was sent home two months later. He finished high school in Brooklyn and went on to college, first to the University of Connecticut and later to Adelphi College in New York. Along the way, he had learned to play guitar and sang cowboy songs whenever he had the oportunity.

The urge to escape from urban culture was too great for Jack to finish school. He left Adelphi and moved to Greenwich Village. Here he moved in coffee house and folk music circles. In 1951, this led to a meeting and the start of a warm friendship with Woody Guthrie. Guthrie was impressed with Elliott's talent and invited the young man to stay with the Guthrie family in the Coney Island section of Brooklyn. The two played and sang for hours each day and Elliott learned many of the fine points of combining guitar playing with other folk instruments.

When the Guthries moved to the Topanga Canyon area of Los Angeles, Elliott went there too. Here he met many other major folk artists, including Bess and Butch Hawes, Guy Carawan, and Derroll Adams. Elliott gained his first professional experience in Southern California at Knott's Berry Farm, acting and playing guitar in the Farm's covered-wagon-encircled amphitheater. He also worked as a "faith-cured cripple" for local revival meetings.

When Elliott met and married actress June Hammerstein, he decided to take her suggestion to go to Europe. His association with Guthrie helped pave the way for acceptance by European audiences. He became a major favorite in England in the mid-1950s and soon this resulted in a recording contract with Topic Records. During 1956 and '57, the Elliotts traveled throughout Europe, appearing in concerts and major clubs and starring on TV. They appeared in Alan Lomax's show, In the Big Rock Candy Mountain, and, joined by Derroll Adams, played to enthusiastic audiences at the Blue Angel in London and later at the Brussels World's Fair.

In 1958 the Elliotts returned to California, but went back to England in 1959. Elliott was then featured on a European tour with The Weavers and Pete Seeger. After his triumphal reception overseas, Elliott once more tried his hand in his home country. This time his engagement at Gerde's Folk City won critical and popular acceptance throughout the U.S. In the years that followed, Elliott became a favorite with U.S. audiences in concerts across the country. He also played at most major festivals in the 1960s, including several appearances at Newport.

By the mid-1960s, Elliott's name appeared on LPs on several labels. On Prestige, he turned out "Guthrie Songs" ('61); "Country Style"; "Ramblin' Jack Elliott" ('62); and "Hootenanny" ('64). His output on Monitor included "Ramblin' Cowboy" and "Jack Elliott Sings Guthrie and Rodgers." In 1964, he became a featured artist on Vanguard label with "Jack Elliott."

ENGLISH, LOGAN: Singer, guitarist, actor. Born Henderson, Kentucky.

The church may have lost a gospel singer and folk music a major performer when Logan English's father retired during Logan's boyhood. Logan spent his first few years in his birthplace of Henderson, Kentucky, where his father was a Baptist preacher. When the boy reached school age, English senior retired from the ministry and moved to a farm in Bourbon County, Kentucky.

So Logan was exposed to the many folk music influences of the region. There were a number of tenants on the farm from the hill country, and they often got together to play stringed instruments and sing. Logan enjoyed these sessions and learned many folk ballads from them. He often listened also to the country music radio shows from Cincinnati. From one of these programs, featuring The Girls of the Golden West, he taught himself how to yodel.

The Cowboy from Brooklyn, Jack Elliott

After finishing high school, Logan went on to attend Georgetown College in Kentucky. For a time, he concentrated on acting and speech rather than on expanding his folk music background. However, his interest in the folk genre revived later, after two years in the Army, when he went to Yale University. His major there continued to be in acting as he worked for his Master of Fine Arts degree in the School of Drama. But the post-World War II folk music boom was beginning and Logan was encouraged to sing many of the old songs he knew for his friends.

After receiving his MFA, he went on to work in both the acting and folk music fields. During the 1950s, he began to perform on the coffee house circuit. Before long he was in demand in many small clubs, including the Cosmo Alley in Hollywood and the Second Fret in Philadelphia. His credits during the 1950s and '60s included Gerde's Folk City and One Sheridan Square in New York, The Unicorn in Hollywood, and appearances in New York's Carnegie Hall and Town Hall.

In the mid-1950s he recorded his first major LP for Folkways, "The Days of '49." In 1957, he cut a 10-inch record for the same label, "Kentucky Ballads." He also recorded a 1957 LP for Riverside, "Gambling Songs." This included such numbers as "My Father Was a Gambler," "Stewball," "The California Gambler," "Jack o' Diamonds," "Stagger Lee," and "The Coon-Can Game."

Coming into the 1960s, he signed for an album on Monitor label, "American Ballads." Released in 1962, it illustrates his range of material, including such songs as "Red Clay Country," "Mule Skinner Blues," "Roll on Columbia," "The Dewy Dens of Yarrow," "Buck-Eye Jim," "Shenandoah," "Little Brown Jug," "He's in the Jailhouse Now" (a song made famous by the original Jimmie Rodgers), "The Kentucky Moonshiner," "My Last Old Dollar Is Gone," "Pretty Saro" and "Mole in the Ground."

During the 1960s, English sang at many major folk festivals. He also recorded the LP "Woody Guthrie Songbag" for Twentieth Century Fox in 1964.

EVANS, DALE (MRS. ROY ROGERS): Singer, actresss, songwriter. Born Uvalde, Texas, October 31, 1912.

The first family in western entertainment in the decades just after World War II were Mr. and Mrs. Roy Rogers. Both Dale and Roy are artists of the first rank, and both have contributed more than their share in humanitarian and religious activities.

The western outlook was natural to Dale, who was born and spent part of her girlhood in Texas. Later her family moved to Osceola, Arkansas, where she attended high school and demonstrated a talent for singing. After a brief marriage (1928-'30) to Thomas Frederick Fox, she went on to concentrate on a career as a vocalist.

During the 1930s, she gradually worked her way to the top as a popular singer. She was featured on a number of radio stations in such cities as Memphis, Dallas, and Louisville. In the late 1930s, she became vocalist with Anson Weeks' band, then one of the top organizations in Chicago. Her growing reputation resulted in a hit engagement at the Chez Paree Night Club in Chicago in 1940. That year she also was signed as a singer on a weekly CBS show called News and Rhythm. As the 1940s went by, she was a guest star on many major radio shows and vocalist on the Edgar Bergen-Charlie McCarthy network show.

Next came the chance to get started in films. In 1943, Dale made her Hollywood debut in "Swing Your Partner." This was the first of many movies over the next twenty years. Her picture credits from 1943 on included "West Side Kid," "Here Comes Elmer," "Hoosier Holiday," "In Old Oklahoma," "Yellow Rose of Texas," "My Pal Trigger," "Sunset in El Dorado," "Bells of San Antonio," "Bells of Coronado," "Pals of the Golden West" and "Don't Fence Me In." Most of the films were with Roy Rogers, whom Dale had married in 1947.

In the 1950s, the team of Roy Rogers and Dale Evans had become number one in the western field. They were starred on the Roy Rogers Show which was one of the top-rated ones on NBC-TV for a number of years. The Rogerses were featured at many rodeos and other major shows across the country. A number of times they helped entertain New York audiences during the World's Championship Rodeo in Madison Square Garden. Their international popularity was well demonstrated by rousing receptions from audiences during their first tour of the British Isles in 1954.

Dale and Roy turned out many records during

the 1950s for RCA Victor. Some were of songs composed by Dale, such as "The Bible Tells Me So," "Aha San Antone," and "Happy Birthday Gentle Savior." They were also represented in the 1960s by a long-time RCA Victor LP best-seller, "Dale Evans and Roy Rogers," and a Capitol LP of religious songs. In addition to songwriting, Dale found time to write several books, including *Angel Unaware* and *Spiritual Diary*. She also turned out a number of articles for national magazines during the 1950s and '60s.

The Rogerses won acclaim during the 1950s and '60s for their charitable work and for their dedication to children. They adopted and raised a large family of their own. Over the years, they received many awards for their efforts, including the Masquer's Club's George Spelvin Award for humanitarian service in 1956, public interest award from the National Safety Council, and citations from the American Red Cross, National Association for Retarded Children, Muscular Dystrophy Association, National Nephrosis Foundation and many religious denominations. (*See also* ROGERS, ROY)

EVERLY BROTHERS: Vocal, instrumental duo, both born Brownie, Kentucky, Don, February 1, 1937; Phil, January 19, 1939.

The late 1950s were not remembered with much joy by many of the country music gentry of Nashville, Tennessee. The initial impact of rock 'n' roll had caused a temporary deflation of the Nashville product. One of the few bright spots was a young singing duo from Kentucky, the Everly Brothers, who bore the Acuff-Rose banner onto both rock 'n' roll and country and western hit charts.

The boys had an impeccable country background. Their parents were Ike and Margaret Everly, country artists well known to southern and midwestern audiences. The boys learned to sing many country standards at an early age and learned the rudiments of the guitar as soon as they could hold an instrument. When Don was six and Phil eight, they made their first public appearance on radio station KMA in Shenandoah, Iowa. After this, the boys regularly joined their parents on performing tours each summer.

The boys decided to strike out on their own when their parents retired just when they themselves finished high school. They moved to Nashville, playing at local clubs and waiting for

their first break. They began to gain notice in the country music capital and, in 1957, had their first record contract. In making the rounds of music publishers for new song material, they met the top songwriting team of Boudleaux and Felice Bryant at Acuff-Rose. Boudleaux played them a new composition, "Bye Bye Love." The boys decided to record it, starting a close association with the Bryants and Acuff-Rose that lasted for many years.

"Bye Bye Love" brought the Everly Brothers national attention, hitting number-one spot in both the popular and country and western charts. Later, they provided Cadence Records with another number-one-ranked song for 1957, "Wake Up Little Susie." The brothers were soon featured on most major TV shows, including the Ed Sullivan Show and Dick Clark's American Bandstand. They had an even greater year, with the Bryants' help, in 1958, with such number-one successes as "All I Have to Do Is Dream" and "Bird Dog." The brothers also scored in 1958 with a non-Bryant song, "This Little Girl of Mine."

The brothers soon showed they could write songs themselves. Their hits included "Cathy's Clown" and a 1959 top 10 success, "Till I Kissed You." Some of their other hits of the late 1950s and early 1960s were "Devoted to You" and "When Will I Be Loved?"

One of the Everlys' best-selling LPs was a Cadence album, "Best of the Everly Brothers." In the early 1960s, the brothers moved to the Los Angeles area and signed a new record contract with Warner Brothers. Their LPs for Warner's included "It's Everly Time"; "Date with the Everly Brothers"; "Top Vocal Duet"; "Instant Party"; "Golden Hits" ('62); "Great Country Hits" ('63) and "Gone, Gone, Gone" ('65).

FIDDLE (VIOLIN): Stringed instrument; smallest member of the violin family.

The word fiddle has been universally used by folk, country and western partisans to describe the stringed instrument called the violin in other segments of the music field. Actually, because of the use of the word violin in the symphonic field, most people assume that violin is the ancient term for the instrument. In truth, fiddle has been the descriptive term for a far longer period.

The exact origins of the fiddle are not clear. However, some experts believe it is derived from an instrument called a ketherah used in ancient Assyria. A similar instrument was adopted by the Greeks, who called it a cithara. Later, the Romans applied the term fidiculae to a special kind of cithara. While the latter didn't resemble what is now called a fiddle, the term eventually came to describe the instrument.

In the Middle Ages, fiddle-like instruments were in use that are now called rebecs. These were bowed instruments with two or three strings stretched over a narrow bridge. Reference to an instrument called a fiddle is found in a Chaucer poem of 1205. Later steps include the guitar fiddle of the same century, minnesinger fiddles of late Renaissance times, and the viols. The viols dominated the bowed instrument picture in Europe from the fifteenth to the seventeenth century and were the direct ancestors of the present day fiddle, or violin.

The fiddle is the smallest and highest pitched of its family. As the Encyclopaedia Britannica describes it, "It consists essentially of a resonant box of peculiar form, over which four strings of different thicknesses are stretched across a bridge standing on the box in such a way that the tension of the strings can be adjusted by means of revolving pegs, to which they are severally attached at one end. The strings are tuned, by means of the pegs, in fifths. . . . To produce other notes of the scale, the length of the strings is varied by 'stopping' them—i.e., by pressing them down with the fingers—on a fingerboard attached to a neck." The pegs are inserted in the head, at the end of the neck. Sounds are produced by setting the strings to vibrate by moving the bow across them.

The great popularity of the fiddle for many centuries in Europe naturally resulted in its entering the North American continent with the first settlers. A blend of fiddle traditions occurred in some cases, as fiddle styles from Britain, Ireland, and Scotland were used in the southern states. Over the years, as the United States developed, new varieties of regional styles arose in various parts of the country. In the twentieth century, for example, a fiddle expert could distinguish the North Georgia sound from that of western North Carolina, East and West Texas, etc. (*See New Lost City Ramblers Songbook*, p. 12.)

The fiddle was the dominant instrument in folk, country and western music for most of the country's history. A solo fiddler could provide all the music needed for a dance, for example. Up until the late 1920s, the fiddle was still the lead instrument in most bands, with the guitar or banjo serving as accompaniment. The fiddle's importance was underlined by the many fiddling competitions that were an important part of fairs, festivals, and other get-togethers. Many legends arose about some of the most outstanding fiddlers or fiddling contests.

In the post-World War II period, the fiddle still was an important folk instrument, but now it served mainly as accompaniment to the guitar.

FLATT, LESTER RAYMOND: Singer, guitarist, songwriter. Born Overton County, Tennessee, June 28, 1914.

The close family ties between folk music and country and western are nowhere better shown than by the careers of Earl Scruggs and Lester Flatt. Playing one of the oldest forms of rural music in America, the style known as "Bluegrass," the team of Flatt & Scruggs and their Foggy Mountain Boys won thunderous applause from the Grand Ole Opry to the coffee house circuit. Symbolically, when the first Newport Folk Festival took place in Rhode Island in

Earl Scruggs (top) and Lester Flatt

[95]

1959, Flatt & Scruggs were there, mingling with such performers as Pete Seeger, Joan Baez, and John Jacob Niles.

Flatt was born and raised in rural Tennessee, attending school in Overton from 1920 to 1928. When he could find time from his chores, he learned to play the guitar, following the traditional "old-timey" style then popular in the country field. During the 1930s, Lester played for local groups, but earned his living working in textile mills. As he perfected his style, more and more of his friends suggested he could make a career in the music field.

In 1939, he finally turned professional, and soon after made his first radio appearance on station WDBJ in Roanoke, Virginia. During the early 1940s he increased his stature with many appearances in various parts of the south and continued radio exposure. The result was a chance to join the Grand Ole Opry in 1944 as a member of Bill Monroe's Bluegrass Boys. The following year, a skilled banjoist from Shelby, North Carolina, joined the show. The newcomer, Earl Scruggs, won attention for his hard-driving banjo playing. Flatt and Scruggs became friends and in 1948 decided to form their own group.

For the next few years, the Flatt & Scruggs troupe toured many parts of the country and were heard on many stations, starting with WCYB, Bristol, Virginia, in 1948 and WROL, Knoxville, in 1949. In the early 1950s, they were featured on stations in Lexington, Kentucky, Tampa, Florida, and Raleigh, North Carolina. They were also asked to appear on the WNOX Tennessee Barn Dance and the WRVA Old Dominion Barn Dance in Richmond, Virginia.

The boys found a surprisingly eager audience throughout the country for their traditional, unamplified kind of country music. Almost from the start, they were represented by best-selling records, many of which they wrote themselves. Their first contract with Mercury Records lasted until 1951. Among the singles issued by the label were "My Cabin in Caroline," "Baby Blue Eyes," "Down the Road," "I'll Never Love Another," "My Litle Girl in Tennessee," "Old Salty Dog Blues," "Pike County Breakdown," "Back to the Cross," "We'll Meet Again Sweetheart," "I'll Never Shed Another Tear," "Foggy Mountain Breakdown" and "Will the Roses Bloom."

In 1951, the boys switched to Columbia Records, an association still going strong in the late 1960s. Among their recordings of the early 1950s were such songs as "Come Back Darling," "The Old Home Town," "I'll Stay Around," "Jimmy Brown, the Newsboy," "I've Lost You," "Earl's Breakdown," "Flinthill Special," "Why Do You Wander," "If I Should Wander Back Tonight," "Dim Lights, Thick Smoke," "Dear Old Dixie," "Reunion in Heaven," "Foggy Mountain Chimes," "Someone Took My Place with You," "Don't This Road Look Rough and Rocky," "Foggy Mountain Special," "Till the End of the World Rolls Around."

The year 1953 saw Flatt & Scruggs rejoin the ranks of the Grand Ole Opry as featured artists. Among the songs heard by Opry fans during the rest of the 1950s were such numbers as "Randy Lynn Rag," "On My Mind," "Blue Ridge Cabin Home," "It Won't Be Long," "Bubbling in My Soul," "Joy Bells," "What's Good for You," "No Doubt About It," "Six White Roses," "A Hundred Years from Now," "Is There Room for Me," "I Won't Be Hangin' Round," "I Don't Care Anymore," "Big Black Train," "Crying Alone," "Foggy Mountain Rock," "Cabin in the Hills," "Someone You Have Forgotten," and "Crying My Eyes Out Over You."

In the late 1950s, Flatt & Scruggs were stars of the first rank in the country and western field. For four straight years, from 1955 to 1958, they were voted number one instrumental group in the nation in the Country & Western Music Jamboree Poll. From 1959 on, the boys became top favorites as well in the folk music field and in popular ranks. They began to appear with regularity in the top parts of the national hit charts beginning in 1959, when they had a top 10 success, "Cabin in the Sky."

They scored with "Go Home" in 1961, then gained universal recognition when they recorded the theme song for 1962's top TV comedy, The Beverly Hillbillies. Their record of "The Ballad of Jed Clampett" remained number one in both country and western and popular polls for many weeks in 1962. The boys followed with two more major hits in '63 and '64, "Pearl, Pearl, Pearl" and "Petticoat Junction." In 1967, they were represented on national hit charts with "California Uptight Band" and "Nashville Cats."

Throughout the 1960s, Flatt & Scruggs and company toured the nation year after year under the banner of Martha White Shows, Inc. The boys also returned regularly to such folk haunts as Newport and the Ash Grove in Los Angeles. Their efforts were also warmly greeted by audiences in Canada, Europe, and the Far East. The 1960s resulted in a landslide of awards from trade polls and recording industry competitions as well as many best-selling albums.

After 25 years, the team of Flatt & Scruggs split up in March 1969. Flatt announced that he would continue to appear at the head of the Foggy Mountain Boys on the Martha White TV program. (*See also* SCRUGGS, EARL)

FLICK, BOB: *See* Brothers Four, The

FOGGY MOUNTAIN BOYS: *See* Flatt, Lester; Scruggs, Earl

FOLEY, BETTY (MRS. BETTY FOLEY CUMMINS): Singer, guitarist. Born Chicago, Illinois, February 3, 1933.

"Foley" has long been one of the royal names in the country and western field. It was only reasonable that the great Red Foley's daughter should also prove to be highly talented.

Betty Foley was born in Chicago, but spent a good part of her youth in Berea, Kentucky. She learned to play guitar at an early age and was an excellent musician during her days at Berea High School. Her father had been instrumental in establishing the Renfro Valley Barn Dance, broadcast weekly from Kentucky to stations across the country. When she was 17, she became a Barn Dance regular; by the time she left the show in 1954, she was a favorite of midwestern audiences.

Betty began recording for Decca while still in her late teens. In 1954, she had a well received number in "As Far As I'm Concerned." She did even better the following year with a number of nationally ranked songs including "Hearts Made of Stone," "Tennessee Whistling Man," and "How About Me." With Red, she scored a top 10 version of "Satisfied Mind" in 1955. In 1956, one of her best sellers was "Sweet Kentucky Rose."

After touring many states, Betty was again featured on nationally syndicated shows during 1956-57. She was a member of the cast of the WLW Midwestern Hayride and the WCKY Cincinnati Show. Among her appearances in 1957 were several on the Grand Ole Opry. That year, she was chosen the Most Promising Female Vocalist in several disk jockey polls.

In 1958, she was featured on the Tennessee Barn Dance, KNOX Knoxville, and the following year on the Louisiana Hayride from Shreveport. With the start of her father's Jubilee U.S.A. ABC network show, she became a regular on the Springfield, Missouri, feature. She also switched from Decca to Bandera, a move that resulted in a top 10 1959 hit, "Old Man."

FOLEY, RED: Singer, musician. Born Berea, Kentucky, June 17, 1910; died Fort Wayne, Indiana, September 19, 1968. Elected to Country Music Hall of Fame, 1967.

As a youngster, Clyde Julian "Red" Foley was one of the shy ones. He would scramble to a favorite blackberry patch in Blue Lick, Kentucky, where he would be unbothered by adults and their talk of sorghum and grain prices and what the Kaiser was doing over there. It was here he brought a battered guitar which his father, who ran the general store, had taken as part payment on an overdue account. By the time he was seven, he could pick out and chord folk tunes properly.

The one-room school and a determined schoolmaster who liked to sing were factors in forcing young Foley to participate in sings. His shyness was tempered by a hickory cane that stood in the corner of the room. His family moved to Berea where his dad took over another store. Part of the stock were dozen-lots of harmonicas—an instrument that fascinated Foley—and he would slip one from its box, play it awhile, then try another one. All were well broken in by the time they were sold.

Foley excelled in track and basketball at Berea High School, winning several cups, ribbons, and trophies. His mother was convinced his voice had great qualities and hired a music coach, a step that was abandoned when Foley skipped the classes for the most part and went along singing in his own way.

It was some surprise when he won the local Atwater-Kent singing contest and went to Louisville to compete for state honors at 17. The Louisville auditorium stage was far removed from the blackberry brambles of Blue Lick, and a classic case of stage fright gripped him when he forgot the words to "Hold Thou My Hand, Dear Lord," a semi-classical hymn chosen because its wide range would show his voice to advantage.

At the impact point of the song, a high sustained note, which then slid down to a lower one, his mind went blank three separate times. Each time he walked over to the pianist and asked what the next words were and then started over again. The fourth time he made it through and won first prize, charming the audience and judges with his unconscious showmanship.

Foley entered Georgetown College where a talent scout for WLS in Chicago spotted him during his first semester in 1932. The scout signed him for immediate work with the WLS National Barn Dance, then in its infancy. His father gave him seventy-five dollars for the trip. He put it in his shoe for safekeeping, got blisters but saved his money.

It was while he was in Chicago that Foley listened to blues and folk music over the radio. Chicago was a mecca for many Negroes from the south and was bursting with new arrivals to be absorbed into the city. Flat-top guitars played Hawaiian style with the neck of a broken bottle, washtub street bands, the soul sounds of a population on the move somewhere in the shifting scene of Chicago, and some of the loneliness, happiness, and despair seeped into young Foley during this period.

In 1937, Foley originated the Renfro Valley show with John Lair. Two years later, he was the first country artist to have a network radio show, Avalon Time, which co-starred Red Skelton. Strings of one-nighters, fair dates, theater engagements and other personal appearances put Foley into gear for later recording success with Decca Records, which signed him to a lifetime contract. With Paul Cohen (now with Kapp Records) supervising for Decca, Foley's best-selling sides included "Foggy River," "Old Shep," "Chattanooga Shoeshine Boy," "Just a Closer Walk with Thee," "Midnight," and "Tennessee Saturday Night."

"Chattanooga Shoeshine Boy" was recorded in Nashville in Owen Bradley's studios, a converted garage, and racked up across-the-board honors and an impressive portion of Foley's twenty-four-million record sales.

Foley turned several hymns written by Thomas A. Dorsey into country standards, including "Take My Hand, Precious Lord" and "There'll Be Peace in the Valley for Me." (Dorsey, who came to Chicago from New Orleans, was originally a talented pianist and risque blues composer. Later, he "saw the light" and became a foremost hymn writer and

close friend to Mahalia Jackson.) In the folk blues area, akin in feeling to the latter two hymns, Foley wrote his own hit, "Blues in My Heart."

Foley was a featured performer on the Grand Ole Opry in the '40s and set up a publishing firm, Home Folks Music, Inc., with the Hill and Range Songs, Inc., combined, as did many country artists in that era. His Ozark Jubilee, originating from Springfield, Missouri, was an ABC-TV production that ran six years and introduced many future stars.

In 1962, Foley was co-starred with Fess Parker on an ABC television network series, Mr. Smith Goes to Washington. In later years, Foley played various personal appearance engagements. He also packaged his own shows for national distribution. His home base in the mid-1960s was Nashville, which is known to have some pretty good blackberry patches near the city limits.

Foley's career came to an end on September 19, 1968, in Fort Wayne, Indiana. He had retired to his hotel room after taking part in two Grand Ole Opry shows on September 18 and died of natural causes during the night.

FOLEY, RICHARD: *See* Brothers Four, The

FOLK SINGERS, THE: *See* Darling, Erik

FORD, TENNESSEE ERNIE: Singer, songwriter, disk jockey, actor, m.c. Born Bristol, Tennessee, February 13, 1919.

The trademark of Ernest Jennings "Tennessee Ernie" Ford was a relaxed air that went with the soothing tones of his deep bass voice. It helped make him one of the most popular performers first in country and western and then in the overall popular entertainment market. That it was more than a pose was shown by Ford's retirement from top-ranked TV programs on several occasions to spend more time with his family. In each case, he found a national audience waiting to verify his star status on his return to the limelight.

Born and raised in Tennessee, Ernie spent many of his boyhood hours listening to country and western musicians, in person or on the radio. He was particularly interested in radio and, during his high school years in Bristol, spent many hours hanging around the local station. This finally won him his first job, as a staff announcer in 1937 at $10 a week. He obviously had a first-rate voice, and in 1938 he went to study at the Cincinnati Conservatory of Music. He returned to the announcing field in 1939, working for stations in Atlanta and Knoxville from 1939 to 1941.

Enlisting in the Air Corps soon after Pearl Harbor, he became a bombardier on heavy bombers and later spent two years as an instructor. He was stationed in California and met and married a girl named Betty Heminger, which helped make up his mind to settle in California after the war. After his discharge, he got back to the Golden State and found a job as a DJ on a San Bernardino station.

He then moved on to an announcing spot with country and western station KXLA in Pasadena. There he soon struck up a warm friendship with veteran band leader Cliffie Stone who had a show on the station. Ernie sometimes joined Cliffie's quartet in a hymn just for the enjoyment of singing.

After a while, Cliffie asked Ernie to join his Saturday night program. Cliffie also saw to it that Capitol Records auditioned Ernie. Capitol signed the newcomer and results were fast in coming. In 1949, Tennessee Ernie had two singles in the top 10 country and western charts, "Mule Train" and a song he wrote with Cliffie Stone, "Smokey Mountain Boogie." The following year things were even better, as Ernie recorded such top 10 hits as "Anticipation Blues," "I'll Never Be Free" (duet with Kay Starr), "The Cry of the Wild Goose" and "Shotgun Boogie." The last-named was an Ernie Ford original that remained number one nationally for many weeks. Two of the records gave Ernie top ranking in the popular music polls.

In short order Ernie became a network radio figure, with his own shows on CBS and ABC over the period from 1950 to 1955. During these years he continued to turn out top 10 hits, including "Mister and Mississippi" ('51); his own composition, "Blackberry Boogie" ('52); "River of No Return" ('54); and "Ballad of Davy Crockett" ('55). In 1955 he recorded a song by his friend Merle Travis that eclipsed anything he had done before, called "Sixteen Tons." This record became number one in both country and western and national polls and made Tennessee Ernie Ford an almost legendary figure. Through 1967, more than 4,000,000 copies of the record had been sold.

By the end of 1955, Ernie was featured on his

Tennessee Ernie Ford

own daytime show on NBC-TV. This won such enthusiastic audience response that NBC started a new nighttime series in September 1956, starring Ernie. Sponsored by Ford Motor Company, the show was consistently among the top-rated ones during its five year existence.

In 1961, Ernie left TV to move to northern California and spend more time with his wife and sons. He moved to a ranch-style home in Portola Valley, 45 miles from San Francisco. Ernie spent much of his time in succeeding years building up his cattle ranch at Eagleville, California.

After a year away from TV, Ernie signed for a new weekday show with ABC-TV, starting in April 1962. Ernie's personal magic quickly moved it to the top ranks of the polls, where it stayed until its three year contract was up in 1965. Once again Ernie returned to spend most of his time in Portola Valley and vicinity.

He continued to give selected public appearances. In May 1965, he played to a sellout audience at the new Melodyland Theatre near Disneyland. The following year, he signed for four more engagements at in-the-round theaters in the Los Angeles and San Francisco regions.

Throughout the 1950s and '60s, Ernie turned out several dozen LP albums. His religious albums were particularly well received, exceeding 10 million sales by the end of the '60s, and providing Ernie with six RIAA Gold Record awards. His output also included such folk music LPs as "Sixteen Tons" ('60) and "This Lusty Land" ('63). Some of his other LPs were: "Hymns"; "Spirituals"; "Nearer the Cross" ('58); "Gather 'Round," "Friend We Have" ('59); "Sing a Hymn" ('60); "Come to the Fair," "Civil War Songs South," "Hymns at Home" ('61); "Sing a Hymn with Me," "Sing a Spiritual with Me," "I Love to Tell the Story," "Favorite Hymns" ('62); "Tennessee Ernie Ford," "We Gather Together," "Long, Long Ago" ('63); "Great Gospel Songs," "Country Hits" ('64); "World's Best Loved Hymns" ('65).

FORD, WHITEY, "THE DUKE OF PADU-CAH": Comedian, instrumentalist (banjo, mandolin, harmonica), m.c. Born DeSoto, Missouri, May 12, 1901.

"I'm goin' back to the wagon, these shoes are killin' me!"

If any sentence can be said to be immortal in the country field, it's this tag line of one of the greatest of all rustic comedians, The Duke of Paducah. Though he delighted audiences for decades on network shows with his humor, his career covered many years as a pioneer musician in the country and western field.

Benjamin Francis "Whitey" Ford was born in Missouri, but his mother died when he was only a year old and he was sent to live with his grandmother in Little Rock, Arkansas. He grew up in Little Rock and attended Peabody Grammar School there. He was interested in music, though no more so than any other boy growing up in an area where singing old songs and playing the banjo or guitar was a major source of leisure. With the country's entry into World War I, young Ford ran away from home to enlist in the Navy in 1918. He stayed in the service for four years.

While a sailor, his interest in music deepened and he perfected his playing on the banjo. When he got out in 1922, he decided to go into the music field, starting his own Dixie Land Jazz Band. During the 1920s, he toured widely with his own band and with all kinds of other organizations. His jobs included medicine shows, tab shows, stage shows, burlesque and dramatic tent shows. Late in the decade, he teamed with

Bobby Van in a banjo act on the national vaudeville circuit.

When vaudeville began to wane, Ford joined one of the first major country and western bands, Otto Gray's Oklahoma Cowboys. His experience with Gray led to a bid from a young up-and-coming radio singer in Chicago. The singer was Gene Autry and he asked Ford to join his group on WLS, Chicago, as m.c., comic (with Frankie Marvin) and banjoist. Once on WLS, Ford also was one of the first cast members of the new WLS Show Boat, that later became the famed network WLS Barn Dance. Ford teamed up with Bob Van in a banjo duo on the Show Boat. During these years, he also acquired the nickname The Duke of Paducah while performing on station KWK, St. Louis, Missouri.

Ford left WLS before the Barn Dance went network. The reason was a chance to m.c. on a new program called Plantation Party over the NBC network. On the show, Ford was almost a one-man gang. As The Duke of Paducah, he was the star comic. In addition, he wrote the entire show and helped work out most of the details of each performance. For nine years, he delighted audiences across the country with his stand-up humor and deft handling of a show that featured many of the top country artists in America. His work on Plantation Party started a personal gag library that totaled, as of 1969, a half million jokes catalogued under 455 different subjects.

The Duke's association with Plantation Party came to an end in 1942 when he left for an overseas trip entertaining the nation's servicemen. After this lengthy tour, he came back to the U. S. to find that his agent had booked him for three guest appearances on the Grand Ole Opry. The audience at Nashville yelled and thundered their approval as did the radio listeners with stacks of mail. The result was a long-term association between the Opry and The Duke that lasted for 16 years. During these years, he was featured in personal appearances in major shows and theaters throughout the U.S. He also was often asked to speak before church groups, college and high school student groups, and at men's clubs.

At the end of the 1950s, The Duke decided to give up the weekly routine of a network TV show. However, he continued to tour, making from 150 to 200 personal appearances a year. He also guested on many TV shows during the 1960s, including the Opry, Red Foley Show, Garry Moore Show, Jimmy Dean Show and Porter Wagoner Show. He also found time, in 1963, to make his second movie, "Country Music on Broadway." (His first, some years earlier, was "Country Farm.")

FRANK, J. L.: Songwriter, promoter, talent agent. Born Rossal, Alabama, April 15, 1900; died Chicago, Illinois, May 4, 1952. Elected to Country Music Hall of Fame, October 1967.

Among the bronze plaques lining the walls of Nashville's Country Music Hall of Fame is one dedicated to J. L. Frank. It carries little significance to casual visitors, but to those involved in producing country and western music it represents one of the prime movers in the field for more than thirty years.

Born and raised in Alabama, J. L. Frank had a natural affinity for country music. He was a born salesman, and after he moved to Chicago in the 1920s he took the first steps toward a career in talent management. He could see the tremendous potential of the infant radio industry, and helped promote the careers of many of the early radio personalities. One of his major efforts revolved around promoting the careers of the great comedy team of Fibber McGee and Molly.

In 1928 he started producing a country show on Chicago's station WLS, a post he maintained until 1935. This brought him in contact with many promising young country and western artists. Among them were a young Oklahoma cowboy singer, Gene Autry, and a new comedian, Smiley Burnette. Frank recognized their ability and started them on the way to national stardom.

During these years, Frank continued to combine talent management with a creative interest in music. He turned out many songs, some of which were recorded by major artists. Among these were "Chapel on the Hill," "Sundown and Sorrow," and "My Main Trail Is Yet to Come."

In 1935, Frank moved his growing talent management business to Louisville, Kentucky. Four years later, sensing the growth of Nashville as the country music capital, he relocated in that city. By then one of the best regarded developers of new talent, he was sought out by many rising country performers. For the next decade, he helped the careers of many artists

of Hall of Fame caliber, including Eddy Arnold, Roy Acuff, and PeeWee King.

Not only did Frank play an important role in advancing the careers of some of the top stars of the 1950s and '60s, he also is credited with innovations that affected the entire entertainment industry. In particular, his early radio promotions included combining the idea of the ruggedness of the cowboy with music. The result was the singing cowboy, a staple to this day in the movie industry.

During a promotional trip to Chicago in May 1952, Frank was stricken and died. His contributions to the field were recognized in October 1967 when he was elected to the CMA Hall of Fame.

FRAZIER, DALLAS: Singer, guitarist, trumpeter, composer. Born Spiro, Oklahoma, 1939.

It isn't unusual for country artists to start young, but it is unusual for them to start with the multifaceted successes of Dallas Frazier. He was a featured performer before he was in his teens and a best-selling songwriter before he was past high school age.

Frazier was born in Oklahoma, but his family moved to California by the time he was grade school age. He was exposed to as much country music in California as he was in Oklahoma, since the Fraziers lived in a farming area near Bakersfield. By the time he was 10, Dallas had started to concentrate on music and could play several instruments by the time he was 12. At this point, he entered a talent contest sponsored by Ferlin Husky and walked off with first prize. He was quickly offered a place with Husky's touring troupe and appeared with Husky throughout the country. Husky brought his young charge to the attention of Capitol Records and Frazier was signed as an artist.

Another result of the Capitol contract was an introduction to Cliffie Stone. Frazier became a regular member of the cast of Stone's Hometown Jamboree TV show. He had the chance to sing and work with such talented people as Billy Strange, Billy Liebert, and Molly Bee. By this time, Frazier was writing music steadily. One song, "Alley Oop," became a major hit in both country and western and popular fields in 1957.

When Cliffie disbanded his show in the late 1950s, Frazier moved to Nashville. Here he continued to star as a performer on radio and TV and increased his songwriting credits. By the late 1960s, he had written more than 300 songs including "Georgia," "Elvira," "Hawg Jaw," "Soakin' Up the Suds," and "Timber I'm Fallin'!"

FRIZZELL, LEFTY: Singer, guitarist, songwriter. Born Corsicana, Texas, March 31, 1928.

Jimmie Rodgers was one of Lefty Frizzell's favorites, perhaps because such Rodgers songs as "Travelin' Blues" fitted Lefty's childhood. The elder Frizzell was an oil well driller whose job took him from one town to another. The nomadic life didn't give young William Orville "Lefty" Frizzell much time to get acquainted with a place, but it did expose him to many different sights and many different sounds of the great southwest.

It isn't surprising that young Lefty Frizzell picked up country and western songs while he was still grade school age. Many of the oil workers enjoyed playing the guitar in their spare time and Lefty soon picked up this skill as well. His voice was good and he tried out for and won a featured spot on a children's program over station KELD, El Dorado, Texas. By the time his family moved to Greenville, Texas, he was a self-assured professional performer at the ripe age of 15. He now added appearances at local dances and county fairs to his radio experience. By the time he was 17, he was playing dance halls and honky tonks in Waco and Dallas.

With his oil field upbringing, Frizzell was handy with his hands. He decided to try out for the Golden Gloves. While he didn't win a title, he scored enough knockdowns with his left hand to gain his nickname of Lefty.

In the late 1940s, Lefty divided his time betwen dance halls and radio shows in New Mexico and West Texas. He felt the time had come to move on in the world and approached Dallas agent Jim Beck for help in gaining a record contract. They worked up a demonstration record of "If You've Got the Money, I've Got the Time." Beck took the demo to Nashville and returned with a contract from Columbia. The song became a hit, starting a long association betwen Lefty Frizzell and the country and western top 10. He followed his first Columbia effort with several songs that won good audience reaction, then hit the number-one spot nationally with "Always Late." In the 1950s, he became a featured member of the Grand Ole Opry.

His hit songs of the early 1950s included the number-one selection "I Want to Be with You Always" and such others as "Look What A Thought Will Do," "Mom and Dad's Waltz," and "Travelin' Blues." The last song was part of a hit album, "Songs of Jimmie Rodgers." Lefty's 1952 output included two top hits, "Don't Stay Away" and "I'm an Old, Old Man." Other Frizzell best-sellers include "Long Black Veil" ('59) and "Saginaw, Michigan" (number one in 1964).

FRUIT JAR DRINKERS: *See* Macon, Uncle Dave

FULLER, JESSE: Singer, instrumentalist (guitar, harmonica, "fotdella"), composer. Born Jonesboro, Georgia, 1896.

Jesse Fuller was forged in the fire of struggle and deprivation. He never knew his father and his mother gave him away to another family when he was only six or seven. Somehow, instead of becoming bitter or despairing, he eventually became a folk artist with a message of hope and beauty for the audiences of the 1950s and '60s.

He began to show an interest in music when staying with a family called Wilson near Macedonia, Georgia. At seven or eight, he suddenly decided to make a mouth bow. Soon after, he made a simple guitar. Though not yet 10, he learned to play many songs by listening to musicians at Saturday night dances. As he recalled in Barbara Dane's article in Sing Out! ("Lone Cat Jesse Fuller," Feb.–March '66, p. 6), "They was really rough. People got killed sometimes."

He finished the third grade before running away from the Wilsons when he was 10. Later he advised other youngsters to gain the advantages of education in his 1964 composition, "Drop Out Song." Somehow, as his nickname "Lone Cat" indicates, Jesse always managed to make it on his own. Even as an uncared-for youngster, his independent spirit always allowed him to make ends meet. After leaving the Wilsons, he grazed cows, worked in a buggy factory, did housework, delivered groceries, worked in a chair factory in Brunswick, Georgia, laid track on the railroads and did many other jobs during his teens. He also attended minstrel and other shows when he could, picking up songs that he could play on the guitar or harmonica. His roster of occupations continued as he neared his twenties. At 18, he worked chopping wood and a few years later earned his keep working for a junk man in Griffin, Georgia.

In his early twenties, he finally left the south for Cincinnati. After a job on a streetcar, he joined the Hagenbeck Wallace Circus as a canvas stretcher. While touring, he went through Michigan where he found he could earn much money by playing his guitar on the streets for soldiers returning from World War I.

When he was 24, he heeded a suggestion to head west by hopping a freight for California. He found the West Coast to his liking and spent most of his years after that in Los Angeles or Oakland. He worked shining shoes near the gate of United Artists Studio in Los Angeles. Such stars as Douglas Fairbanks liked him and got him bit roles in several movies, including "East of Suez," "Thief of Bagdad," and "Hearts of Dixie." Director Raoul Walsh later financed a hotdog stand for Jesse, but Jesse left for a job on the Southern Pacific Railroad.

In the 1930s Jesse was settled in the San Francisco Bay area, working as a construction worker days and playing occasional pick-up music dates in the evenings. Gradually, during the 1930s and '40s, word of his ability began to spread among music enthusiasts in the Bay area. By the late 1940s, both jazz and folk artists in the region often sought him out and he was asked to play at more and more local parties.

In the early 1950s, he began to play steadily at a small club in San Francisco called the Haight Street Barbeque. He also opened a small shoeshine stand on College Avenue in Berkeley, which attracted many avant-garde folk fans. They enjoyed listening to him sing not only conventional folk songs, but some of his own compositions, such as the 1954 "San Francisco Bay Blues."

During these years, Fuller not only composed, he also devised a new kind of instrument he called the fotdella. Essentially a homemade one-man-band rig, it included a right foot pedal to operate a hammer against an arrangement of seven piano strings, a left foot pedal to run a high-hat cymbal or a washboard, and a harness to hold a harmonica and kazoo. While sitting amidst all this, he played a 6- or 12-string guitar with his hands.

In the late 1950s, though Jesse was in his sixties, his musical career really began to blossom. With long-time friend Barbara Dane, he was featured in 1958 at the Ash Grove in Los Angeles. In 1959, he went to the Monterey Jazz Festival uninvited, was set up outside the stands by Festival director Jimmy Lyons, and was one of the star attractions of the event.

In the 1960s, his reputation assumed almost legendary proportions. His songs were played by major folk artists throughout the world. He was asked to perform at concerts and festivals across the country and in Europe. In 1966 he was a sensation in England, starring twice with popular rock groups, the Rolling Stones and the Animals.

His recording efforts also were late in coming. By the mid-1960s, though, his LPs were among the top sellers in the jazz and folk field in many nations. The titles include "Jesse Fuller Working on the Railroad" (World Song Records); "Frisco Bound with Jesse Fuller" (Cavalier Records); "Jesse Fuller, the Lone Cat" (Good Time Jazz Records); and two Prestige LPs, "San Francisco Bay Blues" and "Jesse Fuller's Favorites."

GATEWAY SINGERS, THE: Vocal and instrumental quartet, Jerome Walter, born Chicago, Illinois; Mrs. Elmerlee Thomas ("Mama Lee"), born Oakland, California; Ernie Sheldon, born Brooklyn, New York; Travis Edmondson, born Nogales, Arizona.

It seems proper that The Gateway Singers played such an important part in the folk music ferment that swept the U.S. in the 1950s. One of the best known folk groups of the period, it included performers representing almost every region of the country. Before it disbanded near the start of the next decade, it popularized many of the folk songs in the current repertoire of most performers.

The members of the group hailed from the four corners of the country, but came together in San Francisco. By the time he met the other three, the group's spokesman, bass singer and banjoist Jerry Walter, lived in Palo Alto. He had a long career in show business behind him, having started as a professional radio actor at nine, with such diverse radio credits as Santa Claus and Jack Armstrong, the All-American Boy.

The distaff side was represented by Mrs. Elmerlee Thomas, who was born and raised in Oakland. At the time the Singers formed, she was working as a laboratory technician at the University of California at Berkeley. Her early training included some success as a classical singer.

Lead guitar was provided by Brooklyn-born Sheldon. He too had many years experience, having worked his way from New York to Los Angeles during a thirteen-year career as a singer and guitarist. Rounding out the quartet was the youngest member, Travis Edmondson, born in Arizona but a long-time resident of San Francisco when he met the others. His background included some military service, a job as a truck driver, and college training in anthropology.

The Gateway Singers began performing in San Francisco in 1956. They gained an engagement at the increasingly important San Francisco basement coffee house, the hungry i. Their efforts met wild acclaim from the audiences and their stay was extended for many weeks. Before long, they were written up in many major national publications and had bids for appearances on TV and in many clubs across the country. A recording contract with Decca gave added impetus to their careers as they turned out a number of hit singles and LPs.

One of their best known songs was the title of the Decca LP "Puttin' on the Style." The album included such others as "Sally Don't You Grieve," "Monaco," "Bury Me in My Overalls," and "Rock Island Line."

The group provided two best-selling LPs in 1958, "Gateway Singers at the hungry i" and "Gateway Singers in Hi Fi." The former offered such numbers as "Hey Li-Lee," "Let Me Fly," "Big Rock Candy Mountain," "Rollin' Home," "All Over This World," "Kisses Sweeter Than Wine," "Malagueña Salderosa," "Hard, Ain't It Hard," "Rio Grande," "Fais Do-Do" ("Bon Soir Dame"), "Rock About My Saro Jane." The other LP included "Ballad of Sigmund Freud," "The Fox," "Roving Gambler," "Erie Canal," "Roll Down the Line" and "Oleanna."

Soon after The Gateway Singers disbanded in 1961, Jerome Walter formed a new group called The Gateway Trio. The other Trio members were guitarist Betty Mann and bassist Milt Chapman. The Trio turned out several LPs for Capitol in the early 1960s, including "The Mad, Mad, Mad Gateway Trio" and "The Gateway Trio."

GATEWAY TRIO, THE: *See* Gateway Singers, The

GENTRY, BOBBIE: Singer, guitarist, songwriter. Born Chickasaw County, Mississippi, July 27, 1944.

In early July 1967 six violin players, two cellists, and a pretty, blue-jeaned, guitar-carrying young miss entered Capitol Records' Studio C in Hollywood. The group recorded a song written by the girl and shown to Capitol A&R man Kelly Gordon only a few days before. Within a few weeks after the session, the previously unknown girl had a worldwide reputation as the song, "Ode to Billie Joe," became number one on every major song chart in the country.

Bobbie Gentry wrote the country and western delta blues melody to the song from memories of her very early years in Greenwood, Mississippi. However, though she attended North Greenwood Elementary School, by the time she was high school age she was a full-fledged Californian. Her family moved to Palm Springs where she completed high school at Palm Valley High and then moved on to major in philosophy at UCLA.

She showed an early talent for music and learned to play excellent guitar during her teens. Later she added capability with piano, vibraharp, banjo and bass fiddle. It wasn't too long before music gained the upper hand over philosophy. She enrolled in the Los Angeles Conservatory of Music and studied musical theory, composition, and counterpoint. During these years, she performed with several little theater groups and also worked as a dancer for a time in Las Vegas.

She also composed many of her own songs, based to a great degree on the rhythms of her original home area. After the success of the "Ode to Billie Joe" single in the summer of 1967, many of her other writings were incorporated into an LP of the same title. These included "Chicksaw County Child," "Lazy Willie," "Papa Won't Let Me Go into Town with You," and "Tuesday's Child."

GERLACH, FRED: Singer, guitarist, pianist. Born Detroit, Michigan, 1925.

An interest in performing folk music came late to Fred Gerlach. Once he decided on this approach, he didn't take the easy route. Instead, he picked one of the more difficult instruments to play, the 12-string guitar. It was almost as hard to find such an instrument as to play it, but Gerlach persevered and won a reputation in the 1950s and '60s as one of the finest 12-string artists in the world.

He was born in the Motor City of Detroit, of Yugoslav parentage. He learned to play piano during his youth, but his main interest was in the blues and swing aspects of the popular music of the 1930s and '40s. Music, though, was at first only a hobby; he concentrated on learning drafting techniques in his high school years. With the American entry into World War II, soldiering became his main concern and he served in Germany and the Philippines.

After his discharge, he eventually settled in New York. There he worked as a draftsman, picking up some work on the side as a blues and boogie-woogie pianist. In the 1950s, he became aware of the rising interest among many New Yorkers in folk music. He attended some concerts and coffee house programs and decided he wanted to play this kind of music himself.

The instrument that most appealed to him was a 12-string guitar. As he notes in the liner notes for one of his albums (Audio-Video Productions), "I went into one of the largest musical instrument stores in the country, and the manager assured me that no such instrument existed. . . . In fact, it took me about a year after I had first decided to play a twelve-string before I found one. It wasn't a concentrated search, but it nevertheless indicates the general unavailability of the instrument."

Once he found one, he wasted no time in mastering it. Before long, he got the chance to perform in some of the small folk places in New York. In keeping with his instrumental preference, many of his songs were direct or indirect versions of Huddie Ledbetter's repertoire. In the mid-1950s, he recorded many of these on an Audio-Video Productions LP, "Gallows Pole and Other Folk Songs." Among the titles in the album were "Ham and Eggs," "De Kalb Blues," "Old Hannah," "Fannin Street," "Samson," "This Little Light," "Little Girl," "Motherless Children," "Risin' Sun," "Boll Weevil," "Goin' Down Slow."

During the 1950s and '60s, he made many appearances as a solo performer and in support of other artists. In 1962, he recorded the LP "12 String Guitar" for Folkways Records.

GIBSON, BOB: Singer, guitarist, folk music collector. Born New York, New York, November 16, 1931.

A prime exponent of songs of Ohio and the middle west, Robert "Bob" Gibson inherited a good voice from his father, who worked as a singer for a time. Music was a normal part of the Gibson family, though Bob's upbringing in New York did not expose him to much authentic folk music in his early years. By the time Bob was in high school in the New York area, though, there were many great folk performers appearing in small clubs and this, in turn, resulted in an increasing number of radio broadcasts of songs by such people as Woody Guthrie, Ledbetter, and Burl Ives.

Young Gibson soon was "hooked" by hearing some of this and began to memorize and sing songs of this type for his own pleasure. Though he learned to play both guitar and five-string banjo, he didn't at first consider following a musical career. Starting with free appearances in his teens before school and local groups, he found that the first stage of the post-World War II folk song boom was underway. Soon he was performing before audiences at nightclubs and in concerts.

He began to travel to a number of the North Atlantic states, both to perform and to collect new material. By the early 1950s, he had expanded his collecting chores to several of the midwest states. One of his first albums, on Stinson label, was called "Folksongs of Ohio." It included such songs as "Katey Morey," "Ohio River," "There Was an Old Woman," "Over in the Meadow," "Workin' on a Pushboat," and "Father Grumble."

By the mid-1950s, Bob had achieved a solid reputation as a folk artist. Following his initial TV appearance in 1954 on a Cleveland station, he performed on several network shows in succeeding years. He also won critical praise for an appearance in New York's Carnegie Hall. An LP of this was issued by Riverside. His concert selections included many different types of folk songs, including "Sail Away Ladies," "Michael Row the Boat Ashore," "Marry a Texas Girl," "Day-O," "Go Down to Bimini," "Wheel-a-Matilda," "Good News," "When I Was Single," "You Must Come in at the Door," "Alberta," "The Erie Canal" and "John Riley."

Riverside Records issued two other LPs of Gibson in the 1950s, "Offbeat Folk Songs" and "I Come for to Sing." In 1959, Elektra Records signed him and turned out an LP titled "Ski Songs."

During the 1960s, Gibson continued to perform on campuses and in clubs, extending his travels to take in appearances in most parts of the U.S. He also sang at several major national folk festivals during these years. He was represented in the 1960s by several more Elektra albums, including "Yes I See" and "Bob Gibson and Bob Camp" ('61); and "Where I'm Bound" ('64).

GIBSON, DON: Singer, guitarist, songwriter. Born Shelby, North Carolina, April 3, 1928.

"The song is about 99% of it these days. There is no shortage of good singers, but there is a tremendous shortage of good songs." These words by record executive Don Pierce explain why so many country and western stars also have one or more country standards of their own composing to their credit. They must write their own material to get their foot on the ladder of success.

On the other hand, it is sometimes easier for an artist to make his mark first as a songwriter, for the way to performing success is then wide open. Thus it was with Don Gibson, who did have much professional musical experience, but who first won wide attention as a writer. Unlike some artists, Don went on to prove that he was of the first rank as both performer and composer.

Born and raised in North Carolina, Don took to country music as a duck to water. He could play the guitar before he finished elementary school and was singing for local events before he reached his teens. When he was 14, he turned professional and concentrated on a music career from then on. During the mid-1940s, teenager Gibson performed in an ever-widening circle of towns in the south. He sang on many radio stations and built up a following in many parts of the region.

In the years just after World War II, he moved his base of operations to Knoxville. Before long he was featured on the WNOX Tennessee Barn Dance and Mid-day Merry-Go-Round. By the mid-1950s he had become one of the city's favorite sons. He was the guest of honor at a giant country music concert sponsored by radio station WIVK, and received the key to the city from the mayor.

Don was turning out some increasingly well received records in the early 1950s. But his main forte was songwriting. He wrote songs for many of the top artists of Knoxville and Nashville. An example was the top 10 national hit "Sweet Dreams" as recorded by Faron Young. A few years later, he provided Kitty Wells with a song that was a major hit in both country and western and the popular field, "I Can't Stop Loving You." Like many of Gibson's compositions, the song went on to become an all-time standard.

In 1957, Don was signed to a long-term contract by RCA Victor. The following year, he wrote three hits for himself, the top-10-ranked "Give Myself a Party" and two number-one-ranked songs, "Blue, Blue Day," and "Oh Lonesome Me." From this time forward, the name Gibson was a common one on top 10 hit lists on both the performing and writing ends. While many of his hits were his own songs, he proved his ability as a performer by scoring with many songs authored by others.

His 1959 output included two top 10 hits, "Don't Tell Me Your Troubles" and "Who Cares." He started the 1960s with such originals as "Just One Time" ('60); his own recording of "Sweet Dreams" ('61); and his top 10 rendition of a David-Hampton song, "Sea of Heartbreak." In 1962 he provided Kitty Wells with a hit, "Day Into Night," and had two top 10 records of his own, "I Can Mend Your Broken Heart" and "Lonesome Number One." His successes of the mid-1960s included "Watch Where You're Going" ('65) and "(Yes) I'm Hurting" ('66).

His album output for RCA Victor matched his singles success. His LPs included such titles as "Lonesome Me" ('58); "No One Stands Alone," "That Gibson Boy" ('59); "Look Who's Blue" ('60); "Girls, Guitars," "Sweet Dreams" ('61); "Some Favorites" ('62); "I Wrote a Song" ('63); "God Walks Hills" ('64); "Blue Million Tears" ('65); "The Best of Don Gibson" ('66); "All My Love" ('67); and "King of Country Soul" ('68).

During the '60s, Gibson toured all parts of the country. He was also a frequent visitor to many network TV shows, both popular and country and western.

GILKYSON, TERRY: Singer, guitarist, songwriter. Born near Phoenixville, Pennsylvania, *circa* 1919.

One of the pioneers, in a sense, of the pop folk movement of the 1950s and '60s was a man brought up only four miles from Valley Forge of Revolutionary fame. In the late 1940s, his composition "The Cry of the Wild

Goose" was not only one of the major hits of the decade, but also a stepping stone to national fame for singer Tennessee Ernie Ford.

The composer of "Wild Goose," Hamilton Henry "Terry" Gilkyson, came from an old-line Pennsylvania family. The venerable stone house in which he was born had been built near the Schuylkill River by his great-grandfather. Gilkyson grew up in the region and was enough attracted to music to make it his major at the University of Pennsylvania. However, he grew bored with the formal courses in musical theory, counterpoint, etc., and left school in his sophomore year.

That summer, 1938, he went out west to New Mexico for his vacation. He enjoyed ranch life and liked to listen to some of the cowboy songs sung in the vicinity. Before long, he bought himself a guitar and learned to play it. He decided to stay in the west and got a job at a ranch in the next state over, Arizona. He continued to perfect his singing and to collect new song material. After singing at local clubs, he eventually went to California to try for the big time. By the early 1940s he had begun to achieve a reputation as a performer.

In the 1940s, this resulted in a bid from the Armed Forces Radio Service to do a weekly program on folk music. Terry spent more time researching the subject for the program and greatly increased his stature as a folk music authority. He also guested on some of the major radio shows and his name began to become familiar to audiences throughout the country.

After World War II, Gilkyson toured widely and was featured on radio and TV shows. During the late 1940s and early '50s, he had his own twice-weekly radio show. He sang popular songs, folk songs, and his own compositions. One of the latter was "The Cry of the Wild Goose." Capitol Records executives were impressed with the song and agreed to have it recorded by one of their promising young country performers, Tennessee Ernie Ford. Ford's version won still more notice for the song's composer.

In the late 1940s, Gilkyson signed with Decca Records. Over the next few years, he turned out a number of successful singles and albums. Particularly successful were the 1950-51 albums called "The Solitary Singer." In the first of these, Terry sang "I Know Where I'm Going," "Black Is the Color," "Jennie Jenkins," "Roving Gambler," "The Story of

Creation," "Cotton Eye Joe," "Billy Boy," "Black-Eyed Susie," and "Boll Weevil." In Volume 2, he turned out "The Solitary Singer," "Runnin' Away," "Fast Freight," "The Secret," "Nellie Lou," "The Tick Tock Song," "Mr. Buzzard," and "Everyone's Crazy 'Ceptin' Me."

Later in the 1950s, Gilkyson recorded the LP "Golden Minutes of Folk Music" for Decca. In the 1960s, he signed with Kapp Records. His output on Kapp included the LPs "Remember the Alamo" ('61) and "Wild Goose" ('63).

GLASER, CHUCK: *See* Tompall & the Glaser Brothers

GLASER, JIM: *See* Tompall & the Glaser Brothers

GLASER, TOMPALL: *See* Tompall & the Glaser Brothers

GLAZER, TOM: Singer, instrumentalist (guitar, tuba, bass), author, songwriter, m.c. Born Philadelphia, Pennsylvania, September 3, 1914.

Like many modern folk artists, Tom Glazer's creative efforts go far beyond ballad singing. His compositions have become staple items in both folk and popular domains and his name has appeared on the credit lists of movies and TV specials and, somewhat uniquely, in the field of children's music.

Glazer was first introduced to folk music at home, where his mother often sang traditional ballads to him. While attending grade and high school in Philadelphia, he studied widely in all areas of music, including the classics. He learned a range of instruments during these years, including guitar, string bass, and tuba. In 1929, he made his first professional appearance. His efforts over the next few years included appearing as a musician with Philadelphia groups as well as singing in choirs. When he went to New York to attend the City College, he continued many of these activities.

After three years of college, Glazer left and for the next few years played tuba and bass in military and jazz bands. He also continued his choral work. By the start of the 1940s, he had begun to concentrate more and more on collecting and singing folk music. At first it was a sideline, but in 1943 he became a full-time ballad singer. He gained a reputation as a folk artist in the next few years and also devoted much of his time to developing special material for children. His recording activities in this area won him the Annual Record Music Award for children's records in 1947.

He did not abandon adult audiences during these years. In 1945, he began his own program on ABC radio, "Tom Glazer's Ballad Box," that remained a highly popular show for the two years of its existence. His radio activities expanded, as well, to acting and/or singing on such programs as "We The People," "Listening Post," "True Story" and "Theatre Guild on the Air."

In 1948, Glazer made his Town Hall debut in New York. Over the years, he appeared in this and other major concert halls on many occasions. In addition, he gave many well received concerts for children, appearing as soloist with the Philadelphia Orchestra and the Worcester Festival Children's Concerts. His work with the Philadelphia Orchestra included an appearance at the White House in Washington.

His creative contributions during the 1950s and '60s included acting, singing, and writing for both movies and TV. His movie work included the job of balladeer-narrator for an RKO film, "Sweet Land of Liberty," and composer of the score for the Andy Griffith vehicle "A Face in the Crowd." He also contributed to the Lux-TV Playhouse and CBS TV Workshop. He sang several sea ballads for the CBS Radio Theatre production of Moby Dick.

Glazer's voice was featured on many records in the years after World War II. In the mid-1950s, he shared a Mercury LP called "Olden Ballads" with Richard Dyer-Bennet. Glazer's songs included "Twelve Days of Christmas," "The Sheeling Song," "Hush Little Baby," "Green Sleeves," "Waly Waly," "Uncle Reuben," "Blow the Candles Out," "Black-Eyed Susie," and "Go 'Way from My Window." His records for children were produced for Young People's Records, Inc. Through the 1960s, total sales ran to more than a million.

Glazer's songwriting activities included such diverse numbers as the comic parody "On Top of Spaghetti" and the strident "Skokiaan." His other compositions include: "A Dollar Ain't a Dollar Anymore," "More," "Till We Two Are One," "Ballad for the Babe," "A Worried Man," "Old Soldiers Never Die," "Mama Guitar," "Melody of Love," "Care," and "Don't Weep, Don't Mourn, Don't Worry."

GOBEL, GEORGE: Singer, guitarist, comedian, actor. Born Chicago, Illinois, May 20, 1919.

It's a little hard for TV audiences of the 1950s and '60s to associate George Gobel with country and western music. Yet he got his start in this field and was a major performer in it for close to a decade.

George Leslie Gobel was born and raised in Chicago. While attending grade school, he already was interested in music. He had an excellent voice and sang in school and in his church choir. He also sometimes listened to the country and western programs on radio and memorized some of the songs. By the time he was 12, he had entertained as a soloist in school and church events.

In 1931, he sang on station WLS in the children's choir of the Chicago Episcopal Church. The station's program director was impressed with George's soprano voice and filed the boy's name and address. The following year, he looked George up and asked the boy if he could sing cowboy songs.

The 13-year-old auditioned for the WLS National Barn Dance and was signed for the show. In November 1932 he debuted, singing "Danny Boy." As "The Little Cowboy," he performed on the Barn Dance until 1940. He also toured many of the midwest cities. He might have remained in the country and western field had not World War II intervened. George left the Barn Dance in 1940 to enter the Air Force. While in the service, he began to develop his talents as a comedian.

When he returned to show business in 1946, he concentrated on comedy. He toured widely during the next eight years, appearing at nightclubs across the country. By 1954, his stature as a comedian had increased so much that he gained his own show. The George Gobel Show, which was shown on both NBC-TV and CBS, rapidly became one of the favorites of the viewing public. The result was a host of top awards for George, including an Emmy, the Sylvania Award for 1954-55, Associated Press Man of the Year Award for '54-'55, TV Personality of the Year for 1954-55 and the Look Magazine award for top TV performer of the year. Gobel remained a leading TV artist for the rest of the decade.

In 1956, he branched out into movies with a comedy, "The Birds and the Bees." In 1957, he starred in "I Married a Woman." In the 1960s, George guested on many major TV

[108]

shows and was featured in leading supper clubs from Las Vegas to New York. He also toured on occasion as a star of some of the road companies of hit Broadway shows.

GOODING, CYNTHIA: Singer, guitarist, folk music collector. Born Rochester, Minnesota, August 12, 1924.

One of the most familiar voices to New York radio audiences in the late 1940s and early 1950s was that of Cynthia Gooding. She was often heard on Oscar Brand's folk music show on the New York City station, WNYC, and also had her own radio folk music show for a good number of years.

Cynthia's schooling began in Minnesota and then extended to several private schools in the midwest and Canada. These included Laurel School for Girls in Cleveland, Lake Forest in Illinois, and Branksome Hall, Toronto. When she had completed high school, she decided to go to Mexico instead of to college. Up to this time, Cynthia had little interest in folk music. South of the border, however, she was taken with the beauty of Mexican folk music. She learned guitar-playing along with Spanish and soon began collecting some of the local songs. Her abilities were recognized by folk enthusiasts in Mexico City and she was featured on the city's station XEW in 1945.

In 1947 she returned to the U.S. and settled down in New York. By now she had decided to try for a career in folk music. The first positive result was an engagement at the Soho club in Greenwich Village. She was so well received that she stayed for a year. As her talents became well known to radio audiences, invitations for recitals came from many parts of the country.

Marriage and a family caused her to cut down on her activities in the 1950s and '60s, but she managed to give hundreds of recitals over the years in all the eastern and many midwestern states, and some in Mexico. Her skill in languages led to a varied repertoire that included songs from Spain, Portugal, Italy, Turkey and Mexico as well as Old American and English ballads.

Her linguistic talents merged well with those of another accomplished language specialist, Theodore Bikel, on their Elektra LP, "A Young Man and a Maid." Songs in the album include: "Coplas," "Parle Moi," "Greensleeves," "Laredo," "Mi Jaclito," "Haj Pada Pada," and "A Meidl in di Yoren." Other LPs by Cynthia

Gooding are: "Faithful Lovers and Other Phenomena"; "Italian Folk Songs"; "Mexican Folk Songs"; Turkish, Spanish and Mexican Folk Songs"; and "Queen of Hearts" (early English folk songs).

GOTTLIEB, LOU: *See* Limeliters, The

GRAMMER, BILLY: Singer, guitarist. Born Benton, Illinois, August 28, 1925.

Billy Grammer is one of a group of often unsung heroes of the music world. As a sideman and guitar accompanist, he has helped many country artists shine on records and personal appearances. Any singer knows he needs good backing to show to best advantage, and Billy Grammer has been one of the best staff guitarists in the business. In addition, he has succeeded in breaking through as a star in his own right.

Billy was one of a family of thirteen children. His father, a farmer and coal miner in Franklin County, Illinois, worked hard to provide for his children, but there was often little to go around in the way of food and clothing. Billy decided early in life that he wanted to find a better road to travel. He learned to play the guitar by the time he was in his teens, and performed at local dances.

His persistence paid off in the years after World War II when he showed enough polish to gain a radio job with Connie B. Gay's Radio Ranch on WARL, Arlington, Virginia, in 1947. Connie brought his protege along slowly as he did with many other artists he propelled to stardom. In 1955, when Connie had placed Jimmy Dean on local TV in Washington, D.C., he suggested Billy would make a good addition to the cast. For three and a half years Billy was featured with Jimmy, moving over to CBS network shows with Dean.

Billy's increasing stature resulted in bids to guest on other programs and go on tours throughout the states. He also worked as guitar accompanist for major artists at many recording sessions. Among the people whose shows he appeared on during the 1950s and '60s were Grandpa Jones, Hawkshaw Hawkins, Clyde Moody and T. Texas Tyler.

Billy also led his own bands and won a contract with Monument Records. In 1958, he hit the jackpot with a gold-record number, "Gotta Travel On." One result of his new fame was a contract to join the Grand Ole Opry in 1959.

He continued as a major star of the Opry in the 1960s. Billy followed up his gold record with two more half-million sellers, "Kissing Tree" and "Bonapatre's Retreat." In the 1960s, he switched to Decca, turning out such LPs as "Gospel Guitar Album" and "Billy Grammer Hits" ('64).

Besides starring on TV and radio stations throughout the country in the years following 1958, he also was featured on the Ed Sullivan Show. As of 1968, his credits also included three appearances on Dick Clark's ABC-TV American Bandstand.

GRAND OLE OPRY: Weekly variety show, originating from station WSM, Nashville, Tennessee.

In the days of vaudeville, the goal of all performers was to play the New York Palace Theater. Even in the years of Palace greatness, another institution was beginning to take hold in the south. This one, a radio program in Nashville, was to become the target for all hopefuls in the country and western field. Though the Grand Ole Opry was a radio show, it gained a strong resemblance to the Palace. The show had always been performed before live, enthusiastic audiences and, since 1941, has occupied its own special theater, the Ryman Auditorium in downtown Nashville.

The show began under a different title on November 28, 1925. It was called the WSM Barn Dance and was founded by George D. Hay, known as "The Solemn Ol' Judge." First performer on the program, broadcast 8-9 P.M. on Saturday from Studio A of WSM, was a whiskered fiddler, Uncle Jimmy Thompson, accompanied by his niece, Mrs. Eva Thompson Jones. The show later shifted to Studio B where, in 1927, it finally became known as the Grand Ole Opry. The Opry could not claim the honor of being the first of its kind; that went to the National Barn Dance which started in 1924. But long after the Barn Dance had gone off the air, the Opry was still in existence and the acknowledged mecca of the major stars in the country and western music field.

The Opry had several more temporary homes

The Gully Jumpers, one of the original acts on the 1925 WSM Barn Dance, forerunner of the Grand Ole Opry. Names of the banjoist and pianist are unknown, but three middle performers are Burt Hutcherson, Charles Arrington, and Paul Womack.

before settling down in Ryman Auditorium. These included the Hillsboro Theatre, East Nashville Tabernacle, WSM Studio C, and the War Memorial Building. In 1941, the show moved to Ryman where long lines waited to get in every Saturday night for a show that started at 7:30 and ended at midnight. By the 1960s, the outside of the theater had been turned into a replica of a large red barn with the words Grand Ole Opry spelled out in big white letters.

As the 1960s drew to a close, WSM finally considered building a new home for the show. A study contract was issued to Research Associates, Los Angeles, the firm that planned Disneyland, for a new combined auditorium (4,000 seats) and tourist center to be called Opryland U.S.A.

The first performer to achieve national stardom through the Opry was Uncle Dave Macon, who joined the program in 1926. He held sway until the late 1930s, when such others as Roy Acuff and Ernest Tubb came to the fore. In the 1960s, Acuff and Tubb were still featured with such post-World War II stars as Eddy Arnold, Marty Robbins, Faron Young, Webb Pierce, Ray Price, Flatt & Scruggs, George Hamilton IV, Carl Smith, Skeeter Davis, Kitty Wells, Hank Snow, George Morgan and George Jones. Over the years, the Opry provided a showcase for many major country and western comics as well, including Minnie Pearl, Whitey Ford (The Duke of Paducah), Archie Campbell, Harold Morrison, Stringbean, and Lonnie "Pap" Wilson.

The Opry roster over the years has included almost every country performer listed in this Encyclopedia, and, besides Wilson, mentioned above, such others as Rusty and Doug, Oscar Albright, Alonzo Apple, Bailes Brothers, Bailey Brothers, Rod Brasfield, Hylo Brown, Floyd T. Chance, Lou Childre, Zeke Clements, Honey Bear Collins, Crook Brothers, T. Tommy Cutrer, Don Davis, Lazy Jim Day, Dolores Denning, Anna and Lou Dill, Howdy Forrester, Wally Fowler, Curley Fox, Rusty Gabbard, Red Gale, Hank Garland, Curt Gibson, Marshall Grant, Inez Haines, Sid Harkreader, Curly Harris, Red Hayes, Don Helms, Harold Hens-

Cast of the Grand Ole Opry during the heyday of Uncle Dave Macon—Uncle Dave is sixth from the left in the second row.

All time Opry great Ernest Tubb graces the WSM stage during a broadcast of the 1950s.

ley, Eddie Hill, Salty Holmes, Paul Howard, Van Howard, Marvin Hughes, Randy Hughes, Autry Inman, Louie Innis, Shot Jackson, Cousin Jody, Jerry Johnson, Romonia Jones, Claude Lampley, Cousin Luther, Robert Lunn, Benny Martin, Emory Martin, Jimmy Martin, Clyde Moody, Oak Ridge Quartet, Old Hickory Singers, Luther Perkins, Possum Hunters, Rachel Veech, Wayne Raney, Don Reno, Jimmy Riddle, Jerry Rivers, Texas Ruby, Uncle Rufus, Jack Shook, Dotty Sill, Asher Sizemore, Buddy Sizemore, Ralph Sloan, Tommy Sosebee, Oscar Stone, Carl Story, Gordon Terry, Gabe Tucker, Zeb Turner, Zeke Turner, Staley Walton, Don Warden, June Webb, Lasses White, Roy Wiggins, Cousin Wilbur, Honey Wiles, Chubby Wise, Del Wood, and the York Brothers.

In the late 1950s, the Opry moved from radio to television. In the 1960s, the Opry TV version was widely syndicated throughout the country.

GRAY, CLAUDE: Singer, guitarist, band leader. Born Henderson, Texas, January 26, 1932.

Claude Gray is called "a man you have to

look up to," by his manager, referring both to his successful career as a hit country record artist and his height. At 6 feet 5 inches, he certainly deserved his nickname of "The Tall Texan."

When he was not so tall, growing up in Henderson, Texas, he still bent over to listen to the family radio when such programs as the Saturday night Grand Ole Opry were on. In those days, he looked up to the stars of country and western music and did his best to emulate them. In high school, while other boys spent all their spare time in sports activities, Claude learned to play guitar and began to perform at local events. In the late 1950s, he played many clubs and radio stations in the south and southwest, slowly building up the experience needed to break into the big time.

He signed his first major recording contract with Decca about this time. In 1960, after several successful records, he hit the top 10 national list with "Family Bible." The following year he moved to Mercury and scored with two more top 10 recordings, "I'll Just Have a

[112]

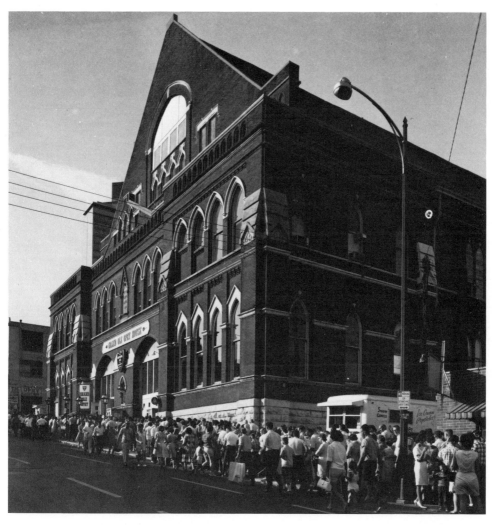

The line starts to form in the early afternoon for a Saturday night Opry show in Nashville.

Cup of Coffee, Then I'll Go" and a song provided by a new young songwriter, Roger Miller, "My Ears Should Burn." Another Gray hit of this period was "Mean Ole Woman."

In the 1960s, Claude settled in Nashville, and appeared on most of the major TV shows produced there. He was, naturally, a frequent guest on the Grand Ole Opry. His tours during these years took him to all parts of the U.S. and Canada. In the mid-'60s, he returned to his old label, Decca. The second time around proved a good one, providing Claude with an all-time best-seller, "I Never Had the One I Wanted."

The year 1966 marked the organization of Claude's first band. Called The Graymen, it comprised Buck Evans on bass, Terry Bethal on steel guitar, and Bob Taylor on drums. The group backed him on his 1968 hit, "Night Life."

GRAYMEN, THE: *See* Gray, Claude

GREENBRIAR BOYS: Bluegrass vocal and instrumental group, formed 1958.

The enthusiasm for Bluegrass-style music that flared up across the country in the 1950s started with the traditional groups, such as Bill Monroe and Flatt & Scruggs. Before long, as in other areas of folk music, city artists began to appear. One of the best of the latter groups was the Greenbriar Boys, formed in 1958 by Bob Yellin, Eric Weissberg and John Herald. Yellin, brought up in New York, studied violin, voice, piano and trumpet in his early years, then picked up the Bluegrass style of 5-string banjo playing in college.

The group gained closer knowledge of the style by touring the rural areas of the south soon after assembling. They appeared in many small clubs and coffee houses and proved their ability by winning the old-time band competition at the Fiddler's Convention in Union Grove, North Carolina, in 1959. That year, the first change occurred in the Greenbriar makeup when Ralph Rinzler replaced Weissberg. Rinzler was no stranger to the group, having helped introduce guitarist Herald, a descendant of poet John Greenleaf Whittier, to folk music some years earlier.

As the 1960s began, the group received favorable critical comment for appearances at concerts and folk festivals and on radio. They added to their laurels by winning the banjo contest at Union Grove two years in a row, 1960 and '61. In the early 1960s, the group added a beauteous lead singer, Miss Dian Edmondson. She appeared with them during several shows on ABC-TV's Hootenanny in 1963-64. She also joined them on one of their first LPs, on the Elektra label, "Dian and the Greenbriar Boys." One of the hit songs in the album was "Green Corn."

In 1964, Rinzler left after accepting a position as folk talent coordinator of the Newport Folk Foundation. His replacement on mandolin was Frank Wakefield, who had heard much Bluegrass music during his youth in the southern hill country. Wakefield also plays rhythm guitar.

Most of the group's recording efforts were on Vanguard label. In the early 1960s, they were one of several folk groups featured on a Vanguard series of LPs, "New Folks." Their contributions included "Stewball," "Katy Cline," and "Rawhide." Later they assisted Joan Baez on her "Volume 2" record for Vanguard, singing with her on "Banks of the Ohio" and "Little Darlin', Pal of Mine."

Their first full album for Vanguard, "The Greenbriar Boys" ('62), included such songs as "We Shall Not Be Moved," "Stay All Night,"

"Down the Road," "Florida Blues," "Other Side of Jordan," and "Coot from Tennessee." Their next LP was "Ragged But Right" (December '64). Some of the songs in the album are: "Sleepy-Eyed John," "Take a Whiff on Me," "Methodist Pie," "A Minor Breakdown," "Roll on John," and "The Blues My Naughty Sweetie Gives to Me." Their third Vanguard LP, issued in 1966, included such numbers as "Alligator Man," "Up to My Neck in High Muddy Water," "The Waggoner's Song," and "Honky Tonk Girl."

GREENE, JACK: Singer, guitarist, drummer, band leader. Born Maryville, Tennessee, January 7, 1930.

When Jack Greene's name began to appear regularly on the hit charts in 1967, some observers called him an overnight sensation. However, as he took pains to point out, he had earned the spotlight only through a long and difficult apprenticeship.

Greene started taking guitar lessons when he was a mere eight years old. In the early 1940s, he played regularly on two local radio shows. During these years, he added the art of drumming to his guitar ability.

By the late 1940s he was living in Atlanta, where he joined with bass player L. M. Bryant and fiddler Speedy Price to form the Cherokee Trio. In 1950, he became the drummer of the Rhythm Ranch Boys, a group that seemed headed for better things. However, Jack had to put his dreams of glory aside to fulfill his obligations to the Army. For the greater part of 1951, he was stationed in Alaska.

After his discharge in 1952, Jack joined another Atlanta group, the Peachtree Cowboys. For a decade, he toured Georgia and other southern states, well thought of in the industry, but seemingly destined for a lifetime career as a sideman.

In June of 1962, though, his career took a decided upturn: he was signed for Ernest Tubb's famed band, the Texas Troubadours. After a while, Jack alternated between drums, guitar, and occasional vocal solos with the band He became a favorite with Troubadour fans. His nickname, The Jolly Giant, came from his six-foot-plus height and his obvious enjoyment of his work.

Jack's association with the Troubadours took him into the bigtime, including performing chores on the Grand Ole Opry. In 1964, he and

[114]

Dottie West won some notice from Opry fans for their rendition of "Love Is No Excuse."

The year 1967 started in much the same way as the previous few for Jack. He was a key member of the Troubadours, and was awarded several solos when the group recorded material for a new LP, "Ernest Tubb Presents the Texas Troubadours." The album hit the charts after its release early in the year. One of Jack's numbers, "The Last Letter," got so many air plays that Decca Records released it as a single. The song hit the top 10 and Jack was suddenly a star.

Jack rounded out 1967 by becoming a Grand Ole Opry regular on December 23.

He quickly consolidated his status with a series of hit releases in 1967 and '68. The first of these was "Don't You Ever Get Tired of Hurting Me." This was followed by "Ever Since My Baby Went Away," "There Goes My Everything," "All the Time," "What Locks the Door" and "You Are My Treasure."

By the end of 1968, Jack was recognized as one of the top stars in country music. He won three awards in the initial Country Music Association poll in 1967: Best Male Vocalist, Best Single Recording, and Best Album. He also won two Grammy nominations for 1967, Best Performance and Best Single of the Year.

GREENWAY, DR. JOHN: Singer, guitarist, folk music collector, educator. Born Pennsylvania, early 1930s.

Protest songs are today so widely sung they are accepted as normal parts of both the popular music picture and the folk music category. Until the late 1950s and the 1960s, though, protest songs were considered a breed apart by popular entertainers as well as folklorists. The efforts of a few scholars, such as John Greenway, in the years after World War II, helped make the family tree of the protest song a proper object of study for folk music historians.

Born and brought up in Pennsylvania, Greenway had a conventional eastern upbringing in which he combined an interest in reading with a healthy appetite for athletics. He entered his teens about the time the post-World War II resurgence of folk music interest took place. He found this kind of music to his liking and, in time, learned to play guitar for accompaniment while he sang some of the ballads gleaned from radio broadcasts and records.

His interest in folklore increased after he matriculated at the University of Pennsylvania in the late 1940s. As an English major, he went on to gain his B.A., M.A., and Ph.D. degrees from the school. He complemented his studies with many other activities, including the writing of a prize-winning play, chess, and track. He was good enough in the last two to win the chess championship of the University and to land a berth on the varsity track team.

During these years, Greenway's curiosity led him to delve into many aspects of folk music. The low regard for protest songs among folklorists helped make him examine this part of the world's music heritage more closely. He collected a great amount of information on the subject which provided the basis for his doctoral dissertation, "American Folksongs of Social and Economic Protest." After receiving his doctorate, he began a career as a teacher of English literature at Pennsylvania, which he continued during the mid-1950s on the faculties of Rutgers University and the University of Denver.

Soon after graduating from Pennsylvania, Greenway revised his doctoral thesis into book form. Published in 1953 by the University of Pennsylvania Press under the title *American Folksongs of Protest*, the book has since become a landmark volume in modern folk music scholarship.

In the mid-1950s, he received a Fulbright Award to study the folksongs of Australia. During 1956 and '57, he traveled widely in the land "down under," taping material by many of the country's traditional singers. On his return to the U.S., he decided to switch his teaching discipline from English to anthropology on the grounds that the latter is more closely associated with the background needed by students of folklore. By the end of the 1950s, he held the title of assistant professor of anthropology at the University of Colorado.

During the late 1950s, Greenway was asked to record his first LP for Folkways Records. Called "Talking Blues," the 1958 album included songs like "Talking Guitar Blues," "Original Talking Blues," "Talking Butcher," "New Talking Blues," "Talking Dust Bowl," "Dry Voters—Wet Drinkers," "Talking Miner," "Talking Union," "Talking Sailor," "Talking Social Worker" and "Talking Inflation Blues." In 1959, Folkways issued a second Greenway LP, "Australian Folksongs and Ballads." A sampling of his efforts from his field work includes "Botany Bay," "The Old Bullock Dray,"

[115]

"The Dying Stockman," "Bluey Brink," "One of the Has-Beens," "Brisbane Ladies," "The Castlereagh River," "Bold Jack Donahue," "Waltzing Matilda," "Ben Hall" and "Wallaby Stew."

In 1961, he worked with the late Aunt Molly Jackson in preparation of her LP for Folkways. Greenway recorded the material shortly after her death.

During the 1950s and '60s, Greenway wrote many articles on various aspects of folklore for many scholarly journals. He served on the staff of the magazine Western Folklore in the 1960s, and in 1964 was named editor of the Journal of American Folklore. The year 1964 saw two more books of his published, *The Inevitable Americans* (Knopf) and *Literature Among the Primitives* (Folklore Associates).

GRIMES, ANNE LAYLIN: Singer, instrumentalist (dulcimer, psaltery, zither, autoharp, banjo, guitar), folk music collector. Born Columbus, Ohio, May 17, 1912.

A family tree rooted deep in Ohio history coupled with a great deal of musical ability helped determine Anne Grimes' lifetime avocation as one of her state's foremost folklorists. The result is one of the finest collections of one state's ballads and folksongs, comprising well over a thousand songs by the mid-1960s.

Both of Anne's parents were highly talented musicians who sang her many traditional songs when she was still a small girl. From her father, one-time Ohio State University law professor Clarence Dewey Laylin, she learned not only many traditional numbers, but how to play several different stringed instruments. Young Anne also had friends and relatives who knew many old songs of the region.

Her interest in folk music increased as she progressed through high school and work for her B.A. at Ohio Wesleyan. After receiving her degree in 1933, she went on to obtain a Bachelor of Music from Ohio State University in 1935. In 1936 she married Dr. James W. Grimes, professor of fine arts at Ohio State. Though the marriage was blessed with five children in ensuing years, Anne managed to find time for a widening amount of effort in the folk music field.

As her collection of material increased, she began to give informal performances for friends and relatives. In 1944, she debuted as a public performer on Ohio State's radio station WOSU.

From then on, she often traveled to folk music events in many parts of the east and midwest. In the 1950s she was in demand to perform at many major festivals, including the Mountain Festival, Asheville, North Carolina, and National Folk Festival in St. Louis, Missouri. Besides traveling for performing reasons, she made many collecting tours of her home state and of some regions in Kentucky, West Virginia, and North Carolina. One of her prime collecting interests in addition to music was the dulcimer. By the mid-1960s, her collection of this relatively rare folk instrument was one of the largest in the world.

Over the years, Anne Grimes wrote a great many articles on folklore for such periodicals as Midwest Folklore, Bulletin of the Ohio Historical Society, and Ohio Music Club News. For a time, she also served as music and dance critic for the Scripps-Howard Columbus *Citizen*. Her reputation by the 1950s had expanded far beyond the borders of her home state. This was recognized in 1954 with an honorable mention from the American Folklore Society's Jo Stafford Research Fellowship. She was also elected to the chairmanship of the Junior Folk Music and Dance Committee of the National Federation of Music Clubs in 1956. In April 1957, she was also elected as president of the Ohio Folklore Society.

She was asked to record many of her songs for the nation's most important folksong repositories. These include the Archive of American Folk Song of the Library of Congress, Ohio Folklore Archive, Ohioiana Library, Ohio Valley Research Project. In 1957, she recorded an album for Folkways Records, "Folk Songs of Ohio." Included on the LP are: "Battle of Point Pleasant," "Logan's Lament," "Lass of Rock Royal," "St. Clair's Defeat," "Portsmouth Fellows," "Christ in the Garden," "The Farmer's Curst Wife," "Boatman's Dance," "Girls of Ohio," "Alphabet Song," "Darling Nelly Gray," "The Underground Railroad," "My Station's Gonna Be Changed," "O Ho! The Copperheads," "The Dying Volunteer," "Ohio Guards," "Ohio River Blues," "Up on the Housetops," and "Old Dan Tucker."

GROOM, DEWEY: Singer, guitarist, band leader, record company executive. Born near Canton, Texas, April 30, 1918.

The word longhorn is closely associated with western lore, Texas, and Dewey Groom. The once plentiful breed of this name was no longer commercially important in the southwest when Dewey was born, but it was fondly remembered by his family and all his neighbors in the East Texas region of his birth. His birthplace was on a farm between the small towns of Mabank and Canton. As Dewey grew up, he had to spend long hours helping with the chores, working in the fields and taking care of the farm animals. It was a hard life, but one lightened by his family's interest in music. His parents were country gospel singers and Dewey joined in as soon as he was old enough to carry a tune.

In his teens, he decided that he wanted to make music his lifelong career. When he was 14, he swapped a prized bull calf for his first guitar. For the next few years, Dewey spent hour after hour learning to play the instrument until he was an excellent musician. By the time he was in his late teens, he was gaining performing experience at local affairs. His progress was interrupted by the outbreak of World War II. Dewey entered the service and spent a good part of the first half of the 1940s in uniform.

After he was discharged, he decided to make a determined bid to become a full-time country artist. His chance came when he heard about a country music talent contest run by the late Pappy Hal Horton. Dewey entered and won first place. His reward was the chance to perform on Dallas station KRLD, with two other artists, Georgia Slim and Big Howdy Forrester. Audience reaction to Dewey was good and it wasn't long before he was a regular on Pappy Hal Horton's KRLD show, Cornbread Matinee.

During the 1950s, Dewey was featured both on the Cornbread Matinee and the new KRLD variety show, Big D Jamboree. He remained with Horton until the latter died. After this Dewey organized a new band, the Texas Longhorns. The eleven-member organization soon became one of the best known in the southwest. As his career prospered, Dewey expanded his operations. He bought the Longhorn Ranch Ballroom in Dallas, a famous landmark once owned by Bob Wills, and operated it successfully. Besides his own organization, he had booked almost every top artist in country and western music into the 18,000-square-foot Ballroom by the late 1960s.

He took another giant step in 1959 by setting up his own record firm, naturally called Longhorn Records. By the mid-1960s, it was one of the first-ranked independent labels in the field, with such artists as Groom himself, Vern Stovall, Leon Rausch and the Texas Playboys, and Janet McBride. Appropriately, one of Stovall's hits of 1967 was a Longhorn record called "Dallas." Groom's other enterprises as of the mid-1960s included a booking agency, the Echo Sound Studio, and the Saran Music Company, all housed in the Longhorn Records building in downtown Dallas.

GUITAR: Stringed instrument, related to the lute family.

The mid-twentieth century can be called, from a musical standpoint, the age of the guitar. The instrument, of course, had vied with the fiddle for decades for domination of folk, country and western music but by World War II had easily become number-one instrument in these fields. After World War II, the onrush of rock 'n' roll made the guitar the primary instrument of popular music as well.

The origins of the guitar, as might be expected, are somewhat hazy. Stringed instruments, of course, are very ancient and can be discerned on ancient sculptures in the Middle East dating back to several thousand years B.C. However, none of these bears any close resemblance to the modern guitar. Some experts believe the guitar evolved from the lute, which in turn originated in the Orient.

The first steps towards development of the modern guitar are believed to have been taken during the 1500s. In the 1600s, paintings from Spain and Italy begin to show instruments with the flat back typical of the guitar instead of the bulging lower section of the lute. Guitarists of the Spanish empire in the New World are credited with introducing the guitar into the Western Hemisphere.

The overall size and shape of guitars have varied widely over the years. In general, however, the instrument can be defined as flat bodied, having a long fretted neck and several strings plucked with a plectrum or a finger. The number of strings has varied over the years from as few as 4 or 5 up to more than 12. Most guitars of today have six strings. The second most common design is the 12-string guitar of Ledbetter fame.

There are many specific kinds of guitar playing styles recognized by musicians, depending on the fingers used, their placement on the strings, and whether or not a pick is used. When the guitar was used mostly for accompaniment, the usual way of playing was with the thumb and two or three fingers. A variation used by early guitar artist Charlie Poole was called thumb-and-roll. In this method the thumb picks out single note runs while the other fingers play chord rolls. (In a roll, the chord notes are played one after the other instead of all at once.)

Maybelle Carter of the Carter Family is credited with innovations that helped make the guitar the lead instrument from the 1930s on. Her approach, as John Cohen wrote in *The New Lost City Ramblers Songbook,* was to use her thumb to "pick out the tune on the lower strings while the index finger brushed up and down across the high strings, articulating both chords and rhythm."

In the 1930s, the use of the flat pick introduced a new element into guitar playing. Another variation introduced by such performers as Merle Travis is, to quote Cohen again, to finger pick "the melody on the high string while the thumb provides a damped or 'choked' base. . . ."

In the 1960s, attention also focused on Bluegrass style. This is a combination of earlier styles using a flat pick or thumb-finger approach for chording and the other fingers for runs.

GUNNING, SARAH: Singer, songwriter. Born Ely Branch, Knox County, Kentucky, 1910.

One of the great names in traditional folk circles for many decades was Aunt Molly Jackson. It surprised some folk enthusiasts of the mid-1960s to discover that Molly had an equally illustrious half-sister, Sarah Elizabeth (Ogan) Gunning, who had been living in obscurity for many years in Detroit. Then it turned out that Jim Garland, who was as famous with folklorists as Aunt Molly, was Sarah's brother. Sarah, as might be surmised, was brought up in a family where music was revered. Her father, a coal miner, union organizer, and Baptist minister, enjoyed leading family sings. Her mother also knew many traditional ballads that she sang and taught to her children. Life in coal mining towns was elemental, though, and Sarah married and began raising a family when she was only 16. Her husband was a miner named Andrew Ogan who had moved to Knox County from Kentucky.

During twelve years of marriage to Ogan, Sarah derived much of her enjoyment of life from singing the old songs. She sang them to her children and in local sings. Her talents finally began to reach the attention of folklorists, some of whom came by on collecting tours to listen to her songs. One of those who became interested was Alan Lomax, who made some records of Sarah between 1935 and 1940, including a number of her original compositions, such as "I Am a Girl of Constant Sorrow."

After her husband's death in 1938, caused by years of working under the difficult mining conditions, Sarah came to know an increasing number of folk artists. Those who enthused over her songs and recordings included Burl Ives, Pete Seeger, Huddie Ledbetter and Woody Guthrie.

In the early 1940s, Sarah had made several trips to New York which led to a second marriage to New York metal polisher Joseph Gunning. With the outbreak of World War II, the Gunnings moved to California where they found work in defense plants. When the war ended, and defense work declined, they moved back east. Instead of returning to New York or the hills of Kentucky, they settled in Detroit in 1946. Sarah's friends had lost track of her and she did not try to pursue a further career in music.

For many years, Sarah sang the old songs just for her own pleasure. The folk music upsurge in the 1950s led to greater interest in traditional singers, causing many collectors to try to track down such artists. In October 1963, this resulted in a visit from Archie Green and Ellen Stekert. They helped bring Sarah's talents to light once more. In late 1963 and early 1964, Sarah delighted audiences at labor meetings, including a union conference at Wayne State University, with her unaccompanied hill country ballads.

In July 1964, she was warmly greeted by audiences at the Newport Folk Festival.

GUTHRIE, ARLO: Singer, guitarist, songwriter. Born Brooklyn, New York, July 10, 1947.

The hit song of the 1967 Newport Folk Festival was a strange ballad called "Alice's Restaurant." The composer had spent a good part of his short life in the odd-seeming locale of Coney Island. But Arlo Guthrie was not another urban folk performer. He had drawn his folk insight from the legitimate background

Arlo Guthrie, heir to the legendary mantle of Woody

bushes out over his ears, sings the song ("Alice's Restaurant") at the beginning and the end of a 20-minute monologue. He strums the tune over and over on his guitar, while he tells why he was arrested for littering on Thanksgiving and describes his adventures at a draft examination.

"Somehow the song and the stories tie together. . . ."

Arlo's ability was recognized by Reprise Records, which signed him to his first record contract in mid-1967. The first release on the label came out in August '67.

GUTHRIE, WOODY: Singer, guitarist, songwriter. Born Okemah, Okfuskee County, Oklahoma, July 14, 1912; died New Jersey, October 4, 1967.

The name of Woody Guthrie strikes fire in the hearts of his ardent folk music followers. His own voice is stilled, but the spirit of this greatest of American folk balladeers lives on in the form of such classic compositions as "This Land Is My Land" and in the performances of his many disciples. Indeed, the so-called "children of Woody Guthrie," including such artists as Bob Dylan, Mark Spoelstra, Phil Ochs, and many others, have altered the course of popular music—as well as folk music—all over the world.

Guthrie was born of pioneer stock, in the Indian country of Oklahoma. His maternal grandmother was one of the first schoolteachers in the county; his grandfather was a pioneer farmer in the region. His father, Charles Edward Guthrie, came from Texas and brought to the family a background of pioneering, prize fighting, and playing guitar and banjo with several cowboy bands.

After marrying Woody's mother, Nora Belle Tanner, Charlie Guthrie settled down to run a trading post and then a real estate office. Things went well for a time and young Woody had an exciting but pleasant atmosphere to grow up in. He was surrounded by folk music—from his grandparents, his father, the neighbors, from Negro singing and even the songs of the many Indian villages in the area. At four, Woody started singing himself and continued to follow this lodestone for the rest of his life.

As Woody reached school age, though, things disintegrated at home. His father's real estate business failed, his sister Clara died in a coal oil stove explosion at home, and his mother had

of a famous father, the great Woody Guthrie.

Growing up as part of the Guthrie environment naturally exposed Arlo to many leading artists, including Pete Seeger and, later on, Bob Dylan. Arlo learned to play guitar at an early age and began performing locally in his teens. In early 1966, he made his professional debut and before long was a steady visitor to college campus folk concerts throughout the east. His talents won sustained applause at such places at the Gaslight in New York City, Club 47 in Cambridge, Massachusetts, and the Second Fret in Philadelphia.

At the end of 1966, he widened his reputation to an international one with a highly successful tour of England in December. In early 1967, he continued to increase his credits, climaxed at mid-year by his Newport appearance. The scene was set for readers of *The New York Times* by John S. Wilson:

"Mr. Guthrie, a slight, wan young man who wears a huge brown felt hat with a turned down brim, under which his long, dark hair to be committed to the State Asylum at Norman. All of this combined to limit Woody's schooling to about the tenth grade. He learned to play harmonica, and when he left home, at 13 or 14, he used it for entertainment and to pick up extra money during his wanderings.

His father, hurt in a fire, was ill in Texas and young Woody "hit the road down south to Houston, Galveston, the Gulf, and back, doing all kinds of odd jobs, hoeing fig orchards, picking grapes, hauling wood, helping carpenters and cement men, working with water well drillers. . . . I carried my harmonica and played in barber shops, at shine stands, in front of shows, around the pool halls, and rattled the bones, done jig dances, sang and played with Negroes, Indians, whites, farmers, town folks, truck drivers and with every kind of a singer you can think of." (*American Folksong/Woody Guthrie,* Oak Publications, N.Y., 1961, p. 3.)

Later, in Pampa, Texas, his father's half-brother Jeff taught Woody to play guitar. The two played for many local events and later performed in their own magic show. After marrying Mary Jenning, Woody took off for

California to try his luck. He worked as a painter during the day and sang in saloons at night. By now he was not only collecting songs, but writing them as well. For most of his life, he wrote one or two songs almost every day, resulting in an estimated published total of more than a thousand compositions.

In California, he joined with a girl named "Lefty Lou" Crissman to form an act called Woody and Lefty Lou. They gained a regular spot on a Los Angeles station, KFVD. After a sojourn on station XELO in Tijuana, Mexico, Woody returned to KFVD as a solo performer. By now he had gained a deep interest in unions and left-wing organizations. He sang for union meetings, migrant groups, etc.

In the late 1930s, he moved to New York where he met many folk artists (including a youngster named Pete Seeger), wrote for the Communist *Daily Worker,* and performed in New England and other eastern states. He also met Alan Lomax, who brought him to Washington to record for the Archive of American Folk Song. Woody turned out enough material, many of them original songs, for twelve records

Woody Guthrie and Leadbelly in concert

[120]

called "Dust Bowl Ballads." Returning to New York, he gained many radio bids and performed on such major shows as Pursuit of Happiness, Cavalcade of America, Back Where I Come From, Pipe Smoking Time and WNYC's Music Festivals.

After a sojourn in California and at the Bonneville Dam, he returned to New York where he joined with such artists as Seeger, Lee Hays, and Millard Lampell in a group called The Almanac Singers. During the early 1940s they toured the entire country, singing at union meetings, radical meetings, and concerts. They also made a number of records, including such songs as "Union Maid," "Talking Union," "Get Thee Behind Me Satan," and "Union Train A Comin'."

With World War II underway, Woody entered the Merchant Marine with his folk song companions Cisco Houston and Jimmy Longhi. He was torpedoed twice during these years, sang and collected material from the British Isles to Russia, and composed still more songs. He was briefly drafted by the Army just before the end of the war.

Returning to New York, Guthrie was asked to record for Moses Asch's new Folkways Records. Over the next decade, Guthrie turned out dozens of LPs for Asch. These included such songs of his as "Goin' Down This Road," "Boomtown Bill," "I Ain't Got No Home in This World Anymore," "Tom Joad," "Jack Hammer John," "Pretty Boy Floyd," "Billy the Kid," "When the Curfew Blows," "Sharecropper Song," "Electricity and All," and "Pastures of Plenty."

His LPs included such titles as "Bound for Glory," "Dust Bowl Ballads" (two LPs), "Woody Guthrie and Cisco Houston," "Guthrie and Leadbelly" ('62); "Ballads of Sacco and Vanzetti" ('61). RCA Victor also issued an LP of his "Dust Bowl Ballads" in '64 and Elektra issued a three-LP album of his "Library of Congress Recordings" the same year. He was also represented on Stinson with an album called "Guthrie, Terry and Stewart."

In the 1950s, Guthrie was already a living legend. He continued composing and writing but a wasting illness, Huntington's Chorea, chained him to a hospital bed in New Jersey for most of these years. Many of the young prospective folk artists of the post-World War II period came to see him for inspiration and such composers as Bob Dylan and Peter La

Farge were considered his spiritual heirs. He passed away in October 1967, after being totally bedridden for a long period. (*See also* ALMANAC SINGERS, THE)

GUY, ATHOL: *See* Seekers, The

HAGGARD, MERLE: Singer, guitarist, songwriter. Born Bakersfield, California, April 6, 1937.

Though most West Coast recording activities in the late 1950s and '60s were based in Southern California, the center for much of the developing country music field in these years remained in the central California town of Bakersfield. The somewhat prosaic San Joaquin Valley city became the base for up-and-coming artists from many parts of the country who flocked there as others did to Nashville.

Bakersfield also had its home grown talent, not the least of whom was Merle Haggard. Born and raised in the city, Merle attended local schools and learned to play excellent guitar by his high school years. In the late 1950s he began to perform in local clubs, gradually building up a following that extended beyond the city area by the early 1960s. Besides playing in clubs and at dances, he was featured on Bakersfield radio stations and also appeared on some of the TV shows emanating from the region.

As his reputation grew throughout the west, Merle gained his first recording contract with Tally Records. In 1965, he had a top 10 nationwide hit with his version of Bill Anderson's "(From Now on All My Friends Are Gonna Be) Strangers." The result was a contract bid from Capitol Records.

His first Capitol LP, "Strangers," became a best-seller. It included five of his own songs including the hit number "I'm Gonna Break Every Heart I Can." His singles output on Capitol for 1966–67 included such songs as "Swinging Doors," "The Girl Turned Ripe," "The Bottle Let Me Down," "The Longer You Wait," "I'm a Lonesome Fugitive," "Someone Told My Story," "I Threw Away the Rose," "Loneliness Is Eating Me Alive," "Branded Man," "You Don't Have Very Far to Go."

Not long after signing with Capitol, Merle married Bakersfield songstress Bonnie Owens. The two combined on Merle's second Capitol LP, "Just Between the Two of Us." (Merle and Bonnie had previously recorded the title song on

Marvel label in 1964.) The album became one of the top 10 LPs of 1966. Later in the year, Merle scored a national hit with his own composition, "Swinging Doors." LP of the same name also was a best-seller. In early 1967, Capitol issued his fourth LP, "I'm a Lonesome Fugitive."

During the mid-1960s, Haggard was featured in personal appearances across the U.S. He also starred on major country TV shows, including Jimmy Dean and Swingin' Country. His ability was recognized by several awards from the First Annual Awards Show of the Academy of Country/Western Music in 1966. Haggard was voted "Most Promising Male Vocalist" and, with his wife, "Best Vocal Group." (*See also* OWENS, BONNIE)

HALL, CONNIE: Singer. Born Walden, Kentucky, June 24, 1929.

The name Pappy Daily often crops up in success stories of country artists. So it was with Connie Hall, who met Daily while he worked as artists-and-repertoire man for Mercury Records. Pappy helped shape her career by changing her contract to a "single artist" contract form.

Connie was born in Kentucky, but spent a good many of her growing-up years in Cincinnati. Her formal education was completed in Cincinnati public schools. While she was in her teens, she already enjoyed singing country music and entertained at local functions. For a while, after finishing her schooling, she worked as a cashier. Then the chance came to sing regularly on station WZIP in Covington, Kentucky, across the river from Cincinnati. She soon had a following among radio listeners in the area that increased still more when she joined the Jimmie Skinner Show on WNOP, Newport, Kentucky, in 1954. For many years after that she was a regular on the Skinner program. In addition, she guested on other radio and TV shows in the area, and for a time served as a weather girl on a local TV station.

In 1959 she signed with Mercury Records. At first, she sang as part of a team with a male singer. Then Pappy Daily gained soloist status for her. A number of her records of the late 1950s became nationwide successes. The most important of her Mercury hits was the 1959 "Bottle Me In." Her other songs for the label included "I'm the Girl in the U.S.A.," "We've

Got Things in Common," and "Where Do We Go from Here" ('58). Her 1959 output included "A Hundred Hearts Or More," "You Deserved Your Invitation," "Third Party at the Table," "Afterdate Rendezvous," "Married to a Friend" and "Heartache Avenue."

At the end of the 1950s, Connie switched to the Decca label. For four years she turned out many well received songs, including "It's Not Wrong," "Poison in Your Hand," "Key to Your World," "Fools Like Me," "Don't Tempt Me," "Fool Me Once," "Yellow Roses" and "Back to Loneliness." Her two Decca LPs were "Connie Hall" and "Country Songs with Connie Hall." In the mid-1960s, Pappy Daily lured her away to his new record company, Musicor. Her first records for the label were "I Wish I Was the Bottle" and "Constantly."

During these years, Connie remained in her home area of Cincinnati with her husband and son. However, she guested on many major shows during the 1960s, including the Grand Ole Opry, Louisiana Hayride, and Midwestern Hayride. Her personal appearances also took her far afield from the midwest to all fifty states and all the provinces of Canada.

HALL, VERA: Singer. Born Livingston, Alabama, 1905; died Livingston, Alabama, January 29, 1964.

The many recordings made in the field of American folk music by the Lomaxes introduced many great and previously unknown artists to the American public. Not the least of these was Vera Hall; Alan Lomax said she "had the loveliest voice I had ever recorded."

Born in rural Alabama, she was subject to the poverty and restrictions of most poor colored families. She began to work at an early age and spent most of her life as a domestic servant. She developed an interest in music while still a child, however, and had already memorized many spirituals, work songs, ballads and blues when in her teens. She sang in her church choir, for her own enjoyment, and at local functions.

The beauty of her singing was recognized by her friends and close neighbors, but there was little thought of it being more than a hobby. However, when John Lomax went through the south and southwest collecting material for the American Archive of Folk Song of the Library of Congress in the 1930s, her name came to his attention. He visited Livingston and recorded dozens of her renditions of such songs as "Soon One Mornin' Death Came Creepin'."

Later his son, Alan Lomax, made more recordings of Miss Hall, who earned her living as a cook and washerwoman. In the 1940s, he asked her to come to New York to perform. Despite the intense opposition of her family, she traveled north and made a deep impression on eastern audiences.

In the 1950s and '60s, her voice was heard on LPs produced by such companies as Folkways, Atlantic, and Prestige. In the late 1950s her health began to fail and she developed cataracts. When she died in her home town of Livingston in 1964, however, she was no longer unknown, but familiar to folk audiences the world over for her original contributions to the art.

HAMBLEN, STUART: Singer, band leader, songwriter. Born Kellyville, Texas, October 20, 1908.

One of the songs that swept the nation in the 1950s was the fast-paced "This Old House." The song, as performed by Rosemary Clooney, was at the top of the popular song lists for weeks in 1954. The song's success brought international fame to its writer, Stuart Hamblen, a man already established as one of the major artists in country and western music.

Hamblen grew up steeped in cowboy tradition in Texas. He already enjoyed singing when he enrolled in McMurray State Teachers College, Abilene, Texas. For a time it seemed as though music would be a hobby as he worked towards his B.A. in the late 1920s. However, the urge to write and sing was too great. Hamblen switched to the music industry before graduation, eventually reaching Southern California in the 1930s. Here he followed in the footsteps of the Sons of the Pioneers, establishing his own group on a local radio station. For a good many years he was featured on several stations, including NBC's Los Angeles outlet, KFI.

By the end of the 1940s, his career embraced a number of records on the Columbia label plus a growing list of song credits for both secular and sacred country and western music. He also appeared in a number of western movies, usually as one of the "bad guys." In 1949, he scored a major national C&W hit with his Columbia recording of his composition, "But I'll Be Chasin' Women." He followed up in 1950 with another top 10 effort, "(Remember Me) I'm the One Who Loves You." Besides

Hamblen's own hit record on Columbia, Ernest Tubb turned out one on Decca label.

Besides music, his interest ranged in many other directions, including horse racing, hunting, and politics. In 1952, he ran for President of the U.S. on the Prohibition Party ticket. He didn't receive too much notice in this role. However, he more than made up for it in the music field with his 1954 recording of "This Old House" for RCA Victor. The following year, Hank Snow presented him with another hit with his RCA Victor version of Hamblen's "Mainliner." During these years, Stuart turned out such other top-ranked songs as "It Is No Secret," "Open Up Your Heart and Let the Sun Shine In," and "The Lord Is Counting on You." Other Hamblen compositions include "Golden River," "My Mary," "Little Old Rag Doll," "Known Only to Him."

Among Hamblen's many recordings were such other songs as "Lonesome Cowboy," "Be My Shepherd," "Beyond the Sunset," "When the Lord Picks Up the Phone," "A Few Things to Remember," "Friends I Know," "Got So Many Million Years," "Desert Sunrise," "Whistler's Dream," "Sunny Side of the Mountain," "Oh How I Cried," "I'll Be Gone," "Hell Train," "That'll Be the Day," "This Book, My Brother," "Old Pappy's New Banjo," and "You Must Be Born Again."

His albums included the Coral LP "Remember Me" ('59) and Columbia's "Spell of the Yukon" ('61). His religious LPs included, for RCA Victor, "Grand Old Hymns" and "It Is No Secret"; for Camden, "Beyond the Sun" ('60); and for Columbia, "Of God I Sing" ('62).

During the late 1950s, Hamblen and his wife, Susie, hosted a TV show on a local Los Angeles station.

HAMILTON, GEORGE, IV: Singer, guitarist, songwriter. Born Winston-Salem, North Carolina, July 19, 1937.

There are a number of unique features in George Hamilton IV's road to country and western stardom. He achieved teenage acclaim in the pop field before turning to country for his main career. He also persevered in gaining his college degree despite a growing national reputation as a performer during his college years.

George heard much good country music during his youth in North Carolina. In addition, he received strong encouragement from his parents as soon as he showed a boyhood interest in music. His father had been an amateur singer with a band during his own high school days and both his parents were fans of the Grand Ole Opry program.

When George reached high school, he had already written a few songs and started to play the guitar. For a while, his interests trended toward rock 'n' roll and he played with bands of this type during his teen years. By the time he completed high school, he had made enough of a name for himself to gain a contract with ABC-Paramount Records. For the 1955–56 school year, he entered the University of North Carolina at Chapel Hill. While there, he clicked with a major national pop hit in 1956, "A Rose and a Baby Ruth." One result of this was a bid to appear regularly on WMAL-TV in Washington, D.C. George refused to give up college, and switched to American University in Washington.

George continued at American University while making himself known to country music fans across the country at the same time. He

George Hamilton IV

began to move into the country field in earnest in 1957 with appearances on such programs as the Jimmy Dean Show in 1957–58. However, he was a major pop star and was in demand for many major network shows. In 1957 he was featured on such TV programs as Arthur Godfrey on CBS-TV, Steve Allen's NBC-TV program, and the Patti Page Show on CBS-TV. In 1959, he appeared several times on Dick Clark's American Bandstand and with Perry Como. That year he also starred in his own show on ABC-TV.

During the late 1950s, George transitioned from the pop to the country field with such hits as "Now and For Always" and "I Know Where I'm Goin'" in '58; "Gee" in '59; and "Why I'm Walkin'" in 1960. His status as a major country artist was recognized by the Grand Ole Opry, which made him a regular on the show in 1959.

During the 1960s, the name George Hamilton IV became a familiar one on country and western hit charts. His first big country hit was the top 10 rated "Before This Day Ends" in 1960 on ABC-Paramount. In 1961, he moved to RCA Victor and soon had a national hit in "Three Steps to a Phone." He had top 10 hits the next three years, starting with his own composition "If You Don't Know I Ain't Gonna Tell You" in 1961 and following with "Abilene" in '63 and "Ft. Worth, Dallas and Houston" in '64.

His LP albums for ABC-Paramount included "George Hamilton IV's Big 15," "George Hamilton IV" and "Sing Me a Sad Song." On RCA Victor, he was represented by the LPs "Abilene" ('63) and "Ft. Worth, Dallas and Houston" ('64). Among the numbers on his LPs were such songs of his own as "If You Don't Know Now," "I've Got a Secret," "Sam," and "Everybody's Baby."

In addition to numerous personal appearances in major cities in the 1960s, he found time for two movies by 1969, "Hootenanny Heart" and "Second Fiddle to a Steel Guitar."

HAMMOND, JOHN, JR.: Singer, guitarist. Born New York, New York, 1943.

The name Hammond is an illustrious one in the annals of American folk musicianship. John Hammond Sr. is a name familiar to many of the major jazz festivals. As a Columbia Records executive and a respected jazz musician, he played a leading role in improving the status of this American idiom. It was thus poetic justice that his son became one of the best white performers of the blues in the 1960s.

John Jr. was born and raised in New York City. He was naturally exposed to many forms of music at home, meeting and listening to some of the foremost exponents of jazz and blues during his youth. By the time he was in high school, he was adept at playing the guitar and harmonica. In his teens, he impressed many of his family's friends with his performance of folk and blues material.

He began to play in local coffee houses in New York. In 1963, he was invited to perform at the Newport Folk Festival and won almost universal acclaim for his efforts. His success with the blues was shown in an item in Leonard Feather's column in Down Beat of March 12, 1964 (quoted in Sing Out!, July '64, by Paul Nelson). Famed Negro jazz musician Bill Henderson was asked by Leonard Feather to listen to a record and tell the name of the artist.

Henderson told Feather, "That's beautiful. Sounds like Brownie McGhee and Sonny Terry . . . I don't think anybody today would be able to duplicate this, because they haven't lived this way. . . ." The record, "Mean Old Frisco," was Hammond's. Other critics were similarly surprised at young Hammond's talents.

The first LP album of Hammond Jr. was released by Vanguard in 1963, titled "John Hammond." In 1964, a second LP was issued, "Big City Blues." The latter contained such songs as "I'm Ready," "My Starter Won't Start," "Barbecue Blues," "I'm a Man," "Barrelhouse Woman," "Midnight Hour Blues," "Backdoor Man," "Live the Life I Love," "No Money Down," "My Babe," "Key to the Highway," and "Baby Won't You Tell Me."

In the mid-1960s, Hammond continued to increase his stature in the folk field, appearing at several major folk festivals in different parts of the country and at more Newport events. His efforts in 1968 included a successful engagement at the Ash Grove in Los Angeles as well as at other coffee houses, and nightclubs in other parts of the country. His Vanguard LPs during this period included "So Many Roads" ('65); "Country Blues" ('66); and "Mirrors" ('67).

HARDEN, ARLEEN: *See* Harden Trio

HARDEN, BOBBY: *See* Harden Trio

HARDEN, ROBBIE: *See* Harden Trio

HARDEN TRIO: Vocal group, Robbie, Arleen, and Bobby Harden. All born England, Arkansas.

For years The Browns, a trio consisting of a brother and two sisters, was among the top 10 vocal groups in country and western music. When The Browns broke up, heir apparent to the throne was the Harden Trio of England, Arkansas. The Hardens grew up in the heart of the Ozarks and were exposed to folk, country and western music as soon as they could understand what music was all about.

In their teens, they began to sing for local dances and gradually began careers as professional singers. Before long they were members of the cast of the Barnyard Frolics radio program broadcast from Little Rock, Arkansas. They soon became local favorites in the region and began to tour other states in the area. In the late 1950s they were featured on the Ozark Jubilee from Springfield, Missouri, and the Louisiana Hayride in Shreveport. Their material ranged from standard country ballads to new songs written by Bobby.

With a growing national reputation under their belts in the 1960s, they were asked to join the Grand Ole Opry. After moving to Nashville, the trio guested on most of the top network TV programs, including the Bill Anderson Show and Stu Phillips Show. They also were featured on WSM radio's Opry Almanac. By the mid-1960s, they had made personal appearances in all fifty states and parts of Canada.

They signed with Columbia Records after arriving in Nashville. Their first release comprised one of Bobby's songs, "Poor Boy," and "Let It Be Me." In 1966, they scored their first top 10 hit with Bobby's "Tippy Toeing." Some of their other hits of this period were "Don't Remind Me," "Seven Days of Crying," and "Husbands and Wives." In 1968 they had a chart hit in "Everybody Wants to Be Somebody Else." The trio split up in 1968, each going out as a single.

HARMONICA: Name given to several simple musical instruments.

The type of harmonica with which most people are familiar is a small wind instrument that produces music through the vibration of small metal reeds. However, the word is also used to describe an instrument (invention is credited to Benjamin Franklin) in which sound is produced by friction upon glass bells. Still another type of harmonica is of the Glockenspiel family in which sound is provided by striking steel reeds with hammers.

The first named, though, is the one used by many folk, country and western artists. Also called the mouth organ, it consists of a series of small reeds, fastened at one end inside a thin metal case. The instrument is played by inhaling or exhaling into mouth holes along the top of the instrument to make the desired reeds vibrate.

It is generally agreed that the harmonica was invented in the early 1800s. An instrument of this type, called the aeolina by its inventor, Sir Charles Wheatstone, was devised in 1829. An instrument closer in design to today's mouth organ was produced in Germany in 1821 by Fredrich Buschmann.

In folk, country and western, the harmonica is mainly used as a supporting instrument. There are performers such as the great Sonny Terry who are solo artists as well. In the popular music domain there have been a number of successful harmonica bands, including Borrah Minnevitch, his successor, Johnny Puleo, and Jerry Murad and his Harmonicats. These groups have occasionally turned out folk, country and western albums.

HARTFORD, JOHN: Singer, banjoist, guitarist, songwriter. Born New York, New York, December 30, 1937.

In the mid-1960s a slim, black-haired Missourian in his late twenties came to Nashville to seek a music career. In this, he was like thousands of other young men who come to town each year. Unlike most of the others, he was not outwardly brash and self-confident, but self-effacing and retiring. However, he had a quiet intensity that won him a job as a disk jockey. A little more than a year later, he was a performer and composer of great promise with a national song hit to his credit, "Gentle on My Mind."

Hartford's songs had unusual polish and sophistication, yet deep country music roots. The former resulted from his upbringing in St. Louis, Missouri. He was born in New York, where his doctor father, a Missourian, was completing his internship. When he was a few weeks old, his family returned to Missouri, where they had ties in the rural parts of the state. In his early years, John spent many hours listening to country radio programs. By the time he was

13, he had learned both fiddle and 5-string banjo. From then on, he often played for local square dances. Later, he added guitar picking to his talents.

When he finished his schooling, he had no good idea of where his future lay. He worked at a number of jobs, including commercial artist and deck hand on the Mississippi River. He continued to play for small affairs or for his own pleasure, but it was strictly a sideline. Along the way, though, he managed to pick up some credits as a radio announcer. He also enjoyed writing verses and sometimes spent hours at this as a form of relaxation.

The years went by and, apart from marriage and the birth of a son, nothing much happened. Then he decided to head for Nashville. As he told one interviewer, ". . . I was working in Southeast Missouri at the time and I wasn't doing too well, moneywise, and I thought, well, you only live once, and a guy can starve to death as easily in Nashville as anywhere else and have more fun doing it, so I just packed up the wife and the little boy and moved to Nashville."

Drawing on his announcing credits, he gained a job on a Nashville station. He began to visit some of the local music firms with some of his own songs. He played some of these for the Glaser Brothers. The Glasers quickly sensed he had something new and different to offer and added his name to their talent agency list. Soon after, Hartford was signed by RCA Victor.

Under the supervision of RCA's Chet Atkins, he recorded a number of his own compositions. The first release, in 1966, consisted of "Tall, Tall Grass" and "Jack's in the Sack." In July '66 his first LP was produced, "John Hartford Looks at Life," including such original compositions as "Eve of My Multiplication," "When the Sky Begins to Fall," "I Shoulda Wore My Birthday Suit," "Corn Cob Blues," "Today," "Front Porch" and "Like Unto a Mockingbird."

Word of his songwriting ability spread throughout Nashville; soon other artists were recording his songs. The Glaser Brothers cut a number of Hartford efforts in 1966 and '67, as did George Hamilton IV, Waylon Jennings, Jack Greene, Patti Page, Billy Grammer and many others.

In 1967, a second Hartford LP was issued, "Earthwords and Music," including the song "Gentle on My Mind." As 1967 came to a close, artist after artist recorded the song. It provided a vocal hit for Glen Campbell on Capitol and an instrumental hit for Floyd Cramer on RCA Victor.

Now an established new star, Hartford started 1968 with a successful new LP, "The Love Album," and a contract from CBS-TV to help prepare the summer replacement for the Smothers Brothers show. In 1969 he was a featured performer on CBS-TV's new Glen Campbell show.

HASSILEV, ALEX: *See* Limeliters, The

HAWES, BESS LOMAX: Singer, guitarist, mandolinist, songwriter, folklorist. Born Austin, Texas, January 21, 1921.

In the 1960s, the effect of the Lomax clan on folk music literally spanned the country. On the East Coast, Alan Lomax continued ably to carry on the tradition of his father, John, by collecting folk songs from all over the world and lecturing on folk music at leading universities. Across the continent, in Santa Monica, California, his younger sister, Bess Hawes, ranked as one of the foremost unofficial authorities on folk music in the west.

Bess naturally grew up in an environment conducive to musical scholarship. Her father had established a reputation as one of the foremost collectors of folk material in the nation and, in general, enjoyed the arts. However, when she was old enough to participate in musical activities, he had left university work to become an official in a Texas bank. Thus she had more exposure to classical music than to folk material during elementary school.

Her family started her on piano lessons and she showed excellent potential as a pianist. By the time she was 10, she had received intensive training in the classics and in basic musical theory. Then several hard blows changed the course of all the Lomaxes. Just as the Depression began to erupt, her mother's death sent Bess to a boarding school in Dallas. In 1932, the effects of the Depression caused cutbacks in the banking field and her father was laid off.

While Bess continued her studies in Dallas, her father and brother Alan embarked on new careers in folk music collecting, based on a book contract from The Macmillan Company. Bess proved a precocious student, walking off with honors in school. At 15, she was able to enter the University of Texas.

By now, folk music was a way of life with the Lomax family and Bess met many of the great artists discovered by her father. These included Leadbelly and the Gant family.

In 1937, she left Texas to join her family, now living in Washington, D.C. She worked on transcribing material from field recordings for her menfolks' second book, *Our Singing Country*. When her father remarried soon after the book was finished, he took her along to Europe on his honeymoon. To keep busy on the trip, Bess bought a second-hand guitar for $15 and taught herself to play it. By the time the journey was over, she already had mastered part of the art of guitar playing.

When the family settled down in the U.S. once more, Bess enrolled in Bryn Mawr College. She soon met many of the folk music artists then living in New York and was welcomed as a talented artist and kindred spirit. Among those with whom she sometimes performed in folk music gatherings were Pete Seeger, Butch Hawes, Earl Robinson, Woody Guthrie and Burl Ives. Soon a new, somewhat amorphous singing group was formed, called The Almanac Singers. She became a part of it and later married one of the group members, Butch Hawes. During these years, she learned a second stringed instrument, the mandolin, with the great Woody Guthrie as her teacher.

When World War II caused the Almanacs

Bess Lomax Hawes

to break up, Bess decided to help the war effort by joining the Office of War Information. She served with the Music Division, helping prepare material for broadcast to Europe and the Near East.

After the war, she and husband Butch Hawes moved to Boston. An informal songfest she gave at a nursery school attended by one of her children resulted in requests from parents for guitar instruction. She then set up her first class and was on the way to a reputation as one of the best folk music teachers in the country.

While in Boston, Bess took an active part in political campaigns. For one of these she wrote "The M.T.A. Song" with Jacqueline Steiner. The song later was made into a national hit by the Kingston Trio.

In the 1950s, when the Hawes family moved to California, she found herself in as much demand as ever as a music instructor. She also was sought out by many major folk artists when they traveled in the west, and received many invitations to perform at both West Coast and national festivals. She accepted many of these, traveling east to Newport for several Folk Festivals in the 1960s. In addition, she was featured at the Berkeley and UCLA Folk Festivals and at other local concerts and festivals in Los Angeles, San Diego, and Newport. Throughout the 1950s and '60s, she was also much in demand for appearances at coffee houses, concerts, and theaters in many parts of the country.

She continued to increase her stature as a teacher, joining the faculty of San Fernando Valley State College. As an instructor in anthropology, she advanced to the rank of associate professor by 1968. In the 1960s, she took on additional teaching responsibilities as a member of the summer faculty of the folk music workshops at Idyllwild School of Music and the Arts, Idyllwild, California. (*See also* HAWES, BUTCH; LOMAX, ALAN; LOMAX, JOHN AVERY)

HAWES, BUTCH: Singer, guitarist, banjoist, fiddler, songwriter, artist. Born Cambridge, Massachusetts, September 21, 1919.

A surname interwoven with many of the best known in folk music during the years just before and after World War II is that of Hawes. The two Hawes brothers often performed as part of the famed Almanac Singers until the group disbanded in the early '40s, and helped write some of the most familiar American songs.

Baldwin "Butch" Hawes is the younger and John Hawes is the elder. (John's nickname is Peter. This often has caused confusion in reports of the time since some authorities assumed John and Peter were two different people.) The Hawes family hailed from Cambridge where the boys grew up. Butch attended third grade with another boy who was to go on to folk music fame: Pete Seeger.

Butch showed talent as an artist and went on to study at the Boston Museum School in the mid-1930s. However, he shared an interest in folk music with his brother and learned to play basic guitar in his teens. "Pete" Hawes went on to New York and played with many other young folk artists, including Pete Seeger. Later he was a charter member of the Almanacs. During a New York visit with John, Butch was introduced to the Almanacs.

Soon after, Butch moved to New York, working as a commercial artist and performing in his spare time with the Almanacs. Butch became a close friend and confidant of Woody Guthrie, who responded by teaching Butch to play banjo and fiddle. Butch also met and married another young member of the group, Bess Lomax, youngest of the children of folklorist John Lomax.

During his association with the Almanacs and afterward, Butch composed many folk and labor union songs. Two of the best known are "UAW-CIO" and "Going Away to Sea, Baby Mine." Some of his songs have been mistakenly ascribed by some critics to Woody Guthrie. Butch also performed with the Almanacs on some of their recordings.

Just after World War II, Butch moved his family back to Cambridge. He and Bess concentrated on raising their three children, though they still found time for some folk music activity. About 1955, they moved to California, settling for a while in Topanga Canyon where the Hawes home was a mecca for many folk artists, including Woody Guthrie and Jack Elliott. In the 1960s, the Haweses' home address was Santa Monica. During this period Butch worked part time as a commercial artist and limited his performing chores mainly to informal gatherings. ("Pete" Hawes moved to Puerto Rico just after World War II and made his home there from then on.)

[128]

HAWKINS, HAROLD F. "HAWKSHAW": Singer, guitarist. Born Huntington, West Virginia, December 22, 1921; died Camden, Tennessee, March 5, 1963.

The Mountaineer State, West Virginia, has produced a goodly share of C&W stars, not the least of whom was Hawkshaw Hawkins. Hawkshaw was born near Wheeling and spent most of his youth there, graduating from Huntington High School. An athletic boy, his interests included baseball, swimming, fishing and hunting. But he also enjoyed music and decided to try to get a guitar. He didn't have much spending money, but after a hunting trip netted him a good share of rabbits, he traded five of them for a guitar.

By the time he was 15, he had mastered the instrument well enough to enter a local amateur contest. The result was a first prize and a $15-a-week job on the local station, WSAZ. By the time World War II erupted, Hawkins had achieved a growing reputation in his home state and had also played on other programs in neighboring states. Hawkshaw entered the service and eventually saw duty in the Pacific. After the Philippines were liberated by MacArthur's forces, Hawkins was stationed in the islands and sang over station WUTM.

In 1946, he was back home in West Virginia again as a featured performer on Wheeling station WWVA. His career now moved rapidly ahead with many personal appearances and his first recording contract with King Records. He soon became one of King's major artists with such records as "Soldier's Last Letter," "Mean Mama Blues," "I'll Get Along Somehow," and "Since You Went Away." He provided King with a top 10 hit in 1952 with "Slow Poke." During the early 1950s, Hawkins also became well known to TV viewers. His activities included a series of shows over WFIL-TV in Philadelphia.

Hawkins remained a regular with the WWVA Jamboree until 1954. He moved to Red Foley's Jubilee U.S.A. show on ABC-TV for the 1954–55 season. In 1955, he heeded the call of the Grand Ole Opry and shifted his base of operations to Nashville as a regular cast member. He was a featured performer on the show and toured the nation with Opry troupes for the rest of his career.

From 1953 on, Hawkins turned out some records for RCA Victor as well as for King. King seemed to be luckier for him, though; most of his major successes were on that label. In 1963, he turned out one of his greatest hits on King, the top 10 national success "Lonesome 7-7203."

Among the hundred-plus songs that he recorded were such numbers as "I'm Kissing Your Picture," "I Love the Way You Said Goodnight," "Counting Tears," "Barbara Allen," "Sunny Side of the Mountain," "Would You Like to Have a Broken Heart," "Doghouse Boogie," "Rattlesnakin' Daddy," "Teardrops from My Eyes," "Pickin' Sweethearts," "Pan American," "Everybody's Got a Girl But Me," "The Love You Steal," "Standing at the End of My World," "All Because of My Jealous Heart," "Oh How I Cried," "Gotta Have Fun," "Patanio," "Got You on My Mind," "It Ain't on the Menu," "A Heartache to Recall" and "Shotgun Boogie."

Hawkshaw's name graced a number of successful albums. These included, on King label, "From Our Vaults" Volumes 1-3; "Hawkshaw Hawkins" (two LPs—'58); and "All New Hawkshaw Hawkins Songs" ('63). He was also represented on Harmony Records with "The Great Hawkshaw Hawkins" ('63) and on RCA's Camden label with "Hawkshaw Hawkins Sings" ('64).

His career was cut short in a 1963 plane crash near Camden, Tennessee, that also cost the lives of Opry stars Patsy Cline and Cowboy Copas, as well as Copas' son-in-law (the plane's pilot), Randy Hughes. Ironically, the mishap occurred as the party neared Nashville after performing at a benefit performance in Kansas City, Kansas, for the family of Cactus Jack Call, who had just died in a car crash.

HAY, GEORGE DEWEY: Editor, reporter, announcer, radio station executive. Born Attica, Indiana, November 9, 1895; died Virginia Beach, Virginia, May 9, 1968. Elected to Country Music Hall of Fame in 1966.

Few people have had a greater impact on the national development of country and western music than the man known as "The Solemn Ol' Judge." His insight into the potential of this form of entertainment led to the start of two of the landmark programs in the field, the National Barn Dance and the Grand Ole Opry.

In his teens, Hay began work in the real estate business. He worked for a number of firms in real estate and general sales until 1920. That year he gained a job as a newsman with the Memphis *Commercial Appeal*. The paper branched out into the infant field of radio, setting up station WMC, one of the pioneer stations of the south. Hay doubled in brass by spending part of his time as radio editor for WMC. In 1923, he suddenly gained a national reputation when he scooped the world with news of the death of President Warren Harding. Within a year, he moved north to Chicago as chief announcer for station WLS.

By now Hay was convinced of the bright future of the medium. He looked for other avenues for his talents, and eventually started a show called the WLS Barn Dance, later known as the National Barn Dance. Before long, the Barn Dance had a top national rating, and a country-wide poll by Radio Digest resulted in Hay's being named as the top announcer in the U.S.

In the fall of 1925, Hay was invited to the dedication of a new 1,000 watt (75-mile range) station in Nashville, which went on the air on October 5, 1925. While in Nashville, Hay was offered the job of director of the new station, WSM, by its owners, the National Life and Accident Insurance Co. (The company still owns WSM.) A month later, he accepted and moved south again.

The continuing success of the WLS Barn Dance made Hay consider a similar show for WSM, but he took no action for a while. Part of his duties involved conducting studio tours; he became fascinated by the anecdotes on fiddle music related by one visitor, 80-year-old Uncle Jimmy Thompson. This gave Hay the incentive to inaugurate the WSM Barn Dance with Thompson as the star. At 8 P.M., November 28, 1925, Thompson fiddled and Hay emceed a

The cornfield setting for this photograph of a pioneer group symbolizes the rural origins of much of our country and folk music. From the WSM Archives, the picture is of the Possum Hunters, performers on the Grand Ole Opry during its first year of existence, 1925. Seated (l. to r.) are: Walter Leggett, Dr. Humphrey Bates, Buster Bates, Staley Walton; standing: Oscar Stone, Aaron Albright.

65-minute program. The Barn Dance was established as a regular WSM feature.

WSM, an NBC network affiliate, carried a number of programs originating in New York. Once such was the NBC Symphony Orchestra. In the scheduling, the Symphony preceded the Barn Dance. One night not long after the Barn Dance began, Hay introduced the program with this historic bit of dialogue:

". . . From here on out, folks, it will be nothing but realism of the realistic kind. You've been up in the clouds with grand opera; now get down to earth with us in a . . . shindig of Grand Ole Opry!"

In January 1926, the show's name officially became the Grand Ole Opry.

Hay expanded the Opry, adding more performers, including Uncle Dave Macon in 1926. Macon, a singer-banjoist, added variety to the hoedown fiddles, jug and string bands. He became and was for many years the leading artist of the show. Other acts Hay introduced in the early years were Paul Warmack and his Gully Jumpers, George Wilkerson and his Fruit Jar Drinkers, the Dixie Dew Drop, Arthur Smith, and his Dixie Liners, Sam and Kirk McGee, and The Delmore Brothers.

Before long, the Opry was extended to three hours of local programming. Hay, as m.c., brought the show to a close with a steamboat

George D. Hay, at left, presides at the historic first broadcast of the WSM Barn Dance in 1925. Star of the show was fiddler Uncle Jimmy Thompson (right).

whistle. He literally "blew the whistle" indicating the end of another Opry radio segment in the middle of a rousing performance that went on for many minutes after the Opry was off the air.

Hay was instrumental in having the station designated a clear-channel station in 1929, and was successful in gaining approval for a maximum power jump to 50,000 watts in 1932. This signal strength permitted WSM to blanket the south and midwest. Listeners were able to hear the Opry as far north as Canada. Through the 1930s and '40s, Hay continued to recruit new talent and encourage trends that resulted in the emergence of name performers from Opry bands, including such artists as Roy Acuff and Eddy Arnold. He evolved formats and types of entertainment now standard throughout the country music field.

In 1951, he retired to live with a daughter, Margaret, in Virginia. In the early 1960s, he made a triumphal return to Nashville to celebrate his election to the Country Music Hall of Fame. From retirement until his death in May 1968, in Virginia Beach, Virginia, he remained on call and on the WSM payroll.

HAYNES, HENRY D.: *See* Homer and Jethro

HAYS, LEE: Singer, songwriter. Born Little Rock Arkansas, 1914.

If it weren't for the Depression, Lee Hays might never have become a folk singer. In fact, he later said he had never even heard the words "folk song" until leaving the south and coming to New York in his early twenties.

He was exposed to folk music, though, in his youth. He started grade school in Arkansas and graduated from high school in Georgia. Older children in the family went on to college, but the Depression thwarted Lee's ambitions. His interest in music helped in his decision to move to New York in 1936. Once in the east, he became interested in folk music and began to sing with local groups. His bass voice won the attention of many first-rate folk artists and over the next four years he sang with many of them, including Woody Guthrie, Leadbelly, Burl Ives, Josh White and Pete Seeger.

In 1940, when Seeger was instrumental in founding The Almanac Singers, Lee Hays was one of the first to join. Surprisingly, his work with this group provided his first income from folk singing. The group, one of the legendary ones of folk music, was broken up by World War II.

When Seeger returned from the service to form The Weavers in 1948, Hays was a key member. He is credited with thinking up the name for the group. Lee remained with The Weavers as a performer and a collaborator on many Weaver hit songs throughout the group's existence. One of the most famous Hays-Seeger compositions is "If I Had a Hammer."

HELLERMAN, FRED: Singer, guitarist, song-writer, musical director. Born New York, New York, May 13, 1927.

One of the reasons for the importance of the Elektra label in the folk music boom of the 1960s was the work of Fred Hellerman. Calling on his background as an artist and composer, he worked with such performers as Theodore Bikel, Judy Collins, and Erik Darling to provide a first-rate catalog.

Hellerman was born and raised in New York, but it took wartime service with the Coast Guard in 1944-45 to start him on a folk music career. To while away his free hours, he taught himself how to play the guitar. By the time he was discharged, he was quite proficient at singing folk songs to his own guitar accompaniment.

As a civilian, he concentrated on getting a college education. He attended New York University, Columbia, and Brooklyn College, graduating from the latter in 1949. But he spent all his free hours away from the campus in the domain of music.

He started playing in local folk music spots in 1946 and found an excellent reception among both folk music fans and other artists. Among those who liked his work was Pete Seeger. With Seeger he was a charter member of a new group called The Weavers. Hellerman remained with the group throughout its existence and helped arrange and compose some of their greatest hits. One of the standards resulting from this was "Kisses Sweeter Than Wine."

With The Weavers, Hellerman traveled throughout the world and was featured in most major folk festivals and on radio. (*See* separate item on The Weavers.)

Over the years, he also learned to play many instruments besides the guitar, including the banjo, recorder, drums, celeste and zither.

In the late 1950s and '60s, his talents were also in demand as both arranger and composer

of special material. Among those for whom he provided this kind of support were Harry Belafonte, Theodore Bikel, and the Kingston Trio. His credits included that of musical director of a play, "The Moon Besieged."

His compositions and adaptations include "Kisses Sweeter Than Wine," "I Never Will Marry," "I'm Just a Country Boy," "Delia," "Darlin' Cora," "The Biggest Ride," "Long About Now," "Come Away Melinda," "The Honey Wind Blows," "Cherries and Plums" and "Healing River."

HELMS, BOBBY: Singer, guitarist, songwriter. Born Bloomington, Indiana, August 15, 1933.

Every Christmas season, one of the names high on any country and western DJ's list is that of Bobby Helms. The reason is his standard recording of "Jingle Bell Rock," which has sold well over a million copies. Bobby isn't a seasonal singer, however, as his many records on best-seller lists over the years have demonstrated.

A product of Indiana, Bobby grew up in Bloomington, attending Bloomington High School. He was already an excellent guitarist in his early years in high school, and in fact was featured on Bloomington's WWTV when he was only 13. He remained a featured performer on the station through 1954 when he switched to the NBC-TV station in town. He became well known throughout the midwest while still in his teens and had the first of his several guest spots on the Grand Ole Opry in 1950.

In the mid-1950s, Bobby's recordings began to receive nationwide attention. In 1957, he finally hit in a big way with two songs that each stayed in the number-one spot for many weeks. The first of these, which was first broadcast to Bloomington audiences, was "Fraulein." The follow-up hit was "My Special Angel." During the next year, he also scored lesser successes with "Just a Little Lonesome," "I Guess I'll Miss the Prom," "Hundred Hearts" and his own composition, "Love My Lady." He scored another gold-record hit in 1958 with "Jacqueline," which was featured in the Columbia movie "The Case Against Brooklyn."

After 1957 Bobby was featured on many network shows, including Jubilee U.S.A., Country America, Ed Sullivan and seven different times, as of 1968, on Dick Clark's American Bandstand. During the 1960s, he guested on such shows as Red Foley and the Patti Page Show.

Some of his other singles were "New River

Train," "Borrowed Dreams," "To My Sorrow," "Let Me Be the One," "I Want to Be with You," "Sorry, My Name Isn't Fred," and "I'm the Man." He also turned out his own compositions, including "Tonight's the Night" ('57) and "I Don't Owe You Nothin'" ('56). Some of the songs of which he was co-writer are "Someone Was Already There," "Mama Gonna Miss You" and "Teach Me."

During the 1950s, Bobby recorded for Decca. One of his more popular Decca LPs was "Bobby Helms Sings." During the early 1960s, he was on Columbia, including the LP "Best of Bobby Helms" ('63). In the mid-1960s, he was featured on Kapp with such LPs as "Sorry, My Name Isn't Fred" and "I'm the Man."

Over the years, Bobby gained eight awards from Cashbox, Billboard, and Western Jamboree magazine. These included the Cashbox award as number one country singer of 1957.

HERALD, JOHN: *See* Greenbriar Boys

HESTER, CAROLYN: Singer, guitarist. Born Waco, Texas, *circa* 1937.

There were few lists of suggested basic albums of folk music of the mid-1960s that did not include one by Carolyn Hester. It was not just her material, but her impressive vocal ability. As *New York Times* critic Robert Shelton stated in a rave review following her first New York concert in the early 1960s, "Miss Hester has a vocal range from rooftop soprano to stunning chest tones."

Besides talent, she showed a great amount of feeling for folk songs, reflecting her southwestern upbringing. A distant relative of President Lyndon Johnson, she was born and spent much of her youth in Texas. She was exposed to many folk and country music influences, though her background was basically in tune with the modern-day world. She began to sing first for her own pleasure and then for small gatherings during her teens.

By the late 1950s, she was able to take advantage of the folk song boom by singing at coffee houses in various parts of the country. Like many other young folk artists of the period, she found her way to New York at the start of the 1960s. Before long, she had scored with local audiences and had a growing reputation with other folksingers. During the first two years of the decade, she sang at most of the folk clubs on the national circuit. She also received

Carolyn Hester

bids to appear in college concerts, and by early 1962 she had been warmly welcomed at the University of Texas, University of Virginia, Yale, Harvard, and elsewhere.

In June 1961 her first LP, "Carolyn Hester," was issued by Tradition Records. This was well received by folk fans, and led to a contract with Columbia Records. Her first Columbia LP, "Carolyn Hester," issued in June 1962, created a national sensation. She was rewarded with ecstatic reviews in all the music trade magazines and in many national newsstand publications, including Time and Hi-Fi Stereo Review. The latter compared her highly favorably with Joan Baez.

During 1962, she was the only native American artist invited to perform at Scotland's Edinburgh Festival. While there, she was asked to appear several times on the British Broadcasting Corporation network. She also toured most of the important British folk clubs. She returned to the U.S. to continued accolades on campuses and in concerts in many major auditoriums. Her English tours resulted in an in-

[133]

vitation from the British government to take part in a sponsored tour of Russian cities in 1963.

During the mid-1960s, she appeared in many parts of the U.S. and Canada. Her engagements included several major folk song festivals. In 1965, she was featured on a Dot Records LP, "That's My Song."

HILL, GOLDIE (MRS. CARL SMITH): Singer, guitarist. Born Karnes County, Texas, January 11, 1933.

"Whatever happened to Goldie Hill?" was a question asked by country and western fans in the 1960s. The answer was that after rocketing to stardom by the time she was 20, she had married the great country artist Carl Smith and retired to raise a new generation of potential country and western stars.

She was brought up in Texas and learned to play the guitar by the time she was in high school. She did not perform professionally during her high school years, but did enjoy singing for her own pleasure or to entertain friends. Though she did not think of following a music career, many of her friends were impressed with her ability and suggested she do so. Finally, at 19, she began singing professionally and was soon an established performer on KWKH's Louisiana Hayride in Shreveport. That same year, 1952, she was signed by Decca Records. Her reputation as a major artist spread through the south and southwest, and in 1953 she was asked to join the Grand Ole Opry.

She scored two major national hits in 1953, "I Let the Stars Get in My Eyes" and "Say, Big Boy." This helped win her the title of number one country and western female vocalist of 1953 from Country Song Roundup magazine. In the next few years, she scored with such other songs as "Yesterday's Girl," "Looking Back to See," "Make Love to Me," "Let Me Be the One," and "Why Talk to My Heart." She was also featured on two Decca LPs, "According to My Heart" and "Hit Parade."

In the mid-1950s, she toured many major cities with major country shows, sharing billing with, among others, Carl Smith. She also guested on many major network TV programs. When Goldie was 24, she married Carl. Soon after she retired to begin a family that consisted, as of 1967, of Lori Lynn, Carl Jr., and Larry Dean. As she wrote in 1967, "We live on a 350-acre ranch fifteen miles from Nashville and raise quarter horses and black angus cows."

Though she was not performing actively in the mid-1960s, she was still often represented across country on C&W stations by her recordings. In 1961, Decca produced another LP of her work titled "Heartaches." The lure of the music field proved strong, however, and in 1967 Goldie again began to make some personal appearances and recordings. (*See also* SMITH, CARL)

HILLBILLY, CAT, THE: *See* Presley, Elvis

HINTON, SAM: Singer, guitarist, educator, marine biologist. Born Tulsa, Oklahoma, March 21, 1917.

When Sam Hinton graduated from high school in Crockett, Texas, he received two books, *American Reptiles* and Carl Sandburg's *American Songbag*. The gifts were to symbolize his lifelong combination of careers as a distinguished scientist and part-time folksinger.

During his boyhood days in Oklahoma and Texas, Sam spent long hours exploring the wonders of nature in his rural surroundings. When he wasn't studying the wildlife and botanical features or going to school, he often sang for pleasure, by himself or with family and friends in local get-togethers. "During my youth," he recalls, "I always sang. It wasn't until I went to college that I found out it was folk music."

This discovery came in 1934 when Sam entered Texas A&M College as a zoology major. Sam remained at Texas A&M for two years, supporting himself with a variety of jobs, including singing, painting signs, and selling snake venom to an eastern manufacturer. The venom came from sixty water moccasins that he maintained for a zoological hobby. In 1936, Sam entered and won a Major Bowes Amateur contest and left school to travel throughout the country with one of the Bowes troupes.

During the next two years, Sam sang his folk songs in 46 states and throughout Canada. Finally tiring of traveling, he moved to Los Angeles and enrolled as a zoology student at UCLA in 1939. Again, singing came in handy to help pay tuition, as did another of Sam's skills, science illustrator. Not long after settling down in Los Angeles, Sam gained a part in the long-run musical comedy "Meet the People." Joining Sam in the cast were such soon-to-be-

[134]

famous individuals as Nanette Fabray, Virginia O'Brien, Doodles Weaver and Jack Gilford.

At UCLA, Sam met and married Leslie Forster, an excellent violinist and soloist with the University's *a capella* choir. Leslie provided Sam with his first introduction to the more formal aspects of music.

After graduating from UCLA in 1940, Sam accepted a position as Director of the Desert Museum in Palm Springs, California. He left there in 1943 to accept a post as Curator of the Aquarium and Museum at the University of California's Scripps Institution of Oceanography at La Jolla. This was the start of a long relationship between Sam and UC San Diego that was still going strong in the late 1960s. In 1964, he was appointed to the post of Assistant Director for the entire University system of the Office of School Relations. This job permitted him to combine his talents as educator, biologist, and singer, since he represented the University in discussions with high schools, junior colleges, and other institutions

Sam Hinton

of learning. During such sessions, he reviewed the University system for prospective students and often sang some of his folk song repertoire.

In 1947, Sam made his first recordings for the Library of Congress Archive of American Folk Song, "Buffalo Boy and The Barnyard Song," an album of Anglo-Irish songs and ballads. In 1950, he made his first commercial recording, "Old Man Atom," for Columbia Records. Among his other singles in the early 1950s were "The Barnyard Song" (two songs, '52); "Country Critters" (four songs, '53); "The Frog Song" and "The Greatest Sound Around" ('54). All of the last named were for Decca Records' Children's Series.

Sam turned out his first LPs in 1952, "Folk Songs of California and the Old West" on Bowmar Records, and nine songs for the two-record RCA album "How the West Was Won." Besides singing in the RCA album, which also featured Bing Crosby, Rosemary Clooney, and Jimmy Driftwood, Sam worked with Alan Lomax and Si Rady in selection and arrangement of the material. His other LP credits on Decca include: "Singing Across the Land" ('55); "A Family Tree of Folk Songs" ('56), and "The Real McCoy" ('57). In the 1960s, Sam was featured on such LPs as "American Folk Songs and Balladeers" (Classics Record Library, '64); "Newport Folk Festival, 1963" (Vanguard); and, on Folkways Records, "The Songs of Men," "Whoever Shall Have Some Peanuts" ('61), and "The Wandering Folksong" ('67).

In addition to his performing chores, Sam taught a number of University courses over the years, mostly in the Extension Division. From 1948 on, he taught courses in biology and folklore and, in 1962 and 1967, special courses on folk music on educational TV. (In 1967, he signed to prepare 13 half-hour shows on folk music for the National Educational TV network.)

From 1958 on, he provided a continuing newspaper feature, "The Ocean World," for the San Diego *Union*. He also co-authored two books on oceanology with Joel Hedgpeth, *Exploring Under the Sea* (Doubleday) and *Common Seashore Animals of Southern California* (Naturegraph).

Sam also was featured as a lecturer in his chosen subjects in many parts of the country, as well as receiving many engagements for campus folk song concerts. From 1957 on, he was featured every year as performer and discussion leader at the Berkeley, California, Folk Festival.

He continued to believe in the enduring nature of folk material despite the breaking of the folk song boom in the mid-1960s. "The Variety headline 'Folk Music is Dead,' made no sense to me," he once said. "In the 1930s, songwriters used themes from Tchaikovsky, Chopin, and other classical composers. When that era disappeared, you could just as well have written the headline, 'Classics are Dead.'"

HOLCOMB, ROSCOE: Singer, banjoist, guitarist. Born Daisy, Kentucky, 1913.

The folk music revival of the 1950s and '60s introduced many previously little known traditional artists to the American public. Not the least of these was Roscoe Holcomb, called "the finest performer of Southern Mountain music on records today" by Jon Pankake and Paul Nelson of the Little Sandy Review (Sing Out!, Feb.–March '63).

Holcomb was born and spent almost his entire life in the mountain region near Hazard, Kentucky. He was introduced to music almost as soon as he could walk, spending some part of every week listening to his friends and relations sing and play banjo, guitar, or dulcimer at local get-togethers. One of his earliest memories was listening to someone play the mouth harp. Little Roscoe sometimes went to outlying farms just to hear an expert on the mouth harp.

By the time he was 10 he had already learned to play the banjo. He was given a homemade banjo by his brother-in-law that lasted him many years. Soon after, he began to accompany a local fiddler. In a year's time, he learned to play and sing some 400 songs. He continued to learn new ballads, work songs, and square dance numbers as he grew up, sometimes adding new verses to them. When he was in his teens, he could play the guitar and other stringed instruments as well as the banjo.

As with most residents of the mountain country, his education was scanty. At an early age he began to work on local farms. After a while he turned to coal mining, the profession he worked at for most of his life. When work in the mines was slow, he often worked on the railroads, setting timber.

Music remained his main relaxation throughout his working life; he played for many parties and other events in the region. Sometimes he received small pay for his work, while other times he played for the enjoyment of it.

During the years between World Wars I and II, Holcomb built up a major reputation in his home area as a square dance musician. He recalled these days for John Cohen's articles in Sing Out!, "Roscoe Holcomb: First Person" (April–May '66, pp. 3-7):

"I've played for square dances 'til the sweat dripped off my elbows. I used to play for square dances a lot. Used a bunch of us get out, maybe we'd go to a party somewhere and after the party was over the moon'd be a-shinin' bright, you know, and we'd all start back home and gang up in the road. Somebody's start his old instrument, guitar or banjer or something or other, and just gang up in the middle of the road and have the awfulest square dance right out in the middle of the highway."

For a while, Roscoe gave up playing the banjo. He was a member of the regular Baptists, who considered music improper in churches. For ten years he laid his instruments aside. However, by the time World War II came, he was once more active in music.

Holcomb continued to mine coal until the region's mine closed down. In the 1950s, he was reduced to working at odd jobs because of lack of work in his area. In 1959, John Cohen heard of him while collecting folk music for Folkways Records. Cohen was extremely impressed with Holcomb's talents and the result was Holcomb's first LP, "Mountain Music of Kentucky." One of the featured songs was Holcomb's "Across the Rocky Mountain," composed from two earlier ballads. A warm friendship resulted, and in 1962 Cohen produced a movie about Holcomb and his music called "The High Lonesome Sound." An LP of the same title was also turned out by Folkways. A third Holcomb LP, "The Music of Roscoe Holcomb and Wade Ward," was introduced by Folkways in 1963.

Folklorists across the country were familiar with Holcomb's music by the early 1960s. Invitations soon came in for him to perform at many concerts and festivals. During the mid-1960s he played at the Newport Folk Festival, University of Chicago Festival, UCLA, University of California at Berkeley, Cornell, and Brandeis. In 1965-66 he won additional applause from European audiences as a member of the touring Festival of American Folk and Country Music.

HOLLEY, DOYLE: *See* Buckaroos, The

HOMER AND JETHRO: Vocal and instrumental duo, comedy team. Both born Knoxville, Tennessee, Homer, July 27; Jethro, March 10.*

In the mid-1960s, Homer and Jethro sang and clowned their way through a series of "corny" commercials for Kellogg's Cereal on network TV. The response to their efforts showed their broad-brush country-style humor to be as effective with "city folk" as with the home folks.

As Homer and Jethro wrote in an RCA Victor press release, "Our home town is Knoxville, Tennessee. We usually don't mention this in our publicity; when we left there, we said we'd keep it quiet if they would. They've been very nice to us through all these years and they have a very big Homer and Jethro club in Knoxville. They use it on us every time we get near the place."

When Homer and Jethro were growing up in Knoxville, they were known, respectively, as Henry D. Haynes and Kenneth C. Burns. When the two joined forces in their early youth, Haynes could play an excellent country guitar and Burns had mastered the mandolin. In 1932,

"Oooh, that's corny," exclaim the zany duo of Homer and Jethro.

when both were child artists, they met and won a regular radio spot on station WNOX in Knoxville. Their brand of country humor with first-rate musicianship caught on with Knoxville audiences and won them wider attention from the music fraternity.

At the end of the 1930s, they were asked to join the Renfro Valley Barn Dance in Mt. Vernon, Kentucky. After several years on the show, the beginning of World War II resulted in temporary dislocation of their careers. Homer (Haynes) was assigned to the medical corps and saw service in the Pacific, while Jethro (Burns) went the other way, as an infantry soldier in Europe.

When the war was over, the boys joined forces at station WLW, Cincinnati, then toured the country with their own tent show. They then settled down for a six-month engagement on station KWTO in Springfield, Missouri.

Next stop in their travels was Chicago, where the boys were made regular cast members of the National Barn Dance. For a decade, almost up to the show's end in 1960, they were featured performers on the WLS program. Now national favorites, the team played before capacity crowds at personal appearances in all parts of the U.S. and Canada. They also guested on almost all major network radio and TV country shows, including the Grand Ole Opry.

The Homer and Jethro specialty was in making hilarious parodies of best-selling popular and country and western songs. From the late 1940s, when they began a long-time association with RCA Victor Records, through the 1960s, this paid off in many best-selling singles and albums. On several occasions, the boys also turned out top 10-selling records, a difficult feat with comedy material. One of the first of these was their 1948 version, with June Carter, of "Baby, It's Cold Outside." In 1953, they scored again with "That Hound Dog in the Window."

The team's success with popular ballads led to an increasing number of engagements in the 1960s in major nightclubs and general audience variety shows. Many of the team's LPs began to appear on the popular song charts as well as those for the country and western field. Their LP output on Victor included "Barefoot Ballads"; "Worst of Homer & Jethro" ('58); "Life

* Verified years of both not available. Thurston Moore gives 1920 for both artists. Other references indicate about 1918 for Homer, 1923 for Jethro.

Can Be Miserable" ('59); "At the Country Club" ('60); "Songs My Mother Never Sang" ('61); "At the Convention," "Playing Straight" ('62); "Zany Songs of the '30's," "Ooh! That's Corny" ('63); "Confucius Say," "Go West," "Fractured Folk Songs" ('64). They also were featured on Camden label with "Homer & Jethro Strike Back" ('62) and "Humorous Side of Country Music" ('63); King Records with "Homer & Jethro" and "Cornier Than Corn" ('63); and Audio Lab with "Musical Madness" ('59).

The boys' main base of operations continued to be in the Chicago area in the mid-1960s. Homer made his home in Lansing, Illinois, and Jethro in Evanston, Illinois.

HOOKER, JOHN LEE: Singer, guitarist. Born Clarksdale, Mississippi, 1917.

A performer of many talents, John Lee Hooker has been claimed by many segments of the blues field. His performances range from traditional country blues to rhythm and blues and commercial rock 'n' roll. His willingness to try such a wide variety of art forms has resulted in his being damned by folk and blues purists as "uneven" and opportunistic. However, few performers can turn out masterpieces every time out, and no critic can deny Hooker's basic ability as a great folk blues artist.

Hooker was born and spent his early years in a region that produced many of the legendary names in country blues. The first wave to gain some recognition included such performers as Sonny Boy Williamson, Mississippi John Hurt, and Big Bill Broonzy. These artists were sometimes looked upon as old fashioned by the next generation, which encompassed such artists as Muddy Waters and John Lee Hooker.

Singing folk blues was thus a living, everyday tradition in John Lee's home area. In an environment where few children had the chance for much schooling or to do much else but work in the fields or at odd jobs, music was one of the few pleasures in life. John Lee followed the usual pattern, working hard at various chores and spending much of his free time singing with friends or performing for local dances or socials.

At 17, John left home, making his way through the country as best he could. For the next decade he led a wandering life, moving from place to place by such expedients as riding the rails or hitching rides on trucks. The De-

pression held sway, and he sometimes earned his supper by singing in the streets. John slowly worked his way north, and by the late 1940s was living near Detroit. Things were picking up in the music field and he found more work performing in small cafes and clubs mostly in the rhythm and blues vein. In 1949, he made some of his first recordings for Modern Records.

During the 1950s, with stepped-up popular interest in both rhythm and blues and rock 'n' roll, his name became increasingly well known. He also had more requests to record for different small companies. Many of these he did under various pseudonyms, including Texas Slim and John Lee Cooker. One of his best received LPs of these years was "John Lee Hooker Sings the Blues" for King Records. In 1953, however, he signed an exclusive contract with the Vee Jay Company.

By the 1960s, he was considered one of the major names in rhythm and blues nationwide. He performed in cities in all parts of the land. His appearances also included a number of blues recitals at various major folk festivals.

After several years for Vee Jay, John eventually went back to singing for a number of labels in the mid-1960s. During his Vee Jay years, he turned out such LPs as "Burnin'," "I'm John Lee Hooker," "Travelin'" ('61); "Folklore" ('62); "Big Soul," "Best of John Lee Hooker" ('63). In 1963, he was featured on Atco label with "Don't Turn Me from Your Door"; on Galaxy Records with "John Lee Hooker"; and on Fortune Records with "Great Blues Album."

HOPKINS, LIGHTNIN': Singer, guitarist, songwriter. Born Leon County, Texas, March 15, 1912.

"Twenty-one years ago, I went to Louisiana to get me a mojo hen and I got me a wife with it. I'm going to try to go back again soon. I might just end up with two wives. . . ." "It's not worth singing [the song "My Babe"] but I'll guitar to it. . . ." These song introductions alternately intrigued and convulsed a packed house at Los Angeles' Ash Grove in March of 1967. The man delivering them, and singing such original comic lines as "I tiptoed to her window just to see how sweet she snored," was one of the legendary names in blues history, Sam "Lightnin'" Hopkins.

He had come a long way from the days of poverty and singing for his supper, but when he delivered some of his country blues, the audience knew he hadn't forgotten the rough spots of his life.

Hopkins was born on a farm in Texas, not far from the city of Houston. There wasn't much chance for schooling and he spent many of his youthful days teaching himself to play the guitar and picking up song material from listening to the world around him. In the early 1920s, he was earning what money he could as a street singer. For many of these years, he played for pennies on buses in Houston.

In the late 1920s, he began to go further afield, playing in dance halls and anyplace else he could gain an audience. Gradually his ability became known to many of the rural record talent scouts then in vogue in the south and southwest. This led to some of his first recordings which helped bring his name to the attention of folklorists in later years.

Like most folk artists, Hopkins managed to keep performing during the Depression years and the 1940s, but it was hard going. The blues recording business, which had begun to flourish in the early 1930s, was cut back sharply by the Depression. Jobs that were available for such artists as Hopkins offered very little money.

With the increased tempo of rhythm and blues and folk music after World War II, this all changed. By this time, Hopkins was well known to experts in the field, if not to the general public. In the 1950s, more and more invitations came Sam's way to sing on folk music

Sam "Lightnin'" Hopkins

[139]

programs, at college concerts, and elsewhere. Along with them came offers from many record companies for recording dates.

The result was a tremendous outpouring of Hopkins recordings from the 1950s on. He was featured on many labels, though most of his work in the '60s was on the Bluesville label of Prestige Records. His 1950 LPs included "Lightnin' Hopkins and the Blues" on Imperial; a two-volume set, "Lightnin' Hopkins," on Time Records; "Lightnin' Strikes" on Vee; "Lightnin' Hopkins" on Folklore ('59); and "Goin' Away," "Gotta Move Your Baby," and "Greatest Hits" on Bluesville. In 1960, he was represented on two Tradition LPs, "Autobiography in Blues" and "Country Blues."

His 1960s output for Bluesville included "Lightnin'" ('61); "Walkin' This Road by Myself," "Blues in My Bottle" ('62); "Lightnin' & Co.," "Smokes Like Lightnin'" ('63); and "Hootin' the Blues" (Prestige—'64). He was also featured on such other labels as Arhoolie ("Lightnin' Sam Hopkins"—'62, "Early Recordings"—'64); Verve ("Fast Life Woman"—'62); Herald ("Lightnin' & the Blues"—'60); and World ("First Meetin'"—'64).

HORTON, JOHNNY: Singer, guitarist. Born Tyler, Texas, April 3, 1929; died November 5, 1960.

Most Americans have an affinity for the automobile. The bond is even closer for most country performers; coming as many do from rural, often poverty-stricken areas, the car represents escape from a life of drudgery. The relationship, though, has had some tragic overtones. Because country artists often perform in small towns, out of the way of regular transportation, such as airlines, the car is often the only way to travel. The combination of long rides and odd hours has resulted in the loss of many major artists in automobile accidents.

Such a mishap ended Johnny Horton's career on November 5, 1960. It occurred just when he seemed on the way to the most important phase of his career, when his recording of "Battle of New Orleans" was a smash hit all over the world.

Horton was raised on a farm and had to work hard at chores as soon as he was old enough to help out his share-cropping parents. His mother had considerable musical talent, and taught Johnny to play the guitar when he was eleven. Johnny was also physically strong and a tal-

ented athlete. His prowess in high school and at Lon Morris Junior College, Jacksonville, Texas, and Kilgore Junior College, Kilgore, Texas, led to offers from many colleges for an athletic scholarship. He finally accepted a basketball bid from Baylor University in Waco, and went there for some time before transferring to the University of Seattle, in Washington. Johnny had a lifelong interest in fishing, and left Seattle for Alaska (without receiving his degree) to work as a fisherman.

In 1950, he went south to Los Angeles where he also worked for a time in the fishing industry. His singing ability caused some of his friends to talk him into entering a contest at Harmony Park Corral, Anaheim, California. He won the contest and also the attention of such people as Cliffie Stone and Tennessee Ernie Ford. (His fishing background earned him the designation "The Singing Fisherman.") He soon gained a spot on KXLA radio in Pasadena. He also was featured on Cliffie Stone's Hometown Jamboree TV show on KLAC for several years.

His growing reputation led to a bid from the Louisiana Hayride in Shreveport, which he accepted in 1955. He became a leading artist on the show in short order and remained one of the Hayride's main attractions for the rest of his life. He also played engagements at county fairs, clubs, etc., throughout the country and had guest shots on many major country shows, including the Grand Ole Opry. In addition, he had his own show Monday nights in the late 1950s over station KLTV, Tyler, Texas.

Soon after Johnny moved to Shreveport, his recordings for Columbia began to hit the top of the song charts. In 1957, he clicked with "I'm Just a One Woman Man." In 1958, he had a top 10 hit, "All Grown Up." The following year, he really began to move with three top 10 hits: "Johnny Reb," "When It's Springtime in Alaska," and the number-one-ranked "Battle of New Orleans." Johnny followed up in 1960 with a top 10 hit of his own composition (written with Tillman Franks), "Sink the Bismarck." He also turned out another 1960 effort that was number one nationwide for many weeks, "North to Alaska."

With his popularity at an all-time high, Johnny was in demand for an increasing number of personal appearances in widely separated parts of the country. On November 5, 1960, he finished a show in Louisiana and got in his car to drive to Nashville, where he was scheduled as a headline act at the disk jockey convention. He was killed instantly, however, in a jarring collision en route.

As happened with other stars, his voice remained widely popular on records. In 1961, he had a top 10 hit, "Sleepy Eyed John." His LPs, which included several issued after his death, also maintained a steady sales pace.

HORTON, VAUGHN: Singer, instrumentalist, songwriter, record producer. Born Broad Top, Pennsylvania, June 6, 1911.

The line separating country and western music from the general run of the popular field is often a thin one. Many of the best-selling songs in the country and western field become even greater hits in the popular market. And, among the top country and western songwriters, many are equally at home in both segments of the field. This certainly is true of Vaughn Horton, whose career as both writer and performer embraced national success both ways.

Horton was born and raised in the eastern state of Pennsylvania, attending Robertsdale High School and Pennsylvania State College. In high school and college, Vaughn played with dance bands and, after graduation, went on to work as a sideman with many of the name bands of the 1930s and '40s. During these years, he began writing his own words and music.

His interest in country music increased with the years. By the 1940s, he was also performing with country and western groups in the eastern part of the country. It wasn't long before he was turning out country and western material that was performed by many other top artists. During the 1940s and '50s, Horton toured with various country and western groups and also was heard on many radio stations in various parts of the country.

One of Horton's first million-selling compositions was in the popular field, "Mockin' Bird Hill." By 1967, he had added eight more gold record songs to his total in both popular and country and western. Thirty more of his several-hundred-song output over the years sold more than half a million each. Two of his early national best-sellers in the country and western field were Jimmy Wakely's 1949 recording of "Til the End of the World" and Little Jimmy Dickens' 1950 "Hillbilly Fever."

Some of Horton's other hits included "Teardrops in My Heart," "Choo Choo Ch'Boogie," "Blossoms in the Springtime," "As long as I'm Dreaming," "Mule Skinner Blues," "Sugarfoot Rag," "Charlie Was a Boxer," "Toolie Oolie Doolie," "Small World," Plantation Boogie," "Address Unknown," "Metro Polka," "Come What May," "Julida Polka," "Breakin' in the Blues," "Baby Brother," "Swiss Lullaby," "Bar Room Polka," "An Old Christmas Card," "Flyin' Eagle Polka," "Heartbreak Trail," "Drina," "You Better Stop Tellin' Lies About Me," "Take Me Home," "Six O'Clock Supper," "Fountain of Youth," "Home Sweet Homesick Blues," "After the Hangover's Over," "Juke Joint Mama," "I Think I'm Gonna Cry Again," "Just a Few Little Miles from Home," "Hoe Cake, Hominy and Sassafras Tea" and "I Wish I Hadn't Told a Lie."

In the 1960s, Horton made his home in New York where he also produced records for many different labels. In 1966-67, he was represented on the song charts with two records by Dick Todd, "Big Wheel Cannonball" and "Pennsylvania Turnpike, I Love You." Horton's brother, Roy, heads the Peer International country music publishing efforts.

HOUSE, SON: Singer, guitarist, songwriter. Born Clarksville, Mississippi, March 21, 1902.

Eddie "Son" House was called the greatest exponent of the country blues, even though few people had ever heard him play and, for more than three decades nobody knew where he was or, indeed, if he was still alive. When he was rediscovered in the folk boom of the 1960s, the almost unanimous opinion of blues enthusiasts was that Son House was still the king of the country blues.

House was born in rural Mississippi, but moved to Tallulah, Louisiana, with his mother when he was seven or eight. His mother was a strict churchgoer and Son would not touch the guitar or sing blues songs in his youth. Those were considered sinful to his congregation. He did, however, sing with the church choir in whatever town he happened to live in.

His father and mother had separated before the move to Louisiana. When Son was old enough to work, he had to help his mother out. From 1916 to 1920, he worked gathering moss in Algiers, Louisiana. The moss was used for stuffing mattresses and furniture. During these years, he heard some news of his father, who played a bass horn for a time in bands that worked Saturday night affairs. This knowledge, though, did not cause Son to become interested in playing an instrument. Later his father became a church deacon and gave up his old ways.

At the start of the 1920s, Son's mother died and he went back to the Clarksville area. He made this home base, but spent a good part of the time working at odd jobs in surrounding states. He plowed, picked and chopped cotton, and once tended cattle. In 1923 he worked briefly in St. Louis, attracted by the high wages of a dollar an hour in the Commonwealth Steel Plant. After eight months, he had had enough of that.

In 1927, he finally decided to play guitar. He was in Matson, Mississippi, one Saturday when he heard two musicians named Willie Wilson and Reuben Lacy and was impressed particularly with Wilson's style. In 1928, Son bought an old guitar for $1.50 and took it to Wilson. Wilson fixed it up and showed Son some of the chords he used. In a little while, Son could play his first song, one learned from Wilson called "Hold Up Sally, Take Your Big Legs Offa Mine." When he played it for Wilson, the latter asked Son to work with him that Saturday night.

Within a short time, House had developed a distinctive style of his own. He also built up a backlog of songs, both from listening to others in the region and from making up his own compositions. In 1930, he met two performers called Willie Brown and Charlie Patton. Patton had made several records for Paramount Records in Grafton, Wisconsin. When Patton was asked to come up north again to make more recordings, he brought House and Brown along.

House recorded several solos, including "Preachin' Blues," "Black Mama," and "Mississippi County Farm" and two with Brown, one of them "Clarksdale Moan." He received $40 for this and returned to Mississippi. He played for country balls for the next few years before his next recording session. The second session occurred in 1932 for Spears Phonograph Co. in Jackson, Mississippi. House provided several originals, including "I Had a Dream Last Night Troubled Me."

After this, House made no more records for many years. He gave up playing for local affairs in the mid-1930s, and soon after stopped playing guitar altogether.

In 1943 he moved to Rochester, New York. After a brief fling at a defense plant job, he moved to the New York Central Railroad as a rivet-heater in a boxcar shop. Then he got a job as a porter in the railroad's Buffalo operation. Later, Willie Brown moved to Buffalo and the two occasionally played together again.

House remained with the New York Central for more than a decade. Finally, he was sought out by the team of Phil Spire, Nick Perls, and Dick Waterman. On Father's Day, 1964, they found him and shortly after House was on the way to nationwide acclaim from blues fans. He was given rousing ovations by audiences at major college campuses throughout the country and at such festivals as the Newport event. He also won new converts to the country blues with his recordings of songs like "Death Letter Blues," "Empire State Express," and "Pearline."

HOUSTON, CISCO: Singer, guitarist, songwriter. Born Wilmington, Delaware, August 18, 1918; died San Bernardino, California, April 29, 1961.

Gilbert "Cisco" Houston was regarded by his fellow artists as one of the greatest American balladeers as well as one of the finest human beings. His great legacy to folk music has been understood clearly only in the years since his untimely passing.

His close friend and long-time traveling companion Woody Guthrie once wrote for Folkways Records, "In my own mind, I see Cisco Houston as one of our manliest and best of our living crop of ballad and folksong singers. H is showman enough to make the grade and to hold any audience anywhere and at any time. I like Cisco as a man, I like him as a person, and as a fun loving, warmhearted, and likeable human being."

Cisco was born in Baltimore but spent only a few years there. His family came from the Carolinas and from Virginia. As a small boy, he heard many folk melodies from one of his grandmothers. When he was just reaching school age, his family moved to Los Angeles. He attended elementary and high school there, finding time to learn to play the guitar before graduating from high school.

Finishing school in the Depression-ridden 1930s, Cisco took his guitar and began his lifetime of wandering. He worked at many odd jobs, first in California and then in Colorado. For a good period in the late 1930s, he was employed as a cowboy on western ranches. This gave him the opportunity to learn firsthand many traditional cowboy songs.

During these years, Cisco performed in many places. He sang for his friends and also in front of audiences in local clubs. On several occasions, he also sang on radio stations in the western region.

In his wanderings, Cisco met or was sought out by many folk musicians. Among them were Woody Guthrie, Huddie Ledbetter, and John Jacob Niles. One of his earliest contacts was with Woody Guthrie. In the late 1930s and early '40s, Guthrie and Cisco toured through many states together, singing at small gatherings, union meetings, and small clubs. On several occasions, Cisco traveled to New York, meeting, among others, Moses Asch, later the founder of Folkways Records.

Despite poor eyesight, Cisco managed to enlist in the Merchant Marine during World War II. He remained in the service throughout the war, surviving three separate torpedoings of ships he was on. During these years, Cisco reached ports throughout the world; in each he picked up new material for his folk repertoire.

After the war, Cisco settled for a while in New York, then moved to Hollywood. He increased his performing pace, singing with many of the most gifted artists in the folk field. Besides working with Ledbetter in the late 1940s and again teaming with Guthrie, Cisco sang with such others as John Jacob Niles, Burl Ives, and Lee Hays, and accompanied many of the top artists in recording sessions. He performed on two of the first LPs issued by Moe Asch's new company in 1948.

Throughout the 1950s, Houston continued to perform before audiences across the nation. He was featured in concerts on college campuses, in churches, in leading nightclubs and in such places as New York's Town Hall and Madison Square Garden. During the 1950s, he was seen or heard on radio and TV, including the American Inventory program and on folk music programs broadcast by Mutual Broadcasting System.

In 1959, Houston toured India under the sponsorship of the State Department and the American National Theatre and Academy. In June of the following year, he served as m.c. for the CBS program Folk Music, U.S.A.

During these years, Cisco turned out recordings for many labels, including Folkways, Stinson, Disc, Coral, Decca and Vanguard. Releases of his performances continued at a steady pace after his death. His Folkways LPs included "Lonesome Valley," "Railroad Songs," "Cowboy Songs," "Hard Traveling," "Cisco Houston Sings," "Songs of the Open Road" and "Songs to Grow On." In 1960, Vanguard issued its first Houston LP, "Cisco Special." In later years, it issued "Songs of Woody Guthrie" ('61) and "I Ain't Got No Home" ('62). In 1964, Disc issued an LP, "Legacy of Cisco Houston."

Over the years, Houston showed himself to be a talented songwriter and arranger as well as performer. Some of his compositions, such as "A Dollar Down," "Bad Man Blunder," and "Ramblin' Gamblin' Man," were included in a commemorative song book, *900 Miles, the Ballads Blues and Folksongs of Cisco Houston,* issued by Oak Publications in 1965.

In 1960, Cisco developed cancer. He died in a hospital in San Bernardino, California. His passing at 42 was mourned not just in obituary columns, but with the more positive tribute of songs to his memory, such as "Fare Thee Well, Cisco" by Tom Paxton, "Cisco Houston Passed This Way," by his protege Peter La Farge, and "Blues for Cisco Houston" by Tom McGrath.

HOUSTON, DAVID: Singer, guitarist. Born Shreveport, Louisiana, December 9, 1938.

If heredity had any bearing on accomplishment, it would seem that a direct descendant of both Sam Houston and General Robert E. Lee would have a good chance to succeed in his chosen field. By the late 1960s, this seemed to be the case for David Houston (his mother's maiden name was Lee) in his choice of country music. His 1966 million-selling record of "Almost Persuaded" won him both Billboard and Cashbox awards for the number-one country record of 1966.

In addition to his illustrious forebears, David had the help of a musical environment in his early years in Bossier City, Louisiana. His parents were both interested in music and one of his father's close friends was a great popular singer of the 1920s, Gene Austin. With Austin's encouragement, David began singing lessons when he was four years old. A few years later, he began taking guitar lessons from his aunt who taught music. He also became proficient at the piano keyboard as well. When he was 12, he auditioned for Horace Logan, producer of the Louisiana Hayride. Logan was impressed and featured young Houston on one show. Some time later, Houston was asked to join the Hayride cast as a regular.

Despite the warm response to his appearance on TV in his teen years, David did not try for a full-time music career until he was attending college. By the late 1950s, he was touring many major cities and playing on TV shows to increasing industry notice.

In the early 1960s, David signed with Epic Records. His first release in 1963, "Mountain of Love," sold more than 300,000 copies and was on the national hit charts for 16 weeks. This performance won him the award from national music trade magazines as the Most Promising Country Performer of 1964.

David came right back in 1965 with a record that had a four-month stay on the charts, "Livin' in a House Full of Love." In 1966, he topped all his previous efforts with "Almost Persuaded." The year 1967 found him scoring once more with his record of "Loser's Cathedral." Other Houston recordings that gained wide acceptance included "Chickashay," "One If for Him," "Sweet, Sweet Judy," and "The Ballad of the Fool Killer."

Through 1967, Epic produced three LPs of Houston's songs, "New Voice from Nashville," "David Houston Sings 12 Great Country Hits," and "Almost Persuaded." The third of these sold well over 200,000 copies. Houston also completed his first movie in 1967, "Cotton-pickin' Chickenpickers," which co-starred him with Sonny Tufts, Del Reeves, Margie Bowes and Maxie Rosenbloom. Houston had a major hit in 1968 with his rendition of "Already It's Heaven."

HOWARD, HARLAN: Songwriter, singer, publisher. Born Harlan County, Kentucky, September 8, 1929.

Although born in fabled Harlan County, Kentucky, young Harlan was raised in and around Detroit, where his parents moved when he was two years old. Their background and the wattage power of WSM's Grand Ole Opry into Detroit provided the boy with country music indoctrination.

His idol, Ernest Tubb, indirectly taught Howard how to write lyrics. Tubb would sing on the Opry and Howard would attempt to write down the lyrics, his quick ear retaining the melodies easily enough. There were gaps in the lyrics and he would fill them in, add new verses, and get a sort of Ernest Tubb song as a result. This led him to try writing his own songs using the earthy three and four chord struc-

tures of his favorite writers, Tubb, Fred Rose, Floyd Tillman and Rex Griffen.

Four years with the paratroopers followed his graduation from high school and it was here that buddies taught him to pick the guitar. He would head directly for Nashville from his Fort Benning, Georgia, base on Friday nights with a buddy, hitchhiking both ways. Sometimes the luck of the thumb was sour and they would report back to the base late for Monday's roll call.

Following his army tour, Howard worked at various jobs in Michigan, Tucson, and finally Los Angeles. It was there that he met Johnny Bond and Tex Ritter, both of whom took an interest in his writing, publishing his songs in their firms. This was in the latter '50s, a period that saw Wynn Stewart, Buck Owens, Bobby Bare, Skeets McDonald and others trying their luck on the California country nightclub and recording circuit.

It was Stewart who recorded Howard's first song, "You Took Her Off My Hands," for Capitol Records, under Ken Nelson's direction. It wasn't long before Columbia's Don Law recorded Charlie Walker with "Pick Me Up on Your Way Down," Howard's first recognized national hit. These were followed with Kitty Wells' "Mommy for a Day" and Ray Price's "Heartaches by the Number," which hit the pop charts with a cover record by Guy Mitchell.

With royalty money coming in nicely, Howard decided to go where the hits were being cut. In June 1960 he moved to Nashville. The first of his 400-plus recordings was made and in both 1961 and 1962 he was awarded Billboard's top country and western songwriter award.

Howard kept up correspondence with country disk jockeys and artists. He regularly covered recording sessions in the various Nashville studios, the Grand Ole Opry and other pipelines of the business. In 1964 he started his own publishing firm, Wilderness Music Publishing Company. As of 1968 he lived in Madison, Tennessee, with his wife, Jan Howard—also a recording artist—and their three sons. Howard, as many others in his circle, remained an avid fisherman in fishing country.

His BMI award hits include: 1959—"Mommy for a Day," "Pick Me Up on Your Way Down," "Heartaches by the Number"; 1960—"Above and Beyond (the Call of Love)," "Three Steps to the Phone," "I Don't Believe I'll Fall in

Love Today," "Odds and Ends (Bits and Pieces)," "Under the Influence of Love," "I Fall to Pieces," "I Wish I Could Fall in Love Today," "Heartbreak USA," "The Blizzard," "Foolin' Around"; 1963—"Don't Call Me from a Honky Tonk," "You Took Her Off My Hands," "Busted," "Second Hand Rose (Second Hand Heart)," "You Comb Her Hair"; 1964—"Your Heart Turned Left"; 1965—"I Won't Forget You," "I've Got a Tiger by the Tail"; 1966—"Streets of Baltimore," "Evil on Your Mind," "It's All Over (But the Crying)."

Howard recorded for RCA Victor, but as of 1969 was not overly anxious to make the personal appearance grind of one-nighters. He preferred to stay at his office, plug his Wilderness songs, stay at home with his family or get lost fishing in one of the nearby lakes. (*See also* HOWARD, JAN)

HOWARD, JAN (MRS. HARLAN HOWARD): Singer. Born West Plains, Missouri, March 13, 1932.

It helps if you're a songwriter to have a wife with a good voice to make demonstration records. On the other hand, it is an equal advantage for such a wife to have a husband who can supply her with best-selling songs, such as Harlan Howard.

The idea of a music career seemed remote when Jan was growing up in West Plains, Missouri. However, she did enjoy listening to country and western music and sang along with records and radio programs as she reached her teens. She began to perform at local affairs, and in time moved to Los Angeles to try to further her musical background.

In California, she met an up-and-coming songwriter named Harlan Howard. It wasn't long before she became Mrs. Howard. She settled down to raise a family which after several years of marriage included three boys. Harlan made use of her singing ability on some demonstration records of new songs. There were plenty of listeners for these disks, for by this time Harlan was one of the most successful songwriters in the business.

One recording executive was as impressed with Mrs. Howard's voice as with the song. In short order, Jan was complementing her housewifely chores with a part-time career as singer and recording artist. For Challenge Records, she turned out a number of hits, such as "Yankee Go Home," "The One You Slip Around With," and "A World I Can't Live In." Her ability was recognized by the jukebox operators of America, who selected her as the Most Promising Country and Western Female Vocalist for 1960. Shortly after, she received similar awards from Billboard and Cashbox.

In the 1960s, she was featured on a number of network TV shows, including appearances on the Grand Ole Opry. As her home schedule permitted, she also made personal appearances in many states and overseas. She was represented on LPs in 1962 with the Wrangler Records "Jan Howard." In the mid-1960s, she signed with Decca Records. Among her successes on the label was the 1966 nationwide top 10 hit, "Evil on Your Mind." The songwriter's name was naturally Harlan Howard. Her 1967 hits included "Roll Over and Play Dead." Her 1968 output for Decca included a hit LP, "Count Your Blessings, Woman." (*See also* HOWARD, HARLAN)

HURT, MISSISSIPPI JOHN: Singer, guitarist. Born Teoc, Carroll County, Mississippi, March 8, 1892; died Grenada, Mississippi, November 2, 1966.

In July 1963, the audience at the Newport

Delta Blues great, Mississippi John Hurt

Folk Festival saw a "ghost." It was a legendary 72-year-old artist who had dropped from sight 35 years earlier and had been thought to have passed away many years before. Within moments, the crowd knew that Mississippi John Hurt was very much alive and very much deserving of all the praise for his few recordings of many years ago. His performance was one of the finest of the Festival and, in appreciation, the officials gave him a new guitar when the Festival ended.

Hurt had first started playing the guitar at nine. His mother gave him a $1.50 Black Anne for a present, and in a short time he taught himself to play it. His home town of Avalon, Mississippi, where he remained almost his entire life, was in a remote part of the country and he had little contact with the folk artists who wandered through Mississippi. As he told one interviewer, he developed his own guitar style. "I taught myself to play the way I thought a guitar should sound."

As he grew older, he learned as many songs as he could from the field hands and other workers in his area. He played for enjoyment, earning his normal meager living from odd jobs. At one time or another, he worked as a field hand picking cotton and corn, worked cattle, spent time on the Mississippi River, was a railroad hand, and, in the 1930s, was on the WPA payroll.

Though he received little money, he played at many local dances and celebrations from the early 1900s on. He occasionally picked up new material from both white and colored itinerant singers who passed through Avalon. In the 1920s, he was able to listen to some of the new crop of country records turned out by major eastern companies. He was greatly interested in the songs of fellow Mississippian Jimmie Rodgers that began to receive attention throughout the south after 1927. In addition to using songs from other sources, Hurt sometimes made up his own, such as the murder ballad "Louis Collins."

Until 1928, practically no one had heard of him outside of Carroll County and a few counties nearby. In that year, Okeh Records' recording director, Tommy Rockwell, was touring Mississippi looking for country artists. Two white musicians suggested that he see Hurt. Rockwell was impressed with John's talent and brought him to Memphis for a recording session. Hurt was paid $240 plus expenses for making eight recordings. Two of these, "Frankie" and "Nobody's Dirty Business," were released. They sold even better than expected and Rockwell sought Hurt out again, this time to bring him to New York. On December 21 and 28 of 1928, Hurt recorded such songs as "Louis Collins," "Candy Man," "Spike Driver Blues," "Stagger Lee Blues" and "Avalon Blues."

Hurt went home to Avalon. He probably would have achieved national success, but the Depression put an end to this record market. Hurt continued to follow his normal pattern of hard work and leisure-time singing for the next three decades. By the time interest in Hurt, based on his fine recordings, was rekindled after World War II, no one could recall where he was. Many folklorists searched for him and finally concluded he had probably died.

Then blues collector Tom Hoskins of Washington, D.C., suddenly realized the connection between Avalon Blues and Hurt. He went to Avalon, Mississippi, in 1963 and found his man. He talked John into going back to Washington with him. In a short time, John had an enthusiastic following at the local Ontario Place coffee house. Later that year, at Newport, he achieved a national reputation. During the mid-1960s, he won praise from audiences at festivals and concerts in many parts of the U.S. He also was once more represented on records. The first new album was "Presenting Mississippi John Hurt: Folk Songs and Blues," produced by Piedmont Records in 1963. A second LP, "Worried Blues," was turned out by the same company in late 1964.

HUSKY, FERLIN: Singer, guitarist, comedian, songwriter. Born Flat River, Missouri, December 3, 1927.

Simon Crum, Terry Preston, Ferlin Husky— these are all the same person, an excellent example of a successful musical split personality. So well has Ferlin Husky developed the rural hayseed character of Crum, in fact, that many country music fans accept Crum as a separate individual. (Ferlin also spelled his last name "Huskey" on earlier recordings.)

The dichotomy affects the records of Ferlin's early history. His birthplace is officially given as Flat River, but biographies also list it as either Hickory Grove or Cantrell, Missouri. There is good reason for this, since Ferlin was born on a farm located at almost equal distance from all three small towns. Husky grew up on the farm, attending rural schools and helping with the chores in his free time.

When still a little boy, he saw an old guitar in a neighbor's barn. Brought up on the guitar and fiddle music of local dances and parties, he immediately wanted to get the instrument. He talked his parents into offering to trade a hen for the guitar, but the neighbors cancelled the deal when the hen would not lay eggs.

Later on, he did get a guitar and learned to play it. Ferlin's career in music eventually got its main push, though, from his ability as an announcer. His succession of disk jockey jobs landed him in Bakersfield, California, in 1949. Ferlin felt his own name sounded made up, so he went under the assumed name of Terry Preston. It was as Preston that he performed at various dates in the Bakersfield area in the late 1940s.

Meanwhile, Husky varied his announcing chores by introducing a new, comic philosopher character as part of his show. Simon Crum quickly caught on with the audience, so much so that Husky's first recording contract with Capitol was to do several sides as Crum.

This led to the chance to record "straight" country songs under the name of Terry Preston in the early 1950s. One of these was a duet with Jean Shepard. The song, "Dear John Letter," became a number-one national hit in 1953. That year, Ferlin wrote an ode to his country music idol, Hank Williams, who had just passed away. This song, "Hank's Song," was released under Ferlin's own name. Its success insured the permanent retirement of Terry Preston, though not Simon Crum.

From 1953 on Husky's career moved steadily ahead. He toured the country and was featured on radio and TV shows in both the popular and country fields. In 1957, he showed his versatility by playing a starring dramatic role in a Kraft TV Theatre play. In 1958, he debuted in the movies in "Country Music Holiday," with Faron Young and Zsa Zsa Gabor as co-stars.

In 1957, he re-recorded a song he had originally made in 1952 as Terry Preston. The 1957 version of "(Since You've) Gone" was one of the major hits of the year. Ferlin also had a top 10 hit in 1957 with "Fallen Star." In 1958, the personality of Simon Crum made a major impact on the nation with the comic hit, "Country Music Is Here to Stay." Husky

Ferlin Husky, alias Simon Crum

started off the 1960s with another number-one nationwide hit, "On the Wings of a Dove."

During the late 1950s and '60s, Husky's LP albums were consistently on the best-seller lists. His output for Capitol included: "Ferlin Husky and His Hush Puppies," "Boulevard of Broken Dreams," "Born to Lose," "Ferlin Husky," "Ferlin Husky's Favorites" ('59); "Gone" ('60); "Walkin' and Hummin'," "Memories of Home" ('61); "Some of My Favorites" ('62); "Heart and Soul of Ferlin Husky," "Hits of Ferlin Husky" ('63); "By Request" ('64); "True, True Lovin'"; "Songs of Music City, U.S.A.," "I Could Sing All Night," "What Am I Gonna Do Now." He also was represented on King label with "Ferlin Husky" ('59).

IAN AND SYLVIA: Vocal and instrumental duo, Ian Tyson, born British Columbia, Canada, September 25, 1933; Sylvia Fricker (Mrs. Tyson), born Chatham, Ontario, September 19, 1940.

"Ian and Sylvia sing close, pretty harmony, synchronizing words and phrases perfectly, although each also soloed several times. Their range of material is impressive; they sang bluegrass, blues, ballads, pop tunes, a striking French-Canadian song and traditional as well as contemporary folk numbers. . . . Every song drew heavy applause, which grew nearly deafening after they forsook the fuzzy microphones (the sound equipment was faulty) at the request of the audience."

Thus did Los Angeles *Times* writer Pete Johnson describe the March 1967 concert of the Canadian folk team of Ian and Sylvia at the Lindy Opera House in Los Angeles. He concluded, "The well-groomed young Canadians have a massive local following, judging from Sunday night's turnout, and judging from their concert performance they deserve it."

The concert demonstrated the hold the team had achieved among folk music fans across the country in a few years' time. Born at opposite ends of Canada, their paths did not cross until 1959. Ian was born and brought up on a farm in British Columbia, Canada's far western province. He left school in his teens to work at a series of jobs. For a while he was a farmhand, then a rodeo performer. He also worked as a lumberjack and commercial artist during the 1950s.

Ian had a strong interest in folk music and learned to play guitar in his teens. As he wandered across Canada, he picked up many folk songs from various parts of the country. By the late 1950s, he occasionally performed at small clubs and coffee houses in Canadian cities.

His journey through Canada eventually took him to Toronto, Ontario, in 1959. Sylvia Fricker was born in Chatham, near Toronto, and spent her school years in that region. She gained an interest in music from her mother, who played organ, directed a local choir, and also taught music. She had an excellent voice which she sometimes put to good use in local events. She enjoyed folk music and spent time at the Purple Onion, a folk music club in Toronto. There she met Ian and the two became friends. They found common interest in folk music and began working together in 1960. They started in local clubs in the Toronto area, then began performing in other cities.

In the early 1960s they began to be featured in coffee houses and clubs in the U.S. Before long they were receiving attention from folk music fans in many parts of America. By 1964,

they were among the best known of the new singing teams of the folk song boom. They signed with Vanguard Records and also were featured on major TV shows, including Jack Linkletter's Hootenanny.

One of their first major hits was "Four Strong Winds," a song written by Ian. The song also served as the title number for their first Vanguard LP. During 1964, Vanguard issued a second album, featuring their Canadian folk song repertoire, "Northern Journey." Their popularity was demonstrated in February 1964, when a capacity audience greeted their concert in New York's Town Hall. The year was successful in another way; on June 26, Ian and Sylvia were married.

In the mid-1960s, despite the bursting of the folk music commercial bubble, their fortunes continued to rise. They were well received in concerts in all parts of the United States and Canada. Their repertoire included such numbers as the Beatles' "She's a Woman," "Catfish Blues"; Sylvia's composition (a major popular hit) "You Were on My Mind"; "Circle Game," "Bill Martin," "Little Beggar Man," and their joint composition, "Mr. Spoons."

IVES, BURL: Singer, guitarist, actor. Born Huntington Township, Jasper County, Illinois, June 14, 1909.

Considered one of the greatest folksingers of the twentieth century, Burl Icle Ivanhoe Ives' talents extended far beyond this one field. He starred in musical comedy in such roles as Cap'n Andy in "Showboat," as an actor in both stage and film dramas, and as a popular entertainer on radio and TV. In addition, his name graced the hit lists of country and western music on more than one occasion.

Folk singing was a tradition handed down through many generations in his family. Some of the songs had been brought from the old country by his English-Irish ancestors when they came to America in the 1600s. One of six children of tenant farmers Frank and Dellie Ives, Burl heard ballads from his family and friends at many rural sings. His grandmother Katie White, in particular, taught him many traditional melodies.

Burl's career as a public performer began when he was four; he sang "Barbara Allen" at an old soldiers' reunion in his home region. By the time he was attending Newton High School, he had mastered the banjo and often sang in school shows and other community events. Despite his obvious musical talent, he was prouder of his ability as a fullback on the high school team. When he graduated high school in 1927, he enrolled in Eastern Illinois Teachers College with the idea of becoming a football coach.

After two years of college, though, he felt the urge to travel. He left school and rambled across the U.S., Canada, and Mexico, making his way by hitching rides or riding the rods. He worked at odd jobs or played his banjo to earn spending money. This trip had a major effect on him, showing him the many facets of the world not available in books. It also provided him with a store of new folk material gathered along the way. At one point, in Mona, Utah, the local police threw him in jail for singing "Foggy Foggy Dew," which they considered a dirty song. During his wanderings, he also taught himself to play guitar.

Returning to the midwest, he enrolled in Indiana State Teachers College, Terre Haute. He worked in a drugstore and sang on local radio to help pay his way. Again he dropped out of school and played professional football, as well as holding down various odd jobs. Finally, in 1937, he made his way to New York, enrolling in New York University to take some formal vocal training while looking for jobs in the entertainment field.

After many months of hand-to-mouth existence, he got his first break playing summer stock in 1938 in Rockridge Theatre, Carmel, New York. This brought him to the attention of librettist-producer George Abbott, who wrote a small part for him into the Broadway show "The Boys from Syracuse." This led to other roles in such shows as "Ah, Wilderness!" and "I Married an Angel" and a personal appearance as a folk artist at New York's Village Vanguard. By now, Ives had made many friends in the folk singing fraternity, including Woody Guthrie and Earl Robinson.

Good reaction to his performances on several NBC and CBS radio shows led to his gaining his own show on CBS in 1940. One of his ballads, "The Wayfarin' Stranger," served as title for the show, which became one of the most popular on the air. His career then was interrupted by an 18-month Army hitch, 1942-44, during which time he starred in Irving Berlin's "This Is the Army."

Discharge in hand, Burl returned to New York to star for many months at the Cafe Society Uptown. He later appeared in the folk song cavalcade "Sing Out, Sweet Land," and won critical raves for his singing of such numbers as "Foggy Foggy Dew" and "Blue-Tailed Fly." His work won him the Donaldson Award as Best Supporting Actor in the 1944-45 Broadway season. Late in '45, he gave his first major concert in New York's Town Hall before a sellout crowd. In 1946, the first movie featuring Ives appeared, a western called "Smoky" in which he played a singing cowboy.

Now one of the best known artists in the country, Burl completed his autobiography, *Wayfarin' Stranger,* and it was published in 1948 by McGraw-Hill. After several more films, Ives returned to Broadway in 1954 to play Cap'n Andy in a revival of "Showboat." In 1955, his dramatic portrayal of Big Daddy in Tennessee Williams' "Cat on a Hot Tin Roof" gained unanimous approval from the critics. Later he repeated the role in the film, which was released in 1958. He followed this with parts in such other movies as "Desire Under the Elms," "The Big Country" (1958), and "Our Man in Havana." His performance in a supporting role in "The Big Country" won him an Academy Award.

Throughout the 1950s and '60s, Ives kept active in many other ways. He compiled many books of folk songs, the first being a collection of 115 songs published in 1953. He continued to work as a singer both in personal appearances and as a guest star on major radio and TV shows. For Decca and Columbia, he also turned out record after record, many of which became major hits. For Decca he provided such albums as "Ballads and Folk Songs," Vols. 1-3 ('49); "Captain Burl Ives' Ark"; "Christmas Day in the Morning"; "Australian Folk Song" ('52); "Coronation Concert"; "Down to the Sea in Ships"; "Folk Songs Dramatic and Humorous"; "Songs of Ireland"; "Men"; "Women"; "Old Time Varieties"; "Christmas Eve with Burl Ives" ('58); and "Cheers with the Charles Singers" ('59). For Columbia, his LPs included "The Return of the Wayfaring Stranger" ('49); "The Wayfaring Stranger"; "Children's Favorites"; "Sings Songs for All Ages"; and "More Folksongs." He was also represented on such other labels as Stinson and United Artists, and made six records of "Historical America in Song" for a series of Encyclopaedia Britannica Films.

In the early 1960s, Ives turned out a series of records that became major hits in both the popular and country and western markets. In 1962, he had three top 10 hits for Decca, "A Little Bitty Tear," "Call Me Mr. In-Between" and "Funny Way of Laughin'." His Decca LPs in the '60s included "Versatile Burl Ives," "Best of Burl Ives" ('61); "Funny Way of Laughin'," "Sunshine in My Soul," "Songs of the West" ('62); "Burl," "Singin' Easy" ('63); "True Love" ('64); "My Gal Sal" ('65). Columbia Records also reissued "The Return of the Wayfaring Stranger" in 1960 and "Wayfaring Stranger" in 1965.

In 1967, Ives returned to Broadway in a short-lived drama, "Dr. Cook's Garden."

JACKSON, AUNT MOLLY: Singer, songwriter, union organizer. Born Clay County, Kentucky, 1880; died September 1, 1960.

". . . After the miners was blacklisted for joining the union, March 5, 1931, the company doctor refused to come to any one of the coal miners' families unless he paid in advance. So I had to nurse all the little children till the last breath left them, and all the light I had was a string in a can lid with a little bacon grease in it. Kerosene was five cents a quart, and I could not get five cents. Thirty-seven babies died in my arms in the last three months of 1931. Their little stomachs busted open; they was mortified inside. Oh, what an awful way for a baby to die. . . ." (Letter from Aunt Molly Jackson to John Greenway, quoted in notes for Folkways Album FH 5457.)

It was with justification that Aunt Molly Jackson could say "I believe I have had more trouble than any other poor woman who has ever been born." Despite this, she remained an indomitable figure to the end, a pioneer in the union movement and a great name in folk music.

She was born Mary Magdalene Garland in Clay County, Kentucky, to a family that had been one of the earliest settlers of the region. For decades before her birth, the Garlands and her other kinfolk, the Robinsons, had wrested a living by working their small farms on land their forebears had cleared. However, the area was found to be rich in coal, a vital ingredient in the booming industrial revolution. In the late 1800s, the coal mines became the most important economic factor in the area and most of the local people ended up working in the mines for starvation wages.

Mary's father worked in the mines. But he also was a preacher and a man who could not abide the terrible conditions his friends and neighbors were enduring. He became a union organizer and fought the coal barons. When Mary was five, she sometimes walked the picket lines with her father, as did her brothers and sisters.

Life was a continuous struggle for existence. In 1886, her mother died of starvation. Two years earlier, in more peaceful times, the four-year-old girl had written her first song based on the theme "love your neighbor." Despite a life of privation, in which she learned hate and bitterness, she still could sing many songs, both her own and traditional ballads, of hope and beauty. However, most of her songs were of sorrow or of strong conviction in behalf of union causes.

She went to jail for her family's union efforts when she was only 10. In the tradition of the hills, she was married off to a man named Jackson when she was only 14. Later on, still in her teens, she became a nurse and spent many of her years waging a futile battle against poverty, disease, and starvation.

As she grew older, life became harder rather than easier. She continued to fight for union causes against terrible odds while the mines claimed one after another of her dear ones. Her father was blinded in a mine accident, as was one of her brothers. Another brother, her husband, and her son were killed in mine accidents. One of her songs, "Poor Miner's Farewell," was written three weeks after her brother's death. Songwriting was one of her few pleasures as well as a weapon in behalf of the miners. In 1910, when she was urging the miners to strike for higher wages, she castigated the mine owner, a man named Colman, in "Hard Times in Colman's Mines." She did not ignore other folk themes, however. She knew and enjoyed singing many of the traditional hill-country ballads, many directly related to English folk songs. In the folk tradition, she wrote new words or changed the tunes slightly to provide new song forms, such as "The Dishonest Miller" and "The Birth of Robin Hood."

Aunt Molly continued to live in Clay County and work in union affairs for a decade after World War I. The Depression brought even greater hardships to an already suffering people. In 1930-31, unemployment, starvation, and riots were the order of the day. Undeclared war existed between mine owners and union organizers as summarized in her 1931 song, "The Death of Harry Simms." By the early 1930s, Aunt Molly had become too great a thorn in the side of local authorities. She was forced to leave Kentucky, and moved to New York.

In New York, other union leaders took up her cause. She sang at labor meetings and her ability came to the attention of folk song enthusiasts. Among those who became interested in her were the Lomaxes, who soon began to record much of her repertoire. During the 1930s and '40s, she made several hundred recordings for the Archive of American Folk Song. She was also sought out by private collectors from colleges and universities for recording sessions or for interviews on some of her folk material.

In the late 1950s, her health began to fail. She continued to write new songs for her beloved laboring class, but she could no longer sing. One of her close friends was folklorist John Greenway, who helped her plan her first commercial album for Folkways Records. It was agreed that Greenway would sing her songs, but she would introduce them with short introductions that also would serve as a brief autobiography. However, a week before taping was to start, she passed away. Greenway completed the album, "The Songs and Stories of Aunt Molly Jackson," which was released in late 1961.

JACKSON, STONEWALL: Singer, guitarist, songwriter. Born Tabor City, North Carolina, November 6, 1932.

"Stonewall" sounds like a nickname, but in Stonewall Jackson's case it's his given name. His father named him after the famed Confederate general, though the latter's real name was Thomas Jonathan. Be that as it may, Stonewall lived up to his name by becoming a hard man to move from the hit charts from 1959 on.

Jackson's early road was not an easy one. His father died when he was two years old and young Stonewall was brought up in the southern part of Georgia. He had few toys, but one was a worn tire-less five-dollar bike. When he was 10, he traded this for an old guitar, one of the important steps in his life. Stonewall took the guitar, and watched some of the older boys

in the neighborhood play. Gradually he figured out the fingering for some of the chords and began to play, himself. Before long, he was singing some of the songs he heard on the radio and on records. In a few years, he went beyond this and started to make up his own songs. Some of these, such as "Don't Be Angry" and "Black Sheep," later became hits for him.

When he was 17, he signed up with the Navy and entered the submarine service. One of his stations was Norfolk, Virginia; it was here that he bought his first good guitar. He played whenever he could and was asked, on several occasions, to entertain the crews. He enjoyed the applause and decided to try for a career in music some day. In 1954, he was discharged and headed home to Georgia.

He continued to write songs and began to figure out how to get started in show business. The obvious goal was the country music capital, Nashville, but he needed a stake. For the next two years he worked on a farm in the summer and logged during the winter. Finally he had enough money saved for the trip to Nashville and he headed there in 1956.

He quickly went to the studios of Acuff-Rose Publishing Company to make some sample records (dubs) of his songs. He intended to take these around to stars of the Grand Ole Opry in hopes that they would record them. He finished the dubs and left while they were being prepared. While he was away, Wesley Rose heard them being played and was quick to ask who'd done them. Rose called Jackson and said he'd arranged an audition with the talent directors. They listened to Jackson and signed him to a long-term contract. Shortly after, Jackson found himself putting his signature to a contract with Columbia Records.

Audiences took to the newcomer right away. Within a short time, he was known to people across the country from his TV appearances. In 1958, he scored his first top 10 hit, "Life to Go." He followed this with the 1959 number-one-rated "Waterloo." The song not only became a top country and western hit, it made the national pop charts as well. As a result, he was starred three times on the coast-to-coast American Bandstand show of Dick Clark.

Jackson continued his winning ways in 1960 with "Why I'm Walkin'." In 1962, he had two best-sellers in "A Wound Time Can't Erase" and "Leona." In 1963, he hit with "Old Showboat" and in 1964 with his own composition, "Don't Be Angry," and the number-one best-selling "B.J. the D.J." Jackson's hits also included "Mary Don't You Weep" and "I Washed My Hands in Muddy Waters."

His Columbia LPs included "Stonewall Jackson" ('59); "Sadness in a Song" and "I Love a Song" ('62); and "Trouble and Me" ('65). In 1967, he scored another top 10 success with "Stamp Out Loneliness." He also turned out a best-selling LP with this title that included such other songs as "Promises and Hearts," "You Can Check on Me," "The Wine Flowed Freely" and "A Man Must Hide to Cry." He scored another chart hit in 1967 with his LP "All's Fair in Love 'n' War."

JACKSON, WANDA: Singer, guitarist, pianist, band leader, songwriter. Born Maud, Oklahoma, October 20, 1937.

The Wanda Jackson story began and reached its initial peak in Oklahoma. But an important influence was the many years spent in California by the Jackson family when she was a girl. It was in Bakersfield, California, that her father gave six-year-old Wanda her first guitar,

an omen of a future revolving around a career in country music.

Times were hard for the Jackson family when Wanda was born in Maud, 50 miles southeast of Oklahoma City, in 1937. Tom Jackson, who had played piano with small bands in Oklahoma in his younger days, worked at whatever odd jobs he could find. In 1941, he put his wife and children and some belongings in his old car and headed for Los Angeles. He learned the barbering trade there, and three months later moved to Bakersfield, some hundred miles to the north.

While he earned his living cutting hair, he encouraged his daughter's interest in music. In 1943, after he gave her the guitar, he spent many hours teaching her the instrument. Before long she not only could play but was making up music of her own. When Wanda reached age 9, she took piano lessons and also learned to read music.

Three years later, the Jacksons returned to Oklahoma, where Tom began working as a used car salesman in Oklahoma City. Soon after, Wanda started classes at Capitol Hill High School. The school was only two blocks

Wanda Jackson poses with her band, The Party Times.

[152]

from station KLPR, which ran a weekly talent program. Wanda and her friends began to attend some of the shows until Wanda got up the nerve to enter one herself.

The 13-year-old girl took first place and was offered a 15-minute daily program of her own. Wanda's singing and guitar playing soon won favor with country fans throughout the city. After a while, the program was so popular that KLPR increased it to a half hour. The show continued to be a vital part of Wanda's life throughout her high school years.

Word of the talented teenager began to reach other country artists. In her junior year, 1954, Wanda received a call from the great Hank Thompson, asking her to record with his group. She agreed and cut several sides, including a duet with Billy Gray called "You Can't Have My Love." The song quickly became one of the top 10 hits nationwide on the Decca label. Wanda was asked to tour the northeast with Hank and was also signed to a Decca contract.

Before concentrating on music, Wanda still wanted to finish school. Diploma received, she was off on tour again for the 1955-56 season, this time with Elvis Presley. In 1956, she signed with one of the top talent agents in the country, Jim Halsey, who soon lined up a new recording contract with Capitol Records and the first of many sensational engagements at Las Vegas. During the late 1950s and throughout the 1960s, she was one of the favorites of visitors to the night spots of Nevada. Capacity audiences attended her multiweek performances at the Golden Nugget, Silver Nugget, Show Boat (all Las Vegas) and Reno's Holiday Hotel.

Besides turning out best-selling singles and LPs for Capitol, Wanda also made her mark as a songwriter. She provided Hank Thompson with a hit song, "Kicking Our Hearts Around." In 1961, she scored nationwide success with two more of her compositions, "Right Or Wrong" and "In the Middle of a Heartache." Some of her other hits of the 1960s were "Let's Have a Party," "Little Charm Bracelet," "Happy, Happy Birthday," "Just Call Me Lonesome," "Candy Man," "Stupid Cupid," "There's a Party Goin' On," "Heartbreak Ahead," "Making Believe," "The Box He Came In," and "Fujiyama Mama." The last-named became a major hit in Japan; turnaway crowds of Japanese came to hear her sing it during one of her international tours. In 1965, record-breaking crowds repeated the process in Germany, where her record of "Santo Domingo" was one of the top hits of that year.

During the 1960s, Wanda toured all fifty states and Canada, Europe and the Far East. Her tours were arranged by her husband, Wendell Goodman, who also packaged her syndicated TV show, "Music Village." Backing Wanda up on the show as well as on tours was her group, The Party Timers. Makeup of The Party Timers in 1966 was Mike Lane, Tex Wilburn, Al Flores and Don Bartlett.

Her LP output included: "Wanda Jackson" ('58); "Rockin' with Wanda" ('60); "Right Or Wrong" ('61); "Lovin' Country Style," "Wonderful Wanda" ('62); "Love Me Forever" ('63); and "Two Sides of Wanda Jackson" ('64). The last of these was one of the best-selling LPs of 1964 and won a nomination for top country LP of the year in the NARAS (National Academy of Recording Arts and Sciences) competition. Her late '60s LPs include "Cream of the Crop," "Salutes the Country Music Hall of Fame," and "The Many Moods of Wanda Jackson" ('69).

JAMES, SKIP: Singer, guitarist, songwriter. Born Bentonia, Mississippi, June 9, 1902.

The mid-1960s saw a great revival of interest in the folk blues, leading to rediscovery of many very talented performers. One was Nehemiah "Skip" James of Mississippi, who had achieved a reputation with folk purists on the basis of a handful of recordings made in 1931.

Skip had the advantage of being born into a musical family, though along with this went the problems of living in the black ghettos of the south. His father, a Baptist minister, could play both organ and guitar. At seven or eight, when Skip became interested in playing the guitar from listening to Bentonia performers Henry Stucky and Rich Griffith, his father was able to help his son learn to play.

The guitar, as noted by Bruce Jackson in Sing Out! magazine ("The Personal Blues of Skip James," Jan. '66, p. 27), cost $2.50. James and the guitar became almost inseparable. Jackson quotes James, reminiscing: "It was just in me, I guess, and I was just graftin' after it. I would just sit still until . . . I didn't have sense enough to know how far to go and how hungry I'd get . . . 'cause my mind was on the music, what I was tryin' to learn."

At 12, when he was starting high school in Yazoo City, Mississippi, he began taking piano lessons, but abandoned them because the $1.50 cost per lesson was too high. Money problems caused him to leave high school before graduation. He worked at odd jobs from Mississippi through Texas and back. He took his guitar along and learned many new songs on the way. In his late teens, he got a sawmill job fifty miles south of Memphis. There he met a dance hall pianist, Will Crabtree, and teamed up with him for a while. He left Crabtree to work in a barrelhouse in Memphis.

In the 1920s, he went back to Mississippi moving to the state capital, Jackson. For most of the decade he remained in Jackson, working at odd jobs and playing at various clubs around town. His musicianship, coupled with some of his original compositions, won him a degree of fame among blues fans in the region. In 1931, his then-roommate, Johnny Temple, and two other friends found that H. C. Spears Music Company of Jackson was looking for new blues talent for Paramount Records.

They talked Skip into auditioning for Spears. Spears and several others listened to Skip play a song called "Devil Blues" and signed him to a two-year contract. Skip was sent to the Paramount studios in Grafton, Wisconsin, two days later. There he spent two days recording 26 songs, including several of his own compositions, such as "Hard Times" and ".22-20." The last named was composed to order on the spot in about three minutes' time.

Not too much happened. Only a few of the songs were released by Paramount. Skip went home to Jackson and for a while completely gave up music. Later in the 1930s, he returned to music briefly by organizing his own gospel quartet. By 1942, when he was ordained a Methodist minister, music had again become a thing of the past for him.

During the 1940s and '50s, Skip worked at various jobs, including timber cutter, tractor operator, and plantation overseer. In 1965, John Fahey, the head of a small label, Takoma Records, and his associates Ed Denson, Bill Barth, and Henry Vestine, went to Mississippi to look for old folk recordings and for Skip. After a lengthy search, Fahey and Barth found him in a hospital in Mississippi.

They taped several songs, including "Devil Blues" and "All Night Long." The material was used to gain financial help from folk enthusiasts in other parts of the country to help pay Skip's medical bills. Soon Skip was given his first singing job in decades at the Bitter Lemon in Memphis. In July 1965, Skip was taken to Newport where he won a standing ovation from the audience.

From then on, he was in demand for concerts and club jobs in many parts of the east. He appeared in short order at Toronto's Mariposa Festival, Ontario Place in Washington, D.C., the Unicorn in Boston, and the Gaslight in New York.

JAMES, SONNY: Singer, guitarist, songwriter. Born Hackleburg, Alabama, May 1, 1929.

It's a rare performer who can claim as enthusiastic a reception from fellow artists as from the general public. Sonny James, for one, has a reputation as a singer's singer. His rapport with the public is equally great, as indicated by song after song on national best-seller lists.

James didn't have to look far for musical encouragement. He was born (real name: Jimmie Loden) into a show business family that toured throughout the south. When he was only four years old, he made his stage debut, singing with his parents and sister at an Alabama convention. Before many more years had passed, he could play the guitar and sing occasional solos with the troupe. When he reached his teens, he had more hours of performing experience behind him than many artists in their twenties.

In the early 1950s, word of Sonny's talents was beginning to circulate around the music field. At this point, though, his career was momentarily slowed by the Korean War. Sonny was sent to Korea and spent fifteen months there. In his spare time he continued to sing to entertain his fellow servicemen or, on some occasions, Korean orphans.

After his discharge, he returned to the tour circuit, playing at fairs and country music shows and on several radio programs. Not long after re-entering civilian life, Sonny was offered a Capitol Records contract by company executive Ken Nelson. As often happened to Nelson finds, it was the beginning of a long and fruitful relationship. In 1957, Sonny scored his first big hit with his top 10 recording of "First Date, First Kiss, First Love." Still leaning towards the youth market, he had an even bigger success late in the year with his record of "Young Love." (In 1962, Dot Records turned out a hit LP of Sonny's, also titled "Young Love.")

For a while things slowed down for Sonny.

[154]

Sonny James

He toured widely and remained a top favorite with audiences, but he did not crack the top 10 for several years. In the mid-1960s, however, he hit his stride again. Almost every release became a national hit. In 1964, he co-authored a song with Bob Tubert that became number one on the charts for a good part of the year, the country standard "You're the Only World I Know." Sonny also had a top 10 hit that year in "Baltimore."

In 1965, Sonny again had a number one hit, "Behind the Tear," and a top success in "I'll Keep Holding On." The following year provided still another number one song, "Take Good Care of Her," and the top 10 hit "True Love's a Blessing" (co-authored with Carole Smith). Keeping his string alive, Sonny turned out such number-one-ranked hits in 1967 as "I'll Never Find Another You" and "Need You." He also made the 1967 charts with "It's the Little Things." His other hits during these years included "The Minute You're Gone" and "Room in Your Heart."

Sonny duplicated his single-record success with many hit LPs. These included "The Minute You're Gone" ('64); "You're the Only World I Know" ('65); "Behind the Tear," "True Love's a Blessing" ('66); "I'll Never Find Another You" ('67); and "Only the Lonely" ('69).

During the late 1950s and through the '60s, Sonny toured all fifty states, Canada, and several other countries. He was joined in his travels by his own group, The Southern Gentlemen. During these years he was featured on such major TV shows as Ed Sullivan, Bob Hope, Swingin' Country, Pat Boone, Star Route, Jimmy Dean, Tennessee Ernie Ford and, naturally, the Grand Ole Opry.

He also appeared in a number of films, including "Second Fiddle to a Steel Guitar," "Las Vegas Hillbillies" (with Jayne Mansfield); "Nashville Rebel," and the 1967 "Hillbilly in a Haunted House." The latter also starred Basil Rathbone and Lon Chaney.

Among Sonny's many awards were three Grammy nominations for his LPs in the 1965 NARAS competition. He won the Record World Magazine Record of the Year Award. In 1966 polls, he won the Number One Artist rating in country and western from Record World. For 1966, Billboard's poll showed him to be rated in the top five of the "Male Artist" category. The Cashbox poll of the experts gave Sonny the number three ranking for 1966.

JAYNE, MITCH: *See* Dillards, The

JEAN, NORMA: Singer, guitarist. Born near Wellston, Oklahoma, January 30, 1938.

In the mid-1960s, one of the most popular country and western shows on national TV was the Porter Wagoner Show. One of the reasons for its popularity was the girl who joined when Porter organized it, Norma Jean. By 1966-67, an estimated 40 million viewers enjoyed her singing in 80 cities across the United States.

Listening to country music was an everyday event in the farm country near Wellston, Oklahoma, where she was born. Little Norma could sing some country songs before she was old enough to read and write. By the time she was of school age, her family had moved to the city—Oklahoma City. She attended public school there and, after she was a little older, began to take guitar lessons from her aunt. She was an apt pupil and could play so well that before she was in her teens she was often engaged to play for square dances in the Oklahoma City area.

She celebrated reaching 13 by auditioning for station KLPR. The result was her own radio show three times a week. Local audiences responded warmly to her talent. Soon she was making personal appearances in country and western shows in the region with such top stars as Leon McAuliff and Billy Gray.

In her late teens, she moved a notch higher, to Springfield, Missouri, to join the cast of Red Foley's Ozark Jubilee in 1958. Her exposure to network TV audiences did nothing to hurt her reputation. In 1960, she was invited to join the cast of the Grand Ole Opry in Nashville. That same year, she met Porter Wagoner during a personal appearance. Porter was greatly impressed with her ability and asked her, soon after, to join the cast of his new filmed TV show. Thus Norma was featured on two top programs during the 1960s.

Norma's work on the Opry was applauded by both country music fans and other cast members. In particular, Marvin Rainwater and Marty Robbins were influential in placing her name before Columbia Records. She was signed to a contract and turned out a number of records for the label during the early 1960s. None of these became major hits, although several did appear on the national charts. In 1963, she changed to RCA Victor and soon chalked up a best-selling recording, "Let's Go All the Way."

In 1964, she turned out a top 10 national hit, "Go Cat Go," and followed with another in 1965, "I Wouldn't Buy a Used Car from Him." She also had countrywide favorites for RCA in such songs as "Put Your Arms Around Her" and "Then Go Home to Her." Some of her other recorded songs of the 1960s were "Lonesome #1," "I'm a Walkin' Advertisement," "You're Driving Me Out of My Mind," "The Shirt," "Please Don't Hurt Me," "Pursuing Happiness," "Conscience, Keep an Eye on Me," and "Don't Let the Doorknob Hit You." In 1966, she teamed with Bobby Bare in a top 10 duet, "Game of Triangles."

She was also represented by a number of LPs on both Columbia and RCA labels. These included "Love's Gonna Live Here," "He Thinks I Still Care," "Happy You, Lonely Me," "Together Again," "Porter Wagoner Show on the Road," "Kitty Wells Tribute" ('66); "Norma

Jean Sings Porter Wagoner" ('67); and "Heaven's a Prayer Away" ('68).

A personal appearance tour during the 1960s took Norma to all fifty states and most of the provinces of Canada.

JENNINGS, WAYLON: Singer, guitarist, disk jockey. Born Littlefield, Texas, June 15, 1937.

One of the rising young stars of the 1960s, Waylon Jennings had plenty of insight into what made the nation's disk jockeys tick. He gained this from personal experience, beginning with a stint as one of the youngest DJs in the nation.

Born and raised in Texas, Waylon, like many southwestern youngsters, had an interest in guitar music almost as soon as he could walk. In his pre-teen years, he learned how to play, though his first interests were not in country music. When he was 12, he gained his first job as a disk jockey over a local station in Littlefield. Throughout his teens, he spun records and occasionally sang himself for home town audiences. He also hosted local talent shows and made personal appearances in towns in his part of Texas. At 17 he began to develop a great interest in country music, whereas before he had concentrated on popular songs.

In 1958 he decided to go further afield, moving to the city of Lubbock, Texas. As before, he worked as a DJ, but in Lubbock he met the national rock 'n' roll star Buddy Holly. He was asked to join Holly's group as electric bass player. For the rest of 1958 and part of '59, Jennings toured with Holly. Then tragedy struck when Holly lost his life in a light-plane crash. The Holly troupe disbanded and Jennings returned to his DJ job in Lubbock. Now, however, he commanded greater respect as a performer and began to make records for small companies in the region.

In the early 1960s, Jennings went west, settling in Phoenix, Arizona. Here he formed his own group, "Waylon Jennings and the Waylors" and played a combination of rock 'n' roll and country and western. The group soon had several lengthy engagements at nightclubs in Phoenix and neighboring Scottsdale and Tempe. In a short period of time they were one of the top entertainment organizations in the area and were starred at one of the largest nightclubs in the southwest, "J.D.'s" in Phoenix.

The group's reputation spread, and many top recording executives made their way to Phoenix

[156]

Waylon Jennings

Wood," "I Wonder Just Where I Went Wrong," "Time to Bum Again," and his top 10 hit of 1966, "That's What You Get for Loving Me." He also was featured on such LPs as "Waylon Jennings Folk-Country," "Leavin' Town," and "Just to Satisfy You."

In 1966, the Stockmen's Association of the Greater Southwest gave him their Pioneer Award for top new country and western act of 1965.

JIM AND JESSE: Bluegrass vocal and instrumental duo, Jim and Jesse McReynolds, both born Coeburn, Virginia, Jim, February 13, 1927; Jesse, July 9, 1929.

Jim and Jesse McReynolds belonged to what might be called the "Bluegrass underground" for some years. They played this traditional style of country music for regional, but appreciative, audiences in the late 1940s and early '50s while more modern approaches dominated the field. When Bluegrass went big-time with the folk song boom, Jim and Jesse and their group, the Virginia Boys, came to the foreground as one of the best Bluegrass troupes in the country.

The brothers had been brought up in the Bluegrass tradition. Their mother and father were talented musicians and often played for dances and get-togethers in their home in Virginia's Clinch Mountains. Their grandfather was one of the best old-time fiddlers in southwestern Virginia and had made some early recordings for RCA Victor.

The boys learned to play stringed instruments in their early years on their family's farm. When they reached their teens, they began to sing at local gatherings with Jesse playing the mandolin and Jim the guitar. It was not too long before they made their radio debut in 1947 on station WNVA, Norton, Virginia. They soon had a good local following and remained on the station until 1952 when they moved on to station WVLK, Lexington, Kentucky. They had made some records for Kentucky Records in the early 1950s; the move brought a new recording contract from Capitol.

Things seemed to be going well when Jesse was called into the service during the Korean War. He served for two years, including a year in Korea. While overseas, Jesse met Charlie Louvin and the two performed for fellow servicemen in Korea.

After Jesse was discharged in 1954, he

to listen to Jennings. One of these was RCA Victor's Nashville officer, Chet Atkins, who came to Phoenix in 1965. Atkins liked what he heard and signed Jennings. The first three recording sessions produced such hits as "That's the Chance I'll Have to Take," "Stop the World and Let Me Off," and "Anita You're Dreaming." With a national reputation in the making, Jennings moved to Nashville in April 1966.

During 1965 and '66 Jennings toured throughout the U.S., playing to cheering fans in all states of the union. He also played engagements in many parts of Mexico and Canada. In Nashville, of course, he was featured on the Grand Ole Opry TV show. In addition, during the mid-1960s, he appeared on ABC-TV's "Anatomy of Pop" special, the Bobby Lord Show, American Swing-Around and Carl Smith's Country Music Hall. He also found time to appear in a movie, "Nashville Rebel."

Some of his other well received songs were "Dark Side of Fame," "Where I Went Wrong," "Look into My Tear Drops," "Norwegian

[157]

Jim and Jesse

teamed up with Jim on the Tennessee Barn Dance on station WNOX, Knoxville. They were also featured with their own group on CBS Network's Saturday Night Country Style. The following year, the boys accepted a bid to join the Swannee River Jamboree, Live Oak, Florida. They also had a daily show on station WNER in Live Oak. In 1957, Jim and Jesse moved again, this time to the Lowndes County Jamboree in Valdosta, Georgia, which remained home base for many years. As of 1960, their Virginia Boys comprised Alfred Donald "Don" McHan, Robert Clark "Bobby" Thompson, and Vassar Clements.

In the early 1960s, the increased national interest in Bluegrass gave new impetus to their careers. They signed with Columbia Records' Epic label and turned out such albums as "Jim and Jesse" ('63); "Bluegrass" ('63); and "Country Church" ('64). Their personal appearances took them further afield, including both country and western and folk concerts. In 1963 they made their first appearance at the Newport Folk Festival, which resulted in a return engagement for the 1966 event.

Their growing popularity resulted in a decision to move to the Nashville area in early 1965. The brothers and their families settled on the Double JJ Ranch in Gallatin, Tennessee. During 1965, they were represented by such well received singles as "Memphis" and "Berry Pickin' in the Country" and an LP, "Johnny B. Goode." Their 1965 credits included a guest spot on the American Sing Along TV Show and the start of regular-cast status with the Grand Ole Opry. The boys taped their first Opry show in November '65, but it wasn't shown nationally until January '66.

The boys scored a top 10 hit in 1966 with "Diesel by the Tail." The LP of the same title was a best-seller of early 1967. Their singles output for '67 included "Thunder Road" and "Tijuana Taxi."

JOHNNIE AND JACK: *See* Anglin, Jack; Wright, Johnny

[158]

JONES BOYS, THE: *See* Jones, George

JONES, GEORGE: Singer, guitarist. Born Saratoga, Texas, September 12, 1931.

In appearance, with his Ivy League crew cut, tie, and jacket, George Jones looks more like a young business executive or matinee idol than a country and western artist. But there can be no doubt of his ability in the latter category from the consistent appearance of his name on hit record lists during the 1950s and '60s.

Jones was born and raised in Saratoga, Texas. Both his parents were talented musically, though both were non-professionals. His mother was a church pianist and his father liked to play the guitar in the hours away from his pipe-fitting job. They encouraged their son's interest in music and gave him his first guitar when he was nine. In a few years George learned to play it well, and entertained at church socials and other local events.

In his late teens, George joined the Marines, serving during the Korean War. When he was discharged, he headed home to Texas and a job as a house painter. He still liked to play his guitar and sing at local events, though he didn't figure on making a living from it. However, his reputation as a performer began to spread to other parts of Texas and came to the attention of veteran music executive H. W. "Pappy" Daily in 1954. Daily, then with the Houston record firm of Starday, heard Jones and thus began a long and close association.

In 1955, Jones scored his first major national hit with "Why Baby Why" on Starday. He turned out other successes for the label, such as "You Gotta Be My Baby," before switching to Mercury Records. His first top 10 hit for Mercury was "Treasure of Love" in 1958. In 1959, he scored with "Who Shot Sam" and a number-one-rated song, nationally, "White Lightnin'." By 1961, he had moved over to the United Artists label for which he turned out a string of major hits during the first part of the 1960s. The first of these was "Window Up Above" in 1961. In 1962, he turned out a number-one best-seller, "She Thinks I Still Care," as well as top 10 successes, "Aching, Breaking Heart" and "A Girl I Used to Know." His 1963 hits for UA were "Not What I Had in Mind," "We Must Have Been Out of Our Minds" (with Melba Montgomery), and "You Comb Her Hair." The

1964 scoreboard included "The Race Is On," "Where Does a Little Tear Come From," and "Your Heart Turned Left."

When Pappy Daily started his own record company, Musicor, George Jones signed with him. The result was five major hits from 1965 to '67: "Take Me," "Things Have Gone to Pieces," and "Love Bug" ('65); "I'm a People" ('66); "You Can't Get There from Here" ('67). Jones also had successes in "Flowers for Mama" and "4033."

During the late 1950s and '60s, Jones was featured on TV and in-person appearances throughout the country and overseas. He formed his own traveling unit called The Jones Boys. His TV engagements in the 1960s included the Jimmy Dean Show, Red Foley Show, and Grand Ole Opry. He also found time to make two movies in the '60s.

By the late 1960s, Jones was represented by dozens of LP albums on all four of the labels he worked for. The Starday catalog included "Crown Prince of Country" ('61); "Fabulous Country Music Sound," and "Greatest Hits" ('62). Mercury LPs were "George Jones Sings" ('60); "Country Church Time," "Country and Western Hits," "Greatest Hits" ('61); "Greatest Hits" ('62); "Sings from the Heart," "Ballad Side," "Duets Country Style" and "Novelty Styles" ('63); "Blue and Lonesome," "Great George Jones," "Salutes Hank Williams," "Number One Male Singer" ('64); and "Heartaches and Tears ('65). The United Artist LPs from 1961 through 1963 cover such titles as "Best of George Jones," "Hits of Country Cousins," "Sings Bob Wills," "My Favorites," "New Favorites" and "Homecoming in Heaven." In 1964, UA also released "Bluegrass Hootenanny," "Grand Ole Opry," "I Get Lonely," "More Favorites," "Sings Like the Dickens," and "What's in Our Hearts."

As of 1969, Jones was one of the few major country artists who had managed to resist the blandishments of Nashville. Instead, he and his wife and two sons lived in a split-level ranch home in the small Texas town of Vidor.

JONES, GRANDPA: Singer, guitarist, banjoist, comic. Born Niagra, Henderson County, Kentucky, October 20, 1913.

About 1924, a sawmill was set up in the woods belonging to the Jones family in Henderson County, Kentucky. The workmen had one guitar among them. They lived in a tent near

[159]

the mill. Because the tent was too damp, they left their precious instrument up at the Joneses' house. What they didn't know was that eleven-year-old Louis Marshall Jones would slip into the room where it was kept and try to play it when no one was around.

Louis longed for a guitar of his own. Finally, gathering together a total capital of seventy-five cents, he gave it to an older brother and begged him to buy an instrument. The brother, who had to more than match Louis' contribution, at last was persuaded. From then on, young Louis spent every spare moment teaching himself to play.

In the late 1920s, his family moved to Akron, Ohio. By this time, Louis could play the guitar quite well. In 1929, now a teenager, he entered a talent contest promoted by Wendall Hall at the local Keith Albee theater. He walked off with first prize, $50 in gold pieces. The money immediately went for a new guitar. The instrument helped Jones gain a number of radio jobs on midwestern stations over the next few years. In 1935, his growing reputation as a musician won him a job with veteran folk-country artist Bradley Kincaid. Jones joined Kincaid's group, then being featured on the National Barn Dance over station WLS, Chicago.

Until this time he had played straight, with no "grandpa" makeup. People began to write to the Barn Dance about the new performer, asking his age. His voice on the radio sounded very old. This gave him the incentive to form a new act, with himself as "Grandpa" even though he was only in his twenties. He put on special makeup, grew a bushy moustache, and affected old-time clothes, including large galluses and boots. In addition, he now concentrated on banjo pickin' —à la Uncle Dave Macon—instead of the guitar. In 1937, with his own band, he debuted in Wheeling, West Virginia. The billing read: "Grandpa Jones and His Grandchildren."

The audience went wild, as audiences still were doing two decades later. His style was described glowingly by Ed Badeaux, associate editor of Sing Out! magazine, in the Dec.-Jan. 1963-64 issue. "Grandpa plays the banjo not with just his hands and arms, but with his whole body. His footwork is as intricate as that of a prize fighter or ballet dancer, and is executed while he is both singing and playing the banjo. When he comes to a banjo solo, the neck of his banjo jets straight up in the air and he arches his body to get the drum as close to the micro-

phone as possible. During his songs, he dances, does stationary road work, and takes frequent jumps and kicks to emphasize and reinforce the humor in the songs."

Grandpa took his new act to Cincinnati in 1938 as part of the cast of the new WLW Boone County Jamboree. He remained on WLW until 1944, when he joined the Army and ended up in Munich, Germany. There, in addition to his regular duties, he played on the Armed Forces Network. After World War II, as so many country artists have done, he made a number of trips to entertain troops abroad. These included two to Europe and one to Korea during the Korean War. In the latter trip, he performed 34 shows in 14 days before 38,000 soldiers. In one performance, he played within 200 yards of the front lines.

Grandpa was mustered out of service in 1946. He was asked to become a regular on the Grand Ole Opry and quickly agreed. More than twenty years later, he was still thrilling Opry audiences. By that time, he lived in Goodlettsville, Tennessee, and the Opry had moved from radio to black-and-white TV to color TV.

Through the 1950s and '60s, Grandpa continued to tour widely. Most of his appearances, usually part of a package show, were on basically country attraction circuits—theaters in the south and southwest, county fairs, etc. However, he also met enthusiastic response in major cities throughout the nation, chalking up performances in almost all the states by the mid-1960s. Accompanying him on his tours was his wife, Ramona, a performer accomplished on several instruments.

Over the years, many songs became particularly associated with him. These included such titles as "Good Ole Mountain Dew," "Old Rattler," "Eight More Miles to Louisville" and "Going Down in Town." These and other songs were among the many records turned out by Jones for such record firms as King, Monument, and Decca. His LP list included "An Evening with Grandpa Jones" on Decca ('63); "Yodeling Hits," "Rafters Ring" ('62), and "Real Folk Songs" ('64) on Monument; and "Rollin' Along," "Other Side of Grandpa Jones" ('50s), and "Do You Remember These Songs" ('63) on King.

JORDANAIRES: Vocal group.

Some of the most often heard voices in the music field belong to the artists that make up the Jordanaires. Each year, millions of records are sold that include their talents. However, a good part of this is "incognito," for the Jordanaires often provide vocal support for solo artists. From the group's founding in 1948 in Springfield, Missouri, through the mid-'60s, it backed such artists as Marty Robbins, Don Gibson, Elvis Presley, Kitty Wells, Patti Page, Ricky Nelson, Connie Francis, Tennessee Ernie Ford and Gene Pitney.

As with most groups, the composition of the Jordanaires varied over the years. As of 1967, the basic quartet consisted of Gordon Stoker, first tenor, born in Gleason, Tennessee; Hoyt Hawkins, baritone, pianist, bassist, born in Paducah, Kentucky; Neal Matthews, second tenor, born in Nashville, Tennessee; and Ray Walker, bass, born in Centerville, Mississippi.

Stoker, one of the first members of the group, learned piano in his youth before spending three years in the Air Force during World War II. He attended Oklahoma Baptist College in Shawnee, Oklahoma, and then majored in psychology and music at George Peabody College in Nashville. While attending Peabody he also worked as a piano accompanist on the Grand Ole Opry station WSM. This eventually led to his role with the Jordanaires.

Hawkins also went to the Jordanaires via George Peabody College, joining the group in 1950. In the 1930s, at the age of 10, he had begun singing in a family quartet over station WPAD in Paducah. Two years in the Army preceded his enrollment in Peabody.

Matthews, who learned to play guitar at 13, served in the Army during the Korean War. Then came a stint at Belmont College in Nashville as a psychology major. In 1953, he joined the Jordanaires.

Walker came to the group with a background that included twelve years as a radio announcer and solo and quartet singer. During his days at David Lipscomb College in Nashville, he sang in a quartet with a fellow undergraduate, Pat Boone. In 1958, he became the fourth member of the Jordanaires. (For some supporting work, the Jordanaires occasionally added the voices of Millie Kirkham and Dolores Dinning.)

The Jordanaires started as singers of barbershop songs and spirituals. They performed in many cities in Tennessee and surrounding states, rapidly winning acceptance and, in 1949, a bid from the Grand Ole Opry. The group extended their popularity to the national level in 1956 by winning on the Arthur Godfrey Talent Scouts program. That same year, they started a long association with Elvis Presley by providing vocal harmony for "I Was the One."

Their work with Elvis included many movies, starting with the 1957 "Loving You." In the late '50s and '60s they were featured on many network TV shows, including Ed Sullivan, Steve Allen, Tennessee Ernie Ford, Tonight, and American Bandstand. Their sound-track credits, as of 1967, totaled 29 films.

Over the years, the Jordanaires collected many awards, including those for providing background accompaniment for such hits as "Battle of New Orleans" and "Big Bad John." In 1965 they won a Grammy for best religious album of the year. Their popularity in the '60s was international. In 1965, they were rated fifth most popular group in Europe; in 1966, they were rated sixth in the top 20.

JOURNEYMEN, THE: Vocal, instrumental group, John Phillips, born Parris Island, South Carolina, August 30, 1941; Scott McKenzie, born Arlington, Virginia; and Richard Weissman, born Philadelphia, Pennsylvania.

The exact reasons for the rapid rise to national attention of folk music in the late 1950s and early '60s and its rapid decline in popularity among the mass audience in the mid-1960s is still being debated. The shifting winds of the mid-1960s did not eliminate folk music, of course, but there came a retrenching that shortened the careers of a number of well regarded groups, including The Journeymen.

For several years, this group was considered one of the most promising of the new crop of the 1960s. Weissman, a noted folklorist and musicologist, studied at the Philadelphia Conservatory of Music, completed college at Goddard in Vermont, and attended Columbia's graduate school of sociology. By the beginning of the 1960s, his skill as a banjoist and guitarist —instruments in which he conducted seminars at New York's School of Folk Music—made him one of the most sought-after accompanists at folk recording sessions.

At one such session, he met Carolina-born John Phillips and his friend Scott McKenzie. They were part of a group known as the Smoothies. Phillips, an allstate basketball and track star in school, had attended the University of Virginia and George Washington University, and received a Presidential appointment to the U.S. Naval Academy. An intramural basketball injury ended his hopes of a Navy career and turned him toward his long-time love of Bluegrass music.

During his travels, he met McKenzie, who had attended a number of prep schools and colleges and had made many popular appearances as a vocalist, including several guest spots on Dick Clark's American Bandstand.

With Phillips as leader, the group made its debut at Gerde's Folk City in the spring of 1961. Frank Werber, who had managed the Kingston Trio, heard them and quickly notified Capitol A&R man Andy Wiswell. Wiswell signed them and set up a session at the firm's New York studios. The first LP was issued in October 1961. Called "The Journeymen," it sold well enough to mark them as coming artists. In 1962, Capitol issued a second LP, "Comin' Attractions," and in 1963, another titled "New Directions."

After the Journeymen broke up, Phillips went on to national fame as Papa John of the top pop group, the Mamas and the Papas.

JUG BAND: Band featuring a jug as one of the instruments.

One of the results of the pop folk fad of the mid-1960s was the rediscovery of a form of old-time music organization called the jug band. These bands were formed in the Negro areas in the south in the ragtime era. One of the instruments was a large jug played by blowing into or across the opening at the top. As Paul Nelson noted in Sing Out! (Dec.-Jan. 1963-64, pp. 8-14), "The jug was used mostly as a novelty item. The main part of the melody was carried by other instruments, usually guitar, kazoo, and harmonica, with banjo, fiddle, washboard and mandolin sometimes added."

The jug band was discovered by the recording industry during the initial emphasis on country music in the mid-1920s. Jug bands that achieved some fame in the 1920s included the Memphis Jug Band, Gus Cannon and his Jug Stompers, the Dixieland Jug Blowers, and the Mississippi Sheiks. One of the first recordings, as related to Paul Nelson by Sam Charters, was made in 1924 by the Old Southern Jug Band led by Clifford Hayes.

When the Depression hit the country music market, the jug bands disappeared from the picture. In the 1950s, some of the urban folk performers began to look into jug band music again. This was heightened by collecting trips

into rural areas by many folklorists.

In the early 1960s, new jug bands began to form, one of the first being Jim Kweskin's Jug Band in 1961. He was soon joined by such other groups as the Even Dozen Jug Band and Dave Van Ronk's Ragtime Jug Stompers. Vanguard turned out an LP of Kweskin's group in 1963, Elektra one of the Even·Dozen Band in 1964, and Mercury recorded Van Ronk's aggregation the same year. Reissues of old-time jug bands were produced in the 1960s by Folkways, Origin Jazz Library ("The Great Jug Bands"), and RBF Records ("The Jug Band").

KAZEE, BUELL: Singer, banjoist, minister, composer, author. Born Burton Fork, Magoffin County, Kentucky, August 29, 1900.

There is an obvious close connection between folk music and religion. Many of the folk standards sung by all manner of artists and groups in the 1950s and 1960s are gospel songs or spirituals or are derived from this genre. Thus, some of the best-known names in folksinging, particularly prior to the mid-twentieth century, have religious or ministerial backgrounds.

A case in point is Bible scholar, minister, and folksinger Buell Hilton Kazee. During his youth in Kentucky, he heard many old ballads and religious songs from his parents and the neighbors. His father, who was in charge of music at their church, made his son a banjo when the boy was five. By the time Buell was old enough to attend the log schoolhouse in the area, he could play and sing many old-time songs.

Buell completed high school in 1920 at the Baptist Magoffin Institute in Salyersville, Kentucky, and went on to nearby Georgetown College. By this time, he was already an ordained minister, having taken up religious studies in 1917. Though some people looked on singing and dancing as sinful, Buell was not troubled by such thoughts. From his teens on, he often performed for local gatherings. By the time he was in college, he had learned to play the piano and guitar as well as banjo.

When Buell gained his degree from Georgetown, he had considerable local repute as a folksinger. In 1925, he was featured in a concert at the University of Kentucky, the first of hundreds of such recitals he was to give.

His college years helped whet his interest in American folk music and he became an avid collector of folk material. This was his major

BUELL KAZEE

Listen To Him Sing and Play
On These Brunswick Records:

No. 206   The Faded Coat of Blue
           Don't Forget Me Little Darling

No. 144 John Hardy
         Roll on John

No. 145 Rock Island
         Old Whisker Bill, The
         Moonshiner

No. 154 Darling Cora
         East Virginia

No. 155 The Ship That's Sailing
         High
         If You Love Your
         Mother(MEET HER IN THE SKIES)

No. 156 The Roving Cowboy
         The Little Mohee

No. 157 The Sporting Bachelors
         The Old Maid

Brunswick Records are Electrically
Recorded and Play on all
Phonographs

75c EACH OF THE ABOVE RECORDS **75c**

TWO GOOD SONGS ON EVERY BRUNSWICK RECORD

A young Buell Kazee is featured on this promotion sheet for some of his recordings of the 1920s.

[163]

hobby throughout his ministerial career. He worked at various places in Kentucky for the Baptist Church before settling down to a 22-year tenure as pastor of the First Baptist Church in Morehead, Kentucky. His church duties included directing the choirs, for some of which he composed original music.

Kazee was one of the pioneer recording artists in the folk music field. During the 1926-30 period, he turned out more than fifty recordings for Brunswick and Vocalion labels. These included many of the best known folk songs, such as "Rock Island Line," "Hobo's Last Ride," "Darling Cora," "East Virginia," "The Little Mohee" and "The Roving Cowboy." These activities came to a close with the collapse of the folk and country market in the early 1930s, due to the Great Depression.

He continued to perform at many folk concerts, however, including recitals at colleges and universities throughout the Appalachian region. In the 1930s, he also recorded some material for the Archive of American Folk Song of the Library of Congress.

Kazee found time to write many articles on religious subjects. He also turned out a book in 1941 titled *Faith Is the Victory*. He never went far afield from his beloved Kentucky, though, and in 1950 moved over to Lexington Baptist College as professor of Old Testament studies. In 1959, Folkways Records once more made Kazee's music available to the general public with the LP "Buell H. Kazee, His Songs and Music." This included some of the songs mentioned above and such others as "Waggoner's Lad," "Yellow Pups," "John Henry," "The Moonshiner," "Cumberland Gap," "Old Grey Mare," "Amazing Grace," "Bread of Heaven," "Eternity," "When Moses" and "The White Pilgrim."

KERR, ANITA: Singer, composer, arranger, pianist, producer. Born Memphis, Tennessee, October 13, 1927.

During the 1950s and '60s, one of the most widely heard groups on records in the country and western field was the Anita Kerr Singers or the Anita Kerr Quartet. The group usually was not the featured name on the record, but provided the vocal background that helped propel many artists' names onto the hit charts. So much a household word had Anita Kerr's name become that some wondered if she really existed. That Anita was for real was well attested to

by music executives, for the one-time nightclub pianist had carved out successes for herself in many areas of music normally dominated by men. She had plenty of musical background to draw on: her mother had a musical show in Memphis when she was a small girl and saw to it that Anita started piano lessons at four. Anita took to music immediately and was already arranging songs for a church group when she was in elementary school. Before she reached high school, she had her own girl trio, the Grilli Sisters, on her mother's program.

Anita's eleven years of piano lessons paid off with a job as staff pianist at a Memphis station when she was 14. She held the job until her high school graduation, whereupon she moved to Nashville, hoping to crack the big time. It was rough going at first, but she managed to make ends meet with jobs in local nightclubs. In 1949 she organized her first group, which included, besides herself as lead, charter members Gil Wright, tenor, and Louis Nunley, baritone. The group won some attention and she was asked to provide an eight-voice choir for a local station. Her arrangements were particularly impressive and led to bids from artists and record companies to turn out special ones. In the years that followed, she provided arrangements for many top-ranked performers, including Floyd Cramer, Chet Atkins, Roy Orbison, Skeeter Davis, Eddy Arnold, Lorne Greene and other country and western artists. She also found her work in demand by such popular stars as Perry Como, Brenda Lee, Brook Benton and Connie Francis.

In 1951, the Anita Kerr Singers were signed to their first solo contract with Decca. Soon after, as a quartet, Anita Kerr's group were often featured on the Arthur Godfrey Show of the 1950s. During the 1950s, the group was asked to provide vocal support to more and more recording sessions in Nashville and other major recording centers. The Anita Kerr Singers also began the first of many tours throughout the U.S. and overseas in the '50s, an operation still in full swing in the late 1960s.

In 1961, Anita was on the Artists and Repertoire staff of RCA Victor in Nashville. She soon added a new laurel to her crown by successfully producing a Skeeter Davis hit LP, "End of the World." Other producing assignments quickly followed in the 1960s. In 1965, Anita moved to Los Angeles where she began freelance production and writing work. She also organized several new groups, including a West Coast version of the Anita Kerr Singers; the Mexicali Singers; and the San Sebastion Strings. All of these were formed under contract to Warner Brothers, before she joined Dot Records.

In December 1966, Anita started a new phase of her career, combining her music with Rod McKuen's poetic lyrics in an album called "The Sea." The album was a major hit in early 1967 and led to a followup called "The Earth" using a 70-piece orchestra.

KILGORE, MERLE: Singer, guitarist, songwriter, disk jockey, actor. Born Chickasha, Oklahoma, August 9, 1934.

Anyone who can write a song that provides gold records for such diverse talents as Webb Pierce and Guy Lombardo figures to have unusual talents. The career of Wyatt Merle Kilgore, only 18 when he turned out that hit composition, "More and More," has borne this out. His successes range from writing to performing, including a number of challenging roles in cowboy films.

Kilgore was born in Oklahoma, but his family soon moved to Shreveport, where Merle attended Creswell Grammar School (1941-48) and Byrd High School (1948-52). He learned to play guitar at an early age and was awarded his first stint as a disk jockey on station KENT in Shreveport when he was 16. This was the first of a number of DJ positions on such other Louisiana stations as KNOE, Monroe, and KZEA, Springhill. While in his teens, Merle began to gain wide notice as a performer throughout his state. Just as impressive were his own compositions that he included in his act. Before long, other artists were singing many of Merle's songs.

While still in high school, Merle was asked to join the cast of the Louisiana Hayride on KWKH Shreveport. An excellent guitarist, he was number one accompanist for many of the top artists appearing on the show. In 1952, Merle also was featured on station KFAZ-TV, Monroe, Louisiana. He continued to perform on the Hayride while starring on KFAZ from 1952 to 1954. The year 1952 also saw his first guest appearance on the Grand Ole Opry, as well as the Big D Jamboree.

Merle wanted to continue his education after high school. He entered Louisiana Tech in 1952 and stayed a year. In 1953, he left to work days for American Optical Company, while he pursued his music career in the evening. In 1954,

"More and More" gave him a national reputation and the incentive to concentrate on music.

Throughout the '50s, he continued to appear on the Hayride and turn out one song after another, including "It Can't Rain All the Time" and "Seeing Double" ('54); "Funny Feeling" ('55); "I've Got a Good Thing Going" ('57); "Tom Dooley Jr.," "Hang Doll" ('58); "Baby Rocked Her Dolly," "It Will Be My First Time," and "Jimmie Bring Sunshine" ('59). In 1959, he had a hit in "Dear Mama." The same year, he provided Johnny Horton with a top 10 seller in "Johnny Reb."

Merle also co-wrote a number of other songs in the '50s including, "Everybody Needs a Little Loving" ('55); "Take the Last Look," "The Wild One" ('57); "Swing Daddy Swing," "Little Pig," "Change of Heart," "You Don't Want to Hold Me," "Old Enough to Love," "We're Talking it Over" ('58); and "I Took a Trip to the Moon" ('59).

Kilgore started off the 1960s in fine style. He had a major hit with his own composition "Love Has Made You Beautiful" in 1960 on Starday label. (He previously recorded for Imperial and D Records.) Two years later, he teamed with Claude King to write "Wolverton Mountain." King's own recording of the song was number one in the nation for many weeks.

During the 1960s, Kilgore toured throughout the country. His engagements included performances at New York's Carnegie Hall and the Hollywood Bowl. He also began to appear in movies, starting with "Country Music on Broadway." His 200-pound, 6-foot-4-inch frame lent itself well to western casting and resulted in a lead role in "Five Card Stud" with Debbie Reynolds. In the mid-1960s, Merle was picked as a featured actor in "Nevada Smith."

Merle switched from Starday to Epic Records in the mid-1960s. (Starday earlier issued a 1964 LP, "Merle Kilgore.") One of Merle's first efforts for Epic was to record his title song for "Nevada Smith."

KINCAID, BRADLEY: Singer, guitarist, songwriter. Born Point Leavell, Kentucky, July 13, 1895.

A pioneering singer on a pioneering station, Bradley Kincaid lays claim to the title of first to introduce folksongs or mountain ballads on radio. Billed as the "Original Authentic Folksong Singer," he set some kind of record on WLS, Chicago, by singing "Barbara Allen" every Saturday night for four straight years. His appearance on the WLS Chicago Barn Dance (later the National Barn Dance) highlighted the close historic relationship between folk music and country and western.

Kincaid was born on a farm in central Kentucky. One of ten children, he was raised in a log-and-frame house. Farm chores took up much of his early youth and he was able to attend Stony Point School in Garrard County only three months out of each year. While still a pre-teener, he could play excellent guitar on an instrument his father got him from a Negro acquaintance. He had gained a backlog of old-time ballads from listening to his parents, relatives, and friends at home sings.

Despite limited opportunity, he did manage to complete two years in the lower (high) school at Berea College. His schooling was interrupted by entry into the Army in 1917. He served for a year in France, then returned to civilian life and home. He completed high school at Berea College in 1922 and enrolled in YMCA College in Chicago.

The move to Chicago resulted in a tryout with station WLS and a singing job beginning in August 1925. He continued to perform regularly on WLS while he went on to take his degree at George Williams College. His interest in folk music continued to grow, and resulted in a series of collecting tours into the rural areas of the border states. His first collecting trip was completed between semesters in 1927. Besides these efforts, he began to compose folk ballads of his own, some of which he introduced on the WLS Barn Dance.

After graduating from college in 1928, Bradley began the first of many tours of the country. From 1928 to 1948, he performed in many parts of the U.S. During the late 1930s and the 1940s, he was one of the favorites on the WLW Midwestern Hayride, Cincinnati. In the 1950s, Kincaid settled in Springfield, Ohio. He devoted most of his time from then on to directing the affairs of station WWSO in which he bought a part interest.

In the mid-1960s, Kincaid recorded many of his best known renditions on a series of LPs for Bluebonnet Records. The albums, which were entitled "The Kentucky Mountain Boy," reached volume 4 as of 1966. Among the songs in these albums are "Methodist Pie," "I Gave My Love a Cherry," "Liza Up a Simmon Tree," "Fatal Derby Day," "Two Little Orphans," "The

Letter Edged in Black," and "The Gypsy's Warning."

KING, CLAUDE: Singer, guitarist, songwriter. Born Shreveport, Louisiana, February 5, 1933.

As part of its claim to top rank in country music right behind Nashville, Shreveport can point to the long, eventful history of the Louisiana Hayride. Equally important, the city can show an impressive list of native sons of top rank, including Faron Young, Carl Belew, and Claude King.

King spent his first few years in Shreveport, but before he reached school age, his family moved to a farm some miles from the city. Country music was often played on his family's radio, but for many years he was far more interested in spending any spare hours playing ball with his friends. As he reached his teens, though, he began to take note of some of the tunes played on the Grand Ole Opry or on station KWKH in Shreveport. When he was 12, his interest became more intense when he bought his first guitar from a neighboring farmer for fifty cents.

During his high school years, Claude became adept at the instrument and entertained for local events. However, music had a strong competitor in the form of athletics. A first-rate football and baseball player, Claude was a regular on school teams and had several scholarship offers when he reached his senior year. After finishing high school, he accepted a bid to the University of Idaho. From there, he returned to Shreveport and attended business college for a while.

By this time, music seemed more attractive to him. He had begun to compose songs of his own and was encouraged by the reactions of friends when he performed his material for them. In the late 1950s, he had an increasing number of engagements in local clubs and soon began to perform on radio and TV. In the 1960s, he really came into his own as both performer and songwriter. His first giant step came in the form of a recording contract with Columbia Records in 1961. Later that year, his name received national attention with several top recordings, including two top 10 hits, "Big River, Big Man," and "The Comancheros."

The year 1962 was an even bigger one for the tall Louisianan. He had a top 10 hit in "The Burning of Atlanta" and his version of "Wolverton Mountain" was number one on the national list for many weeks. For the next few years, things slowed down a bit. But in 1965, Claude scored again with a song he co-wrote with Merle Kilgore, "Tiger Woman." In 1967, the song served as the title number for a best-selling LP. In 1967, Claude had another top 10 success with his rendition of "Laura (What's He Got That I Ain't Got?)."

King's debut album for Columbia, "Meet Claude King," was released in August 1962.

KING, PEEWEE: Singer, band leader, accordionist, songwriter. Born Milwaukee, Wisconsin, February 18, 1914.

Despite his nickname, Frank "PeeWee" King ranks as a giant in the country and western field. As a composer and performer, he turned out some of the all-time classics of country music, including "Tennessee Waltz" and "Slow Poke." As a band leader, he provided the springboard for many famous names in the field, including Ernest Tubb and Eddy Arnold.

He was born and brought up in Milwaukee, where he attended public schools and, from 1928 to 1931, Bay View High School. In 1932, he studied at Vocational Trade School and went on to work as a mechanical draftsman apprentice. However, music had been a normal part of his life, for his father had long played the fiddle for dances and parties in northern Wisconsin. In high school, PeeWee, already an accomplished accordionist and fiddler, had led his own group for school affairs. At 14, he had played on stations WRJN in Racine and WBAY in Green Bay. Thus when the chance came to join the WRJN Badger State Barn Dance in Milwaukee in 1933, he was happy to leave drafting for a music career.

His talent was quickly recognized by other young, aspiring country music artists and he spent 1934 with the Gene Autry Show in

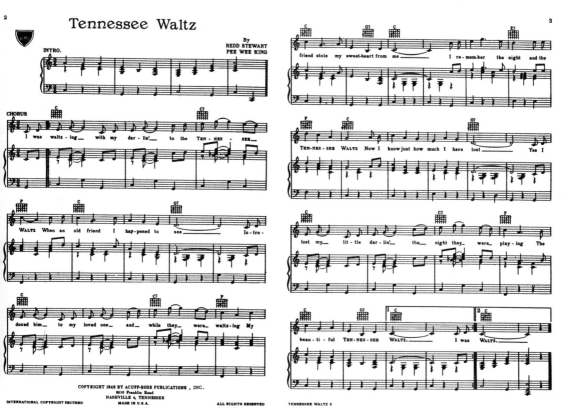

PeeWee King's great standard, "Tennessee Waltz" ("TENNESSEE WALTZ"—Redd Stewart and Pee-Wee King, © 1948 Acuff-Rose Publications, Inc. Used with permission of the publisher.)

Louisville and 1935–36 with the Log Cabin Boys on the Crazy Water Barn Dance, WHAS, Louisville. PeeWee then felt he was ready to go out on his own and formed his Golden West Cowboys. They were heard in short order on a 1936 edition of the Grand Ole Opry. PeeWee appeared regularly on the Opry through 1947, while also heading up his own KNOX Mid-Day Merry-Go-Round in Knoxville from 1937 to 1947. In 1946, many hit records were turned out of PeeWee's own song, "Bonaparte's Retreat."

From 1947 to '57, PeeWee had his own show on WAVE and WAVE-TV in Louisville. During this period, after signing with RCA Victor, he really hit his stride as composer and performer. In 1948, "Tennessee Waltz," which he wrote with Redd Stewart, provided hit records for both PeeWee and Cowboy Copas. Patti Page's recording also reached number one in popular polls. Among songs that achieved success in the next few years that PeeWee wrote or co-authored, were "Slow Poke," "Tennessee Tango," "Walk Me by the River," "A Crazy Waltz," and "River Road Two Step." Over his long career, PeeWee wrote well over 400 songs.

Throughout the 1950s, PeeWee continued to tour the U.S. and other countries as well as star on his own and other major country TV shows. During 1955–57, his WAVE-TV show was given network coverage by NBC. The Pee-Wee King Show from WEWS-TV, Cleveland, also was telecast on ABC-TV. In 1957–58, his show originated from station WBBM-TV in Chicago. Among his record successes during this period were the number-one-placing "Slow Poke" in 1951, "Silver and Gold" in 1952, and "Bimbo" in 1954.

PeeWee's activities in the 1950s won him many awards. From 1950 to 1955, he was voted the number one country and western band leader by Cashbox, Billboard, and Orchestra World. He also was given many BMI songwriter's awards from 1952 to '58. Among the many recordings by King's group during these years were "Woodchopper's Ball," "I'll Be Walking Alone in a Crowd," "Blue Suede Shoes," "Tennessee Dancin' Doll," "Kentucky Waltz," "Sally Goodin'," "Arkansas Traveler," "Billy in the Low Ground," "Blue Grass Waltz," "Oh Monah!" and "Birmingham Bounce." In 1959, PeeWee switched from RCA Victor to Todd records and later joined Starday. One of the first Starday releases was a 1964 LP, "Pee-

Wee King and Redd Stewart."

PeeWee also appeared in a number of westerns, including several Gene Autry films starting with "Gold Mine in the Sky" in 1938. He also worked with Johnny Mack Brown during the 1940s. His 1950s credits included such films as "Riding the Outlaw Trail" ('52) for Columbia.

KIRK, EDDIE: Singer, composer, guitarist. Born Greeley, Colorado, March 21, 1919.

When Eddie Kirk sang western songs, he knew whereof he spoke, for he was born and raised on a cattle ranch. His father, who owned the ranch, made sure his children could rope, ride, and help round up cattle at an early age. Little Eddie used to enjoy listening to the ranch hands tell tall tales of the west and sing the songs of western life. By the time Eddie reached high school age, he knew many of the songs by heart and could accompany himself on the guitar. His singing was good enough to win him a 15-minute daily program on a local station while he was still in his teens.

Anticipating the hit TV show of the 1960s by a couple of decades, he joined a group called the Beverly Hillbillies, led by Glen Rice. He toured a number of the western states with the group and, by 1934, was in Hollywood singing on the radio and appearing in several movies. He still returned to his home state, though, where he not only sang, but fought as a flyweight in a number of amateur fights. Eddie did not hang up his boxing gloves until 1937. In the musical vein, he joined Larry Sunbrock's band in 1935 and appeared in cities throughout the U.S. His yodeling ability won him the National Yodeling Championship in 1935 and '36.

Eddie's touring was suspended with the outbreak of World War II and his entry into the Navy. After D-Day, he settled in Hollywood. His activities included playing the guitar and directing the choir on the Hollywood Barn Dance in the late 1940s. During the same period, he performed on the Gene Autry Show. He also kept busy with film work, appearing in more than a dozen movies.

Eddie did not begin to record on his own until late 1947 when he signed with Capitol. Within a short period of time, though, his efforts won national attention. In 1949, two of Eddie's records became best-sellers, "Candy Kisses" and "The Gods Were Angry with Me." Some of his other successful efforts included

[168]

"Blues Stay Away from Me," recorded with Tennessee Ernie Ford and Merle Travis, "Born to Lose," and "Petals from a Faded Rose."

KIRKLAND, MICHAEL: *See* Brothers Four, The

KWESKIN, JIM: *See* Jug Band

LA FARGE, PETER: Singer, guitarist, songwriter. Born Fountain, Colorado, 1931; died New York, New York, October 27, 1965.

Sensitive and poetic, Peter LaFarge was one of the first of the American "angry young men" who sparked the folk boom of the 1950s and '60s. He functioned on many creative levels, providing some of the best of the "composed" new folk music as well as turning out articles, plays, and poetry in his short lifetime.

As Julius Lester wrote in Sing Out! (Jan. 1966, p. 11), "It is too easy to feel sorrow for a poet who dies young. 'If he had only lived . . .' is the pathetic plaint of those who stand at the grave. But he did live and our sorrow and our tears are wasted on him now. He is beyond us—the audiences that never quite understood him, and the friends who pitied him. . . ."

Of American Indian ancestry, LaFarge grew up in the Rocky Mountain area. He became interested in folk music early in life, and at 14 had his own radio program on a Colorado Springs station. He played many of Woody Guthrie's recordings, which led to a meeting with Guthrie's close friend Cisco Houston. Houston helped LaFarge learn many of the fine points of singing, guitar playing, and, most important, songwriting. Another part of Peter's training came from the man who adopted him, Pulitzer Prize-winning novelist and Indian champion Oliver LaFarge.

LaFarge continued to develop his talents as performer and songwriter during the late 1940s. His career was interrupted by the Korean War. He won five battle stars and suffered a serious head injury before leaving the service. Returning home, he indicated his disdain for physical hurt by working as a rodeo bull-dogger and bronc rider. He also put in some time as a boxer.

Finally, he returned to writing and singing. He performed in local coffee houses, then moved on to star at major folk concerts, including the Newport Folk Festival. His byline

also began to appear on articles on folk music and folk performers in Sing Out! By the early 1960s, many major folk artists were singing and recording his songs, including "Black Stallion," "Ira Hayes," "Coyote," and "As Long as the Grass Shall Grow."

In the early 1960s, LaFarge recorded the first LP of his own material for Columbia Records. He followed up with several more LPs on Folkways label, the first of which was the 1963 "As Long as the Grass Shall Grow." His talents were beginning to win him a reputation as a budding dramatist and author when his life ended in New York in the fall of 1965.

LAMANNO, JOE: *See* Travelers 3

LAMPELL, MILLARD: *See* Almanac Singers, The

LEADBELLY: Singer, guitarist, composer. Born near Mooringsport, Louisiana, January 21,* 1885; died New York, New York, December 6, 1949.

Few names ring in the annals of folk music with greater glory than that of Leadbelly. The self-styled "king of the 12-string guitar players" was a legend in his lifetime. Today there are few folk heroes in the entire world better known than this veteran of many southern prisons. But for all his current fame, for the first 49 years of his life he was unknown and unsung.

Huddie Ledbetter grew up on a farm in the Caddo Lake district near Mooringsport, Louisiana. He was exposed to colored work songs, hymns, and the thrum of voodoo drums almost from his cradle. His Uncle Terrill gave him a concertina when he was barely past the toddling stage, and before long little Huddie could pick out many melodies on the instrument. A few years later, his father bought him a guitar, and this became almost a part of him. In his teens, when he left home to wander through the countryside playing at local affairs, his guitar was almost always in his hands or slung over his shoulder.

In the years near the turn of the century, he spent much time playing on street corners or wandering along the city streets singing for his daily bread. He sang songs he had picked

* Leadbelly gave January 21 as his birthday in talks with John and Alan Lomax in the mid-1930s. However, it is not certain this is the exact date.

up in his travels and others that he had made up on the spot. By now he had grown into a tall, muscled strongman and he was able to find work during the day in construction or cotton picking. Because he was such a fast worker, other field hands nicknamed him Leadbelly. His wanderings took him across Louisiana and into Texas. In 1917 in Dallas, he met another since-famed folk musician, Blind Lemon Jefferson. They teamed up to play for coins on street corners or for slightly better pay in the brothels of East Dallas. One story has it that Huddie took a busman's holiday one night at a traveling carnival. While moving along the midway, he is said to have come upon a man playing a 12-string guitar. One version is that he fell in love with the sound, spent the night listening to the music, then bought himself one the next day. However, Frederic Ramsey, Jr., writing in Sing Out! (March 1965) states he had learned to play it some years earlier.

From World War I through the 1920s and '30s, Huddie continued his same pattern of restless movement across the southwest. He played such songs as "Goodnight Irene" and "Pick a Bale of Cotton" for anyone who would listen. With his fiery temper and huge build, he sometimes got into scrapes that landed him in jail. One jail term in Texas lasted from May 24, 1918, to January 15, 1925. Huddie won his freedom with a song to Governor Pat Neff. He was back in jail again in 1930, though this time in Louisiana. While behind bars, he continued his musical education, picking up new songs from the other inmates. Then, in 1932, his big break came—in jail.

Library of Congress folk song expert Dr. John A. Lomax came to a Louisiana penitentiary to record prison songs and met Huddie. He immediately recognized a great artist, and recorded a plea for freedom by Ledbetter. The recording didn't move Governor O. K. Allen to grant a pardon, but it did increase Lomax's efforts that finally resulted in a good-behavior release in 1934. Huddie arrived in New York with Lomax late in 1934, carrying a beat-up green guitar held together with a piece of string. His first performances in January 1935 won him rave notices and many personal appearance bids.

From then on, the Ledbetter legend was on its way. After his first concerts in New York and at Harvard University, he began a new round of travels. This time he went in relative style, playing with the best known names in the music field before audiences of thousands across the nation. Just a few of the artists with whom he appeared were Sonny Terry, Josh White, Cisco Houston, Big Bill Broonzy and Woody Guthrie. He made many appearances in nightclubs and concert halls and on network radio programs as well. From a financial standpoint, though, he never gained much return for his great talent.

In 1949, he began a series of concerts in Europe. While in Paris, he was stricken with a disease that caused his muscles to atrophy. Huddie returned to New York and died in Bellevue Hospital on December 6. He left behind a recorded legacy of original compositions and traditional folk music that includes "Gray Goose," "Good Morning Blues," "The Midnight Special," "Whoa Back Buck," "Easy Rider," "Keep Your Hands Off Her," "Fannin Street," "New York City," "Goodnight Irene," "Rock Island Line," etc.

LEARY FAMILY: *See* Cooper, Wilma Lee

LEDBETTER, HUDDIE: *See* Leadbelly

LEHRER, TOM: Singer, pianist, author, songwriter, teacher. Born New York, New York, April 9, 1928.

One of the most popular performers on the coffee house and campus circuit of the 1950s and the early '60s was the whimsical Tom Lehrer. He played and sang both folk and popular music to his own piano accompaniment, but his major forte was the comic songs he wrote on many topical subjects from the atom bomb to air pollution.

Thomas Lehrer was born and brought up in New York City. He excelled in school, particularly in technical subjects, but also showed considerable talent as a pianist at a young age. When he completed his high school course, he applied to Harvard as a math major. He was accepted and spent a good part of the 1940s in Cambridge, completing his B.A. and M.A. in mathematics. As one of the top students in his class, he had little trouble gaining a job teaching math at Harvard after graduation. Later, he also gave classes in the subject at Massachusetts Institute of Technology.

In his spare time, however, he continued to entertain himself and his friends with his musical talents. After a while, he began to give concerts in the Boston area. His efforts were well received and soon he was asked to play in other cities. In the 1950s, he started touring the U.S. a good part of the year. His own compositions caught on with college audiences and sophisticated city dwellers. Before long, most folk artists included one or two Lehrer ballads in their repertoires.

Among his songs were such titles as "Be Prepared," "The Irish Ballad," "Poisoning Pigeons in the Park," "We Will All Go Together When We Go," and "Pollution." In the 1950s and '60s, Lehrer was also featured on a number of LPs, including "Songs by Tom Lehrer," "Tom Lehrer Revisited," "More of Tom Lehrer," "An Evening Wasted with Tom Lehrer" and "That Was the Year That Was."

Lehrer wrote special material during the 1950s and '60s for both movies and TV. He was featured on a number of network TV shows as a performer over these years, including the Ed Sullivan Show.

LEWIS, JERRY LEE: Singer, pianist, songwriter. Born Ferriday, Louisiana, September 29, 1935.

Though there's an obvious relationship between country and western and rock 'n' roll, not many performers achieve stardom in both areas. One exception is Elvis Presley; another is Jerry Lee Lewis.

Jerry was born and spent a good part of his childhood in the small town of Ferriday, Louisiana. He went on from grade school to attend the Waxahatchie Bible Institute in Texas. He was already a gifted pianist by the time he was in his teens, and played spirituals for Sunday School groups. As he grew older, though, he became more and more interested in popular music and began to appear in local clubs. For a while after finishing Bible school, he earned his living mainly as a door-to-door salesman of sewing machines.

In the mid-1950s, he formed a small group and managed to get a number of engagements playing for teenage dances. Jerry's name began to be known to the music industry and he was offered a contract from Sun Records, which had been the starting point in 1954–55 for another young artist named Elvis Presley. Jerry scored some success in 1956 with one of his own songs, "End of the Road."

In a short time, Jerry Lee had a number of fast-moving records. His output for 1957 in-cluded two massive hits that made number one on both country and western and popular lists. These were "Great Balls of Fire" and "Whole Lot of Shakin'."

That year, teenagers all over the nation waited in line to hear him. He was featured on major network TV shows, including Ed Sullivan and Dick Clark's American Bandstand, and also appeared in the first of several movies, "Jamboree." At the end of the year, his group was voted the Best Small Combo of 1957 in a poll conducted by Dick Clark.

Jerry continued to hold the national spotlight in 1958 with two top 10 hits, "Breathless" and "High School Confidential." The second of these he co-wrote with R. Hargrave as the title song for his second movie. (His third film was the 1960 "Young and Deadly.") Another of his 1958 records was his own composition, "Lewis Boogie."

Jerry Lee's popularity continued in both C&W and rock 'n' roll into the early 1960s. From then on, though, he slowly phased out of rock 'n' roll and sang mainly in the country category.

Besides the songs mentioned above, Jerry turned out dozens of other recordings. A partial list includes: "Goodnight Irene," "I'll Make It All Up to You," "Crazy Arms," "I'll Be Me," "You Win Again," "Down the Line," "Fools Like Me," "It Hurt Me So," "Return of Jerry Lee," "Lovin' Up a Storm," "Ballad of Billie Joe," "I'll Sail My Ship Alone," "Breakup," "Little Queenie," "Big Blon' Baby," "I Could Never Be Ashamed of You," "Don't Be Cruel," "I'm Feelin' Sorry," "Put Me Down," "Ubangi Stomp," "Jambalaya," "When the Saints Go Marchin' In," "Mean Woman Blues," "Matchbox," and "Let's Talk About Us."

In early 1968, Jerry went off on a new tack, playing the role of Iago in the Los Angeles Music Center musical version of Shakespeare's "Othello." The show received mixed notices, but represented one of the first attempts to apply rock 'n' roll rhythms to the musical theater. His 1968 efforts included the hit LP "Another Time, Another Place" and a top 10 single, "What's Made Milwaukee Famous" (both on Smash Records).

LIGHT CRUST DOUGHBOYS, THE: Vocal and instrumental group, formed early 1930s.

Not too many vocal groups can claim to have made one of their members a state official, much less governor of the state. The Light Crust Doughboys helped play this role in the eventual election of one of its founders, W. Lee "Pappy" O'Daniel, to the governorship of the Lone Star State. But the name of the group is one of the most famous in country & western, so much so that most people outside the State of Texas know its name rather than the name of its political alumnus.

Credit for founding the Doughboys is shared by O'Daniel and Bob Wills of Texas Playboy fame. At the start of the 1930s, Wills and musicians Herman Arnspeiger and Milton Brown toured parts of Texas as the "Wills Fiddle Band." Looking for ways to increase their reputation, the group approached O'Daniel, then on the sales staff of Burrus Mill Company, for a job on Ft. Worth station KFJZ advertising the firm's Light Crust Flour.

O'Daniel's birthplace wasn't Texas, but Malta, Ohio. Christened Wilbert Lee O'Daniel, he first saw the light of Ohio day on March 11, 1890. In his youth, the family moved to Kingman, Kansas, where Lee completed his schooling and began his working career in the early 1920s as a flour salesman for local firms. He moved to Ft. Worth in 1925, gaining a position with Burrus Mill & Elevator Co., "millers of that wonderful Light Crust Flour."

Wills' suggestion met with O'Daniel's favor and the latter promoted the program for Burrus. By the end of 1932, the group had assumed the name Light Crust Doughboys and established itself as one of Ft. Worth's favorite programs. In February, they cut several records for RCA Victor, but most of their output of the 1930s came later on Vocalion label.

In 1933, the Doughboys moved to station WBAP in Ft. Worth, performing daily at 12:30 P.M. Bob Wills left to form his new band about this time and O'Daniel took over as m.c. Still another change took place when Brown quit and was replaced by fiddler Clifford Groves from Kentucky. With their reputation expanding throughout the southwest, the Doughboys signed with Vocalion and turned out dozens of recordings from 1933 to 1935 under O'Daniel's direction.

Some of the Vocalion efforts were: "Beautiful Texas," "On to Victory, Mr. Roosevelt," "Bluebonnet Waltz," "Texas Breakdown," "Memories of Jimmie Rodgers," "Doughboys' Rag," "Texas Rose," "Saturday Night Rag," "Gangster's Moll," "When It's Roundup Time in Heaven,"

"Alamo Waltz," "My Pretty Quadroon," "Carry Me Back to the Lone Prairie," "Milenburg Joys," "Old Rugged Cross," "The Cowboy's Dream," "Kelly Waltz" and "She's Still That Old Sweetheart of Mine."

O'Daniel left the program in 1935 when he resigned from Burrus to form his own firm, Hillbilly Flour Company. Later, though, when he entered politics, he called on the Doughboys to provide musical background for his campaign tours, a factor that was credited with his successful bid for Texas' top position.

He was replaced in the group by Eddie Dunn as m.c. Dunn brought in a number of performers from his own group, including Marvin Montgomery, Dick Reinhart, Bert Dodson and Muryel Campbell. In 1936, still another leader took over, Cecil Brower. The Doughboys, by now an institution, continued to be a vital part of WBAP programming for the rest of the '30s. In 1942, Burrus Mills dropped their sponsorship and the name of the group was changed to "Coffee Grinders" to be synonymous with the new sponsor, Duncan Coffee Co.

The group had enough rapport with their audience that they continued to have support through the war years. However, the new name was not quite as strong as the old, and after World War II the Doughboys title was reassumed, this time with Jack Perry as m.c. The Light Crust Doughboys still exist at this writing. Many changes of personnel have taken place since the late 1940s, and the group has never since equaled the success of the glory days of the 1930s.

Not too much in the way of recordings by the Doughboys is available currently. An LP album, "Lightcrust Doughboys," was issued by Audio Lab in 1959. (*See also* McAULIFF, LEON; WILLS, BOB)

LIMELITERS, THE: Vocal and instrumental trio, Dr. Louis Gottlieb, born Los Angeles, California, 1923, Alex Hassiley, born Paris, France, July 11, 1932; Glenn Yarbrough, born Milwaukee, Wisconsin, January 12, 1930.

One of the most literate of the folk music groups, The Limeliters was the only one to claim a full-fledged Ph.D. as its musical spokesman. The man in question was bespectacled, witty bassist Lou Gottlieb, who earned his degree in musicology from UCLA in 1958.

The group was formed in 1959 at the Cosmo Alley coffee house in Hollywood. Each artist had been working as a single supper club and coffee house act, though Yarbrough and Hassilev had been associated in running a club in Aspen, Colorado, called the Limelite. A few years earlier, Yarbrough had been engaged by the club and became a regular performer there. In time, he and Hassilev joined to buy the lease and run the club themselves.

Hassilev, born in France of Russian parents, had been brought to the U.S. as a boy. By the time he met Yarbrough, he was trying for a career as an actor, having spent some years working in off-Broadway productions. In 1959, Alex got a part in a horror movie in Hollywood and took a singing job at the Cosmo Alley to help pay expenses. Later that year, Yarbrough came to town and sang with Alex. Gottlieb heard them perform one night and suggested they make it a trio.

Gottlieb, by this time, had considerable professional experience. He had been one of the original Gateway Singers, a top folk group of the 1950s, but left after three years to complete

work on his Ph.D. He had already gained a major reputation as an arranger. During the early 1960s he sometimes provided song arrangements for other acts, including "Miss Bailey" and "Good News" for the Kingston Trio.

The three men agreed to start work after Glenn and Alex finished their Cosmo Alley run in late July 1959. They based their name on the title of Glenn and Alex's Aspen club. Combining Gottlieb's arrangements and droll comic interludes with Yarbrough's lyric tenor and Hassilev's command of several languages, they moved to San Francisco to become a smash hit at the hungry i basement nightclub. Their repertoire included such songs as "Gari Gari," "When I First Came to This Land," "The Monks of St. Bernard," "Ya Se Murio El Burro," "The Cumberland Mountain Bear Chase," "Rumeynia, Rumeynia," "The Hammer Song," "Have Some Madeira, M'Deah," "Molly Malone," and the show-stopping comic renditions of "The Ballad of Sigmund Fraud," "Charlie, the Midnight Marauder," and "Mama Don't 'Low."

From that time until the group disbanded in the mid-1960s, it was featured on radio and TV and in concerts throughout the U.S. and the world. These included extended engagements at the Blue Angel, Roundtable, and Village Vanguard in New York and Mister Kelly's in Chicago, and a concert with Eartha Kitt at the Hollywood Bowl. The group also toured the country with Shelley Berman, Chris Connor, and George Shearing, joined Johnny Mathis in a show at the Greek Theater in Los Angeles, and formed an act for a time with comedian Mort Sahl.

The group signed with RCA Victor Records soon after its formation. Limeliter LPs were still finding a wide audience after the group had ceased performing. The list of titles included "The Limeliters" ('60); "Tonight in Person," "Slightly Fabulous" ('61); "Sing Out," "Children's Eyes," "Folk Matinee" ('62); "Our Men in San Francisco," "Makin' a Joyful Noise," "14 14K Folk Songs" ('63); "More of Everything," "Best of The Limeliters," "Leave It to The Limeliters," ('64); "London Concert" ('65).

The Limeliters: from left, Glenn Yarbrough, Alex Hassilev, Dr. Lou Gottlieb

LOCKLIN, HANK: Singer, guitarist, songwriter, public official. Born McLellan, Florida, February 15, 1918.

To go from a farm boy chopping cotton to a star of the Grand Ole Opry is not unusual in country music lore. To do this and then return and win an election as mayor of one's home town, though, is a little extra frosting on any performer's cake.

Henry Locklin had little idea of becoming mayor of McLellan, Florida, when he worked on his family's farm in the 1920s. He did like to sing country songs, though, when he hoed and chopped cotton as part of his weekly chores. Young Hank decided to learn to play the guitar at an age when most boys are just learning their ABC's. He finally gathered enough small change for a down payment on an instrument from the local pawnshop. Though the monthly charges were only $1.50, he found this sum hard to come by and the guitar was repossessed.

He was not yet 10 when this occurred. But he had managed to learn a lot about playing the instrument before returning it. He persevered and got another one on which he worked out some of his early compositions. He began to take part in local dances and sings, moving on to win a number of local contests when he was in his teens. In the 1930s, he performed as often as he could, but times were tough in those Depression years. For a time, he earned his keep by working on road projects of the government Works Project Administration.

He stubbornly refused to give up hopes for a successful musical career. This stubbornness finally paid off with more important dates and his first radio engagements on Florida stations WCOA, Pensacola, and WDLP, Panama City. His star continued to rise with appearances in other cities in the south and air shots on such stations as WALA, Mobile, Alabama; KLEE, Houston, Texas; and KTHS, Hot Springs, Arkansas.

Hank really began to move after World War II. He joined the cast of KWKH Louisiana Hayride in Shreveport soon after that show began. By the early 1950s, he was one of the audience favorites and had signed a record contract with Decca. He moved for a time to Four Star, the label of his first major record hit, the 1953 "Let Me Be the One." Soon after, Hank become a regular on the Grand Ole Opry in Nashville and signed a long-time contract with RCA Victor.

From the mid-1950s on, Hank rapidly became one of the top artists in country music. He scored a top 10 hit in 1957 with "Geisha Girl" and followed up in 1958 with "It's a Little More Like Heaven" and his own composition, "Send Me the Pillow You Dream On." In 1960, his version of Don Robertson's standard, "Please Help Me, I'm Falling," was number one nationally for many weeks. His other best-sellers of the early '60s were "Happy Birthday to Me" ('61) and "Happy Journey" ('62).

During the 1950s and '60s, Hank was represented by many successful LPs. These included two King LPs, "Best of Hank Locklin" and "Encores," and the Wrangler label's "Hank Locklin Favorites." His RCA Victor output included: "Foreign Love" ('58); "Please Help Me" ('60); "Happy Journey," "Hank Locklin," "Tribute to Roy Acuff" ('62); "This Song Is for You" (Camden), "Ways of Life" ('63); "Irish Songs," "Sings Hank Williams" ('64).

Among the songs recorded by Hank in addition to those above are: "Living Alone," "Foreign Car," "Border of the Blues," "I'm a Fool," "Goin' Home All By Myself," "The Rich and the Poor," "How Much," "She's Better Than Most," "The Same Sweet Girl," "Born to Ramble," "Fraulein," "Hiding in My Heart," "Anna Marie," "Blues in Advance," "My Old Home Town," and "Seven Days."

Over the years, Hank's personal appearances took him to all fifty states, Canada, and Europe. He guested on many major TV shows in the 1950s and '60s including ABC's Jamboree U.S.A. In the early 1960s, Hank returned to his home town of McLellan to live, and soon was elected mayor. To complete a boyhood dream, he established his residence on the rambling "Singin' L Ranch," which incorporated the cotton field in which he'd once worked as a child.

LOGAN, HORACE: *See* Louisiana Hayride

LOMAX, ALAN: Singer, author, folk music collector. Born Austin, Texas, January 15, 1915.

The name Lomax is almost synonymous with folk music scholarship in the U.S. First the late John A. Lomax and then his son Alan provided the dynamic force that helped make the Archive of American Folk Song of the Library of Congress one of the most comprehensive in the world. The Archive itself has been of major importance for many scholars, as well as folk artists, who built up much of their repertoire from browsing through the collection. In addition, the discovery or rediscovery of many greatly talented artists is directly traceable to the survey tours of John and Alan Lomax.

Alan spent most of his boyhood in Texas. He went to grade school in Austin and later attended a college preparatory school in Dallas. Alan had been exposed to many folk songs in his youthful home environment. In 1933, he went on his first collecting tour as an observer and sometime helper to his father. The trip made him a confirmed folk music collector in his father's image. Soon after the trip was over, the Lomaxes moved to Washington, D.C., where John Lomax began his monumental work of collecting folk music material for the Library of Congress.

Now that the family was based in the east, young Alan enrolled at Harvard. After one year, though, he went back to Texas, entering the University of Texas, from which he was graduated in 1936. Returning to Washington, he settled down as assistant curator of the Archive in 1937. That year was an eventful one for him; it included a three-month stay in Haiti where he recorded Haitian songs and dances.

In the next half dozen years (he left the Archive in 1942), Alan recorded new and established artists both in Washington and on field trips. Among those with whom he worked were Vera Hall, Horton Barker and, in 1939, the great Leadbelly. During 1939, he also recorded famous jazz pianist Jelly Roll Morton, and began a new folk music series for Columbia Broadcasting's School of the Air, called "Wellsprings of America." Alan played recordings of old and new artists, discussed folk music aspects, and sang some songs himself.

During World War II, Alan was active in government-sponsored morale programs. In 1943 and 1944, he worked for the Office of War Information. He also worked with the Army's Special Services section in 1944 and '45. When the war ended, he accepted an invitation from Decca Records to serve as its director of folk music. His selections helped make the Decca catalog one of the strongest in this field in the late '40s and early 1950s.

Lomax continued to collect and classify folk material in the post-World War II era. He was helped in this by a 1947 Guggenheim grant. He continued his broadcast work with a 1950 program for Mutual Broadcasting, "Your Ballad Man Alan Lomax."

In 1958, Tradition Records issued an LP featuring Lomax's voice called "Texas Folk Songs." Among the album numbers were "Billy Barlow," "Ain't No More Cane on This Brazos," "The Dying Cowboy," "My Little John Henry," "All the Pretty Little Horses," "The Wild Rippling Water," "Black Betty," "Rattlesnake," "Eadie," "Long Summer Days," "Sam Bass," "Lord Lovell" and "Godamighty Drag."

Lomax continued active in the 1960s as an artist and scholar. He performed at a number of festivals, including Newport. He also helped in the direction of some of these, an example being his service as a member of the board of advisors of the American Folk Festival at Asheville, North Carolina. He was one of the founding members of the Newport Folk Foundation and served on the Board of Directors of the Folk Festival for several years starting in 1963. In the 1960s, Kapp Records produced another album of Lomax singing, "Folk Song Saturday Night."

Over the years, Lomax also wrote many books and articles, both scholarly and of popular interest. He worked on a number of books with his father, including *American Ballads and Folk Songs* ('34); *Cowboy Songs and Other Frontier Ballads* (revised edition, '38); *Negro Folk Songs as Sung by Leadbelly* ('36); *Our Singing Country* ('41); and *Folk Song, U.S.A.* ('47). With Sidney Robertson Cowell, he compiled the *American Folk Song and Folk Lore* regional bibliography in 1942. In 1960, Alan was represented by *The Folk Songs of North America in the English Language*.

His activities in the 1950s and '60s included lecturing on folklore at such schools as New York University, Columbia University, University of Indiana, University of Chicago, and the University of Texas. From 1951 to 1957, he served as editor for the Columbia Records World Library of Folk and Primitive Music (17-volume set). Beginning in 1963, he started a comprehensive study in comparative musicology, work he was still engaged in as of 1969. (*See also* HAWES, BESS LOMAX; LOMAX, JOHN AVERY)

LOMAX, JOHN AVERY: Folklorist, folk music collector, educator. Born Goodman, Mississippi, September 23, 1875; died Greenville, Mississippi, January 26, 1948.

The name Lomax is a pioneer name in many ways. Lomax ancestors were among the first settlers of the nation and of the southwest. One of the descendants of this hardy family, John Avery Lomax, helped preserve the musical heritage of pioneer days while himself pioneering the new areas of American folklore scholarship of the twentieth century.

Born in Mississippi and raised in the southwest, John Lomax had an ear for folk ballads of hills and plains from his very early years. When he reached his teens, he began to collect some of this material as best he could. He went around near his home with pencil in hand and listened to farmers, itinerant musicians, and cowboys. He scrawled their lyrics down on an assortment of papers, including the backs of envelopes and pieces of cardboard and wrapping paper. By the time he was in his late teens, he had a considerable pile of these odd-looking manuscripts.

In the mid-1890s, he gathered his belongings making ready to enter the University of Texas at Austin. In among his clothes and some tattered textbooks was his collection of song material. He had no way of knowing that collecting this kind of material was almost unheard of in academic ranks in those years. At the University, he had occasion to show the notes to one of his English professors, Dr. Morgan Callaway, Jr. Dr. Callaway glanced through them and suggested they were of little value.

The disappointed Lomax filed them away and went on to gain his B.A. in 1897. Moving toward a career as an English instructor, he attended a number of schools over the next decade. He took some courses at the University of Chicago in 1903 and 1906 and also continued to attend the University of Texas, receiving his M.A. in 1906. He then moved north to Harvard, having received an Austin Teaching Scholarship, to work toward another Master's in American Literature (1907). In one course given by Barrett Wendell, he received an assignment to bring in examples of native literature. Lomax dug out his old files and this time won the wholehearted attention of his teacher.

Wendell introduced young Lomax to the nation's first-ranked folklorist, George Lyman Kittredge. Kittredge shared Wendell's enthusiasm and both supported further collecting by Lomax. From then on, collecting was an important part of Lomax's life and, in time, the lives of his children. Helped by a Shelden Travelling Fellowship, he went back to the southwest. There he spent three years on its backroads with an Ediphone recording machine to make on-the-spot cylinders of folk melodies.

He returned to the east and, after several rejections, got a publisher. The firm of Sturgis & Walton agreed to produce a book with 122 song texts, 18 with the music. Included in the book was a letter in praise of Lomax's work from Theodore Roosevelt who had been shown the manuscript by Lomax during a Frontier Day Celebration in Cheyenne, Wyoming. Published in 1910, Lomax's *Cowboy Songs and Other Frontier Ballads* was a landmark that compared with the publication in the previous century of Francis James Child's ballad books.

Lomax continued to follow the usual pattern of collectors, earning a living in other ways and pursuing new material in his spare time. From 1903 to 1910, for instance, he had held the title of Associate Professor of English at Texas A&M College. From 1910 to 1917, he was Secretary of the University of Texas in Austin.

For a while, from 1925 to 1932, he varied his pattern by entering the banking business. Though still interested in folk music, his bank work kept him from spending much time on it.

In 1933, he finally embarked on another major collecting tour, this time with his 17-year-old son Alan. The Depression, which resulted in the failure of his bank, was the reason for the tour. To make ends meet, John signed a contract with a publisher for a folk song book. He and Alan built a 350-pound recorder into the back of their car and garnered hundreds of new songs.

These were published by The Macmillan Company in 1934 under the title *American Ballads and Folk Songs*. The raw material collected on the trip was sent to the Library of Congress in Washington. It so impressed Library officials that John Lomax was asked to come to Washington in 1934 as Honorary Consultant and Archivist, Curator of the new Archive of American Folk Song.

During the 1930s and '40s, John and Alan built this collection up into the most impressive in the world. Thousands of songs were added either through field trips or through bringing folk artists to Washington. In time, Alan succeeded his father as curator. In the years between 1934 and his death, John gained a worldwide reputation. He continued to write books on folk music subjects, many with Alan, and lecture before learned and lay groups. The final fruits of his labors were a new awareness of the importance of folk material and the use of the collection as a basis for growth by new folk artists who came to the Library to help increase their knowledge of the field. (*See also* HAWES, BESS LOMAX; LOMAX, ALAN)

LONG, HUBERT: Talent manager. Born Poteet, Texas, December 3, 1923.

Hubert Long picked many berries in his youth in Poteet, Texas, the strawberry capital of the state. He and his brothers and sisters lived with their mother and father, a farmer and oil-hand, in Poteet and later in Freer, Texas, where Hubert went to high school. Then the Long family moved to Corpus Christi, to which Hubert, after a three-year term with the Navy in the Pacific theater, returned to a job as assistant manager of a dime store. What he heard and learned from record salesmen who serviced the store whetted his appetite for the non-strawberry field and he organized a campaign, which worked, to become a regional sales representative for Decca Records and, later, for RCA Victor Records.

While servicing the Houston Fat Stock Show for RCA Victor, Long met Eddy Arnold and the legendary Colonel Tom Parker. Parker, already a star-maker, advised Arnold to hire the dynamic youngster as an advance publicity man, an occupation that Parker had worked at years earlier for tent shows and carnivals. Long did an impressive job for Arnold under Parker's tutelage, and in 1953 set up his own business, the Hubert Long Talent Agency, with Parker's blessing.

Sensing the exploitational explosion that would come for country music, Long started his own publishing firm, Moss Rose Publications, in 1959. He also looked over real estate, checked out the film industry, courted network executives and sponsors, followed the foreign entertainment patterns, kept close to established grass-roots fair dates, and did the myriad things that at some point might have some correlation to the modern company conglomerate he was establishing.

His "Stable of Stars" management took charge of personal appearances as well as film and television activities for many artists, including Ferlin Husky, George Jones, Bill Anderson, Roy Drusky, Del Reeves, David Houston, Charlie Walker, Jan Howard, Jim Edward Brown, Leroy Van Dyke, Margie Bowes, Skeeter

Davis and others. County fairs, nightclubs, television shows, motion picture work, and foreign assignments are a part of "where it is" for country talent. Long gained a reputation for "feeling" the market and exploring market potential, getting good prices for his talent, and building performers' careers.

His appreciation of real estate values put him into the owner's penthouse office of the Capitol Records Building in Nashville. He expanded into producing records with Tommy "Snuff" Garrett, in Hollywood. As with his artists and songwriters, Long built an internal organization with emphasis on employee growth and responsibility. Long represents the newer "inside" breed of manager for country music who has studied, practiced, and learned the field.

LONZO AND OSCAR: Vocal and instrumental comedy duo, revolving around the Sullivan brothers (1945–'67), both born Edmonton, Kentucky, John (Lonzo), born July 7, 1917, died Nashville, Tennessee, June 5, 1967; Rollin (Oscar), born January 19, 1919.

The top comedy duo of the Grand Ole Opry for many years went by the names of Lonzo and Oscar. For the greatest part of this time, it was a brother act, comprising Johnny Sullivan (Lonzo) and his younger (by almost two years) brother, Rollin Sullivan (Oscar). The team did not start as a brother act, however, nor did it end as one.

The Sullivan brothers were both born in Edmonton, Kentucky. Their family was not well off and the boys had to work hard in their early years at many jobs. However, country music was a staple item of relaxation and both Sullivans took to playing and singing when still quite young. By the time they were in their teens, Johnny could play both bass fiddle and guitar and Rollin was on his way to becoming a top mandolin player. The brothers were both performing in small clubs in the region by the end of the 1930s.

Just before World War II, the Sullivans made their radio debut on station WTJS, Jackson, Tennessee. One of their associates was a talented performer named Ken Marvin (born in Haleyville, Alabama, June 27, 1924). Marvin teamed with Rollin to form the original Lonzo and Oscar team, Marvin serving as Lonzo. Marvin and Rollin Sullivan did the first recordings of the comic duo. Among their songs was the na-

The original Lonzo and Oscar comedy team, Ken Marvin (left) and Rollin Sullivan

all parts of the country and overseas, Lonzo and Oscar had many TV credits. These included 24 films of their own show for TV and guest spots on the Kate Smith, Ed Sullivan, and Dave Garroway shows.

The team recorded on many labels over the years, including RCA; Decca; Starday; their own company, Nugget; and, in 1967, Columbia. Their single records included such songs as "If Texas Knew What Arkansas," "I'll Go Chasin' Wimmin," "My Dreams Turned Into a Nightmare," "Ole Buttermilk Sky," "My Adobe Hacienda," "Julie," "Hearts Are Lonely," and "Movin' On." Their repertoire included many original compositions, such as "You Blacked My Blue Eyes Too Often," "Last Old Dollar," "There's a Hole in the Bottom of the Sea," "I Don't Forgive No More," "Take Them Cold Feet Out of My Back," "Cornbread, Lasses and Sassafras Tea," and "She's the Best I Ever Saw."

Their LPs included "Country Comedy Time," Decca Records; and, on Starday, "Lonzo and Oscar" ('61) and "Country Music Time" ('63).

LORD, BOBBY: Singer, guitarist, m.c. Born Sanford, Florida, January 6, 1934.

One of the most promising rhythm singers presented on Paul Whiteman's TV show in the 1950s was a teenager from Florida named Bobby Lord. A bright future was predicted for him. The prediction proved true, though Bobby gained stardom in the country and western field rather than the popular.

Robert Lord returned to his home state to go to the University of Tampa. He had been exposed to country music as a boy, and during his freshman year he drew on this to establish his own TV show, Bobby Lord's Homefolks Show. In the late '50s, he was lured from Tampa to join the cast of Red Foley's new network country and western program, Jubilee U.S.A. For five years, Lord was a featured member of the ABC show originating from Springfield, Missouri.

By this time, Bobby had several popular hits to his credit on Columbia Records, including "Hawkeye" and "Without Your Love." In the early 1960s he recorded for Hickory Records, achieving a hit with "Life Can Have Meaning." In 1965, Harmony Records issued an LP, "Best of Bobby Lord." During the mid-1960s, Bobby was featured on Decca label.

In the 1960s, Bobby guested on many major

tionwide comic hit, written by the Sullivans, "I'm My Own Grandpa."

The careers of the Sullivans came to a halt temporarily when both entered the service. By the mid-1940s, they had been mustered out and joined a band playing on station WAVE, Louisville. Soon after this, Ken Marvin retired and Johnny took over as Lonzo. The brothers then became members of the Eddy Arnold troupe for several years. In 1947, they left Eddy to form their own group. That year, Lonzo and Oscar also became regulars on the Grand Ole Opry. They remained comic mainstays of the show for twenty years, until Johnny's death. Several months after John's passing, the team was reactivated with a new Lonzo, Dave Hooten, of St. Claire, Missouri.

During the 1950s and '60s, the Sullivan brothers toured widely with their own show. Among the members of the show over the years were many Opry stars, including Cousin Jody, Cousin Luther, Smokey Pleacher, and Tommy Warren. In addition to personal appearances in

TV shows, including those of Porter Wagoner, Wilburn Brothers, and Flatt & Scruggs as well as the American Swing-Around. Soon after leaving Springfield, he was asked to move to Nashville as a regular on the Grand Ole Opry.

Once settled in Nashville, a new facet of his career sprang up: he was given his own taped syndicated show. Called the Bobby Lord Show, it featured Jerry Byrd's Band, The Marijohn Singers, and, as guests, many of his co-stars from the Opry. By 1967, the WSM-produced show was featured on stations in all parts of the country.

LOUDERMILK, JOHN D.: Writer, musician, singer. Born Durham, North Carolina, March 31, 1934.

John D. Loudermilk was born the day before April first. His father, a carpenter, helped build the chapel at Duke University in Durham, North Carolina, but could neither read nor write so took his young son down to the grocery store on Saturday afternoons to endorse his pay checks. Some twenty-five years later,

John Loudermilk

Loudermilk was married in that same chapel to Miss Gwen Cooke.

His mother was a moving woman and, Loudermilk recalls, she would pack up pasteboard cartons and have the moving van transport the household to a new home. There were nineteen such moves within the same school district before Loudermilk left home to attend junior college. Prior to that, at the age of eleven, he had his own top-rated country radio show in Durham.

His first music concept was based on what he heard in church, singing to stringed instruments, horns, tambourines, hand clapping and a big bass drum. His country feel developed early when, on Saturday nights, he would soak in a galvanized wash tub placed next to the kitchen stove and, against the fresh-scrubbed linoleum and Ivory soap smells close to the floor, listen to Judge Hay bellow out the preliminary: "The Gra-nd Ol-e O-pry. . . ."

Further influences, particularly during his high school years, were Eddy Arnold, Jimmy Reed, Andres Segovia, Ivory Joe Hunter, Fats Domino, Lloyd Price, and Kahlil Gibran, the Far Eastern philosopher-poet. Following high school, Loudermilk worked at his hometown television station painting sets, playing bass fiddle and performing solo guitar on camera.

Against this backdrop emerged the songwriter whose first effort was a poem set to music, which he played on television to excited listener reaction. One of the listeners was George Hamilton IV, a student at nearby University of North Carolina, who recorded it. The song, "A Rose and a Baby Ruth," made Hamilton a national star.

It was then that Loudermilk went to junior college and wrote Eddie Cochran's first hit, "Sittin' in the Balcony." Offers from Nashville and New York publishers caused Loudermilk to pack and leave for home, where he met Gwen Cooke, a Duke University music major, who decided to drop out and marry him.

He then took the plunge, having some royalty money left, and went to Nashville. There he affiliated with Jim Denny and Cedarwood Music Publishing Company, Inc., met Chet Atkins, and started his current career. He later joined Acuff-Rose Publications, Inc. Results have been "Waterloo," "Language of Love," "Ebony Eyes," "Talk Back Trembling Lips," "Abilene," "Sad Movies," "Norman," "Paper Tiger," "From Nashville with Love," "Thou Shalt Not

Steal," and "Bad News," among scores of songs and recordings.

He was signed as a recording artist by RCA Victor. Unlike most artists, though, he rarely, makes personal appearances. His interests vary: a collection of old railroad dining room lamps; a preoccupation with hurricanes that sees him personally covering each as they boil up the Atlantic Coast; a fascination with bomb shelters (he was recognized by the government for an innovation that safeguarded shelters from one kind of dangerous radiation); a room full of guitars (he composes only on a concert classic model), and people.

LOUISIANA HAYRIDE: Weekly variety show, originating from station KWKH, Shreveport, Louisiana.

The Louisiana Hayride figures in biographies of many of the greatest stars of country and western music. Again and again, the bio will indicate that an artist received his or her first major exposure on this program. Among those who first gained fame on the Hayride are: Elvis Presley, Hank Williams, Johnny Cash, Jim Reeves, T. Texas Tyler, Slim Whitman, Faron Young, George Jones, Wilburn Brothers, Webb Pierce, Floyd Cramer, Kitty Wells, The Browns, Claude King, Johnny Horton, Goldie Hill and Sonny James.

The Hayride began on April 3, 1948, with Horace Logan as program director, a position he held for ten years. The first show featured Johnnie and Jack with Kitty Wells, Bailes Brothers, Four Deacons, Curley Kinsey and the Tennessee Ridge Runners, Harmie Smith and the Ozark Mountaineers, Tex Grinsey and his Texas Playboys and Pappy Covington's band. One of its first cast members to achieve nationwide stardom was Hank Williams, who was with the Hayride from August 7, 1948, to June 3, 1949. His closing number on the Hayride was "Lovesick Blues." Later, Jim Reeves both starred on the show and recorded some of his major hits in the KWKH studios. Elvis Presley appeared on the Hayride in October 1954, and soon after signed a year's contract with the show.

The Hayride was a feature every Saturday night over KWKH and associated stations in the south and southwest until 1958, after which it continued to be heard on KWKH, but not on a regular basis. In the 1960s, the show was made up of guest artists rather than a regular

cast. It returned briefly to a weekly schedule for the summer of 1966.

LOUVIN, CHARLIE: Singer, guitarist, songwriter. Born Rainesville, Alabama, July 7, 1927.

In 1967, one of the best-selling LPs on Capitol was called "I'll Remember Always." The album was a tribute by Charlie Louvin to the memory of his brother Ira with whom he had formed one of the greatest singing teams in country music history. But the record also was testimony to the fact that Charlie Louvin was as successful as a solo performer as he had been in the days of the Louvin Brothers.

The boys were raised on a farm in Henegar, Alabama. Like many rural youths they obtained guitars and learned to play long before reaching high school age, and began performing at local functions by the time they were in their early teens. Music, though, was only a hobby, for they had plenty of chores on the farm to occupy a good part of their time. In the early 1940s, the brothers showed their music potential by winning a talent contest in Chattanooga, Tennessee. Their careers had to wait, however, for they entered the service for the last stages of World War II.

When they returned, things began looking up when Smiling Eddie Hill signed them for station WNOX, Knoxville. They performed regularly on the station's "Mid-Day Merry-Go-Round." Audience interest continued to grow, but once more war intervened when Charlie was recalled to service during the Korean emergency. Charlie returned in the early 1950s to team up with Ira on a Memphis show. The job was still spare time, for they earned most of their living working in the U.S. Post Office.

At this point, their reputation had begun to circulate through the industry. They had made their first record for Decca in the 1940s and then signed with MGM for two years. Their records had received favorable comment, but no hits had resulted. But Ken Nelson, a Capitol Records executive, was impressed with their ability and traveled to Memphis to sign them to a long-term contract. From 1951 on, the brothers (and, later, Charlie Louvin alone) recorded for Capitol.

The Louvin Brothers soon turned out the first of the more than 100 single records they made for Capitol. As the early '50s went by, their audience increased rapidly as more and more DJs played their material. In 1955, they were asked to join the cast of the Grand Ole Opry. Between 1955 and 1963, the Louvin Brothers turned out one hit record after another, including many songs they wrote themselves. Among the latter are "When I Stop Dreaming," "The Weapon of Prayer," and "I Take the Chance." For five straight years, they were voted "Most Programmed Duet" and "Most Programmed Sacred Group" by the nation's country and western disk jockeys.

Among their top hits were three top 10 songs in 1956: "Hoping That You're Hoping," "I Don't Believe You've Met My Baby," and "You're Running Wild." In 1956, they had a best-seller in "My Baby's Gone." In all, 20 LP albums were turned out by the brothers, half of which were of religious songs. During their partnership, the brothers sang before audiences in all parts of the U.S. and Canada and were featured on most major TV country and western shows.

In 1963, Charlie decided to try his hand as a single. In a short time it was evident the Louvins were as good on their own as together. Louvin's

first song, "I Don't Love You Anymore," became a major hit and reached the top 10 in 1964. He followed with many other hit singles, including "Less and Less," "Think I'll Go Somewhere and Cry Myself to Sleep," "You Finally Said Something Good," "Off and On" and a major hit of 1965, "See the Big Man Cry, Mama." After Ira's death in an auto accident on Father's Day, 1965, Charlie paid tribute to his brother by singing many of their hits at each personal performance. In the mid-1960s, his network TV appearances, other than the Grand Ole Opry, included the shows of Porter Wagoner, Bobby Lord, Bill Anderson, Wilburn Brothers, and Flatt & Scruggs, as well as American Swing-Around.

By 1967, Charlie already had four solo LPs to his credit. These were "I Don't Love You Anymore," "Many Moods of Charlie Louvin," "Lonesome Is Me" and "I'll Remember Always." He also continued to appear on nationwide honors lists, starting with a National Academy of Recording Arts and Sciences nomination for the 1965 Grammy award.

In addition to his other chores, Charlie also found time to appear in two movies, "Music City, U.S.A." and "The Golden Guitar."

LOUVIN, IRA: Singer, guitarist, songwriter. Born Rainesville, Alabama, April 21, 1924; died near Jefferson City, Missouri, June 20, 1965.

An automobile accident on Father's Day, 1965, brought the fabulous career of the Louvin Brothers to a close. For more than a decade, the Louvin Brothers had been among the top two or three brother acts in the country music field. Their combined talents had won them 20 BMI awards for songwriting and 18 awards from major trade magazines for their performances.

Ira was three years senior to his brother Charlie. Both boys were born in Rainesville, Alabama, and raised on the family farm. Both learned to play the guitar and sing country songs in their early years. By their teens they were living in Tennessee, still helping their father and singing in their spare time. Ira was in his late teens when the brothers scored their first success by winning a talent contest in Chattanooga. Soon after, both entered the service and went separate ways for a while during World War II.

They returned to team up on WNOX's

The Louvin Brothers

"Mid-Day Merry-Go-Round." In the late '40s, their career blossomed with increasing acceptance as performers by Tennessee audiences. After recording one song for Decca, the boys were signed by MGM Records and turned out a number of songs for that label in 1949-50. The Korean War came along; Charlie went off to the Army while Ira remained behind to perform as a single.

In 1951, Charlie was discharged and the Louvins started anew in Memphis. The boys worked in the U.S. Post Office and moonlighted on their own radio show. The first step towards full-time music careers then appeared in the person of Ken Nelson of Capitol Records who signed the Louvin Brothers to a long-term contract. As their records began to appear regularly on the hit charts, the brothers also began to star on some of the major network country shows. In 1955, they joined the Grand Ole Opry and remained headliners on the show for the next decade.

Many of the more than 100 singles made for Capitol by the brothers were hits, and many of these were drawn from the more than 300 songs written by Ira and Charlie. The 20 LPs of their work issued by Capitol included "Ira and Charlie" and "Family Who Prays" ('58); "Love Ballads" and "Satan Is Real" ('59); "My Baby's Gone" ('60); "Encore" ('61); "The Weapon of Prayer" ('62); "Keep Your Eyes on Jesus" ('63); and "Current Hits" ('64). Besides these albums with Charlie, Ira also turned out one LP as a single.

While the boys still worked together, in 1963, both began to work separately as well. Ira's career was cut tragically short. He and his wife, Florence (who sang under the professional name of Anne Young), were killed in a head-on collision on a Missouri highway on their way back to Nashville from an engagement in Jefferson City. He was buried at Harpeth Memory Gardens on Route 100, fifteen miles west of Nashville. (*See also* LOUVIN, CHARLIE)

LULU BELLE: Singer, guitarist, comedienne. Born Boone, North Carolina, December 24, 1913.

Two of the names best known to country music audiences from the 1930s into the 1950s were Lulu Belle and Scotty. The comedy and singing of this husband-and-wife team were more familiar to fans in some parts of the country than performances of Grand Ole Opry stars, because of the wide network coverage of the National Barn Dance in the 1930s and '40s.

Lulu Belle was the stage name of Myrtle Eleanor Cooper Wiseman. Like Scott Wiseman, she was born and raised in North Carolina. She learned to play guitar by her teens and performed in local events in the late 1920s. For a while she worked as a store clerk before succeeding in show business. In 1932, she auditioned and made the National Barn Dance in Chicago. A year later she teamed with another young Barn Dance member, starting a long career as part of the act they called Lulu Belle and Scotty, and which eventually became, permanently, Mr. and Mrs. Wiseman.

Before long, Lulu Belle and Scotty were favorites of WLS National Barn Dance audiences. In 1934, their records began to receive wide play, beginning with such hits as "Home Coming Time" and "Whippoorwill Time." In the 1930s and '40s, they scored with such other hits as "Mountain Dew," "Empty Christmas Stocking," "Time Will Tell," "In the Doghouse Now," "Have I Told You Lately That I Love You" and "My Heart Cries for You."

Besides starring on the Barn Dance, Lulu Belle and Scotty had a top rated program of their own on WLS, Breakfast in the Blue Ridge, that remained on the station from 1933 to 1958. They held forth on the Barn Dance for almost 25 years, except for a short sojourn in the early 1940s on the Boone County Jamboree on station WLW in Cincinnati. Their presence helped start the Jamboree toward future network status as the Midwestern Hayride.

They later complemented their radio work on the Barn Dance with TV appearances on station WNBQ-TV in Chicago. The WNBQ relationship lasted from 1949 to 1957. Lulu Belle and Scotty also guested on many major country shows, including the Grand Ole Opry, Steve Allen Show (in 1955), and Ozark Jubilee. From 1938 to the mid-1940s, they starred in a number of movies.

In 1958, the Wisemans went into semi-retirement in Scott's home town of Spruce Pine, North Carolina. They continued to be fondly remembered by their fans, as shown by the reception to the Starday LPs of their work released in the 1960s. These included "Lulu Belle and Scotty" ('63) and "Down Memory Lane" ('64). (*See also* WISEMAN, SCOTTY)

LUMAN, BOB: Singer, guitarist. Born Nacogdoches, Texas, April 15, 1937.

As a boy in the almost unpronounceable town

of Nacogdoches, Bobby Glynn Luman spent many weekend hours listening to the Grand Ole Opry on the radio. Like many youngsters in the south and southwest, he had two dreams —to become a star of the Opry, or to become a star athlete.

Bob's father, a school custodian, encouraged him in both, but particularly provided a good example in music. Luman senior was an excellent fiddler, guitarist, and harmonica player, and Bob learned country and western songs by listening to his father. He also learned to play the guitar before he reached high school age.

As Bob grew into his teens, he developed into a strapping 200-pounder, a natural for high school athletics, and, for a time, a baseball career seemed to beckon. By this time, the family had moved to Kilgore, Texas. At the beginning of his junior year, Bob organized his own band and, as the band won increasing attention around town, it nosed out athletics in Bob's estimation.

Bob graduated from Kilgore High in the late 1940s and began to perform in local clubs. He entered a talent contest in Tyler, Texas, and walked off with first prize. This led to more engagements in various Texas towns. Bob's name began to be well known beyond Texas borders, resulting in a bid to guest on the Louisiana Hayride in Shreveport, where he did so well that he was soon asked to become a regular. During the 1950s, Bob was heard on many stations across the country. He also toured almost all fifty states. He signed with Warner Brothers Records and turned out a number of records that sold well, though none made the top 10 national list. In 1960, though, he hit with "Let's Think About Living." The song sold more than a million copies.

During the 1960s, Bob was one of the favorites of national country and western audiences. He turned out many records that made the charts for both Warner Brothers and, in the mid-1960s, Hickory Records. Epic Records signed Bob in the late 1960s. His output for Epic included the 1968 chart hit "Ain't Got Time to Be Unhappy." He guested on most of the major network TV country and western shows during these years, including the Grand Ole Opry, and appeared in the movie "Carnival Rock."

In August 1964, Bob's boyhood dream finally came true. He was asked to become a regular member of the Grand Ole Opry cast.

LUNSFORD, BASCOM LAMAR: Singer, fiddler, banjoist, folk festival organizer and director. Born Mars Hill, North Carolina, March 21, 1882.

The folk festival has played a major role both in preserving much of America's folk heritage and in rekindling widespread interest among new generations for this kind of material. Not all of the festivals have maintained a relatively catholic outlook on the kind of material played, but high standards were always a hallmark of the many festivals organized and/or directed by long-time folklorist Bascom Lunsford.

Lunsford was taught to love folk music when he was a child by his schoolteacher father and musically inclined mother. While he was in grade school, he often sang folksongs at local affairs and school parties. By the time he was high school age, he had a considerable repertoire of traditional music and was accomplished at playing both fiddle and banjo.

Folk music seemed an unlikely way to earn a living, so he pointed toward a profession. After finishing high school at Camp Academy, Leicester, North Carolina, he went on to Rutherford and Trinity Colleges. In 1913, he received his law degree. Law was not completely to his taste, however, and he sought other ways of earning rent money in the following years. For a time he was a teacher. He also worked at such jobs as auctioneer and newspaper editor.

He continued to perform whenever he could and, in 1920, began to collect folk music in earnest after meeting the avid collector Robert W. Gordon. In the 1920s, he and Gordon went on tours throughout the southern hill country collecting songs, meeting performers, and taking part in local dances and other celebrations.

As Lunsford's interest deepened, he began to think of organizing some kind of annual event that would provide a meeting place for folk artists and enthusiasts to exchange information, and also to be a showcase for folk artistry. In 1928, this resulted in his starting the Mountain Dance and Folk Festival at Asheville, North Carolina. Over the years, the festival matured under his direction until it became one of the most important in the country. In the 1960s, this festival was still going strong, attracting hundreds of performers and thousands of listeners.

By the early 1930s, Lunsford had a national reputation among folklorists. He was asked to record some of his songs for the Columbia

University Library in 1935 and he complied by singing 315 of them. Later, John and Alan Lomax asked him to provide material for the Archive of American Folk Song of the Library of Congress. So great was his backlog of material that he sang an additional 400 numbers for the Washington collection, and still had several thousand more in his files.

During the late 1930s, he was director of a group of Appalachian folk dancers and singers who appeared in major cities throughout the U.S. President Franklin D. Roosevelt admired Lunsford's work and asked him to bring a troupe to perform for the King and Queen of England at the White House in 1939.

Lunsford helped the war effort in the mid-1940s and entertained for charitable events. He organized the Annual Folk Festival at Renfro, Kentucky, in 1946, and two years later helped set up the North Carolina State Fair Folk Festival at Raleigh. In 1949, he delighted audiences in London and at the First International Folk Music Festival in Venice.

He continued to expand the folk festival spectrum in the 1950s. In 1952, he directed the first East Carolina Folk Festival at Kenansville, North Carolina.

Despite his many folksong laurels, Lunsford was not represented on many commercially available records. There were a few such LPs available, however, in the 1960s, on Riverside and Folkways. The Riverside LP was called "Minstrel of the Appalachians." It included such songs as "Go to Italy," "I Shall Not Be Moved," "Sundown," "Poor Jesse James," "The Miller's Will," "The Old Man from the North Country," "Sundown," "Fly Around, My Blue Eyed Girl," "Black Jack Davy," "Weeping Willow Tree," "Swing Low, Sweet Chariot," and "The Sailor on the Deep Blue Sea." For Folkways, Lunsford recorded an LP called "Smoky Mountain Ballads," which included "Mr. Garfield," "Jennie Jenkins," "Little Margaret," "On the Banks of the Ohio," "Springfield Mountain," and "The Death of Queen Jane."

LUTE: Stringed instrument of ancient origin.

Many of the art masterpieces of the Renaissance and Middle Ages show people playing the pear-shaped stringed instrument called the lute. The instrument is considered to be of much more ancient origin than this, however. Traces of its development have been discerned in ancient China. Experts believe its use spread from the Chinese to the Arabs who, in turn, introduced it to Europe.

The lute, while pear-shaped when viewed from the front, has a flat upper body surface and a bulbous lower body outline. The neck of the instrument is somewhat shorter than that of the conventional guitar and the pegbox is bent back at an angle. The strings are plucked with the fingers rather than with a pick. Unlike the guitar, it has no bridge.

The modern guitar is considered to be a descendant of the lute. The guitar, from this evolution, took over much of the folk music picture, and by the 1800s, use of the lute was a dying art. A number of folk artists in Europe, most particularly Sven Scholander of Sweden, reintroduced the instrument into modern folk concerts. When Richard Dyer-Bennet visited Scholander in the 1940s, he learned to appreciate the lute and used it in many concerts throuughout the U.S. Country artist Hugh X. Lewis also features lute playing. Several other performers have occasionally used the lute in folk concerts in the post-World War II era, though massive revival of lute-playing is unlikely.

LYNN, JUDY: Singer, songwriter. Born Boise, Idaho, April 12, 1936.

When Judy Lynn appears on stage in a western outfit, she's doin' what comes naturally. Born and brought up in the rugged western terrain of Idaho, she could rope and ride with the best of them when she was still a youngster.

Judy started her singing career early, making her debut before an audience when she was 10. In her teens, she continued to expand her entertainment routines and also appeared as a rider in rodeos. At 16, she was crowned Queen of the Snake River Stampede, Nampa, Idaho, a title that gained her a duet with guest star Gene Autry. In the mid-1950s, she entered and won several beauty contests. Her choice as Miss Idaho led to a runner-up spot in the 1955 Miss America contest.

Following the Miss America contest, Judy achieved a somewhat different title, that of America's Champion Girl Yodeler. By now she was achieving recognition in the music field. Before long, she was appearing in shows throughout the country with many first rank stars, including Rex Allen, Eddie Fisher, Eddy Arnold, Elvis Presley and Red Foley.

In 1957, she shared m.c. honors with Ernest Tubb on the first coast-to-coast Grand Ole Opry telecast. Her abilities won her more honors in the next few years, including a Pioneer magazine award as "Best Western Female Vocalist" and "Best Dressed Western Female" and a Billboard award as "Most Promising Female Vocalist."

By the early 1960s, she had her own TV show, the Judy Lynn Show, featured on many of the nation's stations. In 1962, she signed her first major recording contract with United Artists. In a short time, she had her first top 10 hit, "Footsteps of a Fool." Several other singles for United Artists and, later on, for Pappy Daily's Musicor label, sold in the several-hundred-thousand bracket during the mid-1960s. Among her successes were a number of her own compositions, including "My Father's Voice," "Antique in My Closet," "The Calm Before the Storm," and "Honey Stuff." Through 1967, Judy turned out 12 LP albums, including "Judy Lynn" ('63); "Most Promising Female Vocalist" ('64) and "The Judy Lynn Story" ('65). She is married to promoter John Kelly.

LYNN, LORETTA: Singer, guitarist, band leader. Born Butchers Hollow, Kentucky, April 14, 1935.

The nation's country and western DJs knew whereof they spoke in 1961 when they voted Loretta Lynn the next to reach top ranking. The little lady (5 feet, 2½ inches) from Butchers Hollow, Kentucky, began a string of major hits in 1962 that was still going strong in 1969.

Loretta Webb spent her formative years in the coal mining region of eastern Kentucky. Her home town was two miles east of Van Leer in the Appalachian Mountains. Country and folk music were prime ways of relaxing in that part of the U.S. and Loretta often sang along with parents and friends when she was grade school age. She had plenty of company right at home, for her seven brothers and sisters enjoyed family sings as well.

In her teens, she performed for local functions and sang on radio stations in the region. Then the Webb family moved to Wabash, Indiana, when the Butchers Hollow mines closed down. Loretta continued to gain experience as a country artist. In the late 1950s she moved to Custer, Washington, and sang in nightclubs

Loretta Lynn

and shows throughout the state. She formed her own band for these engagements, which soon included her brother, Jay Lee Webb, on guitar.

During one of the club dates, an executive of Zero Records heard her and quickly got her name on a contract. Soon after, she recorded "I'm a Honky Tonk Girl." The song began to receive many plays nationally, resulting in engagements for Loretta and her group in many major cities, including Nashville.

Before long, the major recording companies were bidding for her services. In the early 1960s, she signed with Decca and moved to Nashville. By 1962, she was represented on the hit charts by the appropriately titled "Success." That year, she won the Cashbox award as "Most Programmed Female Country Star." Loretta continued to turn out top 10 hits, including "'Before I'm Over You" in 1963 and "Wine, Women and Song" in '64. The next year was a banner one, with three major successes, "Blue Kentucky Girl," "Happy Birthday," and "The Home You're Tearing Down." Her 1966 top hits were "Dear Uncle Sam" and

[185]

"You Ain't Woman Enough." She was soon represented by a number of well received LPs, including "Loretta Lynn," "Before I'm Over You," "I Like 'em Country," "Country Christmas," and "Hymns."

Her move to Nashville was naturally accompanied by a bid to join the Grand Ole Opry cast. During the 1960s, her tours covered every part of the country as well as Canada and Europe. She also was a guest star on most of the major TV network country shows.

Her career gained even greater impetus in 1967. She had four major hits, including "If You're Not Gone Too Long," and "Don't Come Home a-Drinkin'." Her album successes for the year included the eighth-ranked best-seller, "Don't Come Home a-Drinkin'," and the eleventh-ranked "You Ain't Woman Enough." Based on these successes, Billboard listed her as "Top Country Female Artist" for 1967, a title she retained in 1968. Her '68 hits included "First City" and "You've Just Stepped In," and LPs "First City" and "Singin' with Feelin'."

MAC ARTHUR, MARGARET CROWL: Singer, autoharpist, folk music collector. Born Chicago, Illinois, 1928.

Margaret MacArthur became an authority on the folk songs of Vermont the long way around.

Though her birthplace was Chicago, by the time she was four the Crowl family had moved to Utah. Her father was a forester and followed the trail of the timber market. In 1934, the family found itself in the Sierra Anchas of Arizona, followed by several more moves to other parts of the southwest. Little Margaret began to take note of the music performed in impromptu after-work get-togethers by the men of the timber camps. Many of them came from the cattle ranches or hill country farms of the border and southwestern states. From them, Margaret learned to love traditional country music and cowboy songs.

Her horizons in folk music were widened still more in 1938 when the family settled in Licking, Missouri. For the next four years, they remained in the heart of the Ozarks region. Here, even more than in the timber camps, singing was an everyday affair. By now, Margaret could sing along with neighbors and friends at local gatherings.

The trail moved out west once more in 1942, this time bringing the family to California. They lived for a while in Salinas in the San Joaquin Valley and in the desert community of Thousand Palms. The next year, it was still another transition to Napoleonville, Louisiana. In 1944, Margaret reached the farthest point east in her life to that date in a move to Monks Corner, South Carolina. During these years of constant change, she picked up a good enough education to qualify for the University of Chicago in 1944. Her roots were still in the southwest, though, and she returned to Arkansas on summer vacations in 1945 and '46. Each time, she added a few new traditional songs to her growing repertoire. In her last year at Chicago, she married a fellow folksinging addict from Canada who was working for an advanced degree in physics.

In 1948, the MacArthurs moved to Marlboro, Vermont, where her wanderings seemed finally to end. The mid-1960s still found her in Vermont with a growing family of four sons and a daughter and a national reputation as a Vermont folklorist. Hardly had she settled into her new home in New England than she began to collect local ballads. She visited with many of the long-time residents of the state, exchanging folk songs and, in time, teaching folk music to local classes.

Her activities included membership in the Green Mountain Folklore Society and the Vermont Historical Society. In 1951, with Barbara Dretzin, she had a folk song program on a local Vermont station.

She finally gained a wider audience for her material in 1963 with completion of a Folkways Record, "Folk Songs of Vermont." Among the songs on the LP are: "The Needle's Eye," "Carrion Crow," "Gypsy Davy," "Jennie Jenkins," "Cherries Are Ripe," "Trot, Trot to Boston," "This Very Unhappy Man," "Aunt Jemima," "The Scolding Wife," "Gorion-Og," "Riddles," "Old Mr. Grumble," "Single Again," "New Hampshire Miller," "What the Old Hen Said," "Mother in the Graveyard," and "Marlboro Merchants."

MAC COLL, EWAN: Singer, songwriter, folk music collector, author. Born Auchterarder, Perthshire, Scotland, January 25, 1915.

Though a voice from across the sea, Ewan MacColl has written so many articles for U.S. publications on folk music, he is considered a part of the American folk scene. In fact, his critical comments and his singing have had an important impact on American folk music.

MacColl literally began his folk education at his parents' feet. Both were performers and taught Ewan many ballads and folk songs of Scotland, Wales, England and Europe. Many folk artists, both relatives and friends of the family, frequented the MacColl home. From such people as Aunt Margaret Logan, Jeannie Robertson, and Harry Cox, young MacColl added to his folk background. He was educated in Scottish and English elementary schools, but began to concentrate on his creative efforts while still in his teens. When he was 19, in 1934, he won his entertainment spurs on a British Broadcasting Corporation program called "Music in the Streets."

From then on, much of his work was done for the BBC. He collected folk music and also wrote special material for many radio programs. By the late 1930s, he already had made a number of appearances as a folk singer in major European cities. After World War II, his reputation with folk experts throughout the world led to requests for recitals or for articles on various aspects of folk music. In the 1950s and '60s, he gave recitals all over England, Europe, and the Iron Curtain countries.

He continued his work for the BBC in the post-World War II era. As noted in Sing Out! in November '64, the MacColl program called "Radio Ballads" provided new dimensions in folk music broadcasts. ". . . We have nothing comparable here. They are usually hour-long programs combining documentary recording and interviews with contemporary ballads created in traditional forms . . . (subject titles include) one on 'boxing' . . . 'Gypsies and Tinkers' and a 'Teen-Agers.' "

MacColl turned out a number of folk records for both English and U.S. labels. The former includes disks on English Decca, H.M.V., and Topic. The Australian record company, Wattle, also featured MacColl performances.

Among the album titles on American labels were "Industrial Songs" on Stinson; "Garland" ('61), "Songs of Robert Burns" ('62—Folk-Lyric); "British Industrial Ballads" ('61—Vanguard). His biggest U.S. output, for Folkways Records, included "Songs of Robert Burns," "Songs of Two Rebellions" ('60); "Child Ballads," "Scottish Songs" ('61); "Broadside Ballads" (2 LPs, '62). MacColl albums were also issued on Tradition and Riverside labels.

With his wife, Peggy Seeger of the famed Seeger family, he was scheduled to tour the U.S. in 1965. A controversy erupted in which MacColl's visa was first refused on political grounds, then finally cleared. By the time the controversy had died down, the tour had been suspended.

His literary output includes three books of collected folksongs: *Scotland Sings, Shuttle and Cage,* and *Personal Choice.*

MACK, WARNER: Singer, guitarist, songwriter. Born Nashville, Tennessee, April 2, 1938.

Like many home state artists, Warner Mack made his way to success in Nashville after a long swing southward. Born in the country music capital in the 1930s, he was soon taken to Mississippi. He began to listen closely to country music radio programs during the years he was attending Carr Central Grade School in Vicksburg. He also started learning guitar and played in school events while a student at Jett High School.

Ewan MacColl

[187]

When he finished high school, Warner performed for a time in local clubs. Before long he had the chance to become a regular on the KWKH Louisiana Hayride. As the 1950s went by, he gained increasing recognition from country and western audiences throughout the south and southwest. He made personal appearances in many parts of the region and also was featured on Red Foley's Ozark Jamboree. He signed with Kapp Records during this period and turned out many records that appeared on the national charts in the late 1950s and early 1960s. These were capsuled in best-selling Kapp LPs, "Warner Mack's Golden Country Hits, Volume 1" ('61) and "Volume 2" ('63).

Warner's real name is MacPherson, reflecting his Scottish ancestry. (His father was a Presbyterian minister.) Unlike many artists, he did not change it purposely to a stage name. At first, he performed under his original name. However, when he began recording, the person preparing the label copy mistook Warner's nickname for his actual surname, hence Mack. Once the records came out this way, Warner decided to keep his new designation.

Mack's following mounted rapidly throughout the states in the early 1960s, resulting in a bid to join the Grand Ole Opry. Warner moved to Nashville and also changed record labels, joining the Decca roster. Though he had done well before, he soon achieved major star status in the mid-1960s with a series of hits. In 1965, he had three top 10 hits, one of which, "The Bridge Washed Out," was number one in the nation for many weeks. The other two were "Sittin' on a Rock" and a song he co-authored, "Sitting in an All Night Cafe." Warner followed up in 1966 with such top 10 hits as "Talkin' to the Wall" and "It Takes a Lot Of Money"; in 1967, with "Drifting Apart," "How Long Will It Take," and "I'd Give the World"; and in 1968, "I'm Gonna Move On." His best-selling LPs include "Driftin' Apart," "The Country Touch," "The Bridge Washed Out," and, with his sister Dean, "Songs We Sing in Church and Home."

In the mid-1960s, Warner had chart hits of two more of his own compositions, "Is It Wrong" and "Surely." These were added to such earlier writings as "Then a Tear Fell," "Last Night," "Yes, There's a Reason," "My Love for You," "If You See Me Cry," "I Wake Up Crying," "Memory Mountain," "The Least Little Thing," "This Little Hurt," "I'll Be Alright in the Morning," and "Blue Mood."

MACON, UNCLE DAVE: Folk, country and western singer, songwriter, banjoist. Born Smart Station, Cannon County, Tennessee, October 7, 1870; died Readyville, Tennessee, March 22, 1952. Elected to Country Music Hall of Fame, 1966.

"Flashing a set of gold false teeth; clad in vest, plug hat and 'gates-a-jar' collar; and packing three banjos all in different tunings, Macon was an overwhelmingly delightful entertainer. Seated in a chair before the microphone, he rapped out clog dance rhythms on the floor with his feet, kicked his legs, flipped and swung his banjo in the air while playing (he termed one of his routines 'Uncle Dave handles a banjo like a monkey handles a peanut'), told jokes and stories, preached, and sang the most amazing variety of American country songs ever to emanate from one performer."

Thus did Jon Pankake and Paul Nelson, editors of the Little Sandy Review, describe one of the all-time greats of country and western music (Sing Out!, Summer 1963). But Uncle Dave was more than just a performer. His repertoire was a folk music scholar's dream. In many cases his singing helped preserve such classics as "Sail Away Ladies," "Hop High Ladies," "The Death of John Henry," "Rolly Trudum," and "Down in the Arkansas." More than one modern folksinger is indebted to Dave Macon for some of his best audience-pleasers.

Macon was born on a farm, but while he was a boy his family bought a hotel in Nashville. A good part of the clientele were show people and little Dave learned much of the lore of the trade. From some of the lodgers, he picked up the technique of playing the 5-string banjo. As he grew older, he added many innovations of his own, eventually becoming one of the greatest banjo players of all time.

Despite his skills, Uncle Dave came close to being a complete unknown. Though he entertained his friends and sang at local functions during his early years, this was only a spare-time hobby. Uncle Dave worked on Tennessee farms as a hired hand and eventually bought his own farm near Readyville, Tennessee. Whenever there was a barn raising or a local dance, Uncle Dave was sure to be there, but hardly a person outside of the county knew he existed. He was two years shy of 50 when a talent scout for Loew's theatres heard him and immediately signed him for a major spot in a Birmingham Loew's Theatre.

Thus it was 1916 before Uncle Dave finally began to make his voice noticed across the south. For the next ten years, he played almost every major city and town in the region. His reputation grew and it was natural that he receive an invitation to the new Grand Ole Opry program in 1926. Within a short time Uncle Dave was the overwhelming favorite of most of the Opry fans. He performed both solo and as lead musician of the famed Fruit Jar Drinkers band. From 1926 through the '40s Uncle Dave was wildly received on the radio show and in concerts across the country.

Many of his most popular songs were those he had either written himself or discovered in his travels. These included "All In, Down and Out Blues," "The Dixie Bee Line," "From Earth to Heaven," "Cumberland Mountain Deer Race," "They're After Me," "Rock About My Saro Jane," "Ain't It a Shame to Keep Your Honey Out in the Rain," and "When the Train Comes Along." Always show-stoppers were his banjo solos, such as "Uncle Dave's Beloved Solos."

Uncle Dave's star waned in the late 1940s, but he remained a member of the Grand Ole Opry cast until his death at the age of 82. By then, only a few of his many recordings were available. In the mid-1960s, interest was revived in his art.

MADDOX, ROSE: Singer, guitarist. Born Boaz, Alabama, December 15, 1926.

The family group is a recurring feature in the history of folk, country and western music. One of the most popular acts of post-World War II decades was the Maddox Brothers and Rose. The team comprised the four Maddox brothers, Cal, Henry, Fred, and Don and their sister, Rose. In time, Rose went her own way to gain recognition as one of the top female vocalists of the 1960s.

The Maddox family grew up in the heartland of country music, Alabama. Their mother, in particular, encouraged their interest in music. Her strong influence was reflected for many years in the selection of songs and the engagements the Maddoxes played. However, the Depression weighed heavily on the family in the early 1930s. Finally, it seemed wise to leave

Alabama. Mrs. Maddox bundled her family, then aged 7 to 16, into a freight car for the long journey to central California. Once settled in the Bakersfield area, the Maddox children helped repair family finances by performing at local events. Their act became more polished as the 1930s progressed and, by the end of the decade, they were well regarded by country and western fans in many parts of the state.

In the early 1950s, the Maddox Brothers and Rose graduated from local appearances in California to regular cast status on the Louisiana Hayride in Shreveport. The combination of Cal on guitar and harmonica, Henry on mandolin, Fred on stand-up bass, Don in comic roles and Rose as lead voice resulted in many song stylings that had audiences asking for more. As their popularity grew from Hayride network exposure, the Maddox Brothers and Rose became one of the most popular groups for one-nighters in the business. In addition to personal appearances, they also performed on most major country and western network shows, including the Grand Ole Opry.

The Brothers and Rose turned out many best-selling records for Columbia, King, and Capitol Records during the 1950s and early '60s. These included such successes as "Philadelphia Lawyer," "Whoa, Sailor," "Tall Man," and the famous "Tramp on the Street." "Tramp on the Street" was one of many sacred and gospel-type recordings featuring a combination of western beat and country material. Their other standards of this kind included "Gathering Flowers for the Master's Bouquet" and "Will There Be Any Stars in My Crown?" Their LP credits included "I'll Write Your Name" on King and "Maddox Brothers and Rose" ('62) on Wrangler.

In the late 1950s, the Maddoxes again moved their base of operations to California. Their appearances ranged from station KTRB in Modesto to the Town Hall Party in Compton. At the start of the 1960s, however, the group disbanded and Rose decided to go out on her own as a single act.

She soon had many notable recordings to her credit on Capitol Records, including the LPs "One Rose" ('60), "Bluegrass" ('62), and "Along with You" ('63). Her 1963 recording of "Sing a Little Song of Heartaches" was second only to Skeeter Davis' for most record sales by a female vocalist. She also teamed with Buck Owens on "We're the Talk of the Town,"

[189]

a recording that was third highest best-seller in the duet and vocal group category for the year. The result was selection in the Cashbox poll as the top country female artist of 1963. Similar awards were given her in Europe and New Zealand.

The year 1964 saw continued success for Rose. She again teamed with Buck Owens on such hits as "Loose Talk" and "Mental Cruelty." At year's end, she and Buck won the top duet award in national disk jockey polls.

MAINER, J. E.: Band leader, banjoist, fiddler. Born Weaversville, North Carolina, July 20, 1898.

One of the pioneer groups of modern country music, J. E. Mainer and his Mountaineers are bracketed with such great old-time names as the Carter Family and Gid Tanner's Skillet Lickers. The best summation of his career, providing some of the flavor of the country music field of the 1920s and '30s, is in a letter from Mainer to John Edwards, founder of the Edwards Collection, reprinted here, in part, with permission.

"I was born in Weaversville, N.C., the year of 1898. Started to play a 5 string banjo when I were 9 years old going to square dances. Me and my brother-in-law, he played the fiddle, he played left-handed. I stayed around home until I were 15 years old then I left home and went to work in a cotton mill at noxeville [Knoxville] Tennessee. Worked there for 7 years then I come to Concord, N.C. Hoboed a fruit train here in Concord, N.C. Got me a job in the cotton mill here. In 1923 Wade come to Concord. I still had my banjo with me and Wade began to learn to play it. He were 17 years old then and he got to where he could play it pertty good by me showing him how to play it. Then I thought I would get me a fiddle, so I sold some seed and sent the money to the seed company and they set me a little old tin fiddle. But I got to where I could play John Henry on it then I went and got me a good fiddle then we would play 2 hours ever' night. In about one year we could play most anything we wanted to. Then we met John Love who played a guitar. We got to going to fiddle conventions and we met Claud [Claude] Moris [Morris] in Old Port, N.C., who played guitar and we all 4 of us sure did love to play. Then we got to winning about all of the prizes wherever we went. Then the Crazy Water

Crystals Co. heard about us and sent for me to come to their office in Charlotte, N.C. and they gave us a job playing for them, advertising for them. We worked over WBT Charlotte for 4 years then they sent us to WWL, New Orleans, Louisiana. We stayed there for a while then they sent for us to come back to Charlotte, then they sent us to Raleigh, N.C.— WPTF—there for 4 years. In this time John Love had married and had a baby then I nicknamed him Daddy John Love and I had nicknamed Claude Morris, Zeke, and the boys is still carrying their nicknames today.

"We made records for the Victor Recording Co. We made some records that were on top for about 4 years, then I left them in Raleigh, N.C., and I got me another bunch and went back to Charlotte on another radio station, WSOC. I had Leonard Stokes and George Morris, Zeke's brother, and my banjo player were Snuffey Jenkins. We stayed there at Charlotte for 4 months then the Crazy Water Crystal Co. wanted me to go to Spartanburg, S.C. and adv. over station WIS. At that time the Monroe Brothers had split up and the old hired han' that had been announcing for them were out of work and the Crazy Water Crystal Co. wanted me to take him in my band and do the announcing for us, so I tuck him in my band. We worked there for 6 years on WIS then me and him got to where we couldn't get along so I left them there and got me another band and went to Greenboro. Played over WBIG, Greenboro, stayed there for 2 years then we went to Birmingham, Alabama, on station WAPI. Worked there for 18 months.

"I had bought me a farm, I decided to work my farm for a while so I stopped playing. But I weren't satisfied so got me another band and went to playing for WEGO here in Concord, N.C. Played here for 2 years then I got a telegram from Chicago, Ill., from Bentson and Doll Advertising Co. They wanted me to go to San Antonio, Texas. I went there and made transcription records for them. My band and the Carter Family were out there at the same time. They sent us to XERT radio station, Montra, Mexico. After our job were done there, they sent me to KMOX, Saint Louis, Missouri. I didn't like the people so well out there so I came back home.

"Well Mr. Edwards, I could sit here and write for a week then couldn't tell you where all I been, but I have played over 140 radio stations, made more personal appearances than any other string band in the South. Made them for 30 years and we were out just about every night, going to some school helping them to raise money for the sponsor.

"I were borned in a one room log house in Buncombe County in the Blue Ridge Mountains of North Carolina. I never will forget one time when we were living in this one room log cabin, that they came up a hard rain in the night and the ditch we had dug above the house to keep the water from running in the house when it rained—it brake over with water and busted the door down. Daddy woke us up— he were cutting a hole in the floor, letting the water out. It were about three feet deep in the house. It tuck Paw and Maw all the next day to get the mud out of the house.

"I can't tell you just what time it were when me and Wade, John Love, Zeke made records for the Victor company, but the first ones we made were in 1935 in Atlanta, Georgia. We made records for them ever' 6 months for 5 years. I got married here in Concord the same year I come here. We had 6 children—2 girls and 4 boys. 2 of the boys and 2 girls were guitar players. Their names were Carolin, and the other were Mary. My old'st boy were J. E. Jr. and Glenn Mainer.

"I took them and went to Johnson City, Tennessee, in 1939. Went to work over radio station WSJS and we went to recording records for the King Recording Co. Worked for them for two years.

"I hope you can read this letter. I didn't have much chance to go to school. When I were at home, only school were 5 miles from where we lived and we had to help Daddy in the fields.

"Well I will close. Let me know if this is what you want."

Exactly.

MAKEBA, MIRIAM: Singer. Born March 4, 1932, Johannesburg, South Africa.

Anyone who has heard Zensi Miriam Makeba sing the "Click" song of her native Xhosa tribe must agree that she is one of the most unique performers of the present day. She is, of course, as much at home with songs from U. S. musicals or the folklore of other lands as she is with those of her native Africa. Harry Belafonte expressed it well in an interview with Newsweek on January 25, 1960: "(She is) easily the most revolutionary talent to appear in any medium in the last decade."

Though of noble lineage, Miriam was born in Prospect Township, an African shantytown outside Johannesburg. Her parents were from the Xhosa tribe, closely related to the Zulus. Her father was a school teacher and her mother worked as a domestic. Music was an important part of her family atmosphere and Miriam loved to sing. When she was grade school age, she was a member of the choir at the Methodist-operated Kilmerton Training School in Pretoria. During a visit of King George VI, she appeared as a soloist in one number.

She remained at Kilmerton for eight years. After this, she went to work as an assistant to her mother. The life of a domestic didn't interest her and she sang as much as she could at dances, weddings, and other local affairs. A male singing group heard of her talent and asked her to accompany them on a tour through South Africa, Rhodesia, and the Belgian Congo in 1954. She remained with the eleven-man group, called the Black Manhattan

Miriam Makeba

[191]

Brothers, for several years. By the late 1950s, she had achieved a rising reputation in South Africa.

Her first starring role was in the Jazz opera "King Kong," which opened in Johannesburg on February 2, 1959. In the role of Joyce, owner of an illegal drinking place called a shebeen, she stopped the show with her singing of "Back of the Moon." The previous year she had taken part in a semi-documentary film, "Come Back Africa," which received wide acclaim at the 1959 Venice Film Festival. This plus her eight-month run in "King Kong" helped bring her to the attention of Harry Belafonte, who brought her to the U. S. in 1959 to appear with his troupe.

Her first TV appearance on the Steve Allen network show on November 30, 1959, won rave notices. This was followed by highly successful appearances in 1960 at the Village Vanguard in New York and clubs in Boston and Los Angeles. From 1960 on, she was often featured on TV and radio; she also turned out a series of well received LPs on RCA Victor, including "Miriam Makeba," "The Voice of Africa," "The World of Miriam Makeba," and "Makeba Sings."

As she reached star status, Miriam's efforts turned more and more to the cause of African freedom. In early 1963, she was an honored guest at the Addis Ababa, Ethiopia, meeting of African leaders. On July 16, 1963, she spoke before the U. N. against apartheid. She addressed that body again on behalf of jailed South African leaders on March 4, 1964. In 1964, she performed in the Independence Day ceremonies in Kenya.

MAKEM, TOMMY: Singer, instrumentalist (banjo, pennywhistle, drums, piccolo, guitar, bagpipes). Born Keady, County Armagh, Ireland, 1932.

Tommy Makem is usually associated by name with The Clancy Brothers. But his career includes many highlights that are purely his own, including selection, based on his solo performance at the Newport Folk Festival, as the most promising young male performer of 1960.

Tommy comes from a long line of Irish folk artists. By the time he was five, he was on stage singing and acting with his parents. Though steeped in folk tradition, in his teens he moved into the pop field for a while. At 15, he formed his own Ceili, which translates as

Irish Country Dance Band. At 17 he had achieved a reputation throughout Ireland as a "pop" vocalist in the American style.

It was at this time that he met up with Liam Clancy, who has recalled the event as follows: "It was . . . beyond that mystical border that separates the blessed subjects of the Queen from the Irish misfortunates that I first met Tommy Makem. I went to a Ceilidhe in Newry town one night in a big dance hall there. I was very embarrassed when the band leader announced, in the midst of the fun and the dancing, that this one poor chap was going to sing and not a person in the hall stopped talking or looked up at the stage. Your man wasn't fazed the slightest. He just sat down and started silently to work on his boot.

"One person looked up and another, and in ten seconds you could hear a pin drop. Then when he had complete attention he began to sing, 'O Me Name Is Dick Darby, I'm a Cobbler.' That was my introduction to Tommy. We both took the 'emigrant ship' to America the next year."

While Liam began on an acting career, Makem pursued his own flamboyant course. It didn't take him long to gain a job as a folk artist in the Circle in the Square in Greenwich Village. Soon after, he was featured in a major Chicago folk nightclub, the Gate of Horn. Makem also made his mark in the theater in the late 1950s. His credits included touring with the Irish Players; a part in "Playboy of the Western World"; and the Broadway show "A Hatful of Rain." He also had a part in the Broadway revival of "Finian's Rainbow."

Meanwhile, he continued pursuing his folk music bent. On occasion, he got together with Liam Clancy and his brothers for an old-time songfest. On his own, he continued to gain more attention, climaxed by his show-stopping effort at the 1960 Newport Folk Festival. His output included both traditional ballads and new material he wrote himself.

Soon after the Newport success, Tommy was asked to join The Clancy Brothers in a new folk song combination. They cut a record on Pat Clancy's own label, Tradition, that won favorable response. Then they scored heavily with New York audiences and critics in an engagement at the Circle in the Square. From then on, The Clancy Brothers and Tommy Makem gathered increased stature with each passing

[192]

year. In 1961, the group completed the first of many LPs on Columbia Records.

During the 1960s, The Clancy Brothers and Tommy Makem were featured on dozens of network TV shows and in concerts all over the world. Though performing together most of the time, they still showed off their individual talents on occasion. Makem, for example, turned out several LPs of his own during the '60s, including "Songs by Tommy Makem" (Tradition —'61) on which he accompanied himself on the pennywhistle. (*See also* CLANCY BROTHERS, THE)

MAPHIS, JOE AND ROSE LEE: Singing and instrumental duo, Joe born Suffolk, Virginia, May 12, 1921; Rose Lee born Baltimore, Maryland, December 29, 1922.

The Old Dominion Barn Dance in Richmond, Virginia, was the meeting place for two young performers in 1948 who became one of the most popular husband-and-wife teams in the post-World War II decades.

Before coming together on the WRVA program, both had been professional artists while in their teens. Otis W. "Joe" Maphis, born and raised near Harpers Ferry, Virginia, learned to play fiddle from his father and entertained at local square dances by the time he was 10. At 16, he was featured on station WBRA in Richmond. Besides fiddle, he also learned to play guitar, mandolin, and bass. Rose Lee started singing and playing guitar before she reached high school age. At 15, she had her own program on a Hagerstown, Maryland, station, billed as "Rose of the Mountains."

For a number of years in the 1940s, Joe was featured on many of the top shows emanating from the midwest, including the Boone County Jamboree, WLW Midwestern Hayride, and Chicago's National Barn Dance. Soon after he and Rose Lee met and married, they moved to California. They appeared on Cliffie Stone's Hometown Jamboree for several years. In the mid-1950s, they were featured on the Town Hall Party from Compton. They remained on the show for 11 years, until the mid-1960s. Besides his duets with Rose Lee on the Party, Joe often teamed with Merle Travis of "16 Tons" fame.

Joe and his wife were often asked to back other major artists during recording sessions in the Los Angeles-Hollywood area. Among those with whom they worked were Ricky Nelson,

Stuart Hamblen, and Tex Ritter. Joe also provided the sound track for such TV shows as FBI Story and Thunder Road.

The Maphis name won applause throughout the world during extensive personal appearances in the 1950s and '60s. Joe and Rose Lee toured all fifty states as well as France, Germany, Spain, the Philippines, Okinawa, Taiwan and Vietnam. In the mid-1960s, their annual travels covered an average of 100,000 miles.

Among the many songs recorded by Joe and Rose Lee were "Twin Banjo Special," "Katy Warren Breakdown," "Your Old Love Letters," "Flying Fingers," "Randy Lynn Rag," "Guitar Rock and Roll," "Tuning Up for the Blues," and "Honky Tonk Down Town." Their LP output included "Fire on the Strings" and the 1964 Starday album "Joe and Rose Lee Maphis."

MARAIS, JOSEF: Singer, guitarist, violinist, songwriter, composer. Born Sir Lowry Pass, South Africa, November 17, 1905.

In the 1940s, American radio audiences were introduced to an exciting new folk music sound, songs of the still mysterious region known as South Africa. The songs were not African songs, but a blend of the English and Dutch cultures that had settled the rich lands at the bottom of the continent. Worries about oppression of native populations and other forms of unrest were still far away and such songs as "Marching to Pretoria" kindled interest in the diamond-rich regions near Johannesburg and in the nature of the romantic-seeming South African veldt.

The man responsible for this was a highly skilled musician and folklorist named Josef Marais. Brought up in South Africa, he early showed talent as a musician. His ability won him a scholarship to the South African College of Music in 1923. He took courses in basic music theory as well as violin. He was to spend several years as a violinist with the Capetown Symphony Orchestra. Though concentrating on classical music, he still had a lively interest in music in general and particularly the folk ballads of the country.

In 1928, Marais went to London to continue his musical studies at the Royal Academy of Music. He expanded his violin technique with such teachers as Otokar Seveik and Jeno Hubay in 1930.

For most of the 1930s, Marais was best known as a classical musician, though he did contribute to folk music scholarship with his translations of Afrikaans (Dutch Boer language) songs into English. His folk music career began in earnest in 1939 when he moved to the U. S. He put his knowledge of South African music to work on a series of programs called "African Trek" for the Blue Network. The show became one of the most popular on the network and was a weekly feature for two years.

In 1941, he became the director of Afrikaans broadcasts for the Office of War Information. Later he was also given charge of OWI Dutch broadcasts. During these years, he met a Dutch girl named Rosa Lily Odette Baruch, also working on U. S. overseas broadcasts, who had considerable musical ability as well as interest in folk music. When he finished his OWI work in 1945, he formed a folk song team with her called Marais and Miranda which soon became one of the most popular of its kind with American audiences. On July 18, 1947, Josef married his partner.

From the late 1940s on, Marais and Miranda were among the most active entertainers in the country. They appeared in concerts throughout the country and were featured on many radio and TV shows. They also turned out many recordings of their songs for Decca Records. After several decades of performing, they were as popular with fans as ever. In December 1967, for example, capacity audiences attended their 20-day run at the Morgan Theater, Santa Monica, California. Critics hailed their singing of such Marais compositions as "Sugarbush," "Pretty Kitty," and "Henrietta's Wedding."

Over the years, Marais' output ranged from popular songs ("The Zulu Warrior," "Around the Corner," "Brandy Leave Me Alone," "The Crickets") to books and symphonic works. His books included *Koos the Hottentot* and *Folk Song Jamboree*. His longer works include an opera, "Tony Beaver"; "African Suite" (written for the Broadway show "Too Late the Phalarope"); "Songs from the Veldt" (14 songs); "Hebraic Rhapsody"; and "The Bangalorey Man" (for children). He made his symphonic debut in 1957 with Franz Allers at New York's Lewisohn Stadium. (*See also* MARAIS, MIRANDA)

MARAIS, MIRANDA: Singer, pianist. Born Amsterdam, The Netherlands, January 9, 1912.

The Office of War Information broadcasts of the early 1940s helped the American war effort. They also helped make the years following World War II brighter by bringing together the two artists who were to become the great man-and-wife folk song team of Marais and Miranda.

Miranda, born Rosa Lily Odette Baruch de la Pardo, had considerable classical music background to bring to the collaboration. Born to a musical family in Amsterdam in 1912, she grew up in an environment of culture and creative curiosity. She was sent to the Barlaeus Gymnasium in Amsterdam and then attended the Muziek Lyceum. She showed considerable talent as a pianist from her first lessons at an early age.

In her teens, she was skilled enough as a pianist to begin accompanying a member of the family, Marcel Baruch de la Pardo. She and Marcel played in most of the major cities of Europe from 1928 to 1935. When the storm clouds of Nazism began to engulf Europe in 1939, she went to America. In 1940, she made her first appearance as a singer.

The following year, she took a position as member of the desk unit for the Voice of America broadcasts to South Africa. Another member of the broadcast team was South Africa-born Joseph Marais. The two became close friends; in 1945, they formed the folk song team of Marais and Miranda. (Both of them became U.S. citizens in 1945.) Their performances were well received, and in 1946 they gave their first major New York recital at Town Hall. The following year, they were married and soon set off on a concert tour throughout the U. S.

Besides concerts, Marais and Miranda were featured on many TV and radio shows during the 1950s and '60s. They recorded on the Decca label and later on Columbia Masterworks. They added new luster to their reputation in 1954 with their first tour of Europe.

During the 1960s, Marais and Miranda made California their home base. They both served on the faculty of the Idyllwild School of Music and Arts, Idyllwild, California. (*See also* MARAIS, JOSEF)

MARTIN, TROY L.: Singer, music executive. Born Danville, Virginia, May 16, 1911.

More than one top country performer can remember the name of Troy Martin with gratitude. As one of the pioneer publishing company executives, he picked material that propelled many an artist to best-selling record ranks and also helped new performers get started in the big time.

An example is Carl Smith. Martin helped Smith land a job on the Grand Ole Opry. However, when Smith's first efforts on Columbia did not move well, the Opry almost dropped the young singer. Martin persuaded the program manager to wait and came up with another song, "I Overlooked an Orchid While Searching for a Rose," that made Carl Smith a national favorite.

Martin learned the ropes the hard way. Born in Danville, Virginia, he left home as a youngster to work as a comedian on the medicine show circuit for $20 a week. After serving his apprenticeship under such men as Doc Marshall and Dr. Butler, he formed his own show. A few years later, he moved into vaudeville, working with such people as Gene Vaughn, Skinny Chandler, Sweet Papa Bozo and Emmett Miller. Miller, Martin recalls, was the first to record the standard, "Love Sick Blues."

Martin continued to work in carnivals, at walkathons, as manager of the side show of the Old Miller Brothers 101 Ranch Wild West Show, and finally in radio. He opened some of the first commercial stations in the south, while also recording for the American Record Company (which featured such performers as Gene Autry, Cliff Carlisle, and the Hoosier Hot Shots).

When World War II came along, Martin volunteered his services to the USO. He played many engagements with such stars as Donald O'Connor, the Mills Brothers, Joe Martin Dancers and Pat Rooney, Sr.

After the war, Martin concentrated on a career in music publishing. For many years he was on the staff of Southern Music and Peer International Music Publishers. On several occasions, songs he had chosen for publication occupied 7 of the top 10 spots in national ratings. He also served for five years as vice president of the Gene Autry Company, owned part of Cedarwood Music, and was president for a time of his own firm, Troy Martin Music, Inc.

In the mid-1960s, he held the post of vice president and executive manager of Hank Snow's Silver Star Music Publishing Company, Inc. Martin's publishing activities were credited with a major role in the development of Nashville into the "Country Music Capital of the World."

Martin's song choices appeared on national hit lists in all categories, from jazz to popular as well as country and western. A partial listing of some of their titles: "Down Yonder," "Don't Let the Stars Get in Your Eyes," "Mocking Bird Hill," "Slippin' Around," "I Gotta Have My Baby Back," "I Love You a Thousand Ways," "Don't Let Me Cross Over," "Walking in the Rain," "If You Got the Money, I Got the Time," and "It Wasn't God Who Made Honky Tonk Angels."

Among his honors over the years were: honorary member of the Senate of Louisiana; Deputy Sheriff, Harris County, Texas; and membership, with Gene Autry, in the Corral Club of Houston, Texas.

MARVIN, KEN: *See* Lonzo and Oscar

MC AULIFF, LEON: Singer, guitarist, band leader, composer. Born Houston, Texas, January 3, 1917.

"Take it away, Leon," was one of several famous trademarks of Bob Wills' Texas Playboys. The phrase referred to Wills' great steel guitar player, Leon McAuliff. It was coined by Wills, appropriately, at a recording session of one of Leon's most notable compositions, "Steel Guitar Rag." The song, which McAuliff notes has been recorded more than 100 different times, also relates to his being credited with introducing the steel guitar into country and western music.

McAuliff spent most of his formative years in Houston, Texas. His interest in the guitar began on Christmas Day, 1931, when he found a seven-dollar Stella guitar under the tree. The 14-year-old took lessons for a while, but quit because he learned faster than his instructor could provide him with new material. He learned so rapidly on his own that he was able to win a summer job on the staff of KPRC radio in Houston in 1932. In 1933, he received his first paycheck as part of a staff band called the Swift Jewel Cowboys.

In September 1933, he moved a notch further ahead by accepting a bid from W. Lee "Pappy" O'Daniel to join The Light Crust Doughboys. One of his fellow Doughboys was Bob Wills. Leon toured with the Doughboys until March 1935, when Bob Wills lured him away to play with the Texas Playboys. His new job resulted in a move with the band to Tulsa, Oklahoma.

which became Leon's main base of operations from then on. Leon played a major role in the rise of the Texas Playboys to one of the country's best known bands. With Wills, Leon co-authored one of the all-time standards in western—and popular—music, "San Antonio Rose."

World War II interrupted Leon's association with the Playboys. Leon joined the U.S. Navy and became a flight instructor during his four-year hitch from 1942 to 1946. Later on, he bought his own plane and flew to his personal appearances in the post-World War II period. (In the mid-1960s, he flew his own twin-engine Cessna 310.) While in the Navy, Leon also played many engagements with the Glenn Miller dance band led by Tex Beneke.

After receiving his discharge, Leon went back to Tulsa and started his own organization called the Western Swing Band. In the late 1940s and early 1950s, they won a wide following with their radio shows over KVOO and KRMG in Tulsa. Gradually, their reputation expanded beyond the southwest to the entire country. After McAuliff became owner and operator of the Cimarron Ballroom in Tulsa, the band's name changed to the Cimarron Boys. During the 1950s and '60s, they played engagements throughout the world. Their appearances in all the fifty states included stops at major nightclubs and ballrooms, country clubs, colleges, resorts, state and county fairs, rodeos, horse shows, and at Armed Forces installations.

For many years in the 1950s and early '60s, McAuliff had his own TV show originating from Tulsa. In the 1960s, the band guested on many major network TV shows, including the Grand Ole Opry; Lawrence Welk; Jubilee U.S.A.; Country America Show (ABC-TV); Town Hall Party, Compton, California; and the Buddy Deane Show, Baltimore, Maryland. From 1956 to 1966, the Cimarron Boys was voted one of the top three country and western bands in major trade magazine polls.

After working with Bob Wills on some 200 Columbia recordings, it was only natural for him to sign with the label for his new band. The organization made 40 records on Columbia in the late 1940s and early 1950s. In the years that followed, he turned out records for such other firms as ABC-Paramount, Dot (1957-59), Starday, Cimarron, and Capitol. In the early '60s, he signed a long-term contract with Capitol. He recorded some of his own hit compositions at

first, including "Steel Guitar Rag," "Panhandle Rag," and Redskin Rag." His newer numbers include "Cozy Inn" ('61), "Faded Love" ('62), and "I Don't Love Nobody" ('63). His LP output included "Take Off" on Dot; "Cozy Inn" on ABC-Paramount; "Mister Western Swing" on Starday; "Swingin' Western Strings" on Cimarron; and "Dancinest Band Around" on Capitol. (*See also* LIGHT CRUST DOUGH-BOYS, THE; WILLS, BOB)

MC CURDY, ED: Singer, guitarist. Born Willow Hill, Pennsylvania, January 11, 1919.

One of the most recorded folk artists of the 1950s and '60s, Ed McCurdy is gifted in far more than this one musical genre. As a composer, for example, he has produced not only folk songs, but pop music and classical compositions as well.

Like many of today's folksingers, McCurdy grew up in the east with minimum exposure to folk music. He attended grade school in a rural area of Pennsylvania, Middle Spring, and went on to graduate from high school at Shippensburg, Pennsylvania. By the time he traveled west to Panhandle A&M College in Goodwell, Oklahoma, he had gained some in-

Ed McCurdy

terest in folk music which became stronger during his one-semester stay at Panhandle and later study at Oklahoma Central State College.

Deciding to make music his career, McCurdy never finished college. He learned to play the guitar and gathered his folk repertoire from records and looking at folk song collections in libraries. His browsing included attention to symphonies, musical comedies, and other facets of music. McCurdy's travels took him to Canada in the mid-1940s, and he made his professional debut on the Canadian Broadcasting system in March 1946. He spent the next several years mainly in Canada, performing on radio and TV and making personal appearances in a number of cities. His Canadian work led to his first LP on the Canadian Whitehall label, "Folk Songs of the Canadian Maritimes and Newfoundland."

In the early 1950s, he was becoming known to U.S. folk fans and he began to perform south of the Canadian border. In 1954, he moved to New York. Soon after, he was asked to provide a musical supplement to Dr. MacEdward Leach's *The Ballad Book,* published by Harper & Brothers. This, in turn, helped result in another McCurdy LP, "The Ballad Record," for Riverside. From then on, McCurdy turned out many folk LPs for several labels during the late 1950s and through the '60s. These included: "Barroom Ballads" on Riverside; "Ballad Singer's Choice" on Tradition; "The Folk Singer" on Dawn; "Ed McCurdy" on Seeco; and a series of LPs for Elektra: "Blood, Booze 'n' Bones"; "Sin Songs, Pro and Con"; "Songs of the Old West"; and a two-LP set, "Ed McCurdy's Treasure Chest."

From 1955 on, McCurdy did much work for the Columbia Broadcasting System's experimental "Camera Three." He also sang on many radio and TV shows and was featured at most of the major folk festivals, including the 1959, 1960, and 1963 events at Newport.

MC DONALD, SKEETS: Singer, guitarist, songwriter. Born Greenway, Arkansas. October 1, 1915; died Inglewood, California, March 1, 1968.

Enos William McDonald had a good grounding in all phases of folk, country and western music during his youth in the Ozark Mountains. Many of the classic folk ballads came from the region he grew up in. But country and western music was equally popular there. Skeets might have been another Jimmy Driftwood, but the pull of such performers as Jimmie Rodgers and Uncle Dave Macon was too strong.

By the time Skeets was in his teens in the early 1930s, he was able to sing many of the country hits of the era. He began to perform for local audiences, then made his way toward the midwest in the 1930s. In 1937, he took a job singing on station WEXL in Royal Oak, Michigan. Later he also sang on two other Michigan stations, WFDF, Flint, and WCAR, Pontiac.

The war years interrupted his midwestern sojourn. When the war was over, he settled in California. For a time, he sang with a group called the Lonesome Cowboys. In the late 1940s, he had established a following in the Los Angeles area and was signed to a recording contract by the new Capitol Records company. In 1952, his Capitol version of "Don't Let the Stars Get in Your Eyes" (a major pop hit for Perry Como) was a top 10 nationwide bestseller in the country and western field.

During the 1950s, Skeets recorded a number of other songs for Capitol, including "Gone and Left Me Blues," "Goin' Steady with the Blues," "You're There," "Yard and a Half of Blues," "Hawaiian Sea Breeze," "Blues in My Mind," "My Room Is Crowded," "Scoot, Sit and Begone," "Riding with the Blues," "Lost Highway," "I'm Sorry Now," "I'm Hurtin'," and "Blues Is Bad News." He was also featured on a Capitol album, "Goin' Steady with the Blues."

Skeets also wrote well over 100 songs during the postwar decades, including "I'm Hurtin'," "Bless Your Little Old Heart," "Baby Brown Eyes" and "A Big Family Trouble."

For several years in the 1950s, Skeets was featured on Cliffie Stone's Hometown Jamboree, broadcast over station KXLA in the Los Angeles region. Afterward, he concentrated on personal appearance tours in various parts of the country.

In the 1960s, Skeets signed a new record contract with Columbia. This resulted in a major 1963 hit, the top 10 recording of "Call Me Mr. Brown." Columbia issued an LP called "Skeets McDonald" in 1964. On March 1, 1968, after returning home from a personal appearance, Skeets died of a heart attack.

MC GEE BROTHERS: Singers, instrumentalists. Both born Franklin, Tennessee, Sam McGee,

May 1, 1894; Kirk McGee, November 4, 1899.

When Grand Ole Opry audiences wildly greeted Uncle Dave Macon's Fruit Jar Drinkers during the pre-World War II days, they were applauding the amazing banjo and guitar artistry of the McGee brothers as well. Long after Uncle Dave had left the Opry stage, the McGee Brothers were among the most popular of the Opry cast.

Like many country artists, they were born and raised on a family farm. The McGee farm was located near Franklin, Tennessee. Their father was an accomplished fiddler and they were exposed to music almost from the time they were born. Almost as soon as they could hold banjos, they were working with their father at local gatherings. In their teens, they played banjo at dances for the princely sum of 10 cents each. As Jon Pankake wrote in Sing Out! (Nov. '64, p. 47), they expanded their string abilities at this time to include effects of Negro syncopated music. The boys had the chance to observe this when the family moved for a short period of time to the central Tennessee town of Perry. As Sam told Pankake, the Negro rhythms "would just ring in my head."

Their introduction to Uncle Dave Macon came in 1923 when they heard him perform on the first professional show the brothers had ever seen. They decided to try out for a job with him and managed to join his troupe in 1924. From then on the brothers accompanied Uncle Dave on tours throughout the U.S. and at recording sessions in New York. When Uncle Dave joined the Opry in 1926, they went along. In a short time, they were sent out as stars of some of the first Opry touring road shows.

In 1930, they formed a combination called the Dixieliners with fiddler Arthur Smith. The threesome achieved great popularity on the Opry and were soon greatly in demand for country shows throughout the south. Their repertoire included many old-time country songs, such as "Whoop 'Em Up, Cindy."

Just before World War II, Smith left and the brothers joined a comedy act called "Sara and Sally." This lasted for several years before they became featured performers in Bill Monroe's Bluegrass band. The brothers remained

Sam McGee, left, and Arthur Smith are shown during the early years of the WSM Grand Ole Opry.

[198]

active on the Opry throughout this period, and by the 1950s were appearing as a separate act. Some of their old-time numbers are available on a Starday LP, "Opry Old Timers."

In the 1960s, the McGees found favor with the growing ranks of folk song fans and were featured at a number of folk festivals. In 1965, they teamed up with Arthur Smith again for a show-stopping appearance at the Newport Folk Festival. (*See also* SMITH, FIDDLIN' ARTHUR)

MC GHEE, BROWNIE: Singer, guitarist, songwriter. Born Knoxville, Tennessee, November 30, 1914.

One of the great country blues artists, Walter Brown McGhee, was born under a relatively lucky star. Unlike many in the field, he had a reasonably happy childhood and a career in music that progressed fairly steadily from mid-1930s beginnings to great artistic (but only moderate financial) success in the years after World War II.

Brownie's earliest years were spent on his father's farm in Kingsport, Tennessee. The family was a close knit one with close musical ties. His father, George McGhee, was a skilled guitarist and singer who often teamed with the boy's uncle, John Evans, a fiddler, to play for local dances and parties. Though George gave up his farm for a while and took his family to live in a series of mill towns in eastern Tennessee, in harvest time he always returned to work at local events with John.

When Brownie was four, he was stricken by poliomyelitis. Luckily, he recovered, though he has walked with a limp ever since. After the illness, Brownie often went with his father and uncle on performing forays. Before he was eight, his uncle rewarded Brownie's growing interest in music by making him a 5-string banjo. Brownie learned to play it and, when he was 8, began to add skill with the piano and guitar to his repertoire.

Soon after, the McGhee family settled for a time in Lenoir City. Here Brownie completed elementary school, sometimes played the organ in Solomon Temple Baptist Church, and later sang in the choir at the Sanctified Baptist Church.

Soon the family moved to Marysville, Tennessee, where Brownie entered high school. When his freshman year was over, he spent his summer vacation entertaining at summer resorts in the Smoky Mountains. Music was beginning to seem more worthwhile than school to Brownie, and in 1928 he quit and earned his living as an itinerant performer. With his guitar slung over one shoulder, he hitched rides throughout Tennessee, playing wherever he could. His jobs in the next few years included stints with medicine shows, minstrel shows, and the Hagg Carnival.

In the early 1930s, he rejoined his family, who were once more on the farm in Kingsport. For the next few years he helped on the farm and sang with a gospel quartet, The Golden Voices, in his spare time. As the rigors of the Depression eased, Brownie moved to the big city of Knoxville in the mid-1930s. Here he formed a series of small bands to play at affairs in the vicinity.

In the late 1930s, things slowed down in Knoxville and Brownie made his way through North Carolina as a street performer. For a while he stayed in Asheville, then went on to Winston-Salem where he formed a team with harmonica player Jordan Webb. After being picked up by police for begging, Brownie moved on to Burlington, heading for Durham, North Carolina. There he met George "Oh Red" Washington, a friend of Webb's. Washington suggested they go to Durham and meet the local Okeh Records talent scout, a man named J. B. Long.

Long was impressed with Brownie and set up his first recording date in Chicago in 1940. Brownie soon was represented by such records as "Step It Up and Go," "Double Trouble," and "Workingman's Blues." His first records were made with Webb, but later Long paired him with another harmonica artist, Sonny Terry.

In the 1940s, Brownie moved to New York where Sonny Terry had already taken up residence. The team of McGhee and Terry soon was a familiar one in local nightclubs and in folk concerts with the great Leadbelly. In 1944, Brownie signed with Savoy Records and the following year with Alert. His recordings included "Sporting Life Blues" for Alert and a major hit on Savoy in 1947, "My Fault."

The next decade found Brownie and Sonny well on their way to a national reputation as major folksingers. Brownie was so well regarded by record company executives that he was signed to record for many different labels. Some of these sessions were with Sonny and,

[199]

PUBLIC LIBRARY
GOSHEN, INDIANA

in some cases, Brownie performed under one of several pseudonyms, including Spider Sam, Big Tom Collins, Henry Johnson, and Blind Boy Williams. Sonny and Brownie were in demand for appearances at clubs and coffee houses throughout the U.S. In addition, Brownie was a member of such Broadway successes as Tennessee Williams' "Cat on a Hot Tin Roof" and Langston Hughes' "Simply Heavenly."

In the 1960s, Brownie and Sonny were featured on many major network shows, including many of the folk music specials. They also accompanied Harry Belafonte on national tours and were featured at major folk festivals, including the one at Newport.

In the 1950s and '60s, Brownie's LP credits included several dozen albums on such labels as Folkways, Savoy, Decca, Jade, King, Verve, Bluesville, and Fantasy. Some of the titles include "Blues," "Traditional Blues" (2 LPs), "Blues and Folksongs" ('58), "On the Road with Burris" ('59)—Folkways; "Brownie's Blues," "Blues and Folk" ('60), "Blues Around My Head" ('61), "Blues in My Soul" ('61), "At the Second Fret" ('63)—Bluesville; "Blues Is My Companion" ('61)—Verve; "Back Country Blues," "Terry and McGhee," "Just a Closer Walk with Thee," "Blues and Shouts" ('62), "At Sugar Hill" ('62)—Fantasy; "Down Home Blues" ('63)—Prestige; and "Work, Play, Faith, Fun" ('60)—SOA Choice. On most of these records, Brownie was joined by Sonny Terry. (*See also* TERRY, SONNY)

MC HAN, DON: *See* Virginia Boys

MC KENZIE, SCOTT: *See* Journeymen, The

MC KUEN, ROD: Singer, actor, composer, author, poet. Born Oakland, California, April 29, 1933.

To say it's hard to pigeonhole Rod McKuen is some kind of understatement. His output in so many different areas is so great it almost seems as though he must be a group rather than one person. In the literary field, he had written four books by 1967 and was working on a fifth. One of his books, *Stanyan Street and Other Sorrows,* sold more than 50,000 copies. According to *The New York Times,* this made it the best-selling book of poetry in twenty years. In music, his output includes many long

works, such as "The Sea," "Something Beyond," "First" and "Second" piano concertos, and "Structures in Jazz."

Despite all this, he remains a figure constantly growing in stature in the folk music field, as both a performer and an artist. In one month in 1965, 79 of his songs were recorded by such singers as Eddy Arnold, the Kingston Trio, The Limelighters, Glenn Yarbrough, Jimmie Rodgers, and French singing star Jacques Brel.

Rod was born in Oakland and spent part of his childhood in Nevada. While still in his teens, he won the *San Francisco Examiner*'s Blue Ribbon Award as most promising radio newcomer. He soon had his own DJ show on station KROW in Oakland. During this same 1951-53 period, he also wrote a syndicated newspaper column, "Scribbling on My Shirtcuff." He already had his first published book, *And Autumn Came,* as of 1950.

Two years in the Army (1953-55) in Japan and Korea failed to slow him down. He starred as a singer at Maxim's Supper Club in Tokyo and found time to perform in six movies for Tono Films, including "The Boy and the General." After his discharge, he continued his movie career under contract to Universal International in four films during 1956-58. In 1959, he moved to New York for a while to compose and conduct music for the CBS Workshop. During his stay in New York, he wrote material for some of the top performers in the U.S. He also scored with city audiences in appearances at the Copacabana, Latin Quarter, and Trude Heller's. Most of the songs he presented were his own compositions.

Before long he was in demand all over the world. He won thunderous applause at such places as the Olympia Music Hall in Paris, the Jockey Club in London, and the casinos of the Riviera. Since then, as both performer and recording artist, he has been one of the top U.S. stars with overseas fans. In the early 1960s, his honors included command performances for President Rhee of Korea and England's Queen Elizabeth, and at two state dinners for the late President John F. Kennedy.

Through 1967, Rod's music output included 900 songs and 29 albums in five languages. These brought him 11 ASCAP awards and the Grand Prix du Disc, Paris. In 1965, he signed with RCA Victor and quickly turned out three LPs, the first of which was "Rod McKuen

Sings His Own." His song hits included "The World I Used to Know," which provided Jimmie Rodgers with a gold record, and the 1967 hit "If You Go Away." Other major McKuen songs include "The Lovers," "Ally, Ally, Oxen Free," "Town and Country," "Oliver Twist," "Two-Ten Six Eighteen," "The Mummy," and "I've Been to Town."

One major project of 1967-68 for Rod was taping all songs written about President Kennedy and his administration. The project was undertaken for the President John F. Kennedy Library at the request of the late Senator Robert Kennedy.

MC MICHEN, CLAYTON "PAPPY": Singer, fiddler, songwriter, comedian, band leader. Born Allatoona, Georgia, January 26, 1900.

One of the country music giants of the early decades of this century, Clayton McMichen, helped make the Skillet Lickers of Gid Tanner a key influence on the development of modern country music. McMichen, along with his friend blind guitarist Riley Puckett, was one of the idols of country boys in all parts of the U.S., serving as a beacon that led some of them to later stardom in the field.

McMichen began as a country boy himself in rural Georgia. The normal pattern of country music get-togethers, square dances, church socials and the like brought an early interest in singing and performing. The fiddle was the main instrument for these affairs, and Clayton learned to play by the time he was high school age. In his teens, he already had a reputation as one of the top fiddlers in the region.

After World War I, McMichen began to perform with local groups in various parts of Georgia. In the early 1920s, he was featured on one of the pioneer country music shows on station WSB in Atlanta. By the mid-1920s, he had settled in Atlanta and played with many of the top artists then in the city, including Tanner and Puckett. When Tanner formed his band soon after making his first recordings in 1924 with Puckett, McMichen joined them. McMichen showed his ability in 1926 by walking off with the first of many national fiddling titles. (He won his last national championship in 1952.)

McMichen's fiddling stood out on such records of Gid Tanner's Skillet Lickers as "Sally Goodin'," "Wreck of the Southern Old 97," and "Down Yonder." McMichen continued to tour and star with the group until 1931, but he formed his own groups in the 1930s and, between bands, played with other major country and western organizations.

By the 1950's he had moved his home base to Louisville. Besides continuing his career as a country artist, he also had his own Dixieland jazz band. Called the Georgia Wildcats, this band was featured on radio and TV in Louisville in the late 1940s and a good part of the 1950s.

In 1954, McMichen retired. A decade later, though, he was sought out by the organizers of the 1964 Newport Folk Festival. He agreed to come out of retirement and his appearance won a heart-felt ovation from the Festival audience. (*See also* TANNER, GID)

MIDWESTERN HAYRIDE: Variety show originating from station WLW, Cincinnati, Ohio.

In any ranking of the major national country and western radio-TV shows, the Midwestern Hayride must be near the top of the list.

Dean Richards, host of the Midwestern Hayride for many years

[201]

Started as a radio show in 1938, it was still going strong as a network TV program twenty years later.

The show started in 1938 as the "Boone County Jamboree" and was broadcast from the Emery Auditorium in Cincinnati. The original cast included Merle Travis and the Drifting Pioneers; Grandpa Jones; Lazy Jim Day; Helen Diller, the Canadian Cowgirl; Louise Massey and the Westerners; Pa and Ma McCormick and the Brown County Revelers; Lafe Harkness; Roy Starkey; Red and Lige Turner; and The Delmore Brothers. In 1939, another act that was one of the most famous in the U. S. country music field was added, Lulu Belle and Scotty.

The radio show continued to attract a major midwestern audience through the 1940s while some of the original cast went on to national stardom and other new stars were developed on the show. In 1945, a new face was added that was to remain one of the show's stars for decades to come: Sally Carson, who was given the performing name of Bonnie Lou.

In 1945, the name of the show was changed to the WLW Midwestern Hayride. Under this name, it switched from radio to TV on Saturday night, February 13, 1948. The show remained a Saturday night fixture on TV through the 1960s. As of 1969, it was shown on four other stations forming the Avco network with WLW, plus syndication on 41 other TV stations across the nation.

Among the other performers featured on the Hayride over the years were Chet Atkins, Homer and Jethro, Bradley Kincaid, Kenny Price and the Hometowners, Dean Richards, Curly Fox and Texas Ruby, Rome Johnstone and the Trailblazers, Natchee (one time partner of Cowboy Copas), Captain Stubby and the Buccaneers, Hugh Cross and his Radio Pals, Hank Penny and his Band, Dean Richards and

Fancy stepping on the Midwestern Hayride is provided by the Midwesterners.

Judy Perkins, Little Jimmy Dickens, the Lucky Pennies, Girls of the Golden West, Zeke and Bill, Charlie Gore, the Midwesterners, and Helen and Billy Scott.

MILLER, JODY: Singer, ukulele player. Born Phoenix, Arizona, November 29, 1941.

Jody Miller is hard to classify. She began singing country and western with her family, gained her first breaks as a folksinger, and scored her first two hits in the popular and country and western fields.

Music was something she grew up with. Her four sisters enjoyed singing from childhood and her father played good country fiddle. It was only natural that Jody took to singing too. From Arizona, where she was born, her family moved to Oklahoma where she went to high school at Blanchard. Soon she joined two friends to form a trio called the Melodies. They attracted the attention of local music fans and were kept busy through most of their high school years with local engagements.

After graduation, Jody decided to go to California to try to make the grade as a solo performer. Three weeks after she arrived, however, an auto accident sent her to the hospital with a broken neck. Lucky to be alive, she returned to Oklahoma to regain her strength.

When she recovered, she began to sing in small clubs in her home region, accompanying herself on the ukulele. She soon was asked to join a local TV variety program, The Tom Paxton Show. She won wider attention from this and went on to sing folk songs at a number of Oklahoma clubs, including The Jester Coffee House in Norman, home of the University. The Limeliters dropped in one night after their own concert at the Oklahoma University Field House. They applauded and suggested she try California once more.

She managed to gain the ear of actor Dale Robertson, who got her an audition at Capitol Records. One of her first records was a 1964 popular hit, "He Walks Like a Man." It helped win her a bid to sing at Italy's San Remo (popular) Song Festival.

Back in the States, Jody was soon represented on hit charts again with "Queen of the House." The song, with a strong country flavor, made the top 10 national ranks for 1965. Her LPs for Capitol included: "Jody Miller" ('65) and "Great Hits of Buck Owens" ('66).

MILLER, ROGER: Singer, instrumentalist (guitar, banjo, piano), songwriter. Born Fort Worth, Texas, January 2, 1936.

In 1965, "King of the Road" took the U.S. by storm. Its lyrics indicated that the writer was familiar with the ins and outs of living on one's uppers, and a look at Roger Miller's early years bears this out. By the time "King of the Road" became an international hit, though, Roger had long since graduated from obscurity to stardom in the country and western field.

Roger Dean Miller was born in Ft. Worth, but was taken to Erick, Oklahoma, when he was a year old. When he was three, his father died and his mother fell seriously ill. He went to live with an aunt and uncle on a farm near Erick and remained there until he was 18.

As he recalls these years, he notes his adopted family was dirt poor. He early learned to shrug off misfortune with a sardonic wit, as evidenced by his comments on his home town: "Erick is so small that the city limits signs are back to back. Its population is 1,500, including rakes and tractors. This school I went to had 37 students, me and 36 Indians. One time we had a school dance and it rained for 36 days straight. During recess we used to play Cowboys and Indians and things got pretty wild from my standpoint."

Most of Roger's education was hard come by. He left school at the end of eighth grade and spent most of his teens doing odd jobs around the region. He worked as a ranch hand, herding cattle and dehorning cows, among other things. He also spent some of his time riding Brahma bulls in rodeos. During these years, however, he did manage to learn to play the guitar and other instruments well.

Roger left Erick to enlist in the Army. He was sent to Korea after basic training, where at first he drove a jeep. His talent as a guitarist and singer eventually paid off, though; he got into Special Services and became part of a hillbilly band entertaining troops. Many of the songs he played were his own creations, and the applause of the soldiers made him feel he might succeed as a musician or writer. He showed his versatility in the group by playing drums and fiddle in addition to guitar.

After his discharge in the mid-1950s, he first tried his hand at being a fireman in Amarillo, Texas. He slept through the alarm of the second fire of his career and was fired

Roger Miller

after two months on the job. Now he felt it was time to make his way as a musician. He went to Nashville with enough money in his pocket for several weeks in a cheap hotel or one night at a good one. He spent the night at the best hotel in town, then got a job as bellhop there the next morning.

Now he worked on writing songs in his spare time. It wasn't easy, for he did not know how to write music. From that day to this, Roger plays or sings the song for someone to put the notes down on paper. He spent months trying his songs out on artists and publishers. Finally Ray Price recorded one of them, "Invitation to the Blues." The song was a hit and Roger was signed to a full-time writing job with the Faron Young organization. He turned out such hits as "You Don't Want My Love," "Hey Little Star," "Lock, Stock and Teardrops," and "In the Summertime."

Roger finally began recording some of his songs in the early 1960s. In 1961, he scored a top 10 hit with "When Two Worlds Collide." This was the only one of his 10 top country

and western hits from 1961 to 1967 that he did not write all by himself. His co-author was country and western great Bill Anderson.

Roger did not score a major hit the next two years, though, and he decided to move to Hollywood to study dramatic acting. He enrolled in an actors' workshop, but withdrew as some of his new records on the Smash label (his first hit was on RCA Victor) began to move. He soon had a number-one national hit in "Dang Me" and another top 10 success, "Chug A Lug." In 1965, Roger really hit his stride. He had four major best-sellers, including "King of the Road." The other three were "Engine, Engine No. 9," "Kansas City Star," and "One Dyin' and A-Buryin'." Roger continued in 1966 with "England Swings" and "Husband and Wives." He also provided Andy Williams with a hit that sold more than two million records, "In the Summer Time." An appearance on Andy's NBC-TV show in late '65 had such excellent viewer reaction that NBC asked him to do his own half-hour special. Aired on January 19, 1966, it drew response enough to cause NBC to plan a fall weekly show featuring Roger. The show went on September 12, 1966, and lasted part of the season. Unfortunately, the show did not continue into 1967.

During 1965 and '66, Roger played to sell out audiences in personal appearances across the country. His engagement at Harrah's at Lake Tahoe brought out so many fans it had to be extended an extra day. He also won ovations in New York and San Francisco.

From 1965 to 1967, Roger gained four gold records for his LPs. These included "Roger Miller/Dang Me"; "The Return of Roger Miller"; "Roger Miller/Golden Hits"; and Roger Miller, The Third Time Around." He also set a new record for Grammy awards, walking off with five in 1965 and six more in 1966 for the unprecedented total of 11. His 1968 output included a hit single of "Little Green Apples."

MITCHELL, PRISCILLA: Singer. Born Marietta, Georgia, September 14, 1941.

Priscilla Mitchell's career seems to revolve around the number two. She maintained two separate identities while recording for two different labels in both country and western and rock 'n' roll fields. She also achieved country and western stardom in duets with Roy Drusky. There was nothing second-rate about their hit recording "Yes, Mr. Peters," though, because it was the number-one song in the country field for much of 1965.

Priscilla's mother actively encouraged her daughter to sing during her youth in Marietta, Georgia. At the age of four, Priscilla made her radio debut on station WFOM in Marietta, singing "Pistol Packin' Mama." As Priscilla grew up, her voice continued to improve as did her poise. During her years at Sprayberry High School, she had many engagements to sing at clubs, on radio programs, and for school affairs. One of the more noteworthy shows from a personal standpoint occurred in June 1957. On the bill was songwriter-singer Jerry Reed Hubbard, who records for RCA Victor. In time, Priscilla became Mrs. Hubbard.

The first record contract for Priscilla was with Smash Records. She sang rock 'n' roll music for this label under the pseudonym of Sadina. By the mid-1960s, she was singing both on Smash and—in the country and western field—on Mercury. By this time, the Hubbards had settled down in Nashville. In addition to her feature recordings, Priscilla worked as a background singer for hundreds of other Nashville recording sessions.

MIZE, BILLY: Singer, guitarist, songwriter, m.c. Born Kansas City, Kansas, April 29, 1932.

Well known to California country and western fans, Billy Mize made his first move toward national prominence in 1967. Billy was voted the Most Promising Vocalist of 1966 in the Academy of Country Music awards poll.

Billy first saw the light of day in Kansas. However, by the time he was of school age, his family had moved to California's San Joaquin Valley. Because that area has absorbed a great influx of people from Oklahoma and other southwestern states, it has many ardent country and western fans, and there is good audience response to country programs from Bakersfield stations. Growing up, Billy often heard country and western music on the radio, and learned to enjoy and sing it.

In high school, Billy excelled in sports, playing on both baseball and football teams. However, unlike most of his fellow athletes, he also joined the school glee club. At 17, he mastered the guitar and began to sing country and western music locally. He found music to his liking and continued to add to his performing experience after high school.

In 1953, he was a member of the group that started the Trading Post Show on station KERO-TV, Bakersfield. Except for two years, he was a regular on the show from September 26, 1953, into the mid-60s. In 1966, he took up the chores of hosting the show.

Meanwhile, Billy was busy in other ways as well. In the 1950s, he signed with Decca Records. His output included several records of his own compositions, including "Who Will Buy the Wine," "I Saw Her First," "It Could Happen" and "Solid Sender." Later he also recorded for Challenge and Liberty before signing with Columbia in the mid-'60s.

During 1966-67, Billy served as host for the nationally syndicated Gene Autry program, Melody Ranch. He also had his own Billy Mize Show in syndication from Bakersfield. In 1967, Billy had a number of successful recordings, including "Lights of Albuquerque."

MOELLER, W. E. "LUCKY": Music executive. Born Okarche, Oklahoma, February 12, 1912.

Having ability as a performer is one thing; exploiting that talent most efficiently is another. The key to success in the music field depends heavily on the management team behind the performer. Thus it's no accident that any list of major commercial performers and their management-booking agency reveals the name Moeller again and again.

The founder of the Moeller agency, W. E. "Lucky" Moeller, grew up in Oklahoma where country and western music was one of the major pleasures of most of the population. Lucky, though interested in listening to it, considered business his main goal in life. When he finished his schooling, he got a job with a bank in the southwest. For twelve years he progressed in the bank until he was one of the officers.

At this point, in the early 1950s, he decided to strike out in a different direction. He left the bank to try his hand at the management side of the entertainment field. In 1954, he moved to Nashville, as president of his own country and western management and booking agency. By the mid-1960s, Moeller Talent was one of the largest of its kind in the world.

As of 1968, the artists under the Moeller banner included such names as Ernie Ashworth, Carl and Pearl Butler, Archie Campbell, Little Jimmy Dickens, Whitey Ford, The Homesteaders, Wade Jackson, Norma Jean, Grandpa Jones, George Morgan, Minnie Pearl, Carl Perkins, Bill Phillips, Webb Pierce, Max Powell, George Riddle, Ben Smathers, Carl Smith, Hank Snow, Red Sovine, Bobbi Staff, Merle Travis, Justin Tubb, Porter Wagoner, Billy Walker, Kitty Wells, Dottie West, Willis Brothers, Bobby Wright, Ruby Wright, and Faron Young.

MONROE, BILL: *See* Monroe Brothers

MONROE BROTHERS: Singers, instrumentalists (guitar, mandolin, fiddle), composers, lyricists. Born Rosine, Kentucky, Bill Monroe, September 13, 1911; Charlie Monroe, June 4, 1903.

In the 1960s, the name associated in most people's minds with Bluegrass music was Flatt & Scruggs. But these talented performers would acknowledge the debt to the man called the "Father of Bluegrass Music," William "Bill" Monroe. Monroe, of course, did not invent the Bluegrass style of playing, but he did more to develop and present this musical form of the border regions to the country than anyone else.

Monroe learned to play stringed instruments at an early age in his home state of Kentucky. By the time he was in his twenties, he had appeared at many county fairs and local dances. Not only was he a talented entertainer, but he also composed many of the tunes he presented.

Bill teamed up with his brother Charlie in the mid-1920s to start a show business career. The Monroe Brothers advanced from local appearances to their first radio broadcasts in 1927. They built up a large following among country music fans of the late 1920s and early 1930s for their Bluegrass arrangements in which Charlie played "houn' dog guitar" and Bill played "potato-bug mandolin."

In the years after World War II, Charlie retired to his Kentucky ranch while Bill carried on the Monroe tradition. Some of their best efforts were chronicled on a Camden LP, "Early Blue Grass Music By the Monroe Brothers." The album includes "New River Train," "No Home, No Place to Pillow My Head," "The Great Speckled Bird," "Once I Had a Darling Mother," "On the Banks of the Ohio," "Rosa Lee McFall," "Bringin' in the Georgia Mail," "Weeping Willow Tree," "Just a Song of Old Kentucky," "Don't Forget me," "I Am Thinking Tonight of the Old Folks,"

The "Father of Bluegrass," Bill Monroe, in action

and "Mother's Not Dead, She's Only Sleeping."

In 1934, Bill scored his first major success as a songwriter with "Kentucky Waltz." The song became a nationwide hit and later helped bring Bill Monroe's group, "The Bluegrass Boys," to the attention of country and western fans. As the 1930s went by, the Monroe troupe was in wide demand for personal appearances and for radio work. During this period, Bill Monroe turned out many instrumental tunes with his trademark of intricate timing and special tuning. Some of these are "Get Up John," "Blue Grass Ramble," and "Memories of You."

The Monroe Brothers remained together for more than a decade, but in 1938 Bill and Charlie decided to go separate ways. Charlie organized his Kentucky Pardners while Bill established his famous Bluegrass Boys. Charlie remained active with his own group until the early 1950s and made many recordings for RCA Victor.

It was Bill Monroe, though, who gained major national attention for the family name

[206]

both during and after World War II. He joined the Grand Ole Opry in 1939 and he and his group remained featured artists on the show for three decades.

Bill Monroe continued to expand his cast of artists and sellout audiences usually greeted his tent shows. Many of the best known names in country and western music were part of the troupe at one time or another. In the 1940s, for example, Sam and Kirk McGee finished the show with a 20-minute "old time" country and western songfest. Among the musicians who played in the Monroe band over the years were Flatt & Scruggs, Clyde Moody, Howdy Forrester, Don Reno, Red Smiley, Jimmy Martin, and Carter Stanley.

For many years, Bill Monroe wrote only music while others provided lyrics, sometimes long after a song became an instrumental hit. In 1942, Monroe began to write words as well. He added lyrics to his "Kentucky Waltz" and in 1951 an Eddy Arnold recording became one of the number one hits of the year. A few years later, Monroe's "Blue Moon of Kentucky" was one song that helped a newcomer, Elvis Presley, on the way to stardom. Other Monroe song hits include "Cheyenne," "Memories of Mother and Dad," "Gotta Travel on," "On the Kentucky Shore," "Uncle Pen" and "Scotland."

In the 1960s, Monroe was still a favorite with audiences and his LP albums continued to sell steadily. With recognition of Bluegrass as a vital part of the folk tradition, Bill was also invited to folk festivals in all parts of the country. He made several appearances at the Newport Festival in the 1960s and was also the guest of honor at the first Bluegrass festival held in the early '60s. Monroe was a guest star, with the Bluegrass Boys, on many network programs of the 1960s, including several appearances on ABC-TV's Hootenanny.

MONROE, CHARLIE: *See* Monroe Brothers.

MONTANA, PATSY: Singer, guitarist, songwriter. Born Hot Springs, Arkansas, October 30, 1914.

In the 1930s and '40s, the WLS National Barn Dance was probably the best known country and western show in most of the country outside the south. One of the prime reasons for this state of affairs was a little lady named Patsy Montana. Her name and her nickname,

"The Yodeling Cowgirl," had a western ring to them, but her origins were a lot closer to the heartland of the Grand Ole Opry than the Chicago based Barn Dance.

Patsy (real name: Rubye Blevins) grew up in Hot Springs, Arkansas, and attended Hope High School there. She continued her education at the University of Western Louisiana. Singing was in her blood, though, and she soon began to spend more and more time perfecting her guitar chording and her repertoire of country and western songs. By the early 1930s, she was on her way to a performing career.

In 1934, she was the lead singer for a quartet called the Prairie Ramblers. The Ramblers, whose members stated they all were born in log cabins in Kentucky, comprised Chick Hurt, Tex Atchison, Jack Taylor, and Salty Holmes. From 1934 through 1948, Patsy and the Ramblers graced many a theater stage and almost every county fair in the nation. From 1935 on, Patsy and the Ramblers were also featured members of the National Barn Dance cast. By this time, Patsy was also known to her friends as Mrs. Paul Rose, after her marriage in 1934.

Patsy began her long recording career in 1933, with such songs as "I Love My Daddy Too" and "When the Flowers of Montana Are Blooming." Her voice was heard on many different labels from 1933 to 1959, including Surf, Columbia, RCA Victor, Vocalion and Decca. Some of her other recordings of the 1930s were "The Wheel of the Wagon Is Broken," "I'm an Old Cowhand," "There's a Ranch in the Sky," "Singing in the Saddle," "A Cowboy Honeymoon," and "Montana." In later decades she turned out such songs as "Old Nevada Moon," "My Million Dollar Smile," "I Only Want a Buddy Not a Sweetheart," "If I Could Only Learn to Yodel," "Little Sweetheart of the Ozarks," "Deep in the Heart of Texas," "Good Night Soldier," and "Leaning on the Old Top Rail."

Patsy also wrote many original songs. Some of her compositions include "My Baby's Lullaby," "Me and My Cowboy Sweetheart," "The Buckaroo," "Cowboy Rhythm," "I'm a Little Cowboy Girl," "The Moon Hangs Low," "My Poncho Pony," "A Cowboy's Gal" and "I've Found My Cowboy Sweetheart."

Her career with the Barn Dance lasted nearly 25 years, finally drawing to a close in 1959. In addition, Patsy was a guest star on other radio and TV shows over the years. During the 1946-47 season, she had her own radio program on ABC called "Wake Up and Smile."

In 1959, Patsy retired temporarily from the entertainment field. Her new job was in the real estate business in Manhattan Beach, California, near Los Angeles. The lure of the theater was too strong, however, and she was once more making personal appearances in the 1960's.

MONTANA SLIM: *See* Carter, Wilf

MONTGOMERY, MELBA: Singer, songwriter. Born Iron City, Tennessee, October 14, 1938.

One of the major stepping stones to country and western success has been the Pet Milk amateur contest. In 1958, the audience jamming Studio C at WSM, Nashville, gave a thunderous ovation to a young brown-haired songstress named Melba Montgomery. Raised on farms in Alabama and Tennessee, she gave the intonation to her country ballads that showed a natural grounding in country music.

The audience reaction mirrored that of the judges who awarded her first prize. Her ability rapidly became known to other country artists and music executives. In short order, Roy Acuff signed her for his Smokey Mountain Gang. She remained with Roy for four years, accompanying the group on tours of all fifty states and on four USO overseas tours to entertain U.S. servicemen at Christmastime.

She recorded for a small label for a while, until she was signed by veteran record executive Pappy Daily, then working for United Artists. She turned out a number of well received singles, some of which were her own compositions. United Artists issued several successful LPs featuring Melba, including "Melba Montgomery" and "Down Home" in 1964 and "I Can't Get Used to Being Lonely" in 1965. She also teamed with another Daily discovery, George Jones, in a number of hit duets. In 1963, she and George scored a top 10 hit for United Artists with Melba's song "We Must Have Been Out of Our Minds."

When Pappy Daily formed his own record company, Musicor, in 1965, both Melba and George Jones signed with him. They continued to turn out hit duets. In 1967, they had one moving up the charts called "Party Pickin'."

MORGAN, GEORGE: Singer, guitarist, songwriter. Born Waverly, Tennessee, June 28, 1925.

A bid to join the Grand Ole Opry usually means a young performer is well on the way to national stardom. Rarely does any new Opry artist begin with the sensational success gained by George Morgan in 1948. Late in the year, George became a member of the Opry cast and soon performed his own song, "Candy Kisses." The song became the biggest country hit of 1949, gaining George record sales of more than 1,000,000 as well as a long-term contract with Columbia Records. But "Candy Kisses" proved a hit for many other artists as well, both in country and western and popular. Joining George's record in the top 10 were versions by Elton Britt, Eddie Kirk, and Cowboy Copas.

George was born and partly raised in Tennessee. To return in glory to Nashville, though, required an apprenticeship in Ohio and West Virginia. George's parents moved to Barberton, Ohio, when he was nearing his teens and he attended the town's high school. George had learned to play guitar by the time he was in his teens, well enough to gain his own program on station WAKR in nearby Akron. He followed this up with his own 15-minute program on a Wooster, Ohio, station.

After finishing high school, George continued his career in music, but the going wasn't easy. He picked up what work he could as a performer, but also added to his income by various jobs including salesman, surveyor, and truck driver. In the mid-1940s, things began to look up when he gained a spot on the WWVA Jamboree in Wheeling, West Virginia. The growth of his popularity in West Virginia was illustrated by a healthy increase in fan mail and bids to perform at major events in the region.

In 1948, he was well enough established for the Grand Ole Opry bid. Once "Candy Kisses" became a country standard, he was assured of top billing on the Opry roster. George demonstrated his ability again and again in 1949 with four more top 10 hit records, "Cry Baby Heart," "Please Don't Let Me Love You," "Rainbow in My Heart," and "Room Full of Roses." He turned out many other best-sellers in the years that followed, including such nationally ranked songs as "Almost" ('52); "I'm in Love Again" (his own composition—

'59); and "You're the Only Good Thing."

After an association with the Opry that lasted from 1948 to 1956, George left for a time to star on his own show on WLAC-TV in Nashville. In 1959, he rejoined the Opry as a regular. During the 1950s and '60s, he guested on many major network shows, including Bobby Lord, Porter Wagoner, Wilburn Brothers, and Country Music Hall.

In the 1960s, he appeared in all fifty states, Canada, and Europe. Besides the songs previously listed, his audiences heard him sing many of his other recorded successes, including "Slipping Around," "You Loved Me Just Enough to Hurt Me," "You're Not Home Yet," "I'm Not Afraid," "Almost," "A Picture That's New," "No Man Should Hurt as Bad as I Do," "You're the Only Star in My Blue Heaven," "Cheap Affair," "Cry of the Lamb," "Ever' So Often," "Wheel of Hurt," "Lonesome Record," "Jesus Savior Pilot Me," "Little Pioneer," "Mansion over the Hilltop," "No One Knows It Better Than Me," "Oh Gentle Shepherd," "Shot in the Dark," "Walking Shoes," and "Whither Thou Goest."

His albums included "Greatest Country and Western Hits," "Morgan, By George," "Slipping Around," "Tender Loving Care," "Red Roses for a Blue Lady," "Candy Kisses" and "George Morgan and Marion Worth" ('64).

In 1966, George ended eighteen years with Columbia Records, switching to the Starday label.

MORRISON, HAROLD: Singer, instrumentalist (guitar, banjo, dobro), songwriter. Born Ava, Missouri, January 30, 1931.

Considering his upbringing in the Ozark Mountains, Harold Morrison came to play the guitar late in life. Brought up on a farm near Ava, Missouri, he didn't start playing until he was 16. At that time, he bought a steel guitar for five dollars, and in a short time was proficient enough to play on some of the smaller stations in the region. In the early 1950s, he moved up to KWTO, Springfield, Missouri, where he added his talents to those of Porter Wagoner.

By the mid-1950s, he was playing on bills with the Lake of the Ozarks Square Dance Group. Some of the Group suggested he learn the 5-string banjo, and join them. Within a few months, he had begun to build a reputation as a banjo player that overshadowed his guitar

playing. Besides playing with the Group, he soon was featured as a banjo player at such places as the Blue Room of New Orleans' Roosevelt Hotel and the Riverside Casino in Reno, Nevada.

Later in the 1950s, he starred on the World's Original WWVA Jamboree in Wheeling, West Virginia. He also began a four-year stint with Red Foley's network show on ABC-TV. By the early 1960s, he was in demand as a featured and supporting artist for both personal tours and recording sessions. His travels throughout the U.S. and Canada were made with such stars as the Wilburn Brothers, Ernest Tubb, Roy Acuff, Johnnie and Jack, Kitty Wells, and Red Foley.

In the early 1960s, he moved to Hendersonville, Tennessee, close to Nashville. This brought him within commuting distance of Nashville, where he became a mainstay of the Grand Ole Opry in the mid-1960s. His network exposure in the 1960s also included regular appearances on the Wilburn Brothers Show.

Morrison extended his activities to songwriting as part of his output for his Decca Records contract. He provided original material for a number of his duets with Jimmy Gately.

MOSER, PROF. ARTUS: Singer, guitarist, folk music collector, educator. Born Swannanoa, North Carolina.

Born and raised in the Swannanoa Valley in the midst of the largest mountain chain in North Carolina, Artus Moser grew up with folk music. All around him in his boyhood new or old versions of traditional songs were sung as a matter of course by the farmers and rugged mountaineers of the area.

Thus he learned many of these tunes without even thinking of them as folk music. One example of a song he mastered as a child is the well known "Sourwood Mountain." As he related in the notes for his Folkways LP "North Carolina Ballads," Sourwood Mountain "is often sung by men out in the hills and mountains when they wish to make their voices echo down the valleys and hollows. When the air is still and they are feeling good, they can sometimes be heard for miles. I've tried it like that several times myself. It is just the thing for mountain singing."

Since folk music was so natural to his surroundings, Moser gave little thought to it as he completed his years in elementary and high school. Afterwards, when he entered the University of North Carolina at Chapel Hill, he gained new insight into the meaning of folklore and the need to preserve this important heritage.

He went on to teaching when he gained his degree. As a professor at Lincoln Memorial University, Harrowgate, Tennessee, in the years just before World War II, he taught folklore to some of his classes, using printed texts to illustrate folk balladry. His pupils, from the rural areas in many cases, quickly demonstrated knowledge of significant versions of the songs from their own upbringing. This experience resulted in Moser's decision to go back into the Great Smoky Mountains and the Blue Ridge region of his state and do his own collecting. Before long, he had compiled an impressive amount of folk material.

Word of his efforts reached the Lomaxes at the Library of Congress Archive of American Folk Song. Professor Moser was asked to contribute to the Archive and he responded by providing more than 300 songs. Because of the importance of his work, he was furnished with a new recording machine in the mid-1940s on which he recorded many regional performers for the Library of Congress collection.

During the 1950s, Moser continued to build his collection of folk material. By the end of the decade, it was considered one of the most complete of its kind in the country. He also performed many of his songs before college groups and at folk festivals, including the traditional folk music event at White Top, North Carolina.

Professor Moser recorded a number of these songs for Folkways in the 1955 "North Carolina Ballads" LP. The album included, besides "Sourwood Mountain," such numbers as "Swannanoa Town," "The Old Man Over the Hill," "Old Grey Mare," "The Two Sisters," "Wildwood Flower," "The False Knight Upon the Road," "Cumberland Gap," "Lord Randal," "Poor Ellen Smith," and "Sweet Rivers."

MOUNTAIN DANCE AND FOLK FESTIVAL: *See* American Folk Festival

MOUNTAIN DULCIMER: *See* Appalachian Dulcimer

MULLICAN, MOON: Singer, organist, pianist, songwriter. Born Polk County, near Corrigan,

Texas, March 27, 1909; died Beaumont, Texas, January 1, 1967.

Aubrey "Moon" Mullican's father owned a rich 87-acre farm and it seemed likely to all concerned that Moon would someday succeed to its management. But when Moon was eight, his father bought a pump-organ that helped change Moon's future. Within a few years, he had worked out a two-finger right-hand style of playing that was to provide the grounds for his claim to the title "King of the Hillbilly Piano Players."

Moon's skill in organ playing continued to improve and he entertained his friends and neighbors on many occasions. He also played for his church when he was in his teens. After a while, he branched out into playing piano for local dances. He took home his first paycheck for a date in Lufkin, Texas, in the late 1920s and decided to make music his occupation.

He moved to Houston, where he began accompanying local folk artists. After a while, he formed his own band and played at clubs and on radio in many places in Louisiana and Texas during the 1930s. For a time, he was featured on station KPBX in Beaumont, Texas. During the 1930s, he also made the first of many records on such labels as Coral, Decca, and King. In 1939, he went to Hollywood for a role in the film "Village Barn Dance." Audiences in California clubs were as impressed with his personal appearances as those in the southwest.

In the 1940s, Mullican returned to home base in Texas. Part of the time, he owned his own nightclubs in Beaumont and Port Arthur. In the mid- and late '40s, he began to move into the big time with hit records of some of his own songs. In 1947, he had a number-one best-seller in "New Jole Blon." The song placed second as "Best Hillbilly Record" of 1947 in polls conducted by Cashbox and the Juke Box Operators association. The following year, he had the third ranked song in these polls, as well as a gold-record-seller, in his composition, "Sweeter Than the Flowers." Mullican hit the top 10 bracket on the charts with another King Record success in 1950, "Goodnight Irene," and topped it that same year with his number-one-placing "I'll Sail My Ship Alone." He had a third major hit in 1950 with "Mona Lisa." Then, in 1951, another Mullican composition (co-authored with W. C. Redbird) closed out his cycle of hits, "Cherokee Boogie."

In the rest of the 1950s and early '60s, Mulli-

[210]

can was active with tours that took him into all the states and overseas as well. He was featured on his own program on KECK, Odessa, Texas, and guested on such shows as Grand Ole Opry, ABC-TV's Jubilee U.S.A., and the Big D Jamboree. Some of his other recordings of these and earlier years were: "Columbus Stockade Blues," "Sugar Beet," "Jole Blon's Sister," "Early Morning Blues," "The Leaves Mustn't Fall," "Well Oh Well," "Sweeter Than the Flowers No. 2," "Moon's Rock," "Pipeliner's Blues," "Jambalaya," "Every Which-Away," and "Moon's Tune."

Moon's long and illustrious career ended in 1967 when he was stricken with a fatal heart attack in Beaumont.

NATIONAL BARN DANCE, THE: Weekly variety show, originating from station WLS, Chicago.

If an award were given for pioneering in the overall field of folk, country and western it would be hard to fault the claim of station WLS, the Prairie Farmer Station, Chicago. In the early 1920s, the station featured Bradley Kincaid, the "Original Authentic Folksong Singer." Kincaid's statement that he was "the first person to introduce folksongs or mountain ballads to radio" (*Folksingers and Folksongs in America,* Ray M. Lawless, p. 130) has thus far not been disputed. And, on April 19, 1924, the station aired a new variety show called the Chicago Barn Dance, first country music jamboree broadcast in the United States. The man who originated the show was George D. Hay; the following year he left Chicago for Nashville where he began another Barn Dance. The latter was to become the Grand Ole Opry.

The WLS Barn Dance grew into one of the major network shows in the country in the 1930s after its beginnings in the Eighth Street Theatre in Chicago. Its title changed, of course, to the National Barn Dance. Over the years, it propelled many artists to national fame, including Gene Autry, who was a cast member 1930-34, Bob Atcher, Johnny Bond, Homer and Jethro, Patsy Montana, Lulu Belle and Scotty, and Red Foley. Foley, in fact, was discovered by a WLS talent scout while a freshman at Georgetown College in Kentucky. The Barn Dance was also proving grounds for a number of famous comedians, including George Gobel, Smiley Burnette, and Pat Buttram.

The Barn Dance began under the auspices of Sears, Roebuck & Co., who owned the station for the first four years of the show's existence. In 1928, national audiences heard all or part of the show every Saturday night between the hours of 7:30 and 12 P.M. Central Standard Time. A familiar cry during those years was "Are you ready, Hezzie?" Thus were introduced the washboard, kazoo, and other instrumentation of the group known as the Hoosier Hot Shots.

Dozens of major country and western performers appeared on the Barn Dance during its decades of existence. In addition to those already mentioned, some of these were: Rex Allen, Arkie the Arkansas Woodchopper, Red Blanchard, Bonnie Blue Eyes, Phyllis Brown, Karl and Harty, Carl Cotner, Hugh Cross, Jenny Lou Carson, Cumberland Ridge Runners, Eddie Dean, Uncle Ezra, Sonny Fleming, Eva Carson Foley, Verne Fredler, Four Hired Hands, Gene and Glenn, Little Genevieve, Dolly Good, Hilltoppers, Jack Holden, Salty Holmes, Dock Hopkins, Hoosier Sod Busters, Don Jacks, Jimmie James, Eileen Jensen, Helen Jensen, Pete Kaye, Joe Kelly, Frank Kettering, Augie Klein, Ray Klein, Bradley Kincaid, John Laird (later founder of the Renfro Valley Barn Dance), Bonnie Linder, Connie Linder, Shorty Long, Bill McCluskey, Clayton McMichen (of Gid Tanner fame), Lilly Mae, Joe Maphis, Maple City Quartet, Sleepy Marlin, Woody Mercer, Curley Miller, Bill Monroe, Wally Moore, Ted Morse, Ted Moss, Bill O'Connor, Hal O'Halloran, Ole Olson, Otto and the Novolodeans, Jimmy Osborne, Lucille Overstake, Tony Pacione, Chubby Parker, Linda Parker, Rocky Porter, The Prairie Ramblers, Lou Prohut, Andy Reynolds, Al Rice, Jerry Richards, Gene Ruppe, The Sage Riders, John Stokes, Tiny Stokes, Captain Stubby and the Buccaneers, Sunshine Sue, Tom Tanner, Cousin Tilford, Rube Transon and his Texas Cowboys, Al Vlodek, Otto Ward, Ozzie Waters, Don White, Colleen Wilson, Grace Wilson, Winnie, Lou and Sally, and George and Sam Workman.

The inroads of rock 'n' roll into the country and western market in the late 1950s helped bring about the end of the National Barn Dance in May 1960.

NATIONAL FOLK FESTIVAL: Folk festival, originated in St. Louis, Missouri.

One of the largest folk festivals in the world,

the National Folk Festival usually played host to upwards of 1,000 performers annually. Founded in St. Louis in the early 1930s, the Festival has been presented in many other major cities, sometimes in connection with special anniversaries. In 1957, for example, it took place in Oklahoma City, Oklahoma, as part of the state's semi-centennial anniversary celebration. Sponsor of the event in St. Louis for most of its existence was a newspaper, the St. Louis *Globe-Democrat*. When held in St. Louis, the Festival usually took place at the Kiel Auditorium. The event was also held in a number of other cities: Chattanooga ('35); Dallas ('36); Chicago ('37); Washington, D.C. ('38-'42); New York ('42—repeat of Washington event); Philadelphia ('43-'46); Cleveland ('47).

In 1959, Festival organizers under the leadership of Sarah Gertrude Knott decided to establish permanent headquarters in Washington, D.C. The new organization is called National Folk Festival Association, Inc. Festivals were held in Washington in 1960, '61, and '62. In 1963, the event was shifted to Devou Park amphitheater in Covington, Kentucky.

The program normally runs three to four days. It covers a wide range, including instrumental presentations—guitar, fiddle, banjo, etc.; folk dances; folk singing; and country and western sessions. Besides presenting general folk material from all over America, the Festival also focuses on songs germane to specific regions or states. The presentations are not limited to the U.S.; folk material is performed from many other nations of the world. Average attendance in recent years has been close to a total of 30,000. Performers range from widely known professional artists to talented amateurs, including leading folklorists.

NEAL, BOB: Performer, music executive. Born Belgian Congo, Africa, October 6, 1917.

Robert Neal may have been prepared for his future career as a top talent finder in country music by his birth in the Belgian Congo, home of many a safari. By the time he was school age, though, he and his missionary parents were back home in the U.S. When he was in his teens, he already was deeply interested in the radio industry that was just growing out of its swaddling clothes in the 1930s.

Bob found a job with a local station and in

the late 1930s was announcing and doing other chores on stations in the midwest.

In the early 1940s, he was an announcer on station WMPS in Memphis, Tennessee. In the post-World War II era, he began to concentrate on work as an advertising sales representative for several stations and as a manager of promising artists. In the early 1950s, while based in Memphis, he became involved in the promotion of country & western music shows. This led to the chance to sign up new talent for the shows. One of the young artists Neal heard in the early '50s was a Mississippi boy named Elvis Presley. In 1954, Neal became the first manager of the artist who was to become one of the all-time greats in the rock 'n' roll idiom. After working with Presley for a while, Neal cooperated in working out the arrangements by which Colonel Tom Parker took over Presley's career.

Soon after, Neal began working with another promising performer, Johnny Cash, and as his first manager helped point Johnny toward future greatness. In 1962, still in Memphis, Neal handled such other artists as Carl Perkins, Roy Orbison, and Jerry Lee Lewis.

Up to this point, Neal had been working for other people. In 1963 he moved to Nashville and set up his own company, Bob Neal Agency, Inc. He was soon busily handling management and bookings for a new crop of stars. By the late 1960s, two of them, Sonny James and Stonewall Jackson, had achieved top status in the nation. Others of note on Neal's roster included Conway Twitty, Nat Stuckey, Pete Drake, Johnny Paycheck, Billy Edd Wheeler, Liz and Lynn Anderson, Leroy Pullins, and Bobby Helms.

NELSON, KEN: Singer, banjoist, radio announcer, record company executive. Born Caledonia, Minnesota, January 19, 1911.

The name Ken Nelson comes up in the biographies of many of the performers listed in this book. As the head of the country and western department of Capitol Records, he has been responsible for starting dozens of artists on the road to fame and fortune. His qualifications for this work include many years as a top-ranked active performer.

Kenneth F. Nelson's music career started when he was just 11. The year was 1922, and he had a job singing in the White City Amusement Park in Chicago. That same year, Ken had his first taste of the business side of the field when he began working in the office of Melrose Brothers Music Publishers in Chicago. While working as a singer and banjoist during the next four years, Ken continued his association with Melrose. In 1925, he broke into the radio field playing a banjo solo on a Chicago station.

In 1926, Ken switched to the publishing firm of a great popular singer of the 1920s, Gene Austin. Austin was impressed with Ken's ability and took the boy to New York to sing and play banjo on a local station. After a year in New York, Ken returned to the Windy City where he formed an orchestra with Lee Gillette called the Campus Kids. Expanding his activities, Ken formed a vocal trio and sang on local stations KYW, WAAF, and WBBM.

After a number of years as a performer, Ken was offered a job on WAAF in 1936. His task was to announce the Symphonic Hour and Chicago Symphony Orchestra concerts. Ken soon worked up a major reputation in the classical field and was ranked as the outstanding classical announcer in Chicago.

In 1940, Ken stepped up a notch, taking over as musical director and program director at station WJJD. He was program director of one of the best known shows in the midwest at the time, Suppertime Frolics, when World War II interrupted his career. After two years as a medic, Ken returned as musical director of WJJD. In 1946, he accepted a bid to moonlight for the fledgling Capitol Records, doing the recording for their transcription service.

Capitol also gave him the chance to make some records for them. In 1948, singing with the Dinning Sisters, Ken scored a national hit with "Buttons and Bows." The record sold more than half a million copies. When Capitol expanded its operations in 1948, Ken went to California to take charge of the transcription department. Capitol continued to be impressed with his understanding of the music field, and in 1951 appointed him head of the country and western department.

Ken Nelson helped build the department into a major factor in the country field and was still going strong in this role as of 1969. Among the hit records he helped set for the company were such million-sellers as Hank Thompson's "Wild Side of Life"; Stan Freberg's "St. George and the Dragonet"; Sonny James' "Young Love"; Gene Vincent's "Be Bop a Lu Lo"; Tommy Sands' "Teen-Age Crush"; and Ferlin

Husky's "Gone." Other best-sellers were "Dear John Letter" with Jean Shepherd and Ferlin Husky; Buck Owens' "I've Got a Tiger By the Tail"; Wanda Jackson's "Right or Wrong"; Tex Ritter's "High Noon"; and Roy Clark's "The Tips of My Fingers."

In addition to his normal chores, Ken also helped organize the Country Music Association. He was elected CMA president for the 1961-63 term.

NELSON, WILLIE: Singer, guitarist, songwriter. Born Fort Worth, Texas, April 30, 1933.

One of the most retiring of people, "Country Willie" Nelson had a resounding impact on the country music field in the 1960s. He started out behind the scenes as a songwriter, but the quality of his songs and his half-whispering style on demonstration records forced him into the limelight as a performer.

Though born in Fort Worth, Willie was raised in the rural central Texas town of Abbott, from whence came the nickname Abbott Willie. He grew up loving the remoteness and peace of farm life. Like many farm boys, he learned to play guitar and took part in after-work sings with his friends. Many of the songs he sang were those he heard on the radio from the Louisiana Hayride or Grand Ole Opry. After a while, though, he began to make up songs of his own.

Still planning an eventual career in farming, he enrolled in Baylor University at Waco, Texas, but left after two years. Soon he began to gain a local reputation as a songwriter. In time, he began to consider a career as a writer. When performers heard some of his material, they agreed that his was a rare talent. His compositions began to be performed by more and more artists. In the late 1950s, he started a career in radio as a disk jockey on a Texas station. For seven years he worked as a DJ in Texas, Oregon, and California. In 1961, his reputation in the industry soared as one song after another showed up on the hit charts. Patsy Cline scored a top 10 hit with Willie's "Crazy," and two other songs reached number one spot across country for many weeks. The latter were Ralph Emery's record of "Hello Fool" (collaborating with Willie on this was Jim Coleman) and Faron Young's version of "Hello Walls." In 1962, Faron Young collaborated with Willie on another hit, "Three Days."

By this time, record executives considered

Willie himself a prime recording prospect. Signed by Liberty Records, he turned out a number of chart hits, including two top 10 successes of 1962, the number-one-ranked record of his composition "Touch Me" and a hit duet with Shirley Collie, "Willingly." Willie was soon making personal appearances in many parts of the country. He was particularly well received in Las Vegas, where he was asked to remain for many weeks.

As his star rose in the country field, Willie moved to Tennessee. He bought his farm in the region near Nashville. In late 1964, he was made a regular cast member of the Grand Ole Opry. He also was signed to a new recording contract, this time by RCA Victor. He recorded such songs as "I Just Can't Let You Say Goodbye," "And So Will You My Love," "The Party's Over," and "Blackjack Country" for RCA in the mid-1960s. The last two of these were chart hits of 1967. He hit in 1968 with "Little Things."

Willie's LP credits in the 1960s included "Willie Nelson" ('63) on Liberty and "Make Way for Willie Nelson" and "Country Willie, His Own Songs" ('67) on RCA Victor.

NEW CHRISTY MINSTRELS: Vocal and instrumental group.

What's in a name? Several million dollars, if the name happens to be New Christy Minstrels. This was the valuation of the marketplace on a title associated with one of the most exciting folk sounds of the 1960s. As is often the case with groups, the personnel of the Minstrels changed several times during its existence, but the general style remained what was expected by the group's fans throughout the world.

The founder of the group was a young San Francisco folk artist named Randy Sparks. Sparks had lined up a number of other singers and instrumentalists in 1961 to apply an up-to-date version of the famed Christy Minstrels of the 1800s. The latter group, headed by Edwin "Pops" Christy, had become legendary. In the years before the Civil War, Christy had led one of the most imitated minstrel troupes in the U.S., credited with introducing many of Stephen Foster's greatest songs.

The New Christy Minstrels differed widely from the older organization. They performed old time folk songs, but with up-to-date arrangements. They did not perform in blackface, and from the start included several female performers. In addition, many of their hit songs were original compositions by Sparks or other members of the troupe. Among the national hits turned out by the group in the early 1960s were "Green, Green," "Today," "Saturday Night," and "Liza Lee."

In 1962 and '63, the group was featured in personal appearance tours across the U.S. and on many major network TV shows, and represented on national hit charts with singles and LPs on the Columbia label. By 1964, the New Christy Minstrels was one of the best known folk groups in the nation. During the summer, the group was featured on its own summer replacement TV show. That same year, the Minstrels performed on the White House steps at the invitation of President Lyndon Johnson.

During 1963 and '64, Randy Sparks had withdrawn as an active performer to concentrate on managing the business affairs of the Minstrels. In 1964, he sold his interest in the group to the management firm of George Greif and Sid Garris for the not insignificant sum of $2,500,000.

Under the new management team, the group continued as a major attraction. In early 1965, the New Christy Minstrels were the toast of Europe during their first overseas tour. The tour took them to England, Holland, and Scandinavia, and they capped the climax with a performance at the San Remo Festival in Italy. They gained top honors at the Festival with their renditions of "Si Piangi, Se Ridi" ("If You Cry, You Laugh") and "Le Colline Sono in Flore" ("The Hills Are Full of Flowers"). Both songs were released on records shortly thereafter and made the top rungs of the Italian hit charts.

The sales count of New Christy Minstrels LPs through 1969 exceeded 11 million. Among the album titles were: "Cowboys and Indians," "Lands of Giants," "Today," "Presenting the New Christy Minstrels," "New Christy Minstrels in Person," "Tall Tales," "Ramblin'," "Merry Christmas!," "Wandering Minstrels," "Chim Chim Cheree," "All Star Hootenanny," "Greatest Hits," "In Italy . . . In Italian," and "New Kick!"

At the start of 1967, the personnel of the Minstrels were as follows: Dave Ellingson, born Ladysmith, Wisconsin; Peter Morse, b. Chicago, Illinois, July 27, 1944; Michael McGinnis, b. near Peoria, Illinois; Mark Holly, b. St.

Petersburg, Florida; Terry Benson (Williams), b. Hollywood, California, June 6, 1947; Kenny Rodgers, b. Texas; Monica Kirby, b. Detroit, Michigan, 1946; Sue Pack, b. Hollywood, California, 1946; and Mike Settle, b. Tulsa, Oklahoma, March 20, 1941.

Settle, who previously sang with the Cumberland Three on tour with Shelley Berman (including a Carnegie Hall concert), was musical director of the group in the mid-'60s. After performing in coffee houses in Oklahoma, he had returned to a feature spot at New York's Bitter End. Prior to joining the Minstrels, several of his original compositions were recorded by major folk groups, including The Limeliters, Peter, Paul and Mary, and The Brothers Four. (*See also* SPARKS, RANDY)

NEW LOST CITY RAMBLERS: Vocal and instrumental group, Mike Seeger, born New York, New York, 1933; Tracy Schwarz, born New York, New York, 1938; John Cohen, born New York, New York, 1932.

A major feature of the folk music renaissance in the decades after World War II was renewed interest in the traditional hill country music. A landmark group in transmitting some of the feeling of old time country music to the urban audiences of the 1960s is the famed New Lost City Ramblers.

The Ramblers came into being in the summer of 1958, sparked by the interest of young Mike Seeger, brother of the renowned Pete Seeger, in collecting old time country songs. In his late teens, Mike had become engrossed in the playing techniques employed by rural artists. He first studied their methods of playing such instruments as fiddle, banjo, guitar, mandolin and autoharp by listening to records in the Library of Congress. During the mid-1950s, he went into the back country with recording equipment to gain first hand experience with the music.

At the time, many other city-bred folk enthusiasts followed similar paths. Among them was mathematician Tom Paley and freelance

Crowd pleasers at many major concerts and folk festivals of the 1960s, the New Lost City Ramblers (l. to r., Mike Seeger, John Cohen, Tracy Schwarz)

photographer John Cohen. Cohen, Paley, and Seeger were acquainted through common folk music activity in the New York area. They compared notes and finally decided to form their own group to concentrate on preserving and extending the traditions of rural folk music.

Their first efforts before audiences in New York and other eastern cities were encouraging. Their first Folkways album, released later in the year, helped extend their reputation throughout the U.S. The songs in the LP, which was titled simply "The New Lost City Ramblers," pretty much set the future style of the group. Basically, as Mike Seeger stated in the album notes, "The songs . . . were recorded by commercial companies and the Library of Congress in the southeastern mountains between 1925 and 1935, and show the first attempts of the hill musicians to 'make a hit' with old traditional songs that had been in the mountains since pioneer days."

The Ramblers' selections had originally been featured by such groups as Gid Tanner and his Skillet Lickers, The Fruit Jar Drinkers, The North Carolina Ramblers, Dr. Smith's Champion Horse Hair Pullers, and The Piedmont Log Rollers. Examples of the LP's contents are: "Tom Cat Blues," "Don't Let Your Deal Go Down," "East Virginia Blues," "Battleship of Maine," "Roving Gambler," "Take a Drink on Me," "It's a Shame to Whip Your Wife on Sunday," "The Old Fish Song," and "Brown's Ferry Blues."

Demands for more recordings and requests for in-person appearances multiplied rapidly as the 1950s gave way to the 1960s. The Ramblers sang in coffee houses and on college campuses across the nation. They were invited to the first Newport Folk Festival in 1959 and returned for most of the succeeding ones in the 1960s. They also performed at other major festivals in the U.S. and abroad. The group also found a steady market for their series of LPs for Folkways. Volume II was issued in 1960, Volume III in 1961, Volume IV in 1962, and Volume V in 1963.

By the time Volume V appeared, Tom Paley had left the group (in August 1962) to concentrate on teaching mathematics. His place was taken by Tracy Schwarz. Schwarz's interest in country music came from listening to country radio programs in New York in the 1940s. At the age of ten he started playing guitar and, in his teens, also mastered fiddle

and banjo. When he went to college in Washington, D.C., in the late 1950s, he played in Bluegrass and country style bands. When he joined the Ramblers, he proved to be as talented and versatile as his predecessor and the ovations for the group were as loud as ever.

New Lost City Ramblers records continued to appear with regularity after Schwarz's arrival. They include, on Folkways, "American Moonshine and Prohibition Songs" ('63), "Gone to the Country" ('64), "Instrumentals" ('64); on Verve/Folkways, "Rural Delivery No. 1," ('65) and "Remembrances" ('67). Their Newport performances are included on several Vanguard LPs, such as "Newport Folk Festival, 1959," "Newport Folk Festival, 1960," and "Country Music at Newport, 1963." (*See also* COHEN, JOHN; PALEY, TOM; SEEGER, MIKE)

NEWMAN, JIMMY: Singer, songwriter, guitarist. Born Big Mamou, Louisiana, August 27, 1927.

The Cajun country of Louisiana has produced many great country songs and artists. Not the least of the latter is Jimmy Newman, whose home town has the ring of many Bayou country hits, such as "Jole Blon," "Jambalaya," and its own namesake, "Big Mamou."

Newman, who is of half-French ancestry, grew up deep in the bayou country. When he was a boy, he memorized some of the country songs then popular with Cajun folk. As he grew older, his interest in performing also grew and he sang at local functions. When he was 19, he decided to concentrate on a career in music. He formed a band and for the next few years sang in small clubs and theaters in the south and southwest.

His next step up the ladder was a bid to host his own show on KPLC radio and TV in Lake Charles, Louisiana. His style of singing, his Cajun "aieee" call that highlighted many of the numbers, caught on with local audiences. His reputation soared throughout Louisiana; in the early 1950s he became a regular on Shreveport's Louisiana Hayride.

Jimmy soon won a recording contract with Dot Records. In 1954, he gained his first national attention with the hit recording of a song he co-wrote with J. Miller, "Cry, Cry Darling." This led to a round of appearances all over the country, and other successful records, including "Seasons of My Heart,"

"Blue Darling," and "Daydreaming." In 1957, he turned out another top seller in "Falling Star." The song was a favorite with Grand Ole Opry TV audiences, Jimmy having joined that show's cast in 1956.

Jimmy continued to improve his record status throughout the 1950s. His two major hits in 1958 and '59 were on another label, MGM. These were "You're Making a Fool Out of Me" ('58) and "Grin and Bear It" ('59). He started out the 1960s with another top 10 song, "A Lovely Work of Art."

In the mid-1960s, Jimmy switched to the Decca label. His record output included many successful songs based on his bayou heritage, including "Big Mamou," "Alligator Man," and "Bayou Talk." He also won applause for such songs as "Everything," "D.J. for a Day," "Angel on Leave," "City of the Angels," and "Back in Circulation." He had two top 10 hits with Decca by '69, "Artificial Rose" in '65 and "Back Pocket Money" in '66.

The year 1966 also rounded out Newman's decade on the Grand Ole Opry. His personal appearances in the mid-'60s took him to all the states and Canadian provinces as well as to most of the countries of Europe.

Jimmy's LP output, as of 1968, included "Songs of Jimmy Newman" ('62) on MGM; "Folk Songs of the Bayou" ('63), "Artificial Rose" ('66), "World of Music" ('67) on Decca; "Crossroads," "Fallen Star," and "Cry, Cry Darling," all on Dot, '66.

NEWPORT FOLK FESTIVAL: Folk festival held in July in Newport, Rhode Island.

The prestige folk festival of the 1960s, at least from the standpoint of national publicity, is the one held at Newport, Rhode Island. By the late 1960s, well over 70,000 people attended the series of concerts, workshops, and study sessions held at the site of the Newport Jazz Festival each July.

The festival originated as a commercial venture, sponsored by George Wein, who had been part of the corporation sponsoring the Newport Jazz Festival beginning in 1954. His goal was to have a comprehensive festival patterned after the traditional ones of the south and southwest. With his co-producer, Albert Grossman, he put on two Folk Festivals in 1959 and 1960.

Among the performers at the initial series of concerts were traditional folk artists and some of the new pop folk groups such as the Kingston Trio. Besides Pete Seeger, other well known artists to perform included Bluegrass banjoist Earl Scruggs, Jimmy Driftwood, Sonny Terry, Brownie McGhee, Frank Warner, Oscar Brand, Leon Bibb, Jean Ritchie, the New Lost City Ramblers, Odetta, and John Jacob Niles. The series attracted a total of about 13,000 onlookers.

The reception was good enough to warrant a second Festival in July 1960. Most of the previous year's performers returned, as well as additional groups of note. The latter included the Tarriers, The Clancy Brothers, The Weavers, Mahalia Jackson, and Theodore Bikel. The Festival also gave national prominence to new performers, such as Joan Baez and Tommy Makem.

The riots at the 1960 jazz event bankrupted Wein's corporation; he had to abandon the Folk Festival, which was a money-losing proposition. In addition, many local residents objected to the event. In 1963, however, discussions between Wein, Pete Seeger, and Theodore Bikel led to reorganization of the Festival on a non-profit basis. Overall supervision of the operation was vested in a group of directors of first rank in the folk music field who also helped administer the Newport Folk Foundation, Inc. The original Board consisted of Seeger, Bikel, Jean Ritchie, Bill Clifton, Erik Darling, Clarence Cooper, and Peter Yarrow. Later Board members included Alan Lomax, Mike Seeger, Oscar Brand, Julius Lester, Ronnie Gilbert, Judy Collins, and Ralph Rinzler. The Foundation receives all profits from the Festival and disburses a certain percentage in the form of grants for folk music research or advancement of one form or another.

The 1963 Festival proved highly successful with 40,000 people attending a three-day series of concerts. In 1964, the audience exceeded 70,000 and in 1965 the figure went over the 80,000 mark. One of the major new names on everyone's lips during these concerts was young Bob Dylan. As of 1969, the Festival seemed set as an annual event, although there were some worries about the unwieldy size of the audiences. (*See also* WEIN, GEORGE)

NILES, JOHN JACOB: Singer, instrumentalist (dulcimer, lute, piano), songwriter, composer, author, folklorist, folk music collector. Born Louisville, Kentucky, April 28, 1892.

One of the giants in the field, John Jacob

Niles has contributed heavily to the art of folk music in a wide range of subjects for more than five decades. Not only did he compile one of the largest folk music collections in the world, he also kept alive the tradition of home-built musical instruments.

Niles was born into a family with deep roots in the tradition of music. His father, a farmer and skilled carpenter, was one of the best known folksingers in the region as well as one of the best square dance callers. His mother played the organ in church and also was an excellent classical pianist. From his father he learned to play several stringed instruments, and he was given a basic grounding in piano by his mother.

He attended the Jefferson County elementary school and went on to DuPont Manual High School in Louisville. When he was still in public school, his father, who was one of the best instrument makers in the area, bought him a three-stringed dulcimer, but informed the boy that he expected him to make his own instruments in the future. John learned to play on this dulcimer, and when he was about 12, replaced it with one he made himself. From then on, John always made his own stringed instruments, including many interesting variations of three- to eight-stringed dulcimers and a number of lutes.

Niles began his folk music collection in high school, devising his own system of musical notation. At 15, he started a notebook of songs from his home region. As related by Ray Lawless (*Folksingers and Folksongs in America*, p. 176), Niles' first paid performance took place about this time "when he accompanied a group of Chatauqua performers in a Saturday afternoon show."

John finished high school in 1909 and took a job as a surveyor. His work took him through the mountains of the Kentucky region and gave him the chance to continue his folk music collecting. By 1910, he had an impressive collection of songs and he began to perform for local churches and other groups.

His budding career as a folk artist was interrupted by World War I. He enlisted in the U.S. Army Air Corps and went to France. In 1918, he almost lost his life in a plane crash. He was partly paralyzed and it took some seven years before he could walk completely normally once more. Instead of returning home, he took his discharge and attended the University of Lyon and the Schola Cantorum

in Paris, improving his background in classical music. In 1919, he returned to the U.S. and continued his studies at the Cincinnati Conservatory of Music. He also soon resumed his spare-time activity of giving folk song concerts.

After two years at the Conservatory, he moved to New York. He supported his folk music work with a variety of jobs, including that of m.c. at the Silver Slipper Club, grooming horses for Ziegfeld Follies extravaganzas, and working as a rose gardener. During the early 1920s, he gave folk concerts at major universities. At Princeton, he met contralto Marion Kerby. The two developed a folk song program and toured widely in the U.S. as well as in most of the countries of Europe.

For several years during this period, Niles also worked as a chauffeur for photographer Doris Ulmann. He drove her throughout the southwest, collecting folk material while she photographed the region. In the late 1920s, the first collections of Niles' material were published. These books, based on his World War I experience, were *Singing Soldiers* ('27) and *Songs My Mother Never Taught Me* ('29). During the 1929-30 period, Niles also wrote a number of short stories for Scribner's magazines. In 1929, another Niles collection was published called *Seven Kentucky Mountain Songs*.

In the 1930s, his reputation continued to grow as he turned out more books, arranged and composed new folk material, and gave upwards of 50 concerts a year. His published collections of the decade included *Songs of the Hill Folk* ('36) and *Ballads, Carols and Tragic Legends from the Southern Appalachian Mountains* ('37). In 1939, he made one of his first major albums for RCA Victor, "Early American Ballads."

In 1940, troubled by Hitler's excesses, he began an oratorio called "Lamentations." The piece was finally completed ten years later and given its initial performance March 14, 1951, at Indiana State Teachers College, Terre Haute. One of the themes of the work, reflecting Niles' Republican background, he states, is a "prayer to deliver the world from the curse of communism." Other long works by Niles are "Rhapsody for the Merry Month of May" and "Mary the Rose."

His recordings of the 1940s included "Early American Carols and Folk Songs" ('40) and "American Folk Lore" ('41). The latter was re-issued on Camden label, with minor changes, in 1954. His concerts, which won critical acclaim for his songs and his sensitive dulcimer playing, continued to draw sellout audiences in the 1940s and '50s. Particularly noteworthy was his 1946 midnight concert at New York's Town Hall, in which a capacity audience heard him sing such favorites as "Black Is the Color of My True Love's Hair," "The Seven Joys of Mary," "The Rovin' Gambler," and "I Wonder as I Wander."

The output of recordings and collections continued through the 1950s and into the '60s. In 1957, RCA Camden issued the LP "John Jacob Niles: 50th Anniversary Album." Niles also turned out several albums on his own Boone-Tolliver label, including "American Folk Love Songs" and "Ballads." He was featured on a number of Tradition LPs, including "I Wonder as I Wander" ('57); "Ballads" (two LPs); and "An Evening with John Jacob Niles" ('60).

Other collections of Niles material issued after World War II included *The Anglo-American Study Book* ('45); *Shape-Note Study Book* ('50) and the massive *Ballad Book of John Jacob Niles*. Among other well known Niles original compositions and arrangements in these books were such songs as "Sweet Little Jesus Boy," "The Cherry Tree," "Froggy Went Courtin'," "Down in Yon Forest," and "You Got to Cross That Lonesome Valley."

In the 1960s, despite his advanced years, Niles remained active as a performer, appearing on many a concert hall and college stage in the eastern U.S. In 1965, RCA Victor issued the LP "John Jacob Niles: Folk Balladeer," and in 1967 Tradition Records presented "The Best of John Jacob Niles."

NORMA JEAN: *See* Jean, Norma

NYE, HERMES: Singer, guitarist, reviewer, author. Born Chicago, Illinois, February 11, 1908.

How to Be a Folksinger; How to Sing and Present Folksongs; or the Folksinger's Guide; or Eggs I Have Laid. This title of Hermes Nye's 1964 book (Oak Publications, New York) gives some insight into the author's personality. He is a man with many years of experience in the field as a singer and collector, but unlike many modern-day folk enthusiasts, he can laugh at himself and the foibles of the folk music set.

Nye was introduced to the folk art as a youngster from listening to his father. Nye Senior, born and raised in Canada, had moved to Chicago by the time the young Hermes was born. In his travels through Canada and Maine, he had picked up many sea shanties, lumberjack songs, and other folk ballads and he often sang them for his family. The Nyes soon moved from Chicago to Topeka, Kansas, where Hermes received most of his pre-college education. Hermes had learned the guitar by the time he finished Topeka High School in 1925. He had also begun to collect new folk songs from books and other sources, an avocation that became a life-long pursuit.

Hermes spent two years at Washburn College. In late 1927, he left school and spent a year in and around Amarillo, Texas. He found Texas much to his liking and determined to make the state his home. First, though, he went back to Kansas to finish college. For the next five years, he attended the University of Kansas at Lawrence, receiving his B.A. in 1930 and Bachelor of Laws in 1933. When he could, he returned to Texas for visits and, after graduation, moved to Dallas.

In Dallas, he began a long career in law, becoming one of the city's prominent legal experts. He also found time for music, writing and working for local music publishing firms. During the 1930s, his interest in folk music remained strong, but it did not serve as a source of income. He collected songs from radio programs, records, and other singers, but his performances were before amateur groups, folklore societies, etc. He was particularly active in the Texas Folklore Society where he associated with such people as the Lomaxes and J. Frank Dobie. Nye occasionally reviewed books for the Society, though most of his reviews were for the Dallas *Times-Herald* and the Southwest Review. Nye also worked with the Whittle Music Company of Dallas.

Nye's career as a public performer began in August 1942, in New Orleans. In the years that followed, he sang in concerts and at festivals in many parts of the country. Among his festival credits were a number of appearances at the Newport event. During the 1950s and '60s, he gave several hundred performances, mostly in the southwest. He also sang many times over stations KSKY and WFAA in Dallas.

His name became familiar to folk enthusiasts around the country by the early 1950s. This helped bring his first record session for Folkways in 1952. Called "Anglo-American Folk Songs," the album included "King Arthur Had Three Sons," "John Peel," "The Mermaid," "Earl Murray," "Earl Richard," "Bailiff's Daughter," and "Greenland Fishery." During the 1950s and '60s, five more LPs of Nye's singing were issued by Folkways. These included: "Ballads of the Civil War" (Volumes I and II); "Texas Folk Songs"; "War Songs, U.S.A."; and "Reliques from Percy and Child." Among the songs in the latter were "Rob Roy," "Robin Hood's Golden Prize," "The Queen's Maries," "Lord Thomas and Fair Elinor," "Glenlogie," "Waly, Waly," "Whittingham Fair" and "The Three Ravens."

Besides his how-to book on folksinging, Nye's book credits include a novel, *Fortune Is a Woman,* published by Signet Books.

O'BRYANT, JOAN: Singer, guitarist, folk song collector, university teacher. Born Wichita, Kansas, September 25, 1923; died Colorado, August 18, 1964.

An automobile accident on a steep mountain road cost the life of one of the nation's major folklorists. In her short span of years, however, Joan O'Bryant accomplished much for folk music. Not the least of her achievements was a strong part in gaining a grant from the University of Wichita regents for an Archive of Midwestern Folklore.

Joan was introduced to folk music by her grandmother and great-grandmother while she was a child. Strangely, the interest in folk songs skipped a generation, for her parents did not sing them. In her grade and high school years, she took lessons in voice and classical music. But folk music continued to enthrall her and she taught herself to play the guitar. In the early 1940s, she began to sing with local groups in recitals throughout the midwest and southwest. During those years, she began to collect folk material from eastern Kansas, Oklahoma, and the Ozarks, an occupation she continued to follow throughout her life.

The start of Joan's singing efforts almost coincided with her enrollment at the University of Wichita in 1942. Her folk music pursuits played a role in her decision to take a leave of absence from Wichita to study at the National University in Mexico City, Mexico, in 1945. While there, she sang over station XEW. In 1946, she returned to Wichita to complete her

Bachelor's degree and went on for an M.A. in 1949. Meanwhile she began teaching folklore at the University in 1948. While doing this, she also found time to complete a novel, *Morning in Exile,* published in 1949.

In the 1950s, her activities expanded to performances on radio and TV and at many folk festivals. In the early 1950s, she had her own show on a Wichita station dealing with folklore and folk music. By the mid-1950s, she held the title of Assistant Professor of English at the University. Typical of her repertoire were the songs she sang at the Ozark Folk Festival in October 1956: "In Kansas," "Careless Love," "Marble Town," "Girls, Quit Your Rowdy Ways."

Folkways Records began recording Joan's performances in 1957. Her first two LPs were "American Ballads and Folksongs" and "Folksongs and Ballads of Kansas." The former included such songs as "Single Girl," "The Lily of the West," "The Cuckoo," "I'm on My Way," "The Texas Rangers," "Tom Sherman's Bar Room," and "Keep Your Hand on the Plow." The second album included: "Molly Bann," "Quantrill," "Old Blue," "Bill," "Zebra Dun," and "Sweet William Died."

Miss O'Bryant was elected president of the Kansas Folklore Society in 1961.

OCHS, PHIL: Singer, clarinetist, guitarist, songwriter. Born El Paso, Texas, December 19, 1940.

When the famous or infamous (depending on your point of view) march against the war in Vietnam took place in Los Angeles during President Johnson's visit in 1967, several folk artists entertained the marchers. Prominent among them was Phil Ochs. It was not an unfamiliar role for Ochs, who sang his own protest songs at every kind of gathering from the stage of Carnegie Hall to the Newport Folk Festival and civil rights marches in the south

There was little to indicate his future career in his early upbringing. Philip David Ochs was born in Texas, but his family soon moved to Ohio. Phil attended public schools in Ohio before he was sent to Staunton Military Academy in Virginia. He was at first more interested in sports and general studies than in either politics or music. He had learned to play the clarinet, though, and followed the general run of popular music. He enrolled as a journalism major at Ohio State University and went on

Phil Ochs

to become editor of a dormitory newspaper, "The Word," and the school's humor magazine, "Sundial."

His roommate, Jim Glover, was inclined toward both folk music and politics. Jim taught Phil how to play guitar and encouraged him to write songs. Said Phil later, "I didn't intend for them to be political. They came out of my subconscious and since I was political by nature, they commented on current events."

After his third year in college, Phil decided music rather than journalism was his goal. He worked his way to New York by performing at small clubs and coffee houses. In New York, he soon became acquainted with such artists as Bob Dylan and Bob Gibson. He was greatly impressed with their work and incorporated some of their musical traits into his own. The resultant blend was uniquely Phil's, an outpouring of original material that marked him as a major new composer and lyricist.

For a while he performed in Greenwich Village coffee houses earning his living by passing the basket to onlookers. Soon, though, many other artists were singing his praises—often literally, through renditions of his writings. He soon was given a recording contract by Elektra Records and was signed up for the first of many cross-country tours. By the mid-1960s, both his own recordings and those of other artists of his songs were often on the best-seller lists. Among those who turned out versions of his material were Peter and Gordon, Judy Collins, The Four Seasons, Anita Bryant, Ian and Sylvia, Pete Seeger, Jim (Jim Glover) and Jean, The Brothers Four, and Joan Baez.

In 1963, he won a thunderous ovation during his first appearance at the Newport Folk Festival. He was invited back to Newport again in 1964, '66, and '67. He was also featured at other festivals across the world, including the 1965 New York Festival, 1965 Canadian Mariposa Folk Festival, 1966 Berkeley Folk Festival, and 1966 Beaulieu Folk Festival in England. In 1966, Phil entertained a sellout crowd in New York's Carnegie Hall with a solo concert. The LP of the concert received little air play, because of its many controversial protest songs, but still became a best-seller.

An example of his protest material was his first topical effort, "The Cuban Invasion" (1961), which implied strong support for Castro. Other protest compositions include "There But for Fortune," "Draft Dodger Rag," State of Mississippi," and "Cops of the World." Elektra LPs included such titles as "All the News That's Fit to Sing," "I Ain't Marching Anymore," and "Carnegie Hall Concert."

His songs, however, were not all protest, ranging from ballads to songs with rock 'n' roll flavor. His importance as an artist of his time was recognized by *Who's Who,* which included him as of 1964.

Phil changed record labels in 1967, signing with Herb Alpert's burgeoning record company, A&M. The first Ochs LP on A&M Records was titled "Pleasures of the Harbor."

O'DANIEL, LEE "PAPPY": *See* Light Crust Doughboys, The

ODETTA: Singer, guitarist. Born Birmingham, Alabama, December 31, 1930.

Until she was almost 20, Odetta knew practically nothing about folk music. When she finally did become interested, classical music lost an average performer and folk music gained a star.

Though known as simply Odetta, she has had a series of last names. She was born

[221]

Odetta Holmes, but soon after her birth her father, a steel worker, died and her mother remarried. Odetta took the surname of her stepfather, Zadock Felious. When she was six, the family took what was to be an important step in her career by moving to Los Angeles.

Odetta's first interest in music came from picking out notes on a piano in her grandmother's home. By the time she reached junior high school, she had a deep desire to gain more musical background. She joined the glee club and also took vocal lessons for a while. She continued her musical activities, with emphasis on classical studies, in Belmont High School. Her work level was high in all subjects, and she won the Bank of America's achievement award on graduation.

Odetta helped finance her night courses at Los Angeles City College by working as a housekeeper during the day. Her major was in classical music. In 1949, she was accepted for the chorus in a Los Angeles production of "Finian's Rainbow." During this period, sev-

eral of her friends were deeply interested in folk music. After hearing some, she decided she preferred it to other musical forms. "I knew I was home," she told one interviewer.

Now she taught herself to play the guitar and began to perform in small folk music establishments. She tried out for a job at San Francisco's hungry i Club, and was accepted, but she never got the chance to go on the bill because of objections from the featured artist. Soon she won a year's engagement at the Tin Angel, and her reputation increased so rapidly that she followed the San Francisco stint with a month's run at the Blue Angel in New York. Here such artists as Pete Seeger and Harry Belafonte were greatly impressed with her talent.

She was asked to return to California to sing the chantey "Santy Anno" in the movie "Cinerama Holiday." For the next two years she was at the Los Angeles Turnabout Theater, and followed this with a hit appearance at the Gate of Horn in Chicago. Her first LP was turned out by Tradition Records in 1956, including such songs as "Joshua," "Deep Blue Sea," and "I'm on My Way." The LP title is "Odetta Sings Ballads and Blues." In 1957, her Gate of Horn engagement was the basis for a second LP, which included "He's Got the Whole World in His Hands," "Take This Hammer," and "Greensleeves."

Now an established performer, Odetta toured the U.S. and Canada in 1958 and '59. Her Town Hall debut in April 1959 won rave notices. In December 1959 she starred on a Belafonte television special, "TV Tonight." In 1960, she signed with Vanguard Records. Her first LP for the new company featured "Water Boy" and "I've Been Driving on Bald Mountain." On May 8, 1960, she again took New York by storm with a recital at Carnegie Hall. In the 1960s, she was a regular performer at the Newport Folk Festival.

Odetta

OHRLIN, GLENN: Singer, guitarist, cowboy. Born Minneapolis, Minnesota, October 26, 1926.

"I was born in Minnesota on Friday, October 26, 1926. As long as I can remember, I wanted to be a rider and when I was about twelve, started working and hanging around stables, dude ranches, stockyards, and what have you, to get experience. Sometimes I'd get a dollar a day, sometimes just the rides."

Thus did Glenn Ohrlin describe one of the two facets of his career: real-life cowboy and rodeo performer and, at the same time, a talented performer of western and folk music. Ohrlin's interest in western music was as deep-rooted as his cowboy desires and may, indeed, have helped turn him in that direction. He got his first guitar at an early age and could play it well before he reached his teens. He learned many traditional cowboy songs in his boyhood and occupied much of his leisure time singing.

In 1943, the 16-year-old Ohrlin got his first chance as a performer at the annual rodeo in Caliente, Nevada. His first contests were in bareback bronco riding. That year and the next, Ohrlin worked as a cowboy on ranches throughout the Rocky Mountain area and in California. Then his career was interrupted by an Army hitch during 1945-46. In 1947, he was back in civilian life as a full-time rodeo rider. His toughness was illustrated by his reaction to a broken back suffered in a fall from a bronc in February 1948. He was in a cast for three months, but came back to work as a bronco rider before the year was out.

Through the 1950s and '60s, he continued to make the rounds of the rodeos. As he did, he often sang for other rodeo people and swapped songs with them. In Nebraska, for instance, he added such songs as "Galway Bay" and "Boston Burglar" from contact with ranchers of Irish lineage. He also picked up such other songs on this tour as "21 Years," "Moonlight and Skies," and "Barbara Allen." When he had the chance, Ohrlin performed at local clubs and dances as well. As he noted, he also entertained his friends ". . . in bars, cars, bunkhouses, motel rooms, cheap hotels, house trailers, camp grounds and rodeo areas—wherever they would listen."

Slowly, in the early 1950s, word about the talent of this singing cowboy began to spread among folk music artists and fans. The process of expanding his audience was speeded up when Ohrlin bought his own 166-acre ranch in Mountain View, Arkansas. Among his neighbors was a noted southwestern folk artist and collector, Jimmy Driftwood. Driftwood soon added his voice to those who suggested that Ohrlin sing at some of the major folk concerts and festivals throughout the country.

By the mid-1950s, Ohrlin was already in demand for appearances on college campuses and in coffee houses. He was well received by many college audiences, including those at the University of Illinois. A result of this was the production of his first album, "The Hell-Bound Train," by the University of Illinois Campus Folksong Club. In the 1960s, Ohrlin was one of the most popular performers at the Newport Folk Festival. In the 1965 Festival, he demonstrated his style at a workshop session, singing such songs as "Zebra Dun" and "Chickens Grow Tall."

OKUN, MILT: Singer, guitarist, banjoist, teacher. Born Brooklyn, New York, December 23, 1923.

Like many urban folk artists of the 1950s and '60s, Milton T. Okun started with a solid classical background. Born and brought up in New York City, Milt was exposed to classical music at home and at school. After graduating from high school, he went on to study music education at the College of the City of New York. He completed his bachelor's degree in the 1940s and then attended the Oberlin Conservatory of Music at Oberlin, Ohio.

His Mus. B. firmly in hand, he went home to New York City and found a job as music teacher at Joseph Pulitzer High School, Jackson Heights, borough of Queens. About this time, his musical horizons began to change as his interest in folk music increased. He learned to play the guitar and banjo and also started to collect folk music from New York and New England. Many songs were provided by his sister-in-law, a well known local square dance caller. Okun soon was functioning both as a performer at local events and as a teacher of folk music.

His activities in the early 1950s included several years as director of the summer Adirondack Folk Song and Dance Festival at Schroon Lake, New York. During the 1950s, he also gave a folk song and ballad course at CCNY's Extension Division. As time went on, he had the opportunity to appear at many concerts and festivals in various cities. Before long, he was turning out records for several labels, including Stinson, Riverside, and Baton.

One of his first LPs was the Stinson "Adirondack Folk Songs and Ballads." This included such numbers as "The Belle of Long Lake," 'The Lass of Glenshee," "The Days of '49," 'Come to the Fair," "Dolan's Ass," "The Fatal

Wedding," "The Gypsy Davy," and "The Banks of Champlain." His other Stinson albums were "Every Inch a Sailor—Fo'c'sle Songs and Shanties," and "I Sing of Canada." The latter included "Donkey Riding," "She's Like a Swallow," "Trinity Cake," "La Poulette Grise," "J'ai Perdu le Do," "Un Canadien Errant," "A Gay Spanish Maid," "Smoky Mountain Bill" and "Vive La Canadienne."

Okun's LP output also included, on Riverside, "Traditional American Love Songs" (with Ellen Stekert) and "Merry Ditties." For Baton Records, he turned out "America's Best Loved Folk Songs." In the early '60s, Okun recorded for Elektra, one of his LPs being "We Sing of the Sea."

His efforts began to turn toward managing and directing in the 1960s. He served as musical director for the Chad Mitchell Trio during this period and also helped shape the careers of Peter, Paul and Mary. His work with the latter group included collaborating on the writing of many songs. In addition, he was music consultant for Elektra on folk records for several years. Okun contributed to the folk song boom of the 1960s by furthering the careers of a number of young artists, including Tom Paxton and other Elektra performers.

OLD DOMINION BARN DANCE: Variety show broadcast on station WRVA, Richmond, Virginia.

The east coast's main entry in the country music variety broadcast field for a number of years was the Old Dominion Barn Dance. In the late 1940s and early '50s, it was one of the six regular attractions on CBS Radio Network's Saturday Night—Country Style.

The program was presided over from its beginning in 1946 until 1957 by Sunshine Sue (real name: Sue Workman). Her contribution to the state of Virginia was recognized in 1949 by Governor William M. Tuck when he crowned her "Queen of the Hillbillies." In 1957, Carlton Haney took over as m.c. of the show.

Among the many famous alumni of the program were Flatt & Scruggs, Joe and Rose Lee Maphis, and Stoney and Wilma Cooper. Other cast regulars over the years were: Slim Bryant, Curley Collins, Sonny Day, Lennie Jones, Benny Kissinger, Mary Klick, Arline Wiltshire Meyers, Daniel L. Pennel, Quincy Snodgrass, The Westernaires Quartet (Pokey Kersey, Zeb Robinson, Irving Gungana, Jimmy

Whitely), Jim Wilson, Craig Wingfield, George Winn, Mac Wiseman, Jean Wright, and Zag, the Ozark Mountain Boy.

ORBISON, ROY: Singer, composer, guitarist. Born Wink, Texas, April 23, 1936.

Wink is a small oil town in Texas and Roy Orbison might have become a solid citizen of the oil industry of that state. He worked the oil rigs as a youngster and followed the logical path of entering North Texas State College as a geology major. It ended there, that pursuit of "black gold." Instead, it is the shining gold reflected from seven- and twelve-inch record grooves that the world identifies with Orbison.

In the true tradition of the idiom, Orbison learned to play the guitar at the age of six, under his father's guidance. As a teenager he was leader of the Wink (Texas) Westerners along with doing a radio show over in Vernon, Texas, on KVWC. At 16, he represented the Lone Star State at the International Lions Convention in Chicago, playing guitar and singing.

While in college he met a fellow student, Pat Boone, who had started tasting recording success with "Two Hearts," on Randy Wood's Dot label, in Tennessee. That encouraged Orbison to convince Sam Phillips of Sun Records in Memphis to record him with "Ooby Dooby," which had a sale of more than 300,000. This was in 1956 and Phillips' hard eye for talent, which helped start careers for Elvis Presley, Jerry Lee Lewis, Bill Justis, Johnny Cash, Carl Perkins and others, was right again.

Another man, Wesley Rose of Acuff-Rose, recognized Orbison's writing talent when the Everly Brothers recorded "Claudette," a hit which was titled after Orbison's wife's name. Rose signed him for personal management and set up a recording contract with Fred Foster's Monument firm which resulted in a running string of chart winners including "Only The Lonely," "Blue Angel," "Running Scared," "Dream Baby," "It's Over," "Crying," "Candy Man," "Mean Woman Blues," and "Pretty Woman."

While Orbison doesn't write all of his own songs for recording himself, he has written many hits for others, including the Everly Brothers, Jerry Lee Lewis, Buddy Knox, and the late Buddy Holly. His schedule has often been so tight that he records while still writing the song in the studio.

Orbison is one of the initial wave of artists of the 1950s who became international stars. He became immensely popular in Europe, particularly in England. His dark hair, dark glasses, and black suits are a personal trademark. Travel in the United States and Canada is done in a 30-foot mobile house containing a TV, shower, parlor, and amenities of the mobile radio-telephone sort.

Like others in Nashville, Roy tried the motion picture field. His first was "Fastest Guitar Alive," produced by MGM Studios shortly after Roy signed with MGM Records. In the 1960s, his goal was to write a movie score and try his hand as a producer.

Old Hickory Lake, Hendersonville, Tennessee, became his home—when he was at home. Part of the furnishings includes gold records for "Only The Lonely" and "Crying," and silver awards for "In Dreams," "Dream Baby," "Running Scared," "It's Over," and "Mean Woman Blues." Three best-selling LPs have been "Roy Orbison's Greatest Hits," "Roy Orbison in Dreams," and "Early Orbison."

OSBORNE BROTHERS: Vocal and instrumental trio, Bob Osborne, born Hyden, Kentucky, December 7, 1931; Sonny Osborne, born Hyden, Kentucky, October 29, 1937; Benny Birchfield, born Isaban, West Virginia, June 6, 1937.

One of the big "discoveries" of the campus folk boom of the 1950s and '60s was Bluegrass music. One of the first country groups to bring this style to college attention was the Osborne Brothers with their highly successful concert at Antioch College, Ohio, in early 1959.

The members of the trio, of course, had been brought up on Bluegrass music in their home states of Kentucky and West Virginia. The Osborne boys had learned to pick out country songs on the 5-string banjo and the mandolin by the time they were high school age. When younger brother Sonny was only 16, he and Bob made their radio debut on WROL, Knoxville. Bob played mandolin and sang high lead (tenor) while Sonny added his baritone voice and 5-string banjo skill.

The brothers left WROL for WJR, Detroit,

Osborne Brothers

[225]

in 1954 and received increasing attention during guest appearances in the midwest. In October 1956 they became featured regulars on the Wheeling Jamboree on WWVA, Wheeling, West Virginia. That same year they signed their first major recording contract with MGM Records. In 1959, they added the 5-string banjo talents of Benny Birchfield. Birchfield, who also plays guitar, became lead singer.

The trio toured widely in the 1960s, guesting on many in-person bills and on network TV country shows. Following their campus debut at Antioch in 1959, they were featured in Bluegrass concerts at many colleges throughout the U.S. in the 1950s and '60s. They often were starred on the Grand Ole Opry beginning in 1959. During the 1960s, the trio remained one of the mainstays of the Wheeling Jamboree. In 1963, the group ended seven years on the MGM label by signing a new contract with Decca.

Among the top-selling records of the Osborne Brothers are: "Each Season Changes You," "Banjo Boys," "Lovey Told Me Goodby," "Fair and Tender Ladies," "Ruby, Are You Mad," "Take This Hammer," "Once More," "Mule Skinner Blues," and "Don't Even Look at Me." LPs to the group's credit include: "Country Picking and Hillside Singing," "Blue Grass Music by The Osbornes," and "Blue Grass Instrumentals."

OWENS, BONNIE: Singer, guitarist, songwriter. Born Blanchard, Oklahoma, October 1, 1933.

The name Owens has become one of the major ones in American country and western music, with Buck Owens perhaps the most successful male vocalist in the 1960s, and Bonnie, formerly his wife, still using the name professionally.

Bonnie was born in Oklahoma, but spent most of her formative years in Arizona. She began to sing in local clubs while in her teens and won notice as one of the best yodelers in the state. She displayed her vocal talents to a wider audience as a member of the "Buck and Britt Show" (Buck refers, of course, to Buck Owens) on station KTYL in Mesa, Arizona. Soon after, both Buck and Bonnie joined a band known as Mac's Skillet Lickers and toured widely through the western states.

The next step was a move to Bakersfield, California, in the early 1960s. There Bonnie, now separated from Buck, sang on both local and syndicated radio and TV shows. She also was featured in personal appearances in many parts of the state. She soon won a record contract from Marvel Records. Her first single for Marvel was "Dear John Letter." Among the artists she met in Bakersfield was an up-and-coming young vocalist-songwriter, Merle Haggard. The two teamed up and, in 1964, turned out a hit record of "Just Between the Two of Us."

In 1965, Bonnie and Merle were signed to long-term contracts by Capitol Records, and not long afterward, they were married. One of their first joint efforts for Capitol was the LP "Just Between the Two of Us." The album included songs written by both Merle and Bonnie. Released in early 1966, the album became one of the top hits of the year.

The Academy of Country/Western Music in 1966 gave Bonnie and Merle its award as "Best Vocal Group." In addition, Bonnie was selected as "Top Female Vocalist."

In March 1966, Merle and Bonnie joined the "Buck Owens Show." As part of the show, they toured all fifty states during the mid-1960s and also performed before audiences in Canada and Europe. (*See also* HAGGARD, MERLE)

OWENS, BUCK: Singer, guitarist, songwriter, band leader. Born Sherman, Texas, August 12, 1929.

The route led west to Bakersfield, California, rather than east to Nashville, for Buck Owens after he left Sherman, Texas, to carve out a career as recording artist, songwriter, and music business entrepreneur. He spent most of his early years in Sherman, but dropped out of school in his early teens. He worked at a series of jobs which eventually led to a sojourn in Arizona.

For a time, Buck earned his keep by hauling produce between Arizona and California's San Joaquin Valley. By this time he was in his late teens and had begun to perform in small clubs in Arizona. Bakersfield, though, was beginning to become a center of country and western activity and Buck decided to move there. By the time he was 21, he was a member of a club band in Bakersfield.

A short while later, he worked with Bill Woods' band in Bakersfield and appeared on the local Chuck Wagon television show. His ability as a guitarist began to gain the attention of other artists who knew the value of a first-rate sideman for recording dates. In the early and mid-1950s, he started to pick up recording session assignments in Hollywood to back such artists as Sonny James, Faron Young, and Wanda Jackson. Capitol Records executives took notice of his musicianship and his budding talent as a songwriter. They signed him as an artist in 1956. In the following three years he advanced rapidly, developing the style and phrasing that broke his first national hit in 1959, the number-one-ranked "Under Your Spell Again."

From that time on, the only direction was up. Buck showed his 1959 success was no fluke by scoring two major hits in 1960, "Above and Beyond" and "Excuse Me (I Think I've Got a Heartache)," a song he co-wrote with Harlan Howard. In 1961, he collaborated with Howard on the top 10 hits "Foolin' Around" and "Under the Influence of Love." He also teamed up with Rose Maddox in a series of duets that produced two more top 10 hits, "Loose Talk" and "Mental Cruelty." For his work with Rose, Buck won the nod from disk jockey polls as part of the top vocal team of the year.

By this time, Buck had engagements lined up in all parts of the nation for himself and his band, The Buckaroos. In the early 1960s, turnaway crowds attended Buck's shows at places ranging from New York's Madison Square Garden and Los Angeles' Olympic Auditorium to dozens of county and state fairs.

Buck had a relatively lean yean in 1962 with only one top 10 hit, "Kickin' Our Hearts Around." Starting in 1963, though, he set a blazing track record with an output through 1968 that included the amazing total of 16 number-one-ranked national hits. In 1963, he had a number-one hit in his recording of his own composition, "Love's Gonna Live Here," as well as two other successes, "Act Naturally" and "You're for Me." His 1964 production included two compositions that made the number-one spot, "I Don't Care" and "My Heart Skips a Beat." The same year, he wrote and recorded the top 10 hit "Together Again." The following year, Buck wrote or collaborated on such national hits as "I've Got a Tiger By the Tail," "Only You," and number-one-ranked "Before You Go." He also scored with "Gonna Have Love" and the number-one-ranked "Buckaroo."

With D. Rich, he wrote the 1966 number-one success "Think of Me." He worked with Rich and Nat Stuckey on the number one hit "Waitin'

in Your Welfare Line," and composed a third top-run success himself, "Open Up Your Heart." The year 1967 resulted in his writing or co-writing number-one-ranked "Sam's Place" and "Where Does the Good Times Go," and the top 10 hit "Your Tender Loving Care." At the end of the year, he held the Billboard titles "Top Country Singles Artist" and "Top Country Male Artist" for 1967. His 1968 score included "How Long Will My Baby Be Gone" and "Sweet Rosie Jones."

Buck was equally successful with his LP efforts. His Capitol albums included such titles as "Buck Owens on the Bandstand," "Buck Owens Sings Tommy Collins" ('63); "Best of Buck Owens," "Together Again," "I Don't Care" ('64); the first-ranked best-selling country and western LP for 1966, "Roll Out the Red Carpet for Buck Owens and His Buckaroos," "Before You Go/No One But You" ('66); "Open Up Your Heart," "Buck Owens and His Buckaroos in Japan," "America's Most Wanted Band" ('67); "It Takes People Like You," and "Best of Buck Owens, Vol. II." Starday also issued a Buck Owens LP, "Fabulous Sound."

Throughout his rise to national reknown, Buck was one of the few country artists who remained "in residence" in California. Besides his performing chores, in the 1960s, he started to build an impressive business empire. By 1967, his interests included Bluebook Music, a song publishing house; radio stations in California and Arizona; booking offices; and property investments.

From his base in California, he continued to take his own show, featuring many top country artists as well as The Buckaroos, further and further afield. In the mid-1960s, he became an international favorite, as popular with crowds abroad as in Bakersfield or Nashville.

OYAMA, CHARLES: *See* Travelers 3

PAINE, JOHN: *See* Brothers Four, The

PALEY, TOM: Singer, guitarist, banjoist. Born New York, New York, March 19, 1928.

A good many of the important folk artists of the post-World War II period have academic backgrounds. Examples are Sam Hinton, a leading oceanographer, Ph.D. Lou Gottlieb, and mathematicians Tom Lehrer and Tom Paley.

Thomas Paley was born into a household where music was prized. However, the emphasis was on classical music, which his mother taught. Growing up in the city, Tom had a bent for science as well as some youthful interest in Bach, Beethoven, and Brahms. He took piano lessons for a time in the classics.

Tom went to a public grammar school in New York. His family moved to Hollywood for a while in the early 1940s, and he attended high school there. However, they returned to New York and Tom graduated from Bronx High School of Science in 1945. It was during these last months at Bronx Science that Tom finally took notice of the folk field. Radio programs and records of the music caught his fancy and he bought and learned to play the banjo and guitar.

During his undergraduate years at the College of the City of New York, he spent much of his spare time practicing and sometimes performing folk music. By the late 1940s, he was considered one of the more talented new performers in the New York area. In 1949, when Jac Holzman was collecting material for a new record company, one of the initial sessions included numbers by Paley. In January 1950, Paley was one of the featured artists at the Leadbelly Memorial Concert in New York's Town Hall.

Paley earned his Bachelor of Science degree from CCNY in 1950 and went to Yale to work for advanced degrees. He was awarded his master's in mathematics in 1952 and went on to earn his doctorate in the later '50s. During these years, he continued to double in brass as a folk performer, appearing at a number of folk festivals and in coffee houses and concerts throughout New England and in Virginia.

Paley settled down to teaching mathematics at several eastern universities, including the University of Connecticut. His teaching work, though, extended to tutoring a number of pupils in banjo and guitar playing.

In 1958, Paley was one of the original members of the New Lost City Ramblers. Along with Mike Seeger and John Cohen, he toured widely during vacation periods and on weekends and also appeared with the group at the Newport Folk Festival. After several years, a research grant plus the pressures of this kind of double schedule led Tom to leave the Ramblers. He was replaced by Tracy Schwarz.

Paley performed on several of the original LPs of the New Lost City Ramblers produced by Folkways Records. He was also featured on an Aravel album, "Tom Paley, Mike Seeger and John Cohen Sing Songs of the New Lost City Ramblers."

In the 1960s, Paley continued to concentrate on teaching while retaining his folk music activities as a pleasant avocation. (*See also* NEW LOST CITY RAMBLERS)

PARTY TIMERS, THE: *See* Jackson, Wanda

PATTERSON, JOE: Singer, instrumentalist ("quills," tambourine). Born Ashford, Alabama, 1898.

One of the great attractions of modern urban folk festivals has been the exposure of audiences not only to little known performers of great ability, but also to new and unusual instruments. At the Newport Folk Festival in 1964, such a treat was provided by "quill" player Joe Patterson. The word "quill" refers to an instrument made of a series of hollow reeds attached together and cut in different lengths to provide different tones. The quill, in other words, was an American folk version of the European pan-pipes or syrinx.

Patterson was born and spent all his life in rural Alabama. At an early age he learned to sing work songs as he worked the fields with his family. He was particularly curious about musical instruments and was entranced when he heard some of his neighbors play simple pan-type instruments made of two or three reeds. As he grew up, he began to make his own instruments, eventually developing one of the most complex of pan-type systems with eight or nine reeds instead of only two or three.

He played for local events for pleasure, most of his life. In the late 1950s, greatly increased collecting efforts by folklorists led to his discovery by the outside world. In time, his ability came to the notice of eminent folk authority Dr. John Quincy Wolfe, professor of English at Southwestern University, Memphis. Dr. Wolfe told Newport Folk Coordinator Ralph Rinzler about Patterson and Ralph traveled to Alabama to meet Joe and record him. This led to Joe's introduction to Newport in 1964.

His style was discussed by Professor Wolfe in an article in the 1964 Newport program, "Quills and Whooping Songs." "The Southern poor white and Negro (discovered) that hollow canes closed at one end and cut to various lengths would produce various musical notes.

[228]

. . . The simplest way (to use these canes) was to hold two, three or four canes against the lower lip so that they could be blown into readily, and to accompany the music of the canes with the voice.

"This came to be known as a whooping-type of music. . . . The musician would utter a musical note, usually in falsetto, and echo the note with one, two or three blasts, usually from one of the canes, then proceed immediately to another whoop in another musical note, and follow with blasts from another of the canes, which he held against his lower lip. . . .

"The most sophisticated use of the quills . . . consisted of a number of canes arranged in a frame and a variety of notes that formed a sort of scale. This is the kind of instrument used by Joe Patterson . . . who is perhaps the last and most accomplished of the musicians using the pan-pipes."

PAXTON, TOM: Singer, guitarist, songwriter. Born Chicago, Illinois, October 31, 1937.

The folk song boom of the 1950s and early 1960s was greeted with raised eyebrows by purists on many levels. Not the least reason was the fact that many of the "folk" songs were not from long time usage, but modern compositions. Still, many of the new songs were hard to distinguish from "classical" folk music. This was particularly true of many of the efforts of Tom Paxton. Pointing to Paxton's work, supporters of the written folk song stressed that the only criterion should be the worth of a song rather than how it was developed.

Paxton spent half his formative years in "folk song country," which may have helped him develop his grass roots style. His first ten years, though, were strictly urban, on Chicago's South Side where Tom's main interests were sports. In 1948, his family moved to the small town of Bristol, Oklahoma, on the road between Tulsa and Oklahoma City. His father died only a few months after the move, but luckily family finances were good enough to keep the wolf from the door. The tragedy did give young Tom some insight into the somber side of life.

In high school, he thought mainly of becoming an actor. When he was 16, an aunt gave him an old guitar and he soon learned to play it. By the time he entered the University of Oklahoma, he was an accomplished player with a new guitar. While majoring in dramatics, Tom suddenly found a deep interest in folk music

after hearing one of Ed McCurdy's albums at a campus party. His first stage appearance as a folksinger was in the school's variety show.

After graduation in 1959, Tom first went into summer stock, starring in "The Spoilers." But acting soon became boring and he decided singing was a better avocation. The final decision was delayed by a six-month Army hitch in 1960.

Out of the service, Paxton headed for New York and soon sang occasionally at the Gaslight folk club on Macdougall Street. He met many dedicated folksingers, both amateur and professional, and rapidly expanded his knowledge of this kind of music. Soon he auditioned as a replacement for one of the members of the Chad Mitchell Trio. He was momentarily selected by the group's director, Milt Okun, but then rejected. However, Okun liked Paxton's style and was even more impressed by one of his compositions, "The Marvelous Toy." Okun urged Paxton to write more material, but Paxton at first preferred to concentrate on

Tom Paxton

[229]

entertaining. In 1961 and '62, he performed at coffee houses throughout the U.S., part of the time in combination with another folksinger, Gil Robbins.

By 1962, though, he gave in to Okun's suggestions and spent more and more time on writing. Before long, Paxton's compositions were played by major folk groups. The Weavers featured his "Ramblin' Boy" in their 1963 Carnegie Hall Concert. By the mid-1960s, he had turned out more than 200 songs, covering a range from love ballads to bitter protest. Some of the most popular are: "The Man Who Built the Bridges," "Every Time," "Bottle of Wine," "What Did You Learn in School Today," "Brand New Baby," and "The Willing Conscript." The first LP on which he sang his own compositions was put out by the Gaslight Club. In 1963, the first Paxton LPs on the Vanguard label appeared.

PAYCHECK, JOHNNY: Singer, songwriter. Born Ohio, May 31, 1941.

One of the more promising country singers of the mid-1960s, Johnny Paycheck, owed his singing career to a chance hearing of a record auditioning one of his compositions. Up to that time, Paycheck had progressed in the music field as a songwriter of great potential.

Born and raised in southern Ohio, Johnny had become a devotee of country music in his boyhood from listening to broadcasts over stations in nearby border states. In the mid-1950s, while in his teens, he began to write songs. In time, he found his way to Nashville to try to place them with leading country artists. After several years of banging on doors, he began to click with some of the top artists in the business. In the early 1960s, many records were turned out by such stars as Webb Pierce, Skeets McDonald, and Sheb Wooley that bore the writing credit of "J. Paycheck."

Though he didn't think of himself as a performer, Paycheck had a good voice. He made his own demonstration records to show off his new songs for various recording stars. This led to bids for him to sing harmony in support of some of the artists at recording sessions. A number of records produced in the early 1960s, by such stars as Faron Young, Ray Price, Roger Miller, and George Jones, have Paycheck's voice in the background.

In November 1964, one of Paycheck's demonstration records was played for record company executive Aubrey Mayhew by an agent of Johnny's. Mayhew quickly sought an introduction to Paycheck and asked if he could manage the young artist. A month later, Paycheck's first release proved Mayhew's hunch was right. The song, "Don't Start Counting on Me," which Paycheck wrote, was on the hit charts for many weeks. An even more enthusiastic reaction greeted Johnny's next release, "The Girl They Talk About." In October 1965, his third effort, "A-ll," quickly was picked as a hit by many of the major country and western stations across the land. The song was high on the charts for many weeks, though it didn't quite make a top 10 rating.

By this time, Paycheck was featured in guest spots on many major TV programs. He also was warmly applauded during personal appearances in many U.S. cities. Mayhew and Paycheck decided it was time to establish a new record label as part of a management and production company for Johnny's activities, including his songwriting efforts. They chose the unusual name of Little Darlin' Records. In 1966, though, it brought them luck as Johnny's record of "The Lovin' Machine" was a top 10 national hit.

PAYNE, JIMMY: Singer, guitarist, songwriter. Born Leachville, Arkansas, April 12, 1936.

A service hitch is not usually considered a blessing. In Jimmy Payne's case, however, it helped pave the way for his later success in the music field. A chance meeting with another soldier who became an important producer was the break that Payne had been looking for.

Jimmy had grown up in rural Missouri, a devoted follower of country and western music. He also enjoyed singing in church and formed a gospel trio in high school with two friends. After finishing high school in the mid-1950s, the boys were given their own Saturday afternoon program on the radio station in Malden, Missouri, called "All Star Gospel Singers." Jimmy enjoyed the program, but pay was low and he had to add to his income by picking cotton during the week.

In 1957, he moved to St. Louis to work as a professional country music performer. He found a number of jobs at local clubs and his career seemed to be moving ahead a little. The Army beckoned at this point and eventually resulted in his being stationed at Fort Lewis, Washington. Jimmy met another young performer, Chuck Glaser of the Glaser Brothers singing group. The two began playing shows in officers' clubs when they had time free from service chores.

At the start of the 1960s, Jimmy entered the All-Army Talent Contest at his base and took top prize. He went to the national contest at Fort Ord, California. He didn't win first prize there, but he gained an important new friend in the person of singer-contestant Bobby Bare.

When Jimmy left the Army, he returned to singing jobs in St. Louis. By now, the Glaser Brothers had become top names in the country music field and had established their own management firm. Jimmy moved to Nashville and Chuck Glaser took over Payne's management and bookings.

Before long, Jimmy was playing dates in many parts of the country with his own group, The Payne Gang. He also began recording for small record firms. Among his first singles were "Ladder to the Sky," "Every Pretty Girl," and "Rusty Old Halo." Among his recordings were some cuts of his own compositions. Before long, he was signed by a major record company, Epic (a division of Columbia). His first efforts included "What Does It Take (to Keep a Woman Like You Satisfied)" and his own "My Most Requested Song." "What Does It Take" made the national charts and won Jimmy his first appearance on the Grand Ole Opry in August 1966.

PAYNE, LEON: Singer, instrumentalist, songwriter. Born Alba, Texas, June 15, 1917.

One of the great country and western songwriters as well as a versatile performer, Leon Roger Payne made it the hard way to a top rung of the music ladder despite a lifetime of darkness. Though he was blind from childhood, he developed his other senses to compensate, in the tradition of Riley Puckett and Doc Watson.

He began attending the Texas School for the Blind in 1924 and continued until 1935. He showed an aptitude for music and began to learn a whole succession of instruments over the years. By his late teens, he could play guitar, piano, organ, trombone and drums. From listening to records and radio programs he developed a good repertoire of country and western songs and began to perform before Texas groups in the mid-1930s.

In 1935, he started his radio career with an appearance on station KWET, Palestine, Texas. His capability as a literal one-man-band led to an increasing number of bids to play with bands in the region. In 1938, he joined Bob Wills and his Texas Playboys, remaining with them for a number of years. He didn't take too many solos in those days, but he began to turn out more and more original songs. For a number of years, despite his blindness, he hitchhiked throughout the state, picking up jobs to play with small groups or as a solo at dances or in clubs. He sang the hit songs of the day, but also wrote his own material. One of these songs from his wandering days became a standard, "Lost Highway."

Between the late 1930s and the early '60s, he wrote an estimated several thousand songs. Some of these he recorded himself in a recording career that began in 1939 and continued for several decades on such labels as Decca, TNT, Starday, Dee, MGM, Bullet, and Capitol. Many of his songs also provided top 10 hits for other leading country artists. Among his top hits were such songs as "I Love You Because," "Blue Side of Lonesome," "Things Have Gone to Pieces," and "Doorstep to Heaven."

During 1948 and '49, Leon joined Jack Rhodes and His Rhythm Boys. In 1949, he left to form his own group, the Lone Star Buddies. In the early 1950s, he was featured with this group on such widely heard shows as the Louisiana Hayride from Shreveport and Dallas' Big D Jamboree. Over the next decade, Leon often sang on the Grand Ole Opry. Despite his early years of hitchhiking, the Opry during these years avoided signing him as a regular because of doubt about his ability to take the lengthy road tours involved.

During the 1950s and early '60s, Leon played on stations all over the country, including WOAI-TV, San Antonio, KGRO, Dallas, KLEE, Houston, KTEM-TV, Temple, Texas, and KMJ, Fresno, California.

From the mid-1950s to the mid-'60s, he was under contract to write songs for the major music publishing firm of Hill and Range. He then was signed to a ten-year pact by Acuff-Rose Music. His performing career was drastically curtailed by a heart attack in 1965. From then on, Leon concentrated on singing his new compositions into his trusty tape recorder.

PEARL, MINNIE: Comedienne, singer. Born Centerville, Tennessee, October 25, 1912. Elected to Country Music Hall of Fame, 1968.

Comedy and satire have always had an important place in country variety shows from the medicine show days to the more sophisticated formats of radio and TV. Thus fans have long flocked to the Grand Ole Opry as much to hear the shrill voice and hayseed humor of Minnie Pearl as to enjoy the guitar and banjo pickin' of the other cast members. And, while the monologues of the "Queen of Country Comedy" always have a rural twang to them, their content is of more general interest, as shown by Minnie Pearl's success with audiences in suave supper clubs and on such network shows as Dinah Shore, Jack Paar, and Tennessee Ernie Ford.

Minnie was born Sarah Ophelia Colley in Centerville, Tennessee. During her youth, she sometimes wandered by a switching station for the railroad some three miles from Centerville.

The name of the station had a more comic ring than her home town and, in later years, she billed herself as being "from Grinder's Switch." A stage career seemed attractive to young Sarah Colley and she majored in stage technique when she enrolled in Ward-Belmont College in Nashville in the late 1920s. The art form that interested her most was dancing; she showed her instructors that she had a great deal of ability in this direction.

Having completed college, she went on to teach dancing for two years. In 1934, she joined the Wayne P. Sewall Producing Company of Atlanta as a dramatic coach. For the next six years, she toured throughout the southern states directing amateur plays in local schools. During her travels, her natural flair for comedy began to assert itself. She found a ready audience for her comic songs and monologues dealing with such subjects as "how to ketch a feller." By the time she left the Sewall organization in 1940, she had switched

Three all time Opry greats ride in a vintage car in a vintage photo: Whitey Ford, "The Duke of Paducah," Roy Acuff; and the lady from Grinder's Switch, Minnie Pearl.

[232]

identities from Sarah Colley to Minnie Pearl.

In 1940, she debuted on the Grand Ole Opry. Though she left for road tours and made guest appearances on other shows, she was still a major prop of the Opry close to thirty years later. Her wide-brimmed straw hat with its topknot of flowers and long length old-style country dress were as much a part of American tradition by the late 1960s as Charlie Chaplin's tramp costume.

During the 1950s and '60s, she played in theaters, on concert stages, and at county fairs across the country. She also starred on variety shows on all three major networks. In 1957, her national reputation was recognized by Ralph Edwards who selected Minnie as the subject for one of his most popular NBC-TV "This Is Your Life" segments. Other honors came Minnie's way in the 1950s and '60s, including selection as Nashville's "Woman of the Year" for 1965.

Minnie's recording efforts over the years were not as widespread, naturally, as those of conventional musicians. She was featured on several LPs, on Everest, Starday, and RCA Victor. Her Everest LP was titled "Minnie Pearl." On RCA, she turned out a number of albums including "Monologue" and "How to Catch a Man." For Starday, she provided the LP "Cousin Minnie" and, in 1966, a top 10 single hit, "Giddyup Go-Answer."

In 1967, Minnie's outside interests included a new food franchise organization called "Minnie Pearl's Chicken System, Inc." She was nominated for the Country Music Hall of Fame in 1968.

PEER, RALPH SYLVESTER: Music publisher, record company executive, producer. Born Kansas City, Missouri, May 22, 1892; died Hollywood, California, January 19, 1960.

One of the phenomena of country and western music was the way in which commercial recording companies acted for a good many years, in effect, as collectors of folk material. Many representatives of recording firms, one of the most notable being Ralph Peer, went into the field and scoured the rural countryside for country performers of talent and for traditional hill country ballads.

In doing this, such men as Peer helped provide the basis for today's sprawling country and western music activity. At the same time, these efforts resulted in the preservation of an important part of this nation's folk heritage. In Peer's case, the experience also served to focus his driving personality on eventual establishment of one of the world's largest music publishing combines.

He was born in Kansas City, Missouri, the son of Abram Peer, a phonograph dealer. The exposure to many kinds of music in his father's shop helped build an interest in the music industry in young Peer during his public school years in the city. When he graduated from high school, he enrolled in Northwestern University, but after two years he left to work in the recording field.

From 1911 to 1919, he was employed by the Columbia Phonograph Company of Kansas City, working up to assistant manager. He then accepted an offer from General Phonograph Corp., in New York, where he served as production director until 1927. His move east also resulted in a position as recording director of Okeh Records starting in 1920. A major pioneer in the so-called "race" category, he cut historic sessions with Mamie Smith and other rhythm and blues artists.

In 1926, Okeh was absorbed by American Recording Corp., which later became Columbia Records, Inc. At this point, Peer joined the Victor Talking Machine Company as recording director. For Victor, he covered the south, sometimes conducting recording activities in a sound truck or in hotel public rooms. He made a point of seeking performers of rural and mountain music, an idiom for which he coined the word "hillbilly." During these years, he discovered some of the most legendary names in country and western music. A partial list of his discoveries includes Jimmie Rodgers, the Original Carter Family, Rabbit Brown, and Willy Smith. Many of his artists came to him from the medicine and tent show circuit.

With Victor participating, he formed Southern Music Publishing Company in 1928. When Victor withdrew in 1932, Peer became president and sole owner. He and his organization popularized and promoted country music, one of the first major concerns to concentrate in this field.

Peer started off with songs in his firm's catalog that have become country standards. Some of the earliest are "Roll Along Kentucky Moon," "I'm Thinking Tonight of My Blue Eyes" ('29); "Mule Skinner Blues" ('31); and "Wabash Cannon Ball" ('33). Over the years, thousands of other titles were added, including such successes as Jimmie Davis' "You Are My Sunshine" in 1942. Devoting his restless energy to a search for new outlets for country music, Peer is credited with setting up the first European offices in the industry. By the late 1950s, he had opened offices in England, France, Australia, Mexico, South Africa, Japan, and the Central and South American countries.

His Southern Music was affiliated with ASCAP. In 1940, he formed another firm, Peer International, that was one of the first major members of the BMI organization. In the mid-1960s, Peer International represented the largest publisher catalog affiliated with BMI.

As his music business flourished, Peer somehow found time for many other interests. He became an authority on international copyright law and set many industry guideposts in the field of performance rights. He also gained recognition in the horticultural field, receiving the Veitch Gold Medal from the Royal Horticultural Society of London (of which he was a member) for his research on the camellia plant. In the years after World War II, he also continued an increasing interest in science, resulting in the collection of an impressive library of science books, with particular emphasis on nuclear subjects.

In 1940, he married Monique Hildborg Thora Alexandra, daughter of a Danish industrialist. After his death in 1960, she carried on the Peer tradition of extending the world-wide horizons of country music. This support helped the growth of the Country Music Association as a strong industry-wide force and also included aid in the assignment of Roy Horton, former CMA board chairman, to help promote international interest in country music.

Peer was a man who didn't look over his shoulder. His successes over seemingly overwhelming opposition amazed the industry time and time again. One New York publisher once commented, "Ralph Peer wrote the book on music publishing, but I'll be damned if I can read his writing."

PENNINGTON, RAY: Singer, band leader, songwriter, A&R man. Born Clay County, Kentucky, 1933.

Songwriting propelled Ray Pennington to the top rungs of the country and western ladder. It also launched a new career as a national recording artist, something that a decade and

a half of performing had failed to do earlier in Ray's life.

Ray was raised on a diet of gospel and country music. His father, Alva Pennington, was the local church choral director. Alva placed his son in the group when Ray was only six. Ray obviously had talent and continued to develop as a singer as he grew up. In his early teens, he was already featured at local get-togethers. At 16, he began singing on television in Cincinnati. In 1952, he formed his own western swing band. For the next decade, he was featured on local TV and in personal appearance tours of Kentucky, Indiana, and the Ohio Valley.

Still, he was mainly known only in the midwest. By the early 1960s, though, he was gaining a reputation with other country artists for his songwriting ability. In 1961, Roy Drusky gained a national hit with his version of a Pennington composition (written with Sonny Thompson), "Three Hearts in a Tangle."

Pennington also showed ability at selecting material for other artists. In the early 1960s,

Ray Pennington

[234]

this was evidenced in his work as A&R executive with King Records. Over a number of years, he was responsible for production of some of the company's most successful records. In 1963, Ray signed a writer's contract with the important Pamper Music firm. Through 1967, he not only provided new song material, but served as production coordinator-arranger and A&R man.

Among his song hits in the mid-'60s were such numbers as "Happy Tracks," "Ramblin' Man," and "Walking on New Grass."

The new aspect of his career started with a performing contract with Capitol Records in 1966. His first record of one of his compositions, "Who's Been Mowing the Lawn (While I Was Gone)," was on the hit charts for a number of weeks. Later, he did even better with "My Heart's Gonna Rise Again." His other recordings for Capitol through mid-1967 were, "I Don't Feel at Home in This House Anymore," "Let Go," "Ramblin' Man," and "The Woman in Town."

PEOPLE'S SONGS, INC.: *See* Seeger, Pete

PERKINS, CARL: Singer, guitarist, songwriter. Born Jackson, Tennessee, April 9, 1932.

A good part of the initial impetus that made rock 'n' roll the number one form of popular music in the late 1950s came from country and western artists. Such performers as Elvis Presley, Jerry Lee Lewis, and the Everly Brothers had strong backgrounds in "traditional" country music before gaining the national limelight in rock 'n' roll. Another good example of this transition is Carl Perkins.

Perkins was born and raised in Tennessee. He developed a good guitar style and was performing in country and western programs when he was in his teens. In the early 1950s, he joined the cast of the Big D Jamboree in Dallas, Texas. As rock 'n' roll began to gain attention, Perkins started to perform this kind of music for youthful audiences. It was not too radical a change, of course, since part of the roots of rock 'n' roll is in country music. By the mid-1950s, he was becoming known to fans throughout the country.

In 1956, Perkins hit the top 10 in both the pop and country and western charts with two of his own compositions. These were "Blue Suede Shoes" on Sun Records and "Boppin' the Blues" (co-authored by C. Griffin) on Sun

label. He was backed on records and during personal appearance tours by his own group, consisting of Clayton "Buck" Perkins, J. B. Jay Perkins, and W. S. Holland. Some of his other best-sellers of the late 1950s were "Pointed Toe Shoes," "Your True Love," and "Match Box."

In the late 1950s and early '60s, Perkins was starred on both popular and country and western shows. He made one appearance on the Perry Como Show and was also featured on Red Foley's ABC-TV network show, Jubilee U.S.A. During these years, he was represented by a number of singles and LPs on Columbia Records.

PERRY, JACK: *See* Light Crust Doughboys, The

PETER, PAUL AND MARY: Vocal and instrumental group, Peter Yarrow, born New York, New York, May 31, 1938; Noel Paul Stookey, born Baltimore, Maryland, November 30, 1937; Mary Ellin Travers, born November 7, 1937.

The team of Peter, Paul and Mary came to the fore at the height of the folk song boom of the early 1960s. They proved their staying power, however, by remaining together as a successful team when the boom was over and many other groups had to disband.

The three took diverse routes to their eventual meeting and combining in New York. Paul Stookey, born and raised in Maryland, began as a rock 'n' roll addict. He learned the electric guitar and used his rock 'n' roll ability to help pay his way through Michigan State University. Another contribution towards his college tuition was his ability to work as an m.c. in local clubs.

He moved to Pennsylvania with his family after graduating from college. He held several odd jobs there, then decided to go to New York to try to make his way in the entertainment field. After months of near-starvation, he found a job in a chemical company and looked for work as a nightclub comic in his spare time. He finally began to catch on and had a growing reputation as a stand-up comedian in Greenwich Village clubs by the end of 1960.

Most of Mary's early years were spent in New York, to which her family had moved from Louisville. She attended local schools and began learning folk music at an early age from such teachers as Charity Bailey. Her interest in folk music deepened when she reached high school and she soon began singing with teenage groups. With a group called the Songswappers, she made two appearances in Carnegie Hall.

After finishing school, she was in the chorus of a Broadway flop, then earned a living at various literary and advertising jobs for a while. She continued to look for a way to enter the music field. In 1961, she met Paul Stookey and the two began to develop a folk music act. Their friend and advisor, Milton Okun, suggested they expand the act to a trio. The search ended with the addition of Peter Yarrow.

Yarrow had won some notice from his performance at the 1960 Newport Folk Festival. His success at Newport had confirmed his decision to go with the music route rather than psychology, in which he had majored at Cornell University. Having learned to play violin and guitar in his youth, he had performed at local events during his college years. After graduation, he toyed with the idea of a job in psychology, but returned to New York and worked with various small folk groups. In May 1960, he gained a spot on a CBS special, Folk Sound, U.S.A., which helped bring about his Newport debut.

The team of Peter, Paul and Mary began performing in the New York area in 1962. Their offerings were quickly snapped up by local audiences. Before the end of the year, they had made their TV debut and were off on a tour of coffee houses in many parts of the country. They signed with Warner Brothers Records and turned out a highly successful 1962 LP, "Peter, Paul and Mary."

With such songs as "Big Boat," "Stranger in Town," and "Blowin' in the Wind," they gained nationwide attention. Their version of the last-named Bob Dylan composition was one of the top hits of 1963. It resulted in their winning the Grammy Award for the Best Folk Music Record of the year. Their LPs "In the Wind" and "Movin'" were both best-sellers that year.

The group was featured on most major TV shows during the mid-1960s and also played concerts and nightclubs across the country. They were closely connected with the Newport Folk Festival, where Yarrow served as one of the founding incorporators of the new non-

profit event in 1963. Yarrow also was a member of the Newport Folk Foundation's first Board of Directors.

One of their big hits of the mid-1960s was "Puff the Magic Dragon," written by Yarrow. Peter and Mary (and Milton Okun as well) collaborated with Stookey on many other original songs. These included "On a Desert Island," "A-Soulin'," "Talking Candy Bar Blues," "Early in the Morning" and "It's Raining."

Their third LP was "Peter, Paul and Mary in Concert," issued by Warner Brothers in 1965.

PHILLIPS, BILL: Singer, guitarist, songwriter. Born Canton, North Carolina, January 28, 1936.

Like many of the boys raised in the rural areas of North Carolina, William Clarence Phillips learned many traditional country ballads almost from the cradle. His interest in country and western music grew stronger as he grew up. He could play good guitar during his junior high and high school years (1947 to 1953) at Bethel High School in Canton.

Though he sometimes played for local audiences during his teens, Bill didn't think at first of a full time career in music. For a while, after finishing high school, he worked for an upholstery firm. His musical ability led to bids to play in local clubs, and after a while he decided to concentrate on this.

Instead of heading toward Nashville or Shreveport, Bill went further south. He settled in Miami, Florida, and began to build his reputation there. In 1955 he joined the cast of the Old South Jamboree on station WMIL, and later he appeared on WMIL-TV as well. He also was featured nightly at the Granada Club. After a number of years in Miami, Bill began to gain a wider audience from personal appearances through the south and from a recording contract with Columbia.

His recordings for Columbia in the late 1950s and early '60s included "Tears That Fall," "Foolish Me," "Sawmill," "You Are the Reason," "Georgiatown Blues," "I Get Enough of These Blues," and his own composition, "There's a Change in Me." During these years, he wrote a number of other songs, including "Falling Back to You" and "My Heartache" in 1958 and "It's Best This Way" in 1959.

Bill's career moved forward in the late '50s with a bid to appear on the Grand Ole Opry. He was also featured on WLAC-TV in Nashville. Harmony Records issued an LP called "Bill Phillips" in 1964. In the mid-1960s, Bill signed a new recording contract with Decca. In 1966, this paid off with a top 10 hit, "Put It Off Until Tomorrow." He followed this up with another hit, "The Words I'm Gonna Have to Eat." Decca also released an album called "Put It Off Until Tomorrow" in 1966.

PHILLIPS, JOHN: *See* Journeymen, The

PIERCE, DON: Producer, record company executive. Born Ballard, Washington, October 10, 1915.

One of the most successful independent record impresarios of the post-World War II period was Washington-born Don Pierce. Don made his way to the top in country and western music, yet had little exposure to it before entering the music field. By the mid-1960s, though, few people, performers or executives, were better versed in country and western lore than Pierce.

Pierce had some interest in music during his youth in a suburb of Seattle. He attended public schools in Ballard and played on his high school tennis and golf teams. Helped by part-time work as a caddy and other odd jobs, Don went through the University of Washington, gaining a degree in business administration.

The outbreak of World War II resulted in his joining the colors as a private. When he was discharged four years later, he held the rank of captain. To celebrate this event, he and several friends drove down to California, playing at various golf courses on the way. One of these was Bel Air Country Club in Los Angeles. Don ended up playing with an avid golfer named Hoagy Carmichael. The encounter helped turn Don's interests toward music.

Soon after, he saw an advertisement in a Los Angeles paper inviting investors in a record company. Little knowing how fragile the company was financially, Don bought in with some money he'd saved during the war. He then went on the road as a record salesman for the firm, Four Star Records. His travels showed that the only records that dealers were interested in were by cowboy T. Texas Tyler. Don became more and more engrossed in this part of the field and began to work with Tyler in producing new records. Many of these became national hits, such as the 1948 top 10

successes "Deck of Cards" and "Dad Gave My Dog Away." Don also worked on such other Tyler hits as "Remember Me," "Filipino Baby," "Divorce Me C.O.D.," and "Bummin' Around."

By 1952, Don was able to sell his share of Four Star at a handsome profit. He entered a partnership with veteran country and western executive H. W. "Pappy" Daily. Daily had started a new label in Houston, called Starday Records, and Don took over as president of the new company. Within a few years Starday was represented by a string of hit records, including "Why, Baby, Why," "A Place for Girls Like You," and "Y'All Come."

At this point, Mercury Records offered an arrangement by which Daily and Pierce would concentrate on producing country and western records for Mercury. It seemed to be a giant step forward. Unfortunately, the inroads of rock 'n' roll caused a temporary depression in the country field. The arrangement, though, did serve to cause Pierce to move his family to Nashville. In 1958, the Mercury agreement was dissolved and Don and Pappy Daily also decided to go their separate ways.

The two divided their copyrights between them and, soon after, Don decided to reactivate the Starday label. The Mercury deal had prevented much activity in Starday. This time, home base for Starday was Nashville. Once things were underway, Starday rapidly increased in strength. Many of the top hits of the 1960s were on Pierce's label. In 1960, for example, Cowboy Copas turned out a number-one-ranked hit called "Alabam." That same year, Don had such top 10 hits as Johnny Cash's "Seasons of My Heart" and Merle Kilgore's "Love Has Made You Beautiful."

Among the other hits in Pierce's catalog were, "Flat Top" (Copas), "Signed, Sealed and Delivered" (Copas) '61; "Second Fiddle (to an Old Guitar)" (Jean Shepard—recorded on Capitol, music published by Starday) '64; number-one-ranked "Giddyup Go" (Red Sovine); "10 Little Bottles" (Johnny Bond) '65; and "Giddyup Go-Answer" (Minnie Pearl) '66.

During the 1960s, Pierce also scored with reissues of the old masters of songs by such artists as Flatt & Scruggs, Dottie West, Roger Miller, and Buck Owens. The move sparked considerable controversy, including complaints from some performers who felt the older recordings were not representative of their later styles. To avid country and music collectors, though, the reissues provided material long out of reach. (*See also* DAILY, PAPPY)

PIERCE, WEBB: Singer, guitarist, songwriter. Born near West Monroe, Louisiana, August 8, 1926.

The name Webb Pierce strikes a responsive chord with Louisianans. Like former governor Jimmie Davis, he is considered as great a state asset as its industry or natural resources. Born and raised in Louisiana, Webb achieved national fame in country music in his home state before moving on to the Grand Ole Opry.

Brought up in a rural area, Webb could play excellent guitar in his teens. As he won notice for performing in local events, he gained his first radio job on station KMLB in Monroe. Encouraged by his reception, he moved on to Shreveport in the late 1940s to try to gain a wider audience. However, for a while he made little progress and had to earn his living as a salesman for Sears, Roebuck. He continued to pick up performing jobs in his spare time and finally won the attention of Horace Logan, program director of station KWKH in Shreveport, sponsor of the new Louisiana Hayride show.

Webb joined the cast, and before long was one of the featured performers. In the early 1950s, his band included many performers who went on to greatness on their own, including Faron Young, Goldie Hill, Jimmy Day, Tommy Hill, and Floyd Cramer. He began to achieve a wider reputation with his first records on the Four Star label. Some of the songs that made the charts were his own compositions.

In 1952, after signing with Decca, his name began to appear on the top rungs of the hit charts. He scored with two top 10 recordings of his own compositions, "That Heart Belongs to Me" and "Wondering," and had a number-one-ranked record in "Back Street Affair." In 1953, he co-wrote the hit "Last Waltz" with M. Freeman, had such other hits as "I'll Go on Alone," "I'm Walking the Dog," "That's Me Without You," and two number-one-ranked hits, "It's Been So Long" and "There Stands the Glass." In 1952–'53 he received the first of many awards, Ranch and Farm magazine's citation as Number One Folk Singer and the Juke Box Operators award as Number One Singer of 1953.

Along with his close friend Red Sovine, he now moved to Nashville as an Opry regular.

The hits continued to pour forth in 1954, such as the number-one-ranked "Slowly" (written with T. Hill), number-one-ranked "More and More," and top 10 "Even Tho" (written with W. Jones and C. Peeples), "Sparkling Brown Eyes," and "You're Not Mine Anymore" (written with the Wilburn Brothers). In 1955, Webb had three number-one songs, "In the Jailhouse Now," " Love, Love, Love," and "I Don't Care," the last co-written with Cindy Walker. In 1956, he teamed with Red Sovine in two hit duets, "Why, Baby, Why" and "Little Rosa." He also hit with "Any Old Time" and "Teen-age Boogie," both original compositions. In the late 1950s, he had such top 10 hits as "Bye Bye Love," "Holiday for Love" (co-authored with Wayne Walker and A. R. Peddy), "Honky Tonk Song," "I'm Tired" ('57); "Falling Back to You," "Tupelo Country Jail" (written with Mel Tillis—'58); and "A Thousand Miles Ago" (written with Mel Tillis—'59).

By the start of the 1960s, Webb had toured throughout the U.S. and Canada and guest-starred on such other network shows as Red Foley's Jubilee U.S.A. His successes of the 1960s included "Fallen Angel," "No Love Have I" ('60); "Let Forgiveness In," "Walking the Streets," "How Do You Talk to a Baby" (written with Wayne Walker), "Sweet Lips" (written with Wayne Walker and Davy Tubb—'61); "All My Love," "Take Time," "Crazy Wild Desire" (written with Mel Tillis—'62); "Sands of Gold" (written with Cliff Parman and Hal Eddy), "Those Wonderful Years" (written with Don Schroeder—'63); and "Memory Number One" ('64).

Through the mid-1960s, Webb had compiled one of the best album sales totals of any popular music performer. His LP titles on Decca included "Webb Pierce"; "Wondering Boy"; "Webb!" and "Just Imagination" ('58); "Bound for the Kingdom," "Webb Pierce" ('59); "Webb with a Beat," "Walking the Streets" ('60); "Golden Favorites," "Fallen Angel" ('61); "Hideaway Heart," "Cross Country" ('62); "I've Got a New Heartache," "Bow Thy Head" ('63); "Sands of Gold," "Webb Pierce Story" (two LP records) ('64); "Memory Number One" ('65).

PILLOW, RAY: Singer, guitarist. Born Lynchburg, Virginia, 1940(?).

A common success story in the entertainment field relates how the hero or heroine wins the major talent contest and goes on to stardom.

In Ray Pillow's case, he lost the contest, but went back home to Virginia and made his way to the top anyway.

Born and raised in Virginia, Ray attended public schools and college there. He had showed his friends and family an excellent voice during his high school years, but he interrupted both studies and possible career ideas to enlist in the Navy for four years in the late 1950s. He returned home in the early 1960s to complete work for a college degree. He continued to work on his singing, and soon after graduation he traveled to the country music capital in Nashville to compete in the National Pet Milk Talent Contest. He lost the contest and his first chance at a recording contract.

Returning to Virginia, he began to sing in local clubs, and before long received the attention of others in the music field. His newly appointed business manager, Joe Taylor, took some of Ray's demonstration material to Capitol Records and quickly gained him a contract. About the same time, Ray was signed to tour in the Martha White Road Shows. He also appeared on the TV and radio shows sponsored by Martha White Flour.

In a short time, he was asked to appear as a guest artist on many major TV shows, including the Porter Wagoner Show, Wilburn Brothers Show, Bobby Lord Show, American Swing-Around and NBC's Swingin' Country. By now he could greet audiences with some of his Capitol successes, including "Left Out," "Take Your Hands Off My Heart," and "Thank You Ma'am." In 1965, Capitol released his first LP, "Presenting Ray Pillow." The next year, Ray teamed with Jean Shepard in a top 10 hit, "I'll Take the Dog." They turned out an LP soon after and another single, "Mr. Do-It-Yourself."

As 1966 went along, Ray's career moved rapidly ahead. He was asked to join the cast of the Grand Ole Opry as a regular. He was also voted the "Most Promising Male Artist of 1966" in polls conducted by Billboard and Cashbox.

Ray was also starred in a movie, "Country Boy." His activities included several business ventures with his manager, such as the Joe Taylor Artist Agency, Shoji Music Publications, and Ming Music, Inc.

PLEASANT VALLEY BOYS, THE: See Robison, Carson

PO' BOYS: See Anderson, Bill

POTGER, KEITH: See Seekers, The

PRAIRIE RAMBLERS: See Montana, Patsy

PRESLEY, ELVIS AARON: Singer, guitarist, actor. Born Tupelo, Mississippi, January 8, 1935.

In October 1954, audiences listening to the Louisiana Hayride heard m.c. Frank Page introduce a new performer. Said Page, "Just a few weeks ago . . . a young man from Memphis, Tennessee, recorded a song on the Sun label and in just a matter of a few weeks that record has skyrocketed right up the charts. It's really doing well all over the country. He is only 19 years old. He has a new, distinctive style . . . Elvis Presley!"

Moments later, Elvis responded with a driving version of "That's All Right, Mama." Soon after, he signed a year's contract with the Hayride at scale—$18 a night. A year later, an Elvis Presley performance was worth more than $18 a minute.

Elvis' career began not too far from Louisiana in the Mississippi city of Tupelo. He was one of twin boys, but his brother died at birth. Even before Elvis was of school age, he sang along with his parents at camp meetings, revivals, and church conventions in the Tupelo region. When he was attending elementary school, he continued his deep interest in singing, and soon added guitar playing to it after his father bought him an instrument.

When Elvis was 13, his family moved to Memphis. During his years at L. C. Humes High there, he often sang in school programs as well as at local dances and church gatherings. He worked at many jobs in his free time, including a stint as usher at Loew's State Theatre in Memphis. After he graduated from high school in 1953, he found a $35-a-week job as a truck driver with the Crown Electric Company.

Music seemed to offer the best alternative to truck driving and Elvis continued to play with local groups. In mid-1953, he decided to cut a record of one of his songs to help him get work in the area. He paid four dollars to use the studios of the Sun Records Company in Memphis. The record helped gain local jobs and also paved the way for a recording contract from Sam Phillips, owner of Sun Records.

Sun recorded a second song of Elvis', "That's All Right, Mama" and released it in 1954. The record didn't make the top 10, but it did well enough to win Presley his first important job with the Louisiana Hayride. It also was vital in another way, bringing Elvis to the attention of talent genius Colonel Tom Parker. Parker, a veteran of the music wars, became Elvis' manager and was the guiding hand in Presley's phenomenal success.

Under Parker's direction, Elvis toured many of the southern states, billed as "The Hillbilly Cat." In 1955, Elvis had two top 10 hits for Sun, "Baby, Let's Play House" and the number-one-ranked "Mystery Train." Rapidly gaining notice as a coming country and western star, Elvis was asked to perform at the annual Country and Western Disk Jockeys Association meeting in Nashville. Steve Sholes, then head of RCA Victor's Specialties Division, was so impressed with Presley's convention appearance, he sought Sam Phillips out and bought Presley's recording contract. He paid Phillips $35,000 for the contract and all masters of unreleased Presley recordings, on Parker's advice.

In a short time, Victor knew Sholes had scored one of the major coups in show business history. Presley had gained a TV guest spot, with Tommy and Jimmy Dorsey, on the Jackie Gleason "Stage Show." He sang his new release, "Heartbreak Hotel." The song quickly became number one in the popular as well as country and western polls. Elvis built up even more frantic enthusiasm from young viewers during five more weekly appearances on the show. Already a national celebrity at 21, he flew to Hollywood where he signed a seven-year, one-picture-a-year contract with Hal Wallis and also was booked for TV appearances on the Milton Berle Show, followed by appearances on the Steve Allen Show and three sensational spots on the Ed Sullivan Show.

Elvis' records continued to burn up the polls. In 1956, he had two more number-one hits, "Hound Dog" and "My Baby Left Me," plus a top 10 hit, "Love Me Tender." In 1957, radios everywhere vibrated to such number-one hits as "Teddy Bear" and "Jailhouse Rock" as well as "All Shook Up" and "Too Much." In 1958, he scored with such songs as "Hard Headed Woman," "I Beg of You," "Don't Be Cruel," and "Wear My Ring Around Your Neck." During these years, Elvis was un-

Elvis Presley

disputed king of popular music, winning the title of Most Popular Male Singer from 1956 through '58 in the Cashbox and American Bandstand polls. In almost every country of Europe, as well, he was the top-rated new vocalist.

In 1958, he left show business to serve in the U.S. Army. Some thought he was only a fad and that Army service would result in his fading from view. If anything, he came out of service even more popular than when he went in. His record sales for 1958 alone exceeded 10 million.

In the 1960s, Elvis returned to performing, though with more emphasis on films and records than on personal appearances. His first four films, "Love Me Tender, "Loving You," "Jailhouse Rock" and "King Creole," had shown him to be a star of the first magnitude. During the '60s, he turned out a series of hit movies, including such films as "Blue Hawaii, "It Happened at the World's Fair" ('63); "Roustabout" ('64); and "Clambake" ('67).

His LP sales were as steady in 1967 as they had been in the late 1950s. They included such titles as "Blue Suede"; "Elvis"; "Loving You"; "Golden Records," "King Creole" ('58); "For LP Fans Only," "Date with Elvis" ('59); "Golden Records, Volume 2," "Elvis Is Back" ('60); "His Hand in Mine," "Something" ('61); "Pot Luck" ('62); "Girls!" "At the World's Fair," "Golden Records, Volume 3" ('63); "Roustabout" ('64); "Clambake" ('67).

Elvis' continuing popularity was again illustrated in the summer of 1967, when his marriage to Priscilla Beaulieu resulted in lead stories in major magazines and newspapers throughout the world.

PRESTON, TERRY: *See* Husky, Ferlin

PRICE, KENNY: Singer, instrumentalist (drums, guitar, banjo, bass fiddle). Born near Florence, Kentucky, May 27, 1931.

In 1966-67, a new name began to appear on national country music hit charts. However, Kenny Price was not unfamiliar to audiences of the Midwestern Hayride, for he had been a program favorite for well over a decade by then.

Born on a farm in northern Kentucky, Kenny attended rural schools and kept busy a good part of the time helping out with the chores. He fell in love with country music at an early age. When he was five, his family bought him a guitar from the Sears, Roebuck catalog. Kenny slowly learned to play and was good enough, in later years, to become a member of his school band. He had a good voice and often sang at local events during his teens.

His goal was not in music. He expected to follow his family heritage and become a farmer. When the Korean War came along, though, he entered the service and this changed his life. He often entertained his friends with guitar playing and singing. While stationed in Korea, this led to their urging him to try out for the Horace Heidt USO show. He won the assignment and racked up considerable performing hours before he was discharged.

Back home again, he decided to see if he could progress in the entertainment field. In 1954 he auditioned for Cincinnati's WLW, and thus started a relationship which was still going strong in the late 1960s. He became a regular on the Midwestern Hayride and his popularity was attested to by a steadily increasing volume of fan mail.

A fellow cast member was Bobby Bobo, who founded his own record firm, Boone Records. Kenny joined a roster that included many well known country & western performers. In 1966, he rewarded Bobo with a top 10 version of a Ray Pennington composition, "Walking on New Grass." He proved this was no fluke in 1967 with another top 10 hit, "Happy Tracks," also by Pennington. He had three other songs on the 1967 charts, as well, including "Pretty Girl, Pretty Clothes, Pretty Sad."

PRICE, RAY: Singer, guitarist, songwriter. Born Perryville, Texas, January 12, 1926.

Texas and Tennessee are the two states that come to mind when the words country and western are spelled out. All roads, of course, lead to Nashville, but a goodly share of Texans have taken it. In the top 10 list of best-selling record artists from 1947 to 1967, for example, Texas has two entrants compared to only one each for eight other states. One is Jim Reeves of Panola and the other "The Cherokee Cowboy," Ray Noble Price.

Ray was born in the tiny town of Perryville in rural Cherokee County, eastern Texas, only one county over from Jim Reeves' home county. Ray spent his younger years in Perryville, but by the time he was high school age, his family had moved to the big city of Dallas. He attended Boude Storey Junior High there during the 1937-38 school year, then went on to Adamson High School in Dallas. After graduation in 1942, he spent several years in the service.

In 1946, back in civilian life, Ray entered North Texas Agricultural College in Arlington. By this time, he had already shown talent as a performer. In addition to his college chores, he appeared at local events, and in 1948 he made his radio debut on the station KRBC Hillbilly Circus in Abilene. Ray remained in college into 1949, still considering a possible career as a rancher or farmer. That year, though, he gained regular status with the Big D Jamboree, broadcast from station KRLD in Dallas.

The die was cast. During 1949 and 1950, Ray began to build a following among listeners to the Big D Jamboree. Parts of the program were broadcast nationally on the CBS network and his name became known to many outside Texas borders. In the early 1950s, he turned out sev-

Ray Price

eral records on the Bullet Label that won plays on country and western stations across the country.

Recognition of his growing potential was fast in coming. In 1952, he was given regular status with the Grand Ole Opry and signed a new record contract with Columbia Records. Columbia knew they had a winner when two of Ray's 1952 recordings made the top 10 lists, "Talk to Your Heart" and "Don't Let the Stars Get in Your Eyes." For a moment, Ray's career dipped as his 1953 output failed to produce a top 10 success. But in 1954, he was off and running with three major hits, "Release Me," "I'll Be There," and "If You Don't, Someone Else Will."

For the balance of the decade, Ray continued to delight Opry audiences as well as in-person crowds in all parts of the U.S. with one hit after another. These included his first number-one national hit in 1956, "Crazy Arms," and "I've Got a New Heartache," "Wasted Words" ('56); "My Shoes Keep Walking Back to You" ('57); "Curtain in the Window," number-one-ranked "City Lights" ('58); "That's What It's

Like to Be Lonesome," "Under Your Spell Again," "Same Old Me" (number one hit), and "Heartaches By the Number." At the end of the year, Ray was voted "Favorite Male Vocalist" in country and western for 1959 by the music trade magazines. They also voted his version of "Heartaches By the Number" as "Best Record of the Year."

Ray continued to be a feature of country and western top 10 lists in the 1960s. In 1960, he turned out "One More Time" and "I Wish I Could Fall in Love Today." In 1961, his hits included "Heart Over Mind" and his own composition, "Soft Rain." (Previous songwriting credits of Ray's included "Give Me More, More, More of Your Kisses" and "I'm Tired.") His other major hits of the 1960s included "Walk Me to the Door," "Make the World Go Away" ('63); "Please Talk to My Heart," "Burning Memories" ('64); "The Other Woman" ('65); and "A Way to Survive" and "Don't You Ever Get Tired of Hurting Me?" ('66).

Ray also held a top place on Columbia's list of best-selling LP artists. The titles included "Ray Price Sings Heart Songs"; "Talk to Your Heart" ('58); "Faith" ('60); "Greatest Hits" ('61); "San Antonio Rose" ('62); "Night Life" ('63); "Love Life" ('64); "Burning Memories" ('65); and "The Other Woman" ('66).

PRIDE, "COUNTRY" CHARLEY: Singer, guitarist. Born Sledge, Mississippi, March 8, 1938.

The color blindness of most true music enthusiasts was demonstrated again in the case of Country Charley Pride whose name began to appear regularly on the country and western hit charts in the mid-1960s. Pride was not the first to break the color bar in the field; Ray Charles had long been successful with country and western fans with his ballads in this field. However, Charles was basically a blues or popular type singer whereas Charley Pride was an all-out country music performer.

Pride became interested in country and western music as a child in Mississippi. Strangely, no one else in the family had any great leanings toward music. But young Charley loved to listen to country music shows on the radio. He memorized many songs and sang them for his own pleasure. When he was 14, he got enough money together to buy his first guitar. Again, from listening to the various picking styles, he selected his own method of playing. By his late teens, he could perform as well as the best country artist, though he only did it for his own amusement.

His main goal in life was to succeed in sports. He was an excellent baseball player and made the grade with the Memphis Red Sox of the Negro American League in the late 1950s. His ability won him a minor league assignment with the Helena, Montana, team. In 1960, he sang between innings of a ball game in Helena and won an ovation. This encouraged him to sing more. His landlady heard him and helped get him a job singing in a Helena club.

Though Charley enjoyed his sideline, dreams of baseball glory still dominated his thinking. Part of the New York Mets chain, he felt sooner or later he would get a big league try out. Even when country and western great Red Sovine heard him perform in the early 1960s, and offered to get him a record company audition, Charley held off. In 1964 he got his tryout, and when he was sent down again he decided to take Sovine's suggestion. Charley went to Nashville and soon had a contract with RCA Victor. At long last, he decided to make music his aim in life.

His first record, "Snakes Crawl at Night," was cut in August 1965, but wasn't released until January 1966. In a short time it was a top chart song, staying on the list for many weeks. Later in the year, he had another hit with "Just Between You and Me." In 1967, he scored with such singles as "Does My Ring Hurt Your Finger" and "I Know One." His first LP, "Country Charley Pride," was one of the major successes of early 1967.

PROFFITT, FRANK: Singer, guitarist, banjo-ist, instrument maker. Born Laurel Bloomery, Tennessee, 1913; died Vilas, North Carolina, November 24, 1965.

The saga of the song "Tom Dooley" was a strange one—on record and in fact. It became a hit for the Kingston Trio in the late 1950s, but not until several years later did the man who was responsible for the song emerge from the shadows of obscurity as one of the great folk artists of the century.

The song had been collected from Frank Proffitt in the late 1930s by folklorists Anne and Frank Warner. For thirty years they had played it and mentioned its origin in Frank's home in the Tennessee-North Carolina hills.

But no one noticed the name Proffitt until it was almost too late for him to gain any rewards from the song.

The Proffitt family moved to the Cracker Neck section of the eastern Tennessee mountains—the Warners wrote in Sing Out! (Oct.–Nov. 1963, p. 7)—just after the Civil War from Wilkes County, North Carolina. When Frank was a boy, his family moved to Reese, North Carolina, a few miles below the Tennessee border. There Wiley Proffitt earned a living as a farmer, cooper, and tinker.

Young Frank grew up in an atmosphere of folk music. His father, his Aunt Nancy Prather, and his Uncle Noah often sang old songs of the hills. Frank's father also made banjos and passed his skills along to his son. The Warners quote some of Frank's reminiscenses of this:

"As a boy I recall going along with Dad to the woods to get the timber for banjo-making. He selected a tree by its appearance and by sounding . . . hitting a tree with a hammer or axe broadsided to tell by the sound if it's straight grained. . . . When the strings were put on and the pegs turned and musical notes begain to fill the cabin, I looked upon my father as the greatest man on earth for creating such a wonderful thing out of a piece of wood, a greasy skin, and some strings."

Young Frank helped his father run the farm. He managed to finish sixth grade in the rural school before he had to devote all his hours to the farm. He continued his deep interest in music and spent most of his few free hours singing or listening to songs. As he grew older, he took more and more part in local gatherings, trading songs with others from the region and playing the banjo. In 1922, he got his first store-bought instrument when he gathered enough premiums from selling goods of the Lee Manufacturing Company to trade them for a guitar.

In 1932, he married Bessie Hicks, daughter of another musical family of the area, and moved to his own farm in Pick Britches Valley. The years passed much as they had before. The Proffitts raised a family of their own, and farmed, and Frank played and sang whenever he could. In 1938, the Warners met Frank's in-laws while passing through the hill country. Nathan Hicks, in turn, introduced them to Frank. In the next few years, the Warners returned to record 120 of Frank's folk songs. One of these was a ballad about a tragedy involving two local people, Tom Dula and Laurie Foster. Other songs bore such titles as "Dan Doo" and "Moonshine."

The Warners' work was interrupted by World War II, but the relationship was resumed afterwards. The major change came after "Tom Dooley" became the nation's number one song. It began in 1960, with a story about Proffitt by J. C. Brown in The Carolina Farmer. The resulting furor resulted in an invitation for Frank to appear at the University of Chicago's first Folk Festival. Frank was one of the hits of the show. Soon after, Folkways issued the first LP of Frank Proffitt. Other invitations poured in, resulting in his first visit to New York and an appearance at the Country Dance Society's Folk Music Camp near Cape Cod, Massachusetts.

In 1962, the second Proffitt album, "Trifling Woman," was released on the Folk Legacy label. In the mid-1960s, Frank reaped well merited applause from audiences at concerts and festivals in many parts of the country. He was a featured performer at the 1964 and '65 Newport Folk Festivals.

Though his name had become famous in many parts of the world besides the U.S., Frank continued to spend most of his time on his beloved farm in North Carolina. In late 1965, after driving his wife 115 miles to a hospital in Charlotte for a needed foot operation, he returned home in seeming good health. He finished his dinner, lay down on his bed, and died in his sleep on November 24. His meaning to folk music lovers throughout the world was reflected in the many Frank Proffitt memorial concerts given during 1966.

PUCKETT, GEORGE RILEY: See Tanner, Gid

RAINWATER, MARVIN: Singer, guitarist, songwriter. Born Wichita, Kansas, July 2, 1925.

More than one of Marvin Rainwater's songs dealt with the animal kingdom. In fact, it was his composition "Gonna Find Me a Bluebird" that helped give him a start as a professional entertainer. The relationship has a certain amount of symbolism, since he probably would have been a Doctor of Veterinary Medicine if he hadn't chosen performing instead.

He was born and raised in Kansas. His environment was not rural, Wichita being a fair sized city, but Marvin did have a folk heritage based to some extent on his part-Indian ancestry. He could play guitar and sing both popular and folk-country ballads by the time he began his pre-veterinary course at Washington State University in Walla Walla, Washington.

After a year, however, his college career was interrupted by World War II. He went into the Navy and spent three years as a pharmacist's mate. He entertained his shipmates from time to time and began to think seriously of going into show business. When he returned to civilian life, he found a job with a small troupe touring the south and southwest. For the next six years, he continued to pick up experience at small clubs, county fairs, and other events. In his spare time he turned out many kinds of compositions, from classical music to country and western songs.

In the mid-1950s he finally got his big break, an opportunity to audition for Arthur Godfrey's CBS-TV Talent Scouts. He sang "Gonna Find Me a Bluebird" and won both a place on the show and first-place prize. Part of his reward was a brief engagement on Godfrey's CBS radio network morning show. Soon after, he had a highly successful stay at the Shamrock Club in Washington, D.C. He joined the cast of the WWVA Jamboree in Wheeling, West Virginia, for a while, and in the late 1950s became a regular on Red Foley's Jubilee U.S.A.

Marvin turned out a number of records in the 1950s and '60s, mostly for MGM. His first MGM sides were two of his own compositions, "Sticks and Stones" and "Albino Stallion." His other originals included such titles as "I Gotta Go Get My Baby" and "I Miss You Already." Some of his other recordings were "Half Breed," "Whole Lotta Woman," "Tennessee Hound Dog Yodel," "What Am I Supposed to Say," "Why Did You Have to Go and Leave Me," "Dem Low Down Blues," "Where Do We Go From Here?" and "Tea Bag Rodeo."

His MGM LPs included "With a Heart with a Beat"; "Songs by Marvin Rainwater"; and "Marvin Rainwater" ('62).

RAUSCH, LEON: Singer, guitarist, band leader. Born Springfield, Missouri, October 2, 1927.

Heir to a great tradition, Leon Rausch grew to musical maturity in the confines of Bob

Wills' Texas Playboys organization. In the late 1960s, he helped perpetuate Wills' contributions to the country & western field by fronting the New Texas Playboys.

Leon was born and raised in Missouri. His family was musically inclined, and when he was 11 he began to play at local dances with his father, from whom he had already learned many country songs. He continued this through his teens until he entered the U.S. Navy during World War II. When he was discharged three years later, he decided to try for a career as a country & western artist.

For several years he performed in and around Springfield. Then he struck out for greener pastures, moving to Tulsa, Oklahoma, in 1955. He joined Bob Wills' band and continued as a regular and sometimes solo artist until 1961. He then joined the group headed by Bob Wills' brother, Johnnie Lee Wills, remaining with Johnnie until 1964. Soon after, Leon organized the New Texas Playboys. This group took Ft. Worth, Texas, as its headquarters and rapidly became a favorite with many of Bob Wills' old fans in the region.

In 1967, the New Texas Playboys signed with Longhorn Records. The reception for such recordings as "I'm So Glad Mom Can't See Me Now" and "Painted Angels" indicated the group had captured much of the excitement of the old-time Playboys.

RAY, WADE: Singer, violinist, guitarist, actor. Born Evansville, Indiana, April 6, 1913.

A child prodigy is usually associated with the classical field, but more than one top-ranked country and western star started in show business at an early age. Few could point to earlier starts than Wade Ray, who began to earn a living on stage when he was five.

Wade was born in Indiana, but his family moved to Boynton, Arkansas, when he was a few years old. His parents recognized his musical inclinations when he was four and his father made him a crude violin from a cigar box. Young Wade quickly learned to use the home-built instrument and progressed to a better one. He could play so well at five that he made his stage debut as "The Youngest Violin Player in the World." In a short time he learned to play the tenor banjo too. For many years when the family was at home, crowds came to the Ray household on Sundays to hear Wade play.

It wasn't long before Ray was widely featured on the Orpheum Vaudeville Circuit in his home region. By the time he was 10, his fans had given him more than 200 violins to show their regard for his talent. He continued to tour many theaters and county fairs during his teens. When he was 18, in 1931, he joined Pappy Cheshire's National Champion Hillbillies on station KMOX in St. Louis. Young Wade found the atmosphere congenial and remained a major cast member on the show until 1943. At that point, he left to join the armed forces.

When he completed his Army service, he moved to Chicago as a member of the Prairie Ramblers on WLS National Barn Dance. In the 1950s, he began to achieve notice as an individual recording artist and performer. His path turned westward to Los Angeles where he was signed for a two-week appearance at the Cowtown in the early 1950s. The response to his engagement was such that the two-week stay turned into a 10-year association. In the 1950s and '60s, Wade became a frequent attraction at major night spots in Las Vegas, Reno, and Lake Tahoe.

Wade's activities on the Coast included a number of movie roles, personal appearances on many TV country and western shows, and many recording sessions. He also served as a regular cast member of the Roy Rogers Show on ABC-TV. His recordings during these years included such hits as "Heart of a Clown," "The Things I Might Have Been," "Walk Softly" and "I Was Just Walking Out the Door."

In the 1960s, Wade became a member of the Grand Ole Opry. In the mid-1960s, he also was featured on NBC-TV's weekly Ernest Tubb Show. Among the songs he introduced via Nashville telecasts were "Two Red, Red Lips," "Have Yourself a Party," "Burning Desire" and "Country Boy."

His album credits include "Country Sun" on ABC label and "Walk Softly" on Camden (both issued '66).

REED, SUSAN: Singer, instrumentalist (zither, Irish harp). Born Columbia, South Carolina, 1927.

Being born into a theatrical family theoretically has the disadvantage of growing up "on the run." Since the work of Susan Karen Reed's father, Daniel Reed, a noted actor, playwright, and director, took him to many different places, she lived and went to school in many different parts of the country. Besides the south, she spent her grade school and high school years in Los Angeles, Hollywood, and New York.

On the other hand, for a prospective folk artist, the life had many advantages. Her parents were interested in folk music and many house guests were folk artists of the first rank. Among them were Carl Sandburg, Huddie Ledbetter, and many of the Irish Abbey Theatre Players. The latter included two highly gifted performers, Ralph Cullinan and Farrell Pelley, who taught her many traditional Irish songs. The Abbey influence helped her direct her first musical efforts toward learning to play the Irish harp. By the time she was in her teens, she was an excellent harpist. Besides the Irish harp, she also mastered the Appalachian autoharp and the zither.

In the early 1940s, the Reed family went to live in New York and Susan was already receiving compliments for her musical ability. She sang with her church choir and also volunteered her services to entertain hospitalized servicemen during the war. In her mid-teens, she began to sing professionally. In 1944, she won rapt attention from audiences at New York's Cafe Society Uptown nightclub.

She followed this up with many engagements across the U.S. in concert halls and clubs. In 1946, she debuted at Town Hall in New York. In the late 1940s and early 1950s, she added credits from radio and TV appearances, including several NBC network shows.

Before long she signed her first recording contract and, through the 1950s, turned out LPs for a number of labels, including RCA Victor, Elektra, and Columbia. Her RCA album, "I Know My Love," featured ballads from many European countries. These included the Irish title song, "I Know My Love," the Italian "Three Gulls," the Scottish-English "Lord Randal," Scottish "Jennie Jenkins," and the rural U.S. "Go 'Way from My Window." Her first Elektra LP titled "Susan Reed" featured such songs as "Black Is the Color," "The Old Woman," "Drill, Ye Tarriers," "Michie Banjo," "Barbara Allen," "A Mighty Ship," "Go 'Way from My Window," "Mother, I Would Marry," "I'm Sad and I'm Lonely" and "Greensleeves." Her other Elektra LPs included "Susan Reed Sings Old Airs" and, 1954, "Old Airs from Ireland, Scotland and England." In 1958, Columbia Records issued a Susan Reed album called "Folk Songs."

REEVES, DEL: Singer, guitarist, songwriter, disk jockey. Born Sparta, North Carolina, July 14, 1933.

Born in the heart of the country music belt, Del Reeves had to go west to gain a bid from the Grand Ole Opry. His years on the Coast brought a close association with the film colony, as well, resulting in roles in such films as "Gold Guitar," "Forty Acre Feud," "Cotton-pickin' Chickenpickers," and "Second Fiddle to a Steel Guitar."

Del was born and raised in North Carolina. He could sing many country and western songs by the time he was in his teens and he performed at a number of local functions. In the 1950s, he headed west to try to break into the music field. He emceed and performed in a number of country shows in California, building up a reputation among both fans and TV executives. In the late 1950s, this resulted in his own TV show. For four years, into the early 1960s, Del fronted the show and became acquainted with many of the top artists in the field. For two years during this period, he was featured on the "Golden Strip" of Las Vegas.

By the beginning of the 1960s, he was beginning to make his mark as a songwriter as well as a performer. He composed many songs with his wife, Ellen, that were recorded by such artists as Roy Drusky, Carl Smith, Rose Maddox and Sheb Wooley.

He also signed as an artist with Decca Records. In 1961, he turned out his first top 10 hit, "Be Quiet Mind." For the next few years, many of his efforts were widely played, but none made best-seller rank. He changed to the United Artists label and soon turned out two of the top country and western records of 1965, "The Belles of Southern Bell" and "Girl on the Billboard." The latter became one of the national favorites of 1965, holding down number one spot for many weeks. During this period, Del turned out several hits that just missed top 10 status, such as "One Bum Town" and "Blame It on My Do Wrong." He made the charmed circle again in 1966 with his recording of "Women Do Funny Things to Me." The year 1966 also saw Del moving to Nashville as a regular on the Grand Ole Opry.

REEVES, JIM: Singer, guitarist, songwriter. Born Panola County, Texas, August 20, 1924; died July 31, 1964. Elected to Country Music Hall of Fame, 1967.

The loyalty of country and western fans to their favorite performers is a phenomenon that is matched in few segments of the music field. This loyalty accounts for the almost personal feeling of loss among Jim Reeves' fans after his death in a plane crash, demonstrated in part by the way they kept subsequently released recordings on the top rungs of the hit charts.

Born in rural Texas, James Reeves was more interested in sports than music as a boy. He already was a standout athlete in elementary school. By the time he entered junior high school in Carthage, Texas, he was marked as a prime prospect for future sports stardom. By this time, he had gained a certain amount of proficiency with the guitar. He had learned to play before entering high school, though he did it in secret for fear of kidding from friends.

In high school, he quickly became a star of the baseball team. At the same time, to earn pin money and to start saving for a hoped-for college education, he performed at local dances and high school events. By his sophomore year at the University of Texas at Austin, he was first string pitcher for the team. Scouts for the St. Louis Cardinals organization were impressed and signed him up. He left college for the Cardinals' Lynchburg, Virginia, farm team.

The team considered him a top prospect and he responded with some excellent pitching performances. Then he injured his leg sliding into second base. The leg did not heal properly and the doctors told him to forget baseball. He turned to entertainment as his only other talent.

Though he enjoyed playing the guitar and singing, Reeves did not think of a career as a musician right away. He did have a good speaking voice and a knowledge of country music. This won him a job as an announcer, and by the early 1950s he was a regular on the staff of station KWKH in Shreveport. He performed occasionally in his spare time and cut some records on the Abbott label. One of these, "Mexican Joe," caught on with the public. To Reeves' surprise, he had a top 10 hit to his credit.

He accepted a bid to join the cast of the Louisiana Hayride that year. His stock went up when he scored a second top 10 success with "Bimbo" on Fairways Records. In 1954, he had a third national hit, his duet with Ginny Wright on Fabor Records, "I Love You." By now he was gaining attention from top music business executives. RCA Victor offered him a contract and he began a relationship that lasted his entire career. From 1955 to 1968, Reeves had one or more top 10 records every year. He scored his initial number-one-ranked national hit in 1955 for RCA with "Yonder Comes a Sucker," his own composition.

By 1955, Reeves had made several guest appearances on the Grand Ole Opry. By the end of the 1950s, he was a regular on the Nashville show. In 1954, he made his first worldwide tour, accompanying a USO group to play for servicemen in Europe. In later years, Reeves made four more tours, performing for American troops throughout the world. In 1957 he was given his own daily show on ABC-TV. He also was featured on most major TV shows, country and western and popular, in the late '50s, including Ed Sullivan, Steve Allen, Dick Clark's American Bandstand, and Jimmy Dean. He continued this pattern in the early 1960s. His travels from 1960 through mid-'64 took him to all fifty states and all parts of the world. In 1962, he received tumultuous welcomes from crowds throughout Africa and Europe. His immense popularity in Europe is shown by his record sales figure in Norway, which topped all other artists. Through 1967, Norwegian fans had provided Jim with 16 gold, silver, platinum and diamond disks.

In his recording career in the U.S., Reeves scored more top 10 hits than any other artist with the exception of Eddy Arnold and Webb Pierce. In 1956, he had "According to My Heart" and "My Lips Are Sealed." His other hits of the 1950s included "Am I Losing You," his own composition, and "Four Walls" ('57); "Anna Marie," "Blue Boy" and number-one-ranked "Billy Bayou" ('58); his all-time best-seller, "He'll Have to Go," and "Home" ('59). Beginning in 1955, Reeves was backed on both records and tours by his own group, The Blue Boys.

Reeves continued into the 1960s with a rush, scoring four top hits in 1960, his own "Am I Losing You"; "I Know One"; "I Missed Me"; and "I'm Getting Better." He turned out ten more top 10 hits between the start of 1961 and mid-'64, "The Blizzard" ('61); "Adios Amigo," "What I Feel in My Heart," "I'm Gonna Change Everything" and "Losing Your Love" ('62); "Guilty," "Is This Me" ('63); number-one-ranked "I Guess I'm Crazy," "Love

Is No Excuse" (with Dottie West), "Welcome to My World" ('64).

In July 1964, returning home to Nashville from an engagement, Reeves met death when his private plane crashed in a thunderstorm. But his voice was not stilled; under direction of his widow, Mary, previously unreleased recordings added to her husband's legend. Jim was represented on the hit charts by many more best-sellers in 1965-67, including three number-one-ranked songs. These included "I Won't Forget You" and number-one songs "Is It Really Over" and "This Is It" in '65 and "Snow Flake" and number-one "Distant Drums" in 1966. His posthumous honors continued in 1967, with number-one-ranked "I Won't Come in While He's There."

The album of "Distant Drums" also was one of the gold-record-sellers for 1966. Jim had scored $1,000,000 in sales for many of his LPs, which included such titles as "Bimbo" ('55); "Jim Reeves" ('57); "Girls I Have Known" ('58); "God Be with You," "Warm the Heart" ('59); "He'll Have to Go," "According to My Heart," "Intimate Side of Jim Reeves" ('60); "To Your Heart," "Tall Tales" ('61); "Country Side," "Touch of Velvet," "We Thank Thee" ('62); "Gentleman Jim," "Good 'n' Country," "International Jim Reeves" ('63); "Kimberley Jim," "Moonlight and Roses," "Have I Told You Lately" ('64); "Jim Reeves Way" ('65); "Yours Sincerely," "Blue Side of Lonesome" ('67); "Touch of Sadness" ('68).

REID, DON: See Statler Brothers

REID, HAROLD: *See* Statler Brothers

REYNOLDS, MALVINA: Singer, guitarist, songwriter. Born Berkeley, California, 1901.

In early 1964, an unusual song made its way to the top of the popular hit charts. Called "Little Boxes," it did not have a particularly new melody nor was the subject of the lyric particularly new—except in music. The words were an ironic commentary on conformity. The composition as a whole capsuled the subject in a way that many articles and learned treatises failed to do.

The song represented a typical post-World War II composed "folk" song. Malvina Reynolds had long been famed in folk music circles for her contributions to this art, but the un-syrupy sentiments of "Little Boxes" brought her to the attention of a national audience.

Malvina's interest in folk material went back to her college days. She received her Ph.D. from the University of California at Berkeley after writing her thesis about a medieval folk tale. In the years that followed, she continued to study many aspects of folklore. She also tried her hand at writing, turning out both fiction and poetry. By the end of the 1930s, though, she still felt she had not yet found her main creative domain.

Her interest in folk music began when she listened to an old 78 rpm record of John Jacob Niles singing "Cherry Tree Carol." In the early 1940s, she began to concentrate on folk music when she got her first guitar. As she recalled in her Oak Publications songbook, "What an instrument that was! A big old F-hole orange crate with a crack in the back. . . ."

After mastering the guitar, she began to write songs in 1943. Slowly word of her talents began to spread until some of her songs were added to the repertoire of The Almanac Singers. In the years that followed, such artists as Pete Seeger and Woody Guthrie often sang some of her compositions.

In the 1950s and '60s, she had achieved recognition as one of the top writers in the modern folk vein. She also was asked to play her guitar and sing her own and other folk songs at festivals in many parts of the country.

Her output in the 1950s included "Magic Penny" ('55); "Bury Me in My Overalls" ('56); "Bring Flowers," "Let Us Come in," "Little Land," "Nobody," "Pied Piper," "We Don't Need the Men" ('58); "Don't Talk to Me of Love," "Faucets Are Dripping," "Oh, Doctor," "Patchwork of Dreams," "Somewhere Between," "The Little Mermaid," "The Miracle," "There'll Come a Time," "We Hate to See Them Go," "Where Is the Little Street" ('59). Two of her best known songs of these years were collaborations. In 1957, she provided the words to Woody Guthrie's music for "Sally, Don't You Grieve" and, with Alan Greene, wrote "Turn Around." (The latter song was used for years in an Eastman Kodak commercial.)

Her 1960 copyrights included "From Way Up Here," written with Pete Seeger ('62) and such others as "Alone," "Dialectic," "Let It Be," "Sausalito Fire," "The Desert" ('60); "Quiet," "Rand Hymn," "Temptation," "The

Emperor's Nightingale," "This World," "Upside Down" ('61); "Andorra," "I Wish You Were Here," "Little Boxes," "You Can't Make a Turtle Come Out" ('62). In 1963, she turned out a song that became a favorite with singers Joan Baez and Bob Dylan. Called "What Have They Done to the Rain," it was an anti-atom bomb message. Like many of her compositions, it reflected her standing as one of the pioneer writers of the post-World War II genre of protest songs.

In 1963, Oak Publications issued a book of her songs titled *Little Boxes and Other handmade Songs by Malvina Reynolds.*

RICE PADDY RANGER: *See* Curless, Dick

RICH, DON: *See* Buckaroos, The

RINZLER, RALPH: Singer, mandolin player, folk music collector, folk festival official. Born New Jersey.

When the Newport Folk Festival was reactivated in the early 1960s after a two-year hiatus, there were many favorable comments on its improved balance. In addition to the "names," the best-selling record artists, there was a good leavening of traditional folk performers providing new insight into the history and meaning of the music. The man responsible for the progress in programming was a young traditional music buff from the urban north, Ralph Rinzler.

Rinzler was born and raised in the New York-New Jersey area. His parents introduced him to classical music at an early age. As he grew up, however, his tastes slowly turned towards the folk genre. He learned to play the mandolin and concentrated on collecting traditional folk song material from books and records.

When he finished school, it looked for a time as though music would remain a sideline. Ralph considered making air transportation his career. As an executive trainee with British Overseas Airways Co., he got his first taste of world travel. In the mid-1950s, though, he decided to give it up in favor of a full-time music career.

During the 1950s, he helped found a New York group devoted to preserving the country's traditional folk heritage. In time, his association with the group, the "Friends of Old-Time Folk Music," helped introduce him to many great old-time folk, country and western artists. He performed in coffee houses and with close friends in the folk field.

In 1959, Ralph was asked to join the Bluegrass group called the Greenbriar Boys. For the next five years, he toured widely with the group and was featured with them on a number of Elektra LPs. His work in traditional music led to a sideline, this time as friend and manager of three top artists, Bill Monroe, Doc Watson, and Tom Ashley, beginning in 1960.

When Newport Folk Festival producer George Wein began looking for someone to search out new talent for the event, Rinzler's name was prominently mentioned by members of the Board of Directors. For a number of years, Rinzler had spent much of his spare time in the field collecting folk material. He was offered the position of Talent and Folklore Coordinator for the Festival and accepted. When he left the Greenbriar Boys in 1964, Frank Wakefield took his place.

From 1964 to 1967, Rinzler spent many months of the year searching out folk and country artists and recording their performances. His average travel per year in this role came to about 12,000 miles. From the standpoint of folklorists and Newport audiences, the results were eminently satisfactory. (*See also* GREENBRIAR BOYS)

RITCHIE FAMILY: Family noted for folk music repertoire through many generations.

The folk music tradition of handing down songs from generation to generation is nowhere more evident than in the history of the Ritchie Family of Kentucky. This family could trace its origins directly to England and, since having always been strongly motivated to sing folk songs, its members could also relate many of their songs to traditional English roots.

The Ritchie family comprised many branches in many parts of the U.S., but the one most important from a folk song standpoint was that located in the Cumberland Mountains of Kentucky. This branch traced its origins to James Ritchie, who came to Virginia from England in 1768 with five brothers. He married a woman whose maiden name was Keith, by whom he had eleven children, including five boys, and he took part in the Revolutionary War.

In the years after the war he moved from Virginia to Buncombe County, North Carolina, and then to Carrs Fork in eastern Kentucky. He died in Carrs Fork and all the family returned to Virginia except his son Crockett. Crockett, considered the main founder of the family's singing traditions, married Susan Grigsby and settled in Hammond's Gap, Kentucky. Crockett, who loved to hunt, party and sing, passed along many traditional songs to his children and to other relations. He also collected new songs from his brothers and from neighbors. Among the songs preserved in this manner were "Nottamun Town" (Nottingham, England), "Lord Bateman," "Old Sally Buck," and "Killy Kranky."

Crockett's children were named Nick, Isom, Hiram, John, Gabe, Elic, Ora, Polly, Oma, Betty, and Nancy. Most of them moved elsewhere, but John married Sylvania Sizemore and remained in the Cumberland area raising ten children of his own (Austin, Nicolas, Ned, Elic, John, Rhoda, Vina, Betts, Anna, and Kizzie). Again, there was a scattering when the children grew up. Austin Ritchie helped continue the family singing tradition after his marriage to Rachel Everidge. Their children also numbered ten: Wash, Joe, Balis, Isaac, Anderson, Mary, Sarah, Martha, Betty Jane, and Polly.

Though many of these children continued to maintain an interest in singing the old songs, Balis Ritchie was the most enthusiastic in this direction. His marriage to Abigail Hall resulted in the twentieth century generations consisting of Raymond, Truman, Balis Wilmer, May, Ollie, Mallie, Una, Kitty, Patty, Edna, Jewel, Opal, Pauline, and Jean Ritchie, the youngest in the family, was to go on to gain worldwide attention among folklorists for herself and for her family.

The family had achieved note among folk music collectors before her birth. One of the pioneer collectors, Cecil Sharp, visited Balis Ritchie and his family in 1917 to mark down many of the songs the Ritchies knew. Balis was born in Clear Creek, Knott County, Kentucky, and lived there for a while after his marriage. He then moved to Hindman, Kentucky, for a time, before settling on a farm near Viper, Kentucky.

Beginning in the 1920s, the family slowly achieved a reputation in academic circles. Though they continued to sing as a hobby, there were more and more visits from folk song collectors. When the Archive of American Folk Song was established in the Library of Congress, the Lomaxes recorded a number of Ritchie Family renditions for the collection.

In the years after World War II, the Ritchies were represented by several LPs, including the Folkways album "The Ritchie Family." The story of the family and words and music for 42 of their songs were recounted by Jean Ritchie in a 1955 book, *Singing Family of the Cumberlands*. The book was re-issued in paperback form by Oak Publications in 1963. (*See also* RITCHIE, JEAN)

RITCHIE, JEAN: Singer, dulcimer player, guitarist, songwriter, author, folk music collector. Born Viper, Crockett County, Kentucky, December 8, 1922.

The youngest member of a family of fourteen musically minded children might seem at a disadvantage. Often, though, the youngest just "tries harder," in any field. In Jean Ritchie's case, she grew up to become the best known of the family name, the catalyst that helped bring international attention to the folk music heritage represented by the large and talented Ritchie clan.

Her birthplace was the tiny hamlet of Viper, deep in the Cumberland Mountains of Kentucky. Her father, Balis Ritchie, had taught school in the nearby town of Dwarf before marrying her mother, Abigail Hall, of Viper. Jean was a pleasant surprise; her mother was 44 when Jean came into the world, and her parents had been married for some 29 years. By the time Jean was born, the Ritchie family had been living on a farm in Viper for close to six years.

Though the house looked more like a dormitory, it was a lively and happy place to be. The children had to help tend the cornfield in summer as soon as they were old enough to lend a hand. When work was done, however, all looked forward to evenings of fun and visits from friends and family. A good part of the time, these hours were devoted to singing and playing the banjo, guitar, dulcimer, and fiddle.

In warm weather, these sings often were held out of doors, but in winter, Jean spent many hours around the fireplace listening to her Granny Katty or other close relatives tell folk tales or ghost stories and sing such ghostly folk songs as "There Was an Old Woman All Skin and Bones" and "My Good Old Man."

As Jean grew up, she learned many new songs

every year from her family and others in the vicinity. Singing was an integral part of life in the Cumberlands. The people sang as they worked in the fields, joined with their neighbors in sings at socials and other events, and sang lustily in church on Sundays. Many of the songs were traditional folk songs handed down and modified by generations of settlers. In the case of the Ritchies, some of the songs the family sang had been brought from England by James Ritchie, Jean's great-great grandfather, in 1768.

Among the songs Jean learned during these years were "Fair Ellender," "Hush Little Baby," "Twilight A-Stealing," "Darby's Ram," "Old King Cole," "Shady Grove," "Somebody," "I'm Goin' to Boston," "I've Been a Foreign Lander," "Maria" and "Old Tyler." These and many other songs made the Ritchie family one of the best known in the entire region for their repertoire. During Jean's childhood, folk music collectors came to the house on several occasions to note down some of the songs her family sang.

She continued to sing and learn new songs as she progressed through grade school and the new high school at Viper. Though it was a spartan existence, the Ritchie children got good educations and many completed college. Before she too went to college, Jean learned to play the dulcimer from her father, one of the best dulcimer players in the region.

In the early 1940s, Jean went to the University of Kentucky in Lexington, from which she received her B.A. in the mid-1940s. In recognition of her scholarship, she was given the Founder's Day Award. She impressed both instructors and classmates with her knowledge of folklore and traditional music. Her interest and reputation in the field increased steadily in the years after graduation from Kentucky. She gave many folk concerts in eastern and southeastern states and also received a Fulbright scholarship to research folk songs in Great Britain.

With the great interest in folk material in the 1950s and '60s, the Ritchie name became known from coast to coast. Besides singing traditional material during these years, she wrote original songs or variations of older songs, including "A Tree in the Valley-O," "The Cuckoo She's a Pretty Bird," "Let the Sun Shine Down on Me" and "What'll I Do with the Baby-O." She also turned out several books of collected folk songs: *The Swapping Song*

Book, From Fair to Fair, and *Folk Songs of the Southern Appalachians.*

Her credits named appearances at many major folk festivals, including those at the University of Chicago, University of California at Berkeley, and the Newport Folk Festivals of 1963, '64, '65, '66, and '67. When the Newport event was reorganized in 1963, she was a member of the original Board of Directors and remained as a member of the Foundation after completing her director's term.

Jean's LP total included albums on several labels. For Elektra, she provided "Jean Ritchie" and for Prestige, "Best of Jean Ritchie" ('61). Her largest LP output was for Folkways, including "Ritchie Family of Kentucky," "Child Ballads in America" (2 LPs—'61), and "Precious Memories" ('62).

In 1955, she paid tribute to her family by writing the autobiographical *Singing Family of the Cumberlands*. The paperback edition of this book was published by Oak Publications, New York, in 1963. (*See also* RITCHIE FAMILY)

RITTER, TEX: Singer, guitarist, songwriter, author, actor. Born Panola County, Texas, January 12, 1906. Elected to Country Music Hall of Fame, 1964.

No one is more closely identified with twentieth century interest in things western than Tex Ritter. His credits as performer and writer cover almost every major phase of western lore from cowboy songs to a pioneering radio program, The Lone Ranger.

His early background gave him a legitimate claim to a cowboy image. Maurice Woodward Ritter was born on Texas land that had been settled by his grandfather in 1830, when Texas was still part of Mexico. In the family tradition, his father ran a thriving spread, raising cotton, corn, peanuts, hogs and cattle. Tex had hardly learned to walk when he began to learn the basics of roping and riding. He grew up in an atmosphere much like that recreated in countless western movies, with cattle roundups and ranch hands spinning tall stories or singing songs in their off-hours in the bunkhouse.

Tex became a skilled rider, and, in his teens, also demonstrated an excellent singing voice. However, he gave little thought to an entertainment career, enrolling in the University of Texas in the early 1920s as a law major. He impressed his classmates and instructors with his knowledge of Texas folklore. He was often asked to talk about the stories and songs he'd learned in his youth. The great interest in this material caused him eventually to work out a combined singing and lecturing program.

Invitations to give the show, called "The Texas Cowboy and His Songs," caused him to wander further and further afield from the University. When one tour took him to Chicago, he settled there for a while and enrolled in Northwestern University to continue his law studies. He sang on local stations and audience acceptance made him think of trying for bigger things in the radio field. After a year in Chicago, he moved on to New York.

It took a lot of persuasion for New York radio programmers to give him a crack at the local air waves. Many doubted that eastern audiences would take to his strong Texas drawl. Finally he got his chance, though, and before long mailbags full of fan mail convinced producers he had something to offer.

From then on, Tex became one of the major factors in both eastern and national radio. As a writer and performer, he had a key part in the original Lone Ranger series. His work won the close attention of radio executives, which quickly resulted in other work. During the 1930s, he performed on such major radio shows as Death Valley Days, Tex Ritter's Camp Fire, and Cowboy Tom's Round Up. During these years, he also turned out the first of many records, starting him on the road toward the top in western singing.

Tex also showed his ability as an actor while living in New York. He was given a major role in a new Theatre Guild play of the 1930s called "Green Grow the Lilacs." This play, written by Lynn Riggs, gave graphic insight into the lives of people in the ranch country of Tex's boyhood. The show provided the basis for the blockbusting Rodgers and Hammerstein musical "Oklahoma!"

In the late 1930s, Hollywood beckoned. Tex moved west once more to become one of the most active performers in movie westerns of the 1940s and '50s. By the early 1950s, he had appeared in more than 50 westerns for Monogram, Columbia, and Universal. When not making films, he toured the country coast to coast with his own company, playing to

Two Grand Ole Opry mainstays, Grant Turner and Tex Ritter, in April '65

[252]

enthusiastic audiences at theaters, rodeos, and state fairs. His personal magnetism continued unabated through the 1960s, though his schedule was not quite as hectic as in earlier years. In the 1950s and '60s he also was featured on many TV shows, both general variety and country and western.

Once settled in California, Tex moved to expand his recording work. In the mid-1940s, he signed with Capitol Records, a relationship still going strong in the late 1960s. His early work for Capitol included such albums as "Children's Songs and Stories by Tex Ritter," "Cowboy Favorites by Tex Ritter," "Tex Ritter and the Dinning Sisters," and "Sunday School for Children." His singles output, including some recordings of his own compositions, covered such titles as "Someone," "There's a Gold Star in Her Window," "There's a New Moon Over My Shoulder," "Jealous Heart," "You Two-Timed Me One Time Too Often," "One Little Tear Drop Too Late," "Have I Told You Lately That I Love You," "Rye Whiskey," "Boll Weevil," "Dallas Darlin'," "Deck of Cards," "Ft. Worth Jail," "You Are My Sunshine," "Bad Brahma Bull," "I've Got Five Dollars and It's Saturday Night," "Pledge of Allegiance," "The Fiery Bear," and "Blood on the Saddle."

In 1948, Tex scored a major national hit with his top 10 recording of "Rock and Rye Rag." His version of "Daddy's Last Letter" was a top 10 success in 1950. With Eddie Dean and H. Sothern, he wrote and recorded the 1961 best-selling "I Dreamed of a Hillbilly Heaven." The year 1967 showed Tex still a hit performer with the best-selling hit "Just Beyond the Moon," and the classic "High Noon."

Tex's LP output on Capitol include such albums as "Songs" ('58); "Blood on the Saddle" ('60); and "Border Affair" ('63).

Tex took an active part in industry affairs and served as an officer of several industry organizations. His great contributions as a performer and his personal integrity were recognized by his election as one of the first six members of the Country Music Hall of Fame in Nashville.

ROBBINS, MARTY: Singer, guitarist, songwriter. Born Glendale, Arizona, September 26, 1925.

First and foremost a country and western artist, Marty Robbins held sway for many years as the idol of the teenage set. Thus his dozens of hits dotted the charts of both country and western and popular fields.

Though he sang rock 'n' roll, gospels, and blues, most of his songs had a strong western flavor, reflecting his boyhood years, of which the first twelve were lived in the small town of Glendale, Arizona. He enjoyed cowboy movies and other normal boyhood pursuits, without having any strong bent toward music. His family moved to Phoenix in 1937 and Marty attended high school there.

When Marty was 19, he signed up for a three-year hitch in the Navy. While serving in the Pacific, he became interested in the guitar and learned how to play. To while away the time he soon began to compose his own songs. After his discharge, he went home to Phoenix with a half-formed idea of continuing his music efforts. A friend of his had a band in a local nightclub and Marty began to appear with him on occasion. The audience reaction was good and he was soon hired as a regular.

By the late 1940s, he was becoming well known among country and western fans in the region. He moved up to having his own radio show which gave way in time to his own TV show, Western Caravan. By the early 1950s, Marty was receiving bids to perform in many other states of the west as well as on West Coast radio and TV. He soon was well enough regarded for several guest shots on the Grand Ole Opry. In 1953, he was asked to become a regular on the Opry, a role in which he was still starring some sixteen years later.

Columbia Records signed him in the early 1950s and many of his records soon showed up on national hit charts. His first really big year was 1953, when two of his own compositions, "I Couldn't Keep from Crying" and "I'll Go on Alone," were top 10 hits. After a one-year hiatus from top 10 ranks, Marty scored once more in 1955 with "That's All Right." From then through 1969, he had one or more national country and western hits every year.

In 1956, he turned out the first of many number-one successes, "Singing the Blues." In 1957, he had three top 10 songs, two of which were number one in the nation a good part of the year. These were "Knee Deep in the Blues," "The Story of My Life," and "White Sport Coat." The last of these, which he wrote, catapulted Marty into overall national fame, hitting number one on every popular poll.

Marty's dual role as country and western and popular favorite picked up steam as the '50s drew to a close with such hits as his 1958 composition "She Was Only Seventeen," the 1958 "Stairway of Love," and his number-one hit composition of 1959, "El Paso."

He started off the 1960s with another national hit, "Big Iron." From 1961 to '67, he added ten more top 10 successes to his score. These included his own compositions, "Don't Worry (Like All the Other Times)" and "It's Your World" ('61); "Devil Woman" ('62); "Beggin' to You" (number one, '63); "One of These Days," "The Cowboy in the Continental Suit" ('64). His hit records by other writers included "Ruby Ann" (number one, '62); "Ribbon of Darkness" (number one, '65); "The Shoe Goes on the Other Foot Tonight" ('66); "Tonight, Carmen" ('67).

During his many years on Columbia Records, Marty had many successful LPs as well. These included "Song of Robbins" ('57); "Marty Robbins," "Song of the Islands" ('58); "Greatest Hits," "Gunfighter Ballads" ('59); "More Gunfighter Ballads" ('60); "More Greatest Hits," "Just Sentimental" ('61); "After Midnight," "Portrait of Marty Robbins," "Devil Woman" ('62); "Hawaii's Calling Me," "Return of Marty Robbins" ('63); "Island Woman," "R.F.D." ('64); "Turn the Lights Down" ('65).

Marty's varied talents led to appearances on most major TV shows in the nation from Ed Sullivan and the Dick Clark American Bandstand to the top country and western shows. His tours also covered all the states and many foreign nations.

ROBERTSON, DON: Singer, instrumentalist (piano, organ, trumpet, trombone, tenor horn), arranger, composer, conductor. Born Peking, China, December 5, 1922.

Few songwriters in the country and western field could claim as many successes as Donald Irwin Robertson. The greatest artists in the post-World War II decades beat a path to his door for new song hits. But Robertson's contributions went beyond this. His background as a skilled musician led to development of several advances in piano styles. These include creation of the "country style" of piano, later popularized by Floyd Cramer, and an adaptation of the Bluegrass banjo pickin' sound for the keyboard.

Don was introduced to music at the age of four by his mother, a talented amateur pianist and poet. The family was then living in China, where Don's father was head of the Department of Medicine at Peking Union Medical College. When Don was five, the family moved to Boston, then Chicago, where Dr. Robertson served as a professor at the University of Chicago. Young Don continued his piano lessons and began composing at seven. His first bent was classical music, particularly since his father often listened to symphonies in the evenings. Don also enjoyed singing hymns during these years in his church choir.

When Don was 9, the family began spending summer vacations at Birchwood Beach in Michigan. Nearby was the home of the Carl Sandburg family. The families became close friends and Don learned many folk and western ballads at Carl's knee as well as receiving instruction in guitar chording.

Don's interest in music continued to increase when he entered high school. In order to join the school band, he learned several brass instruments. Meanwhile, he began to play piano with local dance bands, becoming a professional musician at 14. His father hoped Don would follow in his footsteps and Don did take a pre-med course at the University of Chicago. However, his conflicting emotions finally were resolved in favor of music; he dropped out of college in his fourth year. Soon after, he was working as a musical arranger at station WGN in the Windy City.

In 1945 Don moved to Los Angeles, playing in nightclubs and augmenting his living by making demonstration records of new songs for publishers and songwriters. This eventually led to a job as a demonstration pianist with Capitol Records. Don had written many kinds of music up to this time, including symphonies and jazz compositions. Now he began to concentrate on folk and country material, reflecting the earlier influence of Carl Sandburg.

After many months of turndowns from singers and publishers, Don finally clicked with Hill and Range in 1953. The firm placed three of his songs with such singers as Rosemary Clooney, Eddy Arnold, and Frankie Laine and one, "I Let Her Go," was a mild hit. In 1954, however, Don's career moved into high gear as Eddy Arnold scored a major hit with "I Really Don't Want to Know." The song became a country standard, providing Don with a BMI

Award, a total of more than 50 versions by different recording artists, and sales of more than five million through 1969. Hank Snow also had a hit in '54 with Don's "I Don't Hurt Anymore," which stayed on the charts for half a year.

Don hit with song after song for the balance of the 1950s. His successes included "You're Free to Go" (Carl Smith); "Condemned Without Trial" (Eddy Arnold); "Unfaithful" (Hank Snow); "Go Back You Fool" (Faron Young); "Hummingbird" (Les Paul and Mary Ford); "Born to Be with You" (The Chordettes); "I'm Counting on You" (Elvis Presley, Kitty Wells); and "Please Help Me, I'm Falling" (Hank Locklin). The latter, which gained Don an ASCAP Award, sold more than two million records.

In 1956, Don scored a major hit with his own recording of "The Happy Whistler." During the 1950s and '60s, Don also provided piano or other instrumental backing for many top artists and groups, including Nat Cole, Elvis Presley, Norman Luboff Choir, Kay Starr, Clebanoff Strings, and Jerry Wallace. During these years he wrote twelve songs especially for Elvis Presley, including "Anything That's a Part of You," "There's Always Me," "Marguerita," "They Remind Me Too Much of You," "Love Me Tonight," "No More" and "I'm Yours."

During the 1960s, Don continued to turn out hit compositions. These included "I Love You More and More Each Day" (Al Martino); "Does He Mean That Much to You" (Eddy Arnold); "Ninety Miles an Hour," "I Stepped Over the Line," "The Queen of Draw Poker Town" (Hank Snow); "Wallpaper Roses" (Jerry Wallace); "Go Away" (Nancy Wilson); "Ringo" (Lorne Greene); "Longing to Hold You Again" (Skeeter Davis); "Outskirts of Town," "Watching My World Fall Apart" (The Browns).

RCA Victor issued an LP on which Don played a dozen of his hits, titled, "Heart on My Sleeve." In 1966 he signed a new contract with Victor for recordings under the supervision of A&R producer Chet Atkins.

When the Country Music Hall of Fame was opened in 1967, Don's name was one of those proudly displayed in the "Walkway of Stars."

ROBERTSON, ECK: Fiddler. Born Amarillo, Texas, 1880s.

There must be something invigorating about old-time fiddle playing—so many of these performers lived such long and full lives. A. C. "Eck" Robertson, considered one of the most skilled of the old-time fiddlers, began his career in the 1890s and was still going strong in the 1960s.

Robertson was raised in rural West Texas and learned the fiddle at an early age. He worked at many odd jobs as a boy and played for local socials in his spare time. Word got around when top-flight fiddlers were in the region and he and his brothers walked hundreds of miles on foot to hear them. Eck picked up many pointers from listening to visiting fiddlers and attending major fiddle contests in the region.

By the turn of the century, he was already well regarded as a fiddle player by people in the West Texas region. In the first two decades after 1900, Eck moved around Texas playing in fiddle contests or providing background music for early movies. One of his innovations as he did this was to appear in full western costume. Some folklorists credit him with pioneering the wearing of western garb by country and western artists.

Civil War veteran conventions also provided Eck with employment. At the 1922 meeting in Virginia, Eck met fiddler Henry Gilliland and the two decided to go to New York to try to make records. They managed to get a tryout with Victor. After they had returned home, Victor released some of their numbers. Their rendition of "Sally Goodin'," in particular, has long been considered one of the all-time-great fiddle performances.

Eck's routine changed little through the 1920s. Though Victor wanted to make more Robertson disks, they didn't know where to find him. Finally, in 1930, Ralph Peer located him and a session was held for Eck and his family. This might have launched a major recording career for Robertson, but the Depression intervened.

In the mid-1930s, Eck was featured on a Dallas radio station. He was little known outside Texas, but he was in demand for local events in his home state throughout the 1930s and '40s. He continued to be a major figure at fiddling contests throughout the southwest and won prizes in many of them. In the 1950s, interest in Robertson revived nationally with the new folk music trend. The 1951 Folkways Anthology focused attention on Eck through

[255]

inclusion of his "Brilliancy Medley." At about the time the record was released, Eck was going strong in still another Texas fiddling contest. In 1962, he traveled all the way to Idaho for a contest and won first prize in the old-time fiddler's category.

Eck's virtuosity was emphasized by John Cohen of the New Lost City Ramblers in Sing Out! (April-May 1964, p. 57): "On the record of "Sally Goodin'," one can hear more than a dozen variations on the simple theme. There are syncopated passages, single-string, double-string harmonies, blues notes, drone notes, short rapid grace notes which sound more like piping, and themes played entirely high up on the fingerboard as well as those in the first position."

ROBERTSON, WALT: Singer, guitarist. Born Omaha, Nebraska, 1928.

Born in the midwest, Walter Robertson started out with the wandering urge. As he once noted, he opened the front gate at home when he was 18 months old, and ran a mile and a half down the road before his mother found him—and has been moving around ever since. Though he did eventually settle on Seattle as his home base, his many years of traveling provided him with an impressive collection of folk songs from all parts of the world.

He actually didn't start his ramblings until he was in his teens. Once he started, though, he tried a succession of jobs that almost matched in variety and number the U.S. states and foreign countries he visited. For a while he followed the harvests from Texas to North Dakota to California, shocking wheat and picking peaches and apples. Over the years, he also worked as grocery clerk, lumberjack, U.S. Forest Service firefighter, bank teller, draftsman, carpenter, cab driver, ranch hand, salesman, and counselor in a camp for delinquent boys.

As he reported in the biographical notes for his first Folkways album, "American Northwest Ballads," all along the way he collected folk music and learned to play guitar. He learned ". . . from a foreman I had once when I was fighting forest fires (he only had three fingers on one hand and tuned his guitar a special way), a ship's doctor on a Dutch ship who showed me that the guitar could be a classical instrument, and from a young woman singing to her unborn baby and who didn't know I was listening. . . ."

By the start of the 1950s, he was beginning to build up experience as a singer and guitarist. His performances covered the gamut of locales from small cafes and coffee houses to "sidewalk cafes in Paris, a dusty road in West Virginia, society parties on Philadelphia's main line, in mountain lodges and dude ranches and fancy supper clubs, at revival meetings and on radio and TV."

He found Seattle, Washington, one of the places he enjoyed the most. For a year in the 1950s, he was featured on his own TV show on station KING. As his reputation grew with other folk artists, he also was invited to appear on national hookups from both coasts and also took part in many campus and concert hall hoots. His association with the northwest led to his first Folkways LP. Issued in 1955, "American Northwest Ballads" included such songs as "Wandering," "Puget Sound," "Life Is a Toil," "The Frozen Logger," "I Have Led a Good Life," "The Portland County Jail," "The Mule in the Mines," "Moonshiner," "HooRoo, Johnny," "The Sow Took the Measles," "Sugar Hill," and "Bile Them Cabbage Down."

Soon after completing this LP, he entered the U.S. Army and was assigned to Germany. While there he joined the Seventh Army Repertory Company and acted in such plays as "My Three Angels" and "The Caine Mutiny Court Martial" at army camps in France and Germany. His chores also included providing folk song mood music for the play "The Rainmaker."

After his discharge he returned to Seattle, accepting a job as a writer with Boeing. In his spare time, he continued his activities as a performer in clubs and on TV. He also taught guitar and became a charter member of the new Washington Folklore Society. In 1959, his second Folkways LP, "Walt Robertson," appeared.

ROBINSON, EARL: Singer, guitarist, composer, conductor, teacher. Born Seattle, Washington, July 2, 1910.

Though best known for his film scores, cantatas, and other ambitious works, Earl Robinson also had an illustrious career as a folk performer. In the early 1940s, for example, he was one of the charter members of The Almanac Singers, forerunner of The Weavers and the folk boom of the 1950s.

Robinson gained much of his interest in folk

music from his father, who enjoyed barbershop singing and also played old ballads on the mandolin. From his mother he gained a parallel love for the classics. Her talents were far-ranging: she could play cello, violin, harp, and piano. His interest in music grew during his years at the Lafayette Grade School and West Seattle High School so that he decided to major in music when he entered the University of Washington in 1928.

After several years at college, he took a leave of absence to satisfy a gnawing wanderlust. He started by working his way to China and back as a pianist on a passenger liner. When he got back to the U.S., he departed on a long, catch-as-catch-can trip of the U.S. He worked his way across country and through the south by a variety of odd jobs. These wanderings provided him with a goodly supply of folk material to play on the guitar, which he had mastered some years earlier. Along the way, he became friends with many folk artists, including Woody Guthrie, Leadbelly, Josh White, and Burl Ives. He also met the Lomaxes, who recorded some of his songs for the Archive of American Folk Song of the Library of Congress.

His travels finally took him to New York in 1935, where he worked with a little theater group. As musical director, he provided some original music, acted in some plays, and also sang. At this time he met composer Aaron Copland, under whom he studied later in his career.

Earl returned to the University to gain his degree in music (1938) and his teaching credentials. During this period he composed a cantata called "Ballad for Americans." When he returned to New York, the stirring composition was included in a WPA Federal Theatre revue, "Sing for Your Supper." The cantata was the hit of the show and won Robinson national attention when it was broadcast over CBS radio in 1939. This resulted in his winning a Guggenheim Fellowship the following year.

During 1940, Robinson often sang with the group of itinerant artists who called themselves The Almanac Singers. Most of these artists were featured in the Town Hall presentation by Robinson and Will Geer of the "Cavalcade of American Song." By this time, Robinson had also composed background scores for other Federal Theatre plays, "Processional" and "Life and Death of an American."

Robinson's rapidly rising stature resulted in a bid to move to Hollywood in 1943. For some eight years, he provided music for many films, beginning with Army films and extending to the score for the movie "California" (Paramount) and background scores for "A Walk in the Sun" (Twentieth Century Fox); "The Romance of Rosy Ridge" (MGM); "Man from Texas" (Eagle-Lion); and "The Roosevelt Story" (United Artists).

In 1951, he returned east, settling in Brooklyn. Throughout the 1950s he toured widely, conducting original material and various concerts, continued to compose a wide range of music, lectured, and (beginning in 1957) served as music director of Elisabeth Irwin High School in New York. During tours of the U.S., Canada, and Europe in the '50s and '60s, he continued actively to collect new folk material.

By 1969, he had many cantatas and songs to his credit. The cantatas, some composed for use in films, included "Battle Hymn"; "The Lonesome Train"; "Tower of Babel"; "In the Folded and Quiet Yesterdays"; "The Town Crier"; and "Preamble to Peace." His song credits include "Joe Hill," "The House I Live In" (song for film short, 1945, which won an Academy Award); "The Song of the Free Man," "Hold Fast to Your Dreams," "A Man's a Man For a' That," "Free and Equal Blues," "The Same Boat Brother," "Molly O," and "My Fisherman, My Laddie-O." In 1967, Robinson's output included a concerto for banjo and orchestra commissioned by the Boston Pops.

During his long career, Robinson also found time to write a folk opera, "Sandhog," and a book, *Young Folk*. He also composed the score for a 1956 General Motors film, "Giants in the Land," and for a ballet, "Bouquet for Molly."

In the post-World War II decades, Earl also made a number of folk song recordings for various labels, including Disc, Mercury, Decca, and Folkways. In '57, Folkways issued his LP titled "Walk in the Sun."

ROBISON, CARSON J.: Singer, band leader, songwriter. Born Oswego, Kansas, August 4, 1890; died Pleasant Valley, New York, March 24, 1957.

One of the most familiar voices on New York radio for many years belonged to Carson Robison. He helped build up a strong following for country and western music in the east. His many pioneering efforts made him a figure of national importance to the field.

Robison was exposed to country and folk music from his early years in his home state of Kansas. He sang at local gatherings on many occasions during elementary and high school in the Oswego area. In 1920, a new kind of gadget called radio was beginning to make a faint impact on the midwestern scene. Carson moved to Kansas City that year and was one of the first country and western singers ever to have his voice sent out on the air waves.

Carson built up a strong reputation in the midwest that served as a basis for his next move to New York in 1924. In the big city, he soon began his recording career for RCA Victor, initially as a whistler. Throughout the 1920s and early '30s, he performed on radio and also was featured in vaudeville tours of the east and midwest. Many of the audience favorites by then were songs he had written himself. In 1932, Robison formed his first group, The Buckaroos. The group accompanied him on radio shows, and during the 1930s toured England with him.

During the 1940s and '50s, Carson made his base of operations Pleasant Valley, New York. He eventually named his group of those years The Pleasant Valley Boys. Many of his recordings made the hit brackets during the 1930s and '40s. Probably his biggest success was his MGM top 10 1948 recording of his own composition, "Life Gets Tee-Jus, Don't It?" The song provided hit records for many other artists in the decades that followed. Another Robison comic staple of the 1940s and '50s was "I'm Going Back to Whur I Come From." He also was responsible for a western classic, "Carry Me Back to the Lone Prairie."

Some of Carson's other compositions include, "Barnacle Bill the Sailor," "My Blue Ridge Mountain Home," "Left My Gal in the Mountains," "1942 Turkey in the Straw," "Home Sweet Home on the Prairie," "There's a Bridle Hangin' on the Wall," "The Charms of the City Ain't for Me," "Goin' Back to Texas," "Little Green Valley," "New River Train," "Wreck of the Number Nine," and "Settin' by the Fire."

Robison died on his beloved farm in Pleasant Valley, New York, in early 1957. He had remained active in music up to a short time before his death.

RODGERS, JIMMIE (C.): Singer, guitarist, songwriter. Born Meridian, Mississippi, September 8, 1897; died New York, New York, May 26, 1933. First member elected to the Country Music Hall of Fame, November 3, 1961.

Generations of country music fans and performers have looked back in awe at a figure they knew only from pictures or from records. The most revered name in country music history, an acknowledged founding father of modern country and western patterns, Jimmie Rodgers achieved all this in just a few brief years in the national spotlight.

Born and raised in rural Mississippi, James Charles Rodgers gave little thought to a music career in his youth. Country music was, of course, part of his environment, as were the country blues of the Negro field hands. Singing was one of the few pleasures that relieved the long hours of work for black and white alike. Jimmie took this music for granted, listening or taking part in many informal sessions as he grew to manhood.

In his teens, he worked briefly as a cowboy, but soon left wrangling for his first job on the railroad. Railroading, he felt, would be his life's work. For close to a decade, he worked on the roads as a brakeman. He had learned to play guitar in his youth and sometimes entertained his fellow workers with popular country songs and some songs of his own making. His own compositions were a strangely moving blend of traditional country music, railroad songs, and country blues.

Jimmie might have remained a brakeman were it not for failing health. He had contracted tuberculosis and, by the mid-1920s, found he was not strong enough to continue the rugged life of a trainman.

He formed a company of his own, the Jimmie Rodgers Entertainers, and played rural fairs and tent shows. Some of his performances were in blackface. It was a precarious life. Sometimes crowds were large and money flowed in. Other times the shows were failures or the promoter ran off with the money.

For a while, Jimmie had a small degree of success. But then his finances ran out. However, he got wind of a Victor Talking Machine recording artist audition in the Virginia-Tennessee border city of Bristol. He made his way there at the beginning of August of 1927, and holed up in a cheap hotel on the Virginia side of the main street. Then his group of the time, The Tenneva Ramblers, abandoned him and the future looked bleak. The next day, August 4, he crossed State

The one and only "Singing Brakeman," the late Jimmy Rodgers, was the first artist selected to the Country Music Hall of Fame.

Street onto the Tennessee side*, entering a three-story building at 410 State Street. He met Ralph Peer, the Victor representative, in an upper story and talked him into recording him solo. (Also present at that time was the other great discovery of 1927, the Carter Family.) Peer liked Jimmie's yodeling style and two songs were cut, "Sleep Baby Sleep" and "The Soldier's Sweetheart."

When the records were released a short time after, Victor was literally swamped with orders in a few weeks' time. "The Singing Brakeman" was one of the hottest artists on the company's list by the end of 1927. Jimmie turned out other recordings in 1927, such as "Ben Dewberry's Final Run," "Mother Was a

* August 4 is the date given by RCA Archivists; the date of August 1 is given in the same report.

Lady," and "Blue Yodel #1," with equally dramatic results.

For the rest of his life, Jimmie Rodgers was one of the country's performing royalty. He toured the south and southwest and crowds fought to hear him, touch his clothes, or just get a brief glimpse of his frail form. His records continued to be avidly snapped up by his fans for the few years of life left to him. By early 1933, he had rolled up sales of almost 20 million records. His output included such hits as "Treasure Untold," "My Little Home Down in New Orleans," "Lullaby Yodel," "The Sailor's Plea" ('28); "Hobo Bill's Last Ride," "Yodeling Cowboy Blues," "Mississippi River Blues," "The Land of My Boyhood Dreams," "That's Why I'm Blue," "Jimmie's Texas Blues," "Any Old Time" ('29); "The Mystery of Number Five," "Those Gambler's Blues," "I'm Lonesome Too," "For the Sake of Days Gone By" ('30); "Let Me Be Your Side Track," "My Good Gal's Gone Blues," "T.B. Blues," "The Wonderful City" (with the Carter Family), "When the Cactus Is in Bloom" ('31); "Gambling Barroom Blues," "Roll Along Kentucky Moon," "No Hard Times," "Down the Road to Home" ('32); "Somewhere Down Below the Dixon Line," "Mississippi Delta Blues," "Cowhand's Last Ride," "Old Love Letters" ('33).

One of his most popular efforts was his Blue Yodel. In all, he completed recordings of twelve different Blue Yodel songs before his death. Among his other singles between 1927 and 1933 were "Mule Skinner Blues," "T for Texas," "Travelin' Blues," "One Rose That's Left in My Heart," "The Brakeman's Blues," "Daddy and Home," "My Time Ain't Long," and "Prairie Lullaby."

In addition to his personal appearances, Jimmie sang on several radio programs. He also made a movie short for Columbia Pictures.

His meteoric career had a time limit on it from the beginning. Tuberculosis cures were rare in advanced cases in those years, and Jimmie's health got a little worse with every passing month. Finally, in May 1933, his strength gave out and he passed into the realm of legend. In June 1953, 30,000 people, including most of the major country music artists and executives, assembled in Meridian, Mississippi, for the unveiling of a statue of Jimmie. When the Country Music Hall of Fame came into being some eight years later, his was the first name proposed and accepted for enshrinement in Nashville.

For many years, his old 78 rpm records were prized possessions of country music collectors. Little else was available from shortly after his death until after World War II. But the interest was still there among country music audiences, as shown by the reception of a series of Victor LPs issued in the 1950s and '60s. These included "Never No Mo'"; "Train Whistle Blues" ('59); "My Rough and Rowdy Ways" ('60); "Jimmie the Kid" ('61); "Hall of Fame" ('62); "Short But Brilliant Life" ('63); "My Time Ain't Long" ('64); and "The Best of the Legendary Jimmie Rodgers" ('65).

RODGERS, JIMMIE (F.): Singer, guitarist, songwriter, m.c. Born Camas, Washington, September 18, 1933.

During the late 1950s, few ballad singers could buck the driving beat of rock 'n' roll that dominated the hit charts. An exception was a young man from the state of Washington with an illustrious name, Jimmie Rodgers. Not only did he gain many airplays for his recordings in the folk vein, he also became a national teenage idol as great, in those years, as the most strident rock performer.

James Frederick Rodgers' march to musical success began in his childhood in Camas, Washington, where his piano-teacher mother started giving him lessons at an early age. Jimmie's interest in music grew as he went through elementary and high school in Camas. He was thinking more of a career as a music instructor, though, when he enrolled as a music major at Clark College in Vancouver, Washington. The turning point was to come because of the Korean War, which resulted in Jimmie's enlistment in the Air Force for four years.

Jimmie ended up in Seoul, Korea, where he bought an old guitar for a few dollars to help pass the time. He learned to play and later formed a group called The Rhythm Kings which performed at bases in the Far East and later in the U.S. While stationed outside Nashville, Tennessee, Jimmie gained his first job as a solo singer at the Unique Club in that city. He heard another performer do a song called "Honeycomb." Jimmie liked it and, after arranging it and changing the lyrics to fit his style, he added it to his repertoire.

After his discharge, he returned to Camas and joined a small band that worked in night-clubs in the Portland area. After a while, he decided to leave and try to make his way as a single, specializing in folk-type songs. He could not get bookings for many long months, but finally was signed to appear at the Fort Cafe in Vancouver, Washington. Audience reaction was so favorable that he was held over for a total of 17 weeks.

During this period, a fellow performer, Chuck Miller, caught the act and urged Jimmie to try for a New York recording audition. Jimmie gained a hearing from Roulette Record executives there. They particularly liked "Honeycomb" and had Jimmie tape it for them. Jimmie went back to Camas, but in a short time Roulette called him back to make a commercial version of the song. "Honeycomb" shot to the top of the charts soon after its release, becoming one of the major hits of 1957. Jimmie followed with two more million-sellers that year, "Are You Really Mine" and "Kisses Sweeter Than Wine." He was now nationally known and was asked to appear on many network television shows, including Dick Clark's American Bandstand, Ed Sullivan, Dinah Shore, and Perry Como.

In 1958, Jimmie added two more top 10 hits to his credit, "Oh-Oh, I'm Falling in Love Again" and "Secretly." In the next few years, he scored with such other songs as "Bimbombey," "Woman from Liberia" and "I'm Goin' Home." Jimmie's success in 1958 resulted in his own TV show on NBC network. In 1959, his life was reviewed on NBC's "This Is Your Life." During these years, Jimmie toured extensively throughout the U.S. and overseas, appearing in concerts and nightclubs in almost every major city in America.

As Jimmie's success grew, he moved his family (he married his childhood sweetheart, Colleen McClatchey, in 1957) to Granada Hills, California, at the far end of the San Fernando Valley. The nearness to Hollywood suggested film roles, and in 1960 he made his first movie, for Twentieth Century Fox, "The Little Shepherd of Kingdom Come." His second for Fox, "Back Door to Hell," was released in 1964.

Rodgers switched to Dot Records in 1962 as both performer and artist & repertoire chief for folk music. His efforts for Dot included such songs as "Rainbow at Midnight," "Face in the Crowd," and "No One Will Ever Know." In the mid-1960s he starred in a new syndicated TV show, the "Folk Song World of Jimmie

Rodgers." In 1968, after several years, the show was still going strong in several major cities, including Channel 5 in Los Angeles.

Over the decade 1957-67, Jimmie's total of 30 million record sales included many hit LPs as well as singles. His LP output for Roulette included "Jimmie Rodgers"; "His Golden Year"; "Twilight on the Trail"; "When the Spirit Moves You"; "Folk Song World"; "Folk Songs"; "Best of Folk Tunes" ('61); and "15 Million Seller" ('62). For Dot, Jimmie provided such titles as "No One Will Ever Know" ('62); "Folk Concert," "My Favorite Hymns," "Honeycomb" ('63); "World I Used to Know," "12 Great Hits" ('64); and "Deep Purple" ('65). Jimmie was also represented in 1964 on the Hamilton label with "6 Favorite Hymns/Ballads of Jimmie Rodgers."

In late 1967, Jimmie signed for a new movie, "To Catch a Robber By the Toe." Before he could go to Europe to work on the film, his career was interrupted by a controversial mishap. In the early morning hours of December 2, 1967, Rodgers was found unconscious in his car near a freeway off ramp close to his San Fernando Valley residence.

He apparently had been hit on the head by a blunt instrument, assumed to have been wielded by a robber. Later, it developed that he had been forced to the side of the road by an off-duty police officer for what was claimed to have been erratic driving. When Rodgers got out of his car to discuss the matter, it was claimed he accidentally fell and hit his head. Rodgers, whose memory of events was unclear after his head injury, disputed the Los Angeles Police Department version of the affair in a damage suit later filed against the city.

It was some time, though, before Rodgers was in condition to tell his side. For many weeks, he remained in critical condition. After several operations, he was able to leave the hospital in mid-1968 and resume some of his entertainment activities.

ROGERS, ROY: Singer, guitarist, actor. Born Cincinnati, Ohio, November 5, 1912.

The "King of the Cowboys" almost became the "King of the Bootmakers." Roy's father was a skilled shoemaker, and for a time his son helped him. Luckily for movie audiences the world over, a cross-country trip in a beat-up jalopy helped launch Roy on a fabled Hollywood career.

Roy (real name: Leonard Slye) spent the first seven years of his life in Cincinnati. Then the family moved to a farm in Duck Run, thirteen miles from Portsmouth, Ohio. Roy's mother and three sisters helped keep the farm going while his father worked in a shoe factory in Portsmouth. One of the advantages of living on a farm was that Roy got the chance to learn to ride on a black mare that used to race at the County Fair. This added to his growing interest in the movies of such stars as Buck Jones and Tom Mix shown on Saturday afternoons at the local cinema.

Roy finished grade school in Duck Run and entered high school. He hoped to become a dentist, but family finances were shaky. Before long, they moved back to Cincinnati where teenaged Roy worked with his father in a shoe factory. There Roy met a man who owned a thoroughbred horse farm. He took a liking to Roy and thus gave him the chance to perfect his riding ability.

Meanwhile, one of Roy's sisters married and moved to California. The family yielded to Roy's suggestions and drove out to visit her. In Portsmouth again, Roy dreamed of returning to California, possibly even to work in the movies.

He bought a guitar and soon learned to play. In the late 1920s, he knew enough cowboy songs to sing and double as square dance caller at local dances. In 1930, finding that a distant relative was going to California, Roy hitched a ride as a helper. In Los Angeles, jobs were not easily come by. Roy worked for a while picking peaches, then got a job driving a sand and gravel truck. Roy became a favorite with his co-workers because he entertained them with his singing and guitar playing in the barracks at night. The excellent response made Roy think more seriously about a career as a musician.

He first joined a group of five other musicians called the Rocky Mountaineers. It was enjoyable, but not profitable, so he organized his own group, the International Cowboys. Still the results were not impressive. He broke up this group and soon joined a new one with two other young performers, Tim Spencer and Bob Nolan. They called their act the Sons of the Pioneers. The flavor of this organization was to the liking of local audiences and before long they were more than making ends meet. They soon managed to gain a record date. When one of their first recordings became a major hit, the boys were all on the road to stardom.

The Sons of the Pioneers played more and more engagements in major western cities. They also were signed for a series of radio sketches. Roy began to branch out on his own in small singing roles in cowboy pictures. Hearing that Republic Studios was auditioning for a new cowboy lead, Roy applied for an audition. He was turned down, but sneaked in with a group of extras and got a hearing anyway. He was so impressive that he was signed for the lead in "Under Western Stars." From then on, he—and later his wife, Dale Evans—starred in one western after another. The Sons of the Pioneers, which went on to become one of the most famous western singing groups, often accompanied Roy in his movies.

From the mid-1930s to the 1960s, Rogers starred in well over 100 pictures. His horse Trigger became as well known as the Lone Ranger's Silver. Roy continued to star on radio and had a long-running series with his wife. In the years after World War II, Roy and Dale also starred on their own network TV show.

Roy turned out many hit records over the years for RCA Victor. His Victor albums included "Roy Rogers Souvenir Album," "Roy Rogers Roundup," "Skip to My Lou and Other Square Dances" (with Spade Cooley), and "Roy Rogers and Dale Evans." Some of Roy's single recordings were "You Can't Break My Heart," "Don't Blame It All on Me," "Rock Me to Sleep in My Saddle," "My Chickashay Gal," "Hawaiian Cowboy," "Dusty," "Home on the Range," "Old Fashioned Cowboy," "Stampede," "Smiles Are Made Out of Sunshine," "Frosty the Snow Man," "I'm A-Rollin'," and "Yellow Bonnets and Polka Dot Shoes." (*See also* EVANS, DALE; SONS OF THE PIONEERS)

ROOFTOP SINGERS: Vocal and instrumental group.

The Rooftop Singers could claim a direct link to the bellwether Weavers folk group; the new group was founded by a Weaver alumnus, Erik Darling. Darling played with The Weavers for several years as a replacement for their best known member, Pete Seeger.

He was no stranger to forming groups, having put together The Tarriers in 1956. The Tarriers helped start the ball rolling for "The Banana Boat Song," which later became a nationwide hit for Harry Belafonte. The Rooftop Singers' genesis came some years after, however, in 1962. To his own aptitude on guitar and 5-string banjo, Darling added the skills of guitarist Bill Svanoe and vocalist Lynne Taylor.

Svanoe, who attended Oberlin and the University of Minnesota, spent seven years playing his guitar throughout the U.S. and Europe before joining the Rooftop Singers. Miss Taylor provided a cosmopolitan touch, having impressive jazz and popular credits. These included working with the Benny Goodman Band for a year, feature spots on such TV shows as Steve Allen, Ernie Kovacs, Robert Q. Lewis, and Dick Van Dyke and appearances at the Blue Angel, Birdland, and the "Jazz on a Sunday" series at the Little Theater. In the early '60s, she also showed her folk music abilities in a 28-week engagement at the Village Vanguard.

The group won favorable notice in appearances at concerts and festivals in the eastern states in 1962. Then, at the start of 1963, they scored a nationwide hit with "Walk Right In." The song was featured in their first Vanguard LP, "Rooftop Singers" in April '63. In 1964, Vanguard turned out a second Rooftop Singers album, "Good Time!"

ROSE, FRED: Songwriter, singer, pianist, publisher. Born St. Louis, Missouri, August 24, 1897; died Nashville, Tennessee, December 1, 1954. Elected to Country Music Hall of Fame, 1961.

Fred Rose firmly believed that a person could make a transition from one field to another or one interest to another and did it himself, many times. Though best remembered today as a founder of Acuff-Rose Music Co., he was equally successful as a performer and songwriter.

As a preschooler he became attracted to the piano and by the age of seven he was a self-taught pianist; at ten years of age he was performing professionally. Then, there was the matter of singing: at 15 he left for Chicago—a great talent hub at the time—and started singing and playing in honkytonks and small restaurants. This later led to posh nightclub engagements and a contract with the Brunswick Record Company.

He and another pianist auditioned to cut player piano rolls for the QRS Company; both

One of Fred Rose's many great hits, "Texarkana Baby" ("TEXARKANA BABY"—Fred Rose and Cotton-seed Clark, © 1948, Milene Music, Inc. Used with permission of the publisher).

were selected from among dozens of applicants. The other player was Fats Waller. It went like that with Fred Rose. He had ambition, decision, and self-taught craftsmanship. In the field of songwriting, too, he started at seventeen and in his early twenties had such hits as "Deed I Do," "Honest and Truly," and others going for him. About that time he auditioned, along with more than fifty other pianists, for a job in the nation's top band. He ended up seated at a white grand piano on one side of the band, with Roy Bargy at the other at a second white grand. The group was Paul Whiteman's and the pianists were billed as the "Whiteman Twin Pianos."

After completing the band tour, Rose formed a piano-and-song team with Elmo Tanner, performing over KYW in Chicago. After Tanner left for other interests, Rose started a highly successful series for KYW called Fred Rose's Song Shop, which ran five days a week for more

than a year and led to a CBS network show over Chicago's WBBM. Rose left Chicago at the end of the CBS contract and moved to Nashville where he started his "Song Shop" over WSM in 1933. In mid-1934, he returned to Chicago for a featured spot on NBC during the last year of the city's Century of Progress World's Fair.

From Chicago he went to Nashville, New York, and Hollywood, where he became associated with Gene Autry. He wrote "Be Honest with Me," an Academy nominee, "Tweedle-O-Twill," and "Tears on My Pillow," in Hollywood. And then he left Hollywood, albeit a successful motion picture writer with number-one songs being turned out, to return to Nashville.

During his previous two-year stay in New York, Rose had become a devout Christian Scientist. This helped reinforce his belief in discovering a new "ambition, decision, craftsmanship" goal and moving toward it. His new goal was music publishing, with some emphasis on gospel material. Thus, on returning to Nashville, he joined with Roy Acuff to found Acuff-Rose Publications in 1943. Rose, an ASCAP member, set up his own new operation as a Broadcast Music, Inc. (BMI) affiliated publisher, a rather daring move in those days but one which proved to be a keystone for both organizations.

Rose worked well with people and developed new talent and songwriters. His affinity with both soon put the new firm in business and also led to such Rose songs as "Blues in My Mind," "Fire Ball Mail," "I Can't Go on This Way," "Home in San Antonio," and others that were widely recorded. When business detail started to interfere with his writing and development of new talent in 1945, he brought his son, Wesley, into the company to handle management affairs. Freed to find new talent, he discovered Hank Williams that same year.

His personal interest in people and their future led to associations with Molly O'Day, Boudleaux Bryant, Marty Robbins, Leon Payne and others. As a songwriter he again hit the charts with "Afraid," "Crazy Heart," "Faded Love and Winter Roses," "Foggy River," "I'll Never Stand in Your Way," "It's a Sin," "Kaw Liga," "Roly Poly," "Rose of Ol' Pawnee," "Setting the Woods on Fire," "Sweet Kind of Love," "Take These Chains from My Heart," "Texarkana Baby," and "Waltz of the Wind."

In his drive to create and to help others, Rose would often sit down and think out lyric or music bridges with writers when the song fascinated him. Many country songs were written that way that did not bear his name and, fairly often, did not end up in his publishing company. He collaborated with several writers including Hy Heath, Steve Nelson, Walter Hirsch, Ed G. Nelson, and Gene Autry, reflecting his apprenticeship in New York and Hollywood.

Rose brought a musician's craftsmanship and talent to Nashville, was unstinting in promoting country music and songs regardless of their publisher affiliation, and proved a key influence in gaining Nashville the nickname "Music City, U.S.A." His election to the Country Music Association's Hall of Fame, following his death, rightfully put him among the giants of the industry. (*See also* ACUFF, ROY; ROSE, WESLEY)

ROSE, WESLEY: Music publishing executive, record producer. Born Chicago, Illinois, February 11, 1918.

In the mid-1960s, the acknowledged leader in country and western publishing was the firm of Acuff-Rose. President of the firm, and the man who played a major part in bringing it to this eminence, was Wesley Rose. Though deeply immersed in the music field by this time, he had come close to making his career, instead, in the business end of the oil industry.

Wesley Rose was born into a family with deep country and western roots. His father, Fred, wrote many hit songs in the 1930s and '40s that were performed by the leading country artists of the land. Despite this, young Wesley did not consider a music career at first. After graduating from Bowen High School, Chicago, he went on to Chicago's Walton School of Commerce. After obtaining a B.S. degree in accounting, he accepted a job in the accounting department of the Standard Oil Refinery in Whiting, Indiana.

He was still moving ahead at the refinery, reaching the post of chief accountant in the mid-1940s, when his father started a new music publishing firm with country great Roy Acuff. In 1945, a vacation changed Wesley's career outlook. His trip took him briefly to Nashville to visit his father. Fred Rose asked his son to examine the new company's financial setup.

Wesley's experienced comments brought an invitation to take over the management of Acuff-Rose. He moved to Nashville and was quickly involved in handling sales and promotion details of the compositions of his father, Roy Acuff, and Hank Williams. Wesley was instrumental in expanding the firm's market into the popular field, work that resulted in such national successes as Tony Bennett's record of Hank Williams' "Cold, Cold Heart" and Joni James' version of "Your Cheatin' Heart."

When Hank Williams died on January 1, 1953, Acuff-Rose was faced with the need to attract new songwriters to its roster. By this time, Wesley had learned much about the music field. He applied part of his talents to signing new writers. The result was a list of names in the 1950s that included Marty Robbins, Melvin Endsley, Boudleaux and Felice Bryant, Jenny Lou Carson, John D. Loudermilk, Don Gibson, and Roy Orbison.

After Fred Rose's death in 1954, Wesley had to become involved in new facets of the business. In particular, he had to enter the record producing end, a field in which his father had gained a major reputation. By the mid-1960s, he had become adept at this, as shown by work with his own and other artists for such record firms as Columbia, Warner Bros., MGM, RCA Victor, Epic and Cameo-Parkway.

Wesley's ability to roll with the punch was illustrated by Acuff-Rose's history in the last half of the 1950s. The rock 'n' roll boom had made drastic inroads into country and western markets. Rose's answer to this was to combine the ability of some of his writers with new performing talent. In particular, he helped develop the Everly Brothers' careers, providing them with a series of national hits written by Boudleaux and Felice Bryant.

By the 1960s, Acuff-Rose had expanded in several new directions. The firm had added its own record label, Hickory Records, and a booking agency, Acuff-Rose Artists Corp. Rose also helped pioneer the introduction of country and western material overseas, setting up organizations through the mid-1960s in Brazil, Argentina, Australia, England, Italy, France, Germany, Belgium, Japan, South Africa and Israel.

Besides his own business activities, Rose remained a leader in the overall music industry, keeping up active membership in the National Academy of Recording Arts and Sciences (NARAS), including service for some years as a director; becoming one of the founders and board chairman of the Country Music Association (CMA); and serving as a member of the board of the National Music Publishers Association (NMPA). (*See also* ACUFF, ROY; ROSE, FRED)

RUBIN, MRS. HARRY: Singer, pianist, folk music collector. Born Montreal, Canada, September 1, 1906.

The wealth of material in Jewish, and later Israeli, folk songs, began to interest many scholars in the 1940s. Some of these songs, such as "Hava Nagila," became standard items in the repertoire of many folk artists, from Harry Belafonte to native Israeli singers. This addition to modern folk annals was largely the result of ground work by such folklorists as Ruth Rubin.

Born Ruth Rosenblatt in Montreal, she was exposed to Jewish music and folk songs at an early age, hearing many melodies and songs from her mother, grandfather, and other relatives. She had an excellent voice even as a child, and began singing at concert in her Yiddish school in Montreal at seven. She continued these occasional singing efforts during her years in grammar and high school in Montreal. However, she did not seriously consider a career in folk music at the time.

In the 1920s, she moved across the border to New York. She worked as a secretary for some years and also took night courses at Hunter College and other schools in the city. In 1932, she married Harry Rubin and settled down to raise a family. Her interest in Jewish folklore and music continued as a hobby, but it was not until 1944 that she really devoted time to specializing in the field. She began to give lecture recitals on the subject, first locally and later in other parts of the country. She also eventually returned to her country of birth for a number of concerts.

From 1944 on, she spent more and more time collecting and annotating folk material. She presented articles on some of this material in folk publications, beginning with New York Folklore Quarterly in 1946. Many of her writings appeared in such other journals as the Jewish Music Forum, Journal of American Folklore ('52); Chicago Jewish Forum; London Jewish Quarterly, and the Journal of the International Folk Music Council.

Her contributions to folk scholarship resulted in her election for several years as councillor of the American Folklore Society and the Canadian Folk Music Society. She also served as secretary of the International Folk Music Society and was a member of the New York Folklore Society. In the post-World War II era, she taught at the New School for Social Research.

In 1950, she provided one of the standard works in the field with publication of her *Treasury of Jewish Folk Song*. The book included 110 songs in Hebrew and Yiddish with English translations. In later years, she also authored *Voices of a People, The Story of Yiddish Folksong* and *Singable English Translations (Yiddish Songbook)*.

Beginning in 1945, she also recorded a number of songs herself, mostly for Oriole Records. One of her first LPs was the 1954 Oriole "Jewish Children's Songs and Games" on which Pete Seeger provided banjo accompaniment. Other LPs included Riverside Records' "Yiddish Love Songs" and Prestige International's "Ruth Rubin Sings Yiddish Folk Songs."

RUSH, TOM: Singer, guitarist, songwriter. Born Portsmouth, New Hampshire, February 8, 1941.

One of the major talents of the folk music boom of the mid-1960s, Tom progressed to this genre by way of classical music and rock 'n' roll. His varied musical tastes were shown by his folk concert repertoire which ranged from folk ballads to pop music, rhythm and blues, and country and western.

His classical training began in his grade school years. For nine years he studied classical piano. In high school, however, rock 'n' roll seemed more attractive. So Tom taught himself to play the guitar and then formed his own band, which became a feature of many local high school dances. But Tom's outlook on music changed again after he entered Harvard University in 1960. With friends, he visited local coffee houses. The music hit a responsive chord

Tom Rush

and he began to perform at such places as the Golden Vanity, Club 47, and the Unicorn.

Tom continued his studies toward a degree in English literature, but expanded his folk music engagements as much as possible. During vacations, he worked his way across the U.S. and Europe, performing in local clubs or working at odd jobs. In France, he won much attention in small cabarets and as a street singer. Most of his singing, though, through 1964, was restricted to Boston. His following grew locally and he began to receive bids for major appearances throughout the U.S.

After graduation in 1964, he took advantage of these and appeared at such places as the Brickskeller in Washington, D.C., La Cave in Cleveland, Riverboat in Toronto, Troubador in Los Angeles, The Chessmate in Detroit, and Le Hibou in Ottawa, Canada. His concert engagements took him into most major halls and universities in the mid-1960s, including New York's Town Hall, McCormick Theatre, Chicago, and the Newport and Philadelphia Folk Festivals. TV also called with appearances on such shows as ABC New York's Almanac of Folk Music, CBC-Toronto's Let's Sing Out!, and Upbeat on Cleveland's WEWS.

By the end of 1964, he had recorded LPs for Prestige and Lycornu, including "Got a Mind to Ramble" and "Blues, Songs, Ballads." In 1965, he signed with Elektra. His first two LPs on this label were "Tom Rush" and "Take a Little Walk with Me." His popularity in Boston was reflected in his selection by the folk magazine Boston Broadside as Favorite Male Performer of 1964, '65, and '66. In 1966, Billboard voted him the Most Promising New Male Folk Singer of 1965.

SAINTE-MARIE, BUFFY: Singer, guitarist, songwriter. Birthplace variously given as Canada and Sebago Lake, Maine, February 20, 1941.

When she "plays primitive mouth-bow and sings of 'Cripple Creek,' she sounds like a 100 per cent (folk artist). But then she turns right around and belts out a smoky jazz tune with all the gutty emotion of a Billie Holiday. As her concert continues, she will whisper a little love song. As her concert continues, she then will turn on the audience with sparks in her black eyes and shout angrily in song about the injustices done to her people, or of the cruelty of war. . . ."

[266]

Thus did Life (Dec. 10, 1965, pp. 53-54) describe the versatility of the dark haired, talented Cree Indian girl who promised to become one of the most important performers of the 1960s. She learned of her Cree Indian birth from her foster parents, for she never knew her own parents. Nor was she ever quite certain whether she was born in Canada or the U.S. It is certain, though, that she was adopted when she was a few months old by a couple who were part Micmac Indian, and raised mainly in Wakefield, Massachusetts.

The shy, frail girl did have a warm home, and an interest in music that began in childhood. By her high school years she had taught herself to play the guitar. However, she thought of music mainly as a hobby, majoring in Oriental philosophy at the University of Massachusetts. She laid plans to become a teacher while taking courses at the University and such other institutions as Mt. Holyoke, Smith, and Amherst.

All this was changed by a visit to a guest night hootenanny at The Gaslight Cafe in Greenwich Village in the early 1960s. Buffy performed and greatly impressed one member of the audience, Herb Gart. He became her manager and helped shape a career that won her an income of $100,000 in 1965.

Before long, Buffy was singing at coffee houses and major concert halls throughout the east. She sang some conventional folk songs but as time went on began to write more and more of her material. In addition, she added some unique features to her act. One of her early supporters was a fellow Cree, Patrick Sky; he made and taught her to play the primitive Indian mouth-bow which became a favorite with audiences, including those at the Newport Folk Festival.

The way was not easy, though, particularly because of Buffy's fragile health. In 1963, she contracted bronchial pneumonia. Refusing to give up her singing at such places as the Village Gate in New York and Club 47 in Cambridge, Massachusetts, she almost ruined her voice. During her six-month illness, she took so much codeine she became addicted. She fought this off, but wrote a memorable song about the experience, "Cod'ine." After recuperating, she received her first formal lessons from a vocal coach.

The effectiveness of the training was shown in her very successful concert tour across the U.S. and Canada in 1964. She was also featured on many guest spots on radio and network TV and turned out her first Vanguard LP in May '64, "It's My Way." She turned out another Vanguard album in '65, "Many a Mile."

The '64 LP contained her most controversial composition, written in 1963, "The Universal Soldier." However, as she told Life's reporter, "I have written hundreds of songs, and only a half dozen are of protest. I believe in leaving politics to the experts, only sometimes the experts don't know what's going on." Some of her other often-performed compositions are: "Now That the Buffalo's Gone," "Incest Song," and "It's My Way."

SANDBURG, CARL AUGUST: Author, poet, journalist, singer, guitarist. Born Galesburg, Illinois, January 6, 1878; died Flat Rock, North Carolina, July 22, 1967.

When the majority of people hear Carl Sandburg's name, the only thing that comes to mind is his massive, Pulitzer Prize-winning Lincoln biography. But he is as much a giant in several other creative areas, not the least of which is folk music.

Sandburg's father, a Swedish immigrant, worked as a blacksmith's helper for the Chicago, Burlington & Quincy RR. The family of seven children did not leave much leeway in his paycheck, and by the time Carl was 11 he was already working at the start of a seemingly endless list of jobs. He helped the family finances by sweeping floors and cleaning cuspidors in a law office and delivering papers. He left school at the end of the eighth grade to work as a milkman. During his teens he harvested ice from a frozen lake, sold refreshments, shifted theater scenery, helped in a brickyard, shined shoes, harvested wheat in Kansas, etc. This background plus observance of labor unrest resulted in a strong socialist viewpoint, at least in his early years.

In 1898, he enlisted in the Army for the Spanish-American War, but was stationed in Puerto Rico. When he was discharged, he decided to enroll in Lombard College in Galesburg. He didn't graduate, but did meet Prof. Philip Green Wright, who strongly encouraged his literary efforts. After Sandburg left Lombard in 1902, Wright personally published Carl's first books: two of poetry (*In Reckless Ecstasy*, '04, and *The Plaint of a Rose*, '05) and a book of essays (*Incidentals*, '05).

In 1907, Sandburg became an organizer for the Social Democratic Party in Milwaukee. He wrote socialist-oriented articles and a piece on Lincoln for the Milwaukee *Daily News* in 1909. In 1912, he began a new career as a working journalist, moving to Chicago to work on the *Daily Socialist*. After jobs with different papers over the next few years, he settled down for a 10-year stint as reporter for the Chicago *Daily News* (1917-27). He broke with the Socialist Party over American entry into World War I, which he supported.

Meanwhile, he pursued his writing career in his free time. In 1914, his poem "Chicago" in the magazine "Poetry" won the $200 Helen Haire Levinson prize. By the start of the 1920s, his research on the life of Lincoln was well underway. In 1926, the first two volumes of what was to be a six-volume set on the President were issued by Harcourt: *Abraham Lincoln: The Prairie Years*. The following year, his great interest in folk music was revealed by another book, *American Songbag*. This included 280 songs and ballads Sandburg had collected in his years of wandering. Sandburg took great pleasure in singing these for his family and friends to his own guitar accompaniment.

In 1928, Sandburg decided to concentrate on creative arts and moved his family to the sand dune country of Harbert, Michigan. From the new site, his tremendous output of songs and literature continued. His books included *Good Morning, America* ('28); *Steichen as Photographer* ('29); *Mary Lincoln Wife and Widow* ('32); and *The People, Yes*. The latter has been called one of the great tributes to American citizens. In 1939, he completed his Lincoln saga with *Abraham Lincoln: The War Years,* which brought him the Pulitzer Prize for history in 1940.

From 1941 to 1945, he wrote a syndicated column on politics for the Chicago *Times* and also appeared on radio broadcasts for the Office of War Information. On many of these, he helped the nation's cause during World War II by demonstrating again his ability as a folk singer.

After the war, the Sandburgs moved to Connemara Farm near Flat Rock, North Carolina. Despite his age, Sandburg remained as active as ever until slowed by an intestinal ailment in late 1965.

His post-World War II output included a huge novel, *Remembrance Rock,* in 1948, *Complete Poems* in 1950, which won him the Pulitzer Prize for poetry in 1951, *Always the Young Strangers,* an autobiography, in 1952, and a new compilation of folk songs, *New American Songbook,* in 1951.

During the 1960s, he continued to record and play his folk music and write such poetry books as *Wind Song* ('60); *Harvest Poems* ('60); and *Honey and Salt* ('63). In 1960, an anthology of his work was prepared by Norman Corwin and presented on Broadway with Bette Davis as star. In the 1960s, Sandburg was also featured on many TV shows. His record catalog by this time included LPs on many labels, including Disc, Caedmon, and Lyrichord. Almost to his death, he continued to sing and play folk music for himself and/or friends for at least half an hour a day.

By mid-1966, Sandburg's physical strength had noticeably weakened and he spent much of his time in bed reading. In June 1967, he suffered a heart stroke and finally passed away in his sleep on July 22. The world mourned his passing; President Johnson said, "Carl Sandburg gave us the truest and most enduring of our own greatness. There is no end to the legacy he leaves us."

SCRUGGS, EARL: Banjoist, guitarist, songwriter. Born Cleveland County, North Carolina, January 6, 1924.

"Earl Scruggs, smiling quietly at the massed audience (at the Los Angeles Troubadour), seems completely divorced from the three plastic clawed fingers of his right hand as they scrabble frantically across the five strings of his silvery banjo . . . the undisputed master of his instrument, having created his own style of picking and having invented a modification of the banjo —the Scruggs tuner—which allows the performer to warp and intriguingly distort plucked notes."

"The highest degree of professionalism was shown at the Newport Folk Festival on Saturday night by a group from Nashville, Tennessee . . . Lester Flatt and Earl Scruggs."

These words, the first by Pete Johnson in the Los Angeles *Times* of Friday, February 17, 1967, and the second by Robert Shelton in *The New York Times* in 1960, are typical of dozens of rave notices in papers and magazines across the nation throughout the 1950s and '60s. All attested to the fact that Flatt &

Scruggs were undisputed kings of Bluegrass music in these decades. And all paid particular tribute to the fantastic banjo style of Earl Eugene Scruggs.

It was a style that had been under development from Scruggs' boyhood in rural North Carolina. He had fallen in love with the "old-timey" sound of pre-amplified instrument days from the time he first picked a banjo. This went back to when he was five years old and still a year away from first grade at the Boiling Springs, North Carolina, grammar school. Earl could play some simple tunes on the banjo when he began school in 1930. When he was 10, he had invented his own style of banjo playing, the three-finger approach that became his trademark.

Earl was well known locally as a skilled musician (he also learned the guitar) by the time he left Boiling Springs High School in 1942. In his teens, he worked for a time in a textile mill, but his dreams were of a career in music. He began to gain widespread attention beyond his home locale as he demonstrated his driving banjo style at regional dances and parties.

This helped him gain a job with one of the great names in country and western music, Bill Monroe. Monroe was the number one name in Bluegrass. Recognizing Earl's ability, he made the youth a member of his Bluegrass Boys. In 1944, Earl made his debut on the Grand Ole Opry as part of Monroe's band. He met another talented performer in the group, guitarist and singer Lester Flatt. Earl and Lester remained on the Opry with Monroe until 1948. Becoming fast friends, they decided to form their own group and soon were featured on WCYB, Bristol, Virginia. Almost as soon as the new group started, they had a recording contract with Mercury. The Mercury arrangement lasted until 1951, after which the boys signed a long-term contract with Columbia.

With their Foggy Mountain Boys, Flatt & Scruggs played a number of stations in the south, over the next few years, in Knoxville, Tennessee; Lexington, Kentucky; Tampa, Florida; and Roanoke, Virginia. In 1953, they became regular cast members of the Grand Ole Opry. During the '50s and '60s, the boys traveled under the Opry banner on some tours and also on many shows sponsored by Martha White Mills, Inc. Among the stations on which they played were WTVC, Chattanooga; WATE-TV, Knoxville; WSAZ-TV, Huntington, West Virginia; WTWV, Tupelo, Mississippi; WJTV, Jackson, Mississippi; WHIS-TV, Bluefield, West Virginia; WDXI-TV, Jackson, Tennessee; WBOY-TV, Clarksburg, West Virginia; and WSLS-TV, Roanoke.

In the 1960s, the boys continued to expand their audience, playing on many network TV shows as well as returning regularly to the Newport Folk Festival and major clubs across the country. In 1962, their rendition of the theme song of the number-one TV comedy show The Beverly Hillbillies swept the nation. Between 1962 and 1967, Flatt & Scruggs appeared in one show each year in the series.

Many of the team's best-sellers were written by Scruggs alone or were co-authored by Earl. His own compositions included "Flint Hill Special," named for his home community in North Carolina, "Randy Lynn Rag," "Earl's Breakdown," "Foggy Mountain Special," "Foggy Mountain Chimes," and "Rocky Mountain Rock." Among songs co-authored by him were "Shuckin' the Corn," "Crying My Heart Out Over You," "Someone You Have Forgotten," "I Won't Be Hanging Around," and "Building on Sand."

Among the team's hit LPs on Columbia were: "Foggy Mountain Jamboree," "Foggy Mountain Banjo," "Songs of the Carters" ('61); "Songs of Our Land" ('62); "Hard Travelin'," "Flatt and Scruggs at Carnegie Hall" ('63); "At Vanderbilt University" ('64). They were also represented on other labels, including, on Mercury, "Country Music" ('58); "Original Sound," and "Flatt and Scruggs with the Foggy Mountain Boys" ('64); and on Harmony, "Flatt and Scruggs with the Foggy Mountain Boys" ('60).

By the mid-1960s, Flatt & Scruggs had their own syndicated TV shows on stations throughout the southeast. Management of these and other phases of the team's operations was handled by Mrs. Earl Scruggs. They also had many honors to their credit: Best Instrumental Group, Country and Western Jamboree, 1955 through 1958; 1961, Most Popular Male Stars, Music Reporter; 1962-63, National Academy of Recording Arts and Sciences' nomination for Best Folk, Country and Western Recording; 1963, Most Programmed Vocal Group, Country and Western, Cashbox; 1963, Favorite Country Group, Billboard Outstanding Achievement Award; 1964, Top Vocal Group Award, Record

World; 1964, Most Programmed Group, Cashbox; 1965, Folk Poll Award, Cavalier magazine; 1966, Star Vocal Group, Sound Format.

In early 1969 the team broke up, and Scruggs brought suit to try to prevent Flatt from using the name Foggy Mountain Boys for his group. (*See also* BLUEGRASS; FLATT, LESTER)

SEA ISLAND SINGERS: *See* Carawan, Guy

SEEGER, CHARLES LOUIS (SR.): Educator, author, orchestra conductor, ethno-musicologist. Born Mexico City, Mexico, December 14, 1886.

In the field of musical scholarship, and particularly in folk music studies, there are few reputations as awesome as that of Charles Seeger. To the public in general, his name is not well known. However, the family name Seeger has become familiar to most of the nations of the world because of Seeger's children. Exposure to Charles Seeger's exhaustive research into folk music provided the impetus that made Pete, Mike, and Peggy Seeger become major artists in this field.

Though Charles Seeger was born in Mexico City, his family traced its ancestry back to some of the founding families of New England. He was brought up in Boston and majored in music at Harvard, graduating in 1908. He was well grounded in the classics and established a reputation as a conductor in his early years. This helped bring him a conductorship at the Cologne Opera in 1910-11. He returned to the U.S. to marry Constance de Clyver Edson, December 22, 1911. They had three children, Charles Louis, Jr., John and Peter.

In 1912, the Seeger base of operations was moved to California where Charles Seeger was professor of music at the University from 1912 to 1919. Even in those early years, he was beginning to gain a worldwide reputation for his work in musicology. Besides composing music, he also wrote a text, *Harmonic Structure and Elementary Composition,* published in 1916.

The year 1921 found the Seegers once more on the East Coast. From 1921 to 1933, Dr. Seeger continued his activities as a lecturer in the Institute of Musical Art in New York. While still holding this position, he also began lecturing at the New School for Social Research, remaining there from 1931 through 1935. During 1932, he also assumed the task of editing the American Library of Musicology, which took six years.

By the 1930s, Dr. Seeger was already conducting research into various areas of folk music. He continued his work in more detail in 1935 when he moved to Washington, D.C. He and his second wife, Ruth Crawford Seeger, whom he married November 14, 1931, worked for several years with their close friends John Lomax and his son Alan on material for the Archive of American Folk Song of the Library of Congress. Their efforts included listening to recordings of rural folk artists collected by Library of Congress field researchers and cataloging material on many facets of ethnomusicology gathered by the Archive. This work and their acquaintance with many talented folk performers had a lasting impact on the children of Seeger's second marriage, Michael, Margaret (Peggy), Barbara, Mona, and Penelope (Penny). One of the results of this research was a book co-authored by Seeger and the Lomaxes, *Folk Song U.S.A.*

Seeger held many important government positions during his years in Washington. From 1935 to 1938, he was technical adviser, special skills department, to the Resettlement Administration. From 1938 to 1940, he was assistant to the director of the Federal Music Project of the WPA. From 1941 to 1953, he was Chief of the Music Division of the Pan American Union. His literary output during his years with the Pan American Union included the Union's music series, 1941-50; *Library of Congress Checklist of Recorded Songs* in 1942; *Handbook of Latin American Studies,* 1943-50; *Army Song Book* in 1941; and *Cancionero Popular Americano* in 1950. In 1949-50, Seeger served as a visiting professor at Yale.

In the late 1950s, after his third marriage (to Margaret Adams Taylor, March 10, 1955), he returned to California. He served as a lecturer at the University of California at Los Angeles in 1957 and research associate in 1958. In 1961, he was made consultant to the Institute of Ethno-musicology and regent professor at UCLA.

Though in his eighties, in the late 1960s Seeger pioneered still another development in music research in the form of the Seeger Melograph, a device that permits comparative cross-cultural studies of singing styles. It contains electronic devices that transcribe important properties of music on graph paper. The graphs permit a very sensitive analysis of the properties of different singers that show such things as the difference in vibrato effect between singers from different countries or different cultures. (*See also* SEEGER, MIKE; SEEGER, PEGGY; SEEGER, PETE)

SEEGER, MIKE: Singer, guitarist, banjoist, folk music collector. Born New York, New York, 1933.

The Seeger clan is certainly one of the most amazing in folk music history in this country. What seems to be a dynasty was founded by musicologist and folklorist Dr. Charles Seeger, Sr. His interest in folk music was passed along to his seven children by two wives. His first family of three included the great Pete Seeger. His second brood included Mike, Peggy, and Penny Seeger, all of whom made names for themselves in the folk music field.

Michael, called Mike, the oldest of four children of Charles Seeger's marriage to Ruth Crawford Seeger, spent many of his early years in Washington, D.C. His parents were assisting the Lomaxes in compiling and collecting the Archive of American Folk Music of the Library of Congress. Thus young Mike was exposed to a wide range of folk information and met the many accomplished folk artists who visited the Seeger household. He also had the chance to glean much information over the years from his half-brother Pete.

By the time Mike began high school, he had pretty well decided to continue in the Seeger tradition. For a while he learned the classic Spanish guitar, but when he was 18 he switched to the banjo and the more conventional guitar used in folk music. One of his deep interests was in the country music that laid the foundation for the more urban folk song genre of the post-World War II years. In the early 1950s, he began to travel through the rural parts of the U.S., seeking out old-time performers and collecting traditional folk songs. Though only in his twenties, he contributed greatly to folk research, making tapes of many important songs and bringing many "lost" artists, such as Dock Boggs, back to the attention of current audiences.

By the mid-1950s, Mike was performing at many of the coffee houses and festivals in the U.S. He played not only the guitar, but the banjo, dulcimer, and many other instruments. In 1958 Mike joined with two other artists, John Cohen and Tom Paley, to form the New Lost City Ramblers. In the 1960s, this group was one of the most important on the folk scene, but with Tracy Schwarz replacing Tom Paley.

The New Lost City Ramblers won standing ovations at many concerts throughout the country and were featured performers at the Newport Folk Festival.

The Ramblers sang many of the songs discovered by Mike on his collecting tours and also added to their repertoire from records or from collecting expeditions of the other members. Among the many songs that won sustained applause from audiences were "Oh, Babe It Ain't No Lie," "The Girl I Left Behind," "Lady of Carlisle," "Red Rocking Chair," "Battleship of Maine," "Hopalong Peter," "The Cannonball," "Old Bell Cow," "East Virginia Blues," "Fly Around, My Pretty Little Miss," "The Girl on the Greenbriar Shore," "Freight Train," "Tom Dooley," "Whoop 'Em Up Cindy," and "Arkansas Traveler." These and many other songs were included in their book, *The New Lost City Ramblers,* published by Oak Publications in 1964.

In the 1960s, Mike continued his collecting and performed both solo and with the Ramblers. His activities included annotating many notes on important folk music albums. He also contributed material to Sing Out! magazine. During the 1950s, Mike also began recording for the Folkways label. During the 1950s and '60s, he turned out a number of well received LPs for Folkways, including "Mike Seeger Sings" and "Mike Seeger" ('64). Vanguard Records also issued a Mike Seeger album, "Hello Stranger," in 1964. (*See also* NEW LOST CITY RAMBLERS; SEEGER, CHARLES; SEEGER, PEGGY; SEEGER, PETE)

SEEGER, PEGGY: Singer, guitarist. Born New York, New York, June 17, 1935.

It is hard to find a name more honored or recurrent in modern folk music than that of Seeger. The two broods of the famed ethnomusicologist Charles Seeger, Sr., totaling seven in all, provided at least three great names to the list of performing artists, Pete, Mike, and Peggy. Peggy, second of four children of his second marriage (to Ruth Crawford Seeger), became one of the leading female folk artists of the 1950s and '60s.

The exposure of the Seeger children to all forms of folk music began in the cradle, since Dr. Charles Seeger was continuously collecting and listening to tapes and records from all over the world. As the children grew up in this atmosphere, they were more interested in performing the music than in the analytical pursuits of their parents. As noted by Raymond Lawless, Peggy recalled that the family was not a singing family in the sense of the Ritchie Family but "We always heard songs and we chose our own favorites."

Margaret "Peggy" Seeger was introduced both to folk instruments, including guitar and banjo, and to major folk artists while in grade and high school. Her half-brother Pete and other performers often visited the Seeger household in Washington, D.C., and New York. Her interest in folk music continued to grow when she entered Radcliffe College in the early 1950s. After leaving Radcliffe she went to Europe in the summer of 1955, traveling through Holland, Belgium, France and Italy singing and collecting folk songs.

In 1956, an invitation to perform a role in an English production of "Dark of the Moon" played a key part in her career. It was gained for her by Alan Lomax, son and co-worker of John Lomax, curator of the Archive of American Folk Song of the Library of Congress. The Seeger family had worked closely with the Lomaxes for several years in the 1930s on the Archive. Once in England, Peggy soon joined a folk song quartet which included Scottish folk expert Ewan MacColl. Two years later, she became Mrs. MacColl.

In the interim, she returned to the U.S. in 1957 to perform at concerts, festivals, and clubs in many parts of the country. She was particularly well received at the Gate of Horn in Chicago where she remained for a six-week engagement. That summer, she followed a familiar new-left pattern of the post-World War II era, taking part in the World Youth Festival in Moscow. She journeyed from Russia to Red China, then back through Russia to England. In 1958, she married MacColl and settled in England.

By the late 1950s, she had already turned out a number of recordings. She continued to turn out LPs on various labels through the 1960s both as a solo performer and with her two younger sisters and her husband. Her LPs with sisters Penny and Barbara included "Three Sisters" on International Label and a 10-inch Folkways disk. Her solo LPs included "Songs for You and Me" on International, "Songs of

Courting and Complaint" on Folkways, and "Best of Peggy Seeger" on Prestige. With Ewan MacColl, her work included "Classic Ballads" on Tradition and "Bothy Ballads" on Folkways. (*See also* MacCOLL, EWAN; SEEGER, CHARLES)

SEEGER, PETE: Folksinger, author, composer, musicologist. Born New York, New York, May 3, 1919.

Controversial is perhaps an understatement when applied to Pete Seeger. For years, since his 1955 appearance before the House Un-American Activities Committee, charges and countercharges have flown between Seeger partisans and opponents. In 1963, many prominent folk artists refused to appear on the ABC-TV Hootenanny show because of the alleged blacklist of Seeger.

But one thing is not controversial. Pete Seeger is certainly one of the great names in the annals of folk music in the U.S. as is, indeed, the surname Seeger itself. The name is an honored one in past American history, going back in a direct line to colonial settlers 300 years ago. More directly, Pete Seeger's father, Dr. Charles Seeger, is one of the foremost ethno-musicologists in the world as well as being known as an author, conductor, and educator. Pete Seeger inherited musical talent on his mother's side also; she was a violinist and teacher.

Young Peter R. Seeger went to private schools in Nyack, New York, and Connecticut before entering Harvard. Up to the time he was 16, Pete had little interest in folk music, but a trip with his father to a folk festival in Asheville, North Carolina, changed all that. Though his interest turned this way, he entered Harvard in 1936 as a sociology major. However, in 1938, he abruptly left school to ride the rods or hitchhike all over the U.S. His main goal was to paint and collect songs. In doing this, he made the acquaintance of such other performers as Leadbelly, Woody Guthrie, and Earl Robinson. He also drew closer to his father's friend, Dr. John Lomax, Curator of the Archive of American Folk Song at the Library of Congress. By 1939-40, Seeger was an archive assistant and also went on field trips with the Lomaxes.

In 1940, he was instrumental in founding one of the best known groups in U.S. folk music history, The Almanac Singers. He toured the

Pete Seeger

country for many months with this group and then, for a period of time, just with Woody Guthrie. He and Guthrie sang at labor and migrant meetings and composed labor and anti-fascist songs. In 1942, Seeger was drafted and spent more than three years in the Army, mainly entertaining troops in the Pacific.

After his discharge in December '45, Seeger helped start a form of songwriter's union called People's Songs, Inc. At its pinnacle, the union had 3,000 members, including such luminaries as Sonny Terry, Tom Glazer, Alan Lomax and Guthrie. Part of the activities included hootenannys which were forerunners of the more ambitious hoots of the 1960s. Seeger's projects included a movie short, "And Hear My Banjo Play," in 1946 and a Los Angeles revival of the folk musical "Dark of the Moon."

But the high point of Seeger's career was the beginning of The Weavers quartet in 1948. After debuting at the Village Vanguard in late '49, The Weavers soon took the country by storm, winning many radio, TV, and concert hall appearances. Through 1952, when the group disbanded for a time, some 4,000,000

records were sold of such songs as "On Top of Old Smoky," "Goodnight Irene," and "So Long, It's Been Good to Know You." Before re-forming The Weavers in 1955, Seeger went his own way on concert tours all over the world. His efforts included a series of six concerts at Columbia University, New York, in 1954-55 on "American Folk Music and Its Origins."

His legal troubles with the U.S. government began in 1955 when he took the Fifth Amendment before the House Committee. He was later indicted on ten counts of contempt of Congress, but the charges were dismissed by the U.S. Court of Appeals on May 18, 1962.

Despite all this, Seeger kept busy enough. From 1955 to '57 he was back with The Weavers. He then went on to help revive the Newport Folk Festival in the early 1960s. During this time, he was contributing to Sing Out! magazine and also working on new songs and records. His LP output through the mid-1960s was well over 40 albums. Many of his songs of the 1960s have become standards, including "Where Have All the Flowers Gone," "If I Had a Hammer" (written with Lee Hays), and "Kisses Sweeter Than Wine."

In 1967, he finally returned to American network TV as featured guest on the CBS "Smothers Brothers Comedy Hour." He also had his own show on educational TV in 1968 and '69, called "Rainbow Quest." (*See also* ALMANAC SINGERS; NEWPORT FOLK FESTIVAL; SEEGER, CHARLES; SEEGER, MIKE; SEEGER, PEGGY; WEAVERS, THE)

SEEKERS, THE: Vocal group, Athol Guy, born Melbourne, Australia, January 5, 1940; Judith Durham, born Melbourne, July 7, 1943; Bruce Woodley, born Melbourne, July 25, 1942; Keith Potger, born Colombo, Ceylon, March 2, 1941.

One of the fresh sounds to grace the folk music field of the mid-1960s came from Australia by way of Liverpool, England. It took the form of The Seekers, a personable foursome consisting of three natives of Melbourne and a fourth individual, Keith Potger, who was born on the island of Ceylon in the Indian Ocean. (He had few memories of his exotic birthplace; his family moved to Australia when he was six.)

All four attended school in Melbourne, but did not meet until they began their working careers. Athol and Bruce found a joint interest

The Seekers

in music when they became acquainted in the advertising agency for which both worked. Later they met Judith, who was a secretary for a Melbourne firm, and Keith, who produced radio shows.

They combined forces to sing folk music, ranging from items from Australia and England to Negro spirituals and Woody Guthrie compositions. By spring of 1964, they had made several appearances in local coffee houses. Their style met with quick success with Melbourne folk fans and led to a number of spots on TV shows in the city. Later in 1964, they decided they were ready to try for a wider audience and left for England.

English producers were equally impressed with the new group. The result was an appearance on the top British TV show, "Sunday Night at the Palladium," three weeks after they reached London. Their performance made them one of the most discussed new groups in Eng-

land. They were signed by E. M. I., the major English recording company and main stockholder in Capitol Records in the U.S.

One of their first singles, "I'll Never Find Another You," released in December 1964, became the number one song in England in March 1965. Capitol released it in the U.S., backed with the spiritual "Open Up Them Pearly Gates," and it became a major pop hit in the States as well. American audiences also took to the first LP released by Capitol, "The New Seekers." Soon after, The Seekers turned out another hit, "A World of Our Own." The LP of the same title included such songs as "Leavin' of Liverpool," "Just a Closer Walk with Thee," "Allentown Jail," "Four Strong Winds," "This Land Is Your Land," and such Dylan songs as "Don't Think Twice, It's All Right" and "The Times They Are A-Changin'."

During the rest of the '60's the group made several worldwide tours, touching base in both the U.S. and Australia. In 1967, they scored with another hit, the title song from the movie "Georgy Girl." The reverse side of the record was "When the Stars Begin to Fall." Capitol also released an LP of theirs titled "Georgy Girl."

SETTLE, MIKE: *See* New Christy Minstrels

SHELDON, ERNIE: *See* Gateway Singers, The

SHEPARD, JEAN: Singer, bass player. Born Pauls Valley, Oklahoma, November 21, 1933.

One of the biggest voices on the Grand Ole Opry in the 1960s belonged to a girl just five feet, one inch tall. But blonde, attractive Jean always liked to do things in a big way. Her first choice of a musical instrument was a bass fiddle that was bigger than she was.

She was born in Pauls Valley, Oklahoma, and grew up listening to country music on radio and records. When she was 11, her family moved to the small town of Visalia in California. Before long, Jean had learned to play bass fiddle and had also demonstrated her singing ability at school and in her neighborhood. She soon teamed up with some of the other girls to entertain at picnics, celebrations, and dances. Jean began to receive attention from music fans in nearby towns and cities.

Her singing ability came to the attention of Hank Thompson who was touring through that part of the country in the early 1950s. He was impressed with her voice and brought her to the attention of Ken Nelson of Capitol Records. Nelson, who was responsible for starting many performers on the road to stardom, signed Jean to a contract. Her first single release, called "Crying Steel Guitar Waltz," won many DJ plays across the country. The next record established her as star material. "Dear John Letter," cut with Ferlin Husky, was one of the number-one-rated songs of 1953. After turning out a number of well received but not top 10 records, she hit with two songs in 1955, "Beautiful Lies" and "Satisfied Mind."

During the late 1950s, Jean became a regular in the cast of the Red Foley Saturday night network show originating on KWTO, Missouri. She was featured as a guest artist on many national TV shows and won ovations from crowds at in-person shows across the U.S. After two years with the Foley show, she moved to Nashville as a member of the Grand Ole Opry cast. In the mid-1960s, she delighted Opry

Jean Shepard

audiences with such new hits as "Second Fiddle (to an Old Guitar)" ('64) and, with Ray Pillow, "I'll Take the Dog" ('66).

Jean's popularity was also measured in sales of her LPs in the late '50s and the '60s. These included "Songs of a Love Affair," "Lonesome Love," "This Is Jean Shepard" ('59); "Got You on My Mind" ('61); "Heartaches and Tears" ('62); "Best of Jean Shepard" ('63); "Lighthearted and Blue" ('64).

SHOLES, STEVE: Record company executive. Born Washington, D.C., February 12, 1911; died Nashville, Tennessee, April 22, 1968. Elected to Country Music Hall of Fame, 1967.

The name Steve Sholes means little to the public at large. To people in the music business, however, it brings to mind one of the surest judges of talent in the field, a man instrumental in the success of many of the most important country and western artists in the two decades after World War II.

Stephen Sholes is also closely associated with the growth of RCA Victor. By the mid-1960s, Steve had spent almost four decades with the company. Born in the nation's capital, Steve moved to New Jersey with his family in the 1920s. In 1929, while attending high school in

Camden, New Jersey, he gained a part time job with RCA Victor Records. He left to attend nearby Rutgers University, but found another job waiting for him when he finished college in 1935. In 1937, he was assigned his first Artists and Repertoire position. In this capacity he worked with the division's jazz artists, assisting with selection of material and recording sessions.

When World War II came along, Steve joined the Army in 1943. The military soon drew on his background to help in production of V-disks for distribution to Army special services throughout the world. He helped produce records with organizations and performers ranging from classical cellist Gregor Piatigorsky to the Original Dixieland Band. As part of his job, Steve made the last recordings of the great Fats Waller.

In 1945, Sholes returned to civilian life as Studio and Custom Manager of RCA Victor. Later in the year, he was appointed Manager, Country and Western and Rhythm and Blues Artists and Repertoire. During the next twelve years, he helped develop the RCA country and western roster into one of the most impressive in the field. Among the artists he helped bring to prominence were Chet Atkins, Eddy Arnold, Elton Britt, Hank Snow, Homer and Jethro, The Browns, Hank Locklin, Jim Reeves, Roy Rogers, PeeWee King, Sons of the Pioneers, Al Hirt, and Elvis Presley. He also contributed to development of artists in other categories as well.

Sholes' importance to the company was recognized by a 1957 appointment as Manager of Pop Singles, followed by the same role for Pop Albums in 1958. In 1961, he was promoted to Manager of West Coast Operations, based in Hollywood. In this position, he planned and directed all A&R functions and coordinated activities and policies related to West Coast marketing, sales, custom, recording, and administrative operations. After several years, he returned to the East Coast again as Division Vice President, Popular Artists and Repertoire, RCA Victor, with headquarters in New York City.

On April 22, 1968, while driving from the airport to RCA's Nashville studios, Steve Sholes suffered a fatal heart attack.

SILBER, IRWIN: Editor, author, publisher. Born New York, New York, October 17, 1925.

In the post-World War II decades, folk music magazines blossomed by the score, but few lasted for more than a few issues. Of those that survived, only one, Sing Out!, grew steadily in stature to become, in the mid-1960s, one of the best known folk music publications in the world. The two names most closely associated with the birth and progress of Sing Out! were Moses Asch and the magazine's editor, Irwin Silber.

Silber was born and raised on the Lower East Side of New York's borough of Manhattan. He attended public schools and went on to enroll at Brooklyn College in the early 1940s. His interest in folk music was already strong when he was in his teens, and in 1943 he founded and was director of the American Folksay Group. He continued in this role after receiving his B.A. from Brooklyn College in 1945. In 1947, he switched his attention to the People's Songs organization, remaining as executive director until 1949.

During the late 1940s, Silber worked closely with most of the major folk artists in the New York area, such as Pete Seeger, Woody Guthrie, and Lee Hays. He also worked with Moses Asch, founder of Folkways Records and one of the major forces in presenting folk music in published or recorded form to the American public.

The folk song magazine Sing Out! was started in 1950 as an outgrowth of Asch's recording enterprises. Silber was not the first editor of the publication, but took over after the first few issues. Under his guidance, the magazine slowly developed from a quarterly to a semi-monthly and, in the 1960s, to an even more regular frequency. Over the years, almost every person of stature in the folk music field, on both performing and academic levels, wrote articles for Sing Out! Besides his editing chores, Silber often contributed articles plus a regular column, "Fan the Flames."

In 1960, a book-publishing operation, Oak Publications, was added to the folk song complex. Silber added the job of president of Oak Publications to his other work. In 1967, he was still serving in this position while continuing as editor of Sing Out! (In 1967, Oak Publications was sold to Consolidated Music Co.)

During the '50s and '60s, he also had other strings to his bow. These included editing or writing a number of books and serving as producer and editor of various documentary record albums. Silber's book credits include:

Lift Every Voice, Oak Publications; *Songs of the Civil War*, Columbia University Press; *This Singing Land*, Consolidated; and *Songs of the Great American West*, Macmillan.

SIMAN, E. E. "SI," JR.: Music publisher, talent scout, radio and record executive. Born January 17, 1921.

In 1967, Eddy Arnold had a smash hit in a song called "Somebody Like Me." Arnold's artistry coupled with disk jockey plays and the merit of the song itself were important, but there was another part of the puzzle that helped make the song a hit. This was the music publisher who recognized the song's worth and helped gain the artist's acceptance. The man in question was Si Siman, an old-timer in this and other basic phases of the music business. Over the years, Siman has had a major hand in shaping the careers of many of today's stars as well as placing many songs on the hit lists.

Siman was born and brought up in Springfield where he helped support his family at an early

Si Siman

age. When he was 10, he sold a popsicle to Ralph Foster, general manager of station KWTO, and the result was a start of a career and a long-time business association. In the 1930s, Foster helped young Si learn the ropes of both the radio and music games. Later on, Siman used this background as part-owner of stations KJPW in Waynesville, Missouri, and KCIJ, Shreveport.

By the time Siman was in his twenties, he had racked up considerable experience in finding talent and producing shows on radio. His reputation in the country music field expanded and he moved to California to try his hand at the big time. In the late 1940s and early '50s, he helped produce many of the featured radio country and western shows, including 260 of the early Tennessee Ernie Ford shows and 293 of the Smiley Burnette series.

While keeping at his producing chores, Siman kept an eye out for likely performers. In the late '40s, he met one who played one of the most fabulous guitars in the business. Siman made a record dub of a song called "Canned Heat" and took it to RCA Artists and Repertoire man Steve Sholes. The result was a contract and a long-time association between Chet Atkins and RCA. Soon after, Siman farmed out another of his finds to station KWTO for experience and repeated the performance with Sholes. The latter artist was a fellow Missourian named Porter Wagoner.

In the early 1950s, Siman took another major step. After learning the right approach from publisher Fred Rose, Siman set up his own music publishing firm in association with John Barton Mahaffey. Combining the middle names of both men, they called the company Earl Barton Music, Inc. Within a few years, the company had built up one of the major catalogs in the country field. Among the songs published by the firm are: "Company's Comin'," "Tricks of the Trade," "Somebody Like Me," "Make Believe," "What Would You Do (If Jesus Came to Your House)," and "I'd Like to Be." In 1966, Siman started another music firm with Ronnie Self called Tablerock Music, Inc.

Despite the success of his music publishing firm, Siman kept trying his hand at new producing ventures. In 1960, he was co-executive producer of the first color country music show on network TV. The show, called NBC-TV Five Star Jubilee, featured such stars as Rex Allen, Carl Smith, Tex Ritter, Snooky Lanson, and

Jimmy Wakely. Before this, Siman had helped start the first network TV country music show. Originating on Siman's home station of KWTO as the Ozark Jubilee, it moved on to become a six-year mainstay on ABC-TV as Jubilee U.S.A. The hand-picked m.c. of the show was Red Foley.

Siman is credited with helping the careers of dozens of major performers. On one tour of Georgia, he heard a little girl sing and soon moved her and her family to Springfield. The girl's family name was Rainwater, but she is better known as Brenda Lee. Others whom Siman has promoted include Billy Walker, Bobby Lord, LeRoy Van Dyke, Norma Jean, Sonny Jean, Wanda Jackson, Marvin Rainwater, and Homer and Jethro.

SIMON AND GARFUNKEL: Vocal and instrumental duo, songwriting team, Paul Simon, born Newark, New Jersey, November 5, 1942; Art Garfunkel, born New York, New York, October 13, 1942.

Simon and Garfunkel were ranked among the most unique and sensitive artists in the new urban folk vein of the 1960s before they reached their mid-twenties. As a Los Angeles *Times* reporter wrote on the occasion of their Hollywood Bowl appearance in July 1967, "Their songs are the most literary inhabitants of the pop music charts, delicately exploring the problems of alienation, aging, communication, death and love (in the cities)."

The two met when their families took up residence in the borough of Queens, New York City. Their friendship began in the sixth grade of elementary school and ripened into a singing act when Paul mastered the art of guitar playing. They began to sing at school functions and local gatherings, branching out to weekend club dates when they reached college. (Simon went to Queens College, where he eventually earned a B.A. in English literature, while Garfunkel majored in education and math at Columbia University.)

At the end of their sophomore year, they came on strong with an engagement at Gerde's Folk City in Greenwich Village. Among those who caught their act was Columbia Records executive Tom Wilson, who quickly offered a recording contract. In a matter of days, the boys were in a studio recording their first album, "Wednesday Morning: 3 A.M." It comprised many songs written and arranged by the team. From mid-1964 to early '65, the album sold slowly—between 8,000 and 9,000 copies, mostly to folk addicts. In the meantime, the team separated for a while, with Simon taking off alone for a tour of England in the summer of '65. The tour went well, but not spectacularly.

Nothing sensational seemed to be brewing. But while Simon was abroad, "Sounds of Silence," one of the LP numbers, began to get played on stations in Houston and Miami. A Columbia distributor in Miami advised the home office and the company took the track off the album and underdubbed a 12-string guitar, drums, echo, etc., before releasing the song as a single.

Simon knew nothing about this until he suddenly found that the song had moved to 25th position on the U.S. top 40. He promptly cut short his tour and flew back to the U.S. to resume work with Garfunkel. Requests for appearances came in thick and fast. Over the period from mid-1965 to 1967, the team's concerts covered most of the U.S., the Streets of Paris club in Paris, Edinburgh University, Scotland, etc. Their TV credits soon included Ed Sullivan, Hullaballoo, and many other major network events.

The boys continued to turn out best-selling singles and LPs. Their second LP came out in 1965, called "Sounds of Silence." The third LP was the 1966 "Parsley, Sage, Rosemary and Thyme," which topped the million-dollar gold record mark by mid-'67. Among their major singles hits were "I Am a Rock," "Homeward Bound," "The Dangling Conversation," "A Hazy Shade of Winter," "Christmas Eve, 7 P.M.," and "At the Zoo." In '67, Simon tried a new medium when he was asked to compose a number of songs for the Mike Nichols movie "The Graduate." The song "Mrs. Robinson" from the score was one of 1968's top hits.

SINGING BRAKEMAN, THE: *See* Rodgers, Jimmie C.

SINGLETON, SHELBY: Producer, publisher. Born Waskom, Texas, December 16, 1931.

Shelby Singleton knows the south and its personalities. He put situations together at the right time and helped contribute to the widening base of respect that country music has acquired from nominally pop music areas. Shortly after he saw Marine Corps service in Korea, where he was wounded (he still carries a metal plate in his head as a souvenir), Singleton settled in Shreveport, where he was named local promotion manager for Mercury Records.

A local promotion manager wears many hats. He covers the radio stations to persuade disk jockeys and management of the merits of his records, checks out the music stores and outlets to stimulate sales, and checks over what the competition has going, works with the local promoters who have booked his company's artists for appearances, works with the artists and their management when they get into town, coordinates with the sales force of the local record distributor and national sales personnel, and listens a lot. Singleton listened and learned.

Shreveport was the home of the Louisiana Hayride and saw a lot of recording artists each week. There were established talent, promising youngsters, and both established and upstart record producers. Singleton hustled, acquired skills, and was named Mercury's Southern Regional Sales Manager in a year's time. Another year and he was made a record producer for Mercury in Nashville. Singleton chose to operate out of New York for the most part, picking up still more valuable experience.

He started mixing situations and elements in combinations which provided a Brook Benton hit, "Boll Weevil," and blending current pop numbers with country songs in an array of hits in both fields for both types of acts. He kept in touch with Shreveport, Fort Worth, Nashville, and bus-stop towns between by phone, wire, and hasty trips. If a small company had a record out that was getting great radio play in Houston or Meridian, Mississippi, Singleton knew about it and tried to acquire it for his Mercury operation, usually successfully. His network of contacts over the short span of years sent him new songs, artists, and master recordings.

Some of the results were evidenced in "Walk on By" by LeRoy Van Dyke, which was Van Dyke's second chance for stardom following his southern "Auctioneer" hit of several years previously. When Singleton was recording in the old Owen Bradley studio in Nashville, Atlanta publisher Bill Lowery pointed out a studio musician, Ray Stevens, resulting in "Ahab The Arab." Teddy and Doyle Wilburn brought him a youngster from Michigan who had hit Nashville's music row of publishers with little luck; "Wooden Heart" with Joe

Dowell was the immediate product. Some of the other artists and songs, among many, that the Singleton catalytic action turned into hits were "Hey Paula" by Paul and Paula, "Green Green Grass of Home" with Jerry Lee Lewis, and further hits with Brook Benton, Del Wood, George Jones, Faron Young, Rusty Draper, and Dave Dudley.

Besides supervising recording sessions, Singleton developed Jerry Kennedy, who played great guitar on Nashville sessions, and Jerry Ross as recording directors. Their activities led to the rise of the fortunes of Roger Miller.

In 1966, following a nine-year tenure with the Mercury organization, Singleton resigned to set up his own producing company based in Nashville and New York.

In July 1968, he hit the jackpot with his new operation. He supervised a recording session on his record label, Plantation Records, for an unknown young singer named Jeannie Riley. From this came the satiric hit single, "Harper Valley P.T.A.," that propelled her to stardom in a few months' time and brought record sales for Selby's firm of more than 4 million.

SITAR: Stringed instrument of Indian origin.

In the mid-1960s, one of the surest ways to insure a sellout crowd at a folk or pop festival was to feature a great musician from India, Ravi Shankar. His playing of the ancient Hindu guitar, the sitar, helped start a vogue for the instrument in all segments of western music. Those with whom Shankar was featured in various concerts ranged from the Beatles to country and western artist Chet Atkins.

The sitar is an instrument usually played in the sitting position because of its length. The typical sitar is about five feet long, with roughly 80 per cent of its length consisting of a rectangular-shaped fretted neck. The bottom of the instrument is shaped like the lower section of a conventional guitar but without the double curvature of the sounding box. The number of strings is usually more than on any variation of the conventional guitar. With typical sitars having up to 35 strings, tuning pegs for the strings run the length of the neck.

The sitar is believed to have evolved from a somewhat smaller instrument called the veena. Typically, seven main strings are used to carry the melody with the other strings providing backup. Though considered a classical instrument in India, it still is much more fluidly used than Western classical concepts would permit. Thus there is little written music for the sitar, the artist being left free to improvise varying arrangements to certain classical melodies.

As of the mid-1960s, the growing interest in the sitar's potential was recognized by many new courses in the instrument both among private teachers and in university-level courses.

SKILLET LICKERS: *See* Tanner, Gid

SKINNER, JIMMIE: Singer, guitarist, songwriter, disk jockey. Born near Berea, Kentucky, April 27.

The border state of Kentucky provided Nashville with a good many of the top country music favorites. Despite the continued outflow of artists to the country music capital, there were always plenty of first-rank singers and musicians on programs from Kentucky to Chicago. One of the shows that received less credit than it deserved for the stars it helped develop was Jimmie Skinner's show on WNOP, Newport, Kentucky.

Jimmie, the show's m.c., could claim credentials as both a native-born Kentuckian and a performer of national rank. He was singing country and western music when he was high school age. From performing at local dances, he went on to work as a disk jockey and artist at several stations in the 1940s, including WNOX, Knoxville, and WPEB, Middletown, Ohio.

He also showed talent as a songwriter, turning out his first successful effort in 1941, "Doin' My Time." He followed up with several hundred songs over the next few decades, including "I'm Lonely" ('44); "Will You Be Satisfied That Way" ('48); "There's Nothing About You Special" ('50); "Falling Rain Blues" and "It's All the Same to Me" ('51); and "Riverboat Gambler" (co-authored, '59). Some of his other songs were "John Wesley Hardin," "Let's Say Goodbye Like We Said Hello," and "Two Squares Away."

In the years after World War II, Jimmie was a midwest favorite both as performer and as m.c. of his own show. Among his recorded songs that his radio audiences requested were "Where My Sweet Baby Goes," "On the Wrong Side of the Tracks," "We've Got Things in Common," "Born to Be Wild," "How Long Can You Feel," "Beautiful," "Walkin' My Blues Away," "I Need a Little Lovin' Too" and "Jesus Loves Us Too."

By the mid-1950s, a number of Jimmie's efforts on Mercury label had received many plays across the country. In 1958, he gained national attention with a top 10 recording of his own composition, "I Found My Girl in the U.S.A." The following year, he came up with another national hit, "Dark Hollow."

In the 1950s, Jimmie scored with an LP album for Mercury, "Songs That Make the Juke Box Play." In 1961, he was represented on Decca Records with the LP "Jimmie Skinner." He then signed with Starday Records, which produced the LPs "Kentucky Colonel" ('63) and "Let's Say Goodbye" ('64). Mercury also turned out another LP of his songs in 1964, "Country Blues."

Besides making personal appearances in many cities in the 1960s, particularly in the midwest and border states region, Jimmie also ran his own record store in Cincinnati, the Jimmie Skinner Music Center.

SKY, PAT: Singer, instrumentalist (guitar, banjo, harmonica, mouth-bow), songwriter, author. Born Liveoak Gardens, Georgia, October 2, 1940.

One of the most talented of the young folk artists and writers of the 1960s, Patrick "Pat" Sky also has the distinction of introducing a new kind of instrument to modern folk audiences. This is the Indian mouth-bow, a primitive instrument Sky re-created from memories of his Cree Indian heritage. Pat taught his friend Buffy Sainte-Marie to play the instrument, providing one of the striking parts of her folk concerts.

Pat was born in Georgia, but spent most of his youth in the LaFouche Swamp region of Louisiana. He was exposed to folk and country and western influences from his earliest years. His grandmother loved to sing traditional songs and taught Pat many of them. Some of these songs are still high points of his concerts. Before he was in his teens, he could play several instruments, including banjo, guitar, and harmonica. When he reached high school age, he was already singing both traditional and contemporary songs for audiences in his home area.

Pat went on to college, spent some years in the Army, and then, after leaving the service, decided to concentrate on music. In the early 1960s, he began to sing in small clubs and coffee houses in various parts of the country. His talents were soon recognized by word of mouth from one fan to another and he was encouraged to move on to New York.

He was welcomed into the ranks of coffee house entertainers and soon won over the Greenwich Village audiences. In 1964, many other artists were singing his compositions and echoing his praises. By the end of the year, he had been signed by Vanguard Records. So rapidly had his fame spread that there were orders on hand for his first album before it was on the market. The LP was turned out in June '65 and won immediate critical acclaim. HiFi/Stereo Review called the recording "Very Good" and the performance "Infectious." Called simply "Patrick Sky," it included such songs as "Everytime," "Hangin' Round," "Rattlesnake Mountain," "Come with Me, Love" and "Many a Mile."

The last of these was one of a number of original Sky songs in the album. It also was a song on the way to becoming a classic in the modern folk idiom. Buffy Sainte-Marie used it as the title song for one of her albums. By 1966, this and such other of his compositions as "Separation Blues," "Hangin' Round," "Nectar of God," and "Love Will Endure" were being sung by folk artists throughout the world. Pat's second LP, issued in 1966, duplicated the success of the first.

Pat continued to add to his stature in 1966 with concerts in many parts of the U.S. and overseas. He was also featured on many network TV shows. His 1966 credits included sell-out crowds for solo concerts at New York's Town Hall and Carnegie Hall. An overflow crowd also applauded his Central Park Music Festival concert.

During the year, he wrote songs and a background score and also performed in a film on conservation called "Down the Road." The score, which included the title song, received critical approval when the film was released in early 1967.

SMITH, (FIDDLIN') ARTHUR: *See* Smith, Fiddlin' Arthur

SMITH, ARTHUR: Singer, guitarist, band leader, producer of package music shows, music publisher. Born Clinton, South Carolina, April 1, 1921.

Among the most popular grass roots country music packages of the 1950s and '60s were the Arthur Smith Shows. The shows, a blend of traditional and popular country music and gospel material, played to capacity audiences in fairs and theaters throughout the south and southwest. Radio and TV versions of the shows also had a solid following among audiences in many parts of the country.

The man behind these activities had learned country music from the ground up as a performer and songwriter. Were it not for his youthful enthusiasm for music, though, he might have gone on to a career as an Army or Navy officer. His school performance was far above average. He was president as well as valedictorian of his South Carolina high school class. On graduation, he was offered scholarships from Wofford College; Citadel College, a military school; and the U.S. Naval Academy. But he turned all of these down in favor of organizing a hillbilly band.

As a boy, he grew up in an atmosphere favorable to this choice. His father was an employee and band director of a local textile mill. While Arthur was still in grade school, he performed with this group. The middle one of three brothers, he soon sparked the formation of a country music group with the other two, when he was only in the eighth grade. Two years later the brothers had an RCA Victor recording contract.

In the mid-1930s, Smith performed before many regional audiences and his name became well known to many country fans. In 1937, he debuted on radio, a medium in which he was to excel on many stations in the following years. He also taught music for a while during this period.

The Smith Brothers remained together until the onset of World War II. Each brother went into a different branch of service with Arthur ending up in the U.S. Navy Band. While in service, he composed and recorded a song called "Guitar Boogie" for MGM Records. The record became a major hit, eventually selling more than three million copies. A silver pressing of the song was selected for the American Archive of Folk Song of the Library of Congress.

The Smith group reorganized after the war and expanded to include other acts for various variety programs on WBT radio and WBT-TV in Charlotte, North Carolina. Gospel and hymn singing was an integral part of the format, reflecting Arthur Smith's deep religious feeling.

In 1947 he started teaching Bible classes, something he still devoted time to in the late 1960s despite his other commitments, directing a men's Bible class each week at Providence Baptist Church in Charlotte.

During the 1950s, the Arthur Smith Shows became more diversified with several troupes appearing at engagements in many states. The guest rosters featured many country music greats, but also such varied names as Richard Nixon, E. G. Marshall, evangelist Billy Graham, and duo pianists Ferrante and Teicher.

The entertainment content of the shows included comedy sketches, pop songs, country and western plus one or two hymns per performance. Many of the songs played over the years were originally composed by Arthur Smith, including such titles as "Banjo Buster," "I Saw a Man," "Foolish Questions" and "Shadow of the Cross." Smith remains one of the nation's top gospel song writers, as shown by the makeup of his catalog of more than 200 compositions, of which better than a quarter are in a religious vein.

Smith's contributions to country and gospel music have been recognized by means of many awards. He won Billboard's first annual award in both the folk and country and western categories and also was a recipient of many awards from religious organizations.

In the years after World War II, Smith was active in production of many other major shows in addition to his own. These included the Johnny Cash Show, James Brown Show, Flatt & Scruggs Show, and George Beverly Shea's "Hymntime." He was also featured as an artist on LPs for various labels. His output included "Arthur Smith and the Crossroads Quartet" on Starday ('62) and "Arthur Smith" on Hamilton ('64). In the mid-1960s he recorded for Dot Records, producing the masters in his own studio in Charlotte.

SMITH, CARL: Singer, guitarist. Born Maynardsville, Tennessee, March 15, 1927.

One of the most successful country and western performers of the 1950s and '60s, Carl Smith, got his start cutting grass. At least, it was through the proceeds from this activity that young Carl was able to pay for his guitar lessons in his home town of Maynardsville. By the time he was 13, he felt he was ready to try his hand in an amateur talent contest. The crowd reaction was enough to make him concentrate on becoming a country and western performer.

A few years later, he got his first big chance in Knoxville. One of the regular performers on station WROL needed a replacement and Carl subbed for him. His work was good enough to win him a regular job on the station. His career was interrupted by a hitch in the Navy. After 18 months of service, he got his discharge and returned to WROL in the late 1940s. For a while, he decided to expand his horizons by appearing on other stations, including one in Augusta, Georgia, and another in Asheville, North Carolina.

In the end, though, WROL remained his good luck charm. He returned there to work with Mollie O'Day and Archie Campbell. Audience acceptance was strong and Carl's reputation increased to the point of winning him a bid to join the Grand Ole Opry. His debut came in May 1950, and within a short time he was one of the most popular personalities.

Along with the Opry job came a contract with Columbia Records. One of his first disks, "Let's Live a Little," was one of the major hits of 1951. For the next decade, it was a rare week when a Carl Smith record was not high on the charts. He added two more hits in 1951, "If Teardrops Were Pennies" and "Mr. Moon." His 1952 output included four major hits: the number-one-rated "Just Don't Stand There"; "Are You Teasing Me," "It's a Lovely, Lovely World," and "Our Honeymoon." The following year, Carl gained number-one chart position for a second time with "Hey Joe." Other 1953 hits were "Satisfaction Guaranteed," "This Orchid Means Goodbye," and "Trademark." In 1954, Smith had best-sellers in "Back Up, Buddy," "Doggone It Baby, I'm in Love," and "Loose Talk." The latter was number one on the hit charts for more than 30 weeks. It won Billboard's Triple Crown award and Downbeat Magazine's Best New Western Band of the Year award for Carl. Other major Smith hits included "Kisses Don't Lie" and "There She Goes" ('55); "Why Why" ('57); "Your Name Is Beautiful" ('58); "Ten Thousand Drums" ('59); and "Foggy River" ('68).

Through the 1960s, Carl was featured in person and on TV and radio around the world. His tours took him to all states of the U.S., all of Canada's provinces, and throughout Europe and the Far East. His TV guest spots included Porter Wagoner Shows, Wilburn Brothers Shows, and the Philip Morris Country Music Show. In the mid-1960s, his weekly TV show—Carl Smith's Country Music Hall—was telecast coast-to-coast in Canada. During this period, he also appeared in two movies, "The Badge of Marshal Brennan" and "Buffalo Guns."

Smith's LP album output included: "I Want to Live and Love"; "Great Country and Western Hits"; "Easy to Please"; "The Best of Carl Smith"; "Sunday Down South"; "Smith's the Name"; "Tall, Tall Gentleman"; "Carl Smith's Touch"; and "Kentucky Derby."

In the 1960s, Smith and his talented wife, Goldie Hill, resided with their three children on a large ranch near Nashville. (*See also* HILL, GOLDIE)

SMITH, CONNIE: Singer, Born Elkhart, Indiana, August 14, 1941.

From housewife to winner of almost every award in sight as new country and western vocalist in a little more than a year's time is a neat trick. It was this achievement, naturally, that won Connie Smith the title of "Cinderella Girl of Country Music."

Constance was born and brought up in Indiana in the town made famous by the Alka-Seltzer Company. By the time she was in high school she was already a country music buff, collecting records of the top artists and attending occasional personal appearance concerts of some of them. Though Connie had an excellent voice and sang in local events, she didn't give much thought to trying for a stage career. She still enjoyed singing, even after she married and settled down in the midwest.

This interest led to her entering an amateur contest held near Columbus, Ohio, in 1963. One of those attending the event was country and western artist Bill Anderson. He could tell that Connie was no ordinary amateur contestant, and set about helping her get started in the country field. She agreed to sing with Anderson and it wasn't long before she had many other bids to appear with leading country performers. She also was given a recording contract with RCA Victor.

In 1964, she had a number of records on the hit charts. One of them, her version of Bill Anderson's "Once a Day," was number one in the nation for many weeks. When the year was over, she was voted the "Most Promising Country Female Singer of 1964" by Billboard,

an award she won again in 1965. Connie continued to move up in national stature in 1965 with more hit singles, including top 10 entries "I Can't Remember," "If I Talk to Him," and "Then and Only Then." On June 13, 1965, her talent was recognized by a bid to become a cast regular with the Grand Ole Opry. In 1966, she could sing such new top 10 hits for Opry audiences as "Ain't Had No Lovin' " and "Nobody But a Fool." She was also represented by many best-selling albums, including "Connie Smith," "Cute and Country," "Miss Smith Goes to Nashville," "Great Sacred Songs," "Born to Sing" and "Downtown Country."

During the mid-1960s, she was a guest star on such programs as the Jimmy Dean Show, American Swing-Around, Singin' Country, WGN Barn Dance, Ralph Emery, Bobby Lord, and the Lawrence Welk Show. She also was featured in appearances with Loretta Lynn, George Jones, Bill Anderson, George Morgan, Rex Allen, Jimmy Dean, and Sonny James. She was starred in a number of country movies, such as "Road to Nashville," "Las Vegas Hillbillies," and "Second Fiddle to a Steel Guitar."

Her awards continued to pile up. The Country Music Review voted her the Most Promising Female Singer of 1965. She won a similar award from Cashbox in '65. Record World magazine voted her the "Most Outstanding Female Country and Western Vocalist" for 1966 as did Cashbox. She was also voted the "Best Vocalist, Country and Western Field" by the International Western Market Pioneer Awards.

In 1967, she was represented on the charts by such songs as "I'll Come A Runnin' " and "Cincinnati, Ohio," and in 1968 by "Runaway Little Tears" and "Baby's Back Again."

SMITH, FIDDLIN' ARTHUR: Singer, fiddler, banjoist, songwriter, band leader. Born Dixon County, Tennessee.

The fiddle has always been an important part of country music, though its use has diminished considerably since the 1930s. In past times, the art of fiddle playing was often a family tradition, handed down from father to son as was the case with Fiddlin' Arthur Smith. Smith Senior was a railroader who played fiddle in his spare time for his own enjoyment and for local events. He taught Arthur to play before the boy was in his teens and the two sometimes performed together.

Like his father, Arthur kept his music a

sideline and earned his living working for the railroad. In 1930, though, he met Sam and Kirk McGee, who were impressed with Smith's fiddling skill. Arthur joined the McGee brothers in a trio called the Dixieliners. They began in a small way on local stations, but in a few years' time the trio was featured on WSM's Grand Ole Opry. For seven years, from about 1932 to 1938, Smith toured under WSM sponsorship both as a member of the McGee group and with his own Arthur Smith Trio. Smith's performances often included compositions of his own, such as "Chittlin' Cookin' Time in Cheatham County" and "Dusty Miller." (Some of his songs are derived from older folk tunes.)

In 1936, Smith gained a national reputation with the success of the Smith Trio recording of "There's More Pretty Girls Than One." Late in the decade, he often worked with The Delmore Brothers and helped make many of their best known recordings. Smith continued to perform as a sideman and with small groups of his own during the 1940s and '50s. The average country music fan had lost sight of Smith by the beginning of the 1960s. With the rise of the folk music field, however, many folk buffs became interested in him. He was asked to team up with the McGee brothers again for several appearances at major folk festivals. In July 1965, the three received a rousing ovation for their efforts at the Newport Folk Festival. Smith was represented on several LPs in the '60s, including a Folkways disk, "McGee Brothers and Arthur Smith: Milk 'em in the Evening Blues," and the Starday 1963 album "Fiddlin' Arthur Smith."

Though known mainly for his fiddle playing, Smith was also an excellent banjoist as he demonstrated in such numbers as "I'm Bound to Ride." (*See also* McGEE BROTHERS)

SMITH, HOBART: Singer, banjoist, guitarist, fiddler. Born Smyth County, Virginia, May 10, 1897; died Saltville, Virginia, January 11, 1965.

The 1960s was a time of rediscovery in folk music. Many of the great traditional country music artists existed for most people in the form of recordings made by such collectors as the Lomaxes and the Warners. As folk music interest expanded in the post-World War II era, many of the older artists were brought before audiences throughout the country. The charm and ability of such performers as Hobart Smith was as infectious to college students and big

city groups as it had been for years in rural areas of the country.

Smith's music ability showed up at a very early age. As stated in his Sing Out! autobiography (Jan. 1964, pp. 10-13, based on taped interviews with George Armstrong), "I started playing banjo when I was seven years old. When I was three, I commenced playing on an old fire shovel. . . ."

Both of Smith's parents played banjo and he learned to play from them. When he was seven he could pick out a tune on the banjo, and his father bought him a small, short-necked banjo from the Sears, Roebuck catalog. As he notes, he originally used the "old-timey rapping style" of banjo playing in which individual notes are picked rather than the three-finger picking style of Flatt & Scruggs. Later he concentrated on the double-noting (double-thumbing) style. His father ". . . kept his thumb on the thumb string and that thumb string was just a-going all the time. Now, John Greer came along and went from thumb string to the bottom—double noting—and he was the best man I ever heard on the banjo. And I patterned after him. . . ."

When he was in his early teens, Smith learned to play the guitar from listening to traveling Negro musicians, including Blind Lemon Jefferson. He also learned fiddle playing as a boy from an old colored man.

Smith was raised in an environment of music. He and his father and many of the neighbors played twice a week at the local square dance, and often gathered for an evening at home of singing and playing. In his youth, Smith helped his father run the farm and also ran the family wagon in a local hauling and moving business. He also worked as a painter and, for twelve years, as a butcher with the Olin-Mathieson Company.

During the 1920s, Smith continued active in music in a number of ways. For two years he played and danced in a local minstrel show that played engagements in nearby towns. For a time he had his own band and also played with Clarence Ashley in the late 1920s. As interest in old-style music died down in those years, Smith gave up the banjo. In the early 1930s he played fiddle at local dance halls, providing such music as "Golden Slippers" and "Comin' Around the Mountain."

With his sister, Mrs. Texas Gladden, he played more traditional songs, such as "Coo

Coo Bird," "Claude Allen," "Banging Break-down," "Last Chance," and "Cumberland Gap" at local folk music festivals. During most of the '30s, they were regular performers at the Whitetop, Virginia, event. In 1936, they were heard by Mrs. Eleanor Roosevelt, who invited them to the White House to play for President Roosevelt. In 1941-42, much of their material was recorded for the Library of Congress Archives by Alan Lomax.

For most of the '40s and '50s, Hobart Smith received little notice beyond his Virginia home country. When folk enthusiasts began to search out the old-time musicians, Hobart was one of those contacted. He and his sister won a stand-ing ovation at the 1963 Third University of Chicago Folk Festival in February. That fall, they were asked to give a concert at Chicago's Old Town School of Folk Music. While there, Smith recorded his first LP album for Folk-Legacy Records. Other folk collectors taped in-terviews with Smith. From then on, he was in demand for appearances at nationwide con-certs and at major folk festivals. Just after his performance at the Newport Folk Festival in the summer of 1964, he suffered a stroke that claimed his life in January 1965.

SMOKEY MOUNTAIN BOYS: *See* Acuff, Roy

SMOTHERS BROTHERS: Vocal and instru-mental duo, Thomas "Tommy" Smothers, born New York, New York, February 2, 1937; Rich-ard "Dick" Smothers, born New York, New York, November 20, 1938.

"The Smothers Brothers really are named Smothers and they really are brothers. But the rest of their folk singing act is a big put-on. Tom can't really be 27, he's six. When he steps onstage, cuddling his guitar, his confused, nurs-ery-school eyes peer out from under a shelf of eyebrows and are lit with a small, shim-mering touch of lunacy. And when he speaks, the defiant little-boy words spew out in a bub-bling rush of gags that sound much better than they really are.

"Singing 'Michael, Row the Boat Ashore,' he may break in with 'Hey, Michael, you better get that boat back; you'll lose your deposit.' He introduces 'John Henry' by calling the steel driver 'just a high school dropout'. . . ."

Thus did Newsweek (65:80, March 1, '65) describe one of the most popular folk acts of the 1960s. In 1967, even though the folk boom

of the early '60s had proven to be temporary, the Smothers Brothers rode high as proprietors of one of the most popular variety shows on television.

The brothers were born in New York, but soon moved to the Philippines, where their father, an Army career officer, was stationed. The boys remained there until the Japanese in-vasion during World War II. They and their mother were evacuated to the States, but Major Thomas B. Smothers, Jr., remained and was captured. He later died on a Japanese prison ship.

The boys were brought up in Redondo Beach, California. They attended public schools there and learned to play instruments. Tom became proficient at the guitar and Dick ended up with an unusual choice, the bass fiddle. By their high school graduation, they had worked up an act which was based on using folk music as a foil for comic routines. They played for high school affairs as amateurs, and continued to expand their routines when they entered San Jose State College in the mid-1950s. At the beginning for a brief time they worked with Bobby Blackmore as a trio. After several local appearances won enthusiastic audience response, the boys scored their first major breakthrough with an engagement in The Limelite in Aspen, Colorado.

They were an immediate success with the mostly college crowd and were soon on their way to engagements in all parts of the country. Their tours in the early '60s took them to concert halls, college campuses, and such night-clubs as New York's Basin Street East and the Flamingo Hotel in Las Vegas. They were also featured on many network television shows ranging from several appearances on the Ed Sullivan Show to spots on some of the folk music specials of those years.

Their humor had broad appeal far beyond the boundaries of the folk field. This was well illustrated by the success of their recordings for Mercury Records. Through early 1967, they had turned out nine albums for the label, all of which gained hit status. The titles included "Two Sides of the Smothers Brothers"; "Onion" ('61); "Think Ethnic" ('63); "Curb Your Tongue," "Something I Said" ('64); and "Amer-ican History" ('65).

CBS-TV decided the act had great potential for network programming. The boys were signed for a 1965 situation comedy called "The

[285]

Smothers Brothers Show." In this series, there was no singing—Tom played an angel who, despite his ineptness, helps his brother Dick, a junior publishing executive, on many occasions. The show failed to make the grade, however, because, as Dick stated in a 1967 interview with Sidney Skolsky, "We weren't ourselves. It was a story series . . ." (*Citizen News*, May 19, '67).

CBS refused to give up on them. In early 1967, the boys returned with a variety show to replace a canceled series. This time they performed their comedy routines and played in hilarious skits with their guest stars. The show quickly achieved top ratings and was renewed for the '67-'68 season. In the fall of '67, the Brothers showed their independent thinking by bringing long-blacklisted Pete Seeger back as a star of one of their shows. In '69 the still top-rated show was taken off CBS because of conflict over program censorship between the brothers and the network.

SNOW, HANK: Singer, guitarist. Born Liverpool, Nova Scotia, Canada, May 9, 1914.

Country music's appeal isn't limited to the U.S., as indicated by the many Canadian performers who have achieved stardom. One of the best from north of the border is Hank Snow. Through 1966, only Jim Reeves, Webb Pierce, and Eddy Arnold had more hits.

He originally became interested in country and western music through his love of western movies. In particular, he was partial to Tom Mix. He also received some incentive from his parents' interest in singing. His route to stardom was a rugged one, for he had to go out on his own at the age of 14. A good part of the next four years was spent at sea on fishing schooners. He also had many other trades, including newsboy, insurance salesman, Fuller Brush salesman, and stevedore. One of his early stevedoring jobs, unloading salt from a freighter, provided the $5.95 for his first guitar.

In his late teens, he was singing professionally in small clubs in the Nova Scotia area. This led to his first radio show in 1934, over station CHNS, Halifax, Nova Scotia. As "Hank, the Singing Ranger," he soon built up such a good following that RCA Victor gave him a recording contract in October 1936. While his popularity increased rapidly in Canada over the next few years, he was virtually unknown in the U.S. until the mid-1940s.

In 1944, he made his U.S. performing debut in Dallas in an engagement arranged by Ernest Tubb. For the next few years, he performed occasionally south of the Canadian border, but RCA continued to release his records only in Canada. Finally, in 1949, RCA sent the first of his recordings to U.S. distributors. The response was enough to make RCA issue several more in short order. The popularity of his first records with the U.S. public led to a bid to appear on the Grand Ole Opry in 1950. After this Snow was a mainstay on the U. S. country and western scene and a respected citizen of Nashville.

One of his first hits, "Marriage Vows" ('49), was still under the name "Hank, the Singing Ranger." This changed in 1950, with an output that included two number-one records, "Golden Locket" and "I'm Moving On." Both of these were written by Snow, who continued his writing efforts in 1951 with four hits, including one that made number one, "Rhumba Boogie." The other three were "Bluebird Island," "Music Makin' Mama from Memphis," and "Unwanted Sign on Your Heart."

Throughout the 1950s and '60s, it was a rare year that did not have at least one Hank Snow hit. The 1950s list includes "Fool Such As I," "Gal Who Invented Kissing," "Gold Rush Is Over," "I Went to Your Wedding," and "Lady's Man" (all 1952); "Honeymoon in a Rocket Ship," "Spanish Fire Ball," "When Mexican Joe Met Jole Blon" ('53); "I Don't Hurt Anymore" (number one) and "Let Me Go Lover" ('54); "Cryin', Prayin', Waitin', Hopin'," "Mainliner" and "Yellow Roses" ('55); "Conscience, I'm Guilty," "Stolen Moments" and "These Hands" ('56); "Tangled Mind" ('57); "Chasin' a Rainbow" and "The Last Ride" ('59).

Snow's successes of the 1960s include "Miller's Cave" ('60; "Beggar to a King" ('61); another best-in-the-nation effort, "I've Been Everywhere" ('62); "Ninety Miles an Hour" and "The Man Who Robbed the Bank at Santa Fe" ('63); and "The Wishing Well" ('65).

Reception of Hank's many LP albums was equally impressive. The titles, on Victor and Camden, exceeded several dozen by 1968. Victor LPs included "Country Classics"; "Country Guitar"; "Jamboree"; "Just Keep A-Movin' "; "Sacred Songs" ('58); "When Tragedy Struck" ('59); "Songs of Jimmie Rodgers" ('60); "Souvenirs" ('61); "Sings with The Carters" ('62); "Everywhere," "Railroad Man" ('63); "Songs of Tragedy" ('64); "Favorite Hits" ('65); "Spanish Fire Ball"; "Christmas with Hank Snow" ('67). His Camden output included "Hank, the Singing Ranger" ('60); "Southern Cannonball" ('61); "One and Only Hank Snow" ('62); "Last Ride" ('63); and "Old and Great Songs" ('64).

SOLEMN OL' JUDGE, THE: *See* Hay, George Dewey

SONS OF THE PIONEERS: Vocal and instrumental group.

When anyone thinks of vocal groups in western music, one name stands out above all others: the Sons of the Pioneers. The group is famous not only for its performances, but for the many standards of western music written by its members. Bob Nolan's "Cool Water" and "Tumbling Tumbleweeds," to name just two, are known to almost the entire music audience in the U.S. and in many other countries of the world as well.

The group started from a trio formed in 1930 by Roy Rogers. His two helpmates were Bob Nolan and Tim Spencer. They performed in many western cities and were featured in a

The Sons of the Pioneers as of the mid-1960s: (l. to r.) front, Pat Brady, Lloyd Perryman, Roy Lanham; back, Rusty Richards, Dale Warren.

series of radio sketches in the early '30s. One of their first recordings became a hit and helped propel Roy into his movie career. The group had already named itself Sons of the Pioneers when Roy left, and under Nolan's leadership gained both increased size (to six members) and national repute. In the 1930s and '40s, they turned out many best-selling records and also appeared in many movies, including many of Roy Rogers' efforts. Roy also joined the group for some of their recording sessions.

The Sons' early recordings included work on Decca and Columbia labels. The main share of their output, though, came during a long-term alignment with RCA Victor. Their Decca output included "Cool Water" and "There's a New Moon Over My Shoulder" and, on Columbia, "Open Range Ahead" and "The Devil's Great Grandson." By the late 1940s, they had turned out both albums and hit singles for Victor, including "Blue Prairie," "Cool Water," "Cigarettes, Whusky and Wild, Wild Women," "Room Full of Roses," "Home on the Range," "Lie Low, Little Doggies," and "Have I Told You Lately That I Love You." Early Victor albums included "Cowboy Classics" and "Cowboy Hymns and Spirituals."

In the 1950s, the Pioneers made many appearances throughout the country and in movies and TV. The makeup of the group in the early 1950s was: Bob Nolan, Tim Spencer, the Farr brothers, Hugh and Karl, Lloyd Perryman, and Pat Brady. Nolan was born in northern Canada to American parents and grew up in Tucson, Arizona; Perryman was born in Izzard County, Arkansas; the Farr brothers came from Texas; Tim Spencer came from Webb City, Missouri; and Pat Brady came from Toledo, Ohio. Brady later achieved fame as a comedian in Roy Rogers' movies and TV shows. Spencer retired from the group in 1952, but continued as manager until 1954.

Other members of the group during its long years of existence included Doye O'Dell, Ken Carson, Deuce Spriggins, Tommy Doss, and Ken Curtis.

Sons of the Pioneers LPs continued to find favor with national audiences through the '50s and '60s. In 1966, a number of Bob Nolan's less well known songs were performed on "The Sons of the Pioneers Sing the Songs of Bob Nolan." The album included such songs as "The Boss Is Hangin' Out a Rainbow"; "Night Falls on the Prairie"; "A Sandman Lullaby"; "Song of the Prairie"; "I Follow the Stream"; "At the Rainbow's End"; "One More Ride"; "Following the Sun All Day"; and "Cottage in the Clouds."

In the mid-1960s, the group had five members: senior member Lloyd Perryman (joined 1936), Pat Brady (joined 1937), Rusty Richards, Dale Warren, and Roy Lanham. (*See also* ROGERS, ROY; SPENCER, TIM)

SOUTHERN GENTLEMEN, THE: *See* James, Sonny

SOVINE, RED: Singer, guitarist, songwriter. Born Charleston, West Virginia, July 17, 1918.

One of the underrated country programs of the post-World War II period was the KWKH Louisiana Hayride. From its beginning in early 1948, it was the starting point on the road to stardom for many of the most famous names in modern country music. The fact that a person would establish a reputation, then leave for Nashville, failed to deter the Hayride, for it always found topnotch replacements waiting in the wings. An example is Red Sovine, who became number one man on the Hayride when the great Hank Williams heard the siren call of the country music capital.

Woodrow W. Sovine was born and spent his school years in Charleston, West Virginia. He learned to play guitar at an early age and performed locally in his early teens. When he was 17, he got his first radio job on station WCHS with Jim Pike and the Carolina Tar Heels. He appeared with the band on the Friday night Old Farm Hour on the West Virginia station. The group proved to be popular with local audiences and they soon moved a notch higher by joining the WWVA Jamboree in Wheeling, West Virginia.

After a number of years on the Jamboree, Red decided in 1947 to form his own group, called the Echo Valley Boys. They gained their own show on Red's original station, WCHS. Meanwhile, the Louisiana Hayride had become a major factor on the national country scene, particularly with Hank Williams as number-one star. On June 3, 1949, Hank left and KWKH looked for a replacement. Red Sovine was suggested and he quickly accepted the invitation to move to Shreveport. He not only joined the Hayride with his band, but also took over a 15-minute daily solo program of Hank's called The Johnny Fair Syrup Show.

[288]

From 1949 to 1954, Red was one of the featured performers of the Hayride. He formed close friendships with many rising country stars, including Webb Pierce, who appeared on the show. He and Pierce sometimes sang together and also combined to write songs. In 1954, Red joined Pierce in Nashville, where both became regulars on the Grand Ole Opry. Two years later, they hit the charts with their recording of their own song, "Little Rosa." The same year, 1956, they joined again to record a number-one-rated hit, "Why Baby Why."

Sovine continued to be a major country performer through the 1950s and into the '60s. During these years, he was featured in personal performances in all fifty states and in many parts of Canada and Europe. In 1965, he scored another major hit with "Giddyup Go" on Starday label.

His other successful recordings included "You Used to Be My Baby," "Don't Drop It," "Don't Be the One," "I Hope You Don't Care," "I'm Glad You Found a Place for Me," "The Intoxicated Rat," "How Do You Think I Feel," and "My New Love Affair." His own compositions include "Don't Be the One," "Missing You," "Long Night," "Class of '49," "I Didn't Jump the Fence," "Too Much," and "I Think I Can Sleep Tonight."

His major LPs included "Little Rosa," "Red Sovine," and "Giddyup Go."

SPARKS, RANDY: Singer, guitarist, music executive, producer. Born Leavenworth, Kansas, July 29, 1933.

Sages and poets through the ages have pointed to the value of a good name. Randy Sparks can well agree with them, for he found a good name to be worth $2.5 million. This was the amount he received for the rights to the group he founded called the New Christy Minstrels. Certainly this is one of the top success stories in the annals of the commercial folk field.

Sparks had little idea of this kind of future when he first became interested in folk music in his youth. Born in Kansas, where there was a good body of folk balladry extant, he moved to Oakland, California, as a boy. He attended local schools in the San Francisco Bay region. He could play good guitar by the time he was in high school, and already was performing in local folk music clubs when he began attending the University of California at Berkeley.

With folk music slowly taking hold up and down the Coast in the early 1950s, Randy was able to find more and more places for engagements. As the folk genre became popular on college campuses in the mid-1950s, Randy found himself becoming better known in all parts of the country. In 1956, this led to a contract as a solo artist for Verve Records. He cut a number of records for the label between then and 1961.

Though considered an excellent performer, Randy still was far from the top of the ladder at the start of the '60s. In 1961, he decided it might be rewarding musically to form his own folk group. The result was a combination of some ten performers named after the Edwin "Pops" Christy assemblage of the mid-1800s. Headed by Sparks, the New Christy Minstrels began to tour the U. S. By the end of 1961 they had become one of the top-ranked acts in the music business.

The group was featured in concerts on most major campuses and many clubs and on almost every major network TV show. They also signed with Columbia Records and had many LPs on the hit charts throughout the first half of the decade. In 1962, managerial demands were so heavy that Sparks retired from actively appearing with the Minstrels to concentrate on business affairs. In 1964, the management firm of Greif-Harris proposed the $2.5 million purchase that Randy accepted. Before leaving this association, Sparks had composed a number of top hits that became features of the Minstrels repertoire, including "Today," "Saturday Night," and, with Barry McGuire, "Green, Green." He also had directed the gold-record-award album "Ramblin'."

In the mid-1960s, Randy turned his efforts to developing a new form of folk nightclub and organizing other folk groups. His nightclub effort was called Ledbetter's. Established in 1963 in Westwood, California, near the UCLA campus, it was intended to provide a "live" rehearsal hall for building folk acts. Except for a brief period when it was shut down by a fire, Ledbetter's continued to be a highly popular spot and was still going strong in 1969. A second Ledbetter's was also operated briefly in San Bernardino County (Montclair) in early 1967.

After leaving the Minstrels, Sparks founded the Back Porch Majority for Epic Records and the New Society for RCA Victor. He also wrote for the movies, providing the score for MGM's

"Advance to the Rear" and original material plus lyrics for Soire Sourire's songs in MGM's "The Singing Nun." (*See also* NEW CHRISTY MINSTRELS)

SPENCER, TIM: Singer, guitarist, songwriter, music publisher. Born Webb City, Missouri, July 7, 1908.

It would be hard to think of a singing group that contributed more to western music than the Sons of the Pioneers. The group set standards of performance that helped shape the modern form of this kind of music. In addition, its members wrote some of the all-time standards for both country and western and popular music. One of its founding members and one of its most gifted songwriters was Tim Spencer.

Spencer was exposed to the feeling and the music of a good part of the American west in his boyhood days. He was born and spent the first seven years of his life in rural Missouri. The family then moved to New Mexico where his parents homesteaded 360 acres of land. Some years later the Spencers moved to Oklahoma and then, in 1930, to California. Meanwhile, Tim had gained a deep interest in music. He particularly liked to listen to cowboy songs and to sing them himself. He had a number of performances under his belt by the time he reached the West Coast.

In 1930, Tim met two other young western artists, Roy Rogers and Bob Nolan. They decided to form their own vocal group and selected the name Sons of the Pioneers. At first they sang locally, then gradually expanded their reputation to other parts of California. Before long they were featured in a series of sketches on radio. Roy Rogers left the trio when the opportunity came to star in western movies. However, he recognized the support he could receive from the talented group and they continued to work closely with him in many of his movies. Both Bob Nolan and Tim Spencer provided songs both for the group and for Roy. Through the 1960s, Spencer's output for Roy and the Sons of the Pioneers exceeded 250.

The Sons of the Pioneers became almost a national institution in the years after World War II and Tim Spencer continued to play a major part in this. Besides movies, he and the group toured all parts of the country and played in a number of foreign countries as well. In 1947, surveys by trade publications led to the Sons of the Pioneers being named as the most popular western singing group in the world.

The year 1946 produced one of Spencer's top-selling songs, "Cigarettes, Whusky and Wild, Wild Women." More than a million records of this song were sold. Spencer also won another gold record in 1949, for million-record sales of his composition "Room Full of Roses."

Spencer continued to sing with the group until 1952. He retired as an active member, but managed the Sons of the Pioneers through 1954. That year he left to start a religious publishing house called Manna Music. By the mid-1960s, Manna had become one of the foremost publishers of religious music in the country. Soon after starting the firm, Spencer published a song called "How Great Thou Art" that became a standard in its field. Through 1967, sales of its sheet music had gone well over a million copies. (*See also* SONS OF THE PIONEERS)

STANLEY BROTHERS: Vocal and instrumental duo, Ralph Edmond Stanley, born Stratton, Virginia, February 25, 1927; Carter Glen Stanley, born McClure, Virginia, August 27, 1925, died Bristol, Virginia, December 1, 1966.

The Clinch Mountains of Virginia were home base for many of the best known names in folk, country and western music, including the Stoneman Family and the Carter Family. The region does not come to mind immediately for Bluegrass music, primarily because Bill Monroe of Kentucky made this style of playing nationally famous. However, the Clinch Mountains produced many of the Bluegrass greats of the post-World War II period, not the least of whom were the Stanley Brothers.

Carter and Ralph Stanley were born and spent the greater part of their lives in the region. Their mother was a talented singer and musician and taught her sons vocal harmony almost as soon as they could talk. She also saw to it that they learned to play instruments. In Ralph's case, he took up the banjo while Carter specialized in the guitar.

When the boys were in their teens, they entertained at local events. In 1945, they began to appear in clubs in Bristol, Virginia. During that year, they joined the Farm and Fun Time show on station WCYB, Bristol. They remained as regulars for a good part of the 1950s.

With the increased interest in Bluegrass in the late 1950s and early 1960s, the brothers began to appear in shows in many parts of the country. Their personal appearances took them into 42 states and included county fairs college concerts, coffee houses (including a number of dates at the Ash Grove in Los Angeles), and major folk festivals. As their reputation grew, they also were booked for several European tours. They played to appreciative audiences in such countries as England, Switzerland, Germany, Sweden, and Denmark.

From the late 1940s until Carter's death in a Bristol hospital on December 1, 1966, the brothers recorded many of their renditions on a number of labels. They were among the first country artists to record for the new King label in the late 1940s. They also cut sides for Rich-R-Tone, Columbia, Starday, and Mercury.

Their LP output included: on Starday, "Jacob's Vision" and "Mountain Music Sounds" ('63); on Nashville, "Mountain Son Favorites" and "Carter and Ralph"; on Melodeon, "Carter Brothers' Original Recordings" ('67); and on Mercury, "Stanley Brothers" ('66).

STATLER BROTHERS: Quartet, Don S. Reid, born Staunton, Virginia, June 5, 1945; Harold W. Reid, born Augusta County, Virginia, August 21, 1939; Philip E. Balsley, born Augusta County, Virginia, August 8, 1939; Lew C. DeWitt, born Roanoke County, Virginia, March 8, 1938.

The name Statler Brothers stands for Virginia's number-one vocal group contribution to the country and western field in the 1960s. It also stands for a quartet which includes two brothers and no one named Statler.

All four boys were born and raised in rural Virginia. Listening to country music was a normal avocation among their families and all the boys enjoyed performing for local gatherings during their school years. In the early 1960s, the Reid brothers, Harold and Don, took the lead in forming the new group. Harold provided the bass voice, Don served as m.c. Phil Balsley was the baritone input and Lew DeWitt sang tenor and provided guitar accompaniment. Adding to their potential was the songwriting ability of the Reid brothers and DeWitt.

By the mid-1960s, the Statler Brothers had played a number of major engagements in various parts of Virginia and nearby states.

They signed with Columbia Records and turned out a number of well received songs. In 1965, Lew DeWitt wrote an original composition that made the group nationally famous. Called "Flowers on the Wall," it was a top 10 hit in the country and western polls and number one nationally in popular charts. The LP version of the same title was one of the best-selling albums of 1966. In 1967, the group scored with the oddly titled "You Can't Have Your Kate and Edith Too." Their '67 LP "The Statler Brothers Sing the Big Hits" was also well received.

STEWART, REDD: Guitarist, pianist, fiddler, songwriter. Born Ashland City, Tennessee.

One of the closest relationships in country music over the years was that between band leader PeeWee King and his gifted sideman, Redd Stewart. Stewart for more than two decades provided the King aggregation with solid musical grounding in almost every instrument in the band. Equally important, Stewart teamed with King to write some of the most durable standards in country and western music.

Redd was born in Tennessee, but his family moved to Kentucky when he was little. He attended public school in Louisville. He learned to play piano and guitar while still in grade school and appeared in the Louisville area in the early 1930s. Louisville was a hotbed of country music activity during this period, numbering such rising young stars as PeeWee King and Gene Autry among its radio performers.

Redd played with small groups in town and then became a member of one called the Prairie Riders. Later, when PeeWee King formed his Golden West Cowboys, Redd was asked to join. Redd appeared on the Grand Ole Opry with PeeWee for a number of years. While on the Opry in 1946, Redd and PeeWee collaborated on their first major song hit, the one that helped propel Kay Starr to national fame, "Bonaparte's Retreat."

In 1947, Redd moved with King to PeeWee's own radio show on WAVE radio in Louisville. The show was a weekly feature first on radio then on WAVE-TV for a decade (1947-57). In 1948, Stewart and King collaborated on "Tennessee Waltz," which became one of the top songs of the year. Through the mid-1960s, more than 10,000,000 records of this song, by various performers, were sold. During the 1950s and '60s, Redd toured the country many times with the King band. He and PeeWee King were featured on the 1964 Starday LP "PeeWee King and Redd Stewart."

Redd also turned out some of his own recordings over the years, including the LP "Favorite Old Time Tunes." His single records included "Homestead," "Bonaparte's Retreat," "I'm Getting Tired," "Thy Burdens Are Greater Than Mine," "Gee But I Hate to See Me Go," "When You Are Waltzing with the One You Love," "Tennessee Waltz," and "Slow Poke."

STEWART, WYNN: Singer, guitarist, band leader, songwriter. Born Morrisville, Missouri, June 7, 1934.

As with many country artists, Wynn Stewart's career began with a church song. When he was five, he sang a solo during a Sunday morning church service in his home town of Morrisville. He added to his vocals in the next few years from listening to religious and country records and the entire Grand Ole Opry show on Saturday nights. Before he was in his teens, he had also taught himself to play the guitar.

At 13, he was good enough to appear regularly on station KWTO in Springfield, Missouri. In 1938, his family moved to California and before long Wynn had formed his own band out there. The band performed for benefits and radio shows in Los Angeles and Hollywood. Young Wynn soon followed up with his first recording when he was 15; the following year, he signed his first recording contract with Intro Records in Hollywood.

Wynn continued to pick up experience at local dances and clubs. He formed a new band in 1953 that resulted in still more interest in his work by major entertainment executives. One of his own compositions, "Strollin'," resulted in his first major label contract with Capitol. During the mid-1950s, he and his band turned out such songs for Capitol as "The Waltz of the Angels," "You Took Her Off My Hands," "Keeper of the Keys," and "Hold Back Tomorrow."

In the late 1950s, Wynn left Capitol for Challenge. One of his first recordings for the Challenge subsidiary Jackpot Records was "Above and Beyond." The song, which provided a nationwide hit for Buck Owens in 1960, was a West Coast record success for Wynn. A number of Wynn's Jackpot records featured Harlan Howard's wife, Jan, including such successes as "Wrong Company," "Yankee

Go Home," and "We'll Never Love Again."

Stewart's output on the Challenge label in the early 1960s included a major national hit, the 1960 "Wishful Thinking." His other Challenge records that won good ratings were "Playboy," "Big, Big Love," "Loversville," "Another Day, Another Dollar," "One More Memory" and "One Way to Go."

During the early '60s, Stewart cut down on road trips to star at his own club, the Nashville-Nevada Club in Las Vegas, Nevada. He added other chores to this, including working as a DJ and program director at KTOO radio in Las Vegas and appearing on his own TV show. One of the visitors to the club was recording executive Ken Nelson of Capitol, who offered Stewart a new contract with Capitol. Within a short time, Wynn had turned out a number of well received records for his old label, such as "Half of This, Half of That," "Does He Love You Like I Do?" "I Keep Forgettin'," "Rosalie," and "Angels Don't Lie."

After running the club for two and one-half years, Stewart sold it in the mid-1960s and moved to Hacienda Heights, California. With his new band, The Tourists, he went back on the road, appearing in almost every state of the union. He continued turning out records for Capitol, including "A Pretty World Today," "Ole What's 'er Name; two 1968 top 10 hits, "Something Pretty" and "Love's Gonna Happen to Me," and LPs of the same title; and the LPs "Songs of Wynn Stewart," "In Love," and "Let the Whole World Sing It With Me" ('69).

STONE, CLIFFIE: Singer, band leader, composer, bass violist, comedian, disk jockey, record company executive. Born Burbank, California, March 1, 1917.

California's gift to country and western music, Cliffie Stone (real name: Clifford Gilpin Snyder), learned much about country music at the knee of his father. His father, a talented musician and comic, starred for many years in country shows under the name Herman the Hermit. Over the years Cliffie proved one of the most versatile people in the music business, helping to develop many of the major artists of the 1950s and '60s.

Cliffie began playing a rather non-country instrument—the trombone—at Burbank High School. He was interested in both music and acting in school, picking up a working knowledge of the bass fiddle before graduation. Later on, he combined the two by playing bass in a comedy sketch with Gene Austin as part of Ken Murray's Hollywood Blackouts. He also played comedy for two seasons with the Pasadena Community Playhouse.

For a while, in the mid-1930s, he played bass with some of the leading bands of the popular field, including Anson Weeks and Freddy Slack. Starting in 1935, though, when he began to serve as a country and western disk jockey, his interests swung sharply toward this kind of music. One of his first shows was the Covered Wagon Jubilee on KFVD. During the '30s and '40s, he emceed the Lucky Stars show on KFWB for seven years. In the 1940s, he also led the band and was featured comedian on the CBS network Hollywood Barn Dance. From 1943 to 1947, he was master of ceremonies for 28 western radio shows a week.

With this background, he seemed a natural choice for record consultant on folk artists, a job given him by Capitol Records in 1946. Many of Capitol's major western artists received a helping hand from Cliff, including Tennessee Ernie Ford and Hank Thompson. Cliffie, who formed a new band in 1947, also signed a recording contract with Capitol. Some of the many songs he recorded for the label in the '40s and '50s were "My Pretty Girl," "Spanish Bells," "When My Blue Moon Turns to Gold," "Christmas Waltz," "Cream of Kentucky," "Domino," "Old Joe Clark," "Buffalo Gals," "Blackhawk Waltz," "Blues Stay Away from Me," "Bryant's Boogie," and "Blue Canadian Rockies."

During these years, he also turned out a number of his own compositions with such co-writers as Merle Travis, Eddie Kirk, and Leon McAuliff. These included such often-played songs as "No Vacancy," "Divorce Me C.O.D.," "So Round, So Firm, So Fully Packed," "Steel Guitar Rag" and "Sweet Temptation." Among his Capitol LPs are: "Party's On Me" ('58); "Cliffie Stone Sing-a-long" ('61); and "The Great Hank Williams" ('64).

In the early 1950s, Cliffie headed up his own TV show, Hometown Jamboree, on a local Los Angeles station. The show was one of the staple items of the 1950s and might have gone on for many years more had Cliffie not decided to cut down on his performing chores. The show featured many top artists as guests, but also provided a proving ground for new and talented performers. Among the latter were many names now in the first rank of the country field, including Billy Strange, Billy Liebert, Dallas Frazier, Molly Bee, and Jeanie Black.

In the 1960s, Cliffie concentrated on a series of successful music industry enterprises, including a booking agency and his own publishing firm, Central Songs, Inc., which he sold to Capitol in 1969.

STONEMAN FAMILY: Vocal and instrumental group founded by Ernest V. "Pop" Stoneman, born Monarat, Carroll County, Virginia, May 25, 1893; died Nashville, Tennessee, June 14, 1968.

In the years after World War II, much of traditional country music had been obscured by newer commercial versions. One family that still preserved much of the flavor and content of the old-time ballads and dance tunes was the reknowned Stoneman clan.

The man who built the modern Stoneman musical dynasty was talented, rugged Ernest "Pop" Stoneman. Born in a log cabin in rural Virginia, he grew up in a family whose roots were deep in American history. His great, great, great, great-grandfather had come to America as a cabin boy from England. (His mother's family, named Bowers, had originally emigrated from Germany.)

As in many rural homes, singing the old folk tunes and hymns, or variations of them, was a looked-for pleasure. Young Ernest enjoyed singing and performing from his early youth; thus he learned to play the harmonica and jew's-harp before he was 10, and the banjo and autoharp by the time he was in his teens.

Continuing to improve his skills as he reached manhood, he played at local affairs, but earned his keep in other ways. In the 1920s, the rise of the recording industry changed all this. Word of the collecting efforts of such record representatives as Frank Walker and Ralph Peer began to filter down to many rural artists.

As a result, Stoneman and Peer met and Pop's first record session was set up for the Okeh label. The session took place at the company's studios on September 24, 1924. (Later, Pop sometimes remembered the date, erroneously, as having been in 1925.) The songs were "The Sinking of the Titanic," "The Face That Never Returned," "Freckled Face Mary Jane," and "Me and My Wife." In 1926, Peer set up another session in which Stoneman and his group recorded "Sourwood Mountain." During these

The Stoneman Family on tour: Pop Stoneman, center, with his autoharp

sessions, Pop added guitar playing to his talents.

During the balance of the '20s, Pop toured widely, making personal appearances in many parts of the country. He also continued to turn out new recordings. He taught his wife to play fiddle and added other artists to his group, such as Uncle Eck Dunford. The Stonemans performed with many country music greats from 1926 to 1931, including the Bailes Brothers, Riley Puckett, and Uncle Dave Macon. Among their songs were such titles as "When the Springtime Comes Again," "Say, Darling, Say," "The Black Dog Blues," "New River Train," "Hallelujah Side," "Cumberland Gap," "Hang John Brown," and "Bile Them Cabbage Down." Some of the songs were variations on traditional ballads or original compositions of Pop's.

The Depression had its effect on all country music in the early 1930s. With record dates few and far between and engagements hard to find, the Stonemans settled outside Washington, D.C. Pop got a job in a naval gun factory and with his wife concentrated on raising a family which eventually totaled thirteen children, playing occasional night dates when work was available.

As the children grew up, they learned instruments themselves and joined with their parents in working up song stylings. At the end of World War II, the Stoneman Family began to receive an increasing number of invitations to perform at concerts in many parts of the east and south. Some of the children married and left, but throughout the 1950s and '60s Pop could always count on half a dozen or more

for performing dates. The growth of interest in traditional country music in these decades resulted in new opportunities for the group. They played on many college campuses and at a number of major folk festivals. In 1962, the Stoneman Family made their debut on the Grand Ole Opry and returned several more times in the years that followed.

During these years, new chances to record came from many different labels. In 1957, the group turned out "Banjo Tunes and Songs" for Folkways. Starday issued the LPs "Ernest Stoneman and the Stoneman Family" in 1962 and another Stoneman Family album in 1964. World Pacific issued the LP "Big Ball in Monterey" in 1964. In the mid-1960s, the Stonemans were signed by Columbia Records.

The Family continued to reach new audiences as the 1960s went by. They were equally at home on New York nightclub stages and in county fair settings. They were signed to turn out their own Stoneman Family TV Show for the 1967-68 season. Pop, however, fell ill in early 1968 and died in Nashville, in June.

STONEMAN, POP: *See* Stoneman Family

STOOKEY, PAUL: *See* Peter, Paul and Mary

STOVALL, VERN: Singer, guitarist, songwriter. Born Altus, Oklahoma, October 3, 1928.

More than one country and western star has graduated from the open range to the music field. Vern Stovall also moved from a close association with cattle into the front ranks of the entertainment industry. However, he was prob-

[294]

ably somewhat happier about it, since his "range" was the indoor one of a slaughterhouse.

Stovall started, though, with knowledge of livestock; he was raised on a farm in Oklahoma. Though born at Altus, he was taken to El Rino, on the banks of the South Canadian River, when he was a year old. When he was 10, his family moved to another farm, at Vian, near Muskogee, Oklahoma. Vern had a good voice as a child, and as soon as he was old enough, was a regular member of the church choir. In Vian, he also had many opportunities to sing at local gatherings. During these years, he also mastered the art of guitar playing.

After graduating from high school in 1947, he moved to Sacramento, California, where he found a job in a slaughterhouse. He progressed from menial jobs to the respected one of butcher. All the while, though, his interest in music grew. Whenever he could get work, he sang and played guitar in local clubs. As word of his ability spread, he began to meet some of the top country and western performers who were based in the Golden State.

In 1958 he made the break, moving to Pomona in Southern California, where he joined the group headed by Fred Maddox of Maddox Brothers and Rose. Until 1961, he was a featured member of the band as vocalist and rhythm guitarist. During this time, he met songwriter-musician Bobby George. They decided to collaborate on songs. In 1961, the collaboration extended to a new band formed by Vern, which included such other artists as Phil Baugh and Freddy Rose. The band built up a considerable following in the Los Angeles area from 1961 to 1965.

Meanwhile, many of the Stovall-George compositions began to be picked up by recording artists. The list included "The Long Black Limousine," first recorded by Vern, then by many others, including Bobby Bare and George Hamilton IV; "Who'll Be the One," recorded by Ray Price; and "One More Memory," recorded by Wynn Stewart.

In the early 1960s, Vern gained two new, close friends in the persons of Claude and Janet McBride. Claude had his own small label and produced a number of Stovall sides, including "Country Guitar." The latter, in which Phil Baugh was featured with Vern, began to move nationwide. To gain wider distribution, Claude leased the record to Dewey Groom's Longhorn label. A second hit followed, "One Man Band."

Groom then signed Vern to a long-term contract and Stovall moved to Longhorn's home city of Dallas. His first single for Longhorn was "Breaktime" backed with "Wreck of the Old 88." Soon after, Vern was teamed with Janet McBride in the hit recording "I'm Wild Bill Tonight." In 1967, Vern was represented on the charts with his own composition (co-written by Gene McCoslin) called, appropriately, "Dallas."

STRACKE, WIN: Singer, guitarist. Born Lorraine, Kansas, February 20, 1908.

One of the most popular folk acts on college campuses and in folk concerts of the late 1940s and early '50s was "I Come for to Sing." The group featured the almost legendary name of Big Bill Broonzy. However, even Broonzy's great talents failed to overshadow the bass renditions of midwestern singer Win Stracke.

Win was born in a small town in Kansas. Within a short time, however, his German-born father, a minister, was called to a new pulpit in Chicago. Win thus grew up amid the sights and sounds of the bustling Second City. His parents sang many songs, of both classical and folk origin, from their native Germany. Win learned some of the folk songs, but was even more impressed with the heritage of Bach, Beethoven, Handel and Brahms. He had a good voice and his parents encouraged him to sing serious music. In high school, he was a member of a well known Chicago a capella choir. He kept up his interest in music during his three years at Lake Forest College, near Chicago, in the mid-1920s.

When he left college, he continued to follow a career as a professional singer. He sang with a number of symphony orchestras in the midwest as a soloist and as part of oratorios. With the advent of radio, he sang on a number of classical programs on various stations. In the early 1930s, he was signed as a soloist for the program Hymns of All Churches, which was broadcast over a good many stations across the U.S. and featured Win for eight years.

In his spare time, he still enjoyed singing folk songs, both the old German songs of his youth and American ballads. He numbered many folk artists among his friends in the 1930s, including Burl Ives and Carl Sandburg. They suggested that he had a flair for folk music and should consider giving folk concerts.

His career as a classical singer was interrupted by World War II. He joined the Army and spent four years in many of the battle areas of North Africa and Europe. During these years, he often entertained his fellow soldiers with folk songs. He also learned much about folk music from them, including more about how to play the guitar. After his discharge, he decided to concentrate on folk music from then on. He added more songs to his repertoire by studying folk music books, listening to records, and collecting from other artists.

By 1947, he had given a number of concerts and had a growing reputation as a folk artist. The following year, with Broonzy, Lawrence Lane, and Studs Terkel, he helped form "I Come for to Sing." The first performances of this panorama of American folk music were sponsored by the Renaissance Society of the University of Chicago.

The group continued to tour nationally until the early '50s. In mid-1952, Stracke was featured on an NBC program, America's Music. The show struck paydirt with audiences and developed into a series called The Meaning of America. Besides appearing on this show for several years, Stracke sang on many TV shows throughout the 1950s. He also worked up a program called "A Minstrel's History of the U.S.A." for concerts in many parts of the country.

Many of his favorite songs were included in his 1957 LP, "Americana." Some of these were "Venezuela," "Acres of Clams," "Single Girl," "Dink's Song," "Big Rock Candy Mountain," "Wanderin'," "Paul Bunyan's Manistee," and "Cold Water vs. Rye Whiskey." Later in 1957, Stracke started a school for folk song study called the Old Town School of Folk Music.

Another Stracke LP was issued by Golden Records in 1958. Called "Golden Treasury of Songs America Sings," it included such numbers as "Shenandoah," "Black-Eyed Susie," "Old Dan Tucker," "John Henry," "The Erie Canal," "Kemo Kimo," "Buffalo Gals," "Aunt Rhody," "Elanoy," "Rio Grande," "Hush Little Baby," "Boll Weevil," "Poor Lonesome Cowboy," "Leather Winged Bat," "Cindy," and "One More Day."

In the 1960s, Stracke devoted much of his time to his Old Town School. The school celebrated its first decade with a well established curriculum and faculty and with a growing number of respected alumni. Many major artists visited the school and also gave concerts for Chicago audiences under Stracke's aegis, in-

cluding Jimmy Driftwood, Pete Seeger, and Doc Watson.

STRINGBEAN: Banjoist, singer, comedian. Born Annville, Kentucky, June 17, 1915.

In the great tradition of Uncle Dave Macon, the Grand Ole Opry has always featured first-rate banjo pickers. Not the least of these is the 6 ft. 2 in. performer known as Stringbean, "The Kentucky Wonder." Stringbean is an authentic "godchild" of Uncle Dave, having learned much about banjo playing from him. In recognition of their close relationship, Uncle Dave willed one of his banjos to Stringbean.

Stringbean, born David Akeman and raised on a farm near Annville, had a deep interest in the banjo almost from the cradle. His father was an expert banjo-picker and little David and his four brothers and three sisters enjoyed listening to him and singing along. While going about the chores on the farm, David often thought about his dad's banjo fingering and longed for a banjo of his own. When he was 14, his father gratified this wish and in a short time the boy was one of the best old-time style banjo players in the area.

David began to play at local sings, dances, and holiday programs. At 18, he began playing professionally in the Lexington, Kentucky, region. His ability was quickly recognized and resulted in a bid to play on station WLAP in Lexington in 1935. In the next few years, he began to establish a reputation with many of the best known country performers. He received bids to appear and tour with such artists as Lew Childre, Bill Monroe, Ernest Tubb, Red Foley, and Uncle Dave Macon. In the years after World War II, he not only starred on the Opry, but also performed on Red Foley's NBC programs for a dozen years.

He gained a particularly close friendship with Uncle Dave. Beginning in 1942, he brought his banjo talents to the Opry and was still going strong on the Opry TV show in the late 1960s. A feature of his act was his odd costumes, such as a combination of shirt that extended almost to his knees and pants that started where the shirt ended.

Among his best known single records of the 1950s and '60s were "Run Little Rabbit Run," "I Wonder Where Wanda Went," "Short Life and Trouble," "Train Special 500," "Barnyard Banjo Picking," "Crazy Viet Nam War," "20¢ Cotton and 90¢ Meat," "Hey Old Man," "John

Henry," "Big Ball in Nashville," and "Pretty Little Pink." His LPs on the Starday label included "Salute to Uncle Dave Macon," "Old Time Banjo Picking and Singing," "More Old Time Banjo Picking and Singing," and "Way Back in the Hills of Old Kentucky."

SUMMERS, ANDREW ROWAN: Singer, dulcimer player, musicologist, lawyer. Born Abingdon, Virginia, December 15, 1912.

Perhaps because a lawyer is interested in basics, Andrew Rowan Summers developed a deep interest in the roots of much of the folk music he heard in his native Virginia. His search for the most traditional versions of many of these songs helped preserve much of the English-Scottish ballad structure underlying a good part of this nation's folk music heritage.

He heard many of the traditional hill-country songs during his youth. He enjoyed singing and studied music as well as law when he entered the University of Virginia at the start of the 1930s. After receiving his LL.B. in 1935, he returned to his highland home to practice and to continue his research into the region's folk music. He continued to work as a lawyer in Abingdon into 1940 while also collecting songs and anecdotes from singers and instrumentalists in many parts of the state. His musical activities included performances at the White Top Folk Festival on many occasions.

During one of these festivals, he met an old dulcimer player in his eighties. It was the first time Summers had heard the instrument and he became deeply interested in it. Two years later, when the old dulcimer player died, he willed the instrument to Summers. Summers spent many hours learning to play it until he achieved a style considered the closest modern-day approach to traditional dulcimer folk artistry.

In 1941, he shifted his base of operations to New York where he worked as an editor in Frank Shepard Co. from 1941 to '43. From 1943 to 1945, he was an associate member of the firm of Burroughs and Brown. In 1947, he established his own company, Andrew R. Summers Associates, design specialists and manufacturers. Later on, he also started the Abingdon House antique store.

His residence in New York brought him in contact with many of those sparking the increased interest in folk music. Summers received bids to play at many concerts in the city and in other parts of the country. He also was asked to record some of his material for Folkways Records. His first LP for Folkways was "The Unquiet Grave," produced in 1951. Included in the album were the title song; "Searching for Lambs"; "Pretty Sally"; "The True Lovers' Farewell"; "The Cruel Brother"; "Geordie"; "At the Foot of Yonders Mountain"; and "The House Carpenter."

In 1954, two more Summers LPs appeared. The album titled "The Faulse Ladye" included such songs as "The Ballad of Mary Hamilton," "The Faulse Ladye," "Willie of Hazelgreen," "O Waly, Waly," "Billy Boy," and "The Two Sisters." The album titled "The Lady Gay" included the title song plus "Old Bangum," "Barbara Allen," "The Hangman's Tree," "Two Brothers," "Early One Morning," and "The Cherry Tree Carol."

His next Folkways LP appeared in 1957. Called "Andrew Rowan Sings," it included such numbers as "I Will Give My Love an Apple," "The Death of Queen Jane," "Blackbirds and Thrushes," "Old Mr. Fox," "Shenandoah," "O Death, Rock Me Asleep," "The Three Ravens," and "Lord Thomas and Fair Ellender." In 1961, he was represented by a fourth LP, "The Seeds of Love." In this were "Seeds of Love," "My Mother Chose My Husband," "Plaint for My Lost Youth," "Hares on the Mountain," "The Farmer's Curst Wife," "O No, John, No!" and "Blow away the Dew."

During the 1960s, Rowan continued his collecting work and also sang at many folk concerts and in a number of major folk festivals.

SVANOE, BILL: *See* Rooftop Singers

TANNER, GID: Fiddler, singer, bandleader. Born Thomas Bridge, near Monroe, Georgia, June 6, 1885; died Dacula, Georgia, May 13, 1960.

One group a country and western fan of the 1920s and '30s was sure to know was Gid Tanner and his Skillet Lickers. Tanner organized his band soon after becoming one of the first recorded artists in the country field, and before it disbanded in the 1930s the group made 565 records. Few of these are available today, but those that are stand the test of time surprisingly well. This is evident, for example, from Skillet Licker renditions of "Ida Red" and "On Tanner's Farm" on the RCA Victor LP "Smoky Mountain Ballads."

Like many country greats, James Gideon

Tanner was born on a farm and never completely left farming throughout his life. He maintained his chicken farm in Georgia right up to his death. Young Gid fell in love with local fiddle music almost as soon as he could do chores on his parents' farm. At 14, when an uncle died and left him a fiddle, he lost no time in learning how to play it. In his teens he was already making a reputation for himself playing at local dances and fairs. In the 1920s he began to branch out, taking part successfully in several of the famous fiddle contests of Fiddlin' John Carson.

Thus when Columbia Records' talent scout moved through the area looking for artists to make the firm's first country records, Tanner was a name that he heard much about. He asked Gid to come to New York and Gid took George Riley Puckett with him. The two made their first records on March 7, 1924. The recordings were well enough received that Tanner's name became known across the south. Soon after, he formed his Skillet Lickers. Puckett (born Alpharetta, Georgia, 1890; died College Park, Georgia, July 13, 1946) became lead singer of the band.

Through the late 1920s and the early 1930s, the group was one of the most popular in country music. From 1926 to 1929 it included, besides Tanner and Puckett, Clayton McMichen and Tanner's brother Arthur. McMichen remained with Tanner until 1931. Various other musicians played with the band in the 1930s, including Tanner's son, Gordon, and Jimmie Tarleton. In the 1930s, the Skillet Lickers were featured on radio stations in many parts of the U.S., including Covington, Kentucky; Cleveland, Ohio; Chicago, and Atlanta.

The top hit of the Skillet Lickers was "Down Yonder." Other hits included "The Wreck of the Southern Old 97" and "Sally Goodin'."

A typical arrangement of Tanner's group was given in *Who's Who in Country Music** as follows: "(The band used) two fiddles, often doubling each other at the unison for lead, a back-up guitar and a banjo. All four members sang and Puckett usually took the lead." (*See also* McMICHEN, CLAYTON)

TARLETON, JIMMIE: Singer, guitarist, banjoist, harpist, songwriter. Born Chesterfield County, South Carolina, May 8, 1892.

An amazingly gifted musician, Jimmie Tarle-

* 1965-66 edition, published by Thurston Moore, Colorado.

ton provided American folk and country music with a legend and some of the most famous songs in the folk-country repertoire. Those who heard him play never forgot it, even those who attended some of his performances in the mid-1960s when he came out of a long, enforced retirement. Had Tarleton been born twenty years later, he might have become wealthy and famous in his lifetime. As it was, he settled for a flat fee of $75 for his most famous compositions, "Columbus Stockade Blues" and "Birmingham Jail."

Johnny James Rimbert Tarleton was born on a farm near the Pedee River in Chesterfield County, South Carolina. His parents were both musical. His father played a homemade banjo and taught Jimmie to play when he was six (he was also studying the French harp). His mother sang many old hill-country ballads, including such songs as "Barney McCoy," "Kitty Wells," "Lowe Bonnie," and "Wish I Was a Single Girl Again." Jimmie learned these and sang and recorded them later in life. By the time he was nine, he had also mastered the guitar.

After chores on the farm were done, the family often gathered around to sing and play guitar and banjo. Jimmie enjoyed this and sang

Jimmy Tarleton in the 1920s

solos for friends and neighbors when he was a little boy. As he grew up, he performed at local dances, barn raisings, and other events.

By the time Jimmie was in his teens, he had decided to try to play professionally. He moved north during the World War I decade and worked at odd jobs while performing nights in bars and cafes in New York and nearby Hoboken. After several years of this, he headed west, working as a textile mill hand in Texas, Oklahoma, and Arkansas. In his spare time, he picked up whatever he could in the way of dates at local honkytonks.

In the early 1920s, things were looking up a little for country performers, who were in demand for rural fairs and traveling medicine shows. The mid-1920s found him playing with groups in the Columbus, Georgia, region. In 1926, he teamed up with guitarist-singer Tom Darby. The record industry was beginning to find a market for country records and was looking for new artists. This opened the door to Tarleton and Darby who gained a record date in Atlanta in April 1927. They were asked to come back several more times that year. On November 10, they recorded "Columbus Stockade Blues" and "Birmingham Jail," both written by Jimmie, who had composed the latter some years earlier after spending time in the jail for moonshining. The boys were offered a royalty agreement, but Darby talked Tarleton into settling for $75 for both songs.

Tarleton continued to record for several labels over the next few years, including Columbia (1927-30), RCA Victor in 1932, and American Record Corp. in 1933. He recorded more than 75 songs, many of which were made into major hits by others. During the '20s and early '30s he toured the country with many major artists, including Gid Tanner and the Skillet Lickers, Arthur Smith, The Delmore Brothers, and Jimmie Rodgers.

Life was far from easy, though. In 1932, he was caught riding the rods home from a recording session in New York for RCA Victor. A short term in Atlanta jail resulted in the song "Atlanta Prison Blues." In 1931, he had to work at odd jobs, including a short period as a mill hand in East Rockingham, North Carolina, where he worked with The Dixon Brothers. All three artists traded song material and instrumental techniques.

Since the Depression had ruined much of the country music market, Tarleton retired from an active music career in 1935. For the next twenty years he worked at various jobs, finally ending up in Phoenix City, Alabama, in the mid-1960s. There he was discovered by folk music collectors who wanted to discuss some of his great early country recordings. One collector, Gene Earle, taped some of Tarleton's music in December 1963 for a proposed LP. This, in turn, led to an invitation offered by the owner of the Ash Grove in Los Angeles based on the tapes. In August 1965, Tarleton showed cheering audiences he was still a superlative artist at his week's engagement in Los Angeles.

TARRIERS, THE: *See* Darling, Erik

TAYLOR, LYNNE: *See* Rooftop Singers

TENNESSEE MOUNTAIN BOYS, THE: *See* Wright, Johnny

TENNEVA RAMBLERS, THE: Vocal and instrumental group active in the 1920s.

The Tenneva Ramblers is a group familiar mainly to folk and country record collectors who value some of the band's output of the late 1920s. In their heyday, The Ramblers achieved a form of notoriety in country music lore as the group that broke up with Jimmie Rodgers just before The Singing Brakeman had his historic tryout with Ralph Peer. The Ramblers also auditioned for Peer and cut a number of records in the next few years. Most of these recordings have long been unavailable except for old 78 rpm disks. A few have been reissued as part of vintage collections, such as RCA Victor's "Native American Ballads," which includes one Ramblers selection, "Seven Long Years in Prison."

Members of The Ramblers were: Claud Grant, lead singer and guitar; Jack Grant, mandolin; Jack Pierce, violin; and Claude Slagle, banjo. (*See also* RODGERS, JIMMIE C.)

TERRY, SONNY: Singer, harmonica player. Born near Durham, North Carolina, October 24, 1911.

The lives of millions of people have been brightened by the efforts of many great artists who themselves are plagued by major afflictions. In folk music, many of the greatest performers have been blind. Such people as Doc Watson, Blind Blake, Blind Lemon Jefferson, and Sonny Terry have perhaps come closest to recreating the concept of the ancient troubadours.

Teddell Saunders "Sonny" Terry was born in North Carolina to a poor family. His father

Reuben, owned a small farm twenty miles north-northeast of Durham. He was not born blind, but lost his sight due to an accident when he was very young. He taught himself to play the harmonica during his lonely hours. Before long, he was able to pick out many of the gospel and work songs he could hear around him. While still a boy, he started to play his harmonica in local churches in the south. As he gained mastery over the instrument, he traveled to more and more parts of the country playing hymns and gospels in churches or in church concerts.

In time, he varied his song repertoire so he could play in local clubs or wherever he could earn some money for his music. From his travels, he made mental note of many more folk songs, ranging from ballads to blues. By the early 1930s, folklorists and other folk performers were becoming acquainted with his name. During the 1930s, he started playing before many diverse audiences in concert halls and on college campuses, sometimes accompanying his good friend Leadbelly.

Sonny Terry cups his mouth harp in his hands while Brownie McGhee looks on approvingly.

During the 1940s, he finally started to achieve a national reputation. He toured widely with guitarist Alec Stewart and also with a young artist named Pete Seeger. In 1949, Jac Holzman, founder of Elektra Records, made the first major album of Terry's work. Called "City Blues," it featured Terry and Alec Stewart in such songs as "Little Annie," "Louise Blues," "Down in the Bottom Blues," "Baby, Baby Blues," "Custard Pie," "Kansas City," "Late One Saturday Evening," "Old Woman Blues," "Hard Luck Blues," and "Chain the Lock on My Door." In the years that followed, Sonny was featured on many other albums on various labels. In the 1950s, these included "Folk Blues" on Elektra, "Harmonica and Vocal Solos" and "Washboard Band" on Folkways, "Sonny Terry and His Mouth Harp" on Stinson, and "Mouth-Harp" on Riverside.

His solo LPs of the '60s included "Sonny's Story" ('61) and "Sonny Is King" ('63).

On January 28, 1950, Sonny took part in a Leadbelly Memorial Concert in New York's Town Hall. During the program he teamed up with a close friend of his and Huddie's, Brownie McGhee. During the 1950s, the team of Terry and McGhee became increasingly important on the folk music scene. They were featured in concerts and in coffee houses from coast to coast, including holdover engagements at the hungry i in San Francisco and the Ash Grove in Los Angeles. In the 1960s, McGhee and Terry took part in several of Harry Belafonte's tours through the U. S. and to other parts of the world. McGhee and Terry also were heard —and seen—by coast-to-coast audiences on network TV shows.

Their record output from the mid-1950s into the '60s was extensive, totaling several dozen titles on such labels as Savoy, Fantasy, Folkways, Verve, Blues, Sharp, and Prestige. McGhee and Terry also were featured at many major folk festivals, including several performances at the Newport Folk Festival. (*See also* McGHEE, BROWNIE)

TEXAS LONGHORNS: *See* Groom, Dewey

TEXAS PLAYBOYS: *See* Wills, Bob

TEXAS SLIM: *See* Hooker, John Lee

TEXAS TROUBADOURS: *See* Tubb, Ernest

[300]

THOMAS, MAMA LEE: *See* Gateway Singers, The

THOMPSON, BOBBY: *See* Virgina Boys

THOMPSON, HANK: Singer, guitarist, bandleader, songwriter. Born Waco, Texas, September 3, 1925.

There are many things Texans are proud of, but none rate any higher than a tall, soft-spoken man from Waco called Hank Thompson. Hank helped his home state retain its dominance in the western band field that had started with such greats as Bob Wills and Leon Mc-Auliff. For thirteen consecutive years from 1953 to 1965, Hank's Brazos Valley Boys were voted America's Number One Western Band by almost every major trade magazine, including Billboard and Cashbox. His success was enough to make most Texans forget that for most of these years, Hank lived in Oklahoma.

Hank's youth, however, was all in Texas. Henry William Thompson followed the weekly broadcast of the Grand Ole Opry as a boy and could sing many of the songs from memory. Still, he did not reach for a guitar right away. Instead, he became expert on the harmonica and played well enough to win several amateur contests. In the mid-1930s, he became a staunch follower of western movies. He particularly liked Gene Autry and decided to emulate him.

He asked his parents to get him a guitar. They finally bought one for $4 from a second-hand store as a Christmas present. Young Hank spent all the time he could spare from school and friends to master the instrument. He dreamed of performing before an audience, but had to be satisfied with friends and family for several years.

In the early 1940s, he finally got a job at a local Waco theatre, performing in a Saturday morning youth show broadcast over station WACO. A flour company liked him and sponsored an early show called "Hank the Hired Hand" in 1942. After six months, in January 1943, Hank was graduated from high school

Hank Thompson (center, standing) and his Brazos Valley Boys

[301]

and promptly signed up with the Navy. For the next three years, he carried his guitar across a good part of the U.S. and throughout the South Pacific. His shipmates welcomed his singing to lighten the many hours of sea duty and Hank got much experience playing for men from all parts of the country.

When he was discharged, he went to Princeton University for a while. But the lure of music was too strong; he returned to Waco and won a job on a new station, KWTX. His popularity soared locally and he decided to form his own band. Called the Brazos Valley Boys, they accompanied Hank in shows and dance engagements throughout central Texas. In the Navy, Hank had spent some of his free time composing original songs. He recorded two of these in late 1946 on a local label, "Whoa Sailor!" and "Swing Wide Your Gate of Love." The records sold well and soon Hank found country artists interested in one of his songs, "A Lonely Heart Knows."

Tex Ritter became a Thompson fan and introduced him to Capitol Records executives. Hank was signed to a contract that was the start of an 18-year relationship and total Capitol sales of more than 30 million records. His first recordings for Capitol in 1948 produced two national hits, both Thompson compositions, "Humpty Dumpty Heart" and "Today." In 1949, Hank had two more top 10 hits in a remake of "Whoa Sailor!" and a new composition, "Green Light." Some of his singles during the early 1950s include "Don't Flirt with Me," "Rock in the Ocean," "Standing on the Outside," "Soft Lips," "The Grass Looks Greener," "Humpty Dumpty Boogie," and "Love Thief."

In 1952, Hank scored with "Waiting in the Lobby of Your Heart," co-written with his long-time lead vocalist, Billy Gray. The following year, he and Billy wrote the top 10 hit "Yesterday's Girl" and Hank penned another best-seller, "Rub-A-Dub-Dub." Other top 10 hits of 1952 were "Wake Up Irene" and "No Help Wanted." The year 1954 was another big one, including such top 10 national hits, written or co-authored by Hank, as "Breakin' the Rule," "Honky Tonk Girl," "New Green Light" and "We've Gone Too Far." In addition, the group had a hit record featuring a duet between a new girl vocalist, Wanda Jackson, and Billy Gray called "You're Not Mine Anymore."

During the next seven years, Hank had at least one top 10 success a year except for 1957.

These included "Don't Take It Out on Me" and "Wildwood Flower" ('55); "I'm Not Mad, Just Hurt" ('56); "Squaws Along the Yukon" ('58); "I've Run Out of Tomorrows" (co-authors, L. Compton and V. Mizi—'59); "A Six Pack to Go" (co-authors, J. Lowe and D. Hart—'60); and "Oklahoma Hills" ('61). Only the last one and "Squaws" were not Thompson originals.

Hank had more than a dozen best-selling LPs under the Capitol banner. These included "Songs of the Brazos Valley"; "North of the Rio Grande"; "All Time Hits"; "Hank"; "Hank's Dance Ranch" ('58); "Favorite Waltzes" ('59); "Songs for Rounders"; "Most of All" ('60); "This Broken Heart of Mine"; "An Old Love Affair"; "At The Golden Nugget" ('61); "No. 1 Band" ('62); "Cheyenne Frontier Days"; "Best of Hank Thompson"; "State Fair of Texas" ('63); and "Golden Hits" ('64).

Throughout the 1950s and '60s, Hank and his group were featured on many TV shows and in appearances throughout the country. TV guest performances included the Jimmy Dean Show on ABC-TV, Johnny Carson Show, NBC-TV's Swingin' Country, American Swing-Around, and the WGN Barn Dance. For many years, Hank also had his own regional syndicated TV and radio shows.

The year 1953 saw Hank and his band featured at the state fair of Texas. That same year, he and his family moved into a new lodge on Lake Tenkiller in eastern Oklahoma. As of 1967, he had returned every year to the Texas fair and still lived on the lake. During these years, he also starred six times at the Cheyenne, Wyoming, Frontier Days Rodeo and returned several times to the Golden Nugget in Nevada.

In the mid-1960s, the Brazos Valley Boys averaged 240 personal appearances a year. Their travels took them through Europe and the Far East, to Mexico and to such U.S. spots as the Circle Star Theatre, San Carlos, California, Disneyland, American Royal in Kansas City, Missouri, and dozens of other major theaters.

The year 1966 saw Hank move from Capitol to Warner Brothers. His first single, "Where Is the Circus," made the hit charts, as did the LP of the same name. In 1968 he signed with Dot Records.

THOMPSON, SUE: Singer, guitarist. Born Nevada, Missouri, 1926.

The name of Sue Thompson's home town

was strangely symbolic. Years later, Sue (real name: Eva Sue McKee) was to become one of the most popular performers in such cities as Las Vegas, Reno, and Tahoe.

Country music and western movies were two of the main pleasures of the people from Sue's home area of Missouri. Naturally, from her earliest years, she had a desire to play the guitar and someday sing on the Grand Ole Opry. The chance to play guitar came when she was only seven. A cousin gave her an old instrument and taught her a few chords. During her elementary school years, she sang and played guitar on many occasions in church, at school events, and at town socials.

She continued this pattern when her family moved to San Jose, California, where she attended high school. She soon gained a job as vocalist with a high school band and learned to sing both country and pop songs, depending on the audience. During these years, she got her first break when she won a San Jose talent contest and received a two-week engagement at a local theater.

It wasn't all easy sledding after this. When she finished high school, Sue had to work at various jobs during the day while waiting for opportunities to work in the music field. Her perseverance finally paid off with her first major job as a cast regular on a San Francisco country and pop TV variety show. After several years in the Bay area, she headed south for another successful engagement on a Los Angeles TV show.

The trip to Los Angeles netted her first recording contract with Mercury. She turned out a number of well received sides that brought her to the attention of Nashville country music executives. In the late 1950s, she was signed for several appearances on the Red Foley portion of the Grand Ole Opry.

In 1961, she switched to the Hickory label of Acuff-Rose. Before long, she had a number of chart hits, including "Angel" and "Sad Movies." The latter made number five on national hit lists. In 1962, she scored with "Have a Good Time," which reached the number 15 spot on the popular music lists, and "Willie Can." Some of her other best-sellers for Hickory were "Norman" and "Paper Tiger." She also made such well received LPs as "Meet Sue Thompson," "Two of a Kind," and "Sue Thompson."

During the 1960s, Sue made her home in Las Vegas, Nevada. Much of her performing time was spent in Nevada, but she also was in demand for many national appearances and TV spots. Her credits in the '60s included such shows as Hullabaloo, NBC-TV's Swingin' Country, CBS-TV's Jackie Gleason Show, Dick Clark's American Bandstand and Where the Action Is on ABC, Lloyd Thaxton Show, Hollywood a Go-Go, and 9th Street West.

Her agenda also included regular visits to Hawaii, on a four-times-a-year basis, and a three-week tour of Vietnam to entertain the Armed Forces.

TILLIS, MEL: Singer, guitarist, songwriter. Born Pahokee, Florida, August 8, 1932.

The power behind the throne of country and western music is the songwriter. Without good material, the best performer would have trouble winning gold-record awards. Over the years, one of the best guarantees of success was to have the name of Mel Tillis on the song sheet. However, Mel also succeeded in making an equally impressive reputation for himself as a performer.

Mel was listening intently to country music from his early years in rural Florida. By the time he was in his teens he was already trying to put down words and music of his own. After finishing school, he eventually decided to head to Nashville to try to place some of his songs with major artists. It wasn't long before his ability was recognized and many top artists were recording his material. Between the mid-1950s and the early 1960s, he turned out 350 songs, most of which were recorded by artists of the calibre of Burl Ives, Webb Pierce, and Ray Price. Pierce recorded 35 of Tillis' songs and Ives 11 during this period alone.

One of Mel's first top 10 successes (written with B. Peddy) was Webb Pierce's 1957 version of "Honky Tonk Song." That same year, Pierce duplicated the feat with Mel's "I'm Tired." From then on, it was a rare year in which one or more Tillis songs were not on the best-seller lists.

In 1959, Webb Pierce scored with "A Thousand Miles Ago" and Carl Smith collaborated and recorded "Ten Thousand Days." Ray Price turned out a 1960 top 10 hit, "One More Time," and a '61 success, "Heart Over Mind." The year 1962 provided Mel with three more nationwide hits, Webb Pierce's records of "Crazy Wild Desire" and "Take Time" (co-writer, Marijohn Wilkins), and Little Jimmy Dickens' "The Violet and the Rose" (co-writers, B. Ange and J. Reinfeld). In 1963, Mel's "Detroit City" (recorded by Bobby Bare) was a major hit in both country and national popular fields.

In the late 1950s, Mel also was signed to a recording contract by Columbia Records. During his five-year stay with the label, Mel had a number of records that were best-sellers, such as "The Violet and the Rose" ('62); "Walk on By" ('61); "Georgia Town Blues," and "Sawmill." He then moved over to Decca and had a hit right away with a song co-written with Webb Pierce, "How Come Your Dog Don't Bite Nobody But Me." In the next few years, he also had chart records in "Half Laughing, Half Crying" and "Don't Tell Mama." In the mid-1960s, he left Decca for the Ric label, for which he recorded the hit record "Wine." In 1967, he was recording for Kapp, with such hits on the song charts as "Life Turned Her That Way" and the LP "Life's That Way."

TILLMAN, FLOYD: Singer, instrumentalist (guitar, mandolin, banjo), songwriter. Born Ryan, Oklahoma, December 8, 1914.

The measure of Floyd Tillman's greatness can be gained by listing just a few of the songs turned out by him in more than thirty years as a composer. These include "I Love You So Much It Hurts," "It Makes No Difference Now," "Slippin' Around," "Each Night at Nine," and "I Gotta Have My Baby Back." As he writes, "The return from these are earning the writer an equivalent of more than a million sales and plays a year consistently for 29 years (to 1967)." Another measure of Tillman's stature is the fact that a good percentage of his songs became standards in both country and western and popular music as a whole. In fact, after the songs became hits in the country field, in time 90 per cent of the royalties came from the popular market.

Tillman was born in Oklahoma, but his family moved to Post, Texas, when he was small. He was interested in music by the time he reached his teens and received some training in stringed instruments from his older brothers. At 13, he was a Western Union messenger in Post and, as he told one Billboard reporter, often heard Jimmie Rodgers' records on phonographs while delivering messages. This increased his interest in music and in Rodgers in particular. When he got the chance to see Rodgers in person during a show in Post, it helped make him decide to try for a musical career for himself.

In the early 1930s, he put his skill with guitar, banjo, and mandolin to work as an entertainer in local honkytonks. Soon he joined the first of several groups with whom he played in Houston. For two years he was guitarist with the Mark Clark popular band in that city, but Floyd's interest continued to trend to country music. In the mid-1930s, he left Clark and joined the Blue Ridge Playboys. With the Playboys, he found the impetus to write more of his own material. One of his first compositions was "It Makes No Difference Now." He tried to interest one record company in the song but was told it was too slow. Soon after, though, Dave Kapp of Decca heard it during a Playboy broadcast on a local station and sought Tillman out. The song was recorded on Decca, the first of well over a hundred records made of one of the greatest of all country and western standards.

From that time on, Tillman songs were always in demand among recording artists. (Through 1967, more than 200 of his compositions had been recorded and published.) During the 1930s and '40s, Tillman played with several groups and toured throughout the country. His voice was featured on records on a number of labels, including Decca, Victor, and Columbia. In 1948, he turned out a gold-record version of "I Love You So Much It Hurts" on Columbia. That same year, the song was also number one nationally for many weeks in a recording by Jimmy Wakely and Cowboy Copas.

He scored another double in 1949 with his own recording of "I'll Never Slip Around Again" on Columbia and the Capitol best-selling version by Margaret Whiting and Jimmy Wakely. Whiting and Wakely had earlier scored nationally with Tillman's "Slippin' Around," which was number one for a good part of the year. Tillman's own version and one by Ernest Tubb also were best-sellers. In 1950, a Franklin-Messner recording of "Slipping Around with Joe Blow" brought still more royalties on the theme to Tillman.

In 1961, Tillman was represented on the hit lists with "The Commancheros." An LP album, "The Best of Floyd Tillman," was issued by Harmony Records in 1964.

[304]

TOMPALL & THE GLASER BROTHERS:
Vocal and instrumental trio, all born in or near Spaulding, Nebraska, Tompall Glaser, September 3, 1933; Charles "Chuck" Glaser, February 27, 1936; James "Jim" Glaser, December 16, 1937.

Tompall & the Glaser Brothers is a stage name describing a trio of brothers who have chalked up highly successful music careers singly and together. The boys' father, Louis, was a good guitarist and taught them to play at an early age. Tompall, the oldest, was the first to appear in public, giving his first performance at seven. When younger brothers Chuck and Jim were old enough, they joined Tompall in an act that played for PTA meetings, class picnics, etc.

By the mid-1950s, the boys, now in their teens, had their own TV show in Holdredge, Nebraska. In 1957, a touring Arthur Godfrey Talent Scouts show visited Omaha. The Glasers traveled the 180 miles from Holdredge to try out. They were immediate hits and became regular members of the Godfrey cast for a while. In 1958, the brothers moved to Nashville and were on the Marty Robbins show for a time. Their rapidly expanding reputation as first-rate musicians led to guest spots on other shows, and engagements to back top country and western artists in recording sessions. In 1959, for example, they accompanied Marty Robbins on his top-selling "El Paso" and later backed Claude King's great hit, "Commancheros." They also performed with major artists on tour, appearing with Johnny Cash at his Carnegie Hall concert.

In 1960, the Glasers were featured on the Grand Ole Opry, and in 1962 they became Opry regulars. During the years that followed, they were hits with audiences from coast to coast and overseas. Their 1960 appearances included The Atlantic City Steel Pier, Dick Clark's ABC American Bandstand, several tours of Europe and the Far East, and engagements at the Showboat and Mint Lounge in Las Vegas. One of their first Las Vegas efforts in the early 1960s was in support of Patsy Cline. When Patsy's engagement was over, the Glasers were invited back for 28 days with star billing. By the mid-1960s, the brothers were averaging more than ten days a month touring the U.S. and Canada.

In the late 1950s, the brothers signed with Decca Records. Remaining with the label for nearly eight years, they turned out many songs that made the charts, many of which they wrote themselves. Their Decca hit compositions included "She Loves the Love I Give Her," "A Girl Like You," and "Let Me Down Easy." Other Decca hits were "Teardrops Til Dawn," "Odds and Ends" and "Baby, They're Playing Our Song." One of their hit LPs for Decca was "This Land."

Warner Brothers signed the team in 1966. Two singles that gained national attention on this label were "The Last Thing on My Mind" and "Gone, on the Other Hand."

Their songwriting output, together and singly, produced hits for many artists. Tompall Glaser provided Jimmy Dean with a hit in "Stand Beside Me" and Bobby Bare with a major 1966 success, "Streets of Baltimore." The latter won Tompall a 1966 BMI award. He also provided Jimmy Newman with a hit song in "You're Making a Fool Out of Me." Jimmy Glaser wrote such hits as "Thanks a Lot for Trying Anyway" and "Sitting in an All Night Cafe."

Among the brothers' individual efforts, Jimmy signed as a solo performer for Monument Records, while Chuck worked as a producer for Decca. In his producing capacity, he supervised several Buddy Starcher efforts, including the hit single "History Repeats Itself" and the LP of the same name. In the mid-1960s, Chuck provided career guidance for several artists, including Leon McAuliff, Gordon Terry, Jimmy Payne, and John Hartford.

The Glasers, as of 1969, also had a number of business firms in the entertainment field. Glaser Productions was set up to handle booking and artist guidance. The brothers also had three music publishing firms, Glascap (ASCAP), Glaser Publications (BMI), and Glaco (SESAC). Among the songs published by the firm were "History Repeats Itself," "All Night Cafe," "Streets of Baltimore," "A Taxpayer's Letter," "Stand Beside Me," and "You Take the Future."

TOWN HALL PARTY: Television variety show, originated from Channel 11, Compton, California.

A long-time staple item for Southern California viewers, Town Hall Party, was broadcast from Compton, California, every Saturday night for more than a decade. From its beginning in the fall of 1951 to the early 1960s, it featured such regulars as Johnny Bond, Merle

Travis, and Joe and Rose Lee Maphis, as well as guest stars from other major country shows from all across the nation. For many years, it was written by Johnny Bond and directed by Wesley Tuttle. Other nationally-ranked artists who performed on the show for a number of years included Eddie Dean; Rex Allen, The Arizona Cowboy; Johnny Cash; Lefty Frizzell; Martha Carson; and Tex Ritter.

Dozens of other country and western performers were featured on the show over the years, including Tommy Sands, Wayne Raney, Pee Wee Adams, Les Anderson, Alvis Coker, The Collins Kids, Ted Daffan, Wesley and Marilyn Tuttle, Billy Mize, Tommy Duncan, Freddy Hart, Cousin Herb Henson, Myrna Jory, Fiddlin' Kate, Bonnie Sloan, Tom Tall, Gordon Terry, Slim Willett, and Mac Wiseman.

TRAVELERS 3: Vocal and instrumental group, Pete Apo, born Hawaii; Michael Gene Botta, born Sacramento, California; Charles Oyama, born Honolulu, Hawaii; Joseph Ronald "Joe" Lamanno, born Sacramento, California.

One of the better known folk "trios" of the mid-1960s, the Travelers 3, billed themselves as the "world's first and finest four member trio." The group actually began as a trio in 1959 when Apo, Oyama, and bassist Dick Shirley met at the University of Oregon in Eugene. The group became a foursome in 1964 with the addition of Botta. In 1965, Lamanno joined the group as replacement for Shirley.

The foundation of the Travelers 3 was provided by Apo and Oyama who were both students at the University. Oyama at first was more interested in athletics than music. He was an excellent swimmer as a child, and in his teens was a top boxing prospect. His boxing prowess led to an athletic scholarship at the University of Oregon. While working for his master's degree in educational psychology, he served as swimming and tennis coach and psychologist at a local high school. Apo, who came to Oregon from Lahaina, Maui, also was interested in psychology.

Both Apo and Oyama had found some time for music in their growing-up years. By the time they met, Apo had done some composing and singing and Oyama was a skilled 12-string guitarist. They decided that they had the potential for musical careers and added Shirley to form a trio. They started playing at dances and in clubs in the Eugene area. The reception was good enough for them to decide to devote full time to music, at which point Apo left college with a year to go for his B.A. and Oyama abandoned plans to gain a Ph.D.

During the early 1960s, the group began to branch out, playing engagements in many other parts of the country. Their style initially was basically folk-oriented. Later they also incorporated some of the rhythms of rock 'n' roll. The growing interest in folk-rock in the '60s, spurred by success of such performers as Bob Dylan, also helped increase the Travelers 3 popularity. When the ABC-TV Hootenanny show got underway, the group was featured on four different occasions. Through 1967, they also appeared on such other TV shows as Roy Rogers, Hullabaloo, Mike Douglas, Al Hirt, Regis Philbin, and Let's Sing Out.

In 1962, they were featured on their first major album release, the Elektra LP "Travelers 3." Later that year, Elektra issued a second LP, "Open House." In 1963, they were represented on Elektra with the LP "Live at Last." After adding Botta on drums in '64, they moved to Capitol Records and recorded the LP "New Sounds" in '65.

During the mid-'60s, they played before audiences at many college campuses, including three separate appearances at UCLA, Whittier College, Oregon Technical Institute, Santa Monica City College, and Adams State. They also starred at such folk clubs as the Gate of Horn in Chicago, Shadows in Washington, D.C., Troubadour in Los Angeles, Exodus in Denver, and Buddhi in Oklahoma City. Their nightclub engagements included such places as the Blue Angel in New York, Sherman House in Chicago, Harrah's in Lake Tahoe, Embers in Indianapolis, and a six-month stay in the Shell Bar in Honolulu.

TRAVERS, MARY: *See* Peter, Paul and Mary

TRAVIS, MERLE. Singer, guitarist, songwriter. Born Rosewood, Kentucky, November 29, 1917.

Hard times and Merle Robert Travis went together for a good many of his youthful years in the mining country of Kentucky. In the long run, it proved a blessing of sorts, providing him with the insight for such classics as "Sixteen Tons" and "Dark As a Dungeon."

Merle's father relaxed from the struggle of supporting his family by playing the 5-string banjo. Young Merle loved the music and tried to play the banjo himself. His father gave him an old one when he was six and Merle could play it fairly well in a few years. Later, his brother built a home-made guitar for him. Merle's unusual way of playing the guitar resulted from his applying his banjo technique to the new instrument. He uses his thumb as an accompaniment while the forefinger plays the melody on the higher-pitched strings.

After finishing grade school, Merle quit formal education and began to wander around the local counties playing for square dances, fish fries, and "chitling rags." He improved his guitar playing by observing many Kentucky performers, including Mose Rager and Ike Everly, father of the Everly Brothers.

For a while in his teens, he worked for the Civilian Conservation Corps. As soon as he earned enough to buy a $30 Gretch guitar, he joined a friend hitchhiking around the country. They played on street corners for whatever money passersby would give, and slept in train stations, parked cars, or park benches. His wanderings eventually led him to Evansville, Indiana, in 1935. There he was given a chance to sing at a marathon dance broadcast on the local radio station. A group called the Tennessee Tomcats heard the broadcast and asked him to join them. For some months he toured the midwest with them for a daily wage of 35¢. But this job led to an offer to join a major country group, the Georgia Wildcats.

With the new group, Merle found himself in a featured spot on radio station WLW, Cincinnati. He remained on WLW for six years, moving from the Wildcats to more featured roles on network shows such as Plantation Party. His career was interrupted then by World War II. He enlisted in the Marines. When he was discharged, he settled in California, working with such artists as Cliffie Stone, Tex Ritter, and Wesley Tuttle.

He also gained a recording contract with Capitol Records, turning out such numbers as "No Vacancy," "Divorce Me C.O.D.," "So Round, So Firm, So Fully Packed," and "Cincinnati Lou." His first Capitol album, "Folk Songs of the Hills," included one of his own songs, "Sixteen Tons." Not too much happened with the song until several years later when Tennessee Ernie Ford recorded it. This time, "Sixteen Tons" became the major hit of 1955 and one of the top-selling records of all time. Other hit songs written by Merle are "Smoke,

Smoke, Smoke (That Cigarette)" and "Old Mountain Dew."

During the 1950s, Merle was featured on both local West Coast TV shows and national network shows. In the 1960s, he changed his base of operations to Nashville, where he was featured on the Grand Ole Opry. Throughout the '50s and '60s, his personal appearances took him to every U.S. state, every province of Canada, and most of the nations of the world.

TUBB, ERNEST: Singer, guitarist, composer, publisher. Born Crisp, Texas, February 9, 1914. Elected to Country Music Hall of Fame, 1965.

Ellis County, Texas, is about forty or fifty miles south of Dallas. It was picture-book cottonwoods ranch country when young Ernest Tubb stretched his growing frame and dreamt of becoming a cowboy movie star. A mail-order guitar and self-instruction book were still in his future at that point although he did some singing with the string bands that played dances, mostly square dances, around the county.

At 18, in the mean and lean Depression year of 1932, Tubb got a paying job in San Antonio as a soda jerk. By now he could play guitar, though not as well as he desired. Two years later, still in San Antonio, he talked himself into a singing and picking job at KONO and married Lois Elaine Cook. The year 1935 was a decisive one; he met the gracious widow of Jimmie Rodgers, Carrie. Ernest had never met Rodgers, but The Singing Brakeman's recordings had long ago convinced Tubb to give up his boyhood cowboy star notions. Jimmie became Ernest's ideal as the young Texan copied Rodgers' phrasing for a time and absorbed the already substantial Rodgers lore. In the hot summer of 1935, Ernest's first son, Justin, was born on August 20th.

By 1936, Carrie Rodgers and the Tubbs had become close friends. She not only gave Ernest the original Jimmie Rodgers guitar, but also obtained an RCA Victor recording contract for him. She arranged a theater personal-appearance tour and acted as his manager for a short time. He recorded at the old Texas Hotel in San Antonio, making cuts of "The Passing of Jimmie Rodgers" and "Jimmie Rodgers' Last Thoughts." These were released on RCA Victor's Bluebird label. Things were looking up, but life still consisted of the grind

Birthplace of Ernest Tubb, Texas (photo taken 1947)

of one-night stands and spells of unemployment.

Sadness also was part of these years. A second son, Rodger Dale, was born and died in 1938. Tubb wrote "Our Baby's Book" in his memory; the song remained one of the most requested ones in his repertoire. In 1939, Violet Elaine, "Scooter Bill," was born. (She is now the wife of songwriter and record producer Wayne Walker of Nashville.)

The start of one of the industry's longest and most successful recording affiliations came in 1940 when Tubb was signed by Decca Records. In San Antonio, Texas, on April 4, he recorded two songs he had written, "Blue Eyed Elaine" and "I'll Get Along Somehow." They sold records, enough at any rate for a $20-a-week job at KGKO in Fort Worth. This job, in turn, soon gave him the chance to become identified with a commercial sponsor.

He became known as "The Gold Chain Troubador," for the Gold Chain Flour Company, earning a full $75 a week. But things were discouraging at several personal levels. Tubb seriously considered giving up his career for a defense job where the pay was steady and certain. There was one song he had been playing around with and he decided to record it. It has become his all-time hit, a gold-record-seller, "Walking the Floor Over You." The song

started opening doors, even those to Hollywood.

He made two western movies in 1942. Charles Starrett was the established star in both, and both can still be seen in those very late television showings under the original titles of "Fighting Buckaroo" and "Ridin' West." Hollywood was not exactly shaken by this. But the effort did help gain him a guest appearance late in the year on the Grand Ole Opry. Opry audiences and executives were impressed with him. In 1943, he became a regular member. The following year he appeared in another motion picture, "Jamboree," and in 1947, in the film "Hollywood Barn Dance." Along with better paying personal appearances and thousands of miles of traveling each month, Tubb set a precedent by appearing at Carnegie Hall.

The money was easier and he started expanding business interests, working out a music firm arrangement with Jean and Julian Aberbach of Hill and Range Songs, Inc. He also founded the Ernest Tubb Record Shop in Nashville, now at 417 Broadway near the Opry. Another milestone was the arrangement with WSM for broadcasting the Ernest Tubb Midnight Jamboree show, immediately following the Opry broadcast each Saturday night.

Although Tubb had three songs on the

Ernest Tubb (right) and Hank Snow flank former Tennessee Governor Frank Clement during an Opry telecast.

Billboard Top Ten charts in 1948, it was a bittersweet year; he and Elaine were divorced. He continued having one hit after another in 1949 with a final count of seven songs on the top ten and one a near miss. The latter was "My Tennessee Baby" dedicated to Miss Olene Adams Carter, who soon became Mrs. Tubb. The others were "Blue Christmas," "Don't Rob Another Man's Castle," "Have You Ever Been Lonely," "I'm Bitin' My Fingernails and Thinking of You," "Slippin' Around," "Tennessee Border No. 2" and "Warm Red Wine."

Tubb and Red Foley recorded a duet in 1950, "Goodnight Irene," which gained the top honors for the year. Tubb continued his grueling round of appearances by airplane, car, train and bus, covering more than 100,000 miles a year, playing concerts, honkytonks, parks, everywhere he would be booked with his band, the Texas Troubadours. Daughters Erlene Dale and Olene Gayle were born in 1951 and 1952 before his first Korean and Japanese tour with Hank Snow.

Foul weather and exhaustion brought on a lingering illness that made him leave the Opry until November 1954. Three more children, Ernest Dale Tubb, Jr. (1956), Larry Dean (1958), and Karen Delene (1960), joined the Tubb home at a time when Tubb was successfully recuperating between his still hectic schedules of road trips. His traveling in the 1960s was in his own bus, outfitted for mileage comfort. His recordings of "Thanks a Lot" in 1963, the duet with Loretta Lynn on "Mr. and Mrs. Used to Be" in 1964, and the millionth sale on "Walking the Floor Over You" in 1965, showed his continued popularity. This was acknowledged in 1965 by his election to the coveted Country Music Association's Hall of Fame.

Close to 140 single records were released on Tubb over the years, along with numerous albums. Other hits include "Rainbow at Midnight," "It's Been So Long, Darling," "You Nearly Lose Your Mind," "Women Make a Fool Out of Me," "Take Me Back and Try Me One More Time," "Tomorrow Never Comes," and "Thanks a Lot."

[309]

His LP credits include one on Vocalion label, "Texas Troubadours" ('60). His many Decca albums include such titles as "Ernest Tubb Favorites"; "Daddy of 'Em All"; "Importance of Being Ernest"; "Story of Ernest Tubb" (2 LPs—'59); "Record Shop" ('60); "Golden Favorites," "All Time Hits" ('61); "On Tour" ('62); "Just Call Me Lonesome," "Family Bible" ('63); "Thanks a Lot" ('65).

TUBB, JUSTIN: Singer, guitarist, songwriter. Born San Antonio, Texas, August 20, 1935.

A great deal of entertainment magic seems to go with the name Tubb. It's a magic that carried over from one generation to the next as Justin Wayne Tubb proved a worthy heir to the mantle worn by his Country Music Hall of Fame father, Ernest.

Justin naturally was steeped in country music lore from the cradle. He spent some of his boyhood years in San Antonio before attending Castle Heights Military School at Lebanon, Tennessee, 1944-48. He returned to San Antonio to spend the 1948-49 school year at Poe Junior High, and then completed Brackenridge High School, 1949-52. During his high school years, Justin already showed his potential by playing a mean guitar and singing at school events.

He enrolled in the University of Texas at Austin for the 1952-53 session. But the pull of country music was too great and he left for a disk jockey job at WHIN in Gallatin, Tennessee, during 1953-54. Besides spinning platters, he entertained his audience with his own singing. Many of the songs in his repertoire were his own compositions. It didn't take long for him to prove himself. In 1953, he signed with Decca and soon had a number of records receiving plays across the nation, including his own compositions "Ooh-La-La" and "The Story of My Life."

In 1954, he joined with Goldie Hill on a top 10 hit, "Looking Back to See." He also turned out such records as "Something Called the Blues," "I'm Lookin' for a Date Tonight," "I Miss You," "Sure Fire Kisses," "Fickle Heart," and his own song, "Sufferin' Heart." By now his name was well known nationally and he was asked to become a Grand Ole Opry regular in 1955. He sang such new songs that year as "I Gotta Go Get My Baby," "Chuga-Chuga, Chica-Mauga," "My Heart's Not for You to Play With," "I'm Sorry I Stayed Away So

Long," "All Alone," "Within Your Arms," "Who Will It Be?" and "Pepper Hot Baby." His 1956 output included his own "I'm Just a Fool Enough" and such other records as "You Nearly Lose Your Mind," "Lucky, Lucky Someone Else," and "It Takes a Lot of Heart."

Some of his other recordings of the '50s included his own "I'm a Big Boy Now" and "The Life I Have to Live"; "Miss the Mississippi and You," "Desert Blues," "The Party Is Over," and "If You'll Be My Love" ('57); "Sugar Lips" and his own "Rock It Down to My House" and "Almost Lonely" ('58); and two of his compositions, "I Know You Do" and "Buster's Gang" ('59). Decca also issued an LP of Tubb's work in 1958 called "Country Boy in Love."

Tubb left Decca in 1959, and signed with Starday for 1960-62. (He also turned out one release for Challenge during this period.) In 1962, he went with RCA Victor. During the 1960s, many top performers sang Justin's compositions, including his father, Wilburn Brothers, Faron Young, Webb Pierce, Patsy Cline, Jim Reeves, Mac Wiseman, Skeeter Davis, Cowboy Copas, Red Sovine, Teresa Brewer, Ray Price, and Hank Snow. A number of these were top 10 hits, including Hawkshaw Hawkins' version of "Lonesome 7-7203," a number-one-rated hit of 1963; Faron Young-Margie Singleton with "Keeping Up with the Joneses," and Jim Reeves-Dottie West with "Love Is No Excuse" in 1964.

Justin continued to turn out hit records of his own, such as "Take a Letter Miss Gray" in 1963 and "Dern Ya" in 1964. He also had great success with his LPs in the 1960s, including the 1962 Starday releases "Modern Country Music Sound of Justin Tubb" and "Justin Tubb, Star of the Grand Ole Opry." Other LPs were "Justin Tubb," "Where You're Concerned," and "The Best of Justin Tubb" ('65).

His personal appearances during the 1960s took him to all U.S. states except Alaska, Hawaii, Delaware and Rhode Island and all Canadian provinces except Newfoundland and Prince Edward Island. He also toured Germany. His TV guest spots included the National Barn Dance and WWVA Jamboree.

TUBERT, BOB: Songwriter. Born Worcester, Massachusetts, 1932.

New England and classical music seem an odd combination as background for a major writer of country songs. To make it even stranger, Robert Tubert has turned out material for the popular market, rhythm and blues, and rock 'n' roll as well. And he has written both words and music, despite the fact that he must depend on a professional arranger.

As a boy in Massachusetts, his main interest was in the classics. He had some lessons in classical piano and also tried occasionally to write lyrics to classical music. His interest was mainly in sports during high school, however, and this resulted in a basketball scholarship to Arizona State College in 1950. He did not stay in Arizona, but went on to get his degree as an English major at Southwest Missouri College in Springfield.

After graduation, he got a job as newswriter with Si Siman's pioneering country music station, KWTO. He also served as a stringer, or correspondent, for United Press. While at KWTO, he found a renewed interest in all forms of music. He began to try his hand at writing lyrics and decided to go to New York to gain fame and fortune as a songwriter. Once there, however, he found publishers' doors mainly closed. After struggling for eighteen months as a night clerk, he quit and returned to Springfield.

In a short time, he was trying for a major job opportunity again. This time he scored a breakthrough, becoming script writer of the Ozark Jubilee. He held this position for four years and his association with major artists and executives soon blossomed into collaborations with some of them on songs. This finally paid off with a hit, "Our Winter Love," on which Tubert provided lyrics for Don Cowell's music. In the mid-1960s, Tubert began to score successes both as a collaborator and as solo writer on such songs as the rhythm and blues "Please Don't Hurt Me"; rock 'n' roll "Ring Dang Doo"; and the country and western "Satin Pillows." The last of these was written in collaboration with Sonny James. Tubert and James also turned out "You're the Only World I Know," which provided James with a number-one national best-seller in 1965.

TWITTY, CONWAY: Singer, guitarist, band leader, songwriter. Born Friarspoint, Mississippi.

Much publicity has been given to major rock 'n' roll artists who have moved over from country and western. Less notice has been given

to the trend in the other direction. An example of one of the best known rock 'n' roll performers of the 1950s and early '60s, who switched to top-rated country performer, is Conway Twitty.

Raised in the south and southwest, Twitty (real name: Harold Jenkins) naturally had a great deal of exposure to country and western music in his youth. He lived in Friarspoint, Mississippi, until he was seven when his family moved to Arkansas. Twitty got most of his education in public schools in Arkansas and had already learned to play guitar before he reached his teens.

By the time he was a teenager in the mid-1950s, rock 'n' roll had swept the national pop field. Twitty began to play on local stations, and in a short time had progressed to national rock 'n' roll stardom. He formed his own band and played on almost every major TV show in the country through the latter half of the 1950s and the early '60s. Among the shows on which he starred were Ed Sullivan and Dick Clark's American Bandstand. Besides appearances in all fifty states, Twitty and his group toured Canada, Australia, and Europe.

During these years, Twitty sold more than 16,000,000 records, mostly on MGM label. He made a number of albums, three of which were still available in the mid-1960s, "Hits of Conway Twitty" ('60), "Hit The Road" ('64), and "Conway Twitty" ('65). He also was featured in six movies and wrote title songs and sound track music for three of them: "Platinum High," "Sex Kittens Go to College" and "College Confidential."

In the mid-1960s, Twitty decided to concentrate on country and western music. He settled down in Oklahoma City, Oklahoma, using this as the base for his new band, The Lonely Blue Boys. When the first UHF-TV country music station began operations in Oklahoma City on June 1, 1966, the Conway Twitty Show was a weekly feature. The show, taped on KLPR-TV, was soon shown on other stations via syndication.

Twitty signed with Decca Records for his country output. In 1966 and 1967, he had a number of single records and LPs on Decca that were played on major country stations across the U.S. In 1968 he had a top 10 hit, "Image of Me." The Lonely Blue Boys' List of personal appearances covered every state in the union and several foreign countries as well.

TYLER, T. TEXAS: Singer, guitarist, band leader, songwriter. Born near Mena, Arkansas.

The state of California has been lucky for many entertainers nicknamed Tex, perhaps because of the concentration of movie western production in the Golden State. Among those who gained national reputations in country and western music while based in the far west have been Tex Ritter, Tex Williams, and the man referred to as "The Man with a Million Friends," T. Texas Tyler.

Tyler spent some of his early years in Texas, though he was born across the border in Arkansas. He learned to play guitar by the time he was in his teens and began to perform locally when he was 16. During the 1930s he headed east, appearing on the Major Bowes Amateur Hour in New York and on a radio show in Newport, Rhode Island. During the 1940s he turned his gaze westward again, eventually ending up in the Los Angeles area. During these years he appeared with a number of groups, including the Ozark Ramblers, Dixie Melody Boys, and Oklahoma Melody Boys.

For a time, his career gave way to the demands of the nation and he spent several years in the service during World War II. These years helped provide the background for Tyler's nationwide hit of 1948, his own composition, "Deck of Cards." After receiving his discharge in 1946, Tyler made Hollywood his home ground. He organized his own band which became one of the nation's main country and western groups during the balance of the 1940s and the 1950s. He also signed with the independent Four Star Label in Hollywood. Within a short time, he was the record company's most important meal ticket. Besides "Deck of Cards," he provided Four Star with such top 10 hits as "Dad Gave My Dog Away" (co-written by Tyler) in 1948 and "Bummin' Around" in '53. His efforts in 1948 won him the runner-up spot as best country and western entertainer in the disk jockey-juke box operator poll.

In the late 1940s, Tyler also began to gain stature as a TV performer. He had his own show on Los Angeles TV called "Range Round Up." In 1950, the magazine Country Song Roundup voted Tyler's program the Best Country Music Show for the year. He also appeared in several western films, including the Columbia "Horsemen of the Sierras" (1949). That same year,

Tyler was featured in a show at New York's Carnegie Hall.

During the 1950s and '60s, Tyler continued to record and perform both in person and on TV in many parts of the country. His TV credits included a number of appearances on the Grand Ole Opry. His record output included "Oklahoma Hills," "Home in San Antone," "Honky Tonk Girl," "Beautiful Life," "The Old Country Church," "In the Sweet By and By," "Follow Through," and "Fairweather Baby." Among his own compositions he recorded were "Dear Souvenirs" and "Crawdad Town."

The last two songs were part of an LP he recorded for Don Pierce's Starday label in 1964. (Pierce's successful start in the record field derived from his early association with Tyler in the late 1940s at Four Star.) Titled "Sensational Hits of T. Texas Tyler," the album also included "Texas Boogie Woogie," "Invitations," "My Talk About Leaving," "Just Like Dad," "Injun Joe," "Morning Glory," "It's a Long Road Back Home," "Sunset Years of Life," and "Little Piece of Ground." (*See also* PIERCE, DON)

VAN DYKE, LEROY: Singer, guitarist, songwriter. Born Spring Fork, Missouri, October 4, 1929.

The increased sophistication of country music after 1950 is indicated by the success of such performers as Leroy Frank Van Dyke. Though brought up in a rural area, he and his brothers and sisters all finished both high school and college. This extra polish shows up in his ability to hold his own in many different phases of popular music from country and western shows to "posh" nightclubs.

During Leroy's early years, he performed many chores and odd jobs on his family's farm. He was interested in country music and had learned the guitar by the time he finished high school. However, he didn't think of a musical career when he entered college. His major subjects were animal husbandry and agricultural journalism. For a while he was a local newspaper reporter assigned to farm subjects. He thought for a time of leaving journalism for a job as an auctioneer.

The Korean War helped change his outlook. He spent part of his service career working for Army counterintelligence in the Far East. In his leisure hours, he began to think a little more about what he would do when he left the Army. He had won applause from his Army buddies for his musical ability and he decided to give this a try.

When he returned to the U.S., he entered a number of talent contests. These led to jobs at various small clubs and affairs and, eventually, to his writing a hit song, "Auctioneer." The result was a bid to appear on Arthur Godfrey's TV show. The exposure gained from this helped win a spot on Red Foley's TV show, Jubilee U.S.A. By the late 1950s, he was in demand for shows at county fairs, in major nightclubs, and at many city theaters across the country. His recordings for Mercury began to move up the charts, and in 1961 he hit with a number-one best-seller in both country and western and pop fields, "Walk on By." In 1962, he turned out a second major hit, "If a Woman Answers," and scored with "I've Never Been Loved Before," in 1967 and in 1968 with "Louisville."

VAN RONK, DAVE: Singer, guitarist, band leader, songwriter. Born Brooklyn, New York, June 30, 1936.

One of the best blues singers of the urban folk movement of the 1950s and '60s was Brooklyn-born David Van Ronk. His renditions of such songs as "Willie the Weeper," "Cocaine Blues," and Bad Dream Blues" marked him as one of the most original white performers in this basically Negro idiom. In the mid-1960s, though, he opened new pathways by turning instead to traditional jazz and jug band work. The change was dictated partly by his feeling that it is musically dishonest for a performer to sing blues without living through the harsh conditions that gave rise to them.

His own upbringing was a relatively comfortable one. He attended public schools in Brooklyn and Queens and graduated from Richmond Hill High School. He learned the guitar and initially was much interested in traditional New Orleans jazz. For a while after finishing high school, he performed with jazz groups in New York. He was aware of the growing volume of folk music, but paid little attention to it until 1957, when he worked briefly with Odetta and gained new insight into the folk tradition.

He was particularly attracted to blues material and listened to recordings and performances of many artists. He was deeply interested in some of the renditions of Josh White. Soon he was singing folk music, including a heavy leavening of blues, at local New York spots. He also experimented with other styles of Negro music, including jug playing. In 1958, he and jug player Sam Charters made a jug band record for Lyrichord.

Van Ronk's reputation as a blues singer increased steadily. He played for audiences in many parts of the country and was invited to a number of folk music festivals. In the late 1950s, he signed with Folkways records and turned out two well received LPs, one in 1959 and another in 1961. In 1963, he moved over to the Prestige label and turned out such LPs as "Dave Van Ronk, Folksinger" ('63) and "In the Tradition" ('64). Though much of the material was in the jazz or blues vein, he also showed his ability to perform other kinds of songs with such numbers as "Lady Gay" and "Come All Ye Fair and Tender Ladies."

In the mid-1960s, he began to concentrate more on jazz and jug band material than blues. His performance at the 1964 Newport Folk Festival was mainly jazz in nature. He also formed his own jug band, which featured Sam Charters, called the Ragtime Jug Stompers. In 1964, he signed with Mercury and turned out an LP titled "Ragtime Jug Stompers." His second Mercury LP was turned out in August 1964 and called "Just Dave." He continued to appear in concerts both in the U.S. and abroad. One of his engagements was the 1965 New York Folk Festival in Carnegie Hall.

Van Ronk's performances included some of his own compositions. His writings include "Bad Dream Blues," "Bambee," "If You Leave Me," "Pretty Mama," and "Frankie's Blues."

VIRGINIA BOYS: Jim and Jesse's Band. As of the early 1960s, members were: Alfred Donald "Don" McHan, born Bryson City, North Carolina, July 11, 1933; Robert Clark "Bobby" Thompson, born Converse, South Carolina, July 5, 1937; Vassar Clements, born near Kinard, South Carolina, April 25, 1928. (*See* JIM AND JESSE)

WAGONER, PORTER: Singer, guitarist. Born West Plains, Missouri, August 12, 1930.

Singing and guitar playing during business hours might get some store clerks fired. In Porter Wagoner's case, it opened the door to eventual stardom.

Wagoner's grocery store chores occurred in his home town of West Plains, Missouri. Porter had learned to play the guitar before he reached high school level. He like to listen to country radio programs and mastered many of the lyrics of the top-rated songs for his own enjoyment. In his late teens, he used this ability to while away the hours when business was slow in the market he worked in. His singing was good enough for the market owner to sponsor a 15-minute early morning show featuring him on the local station in the late '40s.

The show not only won new customers, it also demonstrated young Wagoner's audience potential. Porter's work came to the attention of E. E. Siman of station KWTO in Springfield, Missouri. The result was a contract to Porter to sing on a weekly series on the station in the fall of 1951. Not long after, the formation of Red Foley's Ozark Jubilee on the station resulted in another step forward for Wagoner. Foley helped improve Wagoner's style and in a short time Porter was one of the featured artists on the nationally televised show.

As the early 1950s went by, Wagoner received bids to appear in many parts of the country, and audiences signified approval with thunderous applause. In 1955, Porter signed a recording contract with RCA Victor and quickly followed with his first top 10 hit, "Satisfied Mind." Later in the year he proved this was no fluke by scoring with "Eat, Drink and Be Merry." In 1956, another hit was provided with "What Would You Do (If Jesus Came to Your House)?" In 1957, he joined the Grand Ole Opry.

In 1960, a new phase of his career began with the start of his own show. The show was filmed in Nashville and syndicated to 18 stations in its first year, mostly in the southern states. The show continued to build in importance during the 1960s. Joining Wagoner on the regular cast were Norma Jean and Porter's group called The Wagonmasters. By 1967, the show had expanded to 86 stations in all parts of the U.S. and Canada. By that time, Wagoner's popularity resulted in a personal appearance schedule that averaged 230 days a year on the road.

Through the 1960s, Wagoner continued to turn out best-selling records every year. In 1960, he appeared on the charts with "Your Old Love Letters." The following year, two major hits resulted, "Cold Dark Waters Below" and "Misery Loves Company." The latter was ranked number one nationally for many weeks. In 1963, his recording of the Bill Anderson composition "I've Enjoyed as Much of This

as I Can Stand" was in the top 10. The years '64, '65 and '66 provided, respectively, "Sorrow on the Rocks," "Green, Green Grass of Home," and "Skid Row Joe." In 1967, Wagoner's name moved up the charts with another of his prison ballads, "The Cold Hard Facts of Life." His 1968 duets with Polly Parton, "Holding on to "Nothing" and "The Last Thing on My Mind," were top 10 hits.

By 1968, Wagoner was one of the top-selling RCA Victor LP album artists as well. His album list included: "Porter Wagoner" and "Duets with Davis" ('62); "Satisfied Mind" (Camden label) and "Y'All Come" ('63); "Porter Wagoner Show" and "In Person" ('64); "Blue Grass Story" ('65); "Soul of a Convict" ('67); "Just Between You and Me" ('68); "Green Grass of Home" ('68).

WAGONMASTERS, THE: *See* Wagoner, Porter

WAKEFIELD, FRANK: *See* Greenbriar Boys

WAKELY, JIMMY: Singer, movie actor, TV and radio performer. Born Mineola, Arkansas, February 16, 1914.

From log cabin to ranch hand to star of western movies seems a natural progression. With this background, it's not surprising that Jimmy Wakely also proved a natural with the guitar and country and western music.

The log cabin of his birth was in Arkansas, but he spent most of his growing-up years in Oklahoma, where his family moved when he was four. While helping with the chores on the ranch, little Jimmy also managed to begin picking out simple tunes on the guitar when he was seven. By the time he was in high school, he was proficient enough with the instrument to entertain at school affairs. After graduating, he worked on Oklahoma cattle ranches and sometimes won approval from friends for singing.

Finally he was encouraged enough by his reception to try out for an amateur contest at WKY, Oklahoma City. He used this as a stepping-stone to professional work and, in 1937, formed the Wakely Trio with Johnny Bond and Scott Harrel. The Trio was signed for morning airings on WKY. When Gene Autry guested on the program, he liked them well enough to ask them to join his Melody Ranch show on CBS. Once out in Hollywood, Jimmy got the chance to appear in several movies.

In the early 1940s, he left Autry to form his own band. The new organization included many names that became famous in country and western: Cliffie Stone, Spade Cooley, Merle Travis, and Wesley Tuttle. This group too appeared in the 33 pictures Wakely had a part in up to 1943. In 1943, Wakely organized his Saddle Pals trio and starred in a number of Columbia westerns.

In the late 1940s, Jimmy began to make his mark in the recording field as well, first as a single and then in combination with Margaret Whiting. In 1948, his version of "I Love You So Much It Hurts" was number one in the country, and "Signed, Sealed and Delivered" also received wide popularity.

The year 1949 saw Margaret Whiting and Jimmy Wakely become one of the most listened to duos in radio history. They also scored with such national hits as "Slippin' Around," "I'll Never Slip Around Again," and "Til the End of the World." In 1950, their major recordings included "Broken Down Merry-Go-Round," "Let's Go to Church Next Sunday Morning," and "The Gods Were Angry with Me." Jimmy's last major hits of this period (1951) were solos, "Beautiful Brown Eyes" and "My Heart Cries for You." Though the Wakely name has not been on the charts for many years, he still is in the top 20 country and western singers for total national hit recordings.

WALKER, BILLY: Singer, guitarist, songwriter. Born Ralls, Texas, January 14, 1929.

In the little town of Ralls, Texas (population 1,779), it was a tossup as to whether ranching or country and western music was more popular. To hometown boy William Marvin Walker, music won out, though for a time he did work as a ranch hand. His interest in country and western came early, and he learned to play the guitar while still in grade school in Ralls. He figured out his fingering from listening to radio programs and country and western records.

Billy attended grade school in Ralls from 1934 to 1942 by which time he was an excellent, though amateur, performer. His family moved soon after this to New Mexico, where Billy attended Whiteface High School from 1942 to 1946. In 1944, Billy entered an amateur contest and won. One of the prizes was an appearance on a radio program on station KICA, Clovis, New Mexico. He was so well received

that he became a regular on the show, remaining until he finished high school.

For a time, he worked on a ranch. But the lure of a music career was too strong. Billy formed his own band and toured the southwest. He soon achieved considerable notice in the region, resulting in a 1949 bid to join the cast of the Big D Jamboree. From here Billy moved over to the Ranch Time show on a Waco, Texas, station in the early 1950s. Billy's star was steadily rising in the '50s, and he moved up a notch to the famed Louisiana Hayride over station KWKH in Shreveport. In 1954, he won major awards from BMI and Cashbox.

In 1955, Billy, known as "The Travelin' Texan," traveled again, this time to the Ozark Jubilee. He remained one of the stars of the show through 1960, when he was asked to move to the Grand Ole Opry. Walker became a fixture on the Opry show beginning in April 1960.

Billy turned out a number of well received songs in the late 1950s and early 1960s. Many of them were on the hit lists, but none hit the top rungs of the charts until 1962. Then Billy moved all the way to the top with his number-one hit on Columbia, "Charlie's Shoes." He also scored a top 10 success in 1962 with "Willie the Weeper." In 1964, he had two more best-sellers in "Circumstances" and "Cross the Brazos at Waco." He scored in each of the next three years with "Matamoros" ('65); "A Million and One" ('66); and "Del Rio" ('67). The last two of these were on Monument label to which Billy switched in 1965.

Some of Billy's other well known songs of the '50s and '60s were "Forever," "Funny How Time Slips Away," "The Old French Quarter," "Blue Mountain Waltz," "Go Ahead and Make Me Cry," "Let Me Hear from You," "Let's Make Memories Tonight," "Pretend You Just Don't Know Me," "The Record," "Thank You for Calling," and "Whirlpool." Billy also wrote many songs, some of which were hits for other artists. These included "Anything Your Heart Desires," "Make Believe," "Til We Can Make It Come True," "What Makes Me Love You Like I Do?," "It's Doggone Tough on Me," and "Pretend You Just Don't Know Me."

Walker's Columbia LPs include "Hits" ('61); "Greatest Hits" ('63); "Thank You for Calling" ('64); "The Gun, the Gold and the Girl"; and "The Walker Way." He also was featured on a Harmony Records album, "Anything Your

Heart Desires." His personal appearances in the 1950s and '60s took him to all fifty states, Canada, and Europe. His records in the mid-1960s were particularly popular in Germany. He guested on many national TV shows, including the Jimmy Dean Show and Tonight. His credits also include two movies, "Second Fiddle to a Steel Guitar" and "Red River Round-Up."

WALKER, CHARLIE: Singer, disk jockey, sports announcer. Born Collin County, Texas, November 2, 1926.

The voice of Charlie Walker ranks among the most heard ones in the nation. In the southwest, he has long been known to country and western fans as one of the top disk jockeys of the region. But listeners and TV viewers from coast to coast who never listen to this kind of music have eagerly followed play-by-play descriptions of sporting events broadcast by Charlie.

Born and raised in Texas, Charlie had an early love for country music. He was a good musician in his teens and joined Bill Boyd's Cowboy Ramblers in 1943. He also had an excellent announcing style that won him several DJ jobs in the late 1940s. In the early 1950s, he was already one of the better known DJs in the field. Before long, he was on Billboard's list of Top 10 Country Music Disk Jockeys in the U.S., a spot he retained for ten consecutive years.

Besides playing other performers' records, he displayed an excellent vocal style himself. In the mid-1950s, he signed with Columbia Records and turned out a top 10 national hit record in 1958, "Pick Me Up on Your Way Down." For Columbia and, in the mid-1960s, for Epic, he had several more hits, including "Close All the Honky Tonks" and "The Man in the White Suit." In 1965, he had another top 10 hit, "Wild As a Wildcat."

When not attending to broadcasting chores, Walker toured both as m.c. for various country and western shows and as a vocalist. He gained particular popularity in Las Vegas, starring at the Golden Nugget. From 1965 to 1967, he was signed to appear a total of 25 weeks at this casino.

He also won considerable acclaim among his fellow country and western artists for his golfing knowledge and ability. He was in the top brackets for a number of years at the annual Sahara Invitational Tournament in Las Vegas. In 1966, he took top honors among male country music artists in the 1966 Music City Pro-Celebrity Tournament in Nashville. Walker thus knew what he was talking about when he broadcast or telecast major golf events. For four years in the 1960s, he provided the commentary on the Texas Open Golf Tournament for CBS-TV's Wide World of Sports.

In 1967, Charlie was again listed on the hit charts with his Epic recording of "Don't Squeeze My Sharmon."

WALKER, CINDY: Singer, guitarist, songwriter. Born Mexia, Texas.

To 99.99 per cent or more of the U.S. population, the only response to the name of the town of Mexia, Texas, would be "where?" To the professionals in country and western music, the word brings instant recognition as the home of Cindy Walker, one of the top writers in the field.

Songwriting ran in her family. Her grandfather, Prof. F. L. Eiland, was a noted hymn writer whose "Hold to God's Unchanging Hands" is widely used in American churches. Cindy naturally heard cowboy ballads and country music programs from her earliest years. She showed talent almost as soon as she could talk, and at seven had her first entertainment work singing and dancing in the Toy Land Review. She became increasingly interested in show business as she grew older, perfecting her dancing and also learning to play the guitar.

She went on to a career as a dancer, working at Billy Rose's Casa Manana in Fort Worth. Already interested in songwriting, she penned a theme for the show that met with enthusiastic approval when she presented it to the manager. Later, it was played by Paul Whiteman's band on a national hookup.

Cindy had to travel to Los Angeles to break into the recording field. In 1942, her father, a cotton buyer, went there on a business trip and took Cindy and her mother along. Cindy was determined to present a new song she'd written to someone in the recording business. She saw her chance when her father drove past the Crosby Building in Hollywood.

She got out and went up to the office of Larry Crosby. In an almost 1000-1 shot, she talked her way past the front desk and managed to see Bing's brother. Larry listened to the song and agreed to show it to Bing. To do it, though, he asked Cindy to make a demonstration record of the song, "Lone Star Trail," herself. This resulted in a double barreled success. Bing liked the song and recorded it on Decca label. Decca executive Dave Kapp liked Cindy's record and signed her to a contract.

For five years, Cindy worked as a performer and songwriter. She also appeared in several movies. In 1947, though, she decided to concentrate on writing and quit her other chores. The choice paid off as more and more artists recorded her material. Soon her name began to appear regularly on the credit lists for national hits. One of the first to hit the upper brackets of the country and western field was Eddy Arnold's top 10 version of Cindy's "Take Me in Your Arms and Hold Me" in 1950. In 1952, Hank Snow provided another top 10 credit with "Gold Rush Is Over," and in 1953 Cindy worked with Porter Wagoner on a song, "Trademark," that gave Carl Smith a national best-seller.

About this time, Cindy had grown tired of Hollywood, and longed for her own home territory. In 1954, she picked up stakes and moved back to Mexia. From then on, she worked even longer hours as a writer, sending most of her completed songsheets to top artists by mail. The year 1955 provided her with a song that was number one in the nation for many weeks. The hit recording was made by her co-author on "I Don't Care," Webb Pierce. Among Cindy's other top 10 hits in the next decade were "You Don't Know Me," recorded by Eddy Arnold, Stonewall Jackson's version of "Leona" ('62), and two posthumous top 10 hits for Jim Reeves, "This Is It" ('65) and "Distant Drums" ('66).

By the mid-1960s, Cindy had more than 400 published songs to her credit. Among these were such other major hits as "China Doll," "I Was Just Walking Out the Door," "Bubbles in My Beer," "Blue Canadian Rockies," "Thank You for Calling," "In the Misty Moonlight," and "The Night Watch."

WALKER, FRANK BUCKLEY: Recording manager, record company executive. Born Fly Summit, New York, October 24, 1889; died New York, October 16, 1963.

A combination talent scout, record producer, and hard-headed businessman, Frank Walker was one of the industry pioneers who breathed commercial life into the country and western field. Along the way, he helped preserve on records many of the stylings of great traditional folk artists. He is best remembered for his association with Hank Williams. But this was just the frosting on a career that provided many vital folk, country and western milestones.

At first, Walker seemed headed for a purely financial career. After finishing school in upstate New York, he joined the National Savings Bank in Albany in 1908, and remained with the firm until 1912. He then moved to New York City and worked for W. N. Comer & Co. until 1915. At this point, several years in military service provided an important turning-point in his career. Walker attained the rank of Captain in the U.S. Army and took part in some of Pershing's campaigns along the Mexican border. When the U.S. entered World War I, he switched to the Navy and served with that branch from 1917 to 1919.

These years in the service gave young Walker a breathing spell to consider his future. When he left the Navy, he had decided to try to enter the music industry. He became president of an organization called Central Concert Company, and promoted appearances of concert artists in Detroit, Chicago, and St. Louis from 1919 to 1921. With this under his belt, he followed a strong belief in the future importance of the record industry by joining the Columbia Phonograph Company in 1921. It was the start of a long and fruitful association that helped build the firm into one of the major factors in the recording field. By the time Walker left in 1932, he was a vice president and director of the concern.

One of his first activities for Columbia was to travel through the south and audition new artists for the label. He is credited with the important "first" of being the initial representative of a major record company to record traditional folk, country and western in the field. During the 1920s, he lined up many rhythm and blues and country and western artists for Columbia. Among the artists he recorded were Gid Tanner, Charlie Poole, Clarence Ashley, and Riley Puckett. During these years, he discovered the great blues singer Bessie Smith, and made the only recordings of her for Columbia. He also was one of the first to recognize the talent of Huddie Ledbetter, gaining some historic sessions with him for Columbia.

The entire Columbia 14000 blue series and 15000 hillbilly and "old-timey" series were Walker's creation. Creation of separate "race" and "country and western" categories in the record field is also considered to have been originated by Walker. To gain many of these songs, Walker hauled recording equipment into the remotest rural hamlet or farm. During the 1920s, he carried wax disk masters in a Model T or by horse and muleback, in some cases, to accomplish his goals.

Before he left Columbia, Walker established the low-price Okeh series. Soon after he joined RCA Victor in Camden, New Jersey, in 1933, he set up a similar low-cost line called Bluebird. One of his first sessions for Bluebird was devoted to Huddie Ledbetter.

Not only was Walker a superlative discoverer of new talent, he was also an adroit organizer of successful marketing campaigns for the resulting records. He was equally at ease with writers, artists, music publishers, salesmen, distributors, radio station and talent managers, and bookers. He used this ability to exploit the national market for artists in all segments of music during his years with Columbia and RCA. His personal direction, for example, included sessions for such people as Gene Autry, Arturo Toscanini, Glenn Miller, Al Jolson, Ethel Waters, Lawrence Tibbett, Eddy Arnold, Benny Goodman, Eddie Cantor, Paul Whiteman, and Frank Sinatra.

Walker served his country in a new capacity during World War II. At President Roosevelt's request, he organized the V-disc program that helped provide an important morale-builder for the country's Armed Forces.

In 1945, he started a major new record firm. He was appointed general manager and vice-president of Metro-Goldwyn-Mayer's new MGM Records Division. His eye for talent was as sharp as ever; in 1947, he signed a new songwriter and artist who rapidly became one of the greatest in country and western history, Hank Williams. In close association with Williams' publisher, Fred Rose of Acuff-Rose, he helped make the young performer into a music industry legend.

Walker remained the head of MGM Records until 1956 when he went into semi-retirement. However, he remained as a consultant and was active in MGM affairs until his death in 1963. In 1956, he also was appointed vice president of Loew's Inc., a position he occupied until 1963. Over the years, he took a deep interest in industry progress in general. He was one of the founders of the Record Industry Associ-

ation of America (RIAA) and served as its president in 1956.

WALKER, JO: Executive director, Country Music Association. Born Orlinda, Tennessee, February 16, 1924.

Symbolic of the coming of age of country music as a worldwide industry force was the growth and success of the Country Music Association. The CMA, in turn, provided both a focal point for industry effort and a new force to expand the scope of country music through such programs as the Country Music Hall of Fame. A key element in all of this is the organization's executive director, Jo Walker.

Edith Josephine Denning was born and raised in the Grand Ole Opry's home state of Tennessee. After finishing high school, she worked as a secretary at Vultee Aircraft Corporation in Nashville from 1942 to 1945. When World War II ended, she decided to further her education, attending Lambuth College (1946-'48) and Peabody College (1947-'48) in Nashville.

She assumed more authority in the business world in 1951, working as executive secretary at Crescent Amusement Co. in Nashville until 1955. She married Charles Walker, president and general manager of Nashville station WKDA, in October 1954. The happy union was ended by the death of Walker on Labor Day 1967, in a motorcycle accident.

Her close friend, Betty Boles, who introduced her to Walker, also strongly recommended Jo for the job of office manager with the newly formed CMA in 1958. Jo had served as administrative secretary to industry executive G. Edward Friar from 1956 to 1958. She started with CMA on December 8, 1958. When her service began, CMA was a weak fledgling, struggling to survive in its evolution from the old Country Music Disk Jockey's Association.

Within a year, Jo moved up to the title of executive director. Almost singlehandedly, she conducted the routine of business affairs for CMA and helped coordinate plans for its growth. For a time, the depression that hit country music in the mid-1950s threatened to engulf CMA. Thanks partly to Jo's drive and perseverance, CMA weathered that storm to become a thriving organization in the 1960s. In November 1967, Jo was able to transfer her offices to the newly opened Country Music Hall of Fame in Nashville. Her contributions were recognized in the form of many civic and industry awards in the 1960s and selection for listing in *Who's Who in America*.

WALKER, WAYNE P.: Songwriter. Born Quapaw, Oklahoma, December 13, 1925.

Certainly one of the oddest transitions in the music field was Wayne Walker's shift from fire-escape salesman to first-rank country songwriter. Wayne was born in Quapaw, Oklahoma, but his family moved to Kilgore, Texas, soon after his birth. He completed high school in Kilgore, then signed up with the Coast Guard during World War II. During his service years, his family moved to Shreveport, Louisiana. When Wayne was discharged, he returned to Shreveport and soon found the fire-escape salesman's job. In his spare time, though, he satisfied a deep interest in country music by attending the Louisiana Hayride. He had begun to try his hand at songwriting and managed to meet two of the Hayride stars, Webb Pierce and Red Sovine. Both encouraged him to continue his writing efforts. When Webb and Red moved on to Nashville, Wayne soon followed.

In the country music capital, he found a writing niche with Cedarwood Publishing Company. Pierce and other performers began to use Walker's material. Finally, in 1957, Ray Price provided Wayne with his first big hit, "I've Got a New Heartache." That same year, Webb Pierce scored with "Holiday for Love" and Carl Smith with "Why, Why." In 1961, two more Pierce successes were written or co-written by Walker, "How Do You Talk to a Baby?" and "Sweet Lips." Wayne's 1960 score included "Fallen Angel," written with Ben Weisman and B. Raleigh and recorded by Pierce.

The year 1962 was a big one for Wayne. His output included such successes as "Hello Out There" recorded by Carl Belew, "Pride," by Ray Price, "Unloved, Unwanted," by Kitty Wells, and "A Little Heartache" by Eddy Arnold. The year 1963 included Patsy Cline's best-selling record of "Leaving on Your Mind." In 1964, Wayne's roll of hits included "Memory No. 1." by Webb Pierce, "Burning Memories" by Ray Price, and "I Thank My Lucky Stars" by Eddy Arnold.

Through the late 1960s, Walker's total song output exceeded 400. He received 17 BMI awards over the 1957-67 period. Like most songwriters, Walker notes the need for volume output for a professional career. "If I write enough songs, some of them will get recorded, and some of these will sell records. You know the law of averages is bound to work out. I figure a good songwriter can write a song any time he has to. It may not be a good song, but it will be a song. Of course, there are times when I'm in different moods and can write better than at other times, but that is true of any business. This is the business I'm in, and I enjoy it."

WALLER, CHARLIE: *See* Country Gentlemen

WALTER, JEROME: *See* Gateway Singers, The

WARNER, FRANK: Singer, guitarist, banjoist, folk music collector, YMCA executive. Born Selma, Alabama, April 5, 1903.

The renaissance of folk music in the years after World War II owes much to the collectors of old-time music. These people untiringly combed the remote areas of the U.S. to preserve a rich heritage of music that threatened to be obliterated by the march of modern society with its technological advances. In addition, the collectors often brought many previously unknown and deserving artists to the attention of the nation and the world. One of the great contributors in this vein has been Frank Warner (assisted by his wife Anne).

Warner, born and raised in the south, heard much of this music from his early boyhood. He completed part of his grade school education in Selma, later finishing public and high school in other parts of the south, including Jackson, Tennessee, and Durham, North Carolina. Warner enjoyed singing and often took part in informal songfests with friends and neighbors. When he entered Duke University in 1921, he quickly became involved in glee club work, as both a singer and a student glee club officer. In 1924, he made his first solo debut in public at the State Fair in Raleigh. His task was to sing folksongs to help illustrate a lecture on the state's folklore given by Duke Professor Dr. Frank C. Brown.

After graduation from Duke in 1925, he went to New York to study at the New York School of Social Welfare, Columbia University, and the YMCA training schools. He decided to make the YMCA his main career and was assigned to Greensboro, North Carolina, in 1928. His interest in folk music continued and he spent his vacation time wandering through many parts of the country collecting songs and other material. He also spent some of his hours while on YMCA duty entertaining and instructing YMCA members in folk music.

In 1931, he continued his YMCA career in New York. As before, he continued to go into the rural areas whenever he could to collect songs. His travels extended through parts of Canada as well as most of the New England states. In 1935, he married Anne Locker, who shared his enthusiasm for folk material and who accompanied him on vacation tours of this kind. On one such tour in the late 1930s, they discovered a highly talented folk artist and instrument maker named Frank Proffitt. One of the songs they learned from him was to become a nationwide hit in the 1950s. It was called "Tom Dooley."

This was one of many traditional songs the Warners sang at concerts across the U.S. and, in later years, in other countries as well. The Warners were careful to give credit to the musicians who provided them with the material and sometimes were able to gain concert engagements for some of them. After the Kingston Trio, who gained knowledge of the song from other sources, made "Tom Dooley" into a major hit, the Warners labored to bring Frank Proffitt his just recognition. They finally achieved this in the 1960s, and Proffitt starred at many of the major folk festivals.

Frank Warner continued to progress in his YMCA work. In 1952, he was appointed general secretary for operations in Nassau and Suffolk counties, Long Island. He and his wife during the 1950s and '60s also performed in concert halls, at major folk festivals, and on campuses throughout the U.S. In New York, among the places they played were Carnegie Hall and Town Hall.

Frank Warner made several LPs, including "American Folk Songs and Ballads" ('52) and "Songs and Ballads of America's Wars" ('54) on Elektra label, "Songs of the Civil War" on Prestige, and, in 1963, an album for Vanguard.

WATERS, MUDDY: Singer, guitarist, songwriter. Born Rolling Fork, Mississippi, April 4, 1915.

The name Muddy Waters at most folk or blues festivals is usually enough to insure a packed house. Like many other blues performers, he would probably have remained totally unknown were it not for the pursuit of Americana by folk scholars.

Poverty was a normal state of affairs for most of his family and friends in the part of Mississippi where Muddy (real name: McKinley Morganfield) was born. His mother died when he was three and his father, Ollie Morganfield, sent little McKinley to his grandmother's house in Clarksdale, Mississippi. At an early age, Muddy was working as a field hand in the Clarksdale region.

Clarksdale was a hotbed of blues singing and Muddy heard many great artists in his youth. He also listened to many blues renditions by local people, both while they worked and at evening socials and get-togethers. Though he enjoyed singing, Muddy did not get started as a performer until relatively late in life. Though many of his friends could play an instrument before they were in their teens, he didn't start to learn until he was 22.

Soon he began to sing occasionally at Saturday night parties. After several years, he had become one of the more noted performers in a region famed for blues singers. Word of his ability reached folk music collector Alan Lomax who went out to the cotton farm on which Muddy worked to record him for the Library of Congress Archive of American Folk Song. With associate John Work, Lomax recorded two numbers in 1940, "I Be's Troubled" and "Country Blues."

A year later, Muddy finally decided to break away from farm work. He had learned to play the harmonica and joined the Silas Green tent show as an accompanist for blues singers. He didn't last long with the show, but he made up his mind to continue to try to get away from his home region.

In 1943, he headed for Chicago where he soon had a job in a paper mill. For the next few years, he held several other regular jobs while trying to make his way as a performer in the evenings. He met a number of other artists then working in the city, including Big Bill Broonzy. His name began to be mentioned when recording executives were in the market for new blues recording artists.

In 1946, Muddy had his first recording date for Aristocrat Records. He turned out two songs for his first release, "Gypsy Woman" and "Little Anna Mae." Soon after, he provided the label with two big hits, "I Feel Like Going Home" and "I Can't Be Satisfied." He was asked to make some sides for Columbia, but nothing happened with them and he returned to Aristocrat. For the balance of the '40s, he slowly increased his stature in the industry with his own recordings and as a sideman for other artists.

Muddy took the first steps toward major national recognition in the early 1950s when he formed his own band. Their recordings for the Chess label, which had absorbed Aristocrat, found a wide audience among rhythm and blues fans. Muddy began to get contracts to perform at other major cities besides Chicago. His career reached a new high in 1958, when he made a triumphal tour of England.

Most of the band's U.S. engagements in the 1950s and '60s were in southern towns and cities. However, in the 1960s, Muddy began to receive an increasing number of requests to appear at major jazz and folk festivals. His jazz work included a number of well received appearances at Monterey and in Southern California. He was also featured at several of the Newport Folk Festivals. The 1967 Newport audiences, for example, cheered his renditions of his greatest hits, such as "Rollin' Stone," "Got My Mojo Workin'," and "Hoochie Coochie Man."

His LP list for Chess Records included such titles as "The Best of Muddy Waters" ('58); "Muddy Waters at Newport 1960" ('61); and "Folk Singer" ('64).

WATSON, DOC: Singer, guitarist, banjoist. Born Deep Gap, North Carolina, March 2, 1923.

When 13,000 fans applauded Doc Watson at the 1963 Newport Folk Festival, they were honoring not just his ability, but his magnificent spirit. Like Riley Puckett, one of Doc's boyhood musical heroes, Doc had the ability to charm and entertain others despite the great handicap of blindness.

Music, of course, was almost a way of life in the rural area in which he was born. His father, a farmer, led the singing at the local Baptist Church. As he told Ralph Rinzler (Sing Out!, Feb.-March '64), his mother sang the children to sleep with such songs as "Omie Wise," "Katie Morey," "The House Carpenter" and "The FFV." From his grandparents who lived with them, he heard many traditional folk melodies, including "Waggoner's Lad," "Uncloudy Day," and "Tom Dooley."

Young Arthel Watson was introduced to the banjo at the age of six, when a cousin played "Goodbye, Little Bonnie, Goodbye" on a 5-string banjo. The boy longed for such an instrument and finally got one a few years later thanks to his older brother Arnold. Arnold's contribution was to marry; his new brother-in-law presented a homemade banjo to little Doc. With the help of his father, Doc learned to play the instrument, and soon after, his father made him a better one.

A few years later when Doc was attending Raleigh School for the Blind, his father helped him buy a guitar. Soon Doc had mastered the new instrument. From phonograph records, he had learned many songs of such groups as the Carter Family, Skillet Lickers, and other country and western favorites. He and his older brother Lenny harmonized on many of these songs.

When Doc was 17, he earned enough money cutting wood to buy a new guitar from Sears, Roebuck. He used this to play "The Mule Skinner Blues" in his first stage appearance at a fiddlers' convention in Boone, North Caro-

Doc Watson

[321]

lina. From then on, he played at many local affairs. The next year, he joined a group that was sometimes heard over local radio stations.

Most of the music Doc played publicly during the 1940s and '50s was modern country and western, but he continued to play the older songs for his own pleasure. He was in demand for dances and shows in his home area, but virtually unknown outside the region. This all changed in 1960 when a team of eastern recording people came down to record Clarence Ashley's old-time string band. The session led to an invitation for Ashley's group to come to New York for a Friends of Old Time Music concert in early 1961.

Doc's solo spots with the band resulted in an engagement to appear at Gerde's Folk City in December 1962. He received thunderous applause for such songs as "The Storms Are on the Ocean" and "Willie Moore." In 1963, besides appearing at Newport, Doc made his concert debut at Town Hall with Bill Monroe and his Bluegrass Boys. Doc's national reputation continued to increase in the mid-'60s with a series of LPs on Folkways label. These included an album with Jean Ritchie called "Folk City" and "The Watson Family," Volumes I and II. In the latter, Doc was joined by his mother (Mrs. G. D. Watson), his brother Arnold, and Arnold's father-in-law, Gaither Carlton. The album includes such songs as "The House Carpenter," "Bonaparte's Retreat," "Ground Hog," "Darling Corey," "The Train That Carried My Girl from Town," and "Every Day Dirt." Doc also signed with Vanguard Records, resulting in the 1964 LP "Doc Watson."

WEAVERS, THE: Vocal and instrumental group.

One of the basic reasons for the growing popularity of folk music after World War II was the phenomenal success of The Weavers. The group not only propelled one folk song after another onto the hit charts, but also helped make the songs popular standards.

The group was formed in 1948 by Pete Seeger, Lee Hays, Ronnie Gilbert, and Fred Hellerman. (Hays is credited with naming the group.) The last three remained with the group throughout its life span, but at various times three other banjoists—Erik Darling, Frank Hamilton, and Bernie Krause—took Pete Seeger's place.

The Weavers debuted in late 1949 at the Village Vanguard, New York. Almost immediately, they became one of the most popular acts in the entertainment field. Weaver concerts were arranged at theaters, nightclubs, and concert halls throughout the U.S. and the world. The group was featured on network radio and TV shows as well. Their hits of the early 1950s included "On Top of Old Smoky," "Goodnight Irene," and "So Long, It's Been Good to Know You." Best-selling albums appeared on both Decca and Folkways labels.

The group disbanded in 1952, but reformed in 1955. By this time, Congressional inquiries into political views of some of the members resulted in a blacklist on radio and TV. Despite this, they had no trouble finding personal appearance dates across the nation. Pete Seeger left the group permanently in 1957, but he continued working with them on new compositions, such as "Kisses Sweeter Than Wine." In December 1963, The Weavers disbanded permanently after a farewell concert at Chicago's Orchestra Hall. (*See also* Darling, Erik; Hays, Lee; Hellerman, Fred; Seeger, Pete)

WEBB, DEAN: *See* Dillards, The

WEIN, GEORGE: Singer, pianist, band leader, producer of musical events. Born Boston, Massachusetts, October 3, 1925.

In the summer of 1954, a less-than-enthusiastic city of Newport, Rhode Island, played host to a new event, the Newport Jazz Festival. It was to prove a historic milestone, not only for jazz, but for folk, country and western music as well: George Wein, who helped breathe life into the Newport Jazz Festival, was later to be the spark-plug behind the Newport Folk Festival.

Wein was born and brought up in Boston with an early love for music. By his teens, he could play the piano and had developed a deep interest in jazz. During the mid-1940s, he started his public performing career with Dixieland bands in the Boston area. It was the start of many decades of jazz musicianship in which he played with such artists as Ruby Braff and Bud Freeman. In the post-World War II years, he often toured the U.S. and foreign countries with the great jazz musician Thelonius Monk.

The idea of a showcase for jazz occurred to Wein in the early 1950s. As a New Englander, he wanted it to be in this region and finally settled on Newport, Rhode Island. In 1954, he gained the needed organization and produced the first Newport Jazz Festival. After the usual birth pains, the Festival caught on and began to thrive. In the late '50s, Wein decided a festival along similar lines would work for the folk field. In 1959, he made the first effort to prove his point, co-producing the first Newport Folk Festival with Albert B. Grossman.

The show went over well enough to permit production of a second edition in 1960. Unfortunately, a riot which erupted outside the gates during the 1960 Jazz Festival also brought problems that affected the folk event. Wein stepped out as producer of the 1961 Jazz Festival and the Folk Festival was not held that year.

Wein continued with his performing in the early 1960s, and for a time devoted his producing efforts to other areas, such as the first annual Ohio Valley Jazz Festival in Cincinnati in 1962. He still believed in the folk festival concept, however, and called a meeting with Pete Seeger and Theodore Bikel to revive the Newport event. The result was a non-profit foundation with a board of directors composed of leading folk artists and scholars with Wein as board chairman. The Newport Folk Festival was revived in 1963, and by the late 1960s was a thriving, vital part of the folk picture. In addition, the event helped introduce many folk fans to the many great country and western artists who were also invited to perform.

Wein, who was back as producer of the Jazz Festival by 1963, continued to be active in many directions. His 1964 endeavors included production of a general jazz festival presented in Berlin and other European capitals, a Japanese World Jazz Festival, featuring artists from Japan and the U.S., and production of the first annual Pittsburgh Catholic Youth Organization Festival. In 1965, he added a new feather to his cap with the production (with Down Beat) of the first annual Down Beat Jazz Festival in Chicago. His 1966 work included initiation of the Longhorn Jazz Festival in Austin, Texas, and, with the Metropolitan Opera, the first opera festival at Newport. In 1967, he took 24 American jazz groups to Europe for a triumphal series of concerts.

Wein's musical talents were captured in several LPs over the years, including "That Newport Jazz" on Columbia; "Great Moments in Jazz—Re-Created at the Newport Jazz Festival" on RCA Victor; "Jazz at the Modern" on Bethlehem Records; "George Wein in Paris," Smash Records ('63); "With the Newport All Stars," Impulse Records ('63). (*See also* NEWPORT FOLK FESTIVAL)

WEISSBERG, ERIC: *See* Greenbriar Boys

WEISSMAN, RICHARD: *See* Journeymen, The

WELLS, KITTY: Singer, guitarist, songwriter. Born Nashville, Tennessee, August 30, 1919.

It takes only a glance at the list of country music hits from 1952 on to see why Kitty Wells holds the unchallenged title of "Queen of Country Music." From 1952 to 1969, she had 25 songs in the top 10, almost twice the total of the nearest female country and western recording artist.

Kitty, whose real name is Muriel Deason, was born in the country music capital and attended school there, but she had to wander far afield before becoming one of the Opry's top stars. She was a fan of country music almost from the time she learned to talk, and often sang the current hits around her home. When she was 15, she learned to play the guitar and began to perform at local dances. A few years later, in 1936, she started her radio career on station WSIX in Nashville.

In 1938, she married Johnny Wright of the Johnnie and Jack act. She was featured on their show and traveled widely with her husband and the troupe. It was Johnny who gave her a new stage name. During this period, she gained experience as a performer on many country stations, including WCHS, Bluefield, West Virginia; WNOX, Knoxville; WPTF, Raleigh, North Carolina; and WEAS, Decatur, Georgia. She was well thought of by people in the industry, but the job of raising a family kept her from achieving national stardom.

Her ability, though, was enough to win her a guest spot on the Grand Ole Opry in 1947. She then moved to Shreveport where she became one of the top stars of the KWKH Louisiana Hayride. From 1947 to 1952, the name Kitty Wells gained increasing luster with Hayride audiences. Then, in 1952, she signed with Decca Records and turned out the song that rocketed her to top rank in the country music field: "It Wasn't God Who Made Honky

Tonk Angels." The song was number one in the country for many more weeks than any other top song of the year.

This helped bring a bid from the Grand Ole Opry to Kitty and the team of Johnnie and Jack. Once back in her home town, she turned out a number of songs that were high on the charts in 1953, then really began to roll in 1954 and '55 with such hits as "One by One," "As Long as I Live," "Making Believe," and "Lonely Side of Town" ('55). (The first two were duets with Red Foley.) In 1956, she hit the top 10 once more with "Searching Soul." In 1957, she scored with "I'll Always Be Your Fraulein" and "Repeating." She rounded out the decade with such national successes as "I Can't Stop Loving You" ('58); "Amigo's Guitar," and "Mommy for a Day," ('59). She was co-writer of "Amigo's Guitar" with John Loudermilk. Decca recognized her contributions to the company by signing her to a life-time contract in 1959.

The 1960s proved to be no less fruitful. She started off with a major 1960 hit, "Left to Right." In 1961, she turned out a number-one hit, "Heartbreak U.S.A." She really hit her stride in 1962 with such top 10 successes as "Day Into Night," "Unloved, Unwanted," "We Missed You," and "Will Your Lawyer Talk to God." She scored in the mid-1960s with "Password" and "This White Circle on My Finger" ('64); and "Meanwhile, Down at Joe's" and "You Don't Hear" ('65).

Her Decca LPs included "Seasons of My Heart," "Especially for You," "Singing on Sunday," "Winner of Your Heart," "Lonely Street" ('58); "After Dark," "Dust on the Bible" ('59); "Kitty's Choice" ('60); "Golden Favorites" and "Heartbreak U.S.A." ('61); "Queen of Country Music" ('62); "Story of Kitty Wells" ('63); and "Country Music Time" ('64).

During the 1960s, she appeared in person in all the states of the U.S., Canada, the Far East, and Europe. Her TV credits included guest appearances on the Ozark Jubilee, Jimmy Dean Show, Nightlife, and Carl Smith's Country Music Hall. She also appeared in the movie "Second Fiddle to a Steel Guitar."

Her honors included a citation as Outstanding Tennessee Citizen given her by Governor Frank Clement in 1954. She was also voted Best Female Artist in the field by Billboard, Cashbox, and Jamboree magazine in 1957. Billboard's poll also gave her the nod as Favorite Female Vocalist in 1959. (*See also* WRIGHT, JOHNNY)

WEST, DOTTIE: Singer, songwriter. Born Mc-Minnville, Tennessee, October 11, 1932.

Many folk, country and western performers overcome youthful privations and hardships to reach stardom. Dottie West, one of ten children of a low-income farm family, had her share of these. In her case, she not only succeeded in music, but gained a college degree on the way. Her industry was recognized by her school, Tennessee Technological University of Cookeville, in 1966, when it established the "Dottie West Music Scholarship."

During her grade school years, Dottie had to help chop cotton and work in sugar cane fields. By nine, she was a first-rate cook for her family. When she was a little older, she took part-time jobs during school months to help earn money. When vacations came, she worked at full-time jobs if she could find them. Some of the money helped her take music lessons, for she was determined to try to better herself. In high school, she started a new

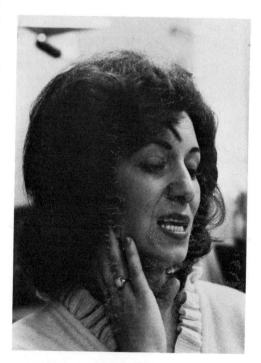

Dottie West

[324]

savings fund to finance a college education.

At the start of the 1950s, her dreams came true as she enrolled in Tennessee Tech as a music major. Though she studied all forms of music, country music remained a prime hobby. During her first week on campus, she met a boy named Bill West who had a similar love of country music. His goal was an engineering degree, but he could play excellent steel guitar and was soon accompanying Dottie at school events. Before long, Dottie and Bill decided to make their duet permanent by getting married.

Both Wests graduated, Bill with an electronics degree and Dottie as a music major. Bill quickly got a job with a Cleveland electronics laboratory and they moved to Ohio. For five years Bill persevered at engineering, and they supplemented their income by appearing as a country music team. They soon were regulars on a local TV show and also played occasional engagements in local clubs.

In the early 1960s, they returned to Tennessee on a visit. While at a relative's place in Nashville, they met some of the executives of Starday Records. Their talents quickly won them a contract with Starday, and the Wests left Cleveland to settle in Nashville. They played on local shows and Dottie switched first to Atlantic label and then to RCA Victor. A little while after the RCA contract, their ability as a songwriting team won them another contract with Tree Publishing Company.

In 1964, Dottie, accompanied by Bill on guitar, cut their composition "Here Comes My Baby" for RCA. The song quickly became a national top 10 hit in the country field. Other artists, such as Perry Como, soon made it a hit on popular charts as well. Dottie also teamed with Jim Reeves for a second major 1964 hit, "Love Is No Excuse." By this time, she was also being seen every week by TV viewers as a regular on the Grand Ole Opry. The Wests turned out another hit composition and record in 1966, "Would You Hold It Against Me?" In 1968 she hit again with "Country Girl."

Some of Dottie's other major recordings were "Before the Ring on Your Finger Turns Green," "Gettin' Married Has Made Us Strangers," "Night Life," "Paper Mansions," "What's Come Over My Baby" and, with son Dale (one of their four children), "Mommie, Can I Still Call Him Daddy?" Her LPs included "Sensational Dottie West" on Starday and "Here Comes My Baby," "Night Life," "Dottie West Sings," "Suffer Time," "Dottie West and the Heartaches," and on RCA "I'll Help You Forget."

In the mid-1960s, Dottie's personal appearances covered all fifty states, Canada, and Europe. Her guest spots on TV included the Jimmy Dean Show, Carl Smith Country Music Hall, and a regular shot on the Faron Young Show. She also appeared in two movies, "Second Fiddle to a Steel Guitar" and "There's A Still on the Hill."

Her recording of "Here Comes My Baby" won her the 1964 Grammy Award for "Most Outstanding Female Performance." On July 10, 1965, her home town of McMinnville celebrated "Dottie West Day."

WEST, HEDY: Singer, banjoist. Born Cartersville, Georgia, April 6, 1938.

A singer of many of the most traditional folk songs, Hedy West, heard her first folk music in her mother's arms in the hill country of western Georgia. Her grandmother played the banjo and sang classic ballads or nonsense songs to the children, and her father, Don West, was one of the best known poets of the south. Other friends and relatives also came to the West home to sing and play, including her Uncle Gus who was one of the most popular fiddlers of the region.

Hedy's parents wanted her to learn music and started her on piano lessons when she was only four. Hedy's interest in music continued to increase as she got older, veering more and more toward the folk idiom. In high school, she taught herself to play the banjo, following her grandmother's example. Soon she was singing some of the old songs at local gatherings. Word of her ability spread beyond Cartersville and she was asked to appear at other folk music events. In 1956, seventeen-year-old Hedy won hearty applause for her singing in a festival at Boone, North Carolina. Two years later, her reputation was further increased when she won first prize in a folk song contest at Nashville, Tennessee.

After this, her career began to move into high gear. She traveled north to play in coffee houses in Chicago and New York. This led to an invitation to appear in a hootenanny run by Sing Out! magazine at Carnegie Hall. Pete Seeger was impressed with her ability and asked her to join him in a two-week engagement at the Village Gate in New York.

Hedy West

Some of her renditions were then included in a Vanguard LP called "New Folks." Soon after, she was featured on her own LP, "Hedy West."

By the mid-1960s, she had sung at most major festivals in the U.S. and given recitals across the country. Audiences were enthralled with her performances of such songs as "Mister Froggie," "Single Girl," "The Wife of Usher's Well," "Lord Thomas and Fair Ellender," "Little Old Man," "Cotton Mill Girl," "Pan of Biscuits," and "The Brown Girl."

In addition to singing, Hedy wrote words and music to classical material or composed her own songs. Her output included music to go with her father's poems, "Anger in the Land." The 1963 country hit by Bobby Bare, "500 Miles Away from Home," is credited to Hedy, Bare, and Charlie Williams.

At the end of the '60s Hedy moved to London, and performed widely in Europe.

WESTERN STRING BAND: *See* McAuliff, Leon

WHEELER, BILLY EDD: Singer, guitarist, songwriter. Born Whitesville, West Virginia, December 9, 1932.

One of the Kingston Trio's big hits of the 1960s was "The Reverend Mister Black." The song of the circuit-riding minister gave some insight into the background of the writer, Billy Edd Wheeler, from the mountainous state of West Virginia.

Both traditional folk songs and country and western music were staple items of Wheeler's youth. He knew many of these songs well during his years of elementary and high school; by the time he was attending college in Kentucky, he could accompany himself on the guitar as well. During his years at Berea College, from which he was graduated with a B.A. degree in the early 1950s, and later on at Yale University, Billy Edd employed his talents to sing at school folk concerts and local events.

During 1955-56, he served as editor of Mountain Life and Work Magazine. He left for a stay in the U.S. Navy as a pilot trainee in 1957 and '58. When he left the Navy, he returned to Berea College as an instructor from 1959 to 1961. He expanded his collection of folk material in these years and also turned out a growing number of original compositions. His increasing stature resulted in a concert of his own folk songs with the Lexington, Kentucky, Symphony Orchestra in 1961. Billy Edd also appeared as an actor in a religious pageant, "Stars in His Crown," in Paducah, Kentucky, in the early '60s.

From 1961 on, he gravitated to full-time performing, singing in concerts in many parts of the country and at fairs and nightclubs. He also turned out a number of recordings on Monitor label, including the LPs "USA" ('61) and "Bluegrass Too."

Among his compositions of the late '50s and 1960s were such songs as "Mary Ann," "Rock Boll Weevil," "High Flying Bird," "The Bachelor," "Wind Spiritual," "Coal Tattoo," "Blue Roses," "On the Outside Looking In," "Ode to the Little Brown Shack Out Back," "Wildcat's Kitten," "The Waltz of Miss Sarah Green," "Lonesome Lovesick Puppy Dog" and "Power of Love."

In the 1960s, Billy Edd entertained at a number of major folk festivals, including the 1965 event in New York City. He was signed by Kapp Records in the mid-'60s and provided them with a top 10 hit in 1965 with his "Ode

[326]

to the Little Brown Shack Out Back." His 1967 composition "Jackson" provided June Carter and Johnny Cash with one of the major country and pop hits of the year.

WHITE, JOSH: Singer, guitarist, songwriter. Born Greenville, South Carolina, February 11, 1908.

Not too many folk artists make *Who's Who in America*. One exception is Josh White, certainly one of the giants of the American folk music scene of the twentieth century. White almost single-handedly carried the message of the importance of the folk song to all corners of the U.S. in the years when this kind of music was considered only a minority interest.

Joshua Daniel White listened closely to the singing of hymns and other songs of his people from his earliest years. His father was a minister and brought his young son along to some of the highly musical services that characterized much of Negro religious life. However, life at home was not too happy and the family split up when Josh was little. He became an assistant to first one and then another of the highly talented, and now legendary, blind minstrels of the Negro south. For ten years he wandered throughout the country as the "eyes" of such performers as Blind Lemon Jefferson, Willie Johnson, John Henry Arnold, and Joel Taggart. His friends taught him many of their songs and provided the best possible instruction in playing the guitar. By the time Josh was in his teens, he was one of the best folk artists in the country, though unknown to the mass of the population.

Then an event occurred that would have ruined the career of lesser men. In the late 1920s, he suffered an accident that paralyzed one of his hands. He could no longer play the guitar. However, he could still sing and act. In 1932, he went to New York and managed to gain the part of Blind Lemon Jefferson in the play "John Henry" that starred Paul Robeson.

Josh continued to exercise his fingers and try to regain their use. For five years he struggled with his infirmity and finally conquered it. In the early 1930s, once more able to play superb guitar, he accompanied many singers including Leroy Carr. By the mid-1930s, he was giving concerts of blues and other folk music on college campuses and occasionally on radio stations. His name became known to audiences in many of the major cities of the country. By the late 1930s, he had played on several network programs, including sessions with a group called the Southernaires on NBC radio.

He began to record for the first of many major record labels in 1931. His first session took place in Chicago and he recorded 28 songs for Columbia. Between the mid-1930s and the 1960s, he turned out several hundred songs and dozens of albums for Decca, Mercury, London, Columbia, Folkways, Stinson, Period, and ABC Paramount. He also recorded many songs for the American Archive of Folk Song of the Library of Congress. His talents were recognized by President Franklin D. Roosevelt who asked White to give a concert at the White House. In 1941, he was asked to make a good-will tour of Mexico for the U.S. with the Golden Gate Quartet.

During the 1940s, White continued to build an international reputation. During 1941-42 he gave many programs with singer Libby Holman. He also was featured at the Cafe Society Uptown in New York for the amazing period of three years. He sang on radio and had long runs at such other clubs as the Village Vanguard and Cafe Society Downtown. In 1944, he had his own 15-minute program over New York station WNEW and also broadcast for the Office of War Information.

During the 1950s and '60s, White continued to tour the U.S. and other countries throughout the world. He took part in many major folk festivals, including those at Newport, and was featured a number of times during 1963-64 on the ABC-TV Hootenanny.

Among his many LPs available in the mid-1960s were such titles as "Josh White and Big Bill Broonzy" on Period and "The Josh White Story, Volumes 1 and 2" on ABC Paramount. On the last two, he sang such songs as "Boll Weevil," "Frankie and Johnny," "House of the Rising Sun," "Hard Time Blues," "Good Morning Blues," "The Gray Goose," "Trouble in Mind," "Sometimes I Feel Like a Motherless Child," "Red River," "I Had a Woman," "Strange Fruit" and "Two Little Fishes and Five Loaves of Bread."

His Stinson LPs included "Josh White Sings" and "Josh White Sings the Blues." He was represented on Decca with "Ballads and Blues" ('58). His London LP, "A Josh White Program," included "Call Me Darling," "Like a Natural Man," "The Lass with the Delicate

[327]

Josh White

Air," "Foggy, Foggy Dew," "Waltzing Matilda," and "He Never Said a Mumbling Word." His Elektra catalog included a number of LPs, "Josh," "Josh at Midnight," "Chain Gang Songs" ('59); "House I Live In" and "Spirituals and Blues" ('61); and "Empty Bed Blues" ('62). Elektra also produced a "25th Anniversary Album," the entire first side of which comprised a musical narrative prepared by Josh. On the second side were such songs as "Black Girl," "Free and Equal Blues," "Live the Life," "Sam Hall," "Where Were You Baby," "Delia's Gone," "Run, Momma, Run" and "You Don't Know My Mind."

His Mercury LPs included "With Josh Jr. and Beverly" ('62), "Beginnings, Volume 1" ('63) and "Beginnings, Volume 2" ('64).

Among the songs Josh is credited with having authored or composed are "The Gray Goose," "I Had a Woman," and "Ball and Chain Blues."

WHITMAN, SLIM: Singer, guitarist. Born Tampa, Florida, January 20, 1924.

More than one of the stars of country and western music has had a strong athletic background. In Slim Whitman's case, he showed great promise as a good hitting pitcher. But music proved the stronger attraction, a choice that provided the country's listeners with some of the major hits of the post-Korean War period.

Otis Dewey Whitman, Jr., was born and raised in Tampa, Florida, along with four brothers and sisters. Though he listened to music on the radio, his main interest was sports. At high school in Tampa, he became a star pitcher on the school baseball team. He didn't pursue an athletic career right away. Instead he worked for a year in a meat packing plant, a job that also introduced him to the future Mrs. Whitman whom he married after a year at the plant.

His marriage almost coincided with the outbreak of World War II. When the war began, Slim got a job as a shipfitter and boilermaker in a Tampa shipyard. In 1943, he left his job and family to enlist in the Navy. While aboard the U.S.S. *Chilton*, his musical abilities finally came to the fore. To combat the boredom between naval operations or ship's chores, he learned the guitar from some of his shipmates. Before long he was alternating as a performer and a boxer at "Happy Hour" events.

When he was discharged in 1945, he returned to the Tampa shipyard. In his spare time, he played baseball. This led to a contract in 1946 with the Plant City Berries of the Orange Belt League. In 1947, his pitching record was 11-1 and his hitting a cool .360. While spending his daytime hours on baseball, he continued to perfect his guitar playing and singing in his leisure time. He performed at local clubs and this, in turn, led to a bid to sing on WDAE in Tampa in 1948.

At this point, Slim decided his future looked rosier in music. His judgment was flawless. His audience grew and he received notice far beyond his home city. In 1949, his abilities were recognized in the form of a recording contract with RCA Victor. One of his first songs for the label, "Casting My Lasso to the Sky," won some national attention. He also increased his national stature in 1949 with an appearance on a Mutual network show with The Light Crust Doughboys.

Soon after, he moved to Shreveport, to become a regular on station KWKH's Louisiana

Slim Whitman

Hayride. First on radio and then on TV, he quickly built up a following among southwestern fans. He also charmed audiences at personal appearances in many of the cities of the south and southwest.

His record career really took off when he signed with Imperial Records in 1952. That year, he scored with a top 10 best-seller, "Keep It a Secret." From then on, his name was often found on best-selling rosters in the 1950s and '60s. In 1953, he had a top 10 hit with "North Wind" and in 1954 he had two, "Secret Love" and "Rose Marie." The year 1965 provided him with another gold record for "More Than Yesterday." Other Whitman hits between 1952 and '67 included "Love Song of the Waterfall," "The Bandera Waltz," "Amateur in Love," "China Doll," and "Indian Love Call." Many of these achieved hit status throughout Europe as well as in Canada, Japan, Australia, Free China, and South Africa. The result was good audience response

to Whitman's trips to many of these countries in the 1960s. In 1968 he had a top 10 hit in "Rainbows Are Back in Style."

Through 1967, the Whitman catalog included several dozen LPs for Imperial, among them "Forever," "Heart Songs & Love Songs," "I'll Walk with God!" "I'm a Lonely Wanderer," "Yodeling Slim Whitman," "Once in a Lifetime," "Million Record Hits," "Just Call Me Lonesome," "Irish Songs," "Country Songs/City Hits," "All Time Favorites," "Annie Laurie," and three LPs titled "Slim Whitman Sings."

WILBURN, TEDDY AND DOYLE (WILBURN BROTHERS): Vocal duo, guitarists, songwriters, music publishers, both born Thayer, Missouri, Doyle, July 7, 1930; Teddy, November 30, 1931.

Many groups or duos in the music field go under the name of "brothers," without the slightest relationship. The Wilburns, though, are authentically titled. In fact, until 1951, the act was known as the Wilburn Family, including two older brothers, Leslie and Lester.

The Wilburns grew up in rural Missouri and the boys were performers at very early ages. In 1938, they began by singing on street corners in Thayer. In a short time, they progressed to more professional performances, appearing in shows in many parts of Missouri, then extending their activities to neighboring states. Their audience rapport was excellent. The older artists with whom they appeared soon spread the word that the Wilburns were rising stars.

In 1941, the Wilburn Family was asked to join the Grand Ole Opry. The boys quickly attracted a national following in the next few years. World War II interfered with their careers, but afterward, they once more starred on the Opry. In 1948, the group moved to Shreveport for a featured spot on the KWKH Louisiana Hayride. They remained until 1951 when the act was once more broken up, this time by the Korean War.

When the act resumed in 1953, it consisted of Teddy (Thurman Theodore) and Doyle (Virgil Doyle). They returned to the Opry and remained regular cast members. Through the mid-1950s, they toured the country and turned out many records that chalked up respectable sales. Their lists of credits during this period included first place in the Arthur Godfrey Talent Scouts TV show. In 1956, they provided Decca

Records with a top 10 hit, "Go Away with Me." From then on, Wilburn Brothers songs were on the best-seller lists regularly. As their reputation increased, the brothers diversified into other parts of the music business. In the late 1950s, all four brothers helped form a new music publishing firm, Sure-Fire Music. The music turned out by the company included a number of songs written by the Wilburns. The brothers had three major hits in 1959, "A Woman's Intuition," "Somebody's Back in Town" and "Which One Is to Blame," the first two of which bore the Sure-Fire imprint.

The 1960s proved even more successful for the brothers than earlier decades. In 1962, they had one of the top hits in the country, "Trouble's Back in Town." The following year, they had many hits, including two in the top 10, "Roll Muddy River" and "Tell Her So." Their mid-'60s top 10 score included "It's Another World" ('65) and "Someone Before Me" ('66). Decca

Records recognized their worth by signing them to a life contract in the mid-'60s.

Some of their other recordings during the '50s and '60s were "Knoxville Girl," "I Can't Keep Away from You," "Mister Love," "Look Around," "Deep Elem Blues," "Cry, Cry Darling," "Always Alone," "You Will Again," and "I'll Sail My Ship Alone." The brothers' songwriting activity included "That's When I Miss You," "I Know You Don't Love Me Anymore," "Need Someone" and "Much Too Often."

During the 1960s, the boys toured all fifty states. They starred on Australian TV for 39 weeks as part of the Roy Acuff Open House show. They were also featured on guest spots on American Bandstand and Jubilee U.S.A. They added to their business enterprises by establishing the Wil-Helm Talent Agency. The agency, formed in conjunction with country artist Smiley Wilson, became one of Nashville's top booking firms. By the mid-'60s, it repre-

Wilburn Brothers Ted (white hat) and Doyle (check shirt) and their group entertain fans in front of the Grand Ole Opry.

sented such stars as Loretta Lynn, Jay Lee Webb, the Osborne Brothers, Harold Morrison, Jean Shepard, Martha Carson, Slim Whitman, and Charlie Louvin.

The Wilburn Brothers turned out many successful LPs during the '50s and '60s. These included "Carefree Moments" on Vocalion ('62) and several dozen albums on Decca. Among the latter were "Wilburn Brothers"; "Wilburn Brothers Sing Folk Songs"; "Big Heartbreak"; "Take Up the Cross"; "Side by Side" ('59); "Sing," "Lovin' in God's Country" ('61); "City Limits" ('62); "Trouble's Back in Town" ('63); and "Never Alone" (64); "Country Gold" ('65); and "Two for the Show" ('67). (*See also* WILBURN FAMILY)

WILBURN FAMILY: Vocal and instrumental family group, all born Thayer, Missouri, Lester Lloyd Wilburn, born May 19, 1924; Leslie Floyd Wilburn, born October 13, 1925; Vinita Geraldine Wilburn, born June 5, 1927; Thurman Theodore "Teddy" Wilburn, born November 30, 1931; Virgil Doyle Wilburn, born July 7, 1930. (*See also* WILBURN, TEDDY AND DOYLE)

WILGUS, D. K., DR.: Folklorist, singer, collector, educator. Born West Mansfield, Ohio, December 1, 1918.

Today the historic traditions that underlie country and western music are recognized by most scholars as being an important part of America's folk music heritage. Not very many years ago, however, country music was looked upon with disdain by most folklorists. One of those responsible for the change in attitude is Professor D. K. Wilgus, now considered one of the world's foremost authorities on country and western music.

Wilgus' interest in country music began in his boyhood in Ohio. He enjoyed listening to "hillbilly" programs and was particularly taken with the style of Bradley Kincaid on the WLS National Barn Dance. (Kincaid was later to become a close friend.) Wilgus memorized some of the songs and sometimes sang them for his own pleasure.

By the time he entered Ohio State University, in 1936, Wilgus had begun to have a vague idea of making country music more than a side interest. As he points out, "Soon after arriving at college, I became possibly the first campus folksinger in the U.S. I made my first appearance in 1936 and sang both on campus and at small clubs in the area during the next few years." Wilgus also began collecting country records in 1936, a move that was to result in an eventual collection of many thousands of records.

While an undergraduate, he tried to interest the school's folk music department in country music. However, the folklorists told him that hillbilly music was not folk. This increased his determination to prove the worth of traditional hill country and rural music.

Wilgus received his B.A. and B.Sc. from Ohio State in 1941. After several years in service, he returned to the school in 1946 as an instructor in English. He completed work on his M.A. in 1947 and then went on for his doctorate. In 1950, he accepted the post of Associate Professor of English at Western Kentucky State College. At his new post, Wilgus became more and more active in folklore activities and intensified his collection of material on both folk and country and western music. In 1953, he founded the Western Kentucky Folklore Archive, which was transferred to UCLA in the 1960s, at which time it contained more than 50,000 items. During his tenure at Western Kentucky, he received his Ph.D. (1954) from Ohio State.

Wilgus occasionally performed at folk festivals and lectured in many parts of the country in the 1950s. His activities included founding the Kentucky Folklore Record (1955), a publication which he edited until 1961. He also was made the record review editor of the Journal of American Folklore in 1959. During these years, many honors came his way for his pioneering efforts, including the Chicago Folklore Prize in 1956, Fellow of the John Simon Guggenheim Foundation, 1957-58, and Fellow of the American Folklore Society beginning in 1961. He also served as secretary-treasurer of the Kentucky Folklore Society from 1951 to 1961, president of the Society, 1961-62, and director of the Society from 1961 on.

He was made a full professor of English and Folklore at Western Kentucky State in 1961. That year, he also received a grant from the school for field work. Four years later, he received a grant for collecting folk music in western Kentucky from the National Science Foundation.

In 1962 Dr. Wilgus wrote, supervised, and took part in the TV film "Hillbilly Music, Lyrics and Legends" for the American Folklore Society and station WKYY. That year also saw a major change in his career; he moved to the West Coast as Associate Professor of English and Anglo-American Folksong at the University of California at Los Angles. (He was made a full professor in 1966.) At UCLA, he became secretary and one of the directors of the newly established John Edwards Memorial Foundation, now considered the most important country and western collection in the nation.

In California, Dr. Wilgus continued his many activities in all aspects of the folk field. In 1963, he helped organize the UCLA Folk Festival and served as director for the '63, '64, and '65 events. In the 1960s, he lectured and sometimes performed at major festivals, including those at Newport, Berkeley, and Monterey. He also provided liner notes and brochures on major folk artists for such record labels as Prestige, Folk-Legacy, Folkways, Vanguard, RCA Victor, and Bluebonnet. For the last-named, he provided the notes for the 1964 and 1966 Bradley Kincaid LPs "The Kentucky Mountain Boy" (Volumes 2 and 4).

Wilgus' bylines during the 1950s and '60s appeared on dozens of articles and reviews in almost every major folklore magazine in the U.S. He also wrote or edited several books, including *Anglo-American Folksong, Scholarship Since 1898* (New Brunswick, N.J., 1959); *Folklore International* (Hatboro, Pa., 1967); and *Folksongs of the Southern United States* (Austin, Texas, 1967).

WILLIAMS, CHARLIE: Singer, actor, disk jockey, songwriter, m.c., music executive. Born Jackson, Mississippi, December 20, 1929.

Diversity is certainly the hallmark of the talented Charlie Williams. In the 1960s, he was one of the top-ranked songwriters on the BMI award list, but also could claim success in music publishing, talent agency operations, and acting.

Charles Williams was born in Mississippi, but spent most of his early life in Texas. During his high school years, he became interested in radio work. This led to his first job on station WELO in Tupelo, Mississippi. He went on to enroll at Texas Christian University, and when he was graduated from college, he went into the Navy. He had considerable talent as an artist and was assigned to a job in a Navy art department.

After his discharge, he returned to Texas.

Once more he diversified, working for a time as a sportswriter for a Fort Worth paper. However, his interest in country and western music eventually won out over writing; he gained a job as a disk jockey on a local station. He soon won a large following among Texas audiences that paved the way for appearances throughout the southwest as master of ceremonies for country music shows. Since he was a good performer, he also took part in these as a singer.

Still restless, however, he moved to California to try his hand as an actor. He enrolled in the nationally known Pasadena Playhouse. During the 1950s and '60s, his acting ability was attested to by offers of roles in many Los Angeles area productions. Among his stage credits were parts in "The Rainmaker," "Death of a Salesman," "An Enemy of the People," "Journey's End," and "The Country Girl."

While studying at the Playhouse, Charlie put his music background to use by signing on as a DJ with station KXLA. For five years he had a daily show. In the 1950s, the station switched to a different format and Charlie moved to station KFOX, Long Beach, California. Besides radio work, Charlie was a familiar figure on Los Angeles television in the 1950s. He guested on Cliffe Stone's Home Town Jamboree and served as m.c. and performer on the Town Hall Party on Channel 11. Much of this time, he also had his own weekly show on Channel 13.

In the late 1950s, Charlie tried his hand at songwriting. This resulted in a collaboration with Johnny Cash on the 1959 gold-record hit "I Got Stripes." Soon after, Charlie was lured away to San Francisco as program director and disk jockey for a new country and western station, KSAY. While there, he performed in "Look Homeward Angel" with the Sausalito Players. By the start of the '60s, however, he was back in Los Angeles and KFOX.

In 1960, he was signed as a writer by Cliffie Stone's Central Songs, Inc. Later, he also served as general manager of the firm. His song output in the '60s provided material for most of the top artists in the field. His hits included "A Million Years or So" ('63) and "500 Miles Away from Home" (with Bobby Bare and Hedy West, '63).

Besides his other activities, he also formed Universal Talent Management with Stew Carnall in the 1960s. The company produced music shows throughout the west and managed such stars as Bobby Bare, The Collins Kids, Sheb Wooley, and Roger Miller.

WILLIAMS, HANK (SR.): Singer, guitarist, songwriter. Born Georgiana, Alabama, September 17, 1923; died January 1, 1953. Elected to Country Music Hall of Fame, 1961.

The two most legendary figures in country music history, Jimmie Rodgers and Hank Williams, Sr., had some surprising parallels in their careers. Both dominated their field as no other artists before or after, each did it in the short span of six years, and each died young. The main difference, in broad terms, is that Rodgers' career began when he was 30 while Williams' ended when he was only 29.

A good capsule description of Williams' short period of personal success is given in a biographical sketch issued by Ren Grevatt Associates. "During the brief span of six years, until his death on New Year's Day of 1953, Williams wrote the most lasting, the most artistically polished, and the most commercially successful of the 100 songs he left.

"Yet, as is true with most creative geniuses during their time on earth, Hank Williams was never quite aware of the true measure of his contribution. His life, like those of his fellow country-music performers of his own time and of today, was that of an itinerant minstrel, traveling the tank towns with his band, returning to Nashville—and his wife and two children—long enough to make a new recording —and hitting the road again."

Williams had an authentic feel for country music, bred from the cradle of his birth on a farm near Georgiana, Alabama. His mother was organist for the family's church and taught her young son many hymns and gospel songs. He accompanied her in song by the time he was six and also was one of the youngest members of the church choir. On his eighth birthday, he was given a guitar as a present. He began to pick out notes, and then chords, any spare moment he had. In a short time, he was able to accompany himself on the guitar. Before he reached his teens, he had a local reputation as one of the best guitar players in the region.

When he was 14, he organized his own band and was soon playing for many hoedowns, square dances, and other local affairs. The group auditioned for the manager of station WSFA, Montgomery, Alabama, and came out with a job. The group, Hank Williams and His Drifting Cowboys, became one of the station's top audience pleasers. For more than a decade, they remained as regulars on WSFA. The move from local favor to nationwide stardom came in 1947. Williams was signed by the veteran record executive Frank Walker, head of the newly established MGM Records. In August 1948, Williams joined the KWKH Louisiana Hayride. One of the first Hayride offerings of Hank and His Drifting Cowboys was a best-seller, "Move It on Over." In 1949, they were asked to join the Grand Ole Opry. From then on, Williams dominated the country music field with half a dozen and more hit records every year, including all of 1953, the year of his death.

His successes in 1949 included the number-one-rated "Love Sick Blues." Other top 10 songs that year included two of his own compositions, "Mind Your Own Business" and "You're Gonna Change," plus "My Bucket's Got a Hole in It" and "Wedding Bells." All four of Williams' gold records for 1950 were his own songs, "I Just Don't Like This Kind of Livin'," "Long Gone Lonesome Blues," "Moaning the Blues," and "Why Don't You Love Me." The same was true of his seven top hits of 1951, "Baby, We're Really in Love," "Cold, Cold Heart," "Crazy Heart," "Dear John," "Hey, Good Lookin'," "Howlin' at the Moon," and "I Can't Help It." "Cold, Cold Heart" provided Tony Bennett with a multi-million-selling hit in the popular field.

Williams scored in 1952 with such songs as the number-one hit "I'll Never Get Out of This World Alive"; his all-time standard composition "Jambalaya"; "Half as Much"; "Honky Tonk Blues"; and "Settin' the Woods on Fire." Though he died on January 1, 1953, his name dominated singles charts throughout the year. The hits included four of his own songs, "Kaw-Liga,"* "I Won't Be Home No More," "Weary Blues from Waitin'," and "Your Cheatin' Heart." He also scored a number-one hit with a Rose-Heath song, "Take These Chains from My Heart."

Williams' death did not remove his voice or his music from public attention. Every year since then, his compositions have been performed by artists in every phase of music and in almost every country in the world. His re-

* One of a number of songs co-written with Fred Rose.

[333]

cordings continue to sell in the hundreds of thousands. In the 1960s alone, several dozen LPs of Williams' recordings of the '40s and '50s were released by MGM. These included: "Lonesome Sound" and "Wait for the Light" ('60); "Hank Williams Greatest Hits" and "Spirit of Hank Williams" ('61); "Greatest Hits, Volume 2," and "On Stage" ('62); "Beyond the Sunset" and "Very Best" ('63); "Greatest Hits, Volume 3," "Lost Highway," "Story of Hank Williams" and "Very Best, Volume 2" ('64); and "Hank Williams" ('65). Earlier LPs still in production in the mid-1960s included "Honky Tonkin'," "I Saw the Light," and 3-LP sets of "Hank Williams" and "Hank Williams, Volume 2."

In 1964, the Hank Williams legend was taken a step further with the start of the recording career of his son, Hank Williams, Jr. In 1961, the first three bronze plaques were dedicated for the new Country Music Hall of Fame in Nashville. The names on them were Jimmie Rodgers, Fred Rose, and Hank Williams.

WILLIAMS, HANK, JR.: Singer. Born Shreveport, Louisiana, May 26, 1949.

The bearer of a name as illustrious as this has a tough row to hoe. Still, there was a good chance the son of the late Hank Williams would inherit some of the skills that made his father one of the legendary figures in country and western music.

Certainly young Hank had plenty of exposure to the greats of the field besides his father. Though born in Shreveport, Hank was taken to the country music capital of Nashville when he was three months old and grew up there. His interests during grade and high school included both music and sports. He made his school varsity in almost every sport: football, basketball, boxing, and swimming.

By the time he was 14, he accompanied his

© COPYRIGHT 1951 BY FRED ROSE MUSIC, INC.
2510 Franklin Road
NASHVILLE 4, TENNESSEE
INTERNATIONAL COPYRIGHT SECURED   MADE IN U. S. A   ALL RIGHTS RESERVED

Music: "Cold, Cold Heart" ("COLD, COLD HEART"—Hank Williams, © 1951 Acuff-Rose Publications, Inc. Used with permission of the publishers.)

mother, Audrey Williams, on tour with her "Caravan of Stars" when school was out. Though record companies were interested, Mrs. Williams turned down contracts for her son until she was sure he wanted to enter the entertainment field. His decision was affirmative and he left regular high school to enroll in Hollywood professional school while continuing his studies with a private tutor.

By 1967, he had already been featured on many major TV shows, including those of Ed Sullivan and Johnny Carson. In 1966, he signed his first contract with MGM and made the top 10 with "Standing in the Shadows." This led to work on his first album with Connie Francis and a part in a new MGM film, "A Time to Sing and a Time to Cry." He also showed additional talent by providing the theme for another MGM movie, "Kiowa Jones."

WILLIAMS, TEX: Singer, songwriter, actor, band leader. Born Ramsey, Fayette County, Illinois, August 23, 1917.

In the 1960s, growing national interest in country and western music was reflected in the inclusion, for the first time, of a western music show as part of the summer "Symphony Under the Stars" series in the Hollywood Bowl. The band selected for this was under the direction of one of the top country and western artists on the Coast, Tex Williams. It was another in a list of firsts for Williams that includes the first million-selling record on the Capitol label and the first president of the Academy of Country and Western Music

Sol Williams was born and raised in rural areas of Illinois. He attended Prairie Mound country school and Bingham, Illinois, high school. As is the case in rural sections across the U.S., country music programs were popular in the area and young Williams was a fan by the time he was grade school age. When he reached high school he was already a versatile performer, and at 13 gained his own song and one-man-band show on station WJBL in Decatur, Illinois. He also played at many local affairs as part of a high school band. When he was 14, he moved to another show on station WDZ, Tuscola, Illinois. Soon after, he decided that music was to be his life interest and he went to Washington and joined a six-piece band called The Reno Racketeers.

Two years later, he moved his base of operations to California. Here he became ac-

Tex Williams

quainted with Tex Ritter and joined Ritter in a movie called "Rollin' Home to Texas." This was the first of many films made by Williams from the late 1930s into the '50s. His companions in some of these were Charles Starrett, Buster Crabbe, and Judy Canova. In the late 1940s and '50s, he worked under the Universal International banner, taking part in some 24 features over this period.

In 1946 he formed a 12-piece band, The Western Caravan, and signed with the fledgling Capitol Records company. His third release for Capitol, "Smoke, Smoke, Smoke," became the first million-seller on the label. Ritter was co-writer of the song with Merle Travis of "16 Tons" fame. Other Capitol recordings of his that were well received were "Rose of the Alamo," "California Polka," "Texas in My Soul," and "Leaf of Love."

In the late 1940s, Tex and his band played to capacity audiences in such places as the Aragon Ballroom in Chicago, Orpheum Theatre in Los Angeles, and Oriental Theatre in Chicago. He continued his record output in the late 1940s and '50s on Capitol, performing with such stars as Jo Stafford, Roberta Lee,

[335]

Dinah Shore, and Tennessee Ernie Ford. In the 1950s he also had his own local TV show on KRCA in Hollywood.

Williams and his group continued touring in the 1950s and '60s as well as appearing on many network TV shows. The latter included the Grand Ole Opry, Spike Jones Show, Jo Stafford Show, National Barn Dance, Swingin' Country (NBC), Gene Autry's Melody Ranch, Jimmy Dean Show on ABC, Midwestern Hayride, and Porter Wagoner Show. Tex also starred for a time on his own NBC network show, Riverside Rancho.

In the early 1960s, Tex was represented on LPs with the Decca album "Tex Williams" ('62) and the Liberty "Tex Williams at the Mint." The latter was recorded live from the stage of the Mint Club in Las Vegas in 1963. Later on, he signed with a new company, Boone Record Co. of Union, Kentucky, and turned out two releases that remained on national charts for 30 weeks. Boone also turned out an LP, "Two Sides of Tex Williams."

WILLIS BROTHERS: Vocal and instrumental trio. Guy Willis, born Alex, Arkansas, July 15, 1915; Skeeter Willis, born Coalton, Oklahoma, December 20, 1917; Vic Willis, born Schulter, Oklahoma, May 31, 1922.

One of the pioneer groups of modern country music, the Willis Brothers rounded out 35 years as stars in 1967. Under the direction of the eldest brother, Guy, the group chalked up many country music firsts. These include being the first group to back Hank Williams (later they accompanied him as The Drifting Cowboys); first featured act on the Jubilee U.S.A. show of the 1950s; and, with other Grand Ole Opry artists, first country & western act to perform in Constitution Hall, Washington, D.C.

James (nicknamed Guy) was born in Arkansas during World War I, but soon after, the family moved to Oklahoma. With his brothers Skeeter and Victor, he grew up in Schulter, Oklahoma. The boys worked at farm chores when not attending elementary or high school.

Country music was integrally bound up with Willis family life. It was as naturally a part of things as plowing and seeding the fields of the boys' childhood, a major pleasure when the day's work was done. The Willis brothers were taking part in evening sings for many years before they reached their teens. By then, they

could play several instruments and became well known in their part of Oklahoma as amateur musicians.

Things were rough in the Depression years of the early 1930s and the boys jumped at the chance to leave farm work behind. They accepted a bid to begin radio careers on station KGEF, Shawnee, Oklahoma, in 1932. Before long, they were recognized as first-rank country performers. During the middle and late 1930s, they began a repeating pattern of radio shows and appearances as part of a country music "package." Their engagements included shows on radio stations in Oklahoma City; Tulsa; Gallup, New Mexico; and, in 1940, the Brush Creek Follies on KMBC, Kansas City, Missouri.

Some of the songs they played were original compositions of Guy's. He began his professional songwriting career in 1932 with "I Miss Old Oklahoma." Between then and the late 1960s, he wrote or co-wrote many others, including "Drive My Blues Away," "You Don't Have to Worry," "My Pillow Knows," "Long Gone," "Poor Boy," "Old Indians Never Die," "Eat a Little More," and "My Heart Is Tired."

World War II temporarily broke up the band. After four years in service, they regrouped and joined the Grand Ole Opry from 1946 to 1949. They became closely identified with Eddy Arnold during these years, remaining an integral part of his touring show from 1946 to 1953. For a while, they also worked closely with the great Hank Williams. In 1947, they began their recording career on Sterling Records. Afterwards, they recorded for many labels, including RCA Victor, Mercury, Coral, and Starday. They also were hired for hundreds of recording dates as studio musicians, backing artists for their own and other labels.

Between 1953 and 1959, they were featured on many radio and TV shows and traveled widely on personal appearance tours. Their credits for the period included the Ozark Jubilee, WLW Midwestern Hayride, and year-long stints from 1956 to 1959 with WRCP-TV and WTVC-TV, Chattanooga, and WABT-TV, Birmingham, Alabama.

In 1960, they rejoined the Grand Ole Opry as featured artists and were still going strong in the late 1960s. During the '60s, USO tours to many parts of the world and many personal dates overseas stamped them as international favorites. Their ports of call included Holland,

Germany, France, Ireland, Newfoundland, Puerto Rico, and the Bahamas.

The brothers' act was based on a blend of all their voices, with each one capable of taking solo lead. A vital part of all Willis Brothers programs has usually been impersonations of other major country artists or groups. Besides acting as master of ceremonies, Guy contributes his ability as a guitarist. Vic plays accordion and doubles on piano, while Skeeter provides fiddle accompaniment.

WILLS, BOB: Band leader, fiddler, songwriter. Born Hall County, Texas, March 6, 1905. Elected to Country Music Hall of Fame, 1968.

"Ah, ha! San Antone" is an exclamation that has become almost a part of the language, much like "by gosh" or "take it easy." Though few people know it when they jokingly say the words, they're paying tribute to one of the most fabulous bands of the southwest. To country and western fans, the wailing delivery of these sounds is a trademark of Bob Wills' Texas Playboys as much as champagne music is of Lawrence Welk.

Unlike the Tijuana Brass, this band was named for the place most of its members hailed from. Robert Wills was brought up on a ranch and learned to ride a horse across the Texas plains at an early age. At 10, he took up the violin on a bet. He grew tired of a cousin's constant repetition of a song he was learning and bet he could play it in less time. Bob took the violin and figured out the melody in a fairly short time. From then on, he borrowed his cousin's fiddle for longer and longer periods.

In his teens, Bob began to play at local events and soon was playing on local stations. By 1933, he was a star fiddler on three different stations in Ft. Worth. That year, he took a major step forward by organizing The Light Crust Doughboys with a guitarist and a singer for a local flour company. The program caught on, and mail praising the group poured in from cities in both Texas and Oklahoma. A few years later, this resulted in a bid to go to Tulsa and form a larger group. Bob agreed, expanded his outfit to 25 musicians, and provided a new name, the Texas Playboys. For ten years, the Playboys were an institution on station KVOO in Tulsa, playing every night but two.

The Playboys brought their string to a close in the mid-'40s in favor of wider horizons. The band was engaged for dances, radio shows, and the like throughout the west and southwest. They were also featured in several movies. Playboy records on the Columbia label were perennially among the best-sellers in both the western and the national arena. Among the major hits spawned by Bob's organization were "Rose of San Antone," "Texas Playboy Rag," "Mexicali Rose," "Take Me Back to Tulsa," "New Worried Mind," and "Yellow Rose of Texas."

The first two of these were also written by Wills. Other Wills songs include: "Lone Star Rag," "Texas Two Step," "Wills Breakdown," and "Betty's Waltz."

The total recorded output of the Playboys through the mid-1960s runs into the hundreds. A few more of the better known Columbia titles are: "Cotton Eyed Joe"; "Bob Wills Special"; "Oozlin' Daddy Blues"; "Ida Red"; "Osage Stomp"; "Oklahoma Rag"; "Bob Wills Boogie"; "Ten Tears"; and "Steel Guitar Stomp." In the 1950s, the Playboys recorded for MGM, turning out such numbers as "Spanish Fandango"; "Little Cowboy Lullaby"; "Cotton Patch Blues"; and "Blues for Dixie."

In the 1960s, Playboy LPs were turned out on both Harmony and Liberty labels. The first group included "Bob Wills Special" and "Home in San Antone." Liberty LPs include "Living Legend"; "Mr. Words and Mr. Music"; and "Bob Wills Sings and Plays."

WILSON, KITTY: Singer, bassist, songwriter. Born Rome, Georgia, December 11, 1927.

Lady bass players are not too common, though there do seem to be more in country and western than other phases of popular music. One of the best bassists in C&W for more than three decades was (Mary K.) Kitty Wilson of the team of Smiley and Kitty Wilson.

It seemed obvious from Kitty's earliest childhood that she was destined for a music career. She attended grade school in Gadsden, Alabama, from 1933 to 1940, but at the age of nine was already performing at local dances and concerts. In 1936, she joined a group called the Moonlight Ramblers and played many engagements in the region around Gadsden. Kitty entered Gadsden High School in 1940, but a few years later cut short her high school career when she met and married another country and western artist, Smiley Wilson.

With Smiley, she joined the Circle 3 Ranch Gang in 1945, moving on to the Louisiana Hayride with her husband in 1949. She had already begun her recording career with Smiley in 1947 with such songs as "Red Silk Stockings and Green Perfume" and "I'm Satisfied with Life." While performing with Smiley over the years on such labels as Apollo, Republic, and K-ARK, she also made solo disks on these labels and on MGM. In 1949, Kitty joined Smiley in their first movie, "Square Dance Jubilee."

In 1951, Kitty joined the cast of the Grand Ole Opry, remaining as a regular for the rest of the decade. Her radio and TV work during the '50s included several years on WLAC-TV starting in 1958. Her recordings during these years included such songs as "I've Found My Own," "Barnyard Blues," "Thunder and Lightning," "Wishful Thinking," "Till Then I'll Remember," and "Come and Knock."

Kitty turned out a number of her own compositions during the 1950s and '60s, including "Sing and Shout," "We Lived It Up," and "I Know." Little Jimmy Dickens recorded a successful version of "We Lived It Up" in 1960. Hank Snow recorded "I Know" in the '60s.

Kitty and Smiley appeared in all fifty states. In 1951, they were first joined by their then seven-year-old daughter, Rita Faye Wilson. Though cutting back on their activities in the mid-'60s, Kitty and Smiley did tour many parts of the U.S. and the world as members of the Ferlin Husky Show. (*See also* WILSON, SMILEY)

WILSON, SMILEY: Singer, guitarist, songwriter, m.c., talent agency executive. Born Etowah County, Alabama, August 23, 1922.

The team of Smiley and Kitty Wilson was one of the most popular to grace the country and western stage from 1942 through the '60s. Both, however, remained stars in their own right, with solo work in several different media.

Hamilton K. Wilson was born and raised in rural Alabama. He attended grade school in Attalla, Alabama, from 1928 to 1936, then went on to Attalla High School from 1936 to 1938. He could already play excellent rhythm guitar by the time he left high school. The result was a start in the music field in 1939 with Tex Bynum's Rogers County Cowboys. After two years with this group, Smiley joined the Rio Grande Cowboys from 1940 to '42. In 1942, Smiley met a pretty young teenage musician from Georgia whom he married that October.

After a wartime interruption, Smiley and Kitty Wilson joined the Circle 3 Ranch Gang in 1945. Smiley toured with the group and played on local stations for three years. He was featured on several records that gained national attention, including "Red Silk Stockings and Green Perfume" and "I'm Satisfied with Life" in 1947 and "Gotta Get to Oklahoma City" and "Everybody's Darlin'" in '48. In 1949, he joined the KWKH Louisiana Hayride in Shreveport. That same year marked the start of his movie activities. His first vehicle, in which he was joined by his wife, was the 1949 "Square Dance Jubilee." Smiley then strapped on his six-shooter for several westerns in 1950 and '51, including "Black Lash," "Vanishing Outpost," "The Phantom," and "Thundering Trails."

Smiley's growing national following was recognized by a bid to join the cast of the Grand Ole Opry in 1950. In addition to his Opry chores, he also was featured on WBRC-TV in Birmingham, Alabama, for the 1952-53 season. Smiley also was featured on station WLAC-TV in Nashville starting in 1958. His recording efforts during these years included such songs as "Barnyard Blues," "I've Found My Own," ('53); "Georgiana Waltz," "TV Set" ('58); "Lady Cop," "Beyond the Next Hilltop" ('59); "Running Bear," "Long as Little Birds Fly" ('60). He also was co-writer of a number of songs, the most popular of which was the 1957 "I Cried in My Dream."

During the 1950s and '60s, Smiley and Kitty appeared as a team on many network shows, including the Opry. They also toured widely during these years, playing for audiences in all fifty states. From 1964 to 1967, they were featured members of the touring Ferlin Husky Show, which traveled to all parts of the U.S. as well as Canada and Mexico. They were often accompanied on these trips by their daughter, singer-autoharpist Rita Faye Wilson. In many appearances, Smiley acted as master of ceremonies as well as performer.

In the mid-1960s, Smiley and Kitty cut their personal appearances to a minimum to spend more time in their home in Hendersonville, Tennessee. They continued to record, turning out an LP on the K-ARK label in 1967. Smiley's work in the 1960s turned more and more to the business side in his role as president of the Wil-Helm Talent Agency. Among the artists represented by the agency, operated by Smiley and the Wilburn Brothers, were Loretta Lynn, Jay Lee Webb, the Osborne Brothers, Martha Carson, and many others. (*See also* WILSON, KITTY)

WISEMAN, SCOTTY: Singer, guitarist, banjoist, teacher, songwriter, part of Lulu Belle and Scotty team. Born Spruce Pine, North Carolina, November 8, 1909.

For more than 25 years, two names that were more familiar to midwesterners than governors or movie stars were those of Lulu Belle and Scotty. Scotty was the nickname* of Scott Wiseman, a talented individual who went on to gain a master's degree and start a new career as a teacher after many years of prominence as a performer.

Born and brought up in the Spruce Pine region of North Carolina, Scotty learned many traditional songs from his family and friends. During his years in Altamont High School, Crossmore, North Carolina, from 1923 to 1927, he perfected his instrumental style on both guitar and banjo. While performing in his spare time, his eye was on a possible career in teaching. He went to Duke University during 1927-28 and then to Fairmont Teachers College, Fairmont, West Virginia, in 1929, from which he received his B.A. degree in 1932.

Scotty had piled up an impressive record as an artist during his school years. In 1927, he made his radio debut on station WRVA, Richmond, Virginia. During his college years in Fairmont, he performed regularly on station WMMN. The result was a chance to join the National Barn Dance in Chicago in 1933. Scotty decided to forego a non-music career for a while and moved to the big city of the midwest.

There he soon married another North Carolinian, Myrtle Eleanor Cooper. Starting in 1933, as Lulu Belle and Scotty, they went on to become an institution on the show. One of their first hits in 1934 was a song Scotty wrote the previous year, "Home Coming Time." It was the first of many best-selling records on such labels as Conqueror, Vocalion, Bluebird, Brunswick, Vogue, Mercury, and KaHill.

Throughout their career, Scotty wrote or co-wrote many songs, including several with his wife. In 1935, he collaborated with Bascom Lunsford on the comic standard "Mountain

* He was also called Skyland Scotty.

Dew." Some of his other compositions were "Empty Christmas Stocking" ('38); "Remember Me" ('40); "Time Will Tell" ('45); "You Don't Love Me Like You Used to Do," "Tell Her You Love Her," "That New Vitamine" ('46); "Dontcha" ('47); "Old Time Bible" ('53); "Tenderly He Watches O'er Me" ('54); "Between You and Me" ('55); "Come As You Are" ('57).

During the late 1930s, the fame of Lulu Belle and Scotty spread far beyond Chicago as network broadcasts of the Barn Dance, personal appearance tours, and records made them national figures. They remained regular cast members of the Barn Dance for most of the years between 1933 and 1958. For a while, in the early 1940s, though, they starred on the Boone County Jamboree on station WLW, Cincinnati, which later became the Midwestern Hayride. In 1949, back in Chicago, they were gracing the TV screen on station WNBQ-TV, an association that lasted until 1957.

Scotty and his wife were guest stars on many major shows during the 1950s, including the Grand Ole Opry in 1950 and 1952 and Red Foley's Ozark Jamboree in 1957-58. In the late 1950s, Scotty began taking courses at Northwestern for an advanced teaching degree. In 1958, he received his M.A. Soon after, the Wisemans settled down in Spruce Pine, North Carolina, where Scotty taught speech at Spruce Pine College.

The team also made several movies in the late '30s and early 1940s, including "Harvest Moon" ('38); "Country Fair" ('39); "Village Barn Dance" ('40); "Swing Your Partner" ('42); "Hi Ya Neighbor," "National Barn Dance" ('43). (*See also* LULU BELLE)

WOODLEY, BRUCE: *See* Seekers, The

WOOLEY, SHEB: Singer, guitarist, actor, songwriter, music publisher. Born Erick, Oklahoma, April 10, 1921.

If diversification is the name of the game, Sheb Wooley rates in the top echelons. In his long career, there were few aspects of the entertainment field he did not essay, from writing comic songs to acting in top-rated western TV shows. Carrying diversification one step further, he was as well known under his original name of Sheb Wooley as by his assumed one of Ben Colder.

PUBLIC LIBRARY
GOSHEN, INDIANA

Sheb could play guitar and sing many country and western songs by the time he finished high school in the southwest. He went on to perform for a time on station WBAP in Ft. Worth, Texas. In 1946, he formed his own western band and toured many western states. During the late '40s he also studied for a while at the Jack Koslyn School of Acting. In 1948, he was given his first major recording contract by MGM Records, an association still going strong twenty years later.

During the '40s, Sheb moved his base of operations to Los Angeles. In 1949, he began work in movies and in TV, while continuing as a singer and songwriter. In the 1950s, his movie credits included "Rocky Mountain," "The Boy from Oklahoma," and "High Noon." The 1960s provided him with roles in such films as "Giant" and "Little Big Horn." When the TV series Rawhide began in the late '50s, Sheb was one of the featured performers.

His songs, many wildly funny, were in the repertoire of country and western artists beginning in the early 1950s. In 1953, Sheb's parody of two hit songs, "When Mexican Joe Met Jole Blon," provided a top 10 hit for Hank Snow. In the late 1950s, Sheb had a major national hit with his recording of his own composition, "Purple People Eater." In 1962, he provided MGM with a number-one-ranked national hit, "That's My Pa." The name Ben Colder came to the fore in the mid-1960s; providing several more major hits for MGM. The Colder imprint was on the 1966 top 10 success "Almost Persuaded #2"; the 1967 single "Purple People Eater #2"; and the 1968 hit "Tie the Tiger Down." Ben also had a best-selling LP of 1967, "Wine, Women and Song."

Wooley-Colder's other compositions included "Blue Guitar," "Too Young to Tango," "Are You Satisfied," "Sweet Chile," "Laughin' the Blues," "Meet Mr. Lonely," and "The Middle of the Night Is My Cryin' Time." A number of these were published by one of the two music publishing firms Sheb owned as of 1968.

WORLD'S ORIGINAL WWVA JAMBOREE:
Variety show, originating from station WWVA, Wheeling, West Virginia.

Still going strong in the late 1960s, the WWVA Jamboree was second only to the Grand Ole Opry in longevity. Its first show in 1926 occurred after the start of the Opry in 1925 and the earlier National Barn Dance in 1924. However, the Barn Dance ceased operation in the 1960s.

Over the years, the Jamboree helped bring many performers into the national spotlight. These included a number of native West Virginians, such as Red Sovine and Hawkshaw Hawkins, as well as such others as George Morgan, the Osborne Brothers, and the Louvin Brothers.

The show's roster over the years also included many performers who already had national ranking by the time they joined WWVA. Among the artists who appeared on the show from 1926 to 1967 were Grandpa Jones, Abbe Neal, Hugh Cross, Elton Britt, Don Reno, Hank Snow, Wayne Raney, Ace Richman and the Sunshine Boys, Roy Scott, Mabelle Seeger, Big Slim, Red Smiley, Chicki Williams, Cy Williams, Dock Williams, Toby Stroud, Dottie Swan, Slim Rogers, Skeeter Bonn, Uncle Charlie Barnette, Red Allen, Johnny Bailes, Red Belcher, Hylo Brown, Bill Browning, Lou Childre, James Carson, Bill Clifton, Betty Cody, Cook Brothers, Don Gibson, Billy Grammer, Hardrock Gunter, Dolph Hewitt, Gene Hooper, Jim and Jesse, Joni Lee, Daisy Mae, Wilma Lee and Stoney Cooper, Lazy Jim Day, Abner Doolittle, Bud Durham, Marion Durham, Crazy Elmer, Shug Fisher, Jimmy Gately, Don Kedwell, Ramblin' Lou, Jimmy Marlin, Curley Miller, Charlie Monroe, Juanita Moore, Lee Moore, and Dusty Owens.

The show was held at the Virginia Theater in Wheeling. By the 1950s, two shows were given each Saturday night with CBS Radio broadcasting every third performance.

WORTH, MARION: Singer, songwriter. Born Birmingham, Alabama, July 4.

In the 1960s, many of the top female country and western artists gave up crinolines or cowboy outfits for contemporary dresses. A prime example is blonde, green-eyed Marion Worth who won ovations trom audiences from Las Vegas, Nevada, to Nashville. Though her dress was modern, her balladry was in the country music tradition.

Listening to the Grand Ole Opry for six hours on Saturday night was a way of life in Marion's home state of Alabama. As a schoolgirl, she memorized many of the ballads from the program and sang them for relatives and friends. After a while, she worked up a singing act with a sister. They began to sing locally during their teens, and in time were featured on a Birmingham radio station. Though a show business career seemed a likelihood, Marion kept up her education, taking college courses in bookkeeping and nursing.

In the late 1950s, Marion was composing her own material as well as singing in clubs in the Birmingham region. She also began looking for the chance to make records. The first label to feature her was Travis Records. In 1960, she scored her first top 10 national hit on Travis, "I Think I Know." Soon after, she signed with Happy Wilson to record for his Guyden label. One of her own songs, "That Is My Kind of Love," provided a second national best-seller in 1960.

In the early 1960s, Marion moved to Nashville and soon was featured on a number of network TV shows. In short order she was also signed as a regular on the Grand Ole Opry. She was featured as well in several appearances on Dick Clark's American Bandstand.

Once in Nashville, she signed with Columbia Records. During the mid-1960s, she scored with several hit singles on Columbia, including "Crazy Arms"; a duet with George Morgan of the country standard "Slippin' Around"; and a perennial Christmas favorite, "Shake Me, I Rattle." She also turned out several hit LPs, including "Hits of Marion Worth" ('65).

During the 1960s, Marion toured the United States, starring at county fairs, in nightclubs, and at the New Frontier Hotel in Las Vegas. Her itinerary included appearances in many Canadian provinces and a number of overseas countries.

WRIGHT, JOHNNY: Singer, guitarist, fiddler, songwriter. Born Mt. Juliet, Tennessee, May 13, 1914.

One of the royal families of country music, the Johnny Wright clan provided country enthusiasts with many great moments for more than three decades. Johnny's wife, Kitty Wells, won the title "Queen of Country Music Singers" while Johnny starred as an individual performer and as half of the team of Johnnie and Jack.

The musical tradition in the Wright family went back several generations. Johnny's grandfather was a champion old-time fiddler in Tennessee, and his father was a gifted 5-string banjoist. Thus he was exposed to many country

music performances during his youth in Mt. Juliet. He sometimes performed for school events during his public school days.

After finishing school, he began to perform in the region. In 1936, he began his first radio engagement on station WSIX, Nashville. One of the members of his show was a talented young singer named Muriel Deason. Johnny decided she needed a new stage name and chose Kitty Wells from a popular song, "I'll Marry Kitty Wells." Two years later, Kitty became Mrs. Johnny Wright.

The WSIX show was the beginning of a long career as a radio performer that included appearances on WCHS, Charleston, West Virginia; WHIS, Bluefield, West Virginia; WNOX, Knoxville; WEAS, Decatur, Georgia; WPTF, Raleigh, North Carolina; and WAPI, Birmingham, Alabama. For most of these engagements, he starred with Jack Anglin, with whom he formed the team of Johnnie and Jack in 1938. With their supporting group, The Tennessee Mountain Boys, they toured widely in the next few years and the period after World War II.

In 1947, the Wrights and Jack Anglin joined the cast of the KWKH Louisiana Hayride in Shreveport. In 1951, Johnnie and Jack scored two major national hits, "Crying Heart Blues" and "Poison Love." In 1952, the team was given the high sign by the Grand Ole Opry and moved to Nashville. Johnnie and Jack had a big year in 1954 with such top 10 national hits as "Beware of It," "Goodnight, Sweetheart, Goodnight" and "I Get So Lonely." Two other top hits were "South of New Orleans" and "The Moon Is High and So Am I." Many of the audience favorites were songs written by Wright and Anglin. During their 25-year association, they wrote more than 100 songs, many of which were best-sellers for other major artists. Their LP output included "Hits of Johnnie and Jack" on RCA Victor ('60); and "Johnnie and Jack" ('63) and "Sincerely" on Camden.

The team came to an end in 1963 when Jack was killed in a car crash. Johnny reorganized The Tennessee Mountain Boys, adding Mrs. Wright and their daughter Ruby, and Bill Phillips. The new troupe was acclaimed on a cross-country tour, the forerunner of many appearances around the United States during the 1960s. In 1965, Johnny scored another top 10 hit with his recording of "Hello Viet

Nam." The song provided the title for a successful LP. Johnny's credits in the 1960s included two other LPs, "Saturday Night" and "Country Music Special." Besides appearing in all fifty states during this period, the Johnny Wright group also traveled to Canada, the Far East, and many parts of Europe.

Some of the other songs recorded by Johnny over the years are: "I Get So Lonely," "Sailor Man," "Leave Our Moon Alone," "Lonely Island Pearl," "That's the Way the Cookie Crumbles," "Sweetie Pie," "Humming Bird," "Baby, It's in the Making," "All the Time," "Pleasure Not a Habit in Mexico," "What Do You Know About Heartaches," "You Can't Divorce My Heart," "Banana Boat Song," "I Want to Be Loved," "I Love You Better Than You Know," "'Love, Love, Love," "Live and Let Live," "Keep the Flag Flying," "Nickels, Quarters and Dimes," "Dear John Letter," "I Don't Claim to Be an Angel," "You Can't Get the Country Out of a Boy," and "Three Ways of Knowing."

Johnny also appeared in a movie, "Second Fiddle to a Steel Guitar." (*See also* ANGLIN, JACK; WELLS, KITTY)

WYNETTE, TAMMY: Singer, guitarist, accordionist, pianist. Born near Tupelo, Mississippi, May 5, 1942.

The year 1967, when she began to receive industry awards as one of the most promising new singers, meant the end of a long, often difficult trail for young Tammy Wynette. Her guitarist father, William Hollis Pugh, died when his daughter was only eight months old. Her mother had to go to Birmingham, Alabama, to earn a living in an aircraft factory, leaving Tammy in the care of her grandparents.

Her early years on her grandparents' farm, she recalls, were much like the life described in the song "Ode to Billie Joe." When she was old enough, she picked and chopped cotton and baled hay along with the hired hands. The fact that her grandfather paid the going pay rate, which served as her allowance, gave her a spirit of independence that served her well in later years.

After World War II ended, her mother returned to help bring her up. By that time, Tammy had received her first taste for music, singing Sacred Harp religious songs with her grandmother. (In this form of singing, notes were sung instead of words.) As she grew older, she wanted to learn to play some of the instruments left her by her father. The collection included guitars, accordion, piano, mandolin and bass fiddle. Her mother let Tammy take music lessons, but tried to persuade her daughter to use music only as a hobby. The lessons went on for five years, ending before Tammy was in her teens.

Tammy's youthful desire to become a performer was strong. However, just before finishing high school, she traded her dreams for marriage and moved to Tupelo, Mississippi, with her husband. After a few months, they returned to a home near her grandparents' house. After her first daughter was born, Tammy learned hair-dressing. She worked for a time in a beauty shop in Tupelo and then as a chiropractor's receptionist.

Her working career was interrupted by new additions to the family. She had a second daughter and was carrying a third child when the marriage broke up.

Tammy moved to Birmingham and worked in a beauty shop until her next child was due. The baby, a girl born prematurely, developed spinal meningitis soon after Tammy brought her home. She nursed the child, helped by her relations, until the baby was sufficiently on the way to recovery for her to go back to work to pay off over $6,000 in bills. Now she looked for something to augment her beauty shop earnings. Her childhood desire for a music career returned and she managed to get a performing role on the Country Boy Eddie Show on WBRC-TV, Birmingham.

She also sang in clubs in several southern cities and found time to write songs with Fred Lehner of station WYAM in Birmingham. When she won several appearances on one of Porter Wagoner's syndicated TV shows, Tammy was sure she could make the grade as a solo artist.

She started to make the rounds of recording companies. She traveled to Nashville and auditioned first for United Artists, then for Hickory and Kapp. Each visit resulted in a little more interest, but no contract. Her Kapp reception was so good she returned to her children in Birmingham expecting a call or letter almost any day. After several months, she tried another time to take Nashville by storm. This time, the executives at Epic Records came through with a contract.

She recorded "Apartment Number Nine" a

[342]

few days later. Within a few months, it was on the way to becoming one of 1967's top hits. She quickly followed with a top 10 success, "Your Good Girl's Gonna Go Bad." Her other hits of 1967 were "Elusive Dreams" (a duet with David Houston) and "I Don't Wanna Play House." Her top 10 single hits of 1968 were "D-I-V-O-R-C-E" and "Take Me to Your World."

As the decade moved to a close, Tammy was set as a star of the Grand Ole Opry. Among the awards that came her way was a nomination for the Top Female Vocalist spot in the Country Music Association 1968 poll.

YARBROUGH, GLENN: Singer, guitarist, songwriter. Born Milwaukee, Wisconsin, January 12, 1930.

From his earliest years, Glenn Yarbrough seemed headed for a singing career, though for a time it looked as though he might be sidetracked by the teaching profession. Born into a prosperous midwest family, he impressed his parents with his vocal ability almost as soon as he was old enough for elementary school. By the time he was eight, he was a soloist with the choir of famed Grace Church in upper Manhattan.

His excellent soprano voice won him a scholarship to the private St. Paul's School in Baltimore. After a year at the school, his voice changed. Luckily, he was a good athlete, a first-stringer on the football team. The result was a continuation of his scholarship in sports instead of music. He was good enough to receive a number of scholarship offers from major universities when his high school graduation approached.

The wanderlust that was to mark his life intervened, however. He decided to take a year off and hitchhike across the United States, Canada, and Mexico. Finally, in 1949, he enrolled at St. John's College in Annapolis. He aimed for a B.A. with some idea of a future in teaching. In 1952, though, he left for three years of Army service, most of which was spent in Korea. In 1955, he returned to college, this time attending Mexico City College where he studied classical Greek and pre-Socratic society.

By now he had decided his goal was to become a professor of philosophy. He returned to New York in 1955 and entered the New School for Social Research. Though he sang for

Glenn Yarbrough

his own pleasure and could, by now, play excellent guitar, he didn't support himself through music, but with a spare-time job as bouncer in a New York hotel.

The following year, music finally returned as the dominating factor in Glenn's life. The owner of Chicago's Gate of Horn Club heard Glenn sing some folk songs at a New York party. After several attempts, the club lured Yarbrough away from his studies with a weekly salary of $150. After this first professional stint, Glenn continued to make the rounds of the growing coffee house circuit. For a while he owned his own coffee house, the Limelite, in Colorado Springs, Colorado, in partnership with actor-singer Alex Hassilev. In May 1959, he joined Hassilev in an engagement at the Cosmo Alley Club near Hollywood and Vine in Los Angeles. There they met another artist, Lou Gottlieb (formerly of The Gateway Singers). The three decided to form a new group called The Limeliters.

From that time until 1963, The Limeliters went on to become one of the best known folk groups in the country. They were featured on TV and in major nightclubs and coffee houses across the country. They also turned out a series of best-selling LPs for RCA Victor.

In 1963, Glenn decided to go out on his own

[343]

again. Within a short time, he had a hit album on RCA Victor. Called "Glenn Yarbrough: Time to Move On," it included such songs as "You Know My Name," "Angel Cake and Wine," "Time to Move On," "Stella's Got a New Dress," "Diamonds of Dew," "San Francisco Bay Blues" and "Four Strong Winds." He followed up with two more successful LPs, "One More Round" and "Come Share My Life." In 1966, he scored with his first nationwide single hit, "Baby the Rain Must Fall." The LP of that title included such other songs as "Lonesome," "She's Too Far Above Me," "The Bull Frog Song," "She," "Long Time Blues," "I've Been to Town" and "Billy Goat Hill." Soon after, RCA released its fifth Yarbrough album, "It's Gonna Be Fine." (In the late '50s, Yarbrough had been featured on an Elektra LP, "Here We Go Baby" and on Tradition with "Come Sit By My Side.")

During the 1960s, Yarbrough's voice was familiar to radio and TV audiences from his many commercials, particularly his "Things go better with Coke" series for Coca-Cola.

As his recording career moved ahead, Glenn added another facet to his work by founding a new publishing firm with Rod McKuen, Stanyan Music Company. A number of Yarbrough's best received songs of the mid-1960s were from the pen of McKuen.

Yarbrough joined Warner Brothers Records in 1968. (See also LIMELITERS, THE)

YARROW, PETER: See Peter, Paul and Mary

YELLIN, BOB See Greenbriar Boys

YOUNG, FARON: Singer, guitarist, actor, songwriter, music publisher. Born Shreveport, Louisiana, Febuary 25, 1932.

One of Faron Young's hit records of the mid-1950s began "Live fast. . . ." It certainly described the secret of Young's success, a round-the-clock devotion to music that made him a top star in his early 20s and one of the most diverse operators in the field a decade later.

Though city-born, Faron moved to the country as a child when his father bought a small dirt farm outside Shreveport. While still in public school, he was given his first guitar. The instrument intrigued him and he spent many hours figuring out chords and fingering with a herd of cattle as an audience. When Faron entered Fair Park High School in Shreveport, he could sing many of the top country hits while providing his own guitar accompani-

ment. It wasn't long before he formed his own band and played at school affairs as well as local fairs and hoedowns.

At the start of 1950s, Faron entered Centenary College in Louisiana. For a while he tried to continue to combine studies with part-time musicianship. However, he had become well known in the region as an exciting performer and the offers of musical advancement were too tempting. He joined station KWKH and soon moved over to the cast of the Louisiana Hayride. Another rising star, Webb Pierce, also was on the Hayride. Pierce took Faron on as a featured vocalist for tours over the entire southern region.

In 1951, Faron was signed by Capitol Records. He quickly turned out two hit recordings, "Tattle Tale Tears" and "Have I Waited Too Long." In 1952, he became a regular cast member of the Grand Ole Opry. His meteoric rise was delayed by the Korean War and Army service: he entered the service in the fall of 1952. No sooner did he finish basic training than he won an Army talent show on ABC-TV. Between 1952 and '54, he toured the world entertaining troops and was starred on the Army's radio recruiting show.

Even before his discharge, Faron was making a dent in the national ratings. In 1953, he had a top 10 recording of his own composition "Goin' Steady" on Capitol. In 1954, he returned to Nashville to rejoin the Opry. He received a royal welcome from a rapidly growing number of fans and soon had another top 10 hit, "If You Ain't Lovin'." He really hit his stride in 1955 with such national successes as "Go Back You Fool," "It's a Great Life," and "Live Fast, Love Hard and Die Young." He was voted "America's Number One Artist of 1955" by Southern Farm and Ranch magazine.

There were very few months in the years that followed when Young was not represented on the national hit charts. In 1956, he had top 10 hits in "I've Got Five Dollars and It's Saturday Night" and "Sweet Dreams." In 1957, he scored with "I Miss You Already." He rounded out the '50s with such hits as "Alone with You" and "That's the Way I Feel" in '58 and the number-one-ranked "Country Girl" in '59. During the '50s, besides touring widely, Faron made his acting debut in several movies, including the 1958 "Country Music Holiday" with Ferlin Husky and Zsa Zsa Gabor. He was also featured in "Daniel Boone" and "Hidden Guns."

[344]

Faron Young

Faron began the 1960s with two top 10 hits he co-authored, "Face to the Wall" (with Billy Anderson) and "Your Old Used to Be" (with Hilda Yoimd). In 1961, he co-authored a hit—"Backtrack"—with Alex Zanetis. He also turned out another number-one-ranked song, "Hidden Walls." He was represented in 1962 with "The Comeback" and "Three Days" (co-author, Willie Nelson) and in early 1963 by "Down by the River."

In 1963, Faron switched from Capitol to Mercury. He continued to provide his new company with national hits, including "The Yellow Bandana" in '63, "You'll Drive Me Back" in '64, "Walk Tall" in '65 and "I Guess I Had Too Much to Dream Last Night" in '67.

Young's output of LPs by the mid-1960s was well over the two dozen mark. The titles on Capitol included "Sweethearts or Strangers"; "This Is Faron Young" ('58); "Talk About Hits" ('59); "Best of Faron Young," "Fan Club Favorites" ('61); "All Time Great Hits" ('63); "Memory Lane" ('64). His Mercury LPs included "This Is Faron"; "Faron Young Aims

at the West" ('63); "Songs for Country Folks," "Dance Favorites" ('64); "Songs of Mountains and Valleys" ('65); "Faron Young's Greatest Hits" and "Faron Young Sings the Best of Jim Reeves" ('66).

During the '60s, Young toured all the states and made several trips to Germany, France, Mexico, and England. By the mid-'60s, he had many other flourishing projects, including his own music publishing firm, Vanadore Music, and his own monthly paper, Music City News. Long an ardent auto racing driver and fan, he was also owner of Sulphur Dell auto track in Nashville. Among his souvenirs was a letter from President Johnson thanking Young for playing at a number of the President's speaking engagements during the 1964 campaign.

ZITHER: Stringed instrument, related to the autoharp.

The ancestry of one of the most ancient instruments, the zither, is traced back to ancient Greece where a similar instrument called a cithara was used. Even earlier versions are credited by some experts to Israel and Phoenicia.

The instrument, which has tones much like a harp, lute, or guitar, has anywhere from 29 to 45 strings stretched over a thin, flat, hollow sounding board. The shape of the board varies widely, some types resembling a small harp and others having either one or both sides of the board rounded. Some types also have a fretted finger board under some of the strings. The zither is usually played with a plectrum, though some musicians use their fingers, and lies flat when played. A version of the zither that is played with a bow is also found in Germany, called the Streichzither.

Most zithers were and are made in Europe. At present, no company makes them in the United States. One American firm, however— the Franz Schwarzler Zither Company, founded in Washington, Missouri, in 1864—was long prominent in their manufacture. The Schwarzler factory ceased operation in 1944.

Different forms of zither have been used for centuries by folk artists in Europe. The instrument was widely used in the United States during the 1800s, though it has been mainly neglected in recent years. It is still a major folk music instrument in such countries as Norway, Denmark, Holland, Germany, Austria, and Switzerland.

A few American artists, such as Susan Reed, played the zither in the 1960s.

Special Articles

Changing Attitudes Toward Folk Music

Sam Hinton

Folk music is many things to many people, and precise definition is impossible. One reason for this is that while we hear a given song or tune, the definition must apply to the processes which produced it. For folk music is not so much a body of art as it is a process, and its characteristics lie not so much in the songs themselves as in the way the songs relate to a community. Much has been written of the fact that twenty-one different definitions, by twenty-one folklorists, are to be found in the *Standard Dictionary of Folklore, Mythology and Legend* (Maria Leach, Editor). But these are not as wildly diverse as might be supposed, and there is a strong thread of agreement that folklore must be defined in terms of the manner of its creation, dissemination, and use, rather than any characteristic of the lore itself.

For myself, I think of folklore as a product of a two-part process. First, a community must treat a song as community property, even though the composer may be very well known to it; there is no standard, authoritative, "correct" version. Each individual may treat the song as he pleases, and the existence of variants and versions becomes a criterion by which a folksong may be recognized as such. Second, these creative efforts result in a full-blown body of folksong if they lie within a traditional framework of poetic and musical style which is representative of the community.

Thus folk music develops through a process of free variation within traditional limits. The origin of the material, which may come from outside the community, does not matter as much as its subsequent treatment. So far as the individual singer is concerned, he does his best with what he has in the way of materials and talent, and whether the result is to be called "folksong" or not is of little concern to him. If his customary medium of expression is part of a well-developed traditional framework, his song is a folksong in that tradition. If his framework is still in the process of "jelling," or if he must choose from among a number of frameworks not native to him, his song is not at that moment a folksong in the fullest sense. (This, by the way, should not be taken to imply any artistic judgment about the song.)

So long as a folksong is truly alive, the dynamic process never ceases. The framework itself is subject to slow change, with new styles constantly being added to, or replacing, old ones. Further, the products of the process are often taken outside their native tradition and imprisoned in print or phonograph recording, and are subject to observation by scholars, classically trained musicians, and the general public, none of whom have been consistent in their attitudes.

The term "folklore" was coined in 1847 by a British scholar, William Thoms. Of course, people had been gathering folk materials for a long while before that, but they called it something else, like "popular antiquities." These early collectors and scholars, including Thoms, had a ready definition for their material: it was the lore of the peasants. The peasants were illiterate members of a society in which literacy was a factor, and a literary tradition existed separately from the folk tradition. A folk musician was felt to be "contaminated" by any contact with the classical or urban popular traditions.

These first collectors, not themselves members of the peasant class, usually saw folk music as something quaint and faintly comic, or as something old and moribund. Some of the greatest of the tragic ballads appeared in books of the type collectively known as "drolleries"; these books bore such titles as *Choyce Drollery* (1656), *Wit Restor'd* (1658), *An Antidote against Melancholy* (1661), *Wit and Drollery* (1682), and the famous series *Pills to Purge Melancholy* (1698–1714).

Such works were intended not for serious study but for entertainment, and their contents were not limited to folk song-poems; many of them contained new poems which ridiculed rustic ways of life, and one is led to infer that the "drollery" of a great ballad like "Chevy Chase" lay in the fact that such a magnificent theme came from the lips of crude unlettered bumpkins.

A number of critics, including Joseph Addison, were able to recognize the dignity and literary value of some of the old ballads, but their attitude was almost entirely backward-looking; a folksong was valuable insofar as it reflected a nobler past. This is illustrated by the great collection published by Thomas Percy in 1765. He showed no lack of respect for the material, but did regard it as the last gasp of an almost-dead tradition. We now know that in 1765 there was a great deal of activity in the living folk tradition, but Reverend (later Bishop) Percy did not listen to living singers but took his material from the crumbling pages of old hand-written manuscripts, and he gave his work the revealing title *Reliques of Ancient English Poetry*.

Many published collections came after Percy. Some collectors (notably Sir Walter Scott) actually listened to folksingers, but even they were chiefly interested in the antiquarian aspects of the songs, and they edited with a heavy hand in order to enhance what they took to be an antique flavor.

The gulf between scholar and folksinger is further illustrated by the fact that while most of the scholars were English, they were very slow to credit England proper with worthwhile folk music of her own. They preferred to find their material in the exotic (and, they probably thought, more primitive) lands of the Celtic tongues—Ireland, Scotland, and Wales.

It must not be supposed that these early works were without value, for they amassed a tremendous quantity of beautiful material, and laid the foundations of later works of impeccable scholarship. The American scholar Francis James Child went through all of these old books, both in published form and in manuscript, in an effort to locate and eliminate the effects of editorial tampering, and his five-volume work, *The English and Scottish Popular Ballads* (1882), has been elevated to the well-deserved eminence of a scholarly classic. But his work, too, was confined to the old songs, and he did not concern himself with the living folksong of his own day.

Back in England, a group of scholars began serious and conscientious collecting of living material in the closing years of the nineteenth century. Cecil Sharp was the best-known member of this group, and his books and notes came to be regarded as models—especially in relation to tunes. His published works contain quite a bit of editing, but in his carefully preserved personal papers he scrupulously retained the unedited originals.

By this time the British and American folklorists were beginning to be a little less suspicious of evidences of literacy, and were accepting as part of the folk tradition songs printed on "broadside" sheets or in "garland" collections. Even so, they insisted upon oral transmission as the chief means of dissemination, and were quick to dismiss any song that might have come from music hall, minstrel show, or vaudeville stage. Their definitions of folk music still did not provide for any music that might be produced by a peasant who had become familiar with "art" music and popular music.

In the United States, mountain singers—bearers of the Anglo-Irish-American folk tradition in its "purest" form—made thousands of commercial phonograph recordings in the 1920s and '30s. Most scholars either dismissed these as worthless "hillbilly" products or, perhaps more often, were not even aware of their existence. D. K. Wilgus was one of the first to recognize their value both as works of art and as materials for serious study. The idea that worthwhile studies may be made of whatever songs a people may sing, even if the songs do not follow previously accepted patterns, began to take root and flourish. Today, many of our leading scholars not only accept change as an integral part of the folk process, but find their most exciting and evocative studies in the nature of the change itself.

Music critics and so-called "serious" musicians have had their own set of attitudes. All too often, their approach has been that folk music is a failing attempt by untrained people to produce GOOD music, and that perhaps folksingers could become REAL singers if they were taught the right way to sing and given the right sorts of songs. Such critics have often indicated that there might, however, be some value in the quaint materials of folksong because some accepted composers have used folk tunes as themes in serious works.

According to this way of thought, if folk music is to be presented at all it must be smoothed out, and its words and music made to conform to accepted classical patterns; and, since folk music is only a simplified version of classical music, anyone properly trained in the latter field can, without additional training, take it upon himself to do the polishing. This is the point of view that has generally prevailed among those responsible for purveying folk music to American school children, who have thus been subjected to a tremendous amount of nonsense. Most folk music published specifically for school use has been so edited as to present a distressingly erroneous picture of the "folk." Arrangements of this sort remind one of the sculptor who, viewing a plaster replica of a great statue, said "It's exactly like the original—except in everything!"

There has been some movement away from all this by a few pioneering composers and educators—notably Zoltán Kodály, following and expanding upon the ideas of Bela Bartók—but the majority of trained art musicians seem to have only one set of musical standards, and continue to apply it to music of all sorts. One still hears the routine distinction between folk (or other) music on the one hand and "art" music on the other, as if the latter were the only sort to which any art were attached.

Perhaps the most varying attitude toward music has been that of the music-consuming general public. The newer mass media are by no means solely responsible for this variation, for styles and fads have risen and fallen all through the centuries, and the regard of the literate social classes for folk music has changed repeatedly. The years since World War II, however, have seen what is probably the greatest boom ever enjoyed by folk music. At the peak of this boom, anything bearing the label "folk music," whether deserved or not, was likely to be a big money-maker. More happily, many folk musicians of unquestioned "authenticity" were able to experience the delight of having their efforts acclaimed by audiences of thousands. Today the furor has somewhat abated, but much of the enthusiasm and a respectable portion of the audience are still there.

The events connected with the popularity of various forms of folk and folk-like music during the last thirty years are fascinating and complex. It seems to me that this popularity arose in response to the difficulty of self-identification in our fast-changing society. Technological and social change are so rapid as to make it hard for an individual to place himself in the stream of cultural tradition, and he may find comfort in the fact that an old song, which he takes to be relatively unchanging, can still speak to him across the years. This may have been coupled with the fact that many young people were becoming dissatisfied with their own society because of its cynical materialism, and they found folk music to be ingenuous and non-commercial.

Whether or not this view is correct, the young folks flocked to folk music with something deeper than a desire for a new and novel fad. Vast numbers of them became performers themselves—and very skillful ones. They found their pleasure not only in the antiquarian aspects of folksong, but in the customary non-authoritarian approach to its performance. They began writing their own songs, at first in imitation of older folk styles but later in new styles, and taking the subjects from their own lives; through all this there was a conscious effort to maintain the non-commercial "innocence" of folksong. Whether these efforts have resulted in a framework that may be called "traditional" is perhaps debatable, but there is no question as to the "creative" approach demanded by our earlier definition of folk music. So this music may certainly still be called "folk music" in some sense, and the farthest-out electronic bands at the least remind us that music of all kinds—folk, popular, "art"—constitutes a continuum or at least a network of intertwining streams, and not a series of separate and unmixed flows.

Biologists have a phrase: "Ontogeny recapitulates phylogeny." This means that an individual animal, in the course of its embryonic or larval development, repeats some of the major steps in the development of the species to which it belongs. The expression is perhaps more poetic than scientific, but in this sense it seems to apply to current attitudes toward folk music, and to the music produced because of these changing attitudes. Young people have broken with their parents' culture, and started a music of their own based upon the folk music of an earlier time. This newer music has gone through some of the stages of the music of the parent culture; there was the folk phase, a modal phase or two, a Baroque phase, an eclectic phase of reaching all over the world for new material and new sounds, and a sort of self-righteous phase of eschewing ALL external influence and attempting to cast off all the chains of tradition. Perhaps the most significant aspect of our times is that one phase has been added to the others without replacing them, and today there is a market (not necessarily in the pejorative commercial sense) for all of them—still including the oldest folk music.

However the attitudes may change, the music goes on its own course. People will sing the way they want to sing no matter what may be written about them. We can rejoice in this fact, and take perhaps more comfort than did the lady ship-passenger who nervously asked her Captain what would happen if they struck one of those dreadful icebergs. The Captain replied: "Don't give it a thought, Madam; the iceberg would go right along just as if nothing had happened."

—Sam Hinton

The Fall—and Rise—of Country Music

BILL ANDERSON

In February 1960, I had been in the country music business only a few months. I was appearing for a week at a Minneapolis nightclub, and I remember it just like it was yesterday.

I was having to do three shows a night, and by Friday my voice was thick and raspy. I had walked up the street from my hotel to a drugstore to try and find something to prevent my coming down with total laryngitis. I was whispering my plight to the pharmacist when I heard coming from the dusty shelves the sound of a radio playing country music.

I must momentarily have glanced up towards the radio, because the druggist suddenly moved back with a startled, almost apologetic, look and mumbled, "Oh . . . somebody's put my radio on that darned 'hillbilly' station again! I'm sorry." And with that he immediately changed frequencies to that of an "easy listening" station. I said nothing, paid for my throat medicine, and left.

In September 1965, I was in New York City to tape a guest appearance on the Jimmy Dean Show, and was walking one night about midnight through Times Square. I was waiting to cross at a light when a bright red convertible pulled up, top down, the radio blaring. The driver broke into a big grin, reached over, and turned up the volume on his set just as the Wilburn Brothers began singing "It's Another World Since I Met You." He began keeping time on the dash with his right hand and he had that "listen everybody . . . it's country music!!" look written all over his face. I smiled and crossed the street, and the shiny red car disappeared into the night.

I don't guess I knew it then, but as I look back now, I realize that these two seemingly insignificant experiences were in reality a reflection of the times . . . a living memory of what things were and what things are and a hopeful insight into the things that are to be.

In 1960, country music in Minneapolis and everywhere else was just beginning to recover from the terrible blow dealt it by the rock 'n' roll stampede of the late 1950s. Country music was still staggering, and in some places its acceptance was to decline even further before it began its upward swing. Minneapolis was one of these places. That "darned hillbilly station" didn't stay that way very long, and for two or three years the Twin Cities had no outlet for country music on radio at all.

But—neither did New York at this time. Nor Chicago. Nor Los Angeles. Nor even Atlanta, Montgomery, Knoxville, or Shreveport . . . the places where country music was born and raised. This is not to say country music couldn't be *heard* in these places, but the fulltime country station was not yet on the scene; it was like admitting you wore last year's fashions to admit you liked country music, and the little old druggists who missed Ernest Tubb, Roy Acuff, and Minnie Pearl went home and listened to the Saturday night Grand Ole Opry from Nashville to satisfy their nostalgia. The radios in their stores stayed on Mantovani.

They talked in 1960 about the "good ole days" of country music. Backstage gab sessions among the entertainers were often about the days when "ole Webb" had 21 straight number-one songs, the least of which sold a quarter of a million records . . . of the days when "ole Hank" was packin' 'em in singing "Lovesick Blues" . . . and the nights when souvenir book and picture sales totaled in the thousands of dollars. How many times did I hear from how many people in how many half-filled halls in how many country music-less cities . . . "Oh, those were the good ole days!"

I notice today, however, that I don't hear too much of that anymore. Our people today are too busy talking about the new Country Music Hall of Fame & Museum in Nashville that's attracting tourists by the thousands; of the record crowds drawn in 1967 at the Grand Ole Opry, now in its 42nd year; of the full-time country radio stations in New York, Chicago, Philadelphia, Los Angeles, Dallas, Atlanta and just about everywhere else. And they're talking about the attendance records broken nearly every week by the Buck Owenses and the George Joneses; about the syndicated country music television shows pulling top ratings in just about every American city; about the big buses, bands, and bankrolls of today's top country music stars.

Times have changed, and they've changed fast . . . and they've changed for the better. They didn't change all by themselves, though. The people you'll meet in these pages are the people who helped to bring these changes about . . . who helped to pick country music up by its sagging bootstraps and put it back onto the American map where it so deservedly belongs.

These people and countless others have done what may well be referred to by the music historians of a future generation as having "turned a tide." These are the people and theirs are the dedicated lives that have made the very day you're reading this one of the "good ole days" of country music.

Because country music is *now* . . . country music is what's *happening* . . . it's *in!*
And you can tell the little old druggist in Minneapolis that I said so.

—Bill Anderson

Country and Pop Music:
Development and Relationship

ED KAHN

The roots of country music go back to a time long before the first settlers came to North America: as the earliest pioneers came across the Atlantic, they brought with them not only their languages and ways of life, but also their musical cultures. As the United States developed and expanded westward, people from different musical backgrounds were thrown together and the new music which developed became distinctively American, although its component elements could be easily seen. In the years before widespread popularity of the phonograph—say about 1910—American rural music had taken on its own distinctive characteristics. A predominantly English, Scottish, and Irish white tradition had lived side by side and often in hybrid combination with an equally viable African-derived Negro tradition. Various commercial influences had been felt for generations as a result of a traveling stage tradition which predated the introduction of the phonograph into the rural areas.

During the early years of this century rural people were increasingly exposed to musical strains foreign to their ears, as the phonograph recordings penetrated into the backwoods of the land. Soon their music was showing strong influences from the sentimental songs of the eighteenth century and the popular airs of the day, as well as ragtime, jazz, and blues. Musical isolation began to break down at a rapid rate.

By the early 1920s, southern rural music was highly reflective of the musical influences that had made an impact over the years, but still it retained a decidedly regional flavor and served as an interesting example of the way in which outside effects are transformed as they are incorporated into a new musical fabric. With the end of the First World War and the return of army people to their civilian lives, there was immediately a new market for musics that had once seemed strange to the rural listener —thus stimulating the movement toward hybrid musics. Also, there was an economic recession. By 1923 the record business was experiencing hard times. Accordingly, Ralph Peer, then an executive at the General Phonograph Corporation in New York City, hit upon the idea of trying to record local talent in order to satisfy a purely local audience. Before this time, apparatus had been too cumbersome to facilitate recording in temporary studios. But now smaller equipment had been developed, and Peer set out on a southern journey.

His first city was Atlanta. In June of 1923, he recorded a number of performers who had a following in the immediate area. One of these was a fiddler who accompanied his own singing and was known as Fiddlin' John Carson. His first recording, "The Little Old Log Cabin in the Lane," was a popular song from the 1870s. On the flip side was "The Old Hen Cackled and the Rooster's Going to Crow," an old-time fiddle favorite which imitated the sounds of the chicken coop. Over Peer's protestations, the local Okeh Records distributor, Polk C. Brockman, insisted that the record would have appeal to an Atlanta audience. With some skepticism Peer had five hundred copies of the recording pressed, but assigned no catalog number as he felt that there would be no more calls for the disk. To his surprise, the initial pressing sold out almost immediately, and General Phonograph realized that there was a vast untapped market for rural music, made by rural musicians, to be sold to a rural audience.

Actually Carson was not the first person to record this kind of music, as Eck Robertson, a Texas fiddler, had recorded for Victor the previous year and Henry Whitter, a millhand from Fries, Virginia, had journeyed to New York to record for Okeh in the spring of 1923. But Whitter's recording was not released until after the success of Carson's record, and Victor never realized that Robertson represented a departure from their more common recordings. Accordingly, Carson's recording must be given credit for beginning the boom in southern white rural music.

Soon other record companies were following Okeh's lead. Colorful old-timers like Ernest V. "Pop" Stoneman, Uncle Dave Macon, and "Aunt" Samantha Bumgarner were also waxing the songs they had learned from tradition. By 1927 electrical recording techniques had supplanted the earlier acoustical methods, and rural recording expeditions throughout the southern regions were becoming commonplace. On one such expedition to Bristol, the town that spans the Virginia-Tennessee border, Ralph Peer, by now working for the Victor Talking Machine Company, found and recorded both the Carter Family and Jimmie Rodgers, "The Singing Brakeman." The regional market that had originally been the reason for these rural recordings began to give way to an ever widening market, so that by the 1930s many of these recordings were being sold around the world.

In the 1930s rural music began to move away from the traditional songs that so strongly marked the 1920s. The reasons for this shift are complex, but for the most part it can be attributed to three pressures. First, the old-timers were running out of traditional songs. Second, the recording executives wanted new compositions on which copyright could be claimed. And third, there was the desire of the industry to expand from a regional into a national and even international market. So the simple accompaniments by one or two instruments began to be replaced by more complex backings, and musicians were often able to make music their livelihood rather than their hobby.

In the west and southwest the large western swing bands such as Bob Wills' Texas Playboys and The Light Crust Doughboys were making their mark. By the time World War II came along, there were highly developed regional styles. But this war, like the earlier one, provided another opportunity for men of different backgrounds to come into contact with each other. Northerners were exposed to southern music and easterners and westerners exchanged musical values. So during and after the

[357]

war a new hybrid music came into being which was known as country and western—signifying just what the name implies. Country—or southeastern—music was merging with the more sophisticated accompaniment of the west to produce musicians like Merle Travis, Webb Pierce, and Hank Williams. The steel guitar, drums, and even horn sections of the western swing band were borrowed to provide backing for the southeastern vocalists who had generally preferred simpler accompaniments. At the same time, the music was moving farther and farther from its folk origins. Regional styles were being displaced by a style which drew upon a variety of sources.

During the late 1950s and early 1960s another significant change took place, but in the independent field of pop music. The earlier easy-going ballad styles of singers like Frank Sinatra, Perry Como, and Dean Martin found increasing competition for airplay from the emerging rock field. By the mid-1960s these ballad singers were receiving little attention on the top 40 format stations around the country and their audience was having trouble finding suitable music on the radio. Gradually these fans began to respond to country music which in turn became more oriented to a "town and country" audience. Singers like Glen Campbell, Roger Miller, George Hamilton IV, and Waylon Jennings began to satisfy the demands of this new "town and country" market. Simultaneously, country singers like Eddy Arnold who had been around for years began to modify their presentation in order to appeal to the new-found audience, and the old pop ballad singers began to record a new uptown "country" music.

Today we are experiencing a whole new development in the music field. Top 40 city groups like the Byrds are using instrumentation that is gaining them popularity among a country music audience, and instruments like the steel guitar that have long been associated exclusively with country music are finding their way into a new top 40 pop music. Boundaries and categories are breaking down as city musicians record country music—using both city and country backings—and country musicians draw increasingly upon city songs and styles in order to expand their audiences.

There is little question that the trend will continue—barring economic conditions that would once again force the music industry to stimulate sales through the cultivation and development of regional talents (if, indeed, vital regional markets still exist in the music business). While the loss of exciting styles of regional music is surely regrettable—and made even more so by the appallingly narrow limits of their documentation—we can look for another new eclectic music to develop drawing upon a wider variety of musical sources than ever before because of the impact of radio, phonograph, and television on what were at one time relatively isolated musical cultures.

—Ed Kahn

Appendices

National Academy of Recording Arts and Sciences

Grammy Awards in Folk, Country and Western Music*

1958

BEST COUNTRY & WESTERN PERFORMANCE
"Tom Dooley"—The Kingston Trio

1959

SONG OF THE YEAR
"The Battle of New Orleans"—Jimmy Driftwood, Composer

BEST COMEDY PERFORMANCE—MUSICAL
"The Battle of Kookamonga"—Homer and Jethro

BEST PERFORMANCE—DOCUMENTARY OR SPOKEN WORD (OTHER THAN COMEDY)
"A Lincoln Portrait"—Carl Sandburg

BEST COUNTRY & WESTERN PERFORMANCE
"The Battle of New Orleans"—Johnny Horton

BEST PERFORMANCE—FOLK
"The Kingston Trio at Large"—The Kingston Trio

BEST ENGINEERING CONTRIBUTION—OTHER THAN CLASSICAL OR NOVELTY
"Belafonte at Carnegie Hall"—Harry Belafonte—Robert Simpson, Engineer

* Awards listed here are only those given for activities in folk, country and western music, or to performers listed in this Encyclopedia.

1960

BEST PERFORMANCE BY A CHORUS
"Songs of the Cowboy"—Norman Luboff Choir

BEST COUNTRY & WESTERN PERFORMANCE
"El Paso"—Marty Robbins

BEST PERFORMANCE—FOLK
"Swing Dat Hammer"—Harry Belafonte

1961

BEST COUNTRY & WESTERN RECORDING
"Big Bad John"—Jimmy Dean

BEST FOLK RECORDING
"Belafonte Folk Singers at Home and Abroad"—Belafonte Folk Singers

1962

BEST PERFORMANCE BY A VOCAL GROUP
"If I Had a Hammer"—Peter, Paul and Mary

BEST PERFORMANCE BY A CHORUS
"Presenting the New Christy Minstrels"—The New Christy Minstrels

BEST COUNTRY & WESTERN RECORDING
"Funny Way of Laughin' "—Burl Ives

BEST FOLK RECORDING
"If I Had a Hammer"—Peter, Paul and Mary

1963

BEST PERFORMANCE BY A VOCAL GROUP
"Blowin' in the Wind"—Peter, Paul and Mary

BEST COUNTRY & WESTERN RECORDING
"Detroit City"—Bobby Bare

BEST FOLK RECORDING
"Blowin' in the Wind"—Peter, Paul and Mary

1964

BEST FOLK RECORDING
"We'll Sing in the Sunshine"—Gale Garnett

BEST GOSPEL OR OTHER RELIGIOUS RECORDING (MUSICAL)
"Great Gospel Songs"—Tennessee Ernie Ford

BEST COUNTRY & WESTERN SINGLE
"Dang Me"—Roger Miller—Jerry Kennedy, A & R Producer

BEST COUNTRY & WESTERN ALBUM
"Dang Me/Chug-A-Lug"—Roger Miller—Jerry Kennedy, A & R Producer

BEST COUNTRY & WESTERN VOCAL PERFORMANCE—FEMALE
"Here Comes My Baby" (single)—Dottie West

BEST COUNTRY & WESTERN VOCAL PERFORMANCE—MALE
"Dang Me" (single)—Roger Miller

BEST COUNTRY & WESTERN SONG
"Dang Me"—Roger Miller, Composer

BEST NEW COUNTRY & WESTERN ARTIST OF 1964
Roger Miller

1965

BEST CONTEMPORARY (R & R) RECORDING
"King of the Road"—Roger Miller (Smash)

BEST CONTEMPORARY (R & R) VOCAL PERFORMANCE—MALE
(SINGLE RECORDS)
"King of the Road"—Roger Miller (Smash)

BEST CONTEMPORARY (R & R) GROUP PERFORMANCE—VOCAL OR
INSTRUMENTAL (SINGLE RECORDS)
"Flowers on the Wall"—Statler Brothers (Columbia)

BEST FOLK RECORDING
"An Evening with Belafonte/Makeba"—Harry Belafonte and Miriam
Makeba (RCA)

BEST GOSPEL OR OTHER RELIGIOUS RECORDING (MUSICAL)
"Southland Favorites"—George Beverly Shea and Anita Kerr Singers
(RCA)

BEST COUNTRY & WESTERN RECORDING—SINGLE (AWARD TO
ARTIST, PLAQUE TO A & R PRODUCER)
"King of the Road"—Roger Miller—Jerry Kennedy, A & R Producer
(Smash)

BEST COUNTRY & WESTERN RECORDING—ALBUM (AWARD TO ARTIST, PLAQUE TO A & R PRODUCER)
"THE RETURN OF ROGER MILLER"—Roger Miller—Jerry Kennedy, A & R Producer (Smash)

BEST COUNTRY & WESTERN VOCAL PERFORMANCE—FEMALE
"QUEEN OF THE HOUSE"—Jody Miller (Capitol)

BEST COUNTRY & WESTERN VOCAL PERFORMANCE—MALE
"KING OF THE ROAD"—Roger Miller (Smash)

BEST COUNTRY & WESTERN SONG (SONGWRITER'S AWARD)
"KING OF THE ROAD"—Roger Miller, Songwriter (Smash)

BEST NEW COUNTRY & WESTERN ARTIST
THE STATLER BROTHERS (Columbia)

1966

BEST PERFORMANCE BY A VOCAL GROUP
"A MAN AND A WOMAN"—Anita Kerr Singers (Warner Bros.)

BEST FOLK RECORDING (AWARD TO ARTIST, PLAQUE TO A & R PRODUCER)
"BLUES IN THE STREET"—Cortelia Clark—Felton Jarvis, A & R Producer (RCA)

BEST SACRED RECORDING (MUSICAL, NON-CLASSICAL) (AWARD TO ARTIST, PLAQUE TO A & R PRODUCER)
"GRAND OLD GOSPEL"—Porter Wagoner & The Blackwood Brothers—Chet Atkins, A & R Producer (RCA)

BEST COUNTRY & WESTERN RECORDING (AWARD TO ARTIST, PLAQUE TO A & R PRODUCER)
"ALMOST PERSUADED"—David Houston—Billy Sherrill, A & R Producer (Epic)

BEST COUNTRY & WESTERN VOCAL PERFORMANCE—FEMALE
"DON'T TOUCH ME" (Single)—Jeanie Seely (Monument)

BEST COUNTRY & WESTERN VOCAL PERFORMANCE—MALE
"ALMOST PERSUADED" (Single)—David Houston (Epic)

BEST COUNTRY & WESTERN SONG (SONGWRITER'S AWARD)
"ALMOST PERSUADED"—Billy Sherrill, Glenn Sutton, Songwriters (Epic)

BEST ALBUM COVER, PHOTOGRAPHY (AWARD TO ART DIRECTOR & PHOTOGRAPHER)
"CONFESSIONS OF A BROKEN MAN"—Porter Wagoner—Robert Jones, Art Director—Les Leverette, Photographer (RCA)

1967

BEST VOCAL PERFORMANCE—FEMALE
"ODE TO BILLIE JOE" (Single)—Bobbie Gentry (Capitol)

BEST VOCAL PERFORMANCE—MALE
"BY THE TIME I GET TO PHOENIX" (Single)—Glen Campbell (Capitol)

BEST INSTRUMENTAL PERFORMANCE
"CHET ATKINS PICKS THE BEST"—Chet Atkins (RCA)

BEST NEW ARTIST
BOBBIE GENTRY (Capitol)

BEST CONTEMPORARY FEMALE SOLO VOCAL PERFORMANCE
"ODE TO BILLIE JOE"—Bobbie Gentry (Capitol)

BEST CONTEMPORARY MALE SOLO VOCAL PERFORMANCE
"BY THE TIME I GET TO PHOENIX"—Glen Campbell (Capitol)

BEST SACRED PERFORMANCE
"HOW GREAT THOU ART"—Elvis Presley (RCA)

BEST GOSPEL PERFORMANCE
"MORE GRAND OLD GOSPEL"—Porter Wagoner & The Blackwood Brothers Quartet (RCA)

BEST FOLK PERFORMANCE
"GENTLE ON MY MIND"—John Hartford (RCA)

BEST COUNTRY & WESTERN RECORDING
"GENTLE ON MY MIND"—Glen Campbell—Al DeLory, A & R (Capitol)

BEST COUNTRY & WESTERN SOLO VOCAL PERFORMANCE—FEMALE
"I DON'T WANNA PLAY HOUSE"—Tammy Wynette (Epic)

BEST COUNTRY & WESTERN SOLO VOCAL PERFORMANCE—MALE
"GENTLE ON MY MIND"—Glen Campbell (Capitol)

BEST COUNTRY & WESTERN PERFORMANCE—DUET, TRIO OR GROUP (VOCAL OR INSTRUMENTAL)
"JACKSON"—Johnny Cash, June Carter (Columbia)

BEST COUNTRY & WESTERN SONG
"GENTLE ON MY MIND"—John Hartford, Songwriter (RCA) (Publisher, Glaser Brothers)

BEST ARRANGEMENT ACCOMPANYING VOCALIST(S) OR INSTRU-MENTALIST(S) (THIS IS AN ARRANGER'S AWARD)
"ODE TO BILLIE JOE"—Bobbie Gentry—Jimmie Haskell, Arranger (Capitol)

BEST ALBUM COVER—PHOTOGRAPHY
"BOB DYLAN'S GREATEST HITS"—Bob Dylan—John Berg and Bob Cato, Art Directors—Roland Scherman, Photographer (Columbia)

1968

ALBUM OF THE YEAR—(AWARDS TO THE ARTIST AND A & R PRO-
  DUCER)
  "By the Time I Get to Phoenix"—Glen Campbell—Al DeLory, Producer
  (Capitol)

SONG OF THE YEAR (SONGWRITERS' AWARD)
  "Little Green Apples"—Bobby Russell (Columbia) (Publisher, Russell-
  Cason Music, Inc.)

BEST ENGINEERING (OTHER THAN CLASSICAL) (ENGINEER'S
  AWARD)
  "Wichita Lineman"—Glen Campbell—Joe Polito, Hugh Davies, Engineers
  (Capitol)

BEST ALBUM NOTES (ANNOTATOR'S AWARD)
  "Johnny Cash at Folsom Prison"—Johnny Cash, Annotator (Columbia)

BEST VOCAL PERFORMANCE—FEMALE
  "Harper Valley P.T.A."—Jeannie C. Riley (Plantation)

BEST VOCAL PERFORMANCE—MALE
  "Folsom Prison Blues"—Johnny Cash (Columbia)

BEST PERFORMANCE, DUO OR GROUP—VOCAL OR INSTRUMENTAL
  "Foggy Mountain Breakdown"—Flatt & Scruggs (Columbia)

BEST SONG (SONGWRITERS' AWARD)
  "Little Green Apples"—Bobby Russell, Songwriter (Smash) (Publisher,
  Russell-Cason Music)

BEST FOLK PERFORMANCE
  "Both Sides Now"—Judy Collins (Elektra)

Record Industry Association of America, Inc.

Gold Record Awards*

Date Awarded	Company	Title	Artist
1958			
Aug. 11	RCA Victor	Hard Headed Woman(S)	Elvis Presley
1959			
Jan. 21	Capitol	Tom Dooley(S)**	Kingston Trio
Feb. 20	Capitol	Hymns	Ernie Ford
1960			
Feb. 17	RCA Victor	Elvis	Elvis Presley
April 18	Capitol	Kingston Trio at Large	Kingston Trio
April 18	Capitol	Kingston Trio	Kingston Trio
Oct. 24	Capitol	Here We Go Again	Kingston Trio
Oct. 24	Capitol	From the hungry i	Kingston Trio
1961			
June 22	Capitol	Sold Out	Kingston Trio
Oct. 10	Capitol	Spirituals	Ernie Ford
Oct. 17	RCA Victor	Elvis' Golden Records	Elvis Presley
Oct. 16	RCA Victor	Belafonte at Carnegie Hall	Harry Belafonte
Dec. 14	Columbia	Big Bad John(S)	Jimmy Dean
Dec. 21	RCA Victor	Blue Hawaii	Elvis Presley
1962			
March 12	Capitol	Star Carol	Ernie Ford
March 22	Capitol	Nearer the Cross	Ernie Ford
March 30	RCA Victor	Can't Help Falling in Love (S)	Elvis Presley

* Folk, country and western field only.
** (S) indicates a single record as opposed to an album.

Gold Record Awards (continued)

Date Awarded	Company	Title	Artist
June 27	Capitol	String Along	Kingston Trio
July 19	ABC-Paramount	I Can't Stop Loving You (S)	Ray Charles
July 19	ABC-Paramount	Modern Sounds in Country & Western Music	Ray Charles
Dec. 10	Warner Bros.	Peter, Paul and Mary	Peter, Paul and Mary
Dec. 10	Warner Bros.	My Son the Folk Singer	Allan Sherman
1963			
March 12	RCA Victor	Calypso	Harry Belafonte
March 12	RCA Victor	G. I. Blues	Elvis Presley
Aug. 13	RCA Victor	Elvis' Christmas Album	Elvis Presley
Aug. 13	RCA Victor	Girls, Girls, Girls	Elvis Presley
Aug. 13	RCA Victor	Belafonte Returns to Carnegie Hall	Harry Belafonte
Aug. 13	RCA Victor	Belafonte	Harry Belafonte
Aug. 23	RCA Victor	Jump-Up Calypso	Harry Belafonte
Aug. 27	Warner Bros.	Moving	Peter, Paul and Mary
Nov. 13	Warner Bros.	In the Wind	Peter, Paul and Mary
1964			
Sept. 4	Capitol	The Best of the Kingston Trio	Kingston Trio
Oct. 16	Columbia	Ramblin'	New Christy Minstrels
Oct. 30	Monument	Oh, Pretty Woman(S)	Roy Orbison
Nov. 2	Columbia	Johnny Horton's Greatest Hits	Johnny Horton
1965			
Jan. 21	Warner Bros.	Peter, Paul and Mary in Concert	Peter, Paul and Mary
Feb. 11	Columbia	Ring of Fire	Johnny Cash
May 19	Smash	King of the Road (S)	Roger Miller
Sept. 1	Smash	Return of Roger Miller	Roger Miller
Sept. 21	Columbia	Gunfire Ballads & Trail Songs	Marty Robbins
1966			
Jan. 29	Vanguard	Joan Baez	Joan Baez
Jan. 29	Vanguard	Joan Baez, Vol. 2	Joan Baez

Gold Record Awards (continued)

Date Awarded	Company	Title	Artist
Jan. 29	Vanguard	Joan Baez in Concert	Joan Baez
Feb. 11	Smash	Golden Hits	Roger Miller
Feb. 14	Columbia	Sounds of Silence(S)	Simon & Garfunkel
March 24	Monument	Roy Orbison's Greatest Hits	Roy Orbison
May 12	RCA Victor	My World	Eddy Arnold
July 20	RCA Victor	The Best of Jim Reeves	Jim Reeves
Aug. 4	Smash	Dang Me	Roger Miller
Aug. 16	Mercury	Think Ethnic	Smothers Brothers
Nov. 1	RCA Victor	Elvis Presley	Elvis Presley
Nov. 1	RCA Victor	Elvis' Golden Records, Vol. 2	Elvis Presley
Nov. 1	RCA Victor	Elvis' Golden Records, Vol. 3	Elvis Presley
Dec. 20	Columbia	Battle of New Orleans (S)	Johnny Horton
1967			
Jan. 19	Epic	Mellow Yellow(S)	Donovan
Feb. 7	Monument	Yakety Sax	Boots Randolph
Feb. 22	Mercury	The Two Sides of the Smothers Brothers	Smothers Brothers
April 10	RCA Victor	An Evening with Belafonte	Harry Belafonte
July 6	Columbia	Parsley, Sage, Rosemary & Thyme	Simon & Garfunkel
July 14	Columbia	I Walk the Line	Johnny Cash
Aug. 14	Capitol	Georgy Girl(S)	The Seekers
Aug. 25	Columbia	Sounds of Silence	Simon & Garfunkel
Aug. 25	Columbia	Blonde on Blonde	Bob Dylan
Aug. 25	Columbia	Highway 61	Bob Dylan
Aug. 25	Columbia	Bringing It All Back Home	Bob Dylan
Sept. 11	Capitol	Ode to Billie Joe(S)	Bobbie Gentry
Oct. 9	Capitol	Ode to Billie Joe	Bobbie Gentry
1968			
Jan. 5	Columbia	Jim Nabors Sings	Jim Nabors
Jan. 5	Columbia	Bob Dylan's Greatest Hits	Bob Dylan
Feb. 16	RCA Victor	How Great Thou Art	Elvis Presley
Feb. 26	RCA Victor	Distant Drums	Jim Reeves

Hall of Fame Members

1961 (limited to deceased)
JIMMIE RODGERS (September 8, 1897–May 26, 1933)
FRED ROSE (August 24, 1897–December 1, 1954)
HANK WILLIAMS (September 17, 1923–January 1, 1953)

1962
ROY ACUFF (September 15, 1903–)

1963
(no winner)

1964
TEX RITTER (January 12, 1906–)

1965
ERNEST TUBB (February 9, 1914–)

1966
EDDY ARNOLD (May 15, 1918–)
JAMES R. (JIM) DENNY (February 28, 1911–August 27, 1963)
JUDGE GEORGE DEWEY HAY (November 9, 1895–May 9, 1968)
UNCLE DAVE MACON (October 7, 1870–March 22, 1952)

1967
RED FOLEY (June 17, 1910–September 19, 1968)
J. L. (JOE) FRANK (April 15, 1900–May 4, 1952)
JIM REEVES (August 20, 1924–July 31, 1964)
STEVE SHOLES (February 12, 1911–April 22, 1968)

1968
BOB WILLS (March 6, 1905–)

Country Music Association Annual Awards

1967

Entertainer of the Year	Eddy Arnold
Single of the Year	"There Goes My Everything"
Album of the Year	"There Goes My Everything"
Song of the Year	"There Goes My Everything"
Male Vocalist of the Year	Jack Greene
Female Vocalist of the Year	Loretta Lynn
Vocal Group of the Year	Stoneman Family
Instrumental Group or Band of the Year	Buck Owens Buckaroos
Instrumentalist of the Year	Chet Atkins
Comedian of the Year	Don Bowman

Second Awards—1968

Entertainer of the Year	Glen Campbell
Single of the Year	"Harper Valley P.T.A."
Album of the Year	"Johnny Cash at Folsom Prison"
Song of the Year	"Honey"
Male Vocalist of the Year	Glen Campbell
Female Vocalist of the Year	Tammy Wynettte
Vocal Group of the Year	Porter Wagoner and Dolly Parton
Instrumental Group or Band of the Year	Buck Owens Buckaroos
Instrumentalist of the Year	Chet Atkins
Comedian of the Year	Ben Colder

Academy of Country and Western Music Awards

1965

Man of the Year	Roger Miller
Top Male Vocalist	Buck Owens
Top Female Vocalist	Bonnie Owens
Best Vocal Group	Merle Haggard and Bonnie Owens
Best Band Leader	Buck Owens
Most Promising Male Vocalist	Merle Haggard
Most Promising Female Vocalist	Kaye Adams
Best Songwriter	Roger Miller
Best TV Personality	Billy Mize
Best Radio Personality	Biff Collie
Best Producer/A&R Man	Ken Nelson
Best Music Publisher	Central Songs, Inc.
Best Nightclub	Palomino Club (Los Angeles)
Best Talent Management	Jack McFadden
Best Publication	Billboard

Sidemen:

Best Steel Guitar	Red Rhodes
Best Fiddle	Billy Armstrong
Best Lead Guitar	Phil Baugh
Best Bass	Bob Morris
Best Piano	Billy Liebert
Best Drums	Muddy Berry

1966

Man of the Year*	Dean Martin
Top Male Vocalist	Merle Haggard
Top Female Vocalist	Bonnie Guitar
Top Vocal Group	Bonnie Owens and Merle Haggard
Band Leader/Band	Buck Owens Buckaroos
Most Promising Male Vocalist	Billie Mize
Most Promising Female Vocalist	Cathy Taylor
Most Promising Vocal Group	Bob Morris and Faye Hardin
Best TV Personality	Billy Mize
Best Radio Personality (tie)	Biff Collie/Bob Kingsley
Best Producer/A&R Man	Ken Nelson
Best Music Publisher	Central Songs, Inc.
Best Country Nightclub	Palomino Club
Best Talent Management/Booking Agent	Jack McFadden
Song of the Year	"Apartment #9" (Bobby Austin/Fuzzy Owen/Johnny Paycheck)

Sidemen:

Lead Guitar	Jimmy Bryant
Steel Guitar (tie)	Tom Brumley/Ralph Mooney
Drums	Jerry Wiggins
Bass	Bob Morris
Fiddle	Billy Armstrong
Piano	Billy Liebert

* Award based on contributions to advancing country music.

1967

Man of the Year	Joey Bishop
Top Male Vocalist	Glen Campbell
Top Female Vocalist	Lynn Anderson
Top Vocal Group	Sons of the Pioneers
Top Duet	Merle Haggard/Bonnie Owens
Band Leader/Band	Bucky Owens Buckaroos
Most Promising Male Vocalist	Jerry Inman
Most Promising Female Vocalist	Bobbie Gentry
Best TV Personality	Billy Mize
Best Radio Personality	Bob Kingsley
Best Country Nightclub	Palomino Club
Song of the Year	"It's Such a Pretty World Today" (Dale Noe/Freeway Music)
Album of the Year *and* Single Record of the Year	"Gentle on My Mind" (Glen Campbell/ A&R: Al DeLorey)

Sidemen:

Lead Guitar	Jimmy Bryant
Steel Guitar	Red Rhodes
Drums	Pee Wee Adams
Bass	Red Wooten
Fiddle	Billy Armstrong
Piano	Earl Ball

Discography

Discography

The goal of this Discography is not to present an exhaustive survey, but to list the most popular or the most representative long-play albums. All of the records listed were available from dealers as of late 1968.

When two numbers are given or where a number or letter precedes the main number [*e.g.*: (7), (S), (D)], the record is available in monaural and stereo or in monaural and electronically reprocessed. The letter "e" following some numbers also indicates the record has been electronically reprocessed to achieve a stereo effect.

Record company abbreviations: Arc Folk (Archive of Folk Music), Arhoo (Arhoolie), Audio Fi (Audio Fidelity), Blues (Bluesway), Buena (Buena Vista), Caed (Caedmon), Cam (Camden), Cap (Capitol), Col (Columbia), Dec (Decca), Elek (Elektra), Fan (Fantasy), Folk Leg (Folk Legacy), Folk (Folkways/Scholastic), GTJ (Good Time Jazz, Ham (Hamilton), Har (Harmony), Heir (Heirloom), Hick (Hickory), Imper (Imperial), Int (International), Lib, (Liberty), Litt (Little Darlin'), Mer (Mercury), Mon (Monitor), Monu (Monument), Musi (Musicor), Nash (Nashville), Pick (Pickwick), Prest (Prestige), RCA (RCA Victor), Riv (Riverside), Rou (Roulette), Sun (Sunset), Tow (Tower), Trad (Tradition), U Artists (United Artists), Van (Vanguard), Verve/Fore (Verve/Forecast), Voc (Vocalion), War (Warner Brothers).

Performers

ACUFF, ROY   Cap (D)T-1870 "Best of Roy Acuff." Hick 109 "King of Country Music." Hick 115 "American Folk Songs." Col HL-7082 "Great Speckled Bird and Other Favorites."

ALLEN, REX   Dec 8776, 78776 "Mister Cowboy." Buena 3307 "16 Favorite Songs." Mer 12324/16324 "Sings and Tells Tales."

ALMANAC SINGERS   War (S) 1330 "Almanac Singers."

ANDERSON, BILL   Dec (7) 4427 "Still." Dec (7) 4646 "From This Pen." Dec (7) 4471 "I Love You Drops."

ANGLIN, EDDY   (*See* Johnnie and Jack)

ARNOLD, EDDY   RCA LPM/LSP 1224 (e) "Any Time." RCA LPM/LSP 3565 "Best of Eddy Arnold." RCA LPM/LSP 3869 "Turn The World Around."

ASHWORTH, ERNIE   Hick 118 "Talk Back Trembling Lips."

ATCHER, BOB   Col CL-2232, CS-9032 "Bob Atcher, Dean of Cowboy Singers." Har HL-7313 "Bob Atcher's Best Early American Folk Songs."

ATKINS, CHET   RCA LPM/LSP 1090 (e) "Session with Chet Atkins." RCA LPM/LSP 2783 "Guitar Country." RCA LPM/LSP 3429 "More of That Guitar Country."

AUTRY, GENE   RCA LPM/LSP 2623 "Gene Autry's Golden Hits." Har 7332 "Gene Autry's Great Hits." Col CL-1575 "Gene Autry's Greatest Hits."

BAEZ, JOAN   Van 9112/2122 "In Concert." Van 9078, 9074/2077, 2097 "Joan Baez" (2 records). Squire (S)33001 "Best of Joan Baez."

BARE, BOBBY   RCA LPM/LSP "Detroit City and Other Hits." RCA LPM/LSP "500 Miles Away from Home." RCA LPM/LSP 3618 "Streets of Baltimore."

BARKER, HORTON   Folk 2362 "Horton Barker."

BEE, MOLLY   MGM E/SE-4423 "Swingin' Country."

BEERS FAMILY   Col CL-2672/CS-9472 "Dumbarton's Drums." Col ML-6105/MS-6705 "Beers Family."

BELAFONTE, HARRY   RCA LPM/LSP 1248 (e) "Calypso." RCA LPM/LSP, RCA LOC/LSO 6006 "Belafonte at Carnegie Hall." RCA LOC/LSO 6007 "Belafonte Returns to Carnegie Hall."

BELEW, CARL   RCA LPM/LSP-3919 "Twelve Shades of Carl Belew." Voc (7) 3774 "Carl Belew." Pick (S)6013 "Another Lonely Night."

BIBB, LEON   Lib 3327/7327 "In Concert." Van 9058 "Tol' My Captain." Van 9041/2042 "Folk Songs."

[378]

BIKEL, THEODORE Elek (7)250 "Folksinger's Choice." Elek (7)230 "On Tour." Elek (7)225 "Best of Theodore Bikel."

BLUE SKY BOYS Starday 269 "Precious Moments." Cam 797 "Blue Sky Boys." Starday 257 "Together Again!"

BOGGS, DOCK Folk 2351 "Dock Boggs." Verve/Fore (S)9025 "Legendary Dock Boggs." Folk 2132, 2392 "Interview" (w. Mike Seeger—Volumes 1 & 2).

BOND, JOHNNY Star (S)147 "Johnny Bond." Star 227 "Songs That Made Him Famous." Har 7308 "Best of Johnny Bond."

BONYUN, BILL Heir AHLP-1 "Songs of Yankee Whaling." Heir 500 "Yankee Legend."

BOWES, MARGIE Dec (7)4816 "Margie Bowes Sings."

BOWMAN, DON RCA LPM/LSP 2831 "Our Man in Trouble." RCA LPM/LSP 3345 "Fresh from the Funny Farm." RCA LPM/LSP 3920 "Funny Folk Flops."

BRAND, OSCAR Trad 1053/2053 "Best of Oscar Brand." Audio Fi 1806, 1824, 1847, 1906/5847 "Bawdy Songs and Backroom Ballads" (4 records). Audio Fi 1971/5971 "Sing-a-Long."

BRITT, ELTON RCA LPM/LSP 1288 "Elton Britt Yodel Songs." RCA LPM 2669 "Best of Britt." ABC (S)521 "Singing Hills."

BROONZY, BIG BILL Arc Folk 213 "Big Bill Broonzy." Folk 3586 "Songs and Story of Big Bill Broonzy." Folk 2326 "Big Bill Broonzy Sings Country Blues."

BROWN, JIM RCA LPM/LSP 3569 "Alone with You." RCA LPM/LSP 3744 "Just Jim." RCA LPM/LSP 3853 "Gems by Jim."

BROWNS, THE RCA LPM/LSP 2144 "Sweet Sounds by the Browns." RCA LPM/LSP 2174 "Town And Country." RCA LPM/LSP 3561 (e) "Best of the Browns."

BURGESS, WILMA Dec (7)4935 "Tear Time." Dec (7)4852 "Misty Blue." Dec (7)4788 "Don't Touch Me."

BUTLER, CARL & PEARL Har HL-7385/HS-11185 "Great Carl Butler Sings." Col CL-2308/CS-9108 "Old and the New." Col CL-2640/CS-9440 "Avenue of Prayer."

CAGLE, BUDDY Imper 9361/12361 "Longtime Traveling." Imper 9348/12348 "Mi Casa, Tu Casa." Imper 9318/12318 "Way You Like It."

CAMPBELL, ARCHIE RCA LPM/LSP 3504 "Have a Laugh on Me." RCA LPM/LSP 3699 "Cockfight And Other Tall Tales." RCA LPM/LSP 3892 "The Golden Years."

CANSLER, LOMAN Folk 5324 "Missouri Songs."

CARAWAN, GUY Folk 3544, 3548, 3552 "Guy Carawan" (3 records).

CARLISLE, BILL Hick (S)129 "Best of Bill Carlisle."

CARSON, MARTHA Cam CAS906 "Martha Carson Sings." Cap T-1507 "Satisfied." Cap T-1607 "Talk with the Lord."

CARTER FAMILY RCA LPM 2772 " 'Mid the Green Fields of Virginia." Col HL7422 "Country Sounds of the Original Carter Family." Col HL7396 "Great Sacred Songs." Cam CAL 586 "Original and Great Carter Family."

CARTER, JUNE Col CL-2728/CS-9528 "Carryin' On" (w. Johnny Cash).

CARTER, MOTHER MAYBELLE Col 2475/CS-9275 "Living Legend." Kapp 1413/3413 "Queen of the Auto-Harp." Smash 27041/67041 "Mother Maybelle."

CARTER, WILF ["MONTANA SLIM"]   Cam CAL/CAS (e) 2171 "No Letter Today." Cam (S)847 "32 Wonderful Years." Starday 300 "Living Legend."

CASH, JOHNNY   Col CL-2053/CS-8853 "Ring of Fire." Col CL-2190/CS-8990 "I Walk the Line." Col CL-1253/CS-8122 "Fabulous Johnny Cash." Col CL-2678/CS-9478 "Johnny Cash's Greatest Hits."

CHANDLER, LEN   Col CL-2459/CS-9259 "To Be a Man."

CHARLES, ROOSEVELT   Van 9136 "Roosevelt Charles."

CLANCY BROTHERS & TOMMY MAKEM   Col CL-1950/CS-8750 "At Carnegie Hall." Col CL-2694/CS-9494 "In Concert." Col CL-2477/CS-9277 "Isn't It Grand Boys?"

CLAYTON, PAUL   Mon (1)8017 "Folk Singer." Trad 1005 "Days of Moby Dick." Folk 2106 "Bay State Ballads."

CLINE, PATSY   Dec (7)4854 "Greatest Hits." Dec (7)4586 "That's How a Heartache Begins." Dec (7)4282 "Sentimentally Yours."

COCHRAN, HANK   RCA LPM/LSP 3303 "Hits from the Heart." RCA LPM/LSP 3431 "Going in Training."

COLLINS, JUDY   Elek (7)320 "In My Life." Elek (7)280 "Judy Collins in Concert." Elek (7)209 "Judy Collins."

COLLINS, TOMMY   Col CL-2510/CS-9310 "Dynamic Tommy Collins." Cap T-1196 "This Is Tommy Collins." Tow (b) T-5021 "Let's Live a Little."

COOPER, WILMA & STONEY   Har HL-7378/HS-11178 "Sunny Side of the Mountain."

COPAS, LLOYD "COWBOY"   Starday 144 "Songs That Made Him Famous." Starday SLP118 "All Time Country Music." Starday 234 "Unforgettable Cowboy Copas."

CRAMER, FLOYD   RCA LPM/LSP 2350 "Last Date." RCA LPM/LSP 3318 "Hits from the Country Hall of Fame." RCA LPM/LSP 2888 "Best of Floyd Cramer."

CURLESS, DICK   Tow (D)T-5025 "Dick Curless." Tow (D)T-5015 "Travelin' Man." Tow (D)T-5005 "Tombstone Every Mile."

DANE, BARBARA   Folk 2468 "Barbara Dane with the Chambers Brothers." Folk 2471 "Barbara Dane Sings the Blues."

DARLING, ERIK   Van 9131 "Train Time." Van 9099 "True Religion." Elek 154 "Erik Darling."

DAVIS, JIMMIE   Dec (7)4495 "Jimmie Davis Sings." Dec (7)8896 "You Are My Sunshine." Dec (7)8953 "Suppertime." Dec (7)4432 "Highway to Heaven."

DAVIS, SKEETER   RCA LPM/LSP 2197 "I'll Sing You a Song." RCA LPM/LSP 2699 "The End of the World." RCA LPM/LSP 3374 "Best of Skeeter Davis."

DEAN, JIMMY   Col CL-2485/CS-9285 "Jimmy Dean's Greatest Hits." Col CL-1735/CS-8535 "Big Bad John." Starday 235 "Bummin' Around."

DELMORE BROTHERS   Some performances included in RCA LPM-6015 "Stars of The Grand Ole Opry."

DEXTER, AL   Har 7293 "Pistol Packin' Mama."

DICKENS, LITTLE JIMMY   Col CL-2551/CS-9351 "Little Jimmy Dickens' Greatest Hits." Col CL-2442/CS-9242 "Bird of Paradise." Har 7311 "Best of Little Jimmy Dickens."

DILLARDS, THE   Elek (7)265 "Live!" Elek (7)232 "Bluegrass." Elek (7) "Pickin' & Fiddlin'."

DIXON, DORSEY   Test 3301 "Dorsey Dixon."

DOLLAR, JOHNNY   Date 3009/4009 "Johnny Dollar."

DONOVAN   Epic LZN-6071/8ZN-171 "Gift from a Flower to a Garden." Epic LN-24239/BN-26239 "Mellow Yellow." Epic LN-24217/BN-26217 "Sunshine Superman." Hick (5)123 "Catch the Wind."

DRAKE, PETE   Smash 27064/67064 "Talking Steel & Singing Strings." Hill (S) 6052 "Are You Sincere?" Starday 180 "Steel Guitar."

DRIFTWOOD, JIMMY   Monu (1)8006 "Voice of the People." Monu (1)8043 "Best of Jimmy Driftwood." Monu (1)8019 "Down in the Arkansas."

DRUSKY, ROY   Dec (7)4340 "It's My Way." Mer MG21052/SR61052 "Roy Drusky's Greatest Hits." Mer MG12326/SR16326 "Songs of the Cities."

DUDLEY, DAVE   Mer 21113/61113 "My Kind of Life." Mer 21046/61046 "Dave Dudley's Greatest Hits." Mer 21028/61028 "Truck Drivin' Son of a Gun."

DYER-BENNET, RICHARD   Dyer-Bennet 1/4 "Richard Dyer-Bennet" (4 records). Dec (7)9102 "Folk Songs & Ballads." Stinson 2 "20th Century Minstrel." Dyer-Bennet 12 "Of Ships & Seafaring Men."

DYLAN, BOB   Col CL-1986/CS-8786 "Freewheelin' Bob Dylan." Col CL-2105/CS-8905 "Times They Are A-Changin'." Col CL-2389/CS-9189 "Highway 61 Revisited." Col KCL-2663/KCS-9463 "Bob Dylan's Greatest Hits."

ELIRAN, RON   Int (S)13063 "Ladino." Int (S)13054 "New Sounds of Israel."

ELLIOTT, JACK   Prest 7453 "Songs of Woody Guthrie." Arc Folk (S)210 "Jack Elliott." Prest 14014 "Ramblin' Jack Elliott."

ENGLISH, LOGAN   Mon (S)388 "American Ballads." Folk 525S "Days of '49." Folk 2136 (10″) "Kentucky Ballads."

EVANS, DALE   (See Roy Rogers)

EVERLY BROTHERS   War (S)513 "Great Country Hits." War (S)1471 "Golden Hits." War (S)1554 "Very Best."

FLATT & SCRUGGS   Col CL-2570/CS-9370 "Greatest Hits." Col CL-2045/CS-8845 "Flatt & Scruggs at Carnegie Hall." Col CL-1564/CS-8364 "Foggy Mountain Banjo." Har 7340 "Great Original Recordings."

FOLEY, RED   Voc (7)1351 "Red Foley." Dec (7)4107 "Golden Favorites." Dec DX (S)-(7)177 "Red Foley Story" (2 records).

FORD, TENNESSEE ERNIE   Cap (D)T-700 "This Lusty Land." Cap T-1380 "16 Tons." Cap (S)T-1005 "Nearer the Cross." Cap (S)T-756 "Hymns."

FRIZZELL, LEFTY   Col CL-2488/CS-9288 "Lefty Frizzell's Greatest Hits." Har 7386/11186 "Great Sound." Col CL-1342 "One and Only Lefty Frizzell."

FULLER, JESSE   Prest (S)7368 "Jesse Fuller Favorites." GTJ 12051/10051 "San Francisco Bay Blues." GTJ 12039/10039 "Lone Cat."

GATEWAY SINGERS, THE   Dec 8742 "Gateway Singers in Hi Fi." Dec 8671 "Gateway Singers at the hungry i."

GERLACH, FRED   Folk 3529 "12 String Guitar."

GIBSON, BOB   Elek (7)239 "Where I'm Bound." Elek (7)207 "Bob Gibson and Bob Camp." Stinson 76 "Ohio Folksongs."

GIBSON, DON   RCA LPM 1743 "Oh Lonesome Me." RCA LPM/LSP 3376 "Best of Don Gibson." RCA LPM/LSP 3594 "Don Gibson with Spanish Guitars."

GILKYSON, TERRY   Kapp 1327/3327 "Wild Goose." Kapp 1216/3216 "Remember the Alamo."

GRAMMER, BILLY   Epic LN-24233/BN-26233 "Sunday Guitar." Dec (7)4642 "Country Guitar." Mon (1)8039 "Travelin' On."

GREENBRIAR BOYS Van (7)9233 "Better Late Than Never." Van (7) 9159 "Ragged But Right." Van 9104 "Greenbriar Boys."

GUNNING, SARAH Folk-Leg Z "Sarah Ogan Gunning."

GUTHRIE, ARLO Reprise (S)6267 "Arlo Guthrie."

GUTHRIE, WOODY RCA LPU-502 "Dust Bowl Ballads." Elek 271/2 "Library of Congress Recordings" (3 records). Folk 2483/4 "Sings with Leadbelly and Others" (2 records).

HAGGARD, MERLE Cap (S)T-2789 "Branded Man." Cap (S)T-2585 "Swinging Doors." Cap (S)T-2373 "Strangers."

HALL, CONNIE Voc (7)3752 "Connie Hall."

HAMBLEN, STUART RCA LPM-1253 "It Is No Secret." Col CL-1588/CS-8388 "Spell of the Yukon."

HAMILTON, GEORGE, IV RCA LPM/LSP 3510 "Coast Country." RCA LPM/LSP 3601 "Steel Rail Blues." RCA LPM/LSP 3752 "Folk Country Classics."

HAMMOND, JOHN Van 9132, 2148 "John Hammond." Van 9153, 79153 "City Blues."

HARDEN TRIO Col CL-2506/CS-9306 "Tippy Toeing." Selections in Col CL-2590/CS-9390 "Welcome to Music City U.S.A."

HARTFORD, JOHN RCA LPM/LSP 3796 "Earth Words and Music." RCA LPM/LSP 3884 "Love Album."

HAWKINS, HAWKSHAW Cam CAL/CAS 931 (e) "Country Gentleman." Cam CAL/CAS 808 (e) "Hawkshaw Hawkins Sings." Har 7301/11044 "Hawkshaw Hawkins."

HELMS, BOBBY Har 7409/11209 "Fraulein." Kapp 1503/3505 "Sorry, My Name Isn't Fred." Dec ED2629 "Bobby Helms."

HESTER, CAROLYN Col CL-1796/CS-8596 "Carolyn Hester." Trad 1043 "Carolyn Hester."

HILL, GOLDIE Voc (7)3800 "Songs." Dec (7)4148 "Heartaches." Dec (7)4219 "According to My Heart."

HINTON, SAM Folk 2400 "The Songs of Men." Folk 2401 "Wandering Folk Song." Dec 8108 "Singing Across the Land."

HOLCOMB, ROSCOE Folk 2368 "Roscoe Holcomb." Folk 2363 "Kentucky and Virginia Traditional Ballads" (w. Ward).

HOMER & JETHRO RCA LPM/LSP 3474 (e) "Best of Homer and Jethro." RCA LPM/LSP 3673 "Wanted for Murder." RCA LPM/LSP 3822 "Nashville Cats."

HOOKER, JOHN LEE Blues (S)6002 "John Lee Hooker at Cafe au Go-Go." Atco 33-151 "Don't Turn Me from Your Door." Chess 1454 "John Lee Hooker Plays and Sings the Blues."

HOPKINS, SAM "LIGHTNIN'" Prest 7370 "My Life in the Blues" (2 records). Trad 1056/2056 "Best of Lightnin' Sam Hopkins." Arhoo 2007 "Early Recordings."

HORTON, JOHNNY Col CL-2299/CS-9099 "I Can't Forget You." Col CL-1596/CS-8396 "Johnny Horton's Greatest Hits." Col CL-1721/CS-8779 "Honky Tonk Man."

HOUSE, SON Verve/Fore 9035 "Blues from the Mississippi Delta." Col CL-2417/CS-2197 "Father." Folk 2467 "Mississippi Delta Blues."

HOUSTON, CISCO Van (7)3006 "Legendary Cisco Houston." Van 9089/2131 "Songs of Woody Guthrie." Folk 2480 "Songs of the Open Road."

HOUSTON, DAVID   Epic LN-24213/BN-26213 "Almost Persuaded." Epic LN-24112/ BN-26112 "New Voice from Nashville." Epic LN-24156/BN-26156 "Twelve Great Hits."

HOWARD, HARLAN   RCA LPM/LSP 3729 "Mr. Songwriter." RCA LPM/LSP 3886 "Down to Earth."

HOWARD, JAN   Dec (7)4931 "This Is Jan Howard." Dec (7)4793 "Evil on Your Mind."

HURT, JOHN   Van (7)9220 "Mississippi John Hurt."

HUSKY, FERLIN   Cap (S)T-1991 "Hits of Ferlin Husky." Cap T-1383 "Gone." Cap (D)T-1880 "Simon Crum."

IAN & SYLVIA   MGM (S)4388 "Lovin' Sound." Van (7) 9154 "Northern Journey." Van 9133/2149 "Four Strong Winds."

IVES, BURL   Dec (7)4850 "Greatest Hits." Dec (7)4279 "Funny Way of Laughin'." Dec DX(S)-(7)167 "Best of Burl Ives" (2 records). Stinson SLP-1 "Original Wayfaring Stranger."

JACKSON, AUNT MOLLY   Folk 5457 "Songs and Stories of Aunt Molly Jackson."

JACKSON, STONEWALL   Col CL-2509/CS-9309 "All's Fair in Love 'n' War." Col CL-2377/CS-9177 "Greatest Hits." Col CL-1391/CS-8186 "Stonewall Jackson."

JACKSON, WANDA   Cap (S)T-2030 "Songs of Wanda Jackson." Cap (S)T-1911 "Love Me Forever." Cap T-1041 "Day Dreaming."

JAMES, SKIP   Van (7)9219 "Skip James Today!" Melo 7321 "Skip James' Greatest."

JEAN, NORMA   RCA LPM/LSP 2961 "Let's Go All the Way." RCA LPM/LSP 3764 "Game of Triangles." RCA LPM/LSP 3836 "Jackson Ain't a Very Big Town."

JENNINGS, WAYLON   RCA LPM/LSP 3660 "Waylon Sings Ol' Harlan." RCA LPM/ LSP 3825 "Love of the Common People." RCA LPM/LSP 3918 "Hangin' On."

JIM & JESSE   Epic LN-24314/BN-26314 "Diesel on My Tail." Epic LN-24031/BN-26031 "Bluegrass Special." Epic LN-24074/BN-26074 "Bluegrass Classics."

JOHNNIE & JACK   Cam CAL/CAS 747(e) "Johnnie and Jack Sing." Cam CAL/CAS 822(e) "Sincerely." Dec (7)4308 "Smiles and Tears."

JONES, GEORGE   U Art 3532/6532 "Golden Hits." Musi 2060/3060 "New Hits— George Jones and the Jones Boys." Starday 150 "Greatest Hits." Nash 2035 "Why Baby Why."

JONES, MARSHALL LOUIS "GRANDPA"   Mon (I)8021 "Real Folk Songs." Dec 4364 "An Evening with Grandpa Jones." Mon 8013 "Rafters Ring."

JORDANAIRES, THE   Col CL-2458/CS-9258 "The Jordanaires."

JOURNEYMEN, THE   Cap (S)T-1951 "New Directions."

KAZEE, BUELL   Folk 3810 "Songs & Music of Buell Kazee."

KERR, ANITA   RCA LPM/LSC-2480 "Hit Sound." Dec 8647 "Four Voices in Hi Fi." War (S)1670 "The Sea."

KILGORE, MERLE   Mer 12316/13661 "Merle Kilgore."

KINCAID, BRADLEY   Bluebonnet 105, 107, 109, 112 "Mountain Ballads & Old Time Songs" (Volumes 1-4).

KING, CLAUDE   Col CL-2415/CS-9215 "Tiger Woman."

KING, FRANK PEEWEE   Cam CAL/CAS 876(e) "Country Barn Dance." Starday 284 "PeeWee King and Redd Stewart." Nash 2042 "Tennessee Waltz and Slowpoke."

KINGSTON TRIO   Cap (S)T-1705, 2280, 2614 "Best of the Kingston Trio" (3 records). Cap T-1107 "From the hungry i." Cap (S)T-2081 "Back in Town."

LA FARGE, PETER   Folk 2535 "On the Warpath." Folk 2533 "Peter La Farge Sings of the Cowboys." Folk 2532 "As Long as the Grass Shall Grow."

LEDBETTER, HUDDIE   Folk 2941/2 "Last Sessions" (4 records). Elek 301/2 "Library of Congress Recordings" (2 records). Cap T-1821 "Ledbetter's Best." RCA LPV-505 "Midnight Special."

LEHRER, TOM   Reprise (S)6199 "Tom Lehrer." Reprise (S)6216 "Songs by Tom Lehrer." Reprise (S)6179 "That Was the Year That Was."

LEWIS, JERRY LEE   Smash 27040/67040 "Jerry Lee Lewis." Smash 27063/67063 "Return of Rock." Smash 27071/67071 "Country Songs."

LIMELITERS, THE   RCA LPM/LSP 2889 "Best of the Limeliters." RCA LPM/LSP "Children's Eyes." Elek (7)180 "The Limeliters."

LOCKLIN, HANK   RCA LPM/LSP 2291(e) "Please Help Me, I'm Falling." RCA LPM/LSP 3559(e) "Best of Hank Locklin." RCA LPM/LSP 3770 "Send Me the Pillow You Dream On."

LOMAX, ALAN   Various albums (Col)—"Columbia World Library of Folk and Primitive Music": *e.g.* KL 213 "Bantu Music"; KL 214 "Folk Music from Japan"; KL 5174 "Folk Music of Southern Italy"; etc. Trad 1029 "Texas Folksongs."

LONZO & OSCAR   Starday 244 "Lonzo & Oscar." Pick (S)6021 "Country Comedy." Dec 4363 "Country Comedy Time."

LORD, BOBBY   Har HL-7322 "Bobby Lord's Best." Hick 126 "Bobby Lord Show."

LOUDERMILK, JOHN   RCA LPM/LSP 3497 "Sings a Bizarre Collection." RCA LPM/LSP 3807 "Suburban Attitudes in Country Verse."

LOUVIN BROTHERS   Cap T-1385 "My Baby's Gone." Cap T-769 "Tragic Songs of Life." Cap (S)T-1721 "Weapon of Prayer."

LOUVIN, CHARLIE   Cap (S)T-2689 "I'll Remember Always." Cap (S)T-2437 "Many Moods of Charlie Louvin." Cap (S)T-2482 "Lonesome Is Me."

LULU BELLE & SCOTTY   Starday 351 "Lulu Belle & Scotty." Starday 206 "Lulu Belle & Scotty."

LUMAN, BOB   Hick 124 "Bob Luman."

LUNSFORD, BASCOM   Folk 2040 (10″) "Smoky Mountain Ballads."

LYNN, JUDY   U Art 3461/6461 "Best of Judy Lynn." Musi 2096/3096 "Judy Lynn Show Plays Again." U Art. 3342/6342 "Most Promising."

LYNN, LORETTA   Dec (7)4842 "Don't Come Home A-Drinkin'." Dec (7)4620 "Songs from My Heart." Dec (7) 4783 "You Ain't Woman Enough."

MACCOLL, EWAN   Folk 8758 "Songs of Robert Burns." Folk 8757 "Scottish Songs." Trad 1015 "Classic Ballads" (w. Pete Seeger).

MACK, WARNER   Kapp 1255-79/3255-79 "Warner Mack" (2 records). Kapp 1440/3440 "Best of Warner Mack." Dec (7)4692 "Bridge Washed Out."

MACON, UNCLE DAVE   Dec 4760 "Uncle Dave Macon." Folk RF-51 "Uncle Dave Macon."

MADDOX, ROSE   Har HL-7312 "Rose Maddox's Best." Cap (S)T-1993 "Along With You." Cap (S)T-1312 "One Rose."

MAINER, J. E.   Arhoo 500 "J. E. Mainer and His Mountaineers."

MAKEBA, MIRIAM   RCA LPM/LSP 2267 "Miriam Makeba." RCA LPM/LSP 2845 "Voice of America." Reprise (S)C253 "In Concert."

MAPHIS, JOE & ROSE LEE Col HL-7180/HS-11032 "Hi Fi Holiday for Banjo." Starday 286 "Joe & Rose Lee Maphis."

MARAIS & MIRANDA Dec 9026/7 "In Person" (2 records). Dec 8791 "Wine of Gaul." Dec (7)8811 "Marais & Miranda Revisit South African Veldt."

McAULIFF, LEON Starday 171 "Western Swing." Cap (S)T-2016 "Dancinest Band." Dot 3689 "Golden Hits."

McCURDY, ED Trad 1051/2051 "Best of Ed McCurdy." Elek 205 "Treasure Chest" (2 records). Trad 1003 "Ballad Singer's Choice."

McGEE BROTHERS Folk 2379 "McGee Brothers and Arthur Smith." Folk FT 1007/FTS 31007 "Milk 'Em in the Evening Blues" (w. A. Smith).

McGHEE, BROWNIE Folk 2421/2 "Traditional Blues" (2 records). Fan 3254 "Sonny Terry & Brownie McGhee." Fan 3317 "Blues & Shouts" (w. Sonny Terry).

McKUEN, ROD RCA LPM/LSP 3508 "The Loner." RCA LPM/LSP 3786 "Through European Windows." RCA LPM/LSP 3863 "Listen to the Warm."

MILLER, JODY Cap (S)T-2446 "Great Hits of Buck Owens." Cap (S)T-2412 "Jody Miller."

MILLER, ROGER Cam CAL/CAS 851 "Roger Miller." Smash 27073/67073 "Golden Hits of Roger Miller." Smash 27075/67075 "Words and Music."

MITCHELL, PRISCILLA Mer 21078/61078 "Roy Drusky & Priscilla Mitchell."

MONROE, BILL Cam CAL-774 "Early Bluegrass Music—Monroe Brothers." Voc (7)3702 "Songs with the Bluegrass Boys." Dec (7)4382 "Bluegrass Special." Dec 4327 "Bill Monroe All Time Favorites."

MONTANA, PATSY Starday 376 "Sweetheart."

MONTGOMERY, MELBA Musi 2097/3097 "Hallelujah Road." U Art 3391/6391 "Being Lonely." U Art 3341/6341 "Melba Montgomery."

MORRISON, HAROLD Dec (7)4680 "Hoss."

MOSER, ARTUS Folk 2112 (10″) "North Carolina Ballads."

MULLICAN, MOON Starday 398 "Moon Mullican's Unforgettable Great Hits." Pick (S)6033 "Good Times."

NELSON, WILLIE RCA LPM/LSP 3418 "Country Willie—His Own Songs." RCA LPM/LSP 3538 "Country Favorites." RCA LPM/LSP-3659 "Concert."

NEW CHRISTY MINSTRELS Col CL-2479/CS-9279 "Greatest Hits." Col CL-2055/CS-8855 "Ramblin'." Col CL-1872/CS-8672 "Presenting the New Christy Minstrels."

NEW LOST CITY RAMBLERS Folk 2396/9 "New Lost City Ramblers" (4 records). Folk 2491 "Gone to the Country." Verve/Fore (S)3018 "Remembrances."

NEWMAN, JIMMY Dec (7)4398 "Folk Songs of the Bayou." Dec (7)4781 "Songs of Jimmy Newman." Dec (7)4221 "Jimmy Newman."

NILES, JOHN JACOB RCA LPU-513 "John Jacob Niles, Folk Balladeer." Trad 1055/2055 "Best of John Jacob Niles." Folk 2373 "Songs by John Jacob Niles." Trad 1046 "Ballads" (2 records).

NYE, HERMES Folk 5249 "War Ballads U.S.A." Folk 2037 (10″) "Anglo-American Folk Songs." Folk 2128 (10″) "Texas Folk Songs."

O'BRYANT, JOAN Folk 2338 "Ballads." Folk 2134 (10″) "Kansas Folk Songs."

OCHS, PHILIP DAVID A&M (4)133 "Pleasures of the Harbor." Elek (7)310 "In Concert." Elek (7)287 "I Ain't Marching Any More."

ODETTA   RCA LPM/LSP 2643 "Odetta Sings Folk Songs." Van (7)3003 "Odetta at Carnegie Hall." Trad 1025 "Odetta at the Gate of Horn."

OHRLIN, GLENN   Campus 301 "Glenn Ohrlin."

OKUN, MILT   Elek (7)182 "We Sing of the Sea." Stinson 82 "Adirondack Songs."

ORBISON, ROY   MGM (S)4322 "Orbison Way." Monu (1)8045 "Roy Orbison's Very Best." Monu (1)8000 "Roy Orbison's Greatest Hits."

OSBORNE BROTHERS   Dec (7)4903 "Osborne Brothers Modern Sounds." Dec (7) 4602 "Voices in Bluegrass." MGM 4018 "Bluegrass Music."

OWENS, BONNIE   Cap (S)T-2660 "All of Me." Cap (S)T-2453 "Between the Two of Us." Cap (S)T-2403 "Bonnie Owens."

OWENS, BUCK   Cap (S)T-2556 "Carnegie Hall Concert." Cap (S)T-2883 "Got a Tiger By the Tail." Cap (S)T-2105 "Best of Buck Owens." Starday (S)324 "Fabulous Sound of Buck Owens."

PALEY, TOM   Elek (7)295 "Tom Paley & Peggy Seeger." (*See also* New Lost City Ramblers)

PAXTON, TOM   Elek (7)317 "Outward Bound." Elek (7)298 "Ain't That News." Elek (7)277 "Tom Paxton."

PAYCHECK, JOHNNY   Litt 4001/8001 "Johnny Paycheck."

PAYNE, LEON   Starday 231, 236 "Leon Payne" (2 records).

PEARL, MINNIE   Sun 1148/1548 "Howdy!" Nash 2043 "Lookin' fer a Feller. Starday 224 "Cousin Minnie Pearl."

PERKINS, CARL   Col CS-8161 "The Big Hits."

PETER, PAUL & MARY   War (S)1700 "Album 1700." War (S)1507 "In the Wind." War (S)1473 "Moving."

PHILLIPS, BILL   Har HL-7309 "Bill Phillips' Best." Dec (7)4897 "Bill Phillips' Style." Dec (7)4792 "Put It Off Until Tomorrow."

PIERCE, WEBB   Dec DX(S)-(7)181 "Webb Pierce Story" (2 records). Dec (7) 4782 "Webb Pierce Choice." Dec (7)4110 "Golden Favorites."

PILLOW, RAY   Cap (S)T-2738 "Even When It's Bad." Cap (S)T-2417 "Ray Pillow."

PRESLEY, ELVIS   RCA LPM/LSP 1707(e), 2075(e), 2765, 3921 "Elvis' Gold Records" (Volumes 1-4).

PRICE, RAY   Col CL-1566/CS-8866 "Ray Price's Greatest Hits." Col CL-2670/ CS-9470 "More Ray Price's Greatest Hits." Col HL-7372/HS-11172 "Collectors' Choice."

PRIDE, COUNTRY CHARLEY   RCA LPM/LSP 3645 "Country Charlie Pride." RCA LPM/LSP 3775 "Pride of Country Music." RCA LPM/LSP 3895 "Country Way."

PROFFITT, FRANK   Folk 2360 "Frank Proffitt." Folk-Leg 1 "Trifling Woman."

RAINWATER, MARVIN   MGM 4046 "Marvin Rainwater."

REED, SUSAN   Elek 116, 126 "Susan Reed" (2 records).

REEVES, DEL   U Art 3571/6571 "Struttin' My Stuff." U Art 3488/6488 "Special Delivery." Pick (S)6029 "Mr. Country Music."

REEVES, JIM   RCA LPM/LSP 2890 "Best of Jim Reeves." RCA LPM/LSP 3482 "Best of Jim Reeves, Vol. II." RCA LPM/LSP 3709(e) "Yours Sincerely."

REYNOLDS, MALVINA   Col CL-2614/CS-9414 "Malvina Reynolds Sings the Truth." Folk 2524 "Malvina Reynolds."

RITCHIE FAMILY   Folk 2316 "Ritchie Family of Kentucky."

RITCHIE, JEAN   Folk 2301/2 "Child Ballads in America" (2 records). Folk 2427 "Precious Memories." Verve/Fore (S)9026 "Jean Ritchie and Doc Watson at Folk City."

RITTER, MAURICE WOODWARD "TEX"   Cap (S)T-2786 "Just Beyond the Moon." Cap (S)T-2595 "Best of Tex Ritter." Cap (D)T-1292 "Blood on the Saddle."

ROBBINS, MARTY   Col CL-2725/CS-9525 "Tonight Carmen." Col CL-1349/CS-8158 "Gunfighter Ballads & Trail Songs." Col CL-1325/CS-8639 "Marty's Greatest Hits." Col CL-1635/CS-8435 "More Greatest Hits."

ROBERTSON, ECK   Selection in RCA "Early American Rural String Bands."

ROBERTSON, WALT   Folk 2330 "Folk Songs." Folk 2046 (10") "American Northwest Ballads."

RODGERS, JIMMIE C.   RCA LPM 1232 "Never No Mo' Blues." RCA LPM 2112 "My Rough and Rowdy Ways." RCA LPM-2531 "Country Music Hall of Fame."

RODGERS, JIMMIE F.   Dot 3815/23815 "Golden Hits." A&M (4)130 "Child of Clay." Rou (S)25179 "15 Million Sellers."

ROGERS, ROY, & DALE EVANS   RCA LPM 1439 "Sweet Hour of Prayer."

ROOFTOP SINGERS   Van (7)9190 "Rainy River." Van (7)9134 "Good Time." Van 9123/2136 "Rooftop Singers."

RUBIN, RUTH   Folk 8740 "Concert." Int 13019 "Yiddish Folk Songs."

RUSH, TOM   Elek (7)308 "Take a Little Walk." Prest (S)7374 "Blues/Songs/Ballads." Elek (7)288 "Tom Rush."

SAINTE-MARIE, BUFFY   Van (7)9250 "Fire, Fleet, Candlelight." Van (7)9171 "Many a Mile." Van (7)9142 "Buffy Sainte-Marie."

SANDBURG, CARL   Caed 2025 "American Songbag" (2 records). Dec 9105 "Cowboy Songs." Lyr 66 "Great Carl Sandburg."

SEEGER, MIKE   Folk 5273 "Tipple, Loom & Rail." Van (7)9150 "Hello Stranger." Folk 2325 "Mike Seeger." (*See also* New Lost City Ramblers)

SEEGER, PEGGY   Prest 14016 "Best of Peggy Seeger." Folk 2049 (10") "Songs of Courting and Complaint." Folk 2005 "Three Sisters."

SEEGER, PETE   Col CL-2616/CS-9416 "Greatest Hits." Col CL-2503/CS-9303 "Dangerous Songs?" Cap (D)T-2718 "Freight Train." Folk 2412 "At Carnegie Hall."

SEEKERS, THE   Cap (D)T-2746 "Best of the Seekers." Cap (S)T-2431 "Georgy Girl." Cap (S)T-2369 "World of Our Own."

SHEPARD, JEAN   Cap (S)T-2765 "Yours Forever." Cap (S)T-2437 "I'll Take the Dog." Cap T-1253 "This Is Jean Shepard."

SIMON & GARFUNKEL   Col CL-2249/CS-9049 "Wednesday Morning: 3 A.M." Col CL-2469/CS-9269 "Sounds of Silence." Col CL-2563/CS-9363 "Parsley, Sage, Rosemary and Thyme."

SINGLETON, MARGIE   U Art 3459/6459 "Margie Singleton."

SKINNER, JIMMIE   Mer 12277/16277 "Country Blues." Dec 4132 "Jimmie Skinner."

SKY, PATRICK   Van (7)90207 "Harvest of Gentle Clang." Van (7)9179 "Patrick Sky."

SMITH, ARTHUR   Dot 3636/25636 "Arthur Smith's Great Hits." Ham (12)134 "Arthur Smith."

SMITH, CARL   Col CL-2610/CS-9410 "Carl Smith's Newest Hits." Col CL-1937/CS-8737 "Greatest Hits." Col HL-7310 "Carl Smith's Best."

[387]

SMITH, CONNIE RCA LPM/LSP 3341 "Connie Smith." RCA LPM/LSP 3444 "Cute 'n' Country." RCA LPM/LSP 3848 "Best of Connie Smith."

SMITH, HOBART Folk-Leg 17 "Hobart Smith."

SMOTHERS BROTHERS Mer 21089/61089 "Golden Hits." Mer 21051/61051 "Mom Always Liked You Best." Mer 20675/60675 "Two Sides of the Smothers Brothers."

SNOW, HANK RCA LPM/LSP 3478(e) "Best of Hank Snow." RCA LPM/LSP 6014(e) "This Is My Story." Cam CAL/CAS 836(e) "Old and Great Songs."

SONS OF THE PIONEERS RCA LPM/LSP 2118 "Cool Water." RCA LPM/LSP (e) 3476(e) "Best of the Sons of the Pioneers." RCA LPM/LSP 3714 "Campfire Favorites."

SOVINE, RED Dec (7)4736 "Music Time." Starday (S)363 "Giddyup Go." Nash 2044 "Dear John Letter." Starday 197 "Red Sovine."

STATLER BROTHERS Col CL-2449/CS-9249 "Flowers on the Wall." Col CL-2719/CS-9519 "Statler Brothers Sing the Big Hits."

STEWART, WYNN Cap (S)T-2737 "It's Such a Prettty World Today." Cap (S)T-2332 "Songs by Wynn Stewart." Hill (S)6050 "Above and Beyond."

STONE, CLIFFIE Cap (S)KAO-1555 "Cliffie Stone Sing-a-long." Cap T-1080 "Party's on Me."

STONEMAN FAMILY MGM (S)4363 "Stonemans." Starday 393 "White Lightning." Folk 2315 "Banjo Tunes and Songs."

STRINGBEAN Starday 142 "Stringbean—Kentucky Wonder."

TERRY, SONNY Arc Folk 106/206 "Sonny Terry." Folk 3821 "New Sound" (w. Brownie McGee and Burris). Stinson 55 "Mouth Harp."

THOMPSON, HANK War (S)1686 "Gold Standard Collection." Cap (S)T-2089 "Hank Thompson's Golden Hits." Cap (S)T-1955 "State Fair of Texas." Cap (D)T-1878 "Best of Hank Thompson."

THOMPSON, SUE Hick 121 "Paper Tiger." Mer 12317/16317 "Country Side of Sue Thompson." Hick 111 "Sue Thompson."

TILLMAN, FLOYD Col HL-7316 "Floyd Tillman's Best." Pick (S)6017 "Greatest Hits of Lovin' Floyd Tillman."

TOMPALL & THE GLASER BROTHERS MGM (S)4465 "Tompall and the Glaser Brothers." Dec (7)4041 "This Land."

TRAVELERS 3 Elek (7)236 "Alive at Last." Elek (7)226 "Open House." Elek (7)216 "Travelers 3."

TRAVIS, MERLE Cap (S)T-1664 "Travis!" Cap T-1391 "Walkin' the Strings." Cap T-891 "Back Home." Cap (D)T-2662 "Best of Merle Travis."

TUBB, ERNEST Dec (7)4772 "Hits Old and New." Dec (7)4046 "All Time Hits." Dec DX(S)–(7)159(8871/2) "Ernest Tubb Story" (2 records). Dec 8553 "Daddy of 'em All."

TUBB, JUSTIN RCA LPM/LSP 3399 "Where You're Concerned." RCA LPM/LSP 3591 "Together and Alone."

TWITTY, CONWAY Dec (7)4828 "Look Into My Teardrops." Dec (7)4724 "Conway Twitty Sings." MGM (S)3849 "Conway Twitty's Hits."

TYLER, T. TEXAS Cap (S)T-2344 "Hits of T. Texas Tyler." Starday (S)379 "T. Texas Tyler's Sensational New Hits." Pick (S)6042 "T. Texas Tyler's Great Hits."

VAN DYKE, LEROY   War (S)1652 "Hits of Leroy Van Dyke." Dot 3693 "Auctioneer." Mer 20682/60682 "Walk on By."

VAN RONK, DAVE   Prest (S)7527 "Dave Van Ronk, Folksinger." Prest 14001 "In the Tradition." Mer 20864/60864 "Ragtime Jug Stompers."

WAGONER, PORTER   RCA LPM/LSP 2706 "Y'all Come." RCA LPM/LSP 3593 "Confessions of a Broken Man." RCA LPM/LSP 3560(e) "Best of Porter Wagoner."

WAKELY, JIMMY   Dot 3711/25711 "Slippin' Around." Dec 8680 "Enter and Rest and Pray." Dec 8409 "Santa Fe Trail."

WALKER, BILLY   Col CL-1935/CS-8735 "Billy Walker's Greatest Hits." Col HL-7410/HS-11210 "Big Country Hits." Col CL-2331/CS-9131 "Gun, Gold and the Girl."

WALKER, CHARLIE   Col HL-7415/HS-11215 "Golden Hits." Epic LN-24153/BN-26153 "Born to Lose."

WALKER, CINDY   Monu (1)8020 "Cindy Walker."

WARNER, FRANK   Van 2150/9130 "Frank Warner."

WATERS, MUDDY   Chess (S)1507 "Brass and the Blues." Chess 1449 "Muddy Waters at Newport." Chess 1427 "Best of Muddy Waters."

WATSON, DOC   Van (7)9239 "Home Again." Folk 2426 "Doc Watson and Jean Ritchie at Folk City." Folk 2366 "Watson Family."

WEAVERS, THE   Dec DX(S)–(7)173 "Best of The Weavers" (2 records). Van 9010 "At Carnegie Hall." Van 9075/2069 "At Carnegie Hall, Volume 2."

WEIN, GEORGE   Impulse (S)31 "George Wein."

WELLS, KITTY   Dec (7)4906 "Together Again" (w. Red Foley). Dec DX(S)–(7)174 "Kitty Wells Story" (2 records). Dec (7)4197 "Queen of Country Music." Dec (7)4108 "Golden Favorites."

WEST, DOTTIE   RCA LPM/LSP 3368 "Here Comes My Baby." RCA LPM/LSP 3587 "Suffer Time." RCA LPM/LSP 3830 "I'll Help You Forget Her."

WEST, HEDY   Van 9124 "Hedy West." Van (7)9162 "Hedy West, Volume 2."

WHEELER, BILLY EDD   Kapp 1479/3479 "Goin' Town and Country." Mon 367 "Bluegrass Too." Mon 354 "U.S.A."

WHITE, JOSH   Elek 123 "25th Anniversary Album." Elek (7)211 "Empty Bed Blues." Dec 8665 "Josh White." Period 1209 "Josh White and Big Bill Broonzy."

WHITMAN, SLIM   Cam CAL/CAS 954(e) "Birmingham Jail." Lib LP-9342/12342 "15th Anniversary Album." Lib LP-9235 "Yodeling." Lib LP-9026/12104 "Country Hits."

WILBURN BROTHERS   Dec (7)4615 "Country Gold." Voc (7)3691 "Carefree Moments." Dec (7)8774 "Side by Side."

WILLIAMS, HANK, JR.   MGM (S)4513 "Best of Hank Williams, Jr." MGM (S)4428 "My Own Way." MGM (S)4260 "Your Cheatin' Heart."

WILLIAMS, HANK, SR.   MGM 4267-4 "Hank Williams' Story" (4 records.) MGM (S) 4168 "Very Best." MGM 3999 "Hank Williams on Stage."

WILLIAMS, SOL "TEX"   Sun 1144/5144 "Tex Williams." Imper 9309/12309 "Voice of Authority." Dec 4295 "Tex Williams."

WILLIS BROTHERS   Starday (S)323 "Give Me Forty Acres." Pick (S)6035 "Sensational Willis Brothers." Nash 2040 "Travelin' and Truck Driver Hits."

WILLS, BOB   Col HL-7036 "Bob Wills Special." Col HL-7304 "Best of Bob Wills and His Texas Playboys." Col HL-7345 "Great Bob Wills."

WISEMAN, SCOTT   (*See* Lulu Belle & Scotty)

WOOLEY, SHEB   MGM (S) 4275 "Very Best of Sheb Wooley." MGM (S)4421 "Big Ben Strikes Again." MGM (S)4173 "Ben Colder."

WORTH, MARION   Col CL-2287/CS-9087 "Marion Worth Sings Marty Robbins." Dec (7)4936 "Woman Needs Love."

WRIGHT, JOHNNY   Dec (7)4846 "Wright Way." Dec (7)4770 "Special." Dec (7) 4968 "Johnny Wright." (*See also* Johnnie & Jack)

YARBROUGH, GLENN   RCA LPM/LSP 2836 "Time to Move On." RCA LPM/ LSP 3422 "Baby, The Rain Must Fall." RCA LPM/LSP 3661 "Live at the hungry i."

YOUNG, FARON   Mer 21047/61047 "Faron Young's Greatest Hits." Cap T-1528 "Hello Walls." Cap T-1450 "Best of Faron Young." Cap (S)T-1245 "Talk About Hits."

Bibliography

Bibliography

Ardmore, J. K., "Ballad of Jimmie (Charles) Rodgers," *Coronet,* July '59, pp. 46–56.

Arnold, Byron, *Folksongs of Alabama,* Univ. of Alabama Press, '50.

Aronowitz, A. G. & Blonsky, M., "Three's Company: Peter, Paul & Mary," *Saturday Evening Post,* May 13, '63, pp. 30ff.

Asch, Moses & Silber, I., eds., *900 Miles—The Ballads, Blues and Folksongs of Cisco Houston,* Oak Publications, N.Y., '65.

Bayard, Samuel Preston, ed., *Hill Country Tunes,* American Folklore Society, Philadelphia, '44.

Billboard Annual Country & Western issues (Oct. '66; Oct. '67; Oct. '68).

Boggs, Dock, "I Always Loved the Lonesome Songs," *Sing Out!,* July '64, pp. 32–37.

Brand, Oscar, *The Ballad Mongers,* Funk & Wagnalls, N.Y., '62.

Bronson, Bertrand Harris, *Traditional Tunes of the Child Ballads,* Vol. 1 (1–53), Vol. 2 (54–113), Princeton Univ. Press, '62.

Broonzy, Big Bill, *Big Bill Blues* (as told to Yannick Bruynoghe), England, '55; revised with additional material, Oak Publications, N.Y., '64.

Charters, Samuel Barclay, *The Country Blues,* Rinehart & Co., N.Y., '59.

Child, James Francis, *English and Scottish Popular Ballads,* Houghton, Mifflin Co., Boston, 1882–98 (10 vols.).

Clancy Brothers and Tommy Maken Songbook, Tiparm Music Publishers, Inc., N. Y., '64

Cohen, John, "Fiddlin' Eck Robertson," *Sing Out!,* April-May '64, pp. 55–59.

———, "Joan Baez," *Sing Out!,* Summer '63, pp. 5–7.

———, "Roscoe Holcomb: First Person," *Sing Out!,* April-May '66, pp. 3–7.

Cohen, John & Seeger, Mike, eds., *The New Lost City Ramblers Song Book,* Oak Publications, N.Y., '64.

Cohen, Norman & Cohen, Anne, "The Legendary Jimmie Tarleton," *Sing Out!,* Sept. '66, pp. 16–19.

Cohn, Lawrence, "Mississippi John Hurt," *Sing Out!,* Nov. '64, pp. 16–21.

Combs, Josiah H. & Shearin, Hubert Gibson, *A Syllabus of Kentucky Folk-Songs,"* Transylvania Printing Co., Lexington, Ky., '11.

"Country Como (Eddy Arnold)," *Time,* May 27, '66, pp. 62ff.

Dane, Barbara, "Lone Cat Jesse Fuller," *Sing Out!,* Dec.-Jan. '63–64, pp. 5–11.

Davis, Arthur Kyle, *Folk Songs of Virginia,* Duke Univ. Press, '49.

de Cormier, Robert, arr., *The Weavers' Song Book,* Harper & Bros., N.Y., '60.

Dylan, Bob, *The Freewheelin' Bob Dylan,* M. Witmark & Sons, N.Y., '64.

Ewen, David, *Songs of America,* Ziff-Davis Publishing Co., N.Y., '47.

Farina, R., "Baez & Dylan, A Generation Sings Out," *Mademoiselle,* Aug. '64, pp. 242ff.

Feldman, Peter F., "In Chicago, It's the Old Town School of Folk Music," *Sing Out!,* Oct.-Nov. '62, pp. 28–31.

Flanders, Helen (Hartness), *Ancient Ballads Traditionally Sung in New England,* Univ. of Pennsylvania Press, '60, '65.

Ford, Ira W., *Traditional Music of America,* Dutton & Co., N.Y., '40.

Friesen, Gordon, "Something New Has Been Added," *Sing Out!,* Oct.-Nov. '63, pp. 12–23.

Gentry, Linnell, *History and Encyclopedia of Country, Western & Gospel Music,* McQuiddy Press, Nashville, Tenn., '61.

Glazer, Tom, *A New Treasury of Folk Songs,* Bantam Books, N.Y., '61.

Goodwin, Mike, "Dave Van Ronk: the Paradox of the Urban Blues Singer," *Sing Out!,* Jan. '64, pp. 26–30.

Grafman, Howard & Manning, B. T., *Folk Music USA,* Citadel Press, N.Y., '62.

Green, Archie, "Dorsey Dixon: Minstrel of the Mills," *Sing Out!,* July '66, pp. 10–12.

Greenway, John, *American Folksongs of Protest,* Univ. of Pennsylvania Press, '53.

Guthrie, Woody, *American Folksong/Woody Guthrie* (ed. Moses Asch), Disc. Co. of America, N.Y., '47; Oak Publications, N.Y., '61.

———, *Born to Win,* Macmillan, N.Y., '65.

Hansen, Barry, "Barbara Dane Sings the Blues," *Sing Out!,* April-May '64, pp. 19–22.

Haworth, Leslie, "Francis J. Child—the Man Behind the Child Ballads," *Sing Out!,* Dec.-Jan. '62, pp. 25–33.

Hemming, R., "Controversy in Song: Chad Mitchell Trio," *Senior Scholastic,* May 18, '63, p. 18.

Henry, Mellinger Edward, *Folk-songs from the Southern Highlands,* Augustin, N.Y., '38.

———, *Songs Sung in the Southern Appalachians,* Mitre Press, London, '34.

Hentoff, Nat, "Profile: Bob Dylan," *New Yorker,* Oct. 24, '64, pp. 61–62.

Hinton, Sam, "Bess Hawes," *Sing Out!,* Sept. '65, pp. 26–30.

House, Son, "I Can Make My Own Songs," *Sing Out!,* July '65, pp. 38–45.

Hubbard, Lester A., *Ballads and Songs from Utah,* Univ. of Utah Press, '61.

"Is This a New Presley?" *Newsweek,* May 30, '60, p. 91.

Ives, Burl, *Wayfaring Stranger,* Whittlesey House, N.Y., '48.

Jackson, Bruce, "The Personal Blues of Skip James," *Sing Out!,* Jan. '66, pp. 26–30.

Keil, Charles, *Urban Blues,* Univ. of Chicago Press, '66.

La Farge, Peter, "Buffy Sainte-Marie," *Sing Out!,* March '65, pp. 34–37.

———, "Pat Sky," *Sing Out!,* July '65, pp. 35ff.

Lawless, Ray McKinley, *Folksingers and Folksongs in America,* Duell, Sloan & Pearce, N.Y., '60; rev. ed., '65.

"Life from the Hearthside, the Beers Family," *Time,* Jan. 6, '67, pp. 38ff.

Lomax, Alan, *The Folk Songs of North America,* Doubleday, Garden City, N.Y., '60.

———, "The Passing of a Great Singer—Vera Hall" (obit.), *Sing Out!,* July '64, p. 30.

Lomax, Alan, ed., *The Penguin Book of American Folk Songs,* Penguin Books, Baltimore, Md., '65.

Lomax, John Avery, *Adventure of a Ballad Hunter,* Macmillan, N.Y., '47.

Lomax, John A. & Alan, *American Ballads and Folk Songs,* Macmillan, N.Y., '34.

————, *Cowboy Songs and Other Frontier Ballads,* Macmillan, N.Y., '38 (orig. ed., Sturgis & Walton, N.Y., '10).

————, *Folksong, U.S.A.,* Duell, Sloan & Pearce, N.Y., '47.

————, *Negro Folk Songs as Sung by Leadbelly,* Macmillan, N.Y., '36.

————, *Our Singing Country,* Macmillan, N.Y., '41.

Lynn Farnol Group, eds., *The ASCAP Biographical Dictionary of Composers, Authors & Publishers, 3rd Edition,* ASCAP, N.Y., '66.

"Man Who Sold Parsley" (Elvis Presley), *Time,* May 16, '60, pp. 61–62.

Moore, Thurston, *Country Music Who's Who,* Heather Publications, Denver, Colo. (1960–67).

Mothner, I., "Big Folk-Singers on Campus: Peter, Paul & Mary," *Look,* July 2, '63, pp. 59–62.

Music City News, Nashville, Tenn. (various issues).

Myrus, Donald, *Ballads, Blues & the Big Beat,* Macmillan, N.Y., '66.

Nelson, Paul, "Jug Band! Jug Band!" *Sing Out!,* Dec.-Jan. '63–64, pp. 8–14.

Nelson, Paul & Pankake, Jon, "Uncle Dave Macon—Country Immortal," *Sing Out!,* Summer '63, pp. 19–21.

Nettl, Bruno, *An Introduction to Folk Music in the United States,* Wayne State Univ. Press, '60.

"Newport Folk Festival '63" (organizing letter), *Sing Out!,* Summer '63, p. 31.

Niles, John Jacob, *The Ballad Book,* Houghton, Mifflin, N.Y., '61.

Nye, Hermes, *How to Be a Folksinger,*" Oak Publications, N.Y., '65.

Ohrlin, Glenn, "Glenn Ohrlin: Cowboy Singer," *Sing Out!,* May '65, pp. 40–44.

Owens, William A., *Texas Folk Songs,* Texas Folklore Society, Austin, Tex., '50.

Pankake, Jon, "Mike Seeger: the Style of Tradition," *Sing Out!,* July '64, pp. 6–11.

————, "Sam and Kirk McGee from Sunny Tennessee," *Sing Out!,* Nov. '64, pp. 46–50.

"Peter La Farge (1931–65)" (obit.), *Sing Out!,* Jan. '66, p. 11.

Pound, Louise, *Folk-Song of Nebraska and the Central West,* Nebraska Academy of Sciences, Lincoln, Neb., Vol. 9, No. 3, '15.

Proffitt, Frank, "Good Memories for Me," *Sing Out!,* Nov. '65, pp. 34–37.

Raim, Walter, *The Josh White Songbook,* Quadrangle Books, Chicago, Ill., '63.

Ramsey, Frederic, Jr., "Leadbelly: A Great Long Time," *Sing Out!,* March '65, pp. 7–24.

Randolph, Vance, *Ozark Folk Songs,* State Historical Society of Missouri, Columbus, Mo., 1946–50 (4 vols.).

————, *The Ozarks,* Vanguard Press, N.Y., '31.

Reynolds, Malvina, *Little Boxes and Other Handmade Songs,* Oak Publications, N.Y., '64.

Ritchie, Jean, *The Dulcimer Book,* Oak Publications, N.Y., '63.

————, *Folk Songs of the Southern Appalachians as Sung by Jean Ritchie,* Oak Publications, N.Y., '65.

————, *Singing Family of the Cumberlands,* Oak Publications, N.Y., '63.

Robinson, Earl, ed., *Young Folk Song Book,* Simon & Schuster, N.Y., '64.

Sandburg, Carl, *The American Songbag,* Harcourt, Brace & Co., N.Y., '27.

Scarborough, Dorothy, *A Song Catcher in the Southern Mountains,* Columbia Univ. Press, '37.

Scruggs, Louise, "A History of America's Favorite Folk Instrument," *Sing Out!,* Dec.-Jan. '63–64, pp. 26–29.

Seeger, Peggy, *Folk Songs of Peggy Seeger,* Oak Publications, N.Y., '64.

Seeger, Pete, *America's Favorite Ballads, Tunes & Songs as Sung by Pete Seeger,* Oak Publications, N.Y., '61.

Sharp, Cecil J., *English Folk Songs from the Southern Appalachians,* Oxford University Press, London, '32 (2 vols.).

Silber, Irwin, "You're Hedy West!" *Sing Out!,* Sept. '64, pp. 29–32.

Silber, Irwin, ed., *Songs of the Great American West,* Macmillan, N.Y., '67.

Smith, Hobart, "I Just Got the Music in My Head," *Sing Out!,* Jan. '64, pp. 10–13.

Solomon, Maynard, ed., *The Joan Baez Songbook,* Ryerson Music Publishers, N.Y., '65.

Stambler, Irwin, *Encyclopedia of Popular Music,* St. Martin's Press, N.Y., '65.

Thomas, Jean, *Ballad Makin' in the Mountains of Kentucky,* Henry Holt, N.Y., '39.

Turner, Gil, "Bob Dylan—A New Voice Singing New Songs," *Sing Out!,* Oct.-Nov. '62, pp. 5–10.

Warner, Frank, *Folk Songs and Ballads of the Eastern Seaboard: From a Collector's Notebook,* Southern Press, Macon, Ga., '64.

———, "Traditional Singers #3: Frank Proffitt," *Sing Out!,* Oct.-Nov. '63, pp. 6–11.

Watson, Doc, "Folksinging Is a Way of Life," *Sing Out!,* Feb.-March '64, pp. 8–12.

Wilgus, D. K., *Anglo-American Folksong Scholarship Since 1898* (discog.), Rutgers Univ. Press, '59.

Wilson, J. S., "Tennessee's Singing Plowboy," *Coronet,* Sept. '55, pp. 32–36.

Yaryan, Bill, "Derroll Adams—Banjo Pickin' Expatriate," *Sing Out!,* Jan. '67, pp. 29–33.

———, "Ramblin' Jack Elliott," *Sing Out!,* Nov. '65, pp. 25–28.